# Complete Essays

of David Hume

Volume 2

# DAVID HUME

# Complete Essays

*Volume 2*

Edited by David Womersley

ALLEN LANE

*an imprint of*

PENGUIN BOOKS

ALLEN LANE

UK | USA | Canada | Ireland | Australia
India | New Zealand | South Africa

Allen Lane is part of the Penguin Random House group of companies
whose addresses can be found at global.penguinrandomhouse.com

Penguin Random House UK,
One Embassy Gardens, 8 Viaduct Gardens, London SW11 7BW

penguin.co.uk

Penguin
Random House
UK

First published 2026
001

Set in 10.2/13.87pt Sabon LT Std
Typeset by Jouve (UK), Milton Keynes
Printed and bound in Great Britain by Clays Ltd, Elcograf S.p.A.

The authorized representative in the EEA is Penguin Random House Ireland,
Morrison Chambers, 32 Nassau Street, Dublin D02 YH68

A CIP catalogue record for this book is available from the British Library

ISBN: 978-0-241-73086-7

# Contents

## Posthumously Published Essays

## Unpublished Essays

## Appendices

# Essays, Moral, Political, and Literary

## Part II

# Essay I

## Of Commerce

The greater part of mankind may be divided into two classes; that of *shallow* thinkers, who fall short of the truth; and that of *abstruse* thinkers, who go beyond it. The latter class are by far the most rare: and I may add, by far the most useful and valuable. They suggest hints, at least, and start difficulties, which they want, perhaps, skill to pursue; but which may produce fine discoveries, when handled by men who have a more just way of thinking. At worst, what they say is uncommon; and if it should cost some pains to comprehend it, one has, however, the pleasure of hearing something that is new. An author is little to be valued, who tells us nothing but what we can learn from every coffee-house conversation.[1]

All people of *shallow* thought are apt to decry even those of *solid* understanding, as *abstruse* thinkers, and metaphysicians, and refiners; and never will allow any thing to be just which is beyond their own weak conceptions. There are some cases, I own, where an extraordinary refinement affords a strong presumption of falsehood, and where no reasoning is to be trusted but what is natural and easy. When a man deliberates concerning his conduct in any *particular* affair, and forms schemes in politics, trade, œconomy, or any business in life, he never ought to draw his arguments too fine, or connect too long a chain of consequences together. Something is sure to happen, that will disconcert his reasoning, and produce an event different from what he expected. But when we reason upon *general* subjects, one may justly affirm, that our speculations can scarcely ever be too fine, provided they be just; and that the difference between a common man and a man of genius is chiefly seen in the shallowness or depth of the principles upon which they proceed. General reasonings seem intricate, merely because they are general; nor is it easy for the bulk of mankind to distinguish, in a great number of particulars, that common circumstance in which they all agree, or to extract it, pure and unmixed, from the other superfluous circumstances. Every judgment or conclusion, with them, is particular. They cannot enlarge their view to those universal propositions, which comprehend under them an infinite number of individuals, and include a whole science in a single theorem. Their eye is confounded with such an extensive prospect; and the conclusions, derived from it, even though clearly expressed, seem intricate and obscure. But however intricate they may seem, it is certain, that general principles, if just and sound, must always prevail in the general course of things, though they may fail in particular cases; and it is the chief business of philosophers to regard the general course of things. I may add, that it is also the chief business of politicians;[2] especially in the domestic government of the state, where the public good, which is, or ought to be their object, depends on the concurrence of a multitude of causes; not, as in foreign politics, on accidents and chances, and the caprices of a few persons. This therefore makes the difference between *particular* deliberations and *general* reasonings, and renders subtility and refinement much more suitable to the latter than to the former.

I thought this introduction necessary before the following discourses on *commerce, money, interest, balance of trade, &c.* where, perhaps, there will occur some principles which are uncommon, and which may seem too refined and subtile for such vulgar subjects. If false, let them be rejected: But no one ought to entertain a prejudice against them, merely because they are out of the common road.

The greatness of a state, and the happiness of its subjects, how independent soever they may be supposed in some respects, are commonly allowed to be inseparable with regard to commerce; and as private men receive greater security, in the possession of their trade and riches, from the power of the public, so the public becomes powerful in proportion to the opulence and extensive commerce of private men. This maxim is true in general; though I cannot forbear thinking, that it may possibly admit of exceptions, and that we often establish it with too little reserve and limitation. There may be some circumstances, where the commerce and riches and luxury of individuals, instead of adding strength to the public, will serve only to thin its armies, and diminish its authority among the neighbouring nations. Man is a very variable being,[3] and susceptible of many different opinions, principles, and rules

4

of conduct. What may be true, while he adheres to one way of thinking, will be found false, when he has embraced an opposite set of manners and opinions.

The bulk of every state may be divided into *husbandmen* and *manufacturers*. The former are employed in the culture of the land; the latter work up the materials furnished by the former, into all the commodities which are necessary or ornamental to human life. As soon as men quit their savage state, where they live chiefly by hunting and fishing, they must fall into these two classes; though the arts of agriculture employ *at first* the most numerous part of the society.* Time and experience improve so much these arts, that the land may easily maintain a much greater number of men, than those who are immediately employed in its culture, or who furnish the more necessary manufactures to such as are so employed.[4]

If these superfluous hands apply themselves to the finer arts, which are commonly denominated the arts of *luxury*, they add to the happiness of the state; since they afford to many the opportunity of receiving enjoyments, with which they would otherwise have been unacquainted. But may not another scheme be proposed for the employment of these superfluous hands? May not the sovereign lay claim to them, and employ them in fleets and armies, to encrease the dominions of the state abroad, and spread its fame over distant nations? It is certain that the fewer desires and wants are found in the proprietors and labourers of land, the fewer hands do they employ; and consequently the superfluities of the land, instead of maintaining tradesmen and manufacturers, may support fleets and armies to a much greater extent, than where a great many arts are required to minister to the luxury of particular persons. Here therefore seems to be a kind of opposition between the greatness of the state and the happiness of the subject. A state is never greater than when all its superfluous hands are employed in the service of the public. The ease and convenience of private persons require, that these hands should be employed in their service. The one can never

---

* Mons. MELON, in his political essay on commerce, asserts, that even at present, if you divide FRANCE into 20 parts, 16 are labourers or peasants; two only artizans; one belonging to the law, church, and military; and one merchants, financiers, and bourgeois. This calculation is certainly very erroneous. In FRANCE, ENGLAND, and indeed most parts of EUROPE, half of the inhabitants live in cities; and even of those who live in the country, a great number are artizans, perhaps above a third.[5]

be satisfied, but at the expence of the other. As the ambition of the sovereign must entrench on the luxury of individuals; so the luxury of individuals must diminish the force, and check the ambition of the sovereign.

Nor is this reasoning merely chimerical;[6] but is founded on history and experience. The republic of SPARTA was certainly more powerful than any state now in the world, consisting of an equal number of people; and this was owing entirely to the want of commerce and luxury. The HELOTES were the labourers: The SPARTANS were the soldiers or gentlemen. It is evident, that the labour of the HELOTES could not have maintained so great a number of SPARTANS, had these latter lived in ease and delicacy, and given employment to a great variety of trades and manufactures. The like policy may be remarked in ROME. And indeed, throughout all ancient history, it is observable, that the smallest republics raised and maintained greater armies, than states consisting of triple the number of inhabitants, are able to support at present. It is computed, that, in all EUROPEAN nations, the proportion between soldiers and people does not exceed one to a hundred.[7] But we read, that the city of ROME alone, with its small territory, raised and maintained, in early times, ten legions against the LATINS.[8] ATHENS, the whole of whose dominions was not larger than YORKSHIRE, sent to the expedition against SICILY near forty thousand men.* DIONYSIUS the elder, it is said, maintained a standing army of a hundred thousand foot and ten thousand horse, besides a large fleet of four hundred sail;† though his territories extended no farther than the city of SYRACUSE, about a third of the island of SICILY, and some sea-port towns and garrisons on the coast of ITALY and ILLYRICUM.[9] It is true, the ancient armies, in time of war, subsisted much upon plunder: But did not the enemy plunder in their turn? which was a more ruinous way of levying a tax, than any other that could be devised. In short, no probable reason can be assigned for the great power of the more ancient states above the modern, but their want of commerce and luxury. Few artizans were maintained by the labour of the farmers, and therefore more soldiers might live upon it. LIVY says, that ROME, in his time, would

---

* THUCYDIDES, lib. vii.[10]

† DIOD. SIC. lib. vii.[11] This account, I own, is somewhat suspicious, not to say worse; chiefly because this army was not composed of citizens, but of mercenary forces.

find it difficult to raise as large an army as that which, in her early days, she sent out against the GAULS and LATINS.* Instead of those soldiers who fought for liberty and empire in CAMILLUS's time, there were, in AUGUSTUS's days, musicians, painters, cooks, players, and tailors; and if the land was equally cultivated at both periods, it could certainly maintain equal numbers in the one profession as in the other. They added nothing to the mere necessaries of life, in the latter period more than in the former.

It is natural on this occasion to ask, whether sovereigns may not return to the maxims of ancient policy, and consult their own interest in this respect, more than the happiness of their subjects? I answer, that it appears to me, almost impossible; and that because ancient policy was violent, and contrary to the more natural and usual course of things. It is well known with what peculiar laws[12] SPARTA was governed, and what a prodigy that republic is justly esteemed by every one, who has considered human nature as it has displayed itself in other nations, and other ages. Were the testimony of history less positive and circumstantial, such a government would appear a mere philosophical whim or fiction, and impossible ever to be reduced to practice. And though the ROMAN and other ancient republics were supported on principles somewhat more natural, yet was there an extraordinary concurrence of circumstances to make them submit to such grievous burthens. They were free states; they were small ones; and the age being martial, all their neighbours were continually in arms. Freedom naturally begets public spirit, especially in small states; and this public spirit, this *amor patriæ*,[13] must encrease, when the public is almost in continual alarm, and men are obliged, every moment, to expose themselves to the greatest dangers for its defence. A continual succession of wars makes every citizen a soldier: He takes the field in his turn: And during his service he is chiefly maintained by himself. This service is indeed equivalent to a heavy tax; yet is it less felt by a people addicted to arms, who fight for honour and revenge more than pay, and are unacquainted with gain and industry as well as pleasure.† Not to mention the great equality of fortunes among the inhabitants of the ancient republics, where every

* TITI LIVII, lib. vii. cap. 24. "Adeo in quæ laboramus," says he, "sola crevimus, divitias luxuriemque."[14]
† See NOTE [O].

field, belonging to a different proprietor, was able to maintain a family, and rendered the numbers of citizens very considerable, even without trade and manufactures.

But though the want of trade and manufactures, among a free and very martial people, may *sometimes* have no other effect than to render the public more powerful, it is certain, that, in the common course of human affairs, it will have a quite contrary tendency. Sovereigns must take mankind as they find them, and cannot pretend to introduce any violent change in their principles and ways of thinking. A long course of time, with a variety of accidents and circumstances, are requisite to produce those great revolutions, which so much diversify the face of human affairs. And the less natural any set of principles are, which support a particular society, the more difficulty will a legislator meet with in raising and cultivating them. It is his best policy to comply with the common bent of mankind, and give it all the improvements of which it is susceptible. Now, according to the most natural course of things, industry and arts and trade encrease the power of the sovereign as well as the happiness of the subjects; and that policy is violent, which aggrandizes the public by the poverty of individuals. This will easily appear from a few considerations, which will present to us the consequences of sloth and barbarity.

Where manufactures and mechanic arts are not cultivated, the bulk of the people must apply themselves to agriculture; and if their skill and industry encrease, there must arise a great superfluity from their labour beyond what suffices to maintain them. They have no temptation, therefore, to encrease their skill and industry; since they cannot exchange that superfluity for any commodities, which may serve either to their pleasure or vanity. A habit of indolence[15] naturally prevails. The greater part of the land lies uncultivated. What is cultivated, yields not its utmost for want of skill and assiduity in the farmers. If at any time the public exigencies require, that great numbers should be employed in the public service, the labour of the people furnishes now no superfluities, by which these numbers can be maintained. The labourers cannot encrease their skill and industry on a sudden. Lands uncultivated cannot be brought into tillage for some years. The armies, mean while, must either make sudden and violent conquests, or disband for want of subsistence. A regular attack or defence, therefore, is not to be expected from such a people, and their soldiers must be as ignorant and unskilful as their farmers and manufacturers.

Every thing in the world is purchased by labour; and our passions are the only causes of labour. When a nation abounds in manufactures and mechanic arts, the proprietors of land, as well as the farmers, study agriculture as a science, and redouble their industry and attention. The superfluity, which arises from their labour, is not lost; but is exchanged with manufactures for those commodities, which men's luxury now makes them covet. By this means, land furnishes a great deal more of the necessaries of life, than what suffices for those who cultivate it. In times of peace and tranquillity, this superfluity goes to the maintenance of manufacturers, and the improvers of liberal arts. But it is easy for the public to convert many of these manufacturers into soldiers, and maintain them by that superfluity, which arises from the labour of the farmers. Accordingly we find, that this is the case in all civilized governments. When the sovereign raises an army, what is the consequence? He imposes a tax. This tax obliges all the people to retrench what is least necessary to their subsistence.[16] Those, who labour in such commodities, must either enlist in the troops, or turn themselves to agriculture, and thereby oblige some labourers to enlist for want of business. And to consider the matter abstractedly, manufactures encrease the power of the state only as they store up so much labour,[17] and that of a kind to which the public may lay claim, without depriving any one of the necessaries of life. The more labour, therefore, is employed beyond mere necessaries, the more powerful is any state; since the persons engaged in that labour may easily be converted to the public service. In a state without manufactures, there may be the same number of hands; but there is not the same quantity of labour, nor of the same kind. All the labour is there bestowed upon necessaries, which can admit of little or no abatement.

Thus the greatness of the sovereign and the happiness of the state are, in a great measure, united with regard to trade and manufactures. It is a violent method, and in most cases impracticable, to oblige the labourer to toil, in order to raise from the land more than what subsists himself and family. Furnish him with manufactures and commodities, and he will do it of himself. Afterwards you will find it easy to seize some part of his superfluous labour, and employ it in the public service, without giving him his wonted return. Being accustomed to industry, he will think this less grievous, than if, at once, you obliged him to an augmentation of labour without any reward. The case is the same with regard to the other members of the state. The greater is the stock of labour of all kinds, the greater quantity may be taken from the heap, without making any sensible alteration in it.

A public granary of corn, a storehouse of cloth, a magazine of arms; all these must be allowed real riches and strength in any state. Trade and industry are really nothing but a stock of labour, which, in times of peace and tranquillity, is employed for the ease and satisfaction of individuals; but in the exigencies of state, may, in part, be turned to public advantage. Could we convert a city into a kind of fortified camp, and infuse into each breast so martial a genius, and such a passion for public good, as to make every one willing to undergo the greatest hardships for the sake of the public; these affections might now, as in ancient times, prove alone a sufficient spur to industry, and support the community. It would then be advantageous, as in camps, to banish all arts and luxury;[18] and, by restrictions on equipage and tables, make the provisions and forage last longer than if the army were loaded with a number of superfluous retainers. But as these principles are too disinterested and too difficult to support, it is requisite to govern men by other passions, and animate them with a spirit of avarice and industry, art and luxury. The camp is, in this case, loaded with a superfluous retinue; but the provisions flow in proportionably larger. The harmony of the whole is still supported; and the natural bent of the mind being more complied with, individuals, as well as the public, find their account in the observance of those maxims.

The same method of reasoning will let us see the advantage of *foreign* commerce,[19] in augmenting the power of the state, as well as the riches and happiness of the subject. It encreases the stock of labour in the nation; and the sovereign may convert what share of it he finds necessary to the service of the public. Foreign trade, by its imports, furnishes materials for new manufactures; and by its exports, it produces labour in particular commodities, which could not be consumed at home. In short, a kingdom, that has a large import and export, must abound more with industry, and that employed upon delicacies and luxuries, than a kingdom which rests contented with its native commodities.[20] It is, therefore, more powerful, as well as richer and happier.[21] The individuals reap the benefit of these commodities, so far as they gratify the senses and appetites. And the public is also a gainer, while a greater stock of labour is, by this means, stored up against any public exigency; that is, a greater number of laborious men are maintained, who may be diverted to the public service, without robbing any one of the necessaries, or even the chief conveniencies of life.

If we consult history, we shall find, that, in most nations, foreign trade has preceded any refinement in home manufactures, and given birth to domestic luxury.[22] The temptation is stronger to make use of foreign commodities, which are ready for use, and which are entirely new to us, than to make improvements on any domestic commodity, which always advance by slow degrees, and never affect us by their novelty. The profit is also very great, in exporting what is superfluous at home, and what bears no price, to foreign nations, whose soil or climate is not favourable to that commodity. Thus men become acquainted with the *pleasures* of luxury and the *profits* of commerce; and their *delicacy* and *industry*, being once awakened, carry them on to farther improvements, in every branch of domestic as well as foreign trade. And this perhaps is the chief advantage which arises from a commerce with strangers. It rouses men from their indolence; and presenting the gayer and more opulent part of the nation with objects of luxury, which they never before dreamed of, raises in them a desire of a more splendid way of life than what their ancestors enjoyed. And at the same time, the few merchants, who possess the secret of this importation and exportation, make great profits; and becoming rivals in wealth to the ancient nobility, tempt other adventurers to become their rivals in commerce. Imitation soon diffuses all those arts; while domestic manufactures emulate the foreign in their improvements, and work up every home commodity to the utmost perfection of which it is susceptible. Their own steel and iron, in such laborious hands, become equal to the gold and rubies of the INDIES.

When the affairs of the society are once brought to this situation, a nation may lose most of its foreign trade, and yet continue a great and powerful people. If strangers will not take any particular commodity of ours, we must cease to labour in it. The same hands will turn themselves towards some refinement in other commodities, which may be wanted at home. And there must always be materials for them to work upon; till every person in the state, who possesses riches, enjoys as great plenty of home commodities, and those in as great perfection, as he desires;

which can never possibly happen. CHINA is represented as one of the most flourishing empires in the world; though it has very little commerce beyond its own territories.[23]

It will not, I hope, be considered as a superfluous digression, if I here observe, that, as the multitude of mechanical arts is advantageous, so is the great number of persons to whose share the productions of these arts fall. A too great disproportion among the citizens weakens any state. Every person, if possible, ought to enjoy the fruits of his labour, in a full possession of all the necessaries, and many of the conveniencies of life. No one can doubt, but such an equality is most suitable to human nature, and diminishes much less from the *happiness* of the rich than it adds to that of the poor. It also augments the *power of the state*, and makes any extraordinary taxes or impositions be paid with more chearfulness. Where the riches are engrossed by a few, these must contribute very largely to the supplying of the public necessities. But when the riches are dispersed among multitudes, the burthen feels light on every shoulder, and the taxes make not a very sensible difference on any one's way of living.

Add to this, that, where the riches are in few hands, these must enjoy all the power, and will readily conspire to lay the whole burthen on the poor, and oppress them still farther, to the discouragement of all industry.

In this circumstance consists the great advantage of ENGLAND above any nation at present in the world, or that appears in the records of any story. It is true, the ENGLISH feel some disadvantages in foreign trade by the high price of labour, which is in part the effect of the riches of their artisans, as well as of the plenty of money: But as foreign trade is not the most material circumstance, it is not to be put in competition with the happiness of so many millions. And if there were no more to endear to them that free government under which they live, this alone were sufficient. The poverty of the common people is a natural, if not an infallible effect of absolute monarchy; though I doubt, whether it be always true, on the other hand, that their riches are an infallible result of liberty. Liberty must be attended with particular accidents, and a certain turn of thinking, in order to produce that effect. Lord BACON, accounting for the great advantages obtained by the ENGLISH in their wars with FRANCE, ascribes them chiefly to the superior ease and plenty of the common people amongst the former; yet the government of the two kingdoms was, at that time, pretty much alike.[24] Where the labourers and artisans are accustomed to work for low wages, and to retain but a small part of the fruits of their labour, it is difficult for them, even in a free government, to better their condition, or conspire among themselves to heighten their wages. But even where they are accustomed to a more plentiful way of life, it is easy for the rich, in an arbitrary government, to conspire against *them*, and throw the whole burthen of the taxes on their shoulders.

It may seem an odd position, that the poverty of the common people in FRANCE, ITALY, and SPAIN, is, in some measure, owing to the superior riches of the soil and happiness of the climate; yet there want not reasons to justify this paradox.[25] In such a fine mould or soil as that of those more southern regions, agriculture is an easy art; and one man, with a couple of sorry horses, will be able, in a season, to cultivate as much land as will pay a pretty considerable rent to the proprietor. All the art, which the farmer knows, is to leave his ground fallow for a year, as soon as it is exhausted; and the warmth of the sun alone and temperature of the climate enrich it, and restore its fertility. Such poor peasants, therefore, require only a simple maintenance for their labour. They have no stock or riches, which claim more; and at the same time, they are for ever dependant on their landlord, who gives no leases, nor fears that his land will be spoiled by the ill methods of cultivation. In ENGLAND, the land is rich, but coarse; must be cultivated at a great expence; and produces slender crops, when not carefully managed, and by a method which gives not the full profit but in a course of several years. A farmer, therefore, in ENGLAND must have a considerable stock, and a long lease; which beget proportional profits. The fine vineyards of CHAMPAGNE and BURGUNDY, that often yield to the landlord above five pounds *per* acre, are cultivated by peasants, who have scarcely bread: The reason is, that such peasants need no stock but their own limbs, with instruments of husbandry, which they can buy for twenty shillings. The farmers are commonly in some better circumstances in those countries. But the grasiers are most at their ease of all those who cultivate the land. The reason is still the same. Men must have profits proportionable to their expence and hazard. Where so considerable a number of the labouring poor as the peasants and farmers are in very low circumstances, all the rest must partake of their poverty, whether the government of that nation be monarchical or republican.

We may form a similar remark with regard to the general history of mankind. What is the reason, why no people, living between the tropics, could ever yet attain to any art or civility, or reach even any police[26] in their government, and any military discipline; while few nations in the temperate climates have been altogether deprived of these advantages? It is probable that one cause of this phænomenon is the warmth and equality of weather in the torrid zone, which render clothes and houses less requisite for the inhabitants, and thereby remove, in part, that necessity, which is the great spur to industry and invention. *Curis acuens mortalia corda.*[27] Not to mention, that the fewer goods or possessions of this kind any people enjoy, the fewer quarrels are likely to arise amongst them, and the less necessity will there be for a settled police or regular authority to protect and defend them from foreign enemies, or from each other.

# NOTES

## Note [O]

The more ancient ROMANS lived in perpetual war with all their neighbours: And in old LATIN, the term *hostis*, expressed both a stranger and an enemy. This is remarked by CICERO; but by him is ascribed to the humanity of his ancestors, who softened, as much as possible, the denomination of an enemy, by calling him by the same appellation which signified a stranger. *De Off.* lib. ii.[28] It is however much more probable, from the manners of the times, that the ferocity of those people was so great as to make them regard all strangers as enemies, and call them by the same name. It is not, besides, consistent with the most common maxims of policy or of nature, that any state should regard its public enemies with a friendly eye, or preserve any such sentiments for them as the ROMAN orator would ascribe to his ancestors. Not to mention, that the early ROMANS really exercised piracy, as we learn from their first treaties with CARTHAGE, preserved by POLYBIUS, lib. iii.[29] and consequently, like the SALLEE and ALGERINE rovers,[30] were actually at war with most nations, and a stranger and an enemy were with them almost synonimous.

# Essay II

## *Of Refinement in the Arts*

Luxury is a word of an uncertain signification, and may be taken in a good as well as in a bad sense. In general, it means great refinement in the gratification of the senses; and any degree of it may be innocent or blameable, according to the age, or country, or condition of the person. The bounds between the virtue and the vice[1] cannot here be exactly fixed, more than in other moral subjects. To imagine, that the gratifying of any sense, or the indulging of any delicacy in meat, drink, or apparel, is of itself a vice, can never enter into a head, that is not disordered by the frenzies of enthusiasm. I have, indeed, heard of a monk abroad, who, because the windows of his cell opened upon a noble prospect, made a *covenant with his eyes* never to turn that way, or receive so sensual a gratification.[2] And such is the crime of drinking CHAMPAGNE or BUR-GUNDY, preferably to small beer or porter. These indulgences are only vices, when they are pursued at the expence of some virtue, as liber-ality or charity; in like manner as they are follies, when for them a man ruins his fortune, and reduces himself to want and beggary. Where they entrench upon no virtue, but leave ample subject[3] whence to provide for friends, family, and every proper object of generosity or compassion, they are entirely innocent, and have in every age been acknowledged such by almost all moralists. To be entirely occupied with the luxury of the table, for instance, without any relish for the pleasures of ambition, study, or conversation, is a mark of stupidity, and is incompatible with any vigour of temper or genius. To confine one's expence entirely to such a gratification, without regard to friends or family, is an indication of a heart destitute of humanity or benevolence. But if a man reserve time sufficient for all laudable pursuits, and money sufficient for all generous purposes, he is free from every shadow of blame or reproach.

Since luxury may be considered either as innocent or blameable, one may be surprized at those preposterous opinions, which have been entertained concerning it; while men of libertine principles bestow praises even on vicious luxury, and represent it as highly advantageous to society;[4] and on the other hand, men of severe morals blame even the most innocent luxury, and represent it as the source of all the corruptions, disorders, and factions, incident to civil government. We shall here endeavour to correct both these extremes, by proving, *first*, that the ages of refinement are both the happiest and most virtuous; *secondly*, that wherever luxury ceases to be innocent, it also ceases to be beneficial; and when carried a degree too far, is a quality pernicious, though perhaps not the most pernicious, to political society.

To prove the first point, we need but consider the effects of refinement both on *private* and on *public* life. Human happiness, according to the most received notions, seems to consist in three ingredients; action, pleasure, and indolence: And though these ingredients ought to be mixed in different proportions, according to the particular disposition of the person; yet no one ingredient can be entirely wanting, without destroying, in some measure, the relish of the whole composition. Indolence or repose, indeed, seems not of itself to contribute much to our enjoyment; but, like sleep, is requisite as an indulgence to the weakness of human nature, which cannot support an uninterrupted course of business or pleasure. That quick march of the spirits, which takes a man from himself, and chiefly gives satisfaction, does in the end exhaust the mind, and requires some intervals of repose, which, though agreeable for a moment, yet, if prolonged, beget a languor and lethargy, that destroys all enjoyment. Education, custom, and example, have a mighty influence in turning the mind to any of these pursuits; and it must be owned, that, where they promote a relish for action and pleasure, they are so far favourable to human happiness. In times when industry and the arts flourish, men are kept in perpetual occupation, and enjoy, as their reward, the occupation itself, as well as those pleasures which are the fruit of their labour. The mind acquires new vigour; enlarges its powers and faculties; and by an assiduity in honest industry, both satisfies its natural appetites, and prevents the growth of unnatural ones, which commonly spring up, when nourished by ease and idleness. Banish those arts from society, you deprive men both of action and of pleasure; and leaving nothing but indolence in their place, you even destroy the relish of indolence, which never is agreeable, but when it succeeds to labour, and recruits the spirits, exhausted by too much application and fatigue.

Another advantage of industry and of refinements in the mechanical arts, is, that they commonly produce some refinements in the liberal; nor can one be carried to perfection, without being accompanied, in some degree, with the other. The same age, which produces great philosophers and politicians, renowned generals and poets, usually abounds with skilful weavers, and ship-carpenters. We cannot reasonably expect, that a piece of woollen cloth will be wrought to perfection in a nation, which is ignorant of astronomy, or where ethics are neglected.[5] The spirit of the age affects all the arts; and the minds of men, being once roused from their lethargy, and put into a fermentation, turn themselves on all sides, and carry improvements into every art and science. Profound ignorance is totally banished, and men enjoy the privilege of rational creatures, to think as well as to act, to cultivate the pleasures of the mind as well as those of the body.

The more these refined arts advance, the more sociable men become: nor is it possible, that, when enriched with science, and possessed of a fund of conversation, they should be contented to remain in solitude, or live with their fellow-citizens in that distant manner, which is peculiar to ignorant and barbarous nations. They flock into cities; love to receive and communicate knowledge; to show their wit or their breeding; their taste in conversation or living, in clothes or furniture. Curiosity allures the wise; vanity the foolish; and pleasure both. Particular clubs and societies are every where formed: Both sexes meet in an easy and sociable manner; and the tempers of men, as well as their behaviour, refine apace. So that, beside the improvements which they receive from knowledge and the liberal arts, it is impossible but they must feel an encrease of humanity, from the very habit of conversing together, and contributing to each other's pleasure and entertainment. Thus *industry*, *knowledge*, and *humanity*, are linked together by an indissoluble chain, and are found, from experience as well as reason, to be peculiar to the more polished, and, what are commonly denominated, the more luxurious ages.

Nor are these advantages attended with disadvantages, that bear any proportion to them. The more men refine upon pleasure, the less will they indulge in excesses of any kind; because nothing is more destructive to true pleasure than such excesses. One may safely affirm, that the

TARTARS are oftener guilty of beastly gluttony, when they feast on their dead horses, than EUROPEAN courtiers with all their refinements of cookery.[6] And if libertine love, or even infidelity to the marriage-bed, be more frequent in polite ages, when it is often regarded only as a piece of gallantry; drunkenness, on the other hand, is much less common: A vice more odious, and more pernicious both to mind and body. And in this matter I would appeal, not only to an OVID or a PETRONIUS, but to a SENECA or a CATO. We know, that CÆSAR, during CATILINE's conspiracy, being necessitated to put into CATO's hands a *billet-doux*, which discovered an intrigue with SERVILIA, CATO's own sister, that stern philosopher threw it back to him with indignation; and in the bitterness of his wrath, gave him the appellation of drunkard, as a term more opprobrious than that with which he could more justly have reproached him.[7]

But industry, knowledge, and humanity, are not advantageous in private life alone: They diffuse their beneficial influence on the *public*, and render the government as great and flourishing as they make individuals happy and prosperous. The encrease and consumption of all the commodities, which serve to the ornament and pleasure of life, are advantageous to society; because, at the same time that they multiply those innocent gratifications to individuals, they are a kind of *storehouse* of labour, which, in the exigencies of state, may be turned to the public service.[8] In a nation, where there is no demand for such superfluities, men sink into indolence, lose all enjoyment of life, and are useless to the public, which cannot maintain or support its fleets and armies, from the industry of such slothful members.

The bounds of all the EUROPEAN kingdoms are, at present, nearly the same they were two hundred years ago: But what a difference is there in the power and grandeur of those kingdoms? Which can be ascribed to nothing but the encrease of art and industry. When CHARLES VIII. of FRANCE invaded ITALY, he carried with him about 20,000 men: Yet this armament so exhausted the nation, as we learn from GUICCIARDIN, that for some years it was not able to make so great an effort.[9] The late king of FRANCE,[10] in time of war, kept in pay above 400,000 men;[11]* though from MAZARINE's death[12] to his own, he was engaged in a course of wars that lasted near thirty years.

---

* The inscription on the PLACE-DE-VENDOME says 440,000.

This industry is much promoted by the knowledge inseparable from ages of art and refinement; as, on the other hand, this knowledge enables the public to make the best advantage of the industry of its subjects. Laws, order, police,[13] discipline; these can never be carried to any degree of perfection, before human reason has refined itself by exercise, and by an application to the more vulgar arts, at least, of commerce and manufacture. Can we expect, that a government will be well modelled by a people, who know not how to make a spinning-wheel, or to employ a loom to advantage? Not to mention, that all ignorant ages are infested with superstition, which throws the government off its bias,[14] and disturbs men in the pursuit of their interest and happiness.

Knowledge in the arts of government naturally begets mildness and moderation, by instructing men in the advantages of humane maxims above rigour and severity, which drive subjects into rebellion, and make the return to submission impracticable, by cutting off all hopes of pardon. When the tempers of men are softened as well as their knowledge improved, this humanity appears still more conspicuous, and is the chief characteristic which distinguishes a civilized age from times of barbarity and ignorance. Factions are then less inveterate, revolutions less tragical, authority less severe, and seditions less frequent. Even foreign wars abate of their cruelty; and after the field of battle, where honour and interest steel men against compassion as well as fear, the combatants divest themselves of the brute, and resume the man.

Nor need we fear, that men, by losing their ferocity, will lose their martial spirit, or become less undaunted and vigorous in defence of their country or their liberty. The arts have no such effect in enervating either the mind or body. On the contrary, industry, their inseparable attendant, adds new force to both. And if anger, which is said to be the whetstone of courage,[15] loses somewhat of its asperity, by politeness and refinement; a sense of honour, which is a stronger, more constant, and more governable principle, acquires fresh vigour by that elevation of genius which arises from knowledge and a good education. Add to this, that courage can neither have any duration, nor be of any use, when not accompanied with discipline and martial skill, which are seldom found among a barbarous people. The ancients remarked, that DATAMES[16] was the only barbarian that ever knew the art of war. And PYRRHUS,[17] seeing the ROMANS marshal their army with some art and skill, said with surprize, *These barbarians have nothing barbarous in their discipline!* It is observable, that, as the old ROMANS, by applying themselves solely to war, were almost the only uncivilized people that ever possessed military discipline; so the modern ITALIANS are the only civilized people, among EUROPEANS, that ever wanted courage and a martial spirit.[18] Those who would ascribe this effeminacy of the ITALIANS to their luxury, or politeness, or application to the arts, need but consider the FRENCH and ENGLISH, whose bravery is as uncontestable, as their love for the arts, and their assiduity in commerce. The ITALIAN historians[19] give us a more satisfactory reason for this degeneracy of their countrymen. They shew us how the sword was dropped at once by all the ITALIAN sovereigns; while the VENETIAN aristocracy was jealous of its subjects, the FLORENTINE democracy applied itself entirely to commerce; ROME was governed by priests, and NAPLES by women. War then became the business of soldiers of fortune, who spared one another, and to the astonishment of the world, could engage a whole day in what they called a battle, and return at night to their camp, without the least bloodshed.[20]

What has chiefly induced severe moralists to declaim against refinement in the arts, is the example of ancient ROME, which, joining, to its poverty and rusticity, virtue and public spirit, rose to such a surprizing height of grandeur and liberty; but having learned from its conquered provinces the ASIATIC luxury, fell into every kind of corruption; whence arose sedition and civil wars, attended at last with the total loss of liberty. All the LATIN classics,[21] whom we peruse in our infancy, are full of these sentiments, and universally ascribe the ruin of their state to the arts and riches imported from the East: Insomuch that SALLUST represents a taste for painting as a vice, no less than lewdness and drinking.[22] And so popular were these sentiments, during the later ages of the republic, that this author abounds in praises of the old rigid ROMAN virtue, though himself the most egregious instance of modern luxury and corruption; speaks contemptuously of the GRECIAN eloquence, though the most elegant writer in the world; nay, employs preposterous digressions and declamations to this purpose, though a model of taste and correctness.[23]

But it would be easy to prove, that these writers mistook the cause of the disorders in the ROMAN state, and ascribed to luxury and the arts, what really proceeded from an ill modelled government,[24] and the unlimited extent of conquests. Refinement on the pleasures and conveniencies of life has no natural tendency to beget venality and corruption.

The value, which all men put upon any particular pleasure, depends on comparison and experience; nor is a porter less greedy of money, which he spends on bacon and brandy, than a courtier, who purchases champagne and ortolans.[25] Riches are valuable at all times, and to all men; because they always purchase pleasures, such as men are accustomed to, and desire: Nor can any thing restrain or regulate the love of money, but a sense of honour and virtue; which, if it be not nearly equal at all times, will naturally abound most in ages of knowledge and refinement.[26]

Of all EUROPEAN kingdoms, POLAND seems the most defective in the arts of war as well as peace, mechanical as well as liberal; yet it is there that venality and corruption do most prevail. The nobles seem to have preserved their crown elective for no other purpose, than regularly to sell it to the highest bidder. This is almost the only species of commerce, with which that people are acquainted.[27]

The liberties of ENGLAND, so far from decaying since the improvements in the arts, have never flourished so much as during that period. And though corruption may seem to encrease of late years; this is chiefly to be ascribed to our established liberty,[28] when our princes have found the impossibility of governing without parliaments,[29] or of terrifying parliaments by the phantom of prerogative.[30] Not to mention, that this corruption or venality prevails much more among the electors than the elected; and therefore cannot justly be ascribed to any refinements in luxury.

If we consider the matter in a proper light, we shall find, that a progress in the arts is rather favourable to liberty, and has a natural tendency to preserve, if not produce a free government.[31] In rude unpolished nations, where the arts are neglected, all labour is bestowed on the cultivation of the ground; and the whole society is divided into two classes, proprietors of land, and their vassals or tenants.[32] The latter are necessarily dependent, and fitted for slavery and subjection; especially where they possess no riches, and are not valued for their knowledge in agriculture; as must always be the case where the arts are neglected. The former naturally erect themselves into petty tyrants; and must either submit to an absolute master, for the sake of peace and order; or if they will preserve their independency, like the ancient barons, they must fall into feuds and contests among themselves, and throw the whole society into such confusion, as is perhaps worse than the most despotic government. But where luxury nourishes commerce and industry, the peasants, by a proper cultivation of the land, become rich and independent; while the tradesmen and merchants acquire a share of the property, and draw authority and consideration to that middling rank of men, who are the best and firmest basis of public liberty. These submit not to slavery, like the peasants, from poverty and meanness of spirit; and having no hopes of tyrannizing over others, like the barons, they are not tempted, for the sake of that gratification, to submit to the tyranny of their sovereign. They covet equal laws, which may secure their property, and preserve them from monarchical, as well as aristocratical tyranny.

The lower house is the support of our popular government; and all the world acknowledges, that it owed its chief influence and consideration to the encrease of commerce, which threw such a balance of property into the hands of the commons.[33] How inconsistent then is it to blame so violently a refinement in the arts, and to represent it as the bane of liberty and public spirit!

To declaim against present times, and magnify the virtue of remote ancestors, is a propensity almost inherent in human nature:[34] And as the sentiments and opinions of civilized ages alone are transmitted to posterity, hence it is that we meet with so many severe judgments pronounced against luxury, and even science; and hence it is that at present we give so ready an assent to them. But the fallacy is easily perceived, by comparing different nations that are contemporaries; where we both judge more impartially, and can better set in opposition those manners, with which we are sufficiently acquainted. Treachery and cruelty, the most pernicious and most odious of all vices, seem peculiar to uncivilized ages; and by the refined GREEKS and ROMANS were ascribed to all the barbarous nations, which surrounded them. They might justly, therefore, have presumed, that their own ancestors, so highly celebrated, possessed no greater virtue, and were as much inferior to their posterity in honour and humanity, as in taste and science. An ancient FRANK or SAXON may be highly extolled: But I believe every man would think his life or fortune much less secure in the hands of a MOOR or TARTAR, than in those of a FRENCH or ENGLISH gentleman, the rank of men the most civilized in the most civilized nations.

We come now to the *second* position which we proposed to illustrate, to wit, that, as innocent luxury, or a refinement in the arts and conveniencies of life, is advantageous to the public; so wherever luxury ceases to be innocent, it also ceases to be beneficial; and when carried a degree farther, begins to be a quality pernicious, though, perhaps, not the most pernicious, to political society.

Let us consider what we call vicious luxury. No gratification, however sensual, can of itself be esteemed vicious. A gratification is only vicious, when it engrosses all a man's expence, and leaves no ability for such acts of duty and generosity as are required by his situation and fortune. Suppose, that he correct the vice, and employ part of his expence in the education of his children, in the support of his friends, and in relieving the poor; would any prejudice result to society? On the contrary, the same consumption would arise; and that labour, which, at present, is employed only in producing a slender gratification to one man, would relieve the necessitous, and bestow satisfaction on hundreds. The same care and toil that raise a dish of peas at CHRISTMAS,[35] would give bread to a whole family during six months. To say, that, without a vicious luxury, the labour would not have been employed at all, is only to say, that there is some other defect in human nature, such as indolence, selfishness, inattention to others, for which luxury, in some measure, provides a remedy; as one poison may be an antidote to another. But virtue, like wholesome food, is better than poisons, however corrected.

Suppose the same number of men, that are at present in GREAT BRITAIN, with the same soil and climate; I ask, is it not possible for them to be happier, by the most perfect way of life that can be imagined, and by the greatest reformation that Omnipotence itself could work in their temper and disposition? To assert, that they cannot, appears evidently ridiculous. As the land is able to maintain more than all its present inhabitants, they could never, in such a UTOPIAN state, feel any other ills than those which arise from bodily sickness; and these are not the half of human miseries. All other ills spring from some vice, either in ourselves or others; and even many of our diseases proceed from the same origin. Remove the vices, and the ills follow. You must only take care to remove all the vices. If you remove part, you may render the matter worse. By banishing *vicious* luxury, without curing sloth and an indifference to others, you only diminish industry in the state, and add nothing to men's charity or their generosity. Let us, therefore, rest contented with asserting, that two opposite vices in a state may be more advantageous than either of them alone; but let us never pronounce vice in itself advantageous. Is it not very inconsistent for an author to assert in one page, that moral distinctions are inventions of politicians for public interest; and in the next page maintain, that vice is advantageous to the public?* And indeed it seems upon any system of morality, little less than a contradiction in terms,[36] to talk of a vice, which is in general beneficial to society.[37]

I thought this reasoning necessary, in order to give some light to a philosophical question, which has been much disputed in ENGLAND. I call it a *philosophical* question, not a *political* one. For whatever may be the consequence of such a miraculous transformation of mankind, as would endow them with every species of virtue, and free them from every species of vice; this concerns not the magistrate, who aims only at possibilities. He cannot cure every vice by substituting a virtue in its place. Very often he can only cure one vice by another; and in that case, he ought to prefer what is least pernicious to society. Luxury, when excessive, is the source of many ills; but is in general preferable to sloth and idleness, which would commonly succeed in its place, and are more hurtful both to private persons and to the public. When sloth reigns, a mean uncultivated way of life prevails amongst individuals, without society, without enjoyment. And if the sovereign, in such a situation, demands the service of his subjects, the labour of the state suffices only to furnish the necessaries of life to the labourers, and can afford nothing to those who are employed in the public service.

* Fable of the Bees.[38]

# Essay III

## *Of Money*

Money is not, properly speaking, one of the subjects of commerce; but only the instrument which men have agreed upon to facilitate the exchange of one commodity for another. It is none of the wheels of trade: It is the oil which renders the motion of the wheels more smooth and easy.[1] If we consider any one kingdom by itself, it is evident, that the greater or less plenty of money is of no consequence;[2] since the prices of commodities are always proportioned to the plenty of money, and a crown in HARRY VII.'s[3] time served the same purpose as a pound does at present. It is only the *public* which draws any advantage from the greater plenty of money; and that only in its wars and negociations with foreign states. And this is the reason, why all rich and trading countries from CARTHAGE to GREAT BRITAIN and HOLLAND, have employed mercenary troops,[4] which they hired from their poorer neighbours. Were they to make use of their native subjects, they would find less advantage from their superior riches, and from their great plenty of gold and silver; since the pay of all their servants must rise in proportion to the public opulence. Our small army of 20,000 men is maintained at as great expence as a FRENCH army twice as numerous.[5] The ENGLISH fleet, during the late war,[6] required as much money to support it as all the ROMAN legions, which kept the whole world in subjection, during the time of the emperors.*

The greater number of people and their greater industry are serviceable in all cases; at home and abroad, in private, and in public. But the greater plenty of money, is very limited in its use, and may even sometimes be a loss to a nation in its commerce with foreigners.

There seems to be a happy concurrence of causes in human affairs,

* See NOTE [P].

which checks the growth of trade and riches, and hinders them from being confined entirely to one people; as might naturally at first be dreaded from the advantages of an established commerce.[7] Where one nation has gotten the start of another in trade, it is very difficult for the latter to regain the ground it has lost; because of the superior industry and skill of the former, and the greater stocks, of which its merchants are possessed, and which enable them to trade on so much smaller profits. But these advantages are compensated, in some measure, by the low price of labour in every nation which has not an extensive commerce, and does not much abound in gold and silver. Manufactures, therefore gradually shift their places, leaving those countries and provinces which they have already enriched, and flying to others, whither they are allured by the cheapness of provisions and labour; till they have enriched these also, and are again banished by the same causes. And, in general, we may observe, that the dearness of every thing, from plenty of money, is a disadvantage, which attends an established commerce, and sets bounds to it in every country, by enabling the poorer states to undersel the richer in all foreign markets.

This has made me entertain a doubt concerning the benefit of *banks* and *paper-credit*, which are so generally esteemed advantageous to every nation.[8] That provisions and labour should become dear by the encrease of trade and money, is, in many respects, an inconvenience; but an inconvenience that is unavoidable, and the effect of that public wealth and prosperity which are the end of all our wishes. It is compensated by the advantages, which we reap from the possession of these precious metals, and the weight, which they give the nation in all foreign wars and negociations. But there appears no reason for encreasing that inconvenience by a counterfeit money, which foreigners will not accept of in any payment, and which any great disorder in the state will reduce to nothing. There are, it is true, many people in every rich state, who having large sums of money, would prefer paper with good security; as being of more easy transport and more safe custody.[9] If the public provide not a bank, private bankers will take advantage of this circumstance; as the goldsmiths formerly did in LONDON, or as the bankers do at present in DUBLIN: And therefore it is better, it may be thought, that a public company should enjoy the benefit of that paper-credit, which always will have place in every opulent kingdom. But to endeavour artificially to encrease such a credit, can never be the interest of any trading nation; but must lay them under disadvantages, by encreasing money beyond its natural proportion to labour and commodities, and thereby heightening their price to the merchant and manufacturer. And in this view, it must be allowed, that no bank could be more advantageous, than such a one as locked up all the money it received,* and never augmented the circulating coin, as is usual, by returning part of its treasure into commerce. A public bank, by this expedient, might cut off much of the dealings of private bankers and money-jobbers; and though the state bore the charge of salaries to the directors and tellers of this bank (for, according to the preceding supposition, it would have no profit from its dealings), the national advantage, resulting from the low price of labour and the destruction of paper-credit, would be a sufficient compensation. Not to mention, that so large a sum, lying ready at command, would be a convenience in times of great public danger and distress; and what part of it was used might be replaced at leisure, when peace and tranquillity was restored to the nation.

But of this subject of paper credit we shall treat more largely hereafter.[10] And I shall finish this essay on money, by proposing and explaining two observations, which may, perhaps, serve to employ the thoughts of our speculative politicians.

It was a shrewd observation of ANACHARSIS† the SCYTHIAN, who had never seen money in his own country, that gold and silver seemed to him of no use to the GREEKS, but to assist them in numeration and arithmetic. It is indeed evident, that money is nothing but the representation of labour and commodities, and serves only as a method of rating or estimating them.[11] Where coin is in greater plenty; as a greater quantity of it is required to represent the same quantity of goods; it can have no effect, either good or bad, taking a nation within itself; any more than it would make an alteration on a merchant's books, if, instead of the ARABIAN method of notation, which requires few characters, he should make use of the ROMAN, which requires a great many. Nay, the greater quantity of money, like the ROMAN characters, is rather inconvenient, and requires greater trouble both to keep and transport it. But notwithstanding this conclusion, which must be allowed just, it is certain, that, since the discovery of the mines in AMERICA, industry has encreased in

* This is the case with the bank of AMSTERDAM.[12]
† PLUT. *Quomodo quis suos profectus in virtute sentire possit.*[13]

all the nations of EUROPE, except in the possessors of those mines; and this may justly be ascribed, amongst other reasons, to the encrease of gold and silver.[14] Accordingly we find, that, in every kingdom, into which money begins to flow in greater abundance than formerly, every thing takes a new face: labour and industry gain life; the merchant becomes more enterprising, the manufacturer more diligent and skilful, and even the farmer follows his plough with greater alacrity and attention. This is not easily to be accounted for, if we consider only the influence which a greater abundance of coin has in the kingdom itself, by heightening the price of commodities, and obliging every one to pay a greater number of these little yellow or white pieces for every thing he purchases. And as to foreign trade, it appears, that great plenty of money is rather disadvantageous, by raising the price of every kind of labour.

To account, then, for this phenomenon, we must consider, that though the high price of commodities be a necessary consequence of the encrease of gold and silver, yet it follows not immediately upon that encrease;[15] but some time is required before the money circulates through the whole state, and makes its effect be felt on all ranks of people. At first, no alteration is perceived; by degrees the price rises, first of one commodity, then of another; till the whole at last reaches a just proportion with the new quantity of specie[16] which is in the kingdom. In my opinion, it is only in this interval or intermediate situation, between the acquisition of money and rise of prices, that the encreasing quantity of gold and silver is favourable to industry. When any quantity of money is imported into a nation, it is not at first dispersed into many hands; but is confined to the coffers of a few persons, who immediately seek to employ it to advantage. Here are a set of manufacturers or merchants, we shall suppose, who have received returns of gold and silver for goods which they sent to CADIZ.[17] They are thereby enabled to employ more workmen than formerly, who never dream of demanding higher wages, but are glad of employment from such good paymasters. If workmen become scarce, the manufacturer gives higher wages, but at first requires an encrease of labour; and this is willingly submitted to by the artisan, who can now eat and drink better, to compensate his additional toil and fatigue. He carries his money to market, where he finds every thing at the same price as formerly, but returns with greater quantity and of better kinds, for the use of his family. The farmer and gardener, finding, that all their commodities are taken off, apply themselves with alacrity to the raising more; and at the same time can afford to take better and more cloths from their tradesmen, whose price is the same as formerly, and their industry only whetted by so much new gain. It is easy to trace the money in its progress through the whole commonwealth; where we shall find, that it must first quicken the diligence of every individual, before it encrease the price of labour.

And that the specie may encrease to a considerable pitch, before it have this latter effect, appears, amongst other instances, from the frequent operations of the FRENCH king on the money; where it was always found, that the augmenting of the numerary value did not produce a proportional rise of the prices, at least for some time. In the last year of LOUIS XIV. money was raised three-sevenths, but prices augmented only one. Corn in FRANCE is now sold at the same price, or for the same number of livres, it was in 1683; though silver was then at 30 livres the mark, and is now at 50.* Not to mention the great addition of gold and silver, which may have come into that kingdom since the former period.

From the whole of this reasoning we may conclude, that it is of no manner of consequence, with regard to the domestic happiness of a state, whether money be in a greater or less quantity.[18] The good policy of the magistrate consists only in keeping it, if possible, still encreasing; because, by that means, he keeps alive a spirit of industry in the nation, and encreases the stock of labour, in which consists all real power and riches. A nation, whose money decreases, is actually, at that time, weaker and more miserable than another nation, which possesses no more money, but is on the encreasing hand. This will be easily accounted for, if we consider, that the alterations in the quantity of money, either on one side or the other, are not immediately attended with proportionable alterations in the price of commodities. There is always an interval before matters be adjusted to their new situation; and this interval is as pernicious to industry, when gold and silver are diminishing, as it is advantageous when these metals are encreasing. The workman has not the same employment from the manufacturer and merchant; though he pays the same price for every thing in the market. The farmer cannot dispose of his corn and cattle; though he must pay the same rent to his landlord. The poverty, and beggary, and sloth, which must ensue, are easily foreseen.

* See NOTE [Q].

II. The second observation which I proposed to make with regard to money, may be explained after the following manner. There are some kingdoms, and many provinces in EUROPE, (and all of them were once in the same condition) where money is so scarce, that the landlord can get none at all from his tenants; but is obliged to take his rent in kind, and either to consume it himself, or transport it to places where he may find a market. In those countries, the prince can levy few or no taxes, but in the same manner: And as he will receive small benefit from impositions so paid, it is evident that such a kingdom has little force even at home; and cannot maintain fleets and armies to the same extent, as if every part of it abounded in gold and silver. There is surely a greater disproportion between the force of GERMANY, at present, and what it was three centuries ago,* than there is in its industry, people, and manufactures.[19] The AUSTRIAN dominions in the empire are in general well peopled and well cultivated, and are of great extent; but have not a proportionable weight in the balance of EUROPE; proceeding, as is commonly supposed, from the scarcity of money. How do all these facts agree with that principle of reason, that the quantity of gold and silver is in itself altogether indifferent? According to that principle wherever a sovereign has numbers of subjects, and these have plenty of commodities, he should of course be great and powerful, and they rich and happy, independent of the greater or lesser abundance of the precious metals. These admit of divisions and subdivisions to a great extent; and where the pieces might become so small as to be in danger of being lost, it is easy to mix the gold or silver with a baser metal, as is practised in some countries of EUROPE; and by that means raise the pieces to a bulk more sensible and convenient. They still serve the same purposes of exchange, whatever their number may be, or whatever colour they may be supposed to have.

To these difficulties I answer, that the effect, here supposed to flow from scarcity of money, really arises from the manners and customs of the people; and that we mistake, as is too usual, a collateral effect for a cause. The contradiction is only apparent; but it requires some thought and reflection to discover the principles, by which we can reconcile *reason* to *experience*.

---

* The ITALIANS gave to the Emperor MAXIMILIAN, the nickname of POCCI-DANARI.[20] None of the enterprises of that prince ever succeeded, for want of money.

It seems a maxim almost self-evident, that the prices of every thing depend on the proportion between commodities and money, and that any considerable alteration on either has the same effect, either of heightening or lowering the price. Encrease the commodities, they become cheaper; encrease the money, they rise in their value. As, on the other hand, a diminution of the former, and that of the latter, have contrary tendencies.

It is also evident, that the prices do not so much depend on the absolute quantity of commodities and that of money, which are in a nation, as on that of the commodities, which come or may come to market, and of the money which circulates. If the coin be locked up in chests, it is the same thing with regard to prices, as if it were annihilated;[21] if the commodities be hoarded in magazines and granaries, a like effect follows. As the money and commodities, in these cases, never meet, they cannot affect each other. Were we, at any time, to form conjectures concerning the price of provisions, the corn, which the farmer must reserve for feed and for the maintenance of himself and family, ought never to enter into the estimation. It is only the overplus, compared to the demand, that determines the value.

To apply these principles, we must consider, that, in the first and more uncultivated ages of any state, ere fancy has confounded her wants with those of nature, men, content with the produce of their own fields, or with those rude improvements which they themselves can work upon them, have little occasion for exchange, at least for money, which, by agreement, is the common measure of exchange. The wool of the farmer's own flock, spun in his own family, and wrought by a neighbouring weaver, who receives his payment in corn or wool, suffices for furniture and cloathing. The carpenter, the smith, the mason, the tailor, are retained by wages of a like nature; and the landlord himself, dwelling in the neighbourhood, is content to receive his rent in the commodities raised by the farmer. The greater part of these he consumes at home, in rustic hospitality: The rest, perhaps, he disposes of for money to the neighbouring town, whence he draws the few materials of his expence and luxury.

But after men begin to refine on all these enjoyments, and live not always at home, nor are content with what can be raised in their neighbourhood, there is more exchange and commerce of all kinds, and more money enters into that exchange. The tradesmen will not be paid in corn; because they want something more than barely to eat. The farmer goes beyond his own parish for the commodities he purchases, and cannot always carry his commodities to the merchant who supplies him. The landlord lives in the capital, or in a foreign country; and demands his rent in gold and silver, which can easily be transported to him. Great undertakers, and manufacturers, and merchants, arise in every commodity; and these can conveniently deal in nothing but in specie. And consequently, in this situation of society, the coin enters into many more contracts, and by that means is much more employed than in the former.

The necessary effect is, that, provided the money encrease not in the nation, every thing must become much cheaper in times of industry and refinement, than in rude, uncultivated ages. It is the proportion between the circulating money, and the commodities in the market, which determines the prices. Goods, that are consumed at home, or exchanged with other goods in the neighbourhood, never come to market; they affect not in the least the current specie; with regard to it they are as if totally annihilated; and consequently this method of using them sinks the proportion on the side of the commodities, and encreases the prices. But after money enters into all contracts and sales, and is every where the measure of exchange, the same national cash has a much greater task to perform; all commodities are then in the market; the sphere of circulation is enlarged; it is the same case as if that individual sum were to serve a larger kingdom; and therefore, the proportion being here lessened on the side of the money, every thing must become cheaper, and the prices gradually fall.

By the most exact computations, that have been formed all over EUROPE, after making allowance for the alteration in the numerary value or the denomination, it is found, that the prices of all things have only risen three, or at most, four times, since the discovery of the WEST INDIES.[22] But will any one assert, that there is not much more than four times the coin in EUROPE, that was in the fifteenth century, and the centuries preceding it? The SPANIARDS and PORTUGUESE from their mines, the ENGLISH, FRENCH, and DUTCH, by their AFRICAN trade,[23] and by their interlopers in the WEST INDIES, bring home about six millions a year, of which not above a third goes to the EAST-INDIES. This sum alone, in ten years, would probably double the ancient stock of money in EUROPE. And no other satisfactory reason can be given, why all prices have not risen to a much more exorbitant height, except that which is derived from a change of customs and manners. Besides that more commodities are produced by additional industry, the same commodities come more to market, after men depart from their ancient simplicity of manners. And though this encrease has not been equal to that of money, it has, however, been considerable, and has preserved the proportion between coin and commodities nearer the ancient standard.

Were the question proposed, Which of these methods of living in the people, the simple or refined, is the most advantageous to the state or public? I should, without much scruple, prefer the latter, in a view to politics at least; and should produce this as an additional reason for the encouragement of trade and manufactures.[24]

While men live in the ancient simple manner, and supply all their necessaries from domestic industry or from the neighbourhood, the sovereign can levy no taxes in money from a considerable part of his subjects; and if he will impose on them any burthens, he must take payment in commodities, with which alone they abound; a method attended with such great and obvious inconveniencies, that they need not here be insisted on. All the money he can pretend to raise, must be from his principal cities, where alone it circulates; and these, it is evident, cannot afford him so much as the whole state could, did gold and silver circulate throughout the whole. But besides this obvious diminution of the revenue, there is another cause of the poverty of the public in such a situation. Not only the sovereign receives less money, but the same money goes not so far as in times of industry and general commerce. Every thing is dearer, where the gold and silver are supposed equal; and that because fewer commodities come to market, and the whole coin bears a higher proportion to what is to be purchased by it; whence alone the prices of every thing are fixed and determined.

Here then we may learn the fallacy of the remark, often to be met with in historians,[25] and even in common conversation, that any particular state is weak, though fertile, populous, and well cultivated, merely because it wants money. It appears, that the want of money can never injure any state within itself: For men and commodities are the real strength of any community. It is the simple manner of living which here hurts the public, by confining the gold and silver to few hands, and preventing its universal diffusion and circulation. On the contrary, industry and refinements of all kinds incorporate it with the whole state, however

33

small its quantity may be: They digest it into every vein, so to speak;[26] and make it enter into every transaction and contract. No hand is entirely empty of it. And as the prices of every thing fall by that means, the sovereign has a double advantage: He may draw money by his taxes from every part of the state; and what he receives, goes farther in every purchase and payment.

We may infer, from a comparison of prices, that money is not more plentiful in CHINA, than it was in EUROPE three centuries ago: But what immense power is that empire possessed of, if we may judge by the civil and military establishment maintained by it?[27] POLYBIUS* tells us, that provisions were so cheap in ITALY during his time, that in some places the stated price for a meal at the inns was a *semis* a head, little more than a farthing![28] Yet the ROMAN power had even then subdued the whole known world. About a century before that period, the CARTHAGINIAN ambassador said, by way of raillery, that no people lived more sociably amongst themselves than the ROMANS; for that, in every entertainment, which, as foreign ministers, they received, they still observed the same plate at every table.† The absolute quantity of the precious metals is a matter of great indifference. There are only two circumstances of any importance, namely, their gradual encrease, and their thorough concoction[29] and circulation through the state; and the influence of both these circumstances has here been explained.

In the following Essay we shall see an instance of a like fallacy as that above mentioned; where a collateral effect is taken for a cause, and where a consequence is ascribed to the plenty of money; though it be really owing to a change in the manners and customs of the people.

## NOTES

## Note [P]

A private soldier in the ROMAN infantry had a denarius a day, somewhat less than eightpence. The ROMAN emperors had commonly 25 legions in pay, which allowing 5000 men to a legion, makes 125,000. TACIT. *Ann.* lib. iv.[30] It is true, there were also auxiliaries to the legions; but their numbers are uncertain, as

---

* Lib. ii. cap. 15.[31]
† PLIN. lib. xxxiii. cap. 11.[32]

well as their pay. To consider only the legionaries, the pay of the private men could not exceed 1,600,000 pounds. Now, the parliament in the last war commonly allowed for the fleet 2,500,000. We have therefore 900,000 over for the officers and other expences of the ROMAN legions. There seem to have been but few officers in the ROMAN armies, in comparison of what are employed in all our modern troops, except some SWISS corps. And these officers had very small pay: A centurion, for instance, only double a common soldier. And as the soldiers from their pay (TACIT. *Ann.* lib. i.)[33] bought their own cloaths, arms, tents, and baggage; this must also diminish considerably the other charges of the army. So little expensive[34] was that mighty government, and so easy was its yoke over the world. And, indeed, this is the more natural conclusion from the foregoing calculations. For money, after the conquest of ÆGYPT, seems to have been nearly in as great plenty at ROME, as it is at present in the richest of the EUROPEAN kingdoms.[35]

# Note [Q]

These facts I give upon the authority of Mons. du TOT[36] in his *Reflections politiques*, an author of reputation. Though I must confess, that the facts which he advances on other occasions, are often so suspicious, as to make his authority less in this matter. However, the general observation, that the augmenting of the money in FRANCE does not at first proportionably augment the prices, is certainly just.

By the by, this seems to be one of the best reasons which can be given, for a gradual and universal encrease of the denomination of money, though it has been entirely overlooked in all those volumes which have been written on that question by MELON,[37] Du TOT, and PARIS de VERNEY.[38] Were all our money, for instance, recoined, and a penny's worth of silver taken from every shilling, the new shilling would probably purchase every thing that could have been bought by the old; the prices of every thing would thereby be insensibly diminished; foreign trade enlivened; and domestic industry, by the circulation of a great number of pounds and shillings, would receive some encrease and encouragement. In executing such a project, it would be better to make the new shilling pass for 24 halfpence, in order to preserve the illusion, and make it be taken for the same. And as a recoinage of our silver begins to be requisite, by the continual wearing of our shillings and sixpences, it may be doubtful, whether we ought to imitate the example in King WILLIAM's reign, when the clipt money was raised to the old standard.[39]

# Essay IV

## *Of Interest*

Nothing is esteemed a more certain sign of the flourishing condition of any nation than the lowness of interest: And with reason; though I believe the cause is somewhat different from what is commonly apprehended. Lowness of interest is generally ascribed to plenty of money.[1] But money, however plentiful, has no other effect, *if fixed*, than to raise the price of labour. Silver is more common than gold; and therefore you receive a greater quantity of it for the same commodities. But do you pay less interest for it? Interest in BATAVIA[2] and JAMAICA is at 10 *per cent.* in PORTUGAL at 6; though these places, as we may learn from the prices of every thing, abound more in gold and silver than either LONDON or AMSTERDAM.

Were all the gold in ENGLAND annihilated at once, and one and twenty shillings substituted in the place of every guinea, would money be more plentiful or interest lower? No surely: We should only use silver instead of gold. Were gold rendered as common as silver, and silver as common as copper; would money be more plentiful or interest lower? We may assuredly give the same answer. Our shillings would then be yellow, and our halfpence white; and we should have no guineas. No other difference would ever be observed; no alteration on commerce, manufactures, navigation, or interest; unless we imagine, that the colour of the metal is of any consequence.

Now, what is so visible in these greater variations of scarcity or abundance in the precious metals, must hold in all inferior changes. If the multiplying of gold and silver fifteen times makes no difference, much less can the doubling or tripling them. All augmentation has no other effect than to heighten the price of labour and commodities; and even this variation is little more than that of a name. In the progress towards these changes, the augmentation may have some influence, by exciting industry; but after the prices are settled, suitably to the new abundance of gold and silver, it has no manner of influence.

An effect always holds proportion with its cause.[3] Prices have risen near four times since the discovery of the INDIES; and it is probable gold and silver have multiplied much more: But interest has not fallen much above half. The rate of interest, therefore, is not derived from the quantity of the precious metals.[4]

Money having chiefly a fictitious value, the greater or less plenty of it is of no consequence, if we consider a nation within itself; and the quantity of specie,[5] when once fixed, though ever so large, has no other effect, than to oblige every one to tell out a greater number of those shining bits of metal, for clothes, furniture or equipage, without encreasing any one convenience of life. If a man borrow money to build a house, he then carries home a greater load; because the stone, timber, lead, glass, &c. with the labour of the masons and carpenters, are represented by a greater quantity of gold and silver. But as these metals are considered chiefly as representations, there can no alteration arise, from their bulk or quantity, their weight or colour, either upon their real value or their interest. The same interest, in all cases, bears the same proportion to the sum. And if you lent me so much labour and so many commodities; by receiving five *per cent.* you always receive proportional labour and commodities, however represented, whether by yellow or white coin, whether by a pound or an ounce. It is in vain, therefore, to look for the cause of the fall or rise of interest in the greater or less quantity of gold and silver, which is fixed in any nation.

High interest arises from *three* circumstances: A great demand for borrowing; little riches to supply that demand; and great profits arising from commerce:[6] And these circumstances are a clear proof of the small advance of commerce and industry,[7] not of the scarcity of gold and silver. Low interest, on the other hand, proceeds from the three opposite circumstances: A small demand for borrowing; great riches to supply that demand; and small profits arising from commerce: And these circumstances are all connected together, and proceed from the encrease of industry and commerce, not of gold and silver. We shall endeavour to prove these points; and shall begin with the causes and the effects of a great or small demand for borrowing.

When a people have emerged ever so little from a savage state, and their numbers have encreased beyond the original multitude, there must immediately arise an inequality of property; and while some possess large tracts of land, others are confined within narrow limits, and some are entirely without any landed property. Those who possess more land than they can labour, employ those who possess none, and agree to receive a determinate part of the product. Thus the *landed* interest is immediately established; nor is there any settled government, however rude, in which affairs are not on this footing. Of these proprietors of land, some must presently discover themselves to be of different tempers from others; and while one would willingly store up the produce of his land for futurity, another desires to consume at present what should suffice for many years. But as the spending of a settled revenue is a way of life entirely without occupation; men have so much need of somewhat to fix and engage them, that pleasures, such as they are, will be the pursuit of the greater part of the landholders, and the prodigals among them will always be more numerous than the misers. In a state, therefore, where there is nothing but a landed interest, as there is little frugality, the borrowers must be very numerous, and the rate of interest must hold proportion to it. The difference depends not on the quantity of money, but on the habits and manners which prevail. By this alone the demand for borrowing is encreased or diminished. Were money so plentiful as to make an egg be sold for sixpence; so long as there are only landed gentry and peasants in the state, the borrowers must be numerous, and interest high. The rent for the same farm would be heavier and more bulky: But the same idleness of the landlord, with the higher price of commodities, would dissipate it in the same time, and produce the same necessity and demand for borrowing.

Nor is the case different with regard to the *second* circumstance which we proposed to consider, namely, the great or little riches to supply the demand. This effect also depends on the habits and way of living of the people, not on the quantity of gold and silver. In order to have, in any state, a great number of lenders, it is not sufficient nor requisite, that there be great abundance of the precious metals. It is only requisite, that the property or command of that quantity, which is in the state, whether great or small, should be collected in particular hands, so as to form considerable sums, or compose a great monied interest. This begets a number of lenders, and sinks the rate of usury; and this I shall venture to affirm, depends not on the quantity of specie, but on particular manners and customs, which make the specie gather into separate sums or masses of considerable value.

For suppose, that, by miracle, every man in GREAT BRITAIN should have five pounds slipt into his pocket in one night; this would much more than double the whole money that is at present in the kingdom; yet there would not next day, nor for some time, be any more lenders, nor any variation in the interest. And were there nothing but landlords and peasants in the state, this money, however abundant, could never gather into sums; and would only serve to encrease the prices of every thing, without any farther consequence. The prodigal landlord dissipates it, as fast as he receives it; and the beggarly peasant has no means, nor view, nor ambition of obtaining above a bare livelihood. The overplus of borrowers above that of lenders continuing still the same, there will follow no reduction of interest. That depends upon another principle; and must proceed from an encrease of industry and frugality, of arts and commerce.

Every thing useful to the life of man arises from the ground; but few things arise in that condition which is requisite to render them useful. There must, therefore, beside the peasants and the proprietors of land, be another rank of men, who receiving from the former the rude materials, work them into their proper form, and retain part for their own use and subsistence. In the infancy of society, these contracts between the artisans and the peasants, and between one species of artisans and another are commonly entered into immediately by the persons themselves, who, being neighbours, are easily acquainted with each other's necessities, and can lend their mutual assistance to supply them. But when men's industry encreases, and their views enlarge, it is found, that the most remote parts of the state can assist each other as well as the more contiguous, and that this intercourse of good offices may be carried on to the greatest extent and intricacy. Hence the origin of *merchants*, one of the most useful races of men, who serve as agents between those parts of the state, that are wholly unacquainted, and are ignorant of each other's necessities. Here are in a city fifty workmen in silk and linen, and a thousand customers; and these two ranks of men, so necessary to each other, can never rightly meet, till one man erects a shop, to which all the workmen and all the customers repair. In this province, grass rises in abundance: The inhabitants abound in cheese, and butter, and cattle; but want bread and corn, which, in a neighbouring province, are in too great abundance for the use of the inhabitants. One man discovers this. He brings corn from the one province and returns with cattle; and supplying the wants of both, he is, so far, a common benefactor. As the people encrease in numbers and industry, the difficulty of their intercourse encreases: The business of the agency or merchandize becomes more intricate; and divides, subdivides, compounds, and mixes to a greater variety. In all these transactions, it is necessary, and reasonable, that a considerable part of the commodities and labour should belong to the merchant, to whom, in a great measure, they are owing. And these commodities he will sometimes preserve in kind, or more commonly convert into money, which is their common representation. If gold and silver have encreased in the state together with the industry, it will require a great quantity of these metals to represent a great quantity of commodities and labour. If industry alone has encreased, the prices of every thing must sink, and a small quantity of specie will serve as a representation.

There is no craving or demand of the human mind more constant and insatiable than that for exercise and employment; and this desire seems the foundation of most of our passions and pursuits. Deprive a man of all business and serious occupation, he runs restless from one amusement to another; and the weight and oppression, which he feels from idleness, is so great, that he forgets the ruin which must follow him from his immoderate expences. Give him a more harmless way of employing his mind or body, he is satisfied, and feels no longer that insatiable thirst after pleasure. But if the employment you give him be lucrative, especially if the profit be attached to every particular exertion of industry, he has gain so often in his eye, that he acquires, by degrees, a passion for it, and knows no such pleasure as that of seeing the daily encrease of his fortune. And this is the reason why trade encreases frugality, and why, among merchants, there is the same overplus of misers above prodigals, as, among the possessors of land, there is the contrary.

Commerce encreases industry, by conveying it readily from one member of the state to another, and allowing none of it to perish or become useless. It encreases frugality, by giving occupation to men, and employing them in the arts of gain, which soon engage their affection, and remove all relish for pleasure and expence. It is an infallible consequence of all industrious professions, to beget frugality, and make the love of gain prevail over the love of pleasure. Among lawyers and physicians who have any practice, there are many more who live within their income, than who exceed it, or even live up to it. But lawyers and physicians beget no industry; and it is even at the expence of others they acquire their riches; so that they are sure to diminish the possessions of some of their fellow-citizens, as fast as they encrease their own. Merchants, on the contrary, beget industry, by serving as canals to convey it through every corner of the state: And at the same time, by their frugality, they acquire great power over that industry, and collect a large property in the labour and commodities, which they are the chief instruments in producing. There is no other profession, therefore, except merchandize, which can make the monied interest considerable, or, in other words, can encrease industry, and, by also encreasing frugality, give a great command of that industry to particular members of the society. Without commerce, the state must consist chiefly of landed gentry, whose prodigality and expence make a continual demand for borrowing; and of peasants, who have no sums to supply that demand. The money never gathers into large stocks or sums, which can be lent at interest. It is dispersed into numberless hands, who either squander it in idle show and magnificence, or employ it in the purchase of the common necessaries of life. Commerce alone assembles it into considerable sums; and this effect it has merely from the industry which it begets, and the frugality which it inspires, independent of that particular quantity of precious metal which may circulate in the state.

Thus an encrease of commerce, by a necessary consequence, raises a great number of lenders, and by that means produces lowness of interest. We must now consider how far this encrease of commerce diminishes the profits arising from that profession, and gives rise to the *third* circumstance requisite to produce lowness of interest.

It may be proper to observe on this head, that low interest and low profits of merchandize are two events, that mutually forward each other, and are both originally derived from that extensive commerce, which produces opulent merchants, and renders the monied interest considerable. Where merchants possess great stocks, whether represented by few or many pieces of metal, it must frequently happen, that, when they either become tired of business, or leave heirs unwilling or unfit to engage in commerce, a great proportion of these riches naturally seeks an annual and secure revenue. The plenty diminishes the price, and makes the lenders accept of a low interest. This consideration obliges many to keep their stock employed in trade, and rather be content with low profits than dispose of their money at an undervalue. On the other hand, when commerce has become extensive, and employs large stocks, there must arise rivalships among the merchants, which diminish the profits of trade, at the same time that they encrease the trade itself. The low profits of merchandize induce the merchants to accept more willingly of a low interest, when they leave off business, and begin to indulge themselves in ease and indolence. It is needless, therefore, to enquire which of these circumstances, to wit, *low interest or low profits*, is the cause, and which the effect? They both arise from an extensive commerce, and mutually forward each other. No man will accept of low profits, where he can have high interest; and no man will accept of low interest, where he can have high profits. An extensive commerce, by producing large stocks, diminishes both interest and profits; and is always assisted, in its diminution of the one, by the proportional sinking of the other. I may add, that, as low profits arise from the encrease of commerce and industry, they serve in their turn to its farther encrease, by rendering the commodities cheaper, encouraging the consumption, and heightening the industry. And thus, if we consider the whole con-nexion of causes and effects, interest is the barometer of the state, and its lowness is a sign almost infallible of the flourishing condition of a people. It proves the encrease of industry, and its prompt circulation through the whole state, little inferior to a demonstration. And though, perhaps, it may not be impossible but a sudden and a great check to commerce may have a momentary effect of the same kind, by throwing so many stocks out of trade; it must be attended with such misery and want of employment in the poor, that, besides its short duration, it will not be possible to mistake the one case for the other.

Those who have asserted, that the plenty of money was the cause of low interest, seem to have taken a collateral effect for a cause; since the same industry, which sinks the interest, commonly acquires great abundance of the precious metals. A variety of fine manufactures, with vigilant enterprising merchants, will soon draw money to a state, if it be any where to be found in the world. The same cause, by multiplying the conveniencies of life, and encreasing industry, collects great riches into the hands of persons, who are not proprietors of land, and produces, by that means, a lowness of interest. But though both these effects, plenty of money and low interest, naturally arise from commerce and indus-try, they are altogether independent of each other. For suppose a nation removed into the *Pacific* ocean, without any foreign commerce, or any knowledge of navigation: Suppose, that this nation possesses always the same stock of coin, but is continually encreasing in its numbers and industry: It is evident, that the price of every commodity must gradually diminish in that kingdom; since it is the proportion between money and any species of goods, which fixes their mutual value; and, upon the present supposition, the conveniencies of life become every day more abundant, without any alteration in the current specie. A less quantity of money, therefore, among this people, will make a rich man, during the times of industry, than would suffice to that purpose, in ignorant and slothful ages. Less money will build a house, portion a daughter, buy an estate, support a manufactory, or maintain a family and equipage. These are the uses for which men borrow money; and therefore, the greater or less quantity of it in a state has no influence on the interest. But it is evident, that the greater or less stock of labour and commodities must have a great influence; since we really and in effect borrow these, when we take money upon interest. It is true, when commerce is extended all over the globe, the most industrious nations always abound most with the precious metals: So that low interest and plenty of money are in fact almost inseparable. But still it is of consequence to know the principle whence any phenomenon arises, and to distinguish between a cause and a concomitant effect.[8] Besides that the speculation is curious, it may frequently be of use in the conduct of public affairs. At least, it must be owned, that nothing can be of more use than to improve, by practice, the method of reasoning on these subjects, which of all others are the most important; though they are commonly treated in the loosest and most careless manner.

Another reason of this popular mistake with regard to the cause of low interest, seems to be the instance of some nations; where, after a sudden acquisition of money or of the precious metals, by means of foreign conquest, the interest has fallen, not only among them, but in all the neighbouring states, as soon as that money was dispersed, and had insinuated itself into every corner. Thus, interest in SPAIN fell near a half immediately after the discovery of the WEST INDIES, as we are informed by GARCILASSO DE LA VEGA:[9] And it has been ever since gradually sinking in every kingdom of EUROPE. Interest in ROME, after the conquest of EGYPT, fell from 6 to 4 *per cent.* as we learn from DION.*

* Lib. ii.[10]

The causes of the sinking of interest, upon such an event, seem different in the conquering country and in the neighbouring states; but in neither of them can we justly ascribe that effect merely to the encrease of gold and silver.

In the conquering country, it is natural to imagine, that this new acquisition of money will fall into a few hands, and be gathered into large sums, which seek a secure revenue, either by the purchase of land or by interest; and consequently the same effect follows, for a little time, as if there had been a great accession of industry and commerce. The encrease of lenders above the borrowers sinks the interest; and so much the faster, if those, who have acquired those large sums, find no industry or commerce in the state, and no method of employing their money but by lending it at interest. But after this new mass of gold and silver has been digested, and has circulated through the whole state, affairs will soon return to their former situation; while the landlords and new money-holders, living idly, squander above their income; and the former daily contract debt, and the latter encroach on their stock till its final extinction. The whole money may still be in the state, and make itself felt by the encrease of prices: But not being now collected into any large masses or stocks, the disproportion between the borrowers and lenders is the same as formerly, and consequently the high interest returns.

Accordingly we find, in ROME, that, so early as TIBERIUS's time, interest had again mounted to 6 *per cent.*\* though no accident had happened to drain the empire of money. In TRAJAN's time, money lent on mortgages in ITALY, bore 6 *per cent.*;† on common securities in BITHYNIA, 12.‡ And if interest in SPAIN has not risen to its old pitch; this can be ascribed to nothing but the continuance of the same cause that sunk it, to wit, the large fortunes continually made in the INDIES, which come over to SPAIN from time to time, and supply the demand of the borrowers. By this accidental and extraneous cause, more money is to be lent in SPAIN, that is, more money is collected into large sums than would otherwise be found in a state, where there are so little commerce and industry.

---

\* COLUMELLA, lib. iii. cap. 3.[11]
† PLINII epist. lib. vii. ep. 18.[12]
‡ Id. lib. x. ep. 62.[13]

As to the reduction of interest, which has followed in ENGLAND, FRANCE, and other kingdoms of EUROPE, that have no mines, it has been gradual; and has not proceeded from the encrease of money, considered merely in itself; but from that of industry, which is the natural effect of the former encrease, in that interval, before it raises the price of labour and provisions. For to return to the foregoing supposition; if the industry of ENGLAND had risen as much from other causes, (and that rise might easily have happened, though the stock of money had remained the same) must not all the same consequences have followed, which we observe at present? The same people would, in that case, be found in the kingdom, the same commodities, the same industry, manufactures, and commerce; and consequently the same merchants, with the same stocks, that is, with the same command over labour and commodities, only represented by a smaller number of white or yellow pieces; which being a circumstance of no moment, would only affect the waggoner, porter, and trunk-maker. Luxury, therefore, manufactures, arts, industry, frugality, flourishing equally as at present, it is evident, that interest must also have been as low; since that is the necessary result of all these circumstances; so far as they determine the profits of commerce, and the proportion between the borrowers and lenders in any state.

# Essay V

## *Of the Balance of Trade*

It is very usual, in nations ignorant of the nature of commerce, to pro-hibit the exportation of commodities, and to preserve among themselves whatever they think valuable and useful. They do not consider, that, in this prohibition, they act directly contrary to their intention; and that the more is exported of any commodity, the more will be raised at home, of which they themselves will always have the first offer.

It is well known to the learned, that the ancient laws of ATHENS rendered the exportation of figs criminal; that being supposed a spe-cies of fruit so excellent in ATTICA, that the ATHENIANS deemed it too delicious for the palate of any foreigner. And in this ridiculous prohib-ition they were so much in earnest, that informers were thence called *sycophants* among them, from two GREEK words, which signify *figs* and *discoverer.*\*[1] There are proofs in many old acts of parliament of the same ignorance in the nature of commerce, particularly in the reign of EDWARD III.[2] And to this day, in FRANCE, the exportation of corn is almost always prohibited; in order, as they say, to prevent famines; though it is evident, that nothing contributes more to the frequent famines, which so much distress that fertile country.

The same jealous fear, with regard to money, has also prevailed among several nations; and it required both reason and experience to convince any people, that these prohibitions serve to no other purpose than to raise the exchange against them, and produce a still greater exportation.[3]

These errors, one may say, are gross and palpable: But there still prevails, even in nations well acquainted with commerce, a strong jeal-ousy with regard to the balance of trade, and a fear, that all their gold

---

\* PLUT. *De Curiositate.*

46

and silver may be leaving them. This seems to me, almost in every case, a groundless apprehension; and I should as soon dread, that all our springs and rivers should be exhausted, as that money should abandon a kingdom where there are people and industry. Let us carefully preserve these latter advantages; and we need never be apprehensive of losing the former.

It is easy to observe, that all calculations concerning the balance of trade are founded on very uncertain facts and suppositions. The customhouse books[4] are allowed to be an insufficient ground of reasoning; nor is the rate of exchange much better; unless we consider it with all nations, and know also the proportions of the several sums remitted; which one may safely pronounce impossible. Every man, who has ever reasoned on this subject, has always proved his theory, whatever it was, by facts and calculations, and by an enumeration of all the commodities sent to all foreign kingdoms.

The writings of Mr. GEE[5] struck the nation with an universal panic, when they saw it plainly demonstrated, by a detail of particulars, that the balance was against them for so considerable a sum as must leave them without a single shilling in five or six years. But luckily, twenty years have since elapsed, with an expensive foreign war;[6] yet is it commonly supposed, that money is still more plentiful among us than in any former period.

Nothing can be more entertaining on this head than Dr. SWIFT;[7] an author so quick in discerning the mistakes and absurdities of others. He says, in his *short view of the state of* IRELAND, that the whole cash of that kingdom formerly amounted but to 500,000*l.*; that out of this the IRISH remitted every year a neat million to ENGLAND, and had scarcely any other source from which they could compensate themselves, and little other foreign trade than the importation of FRENCH wines, for which they paid ready money. The consequence of this situation, which must be owned to be disadvantageous, was, that, in a course of three years, the current money of IRELAND, from 500,000*l.* was reduced to less than two. And at present, I suppose, in a course of 30 years it is absolutely nothing. Yet I know not how, that opinion of the advance of riches in IRELAND, which gave the Doctor so much indignation, seems still to continue, and gain ground with every body.

In short, this apprehension of the wrong balance of trade, appears of such a nature, that it discovers itself, wherever one is out of humour with the ministry, or is in low spirits; and as it can never be refuted by a particular detail of all the exports, which counterbalance the imports, it may here be proper to form a general argument, that may prove the impossibility of this event, as long as we preserve our people and our industry.

Suppose four-fifths of all the money in GREAT BRITAIN to be annihilated in one night, and the nation reduced to the same condition, with regard to specie,[8] as in the reigns of the HARRYS and EDWARDS,[9] what would be the consequence? Must not the price of all labour and commodities sink in proportion, and every thing be sold as cheap as they were in those ages? What nation could then dispute with us in any foreign market, or pretend to navigate or to sell manufactures at the same price, which to us would afford sufficient profit? In how little time, therefore, must this bring back the money which we had lost, and raise us to the level of all the neighbouring nations? Where, after we have arrived, we immediately lose the advantage of the cheapness of labour and commodities; and the farther flowing in of money is stopped by our fulness and repletion.

Again, suppose, that all the money of GREAT BRITAIN were multiplied fivefold in a night, must not the contrary effect follow? Must not all labour and commodities rise to such an exorbitant height, that no neighbouring nations could afford to buy from us; while their commodities, on the other hand, became comparatively so cheap, that, in spite of all the laws which could be formed, they would be run in upon us, and our money flow out; till we fall to a level with foreigners, and lose that great superiority of riches, which had laid us under such disadvantages?

Now, it is evident, that the same causes, which would correct these exorbitant inequalities, were they to happen miraculously, must prevent their happening in the common course of nature, and must for ever, in all neighbouring nations, preserve money nearly proportionable to the art and industry of each nation. All water, wherever it communicates, remains always at a level. Ask naturalists[10] the reason; they tell you, that, were it to be raised in any one place, the superior gravity of that part not being balanced, must depress it, till it meet a counterpoise; and that the same cause, which redresses the inequality when it happens, must for ever prevent it, without some violent external operation.*

---

* There is another cause, though more limited in its operation, which checks the wrong balance of trade, to every particular nation to which the kingdom trades. When we import

Can one imagine, that it had ever been possible, by any laws, or even by any art or industry, to have kept all the money in SPAIN, which the galleons have brought from the INDIES?[11] Or that all commodities could be sold in FRANCE for a tenth of the price which they would yield on the other side of the PYRENEES, without finding their way thither, and draining from that immense treasure? What other reason, indeed, is there, why all nations, at present, gain in their trade with SPAIN and PORTUGAL; but because it is impossible to heap up money, more than any fluid, beyond its proper level? The sovereigns of these countries have shown, that they wanted not inclination to keep their gold and silver to themselves, had it been in any degree practicable.

But as any body of water may be raised above the level of the surrounding element, if the former has no communication with the latter;[12] so in money, if the communication be cut off, by any material or physical impediment, (for all laws alone are ineffectual) there may, in such a case, be a very great inequality of money. Thus the immense distance of CHINA, together with the monopolies of our INDIA companies, obstructing the communication, preserve in EUROPE the gold and silver, especially the latter, in much greater plenty than they are found in that kingdom. But, notwithstanding this great obstruction, the force of the causes abovementioned is still evident. The skill and ingenuity of EUROPE in general surpasses perhaps that of CHINA, with regard to manual arts and manufactures; yet are we never able to trade thither without great disadvantage. And were it not for the continual recruits, which we receive from AMERICA, money would soon sink in EUROPE, and rise in CHINA, till it came nearly to a level in both places. Nor can any reasonable man doubt, but that industrious nation, were they as near us as POLAND or BARBARY, would drain us of the overplus of our specie, and draw to themselves a larger share of the WEST INDIAN treasures. We need not have recourse to a physical attraction, in order to explain the necessity of this operation. There is a moral attraction, arising from the interests and passions of men, which is full as potent and infallible.

---

more goods than we export, the exchange turns against us, and this becomes a new encouragement to export; as much as the charge of carriage and insurance of the money which becomes due would amount to. For the exchange can never rise but a little higher than that sum.

How is the balance kept in the provinces of every kingdom among themselves, but by the force of this principle, which makes it impossible for money to lose its level, and either to rise or sink beyond the proportion of the labour and commodities which are in each province? Did not long experience make people easy on this head, what a fund of gloomy reflections might calculations afford to a melancholy YORKSHIREMAN, while he computed and magnified the sums drawn to LONDON by taxes, absentees, commodities, and found on comparison the opposite articles so much inferior? And no doubt, had the *Heptarchy*[13] subsisted in ENGLAND, the legislature of each state had been continually alarmed by the fear of a wrong balance; and as it is probable that the mutual hatred of these states would have been extremely violent on account of their close neighbourhood, they would have loaded and oppressed all commerce, by a jealous and superfluous caution. Since the union has removed the barriers between SCOTLAND and ENGLAND, which of these nations gains from the other by this free commerce? Or if the former kingdom has received any encrease of riches, can it reasonably be accounted for by any thing but the encrease of its art and industry?[14] It was a common apprehension in ENGLAND, before the union, as we learn from L'ABBE DU BOS,*[15] that SCOTLAND would soon drain them of their treasure, were an open trade allowed; and on the other side the TWEED[16] a contrary apprehension prevailed: With what justice in both, time has shown.

What happens in small portions of mankind, must take place in greater. The provinces of the ROMAN empire, no doubt, kept their balance with each other, and with ITALY, independent of the legislature; as much as the several counties of GREAT BRITAIN, or the several parishes of each county. And any man who travels over EUROPE at this day,[17] may see, by the prices of commodities, that money, in spite of the absurd jealousy of princes and states, has brought itself nearly to a level; and that the difference between one kingdom and another is not greater in this respect, than it is often between different provinces of the same kingdom. Men naturally flock to capital cities, sea-ports, and navigable rivers. There we find more men, more industry, more commodities, and consequently more money; but still the latter difference holds proportion with the former, and the level is preserved.†

* *Les interets d'* ANGLETERRE *mal-entendus.*
† See NOTE [R].

Our jealousy and our hatred of FRANCE are without bounds; and the former sentiment, at least, must be acknowledged reasonable and well-grounded. These passions have occasioned innumerable barriers and obstructions upon commerce, where we are accused of being commonly the aggressors. But what have we gained by the bargain? We lost the FRENCH market for our woollen manufactures, and transferred the commerce of wine to SPAIN and PORTUGAL, where we buy worse liquor at a higher price. There are few ENGLISHMEN who would not think their country absolutely ruined, were FRENCH wines sold in ENGLAND so cheap and in such abundance as to supplant, in some measure, all ale, and home-brewed liquors: But would we lay aside prejudice, it would not be difficult to prove, that nothing could be more innocent, perhaps advantageous. Each new acre of vineyard planted in FRANCE, in order to supply ENGLAND with wine, would make it requisite for the FRENCH to take the produce of an ENGLISH acre, sown in wheat or barley, in order to subsist themselves; and it is evident, that we should thereby get command of the better commodity.[18]

There are many edicts of the FRENCH king, prohibiting the planting of new vineyards, and ordering all those which are lately planted to be grubbed up:[19] So sensible are they, in that country, of the superior value of corn, above every other product.[20]

Mareschal VAUBAN[21] complains often, and with reason, of the absurd duties which load the entry of those wines of LANGUEDOC, GUIENNE, and other southern provinces, that are imported into BRITANNY and NORMANDY. He entertained no doubt but these latter provinces could preserve their balance, notwithstanding the open commerce which he recommends. And it is evident, that a few leagues more navigation to ENGLAND would make no difference; or if it did, that it must operate alike on the commodities of both kingdoms.

There is indeed one expedient by which it is possible to sink, and another by which we may raise money beyond its natural level in any kingdom; but these cases, when examined, will be found to resolve into our general theory, and to bring additional authority to it.

I scarcely know any method of sinking money below its level, but those institutions of banks, funds, and paper-credit,[22] which are so much practised in this kingdom. These render paper equivalent to money, circulate it throughout the whole state, make it supply the place of gold and silver, raise proportionably the price of labour and commodities, and by that means either banish a great part of those precious metals,[23] or prevent their farther encrease. What can be more short-sighted than our reasonings on this head? We fancy, because an individual would be much richer, were his stock of money doubled, that the same good effect would follow were the money of every one encreased; not considering, that this would raise as much the price of every commodity, and reduce every man, in time, to the same condition as before. It is only in our public negociations and transactions with foreigners, that a greater stock of money is advantageous; and as our paper is there absolutely insignificant, we feel, by its means, all the ill effects arising from a great abundance of money, without reaping any of the advantages.*

Suppose that there are 12 millions of paper, which circulate in the kingdom as money, (for we are not to imagine, that all our enormous funds are employed in that shape) and suppose the real cash of the kingdom to be 18 millions: Here is a state which is found by experience to be able to hold a stock of 30 millions. I say, if it be able to hold it, it must of necessity have acquired it in gold and silver, had we not obstructed the entrance of these metals by this new invention of paper. *Whence would it have acquired that sum?* From all the kingdoms of the world. *But why?* Because, if you remove these 12 millions, money in this state is below its level, compared with our neighbours; and we must immediately draw from all of them, till we be full and saturate, so to speak, and can hold no more. By our present politics, we are as careful to stuff the nation with this fine commodity of bank-bills and chequer-notes,[24] as if we were afraid of being overburthened with the precious metals.

It is not to be doubted, but the great plenty of bullion in FRANCE is, in a great measure, owing to the want of paper-credit. The FRENCH have no banks:[25] Merchants bills do not there circulate as with us: Usury or lending on interest is not directly permitted; so that many have large sums in their coffers: Great quantities of plate are used in private houses; and all the churches are full of it. By this means, provisions and labour still remain cheaper among them, than in nations that are not half so

---

* We observed in Essay III.[26] that money, when encreasing, gives encouragement to industry, during the interval between the encrease of money and rise of the prices. A good effect of this nature may follow too from paper-credit; but it is dangerous to precipitate matters, at the risk of losing all by the failing of that credit, as must happen upon any violent shock in public affairs.

rich in gold and silver. The advantages of this situation, in point of trade as well as in great public emergencies, are too evident to be disputed.

The same fashion a few years ago prevailed in GENOA, which still has place in ENGLAND and HOLLAND, of using services of CHINA-ware instead of plate; but the senate, foreseeing the consequence, prohibited the use of that brittle commodity beyond a certain extent; while the use of silver-plate was left unlimited.[27] And I suppose, in their late distresses, they felt the good effect of this ordinance. Our tax on plate is, perhaps, in this view, somewhat impolitic.[28]

Before the introduction of paper-money into our colonies,[29] they had gold and silver sufficient for their circulation. Since the introduction of that commodity, the least inconveniency that has followed is the total banishment of the precious metals. And after the abolition of paper, can it be doubted but money will return, while these colonies possess manufactures and commodities, the only thing valuable in commerce, and for whose sake alone all men desire money.

What pity LYCURGUS[30] did not think of paper-credit, when he wanted to banish gold and silver from SPARTA! It would have served his purpose better than the lumps of iron he made use of as money; and would also have prevented more effectually all commerce with strangers, as being of so much less real and intrinsic value.

It must, however, be confessed, that, as all these questions of trade and money are extremely complicated, there are certain lights, in which this subject may be placed, so as to represent the advantages of paper-credit and banks to be superior to their disadvantages. That they banish specie[31] and bullion from a state is undoubtedly true; and whoever looks no farther than this circumstance does well to condemn them; but specie and bullion are not of so great consequence as not to admit of a compensation, and even an overbalance from the encrease of industry and of credit, which may be promoted by the right use of paper-money. It is well known of what advantage it is to a merchant to be able to discount his bills upon occasion; and every thing that facilitates this species of traffic is favourable to the general commerce of a state. But private bankers are enabled to give such credit by the credit they receive from the depositing of money in their shops; and the bank of ENGLAND in the same manner, from the liberty it has to issue its notes in all payments. There was an invention of this kind, which was fallen upon some years ago by the banks of EDINBURGH; and which, as it is one of the most ingenious ideas that has been executed in commerce, has also been thought advantageous to SCOTLAND. It is there called a BANK-CREDIT; and is of this nature.[32] A man goes to the bank and finds surety to the amount, we shall suppose, of a thousand pounds. This money, or any part of it, he has the liberty of drawing out whenever he pleases, and he pays only the ordinary interest for it, while it is in his hands. He may, when he pleases, repay any sum so small as twenty pounds,[33] and the interest is discounted from the very day of the repayment. The advantages, resulting from this contrivance, are manifold. As a man may find surety nearly to the amount of his substance, and his bank-credit is equivalent to ready money, a merchant does hereby in a manner coin his houses, his household furniture, the goods in his warehouse, the foreign debts due to him, his ships at sea; and can, upon occasion, employ them in all payments, as if they were the current money of the country. If a man borrow a thousand pounds from a private hand, besides that it is not always to be found when required, he pays interest for it, whether he be using it or not: His bank-credit costs him nothing except during the very moment, in which it is of service to him: And this circumstance is of equal advantage as if he had borrowed money at much lower interest. Merchants, likewise, from this invention, acquire a great facility in supporting each other's credit, which is a considerable security against bankruptcies. A man, when his own bank-credit is exhausted, goes to any of his neighbours who is not in the same condition; and he gets the money, which he replaces at his convenience.

After this practice had taken place during some years at EDINBURGH, several companies of merchants at GLASGOW carried the matter farther.[34] They associated themselves into different banks, and issued notes so low as ten shillings, which they used in all payments for goods, manufactures, tradesmen's labour of all kinds; and these notes, from the established credit of the companies, passed as money in all payments throughout the country. By this means, a stock of five thousand pounds was able to perform the same operations as if it were six or seven; and merchants were thereby enabled to trade to a greater extent, and to require less profit in all their transactions. But whatever other advantages result from these inventions, it must still be allowed that, besides giving too great facility to credit, which is dangerous, they banish the precious metals; and nothing can be a more evident proof of it, than a comparison of the past and present condition of SCOTLAND in that particular. It was found, upon the recoinage made after the union,[35] that there was near a million of specie[36] in that country: But notwithstanding the great encrease of riches, commerce and manufactures of all kinds, it is thought, that, even where there is no extraordinary drain made by ENGLAND, the current specie will not now amount to a third of that sum.[37]

But as our projects of paper-credit are almost the only expedient, by which we can sink money below its level; so, in my opinion, the only expedient, by which we can raise money above it, is a practice which we should all exclaim against as destructive, namely, the gathering of large sums into a public treasure, locking them up, and absolutely preventing their circulation. The fluid, not communicating with the neighbouring element, may, by such an artifice, be raised to what height we please. To prove this, we need only return to our first supposition, of annihilating the half or any part of our cash; where we found, that the immediate consequence of such an event would be the attraction of an equal sum from all the neighbouring kingdoms. Nor does there seem to be any necessary bounds set, by the nature of things, to this practice of hoarding. A small city, like GENEVA, continuing this policy for ages, might engross nine tenths of the money of EUROPE. There seems, indeed, in the nature of man, an invincible obstacle to that immense growth of riches. A weak state, with an enormous treasure, will soon become a prey to some of its poorer, but more powerful neighbours. A great state would dissipate its wealth in dangerous and ill-concerted projects; and probably destroy, with it, what is much more valuable, the industry, morals, and numbers of its people. The fluid, in this case, raised to too great a height, bursts and destroys the vessel that contains it; and mixing itself with the surrounding element, soon falls to its proper level.

So little are we commonly acquainted with this principle, that, though all historians agree in relating uniformly so recent an event, as the immense treasure amassed by HARRY VII.[38] (which they make amount to 2,700,000 pounds,) we rather reject their concurring testimony, than admit of a fact, which agrees so ill with our inveterate prejudices. It is indeed probable, that this sum might be three-fourths of all the money in ENGLAND. But where is the difficulty in conceiving, that such a sum might be amassed in twenty years, by a cunning, rapacious, frugal, and almost absolute monarch? Nor is it probable, that the diminution of circulating money was ever sensibly felt by the people, or ever did them any prejudice. The sinking of the prices of all commodities would immediately replace it, by giving ENGLAND the advantage in its commerce with the neighbouring kingdoms.

Have we not an instance, in the small republic of ATHENS with its allies, who, in about fifty years, between the MEDIAN and PELOPON-NESIAN wars,[39] amassed a sum not much inferior to that of HARRY VII.? For all the GREEK historians* and orators† agree, that the ATHENIANS collected in the citadel more than 10,000 talents, which they afterwards dissipated to their own ruin, in rash and imprudent enterprizes. But when this money was set a running, and began to communicate with the surrounding fluid; what was the consequence? Did it remain in the state? No. For we find, by the memorable *census* mentioned by DEMOS-THENES‡ and POLYBIUS,§ that, in about fifty years afterwards, the whole value of the republic, comprehending lands, houses, commodities, slaves, and money, was less than 6000 talents.

What an ambitious high-spirited people was this, to collect and keep in their treasury, with a view to conquests, a sum, which it was every day in the power of the citizens, by a single vote, to distribute among themselves, and which would have gone near to triple the riches of every individual! For we must observe, that the numbers and private riches of the ATHENIANS are said, by ancient writers, to have been no greater at the beginning of the PELOPONNESIAN war, than at the beginning of the MACEDONIAN.

Money was little more plentiful in GREECE during the age of PHILIP and PERSEUS, than in ENGLAND during that of HARRY VII.: Yet these two monarchs in thirty years¶ collected from the small kingdom of MACE-DON, a larger treasure than that of the ENGLISH monarch. PAULUS ÆMILIUS brought to ROME about 1,700,000 pounds *Sterling*.** PLINY says, 2,400,000.†† And that was but a part of the MACEDONIAN treasure. The rest was dissipated by the resistance and flight of PERSEUS.‡‡

We may learn from STANIAN,[40] that the canton of BERNE had 300,000

---

* THUCYDIDES, lib. ii. and DIOD. SIC. lib. xii.[41]
† *Vid. ÆSCHINIS et* DEMOSTHENIS *Epist.*[42]
‡ Περι Συμμοριας.[43]
§ Lib. ii. cap. 62.[44]
¶ TITI LIVII, lib. xlv. cap. 40.[45]
** VEL. PATERC. lib. i. cap. 9.[46]
†† Lib. xxxiii. cap. 3.[47]
‡‡ TITI LIVII, *ibid.*[48]

pounds lent at interest, and had above six times as much in their treasury. Here then is a sum hoarded of 1,800,000 pounds *Sterling*, which is at least quadruple what should naturally circulate in such a petty state; and yet no one, who travels in the PAIS DE VAUX, or any part of that canton, observes any want of money more than could be supposed in a country of that extent, soil, and situation. On the contrary, there are scarce any inland provinces in the continent of FRANCE or GERMANY, where the inhabitants are at this time so opulent, though that canton has vastly encreased its treasure since 1714, the time when STANIAN wrote his judicious account of SWITZERLAND.*

The account given by APPIAN† of the treasure of the PTOLEMIES,[49] is so prodigious, that one cannot admit of it; and so much the less, because the historian says, that the other successors of ALEXANDER were also frugal, and had many of them treasures not much inferior. For this saving humour of the neighbouring princes must necessarily have checked the frugality of the EGYPTIAN monarchs, according to the foregoing theory. The sum he mentions is 740,000 talents, or 191,166,666 pounds 13 shillings and 4 pence, according to Dr. ARBUTHNOT's computation.[50] And yet APPIAN says, that he extracted his account from the public records; and he was himself a native of ALEXANDRIA.

From these principles we may learn what judgment we ought to form of those numberless bars, obstructions, and imposts, which all nations of Europe, and none more than ENGLAND, have put upon trade; from an exorbitant desire of amassing money, which never will heap up beyond its level, while it circulates; or from an ill-grounded apprehension of losing their specie, which never will sink below it. Could any thing scatter our riches, it would be such impolitic contrivances. But this general ill effect, however, results from them, that they deprive neighbouring nations of that free communication and exchange which the Author of the world has intended,[51] by giving them soils, climates, and geniuses, so different from each other.

Our modern politics embrace the only method of banishing money, the using of paper-credit; they reject the only method of amassing it,

---

* The poverty which STANIAN speaks of is only to be seen in the most mountainous cantons, where there is no commodity to bring money. And even there the people are not poorer than in the diocese of SALTSBURGH on the one hand, or SAVOY on the other.
† *Proem.*[52]

the practice of hoarding; and they adopt a hundred contrivances, which serve to no purpose but to check industry, and rob ourselves and our neighbours of the common benefits of art and nature.

All taxes, however, upon foreign commodities, are not to be regarded as prejudicial or useless, but those only which are founded on the jealousy above-mentioned. A tax on German linen encourages home manufactures, and thereby multiplies our people and industry. A tax on brandy encreases the sale of rum, and supports our southern colonies. And as it is necessary, that imposts should be levied, for the support of government, it may be thought more convenient to lay them on foreign commodities, which can easily be intercepted at the port, and subjected to the impost. We ought, however, always to remember the maxim of Dr. SWIFT, That, in the arithmetic of the customs, two and two make not four, but often make only one.[53] It can scarcely be doubted, but if the duties on wine were lowered to a third, they would yield much more to the government than at present: Our people might thereby afford to drink commonly a better and more wholesome liquor; and no prejudice would ensue to the balance of trade, of which we are so jealous. The manufacture of ale beyond the agriculture is but inconsiderable, and gives employment to few hands. The transport of wine and corn would not be much inferior.

But are there not frequent instances, you will say, of states and kingdoms, which were formerly rich and opulent, and are now poor and beggarly? Has not the money left them, with which they formerly abounded? I answer, If they lose their trade, industry, and people, they cannot expect to keep their gold and silver: For these precious metals will hold proportion to the former advantages. When LISBON and AMSTERDAM got the EAST-INDIA trade from VENICE and GENOA, they also got the profits and money which arose from it. Where the seat of government is transferred, where expensive armies are maintained at a distance, where great funds are possessed by foreigners; there naturally follows from these causes a diminution of the specie. But these, we may observe, are violent and forcible methods of carrying away money, and are in time commonly attended with the transport of people and industry. But where these remain, and the drain is not continued, the money always finds its way back again, by a hundred canals, of which we have no notion or suspicion. What immense treasures have been spent, by so many nations, in FLANDERS, since the revolution, in the course of three long wars?[54] More money perhaps than the half of what is at present in EUROPE. But what has now become of it? Is it in the narrow compass of the AUSTRIAN provinces? No, surely: It has most of it returned to the several countries whence it came, and has followed that art and industry, by which at first it was acquired. For above a thousand years, the money of EUROPE has been flowing to ROME,[55] by an open and sensible current; but it has been emptied by many secret and insensible canals: And the want of industry and commerce renders at present the papal dominions the poorest territory in all ITALY.

In short, a government has great reason to preserve with care its people and its manufactures. Its money, it may safely trust to the course of human affairs, without fear or jealousy. Or if it ever give attention to this latter circumstance, it ought only to be so far as it affects the former.

## NOTES

## Note [R]

It must carefully be remarked, that throughout this discourse, wherever I speak of the level of money, I mean always its proportional level to the commodities, labour, industry, and skill, which is in the several states. And I assert, that where these advantages are double, triple, quadruple, to what they are in the neighbouring states, the money infallibly will also be double, triple, quadruple. The only circumstance that can obstruct the exactness of these proportions, is the expence of transporting the commodities from one place to another; and this expence is sometimes unequal. Thus the corn, cattle, cheese, butter, of DERBY-SHIRE, cannot draw the money of LONDON, so much as the manufactures of LONDON draw the money of DERBYSHIRE. But this objection is only a seeming one: For so far as the transport of commodities is expensive, so far is the communication between the places obstructed and imperfect.[56]

# Essay VI

## *Of the Jealousy of Trade*

Having endeavoured to remove one species of ill-founded jealousy,[1] which is so prevalent among commercial nations, it may not be amiss to mention another, which seems equally groundless. Nothing is more usual, among states which have made some advances in commerce, than to look on the progress of their neighbours with a suspicious eye, to consider all trading states as their rivals, and to suppose that it is impossible for any of them to flourish, but at their expence. In opposition to this narrow and malignant opinion,[2] I will venture to assert, that the encrease of riches and commerce in any one nation, instead of hurting, commonly promotes the riches and commerce of all its neighbours; and that a state can scarcely carry its trade and industry very far, where all the surrounding states are buried in ignorance, sloth, and barbarism.

It is obvious, that the domestic industry of a people cannot be hurt by the greatest prosperity of their neighbours; and as this branch of commerce is undoubtedly the most important in any extensive kingdom, we are so far removed from all reason of jealousy. But I go farther, and observe, that where an open communication is preserved among nations, it is impossible but the domestic industry of every one must receive an encrease from the improvements of the others. Compare the situation of GREAT BRITAIN at present, with what it was two centuries ago. All the arts both of agriculture and manufactures were then extremely rude and imperfect. Every improvement, which we have since made, has arisen from our imitation of foreigners; and we ought so far to esteem it happy, that they had previously made advances in arts and ingenuity. But this intercourse is still upheld to our great advantage: Notwithstanding the advanced state of our manufactures, we daily adopt, in every art, the inventions and improvements of our neighbours. The commodity is first imported from abroad, to our great discontent, while we imagine that it drains us of our money: Afterwards, the art itself is gradually imported, to our visible advantage: Yet we continue still to repine,[3] that our neighbours should possess any art, industry, and invention; forgetting that, had they not first instructed us, we should have been at present barbarians; and did they not still continue their instructions, the arts must fall into a state of languor, and lose that emulation and novelty, which contribute so much to their advancement.

The encrease of domestic industry lays the foundation of foreign commerce. Where a great number of commodities are raised and perfected for the home-market, there will always be found some which can be exported with advantage. But if our neighbours have no art or cultivation, they cannot take them; because they will have nothing to give in exchange. In this respect, states are in the same condition as individuals. A single man can scarcely be industrious, where all his fellow-citizens are idle. The riches of the several members of a community contribute to encrease my riches, whatever profession I may follow. They consume the produce of my industry, and afford me the produce of theirs in return.

Nor needs any state entertain apprehensions, that their neighbours will improve to such a degree in every art and manufacture, as to have no demand from them. Nature, by giving a diversity of geniuses, climates, and soils, to different nations, has secured their mutual intercourse and commerce, as long as they all remain industrious and civilized.[4] Nay, the more the arts encrease in any state, the more will be its demands from its industrious neighbours. The inhabitants, having become opulent and skilful, desire to have every commodity in the utmost perfection; and as they have plenty of commodities to give in exchange, they make large importations from every foreign country. The industry of the nations, from whom they import, receives encouragement: Their own is also encreased, by the sale of the commodities which they give in exchange.

But what if a nation has any staple commodity, such as the woollen manufacture is in ENGLAND? Must not the interfering of our neighbours in that manufacture be a loss to us? I answer, that, when any commodity is denominated the staple of a kingdom, it is supposed that this kingdom has some peculiar and natural advantages for raising the commodity; and if, notwithstanding these advantages, they lose such a manufacture, they ought to blame their own idleness, or bad government, not the industry of their neighbours. It ought also to be considered, that, by the encrease of industry among the neighbouring nations, the consumption of every particular species of commodity is also encreased; and though foreign manufactures interfere with them in the market, the demand for their product may still continue, or even encrease. And should it diminish, ought the consequence to be esteemed so fatal? If the spirit of industry be preserved, it may easily be diverted from one branch to another; and the manufacturers of wool, for instance, be employed in linen, silk, iron, or any other commodities, for which there appears to be a demand. We need not apprehend, that all the objects of industry will be exhausted, or that our manufacturers, while they remain on an equal footing with those of our neighbours, will be in danger of wanting employment. The emulation among rival nations serves rather to keep industry alive in all of them: And any people is happier who possess a variety of manufactures, than if they enjoyed one single great manufacture, in which they are all employed. Their situation is less precarious; and they will feel less sensibly those revolutions and uncertainties, to which every particular branch of commerce will always be exposed.

The only commercial state, that ought to dread the improvements and industry of their neighbours, is such a one as the DUTCH, who enjoying no extent of land, nor possessing any number of native commodities, flourish only by their being the brokers, and factors, and carriers of others. Such a people may naturally apprehend, that, as soon as the neighbouring states come to know and pursue their interest, they will take into their own hands the management of their affairs, and deprive their brokers of that profit, which they formerly reaped from it. But though this consequence may naturally be dreaded, it is very long before it takes place; and by art and industry it may be warded off for many generations, if not wholly eluded. The advantage of superior stocks and correspondence is so great, that it is not easily overcome; and as all the transactions encrease by the encrease of industry in the neighbouring states, even a people whose commerce stands on this precarious basis, may at first reap a considerable profit from the flourishing condition of their neighbours. The DUTCH, having mortgaged all their revenues, make not such a figure in political transactions as formerly;[5] but their commerce is surely equal to what it was in the middle of the last century, when they were reckoned among the great powers of EUROPE.

Were our narrow and malignant politics[6] to meet with success, we should reduce all our neighbouring nations to the same state of sloth and ignorance that prevails in MOROCCO and the coast of BARBARY. But what would be the consequence? They could send us no commodities: They could take none from us: Our domestic commerce itself would languish for want of emulation, example, and instruction: And we ourselves should soon fall into the same abject condition, to which we had reduced them. I shall therefore venture to acknowledge, that, not only as a man, but as a BRITISH subject, I pray for the flourishing commerce of GERMANY, SPAIN, ITALY, and even FRANCE itself.[7] I am at least certain, that GREAT BRITAIN, and all those nations, would flourish more, did their sovereigns and ministers adopt such enlarged and benevolent sentiments towards each other.

# Essay VII

## *Of the Balance of Power*

It is a question whether the *idea* of the balance of power be owing entirely to modern policy, or whether the *phrase* only has been invented in these later ages? It is certain, that XENOPHON,* in his Institution of CYRUS, represents the combination of the ASIATIC powers to have arisen from a jealousy of the encreasing force of the MEDES and PERSIANS; and though that elegant composition should be supposed altogether a romance, this sentiment, ascribed by the author to the eastern princes, is at least a proof of the prevailing notion of ancient times.

In all the politics of GREECE, the anxiety, with regard to the balance of power, is apparent, and is expressly pointed out to us, even by the ancient historians. THUCYDIDES† represents the league, which was formed against ATHENS, and which produced the PELOPONNESIAN war, as entirely owing to this principle. And after the decline of ATHENS, when the THEBANS and LACEDEMONIANS disputed for sovereignty, we find, that the ATHENIANS (as well as many other republics) always threw themselves into the lighter scale, and endeavoured to preserve the balance. They supported THEBES against SPARTA, till the great victory gained by EPAMINONDAS at LEUCTRA;[1] after which they immediately went over to the conquered, from generosity, as they pretended, but in reality from their jealousy of the conquerors.‡

Whoever will read DEMOSTHENES's oration for the MEGALO-POLITANS, may see the utmost refinements on this principle, that ever entered into the head of a VENETIAN or ENGLISH speculatist.[2] And upon the first rise of the MACEDONIAN power, this orator immediately

* Lib. i.[3]
† Lib. i.[4]
‡ XENOPH. Hist. GRAEC. lib. vi. & vii.

discovered the danger, sounded the alarm throughout all GREECE, and at last assembled that confederacy under the banners of ATHENS, which fought the great and decisive battle of CHAERONEA.[5]

It is true, the GRECIAN wars are regarded by historians as wars of emulation rather than of politics; and each state seems to have had more in view the honour of leading the rest, than any well-grounded hopes of authority and dominion. If we consider, indeed, the small number of inhabitants in any one republic, compared to the whole, the great difficulty of forming sieges in those times, and the extraordinary bravery and discipline of every freeman among that noble people; we shall conclude, that the balance of power was, of itself, sufficiently secured in GREECE, and needed not to have been guarded with that caution which may be requisite in other ages. But whether we ascribe the shifting of sides in all the GRECIAN republics to *jealous emulation* or *cautious politics*, the effects were alike, and every prevailing power was sure to meet with a confederacy against it, and that often composed of its former friends and allies.

The same principle, call it envy or prudence, which produced the *Ostracism* of ATHENS,[6] and *Petalism* of SYRACUSE,[7] and expelled every citizen whose fame or power overtopped the rest; the same principle, I say, naturally discovered itself in foreign politics, and soon raised enemies to the leading state, however moderate in the exercise of its authority.

The PERSIAN monarch was really, in his force, a petty prince, compared to the GRECIAN republics; and therefore it behoved him, from views of safety more than from emulation, to interest himself in their quarrels, and to support the weaker side in every contest. This was the advice given by ALCIBIADES to TISSAPHERNES,* and it prolonged near a century the date of the PERSIAN empire; till the neglect of it for a moment, after the first appearance of the aspiring genius of PHILIP,[8] brought that lofty and frail edifice to the ground, with a rapidity of which there are few instances in the history of mankind.

The successors of ALEXANDER[9] showed great jealousy of the balance of power; a jealousy founded on true politics and prudence, and which preserved distinct for several ages the partition made after the death of that famous conqueror. The fortune and ambition of ANTIGONUS†

* THUCYD. lib. viii.[10]
† DIOD. SIC. lib. xx.[11]

threatened them anew with a universal monarchy; but their combination, and their victory at IPSUS[12] saved them. And in subsequent times, we find, that, as the Eastern princes considered the GREEKS and MACEDONIANS as the only real military force, with whom they had any intercourse, they kept always a watchful eye over that part of the world. The PTOLEMIES,[13] in particular, supported first ARATUS and the ACHAEANS, and then CLEOMENES king of SPARTA, from no other view than as a counterbalance to the MACEDONIAN monarchs. For this is the account which POLYBIUS gives of the EGYPTIAN politics.*

The reason, why it is supposed, that the ancients were entirely ignorant of the *balance of power*, seems to be drawn from the ROMAN history more than the GRECIAN; and as the transactions of the former are generally more familiar to us, we have thence formed all our conclusions. It must be owned, that the ROMANS never met with any such general combination or confederacy against them, as might naturally have been expected from their rapid conquests and declared ambition; but were allowed peaceably to subdue their neighbours, one after another, till they extended their dominion over the whole known world. Not to mention the fabulous history of their ITALIC wars;[14] there was, upon HANNIBAL's invasion of the ROMAN state,[15] a remarkable crisis, which ought to have called up the attention of all civilized nations. It appeared afterwards (nor was it difficult to be observed at the time)† that this was a contest for universal empire; yet no prince or state seems to have been in the least alarmed about the event or issue of the quarrel. PHILIP of MACEDON[16] remained neuter, till he saw the victories of HANNIBAL; and then most imprudently formed an alliance with the conqueror, upon terms still more imprudent. He stipulated, that he was to assist the CARTHAGINIAN state in their conquest of ITALY; after which they engaged to send over forces into GREECE, to assist him in subduing the GRECIAN commonwealths.‡

The RHODIAN and ACHAEAN republics are much celebrated by ancient historians for their wisdom and sound policy;[17] yet both of them assisted the ROMANS in their wars against PHILIP and ANTIOCHUS.

---

* Lib. ii. cap. 51.[18]

† It was observed by some, as appears by the speech of AGELAUS of NAUPACTUM, in the general congress of GREECE. See POLYB. lib. v. cap. 104.[19]

‡ TITI LIVII, lib. xxiii. cap. 33.[20]

And what may be esteemed still a stronger proof, that this maxim was not generally known in those ages; no ancient author has remarked the imprudence of these measures, nor has even blamed that absurd treaty above-mentioned, made by PHILIP with the CARTHAGINIANS. Princes and statesmen, in all ages, may, before-hand, be blinded in their reasonings with regard to events: But it is somewhat extraordinary, that historians, afterwards, should not form a sounder judgment of them.

MASSINISSA, ATTALUS, PRUSIAS, in gratifying their private passions, were, all of them, the instruments of the Roman greatness; and never seem to have suspected, that they were forging their own chains, while they advanced the conquests of their ally. A simple treaty and agreement between MASSINISSA and the CARTHAGINIANS, so much required by mutual interest, barred the ROMANS from all entrance into AFRICA, and preserved liberty to mankind.[21]

The only prince we meet with in the ROMAN history, who seems to have understood the balance of power, is HIERO king of SYRACUSE. Though the ally of ROME, he sent assistance to the CARTHAG-INIANS, during the war of the auxiliaries;[22] "Esteeming it requisite," says POLYBIUS,* "both in order to retain his dominions in SICILY, and to preserve the ROMAN friendship, that CARTHAGE should be safe; lest by its fall the remaining power should be able, without contrast or opposition, to execute every purpose and undertaking. And here he acted with great wisdom and prudence. For that is never, on any account, to be overlooked; nor ought such a force ever to be thrown into one hand, as to incapacitate the neighbouring states from defending their rights against it." Here is the aim of modern politics pointed out in express terms.

In short, the maxim of preserving the balance of power is founded so much on common sense and obvious reasoning, that it is impossible it could altogether have escaped antiquity, where we find, in other particulars, so many marks of deep penetration and discernment. If it was not so generally known and acknowledged as at present, it had, at least, an influence on all the wiser and more experienced princes and politicians. And indeed, even at present, however generally known and acknowledged among speculative reasoners, it has not, in practice, an authority much more extensive among those who govern the world.

* Lib. i. cap. 83.[23]

After the fall of the ROMAN empire, the form of government, established by the northern conquerors, incapacitated them, in a great measure, for farther conquests, and long maintained each state in its proper boundaries. But when vassalage and the feudal militia were abolished, mankind were anew alarmed by the danger of universal monarchy, from the union of so many kingdoms and principalities in the person of the emperor CHARLES.[24] But the power of the house of AUSTRIA, founded on extensive but divided dominions, and their riches, derived chiefly from mines of gold and silver,[25] were more likely to decay, of themselves, from internal defects, than to overthrow all the bulwarks raised against them. In less than a century, the force of that violent and haughty race was shattered, their opulence dissipated, their splendor eclipsed. A new power succeeded,[26] more formidable to the liberties of EUROPE, possessing all the advantages of the former, and labouring under none of its defects, except a share of that spirit of bigotry and persecution, with which the house of AUSTRIA was so long, and still is so much infatuated.[27]

In the general wars,[28] maintained against this ambitious power, GREAT BRITAIN has stood foremost; and she still maintains her station. Beside her advantages of riches and situation, her people are animated with such a national spirit, and are so fully sensible of the blessings of their government, that we may hope their vigour never will languish in so necessary and so just a cause. On the contrary, if we may judge by the past, their passionate ardour seems rather to require some moderation; and they have oftener erred from a laudable excess than from a blameable deficiency.

In the *first* place, we seem to have been more possessed with the ancient GREEK spirit of jealous emulation, than actuated by the prudent views of modern politics. Our wars with FRANCE have been begun with justice, and even, perhaps, from necessity; but have always been too far pushed from obstinacy and passion.[29] The same peace, which was afterwards made at RYSWICK in 1697,[30] was offered so early as the year ninety-two; that concluded at UTRECHT[31] in 1712 might have been finished on as good conditions at GERTRUYTENBERG in the year eight; and we might have given at FRANKFORT, in 1743, the same terms, which we were glad to accept of at AIX-LA-CHAPELLE[32] in the year forty-eight. Here then we see, that above half of our wars with FRANCE, and all our public debts, are owing more to our own imprudent vehemence, than to the ambition of our neighbours.[33]

In the *second* place, we are so declared in our opposition to FRENCH power, and so alert in defence of our allies, that they always reckon upon our force as upon their own; and expecting to carry on war at our expence, refuse all reasonable terms of accommodation. *Habent subjectos, tanquam suos; viles, ut alienos.*[34] All the world knows, that the factious vote of the House of Commons, in the beginning of the last parliament, with the professed humour of the nation, made the queen of HUNGARY inflexible in her terms, and prevented that agreement with PRUSSIA, which would immediately have restored the general tranquillity of EUROPE.[35]

In the *third* place, we are such true combatants, that, when once engaged, we lose all concern for ourselves and our posterity, and consider only how we may best annoy the enemy. To mortgage our revenues at so deep a rate, in wars, where we were only accessories, was surely the most fatal delusion, that a nation, which had any pretension to politics and prudence, has ever yet been guilty of. That remedy of funding,[36] if it be a remedy, and not rather a poison, ought, in all reason, to be reserved to the last extremity; and no evil, but the greatest and most urgent, should ever induce us to embrace so dangerous an expedient.

These excesses, to which we have been carried, are prejudicial; and may, perhaps, in time, become still more prejudicial another way, by begetting, as is usual, the opposite extreme, and rendering us totally careless and supine with regard to the fate of EUROPE. The ATHENIANS, from the most bustling, intriguing, warlike people of GREECE, finding their error in thrusting themselves into every quarrel, abandoned all attention to foreign affairs; and in no contest ever took part on either side, except by their flatteries and complaisance to the victor.

Enormous monarchies are, probably, destructive to human nature; in their progress, in their continuance,* and even in their downfal, which never can be very distant from their establishment. The military genius, which aggrandized the monarchy, soon leaves the court, the capital, and the center of such a government; while the wars are carried on at a great distance, and interest so small a part of the state. The ancient nobility, whose affections attach them to their sovereign, live all at court; and never will accept of military employments, which would carry them to remote and barbarous frontiers, where they are

---

* If the ROMAN empire was of advantage, it could only proceed from this, that mankind were generally in a very disorderly, uncivilized condition, before its establishment.[37]

distant both from their pleasures and their fortune. The arms of the state, must, therefore, be entrusted to mercenary strangers, without zeal, without attachment, without honour; ready on every occasion to turn them against the prince, and join each desperate malcontent, who offers pay and plunder.[38] This is the necessary progress of human affairs: Thus human nature checks itself in its airy elevation: Thus ambition blindly labours for the destruction of the conqueror, of his family, and of every thing near and dear to him. The BOURBONS, trusting to the support of their brave, faithful, and affectionate nobility, would push their advantage, without reserve or limitation. These, while fired with glory and emulation, can bear the fatigues and dangers of war; but never would submit to languish in the garrisons of HUNGARY or LITHUANIA, forgot at court, and sacrificed to the intrigues of every minion or mistress, who approaches the prince. The troops are filled with CRAVATES and TARTARS, HUSSARS and COSSACS;[39] intermingled, perhaps, with a few soldiers of fortune from the better provinces: And the melancholy fate of the ROMAN emperors, from the same cause, is renewed over and over again, till the final dissolution of the monarchy.

# Essay VIII

## *Of Taxes*

There is a prevailing maxim, among some reasoners,[1] *that every new tax creates a new ability in the subject to bear it, and that each encrease of public burdens encreases proportionably the industry of the people.* This maxim is of such a nature as is most likely to be abused; and is so much the more dangerous, as its truth cannot be altogether denied: but it must be owned, when kept within certain bounds, to have some foundation in reason and experience.

When a tax is laid upon commodities, which are consumed by the common people, the necessary consequence may seem to be, either that the poor must retrench something from their way of living, or raise their wages, so as to make the burden of the tax fall entirely upon the rich. But there is a third consequence, which often follows upon taxes, namely, that the poor encrease their industry, perform more work, and live as well as before, without demanding more for their labour. Where taxes are moderate, are laid on gradually, and affect not the necessaries of life, this consequence naturally follows; and it is certain, that such difficulties often serve to excite the industry of a people, and render them more opulent and laborious, than others, who enjoy the greatest advantages. For we may observe, as a parallel instance, that the most commercial nations have not always possessed the greatest extent of fertile land; but, on the contrary, that they have laboured under many natural disadvantages.[2] TYRE, ATHENS, CARTHAGE, RHODES, GENOA, VENICE, HOLLAND,[3] are strong examples to this purpose. And in all history, we find only three instances of large and fertile countries, which have possessed much trade; the NETHERLANDS, ENGLAND, and FRANCE. The two former seem to have been allured by the advantages of their maritime situation, and the necessity they lay under of frequenting foreign ports, in order to procure what their own climate refused them. And as to FRANCE, trade has come late into that kingdom,[4] and seems to have been the effect of reflection and observation in an ingenious and enterprizing people, who remarked the riches acquired by such of the neighbouring nations as cultivated navigation and commerce.

The places mentioned by CICERO,* as possessed of the greatest commerce in his time, are ALEXANDRIA, COLCHUS, TYRE, SIDON, ANDROS, CYPRUS, PAMPHYLIA, LYCIA, RHODES, CHIOS, BYZANTIUM, LESBOS, SMYRNA, MILETUM, COOS. All these, except ALEXANDRIA, were either small islands, or narrow territories. And that city owed its trade entirely to the happiness of its situation.

Since therefore some natural necessities or disadvantages may be thought favourable to industry, why may not artificial burdens have the same effect? Sir WILLIAM TEMPLE,† we may observe, ascribes the industry of the DUTCH entirely to necessity, proceeding from their natural disadvantages; and illustrates his doctrine by a striking comparison with IRELAND; "where," says he, "by the largeness and plenty of the soil, and scarcity of people, all things necessary to life are so cheap, that an industrious man, by two days labour, may gain enough to feed him the rest of the week. Which I take to be a very plain ground of the laziness attributed to the people. For men naturally prefer ease before labour, and will not take pains if they can live idle; though when, by necessity, they have been inured to it, they cannot leave it, being grown a custom necessary to their health, and to their very entertainment. Nor perhaps is the change harder, from constant ease to labour, than from constant labour to ease." After which the author proceeds to confirm his doctrine, by enumerating, as above, the places where trade has most flourished, in ancient and modern times; and which are commonly observed to be such narrow confined territories, as beget a necessity for industry.[5]

The best taxes are such as are levied upon consumptions,[6] especially those of luxury;[7] because such taxes are least felt by the people.[8] They seem, in some measure, voluntary;[9] since a man may chuse how far he will use the commodity which is taxed: They are paid gradually and insensibly:[10] They naturally produce sobriety and frugality,[11] if judiciously imposed: And being confounded with the natural price of the

* Epist. ad ATT. lib. ix. ep. 11.[12]
† Account of the NETHERLANDS, chap. 6.[13]

commodity, they are scarcely perceived by the consumers. Their only disadvantage is, that they are expensive in the levying.[14]

Taxes upon possessions are levied without expence; but have every other disadvantage. Most states, however, are obliged to have recourse to them, in order to supply the deficiencies of the other.[15]

But the most pernicious of all taxes are the arbitrary.[16] They are commonly converted, by their management, into punishments on industry; and also, by their unavoidable inequality, are more grievous, than by the real burden which they impose. It is surprising, therefore, to see them have place among any civilized people.

In general, all poll-taxes,[17] even when not arbitrary, which they commonly are, may be esteemed dangerous: Because it is so easy for the sovereign to add a little more, and a little more, to the sum demanded, that these taxes are apt to become altogether oppressive and intolerable. On the other hand, a duty upon commodities checks itself;[18] and a prince will soon find, that an encrease of the impost is no encrease of his revenue. It is not easy, therefore, for a people to be altogether ruined by such taxes.

Historians inform us, that one of the chief causes of the destruction of the ROMAN state, was the alteration, which CONSTANTINE introduced into the finances, by substituting an universal poll-tax, in lieu of almost all the tithes, customs, and excises, which formerly composed the revenue of the *empire*.[19] The people, in all the provinces, were so grinded and oppressed by the *publicans*,[20] that they were glad to take refuge under the conquering arms of the barbarians; whose dominion, as they had fewer necessities and less art, was found preferable to the refined tyranny of the ROMANS.

It is an opinion, zealously promoted by some political writers, that, since all taxes, as they pretend, fall ultimately upon land, it were better to lay them originally there, and abolish every duty upon consumptions.[21] But it is denied, that all taxes fall ultimately upon land. If a duty be laid upon any commodity, consumed by an artisan, he has two obvious expedients for paying it; he may retrench somewhat of his expence, or he may encrease his labour. Both these resources are more easy and natural, than that of heightening his wages.[22] We see, that, in years of scarcity, the weaver either consumes less or labours more, or employs both these expedients of frugality and industry, by which he is enabled to reach the end of the year. It is but just, that he should subject himself to the same hardships, if they deserve the name, for the sake of the publick, which gives him protection.[23] By what contrivance can he raise the price of his labour? The manufacturer who employs him, will not give him more: Neither can he, because the merchant, who exports the cloth, cannot raise its price, being limited by the price which it yields in foreign markets. Every man, to be sure, is desirous of pushing off from himself the burden of any tax, which is imposed, and of laying it upon others: But as every man has the same inclination, and is upon the defensive; no set of men can be supposed to prevail altogether in this contest. And why the landed gentleman should be the victim of the whole, and should not be able to defend himself, as well as others are, I cannot readily imagine. All tradesmen, indeed, would willingly prey upon him, and divide him among them, if they could: But this inclination they always have, though no taxes were levied; and the same methods, by which he guards against the imposition of tradesmen before taxes, will serve him afterwards, and make them share the burden with him. They must be very heavy taxes, indeed, and very injudiciously levied, which the artizan will not, of himself, be enabled to pay, by superior industry and frugality, without raising the price of his labour.

I shall conclude this subject with observing, that we have, with regard to taxes, an instance of what frequently happens in political institutions, that the consequences of things are diametrically opposite to what we should expect on the first appearance. It is regarded as a fundamental maxim of the TURKISH government, that the *Grand Signior*,[24] though absolute master of the lives and fortunes of each individual, has no authority to impose a new tax; and every OTTOMAN prince, who has made such an attempt, either has been obliged to retract, or has found the fatal effects of his perseverance.[25] One would imagine, that this prejudice or established opinion were the firmest barrier in the world against oppression; yet it is certain, that its effect is quite contrary. The emperor, having no regular method of encreasing his revenue, must allow all the bashaws and governors to oppress and abuse the subjects: And these he squeezes after their return from their government. Whereas, if he could impose a new tax, like our EUROPEAN princes, his interest would so far be united with that of his people, that he would immediately feel the bad effects of these disorderly levies of money, and would find, that a pound, raised by a general imposition, would have less pernicious effects, than a shilling taken in so unequal and arbitrary a manner.

# Essay IX

## *Of Public Credit*

It appears to have been the common practice of antiquity, to make pro-vision, during peace, for the necessities of war, and to hoard up treasures before-hand,[1] as the instruments either of conquest or defence; without trusting to extraordinary impositions, much less to borrowing, in times of disorder and confusion. Besides the immense sums above mentioned,* which were amassed by ATHENS, and by the PTOLEMIES,[2] and other successors of ALEXANDER; we learn from PLATO,† that the frugal LACEDEMONIANS had also collected a great treasure; and ARRIAN‡ and PLUTARCH§ take notice of the riches which ALEXANDER got possession of on the conquest of SUSA and ECBATANA, and which were reserved, some of them, from the time of CYRUS. If I remember right, the scripture also mentions the treasure of HEZEKIAH and the JEWISH princes;[3] as pro-fane history does that of PHILIP and PERSEUS, kings of MACEDON.[4] The ancient republics of GAUL had commonly large sums in reserve.¶ Every one knows the treasure seized in ROME by JULIUS CÆSAR, during the civil wars:[5] and we find afterwards, that the wiser emperors, AUGUSTUS, TIBERIUS, VESPASIAN, SEVERUS, &c. always discovered[6] the prudent foresight, of saving great sums against any public exigency.[7]

On the contrary, our modern expedient, which has become very gen-eral, is to mortgage the public revenues, and to trust that posterity will pay off the incumbrances contracted by their ancestors: And they,

---

* Essay V.[8]
† ALCIB. I.[9]
‡ Lib. iii.[10]
§ PLUT. *in vita* ALEX.[11] He makes these treasures amount to 80,000 talents, or about 55 millions sterl. QUINTUS CURTIUS (lib. v. cap. 2.) says, that ALEXANDER found in SUSA above 50,000 talents.
¶ STRABO, lib. iv.[12]

having before their eyes, so good an example of their wise fathers, have the same prudent reliance on *their* posterity; who, at last, from necessity more than choice, are obliged to place the same confidence in a new posterity. But not to waste time in declaiming against a practice which appears ruinous, beyond all controversy; it seems pretty apparent, that the ancient maxims are, in this respect, more prudent than the modern;[13] even though the latter had been confined within some reasonable bounds, and had ever, in any instance, been attended with such frugality, in time of peace, as to discharge the debts incurred by an expensive war. For why should the case be so different between the public and an individual, as to make us establish different maxims of conduct for each? If the funds of the former be greater, its necessary expences are proportionably larger; if its resources be more numerous, they are not infinite; and as its frame should be calculated for a much longer duration than the date of a single life, or even of a family, it should embrace maxims, large, durable, and generous, agreeably to the supposed extent of its existence. To trust to chances and temporary expedients, is, indeed, what the necessity of human affairs frequently renders unavoidable; but whoever voluntarily depend on such resources, have not necessity, but their own folly, to accuse for their misfortunes, when any such befal them.

If the abuses of treasures be dangerous, either by engaging the state in rash enterprizes, or making it neglect military discipline, in confidence of its riches; the abuses of mortgaging are more certain and inevitable; poverty, impotence, and subjection to foreign powers.

According to modern policy war is attended with every destructive circumstance; loss of men, encrease of taxes, decay of commerce, dissipation of money, devastation by sea and land. According to ancient maxims, the opening of the public treasure, as it produced an uncommon affluence of gold and silver, served as a temporary encouragement to industry, and atoned, in some degree, for the inevitable calamities of war.

It is very tempting to a minister to employ such an expedient, as enables him to make a great figure during his administration, without overburthening the people with taxes, or exciting any immediate clamours against himself. The practice, therefore, of contracting debt will almost infallibly be abused, in every government. It would scarcely be more imprudent to give a prodigal son a credit in every banker's shop in London, than to impower a statesman to draw bills, in this manner, upon posterity.[14]

What then shall we say to the new paradox, that public incumbrances, are, of themselves, advantageous, independent of the necessity of contracting them; and that any state, even though it were not pressed by a foreign enemy, could not possibly have embraced a wiser expedient for promoting commerce and riches, than to create funds, and debts, and taxes, without limitation?[15] Reasonings, such as these, might naturally have passed for trials of wit among rhetoricians, like the panegyrics on folly and a fever, on BUSIRIS and NERO,[16] had we not seen such absurd maxims patronized by great ministers, and by a whole party[17] among us.

Let us examine the consequences of public debts, both in our domestic management, by their influence on commerce and industry; and in our foreign transactions, by their effect on wars and negociations.

Public securities are with us become a kind of money, and pass as readily at the current price as gold or silver. Wherever any profitable undertaking offers itself, how expensive soever, there are never wanting hands enow to embrace it; nor need a trader, who has sums in the public stocks, fear to launch out into the most extensive trade; since he is possessed of funds, which will answer the most sudden demand that can be made upon him. No merchant thinks it necessary to keep by him any considerable cash. Bank-stock, or India-bonds,[18] especially the latter, serve all the same purposes; because he can dispose of them, or pledge them to a banker, in a quarter of an hour; and at the same time they are not idle, even when in his scritoire,[19] but bring him in a constant revenue. In short, our national debts furnish merchants with a species of money, that is continually multiplying in their hands, and produces sure gain, besides the profits of their commerce. This must enable them to trade upon less profit. The small profit of the merchant renders the commodity cheaper, causes a greater consumption, quickens the labour of the common people, and helps to spread arts and industry throughout the whole society.[20]

There are also, we may observe, in ENGLAND and in all states, which have both commerce and public debts, a set of men, who are half merchants, half stock-holders, and may be supposed willing to trade for small profits; because commerce is not their principal or sole support, and their revenues in the funds are a sure resource for themselves and their families. Were there no funds, great merchants would have no expedient for realizing or securing any part of their profit, but by making purchases of land; and land has many disadvantages in comparison of funds. Requiring more care and inspection, it divides the time and attention of the merchant; upon any tempting offer or extraordinary accident in trade, it is not so easily converted into money; and as it attracts too much, both by the many natural pleasures it affords, and the authority it gives, it soon converts the citizen into the country gentleman. More men, therefore, with large stocks and incomes, may naturally be supposed to continue in trade, where there are public debts; and this, it must be owned, is of some advantage to commerce, by diminishing its profits, promoting circulation, and encouraging industry.

But, in opposition to these two favourable circumstances, perhaps of no very great importance, weigh the many disadvantages which attend our public debts, in the whole *interior* œconomy of the state: You will find no comparison between the ill and the good which result from them.

*First*, It is certain, that national debts cause a mighty confluence of people and riches to the capital, by the great sums, levied in the provinces to pay the interest; and perhaps, too, by the advantages in trade above mentioned, which they give the merchants in the capital above the rest of the kingdom. The question is, whether, in our case, it be for the public interest, that so many privileges should be conferred on LONDON, which has already arrived at such an enormous size,[21] and seems still encreasing? Some men are apprehensive of the consequences. For my own part, I cannot forbear thinking, that, though the head is undoubtedly too large for the body, yet that great city is so happily situated, that its excessive bulk causes less inconvenience than even a smaller capital to a greater kingdom. There is more difference between the prices of all provisions in PARIS and LANGUEDOC, than between those in LONDON and YORKSHIRE. The immense greatness, indeed, of LONDON, under a government which admits not of discretionary power, renders the people factious, mutinous, seditious, and even perhaps rebellious. But to this evil the national debts themselves tend to provide a remedy. The first visible eruption, or even immediate danger, of public disorders must alarm all the stock-holders, whose property is the most precarious of any; and will make them fly to the support of government, whether menaced by Jacobitish violence[22] or democratical frenzy.[23]

*Secondly*, Public stocks, being a kind of paper-credit, have all the disadvantages attending that species of money. They banish gold and silver from the most considerable commerce of the state, reduce them to common circulation, and by that means render all provisions and labour dearer than otherwise they would be.

*Thirdly*, The taxes, which are levied to pay the interests of these debts, are apt either to heighten the price of labour, or be an oppression on the poorer sort.

*Fourthly*, As foreigners possess a great share of our national funds,[24] they render the public, in a manner, tributary to them, and may in time occasion the transport of our people and our industry.

*Fifthly*, The greater part of the public stock being always in the hands of idle people, who live on their revenue, our funds, in that view, give great encouragement to an useless and unactive life.

But though the injury, that arises to commerce and industry from our public funds, will appear, upon balancing the whole, not inconsiderable, it is trivial, in comparison of the prejudice that results to the state considered as a body politic, which must support itself in the society of nations,[25] and have various transactions with other states in wars and negociations. The ill, there, is pure and unmixed, without any favourable circumstance to atone for it; and it is an ill too of a nature the highest and most important.

We have, indeed, been told, that the public is no weaker upon account of its debts; since they are mostly due among ourselves, and bring as much property to one as they take from another. It is like transferring money from the right hand to the left; which leaves the person neither richer nor poorer than before.[26] Such loose reasonings and specious comparisons will always pass, where we judge not upon principles. I ask, Is it possible, in the nature of things, to overburthen a nation with taxes, even where the sovereign resides among them? The very doubt seems extravagant; since it is requisite, in every community, that there be a certain proportion observed between the laborious and the idle part of it. But if all our present taxes be mortgaged, must we not invent new ones? And may not this matter be carried to a length that is ruinous and destructive?

In every nation, there are always some methods of levying money more easy than others, agreeably to the way of living of the people, and the commodities they make use of. In GREAT BRITAIN, the excises upon malt and beer afford a large revenue; because the operations of malting and brewing are tedious, and are impossible to be concealed; and at the same time, these commodities are not so absolutely necessary to life, as that the raising of their price would very much affect the poorer sort. These taxes being all mortgaged, what difficulty to find new ones! what vexation and ruin of the poor!

Duties upon consumptions are more equal and easy than those upon possessions.[27] What a loss to the public, that the former are all exhausted, and that we must have recourse to the more grievous method of levying taxes!

Were all the proprietors of land only stewards to the public, must not necessity force them to practise all the arts of oppression used by stewards; where the absence or negligence of the proprietor render them secure against enquiry?

It will scarcely be asserted, that no bounds ought ever to be set to national debts; and that the public would be no weaker, were twelve or fifteen shillings in the pound, land-tax, mortgaged, with all the present customs and excises. There is something, therefore, in the case, beside the mere transferring of property from the one hand to another. In 500 years, the posterity of those now in the coaches, and of those upon the boxes, will probably have changed places, without affecting the public by these revolutions.

Suppose the public once fairly brought to that condition, to which it is hastening with such amazing rapidity; suppose the land to be taxed eighteen or nineteen shillings in the pound; for it can never bear the whole twenty; suppose all the excises and customs to be screwed up to the utmost which the nation can bear, without entirely losing its commerce and industry; and suppose that all those funds are mortgaged to perpetuity, and that the invention and wit of all our projectors can find no new imposition, which may serve as the foundation of a new loan; and let us consider the necessary consequences of this situation. Though the imperfect state of our political knowledge, and the narrow capacities of men, make it difficult to foretel the effects which will result from any untried measure, the seeds of ruin are here scattered with such profusion as not to escape the eye of the most careless observer.

In this unnatural state of society, the only persons, who possess any revenue beyond the immediate effects of their industry, are the stockholders, who draw almost all the rent of the land and houses, besides the produce of all the customs and excises. These are men, who have no connexions with the state,[28] who can enjoy their revenue in any part of the globe in which they chuse to reside, who will naturally bury themselves in the capital or in great cities, and who will sink into the lethargy of a stupid and pampered luxury, without spirit, ambition, or enjoyment. Adieu to all ideas of nobility, gentry, and family.[29] The stocks can be transferred in an instant, and being in such a fluctuating state, will seldom be transmitted during three generations from father to son. Or were they to remain ever so long in one family, they convey no hereditary authority or credit to the possessor; and by this means, the several ranks of men, which form a kind of independent magistracy in a state, instituted by the hand of nature, are entirely lost; and every man in authority derives his influence from the commission alone of the sovereign.[30] No expedient remains for preventing or suppressing insurrections, but mercenary armies:[31] No expedient at all remains for resisting tyranny: Elections are swayed by bribery and corruption alone:[32] And the middle power between king and people being totally removed, a grievous despotism must infallibly prevail. The landholders, despised for their poverty, and hated for their oppressions, will be utterly unable to make any opposition to it.

Though a resolution should be formed by the legislature never to impose any tax which hurts commerce and discourages industry, it will be impossible for men, in subjects of such extreme delicacy, to reason so justly as never to be mistaken, or amidst difficulties so urgent, never to be seduced from their resolution. The continual fluctuations in commerce require continual alterations in the nature of the taxes; which exposes the legislature every moment to the danger both of wilful and involuntary error. And any great blow given to trade, whether by injudicious taxes or by other accidents, throws the whole system of government into confusion.

But what expedient can the public now employ, even supposing trade to continue in the most flourishing condition, in order to support its foreign wars and enterprizes, and to defend its own honour and interests, or those of its allies? I do not ask how the public is to exert such a prodigious power as it has maintained during our late wars;[33] where we have so much exceeded, not only our own natural strength, but even that of the greatest empires. This extravagance is the abuse complained of, as the source of all the dangers, to which we are at present exposed. But since we must still suppose great commerce and opulence to remain, even after every fund is mortgaged; these riches must be defended by proportional power; and whence is the public to derive the revenue which supports it? It must plainly be from a continual taxation of the annuitants, or, which is the same thing, from mortgaging anew, on every exigency, a certain part of their annuities; and thus making them contribute to their own defence, and to that of the nation. But the difficulties, attending this system of policy, will easily appear, whether we suppose the king to have become absolute master, or to be still controuled by national councils, in which the annuitants themselves must necessarily bear the principal sway.

If the prince has become absolute, as may naturally be expected from this situation of affairs, it is so easy for him to encrease his exactions upon the annuitants, which amount only to the retaining money in his own hands, that this species of property would soon lose all its credit, and the whole income of every individual in the state must lie entirely at the mercy of the sovereign: A degree of despotism, which no oriental monarchy has ever yet attained. If, on the contrary, the consent of the annuitants[34] be requisite for every taxation, they will never be persuaded to contribute sufficiently even to the support of government; as the diminution of their revenue must in that case be very sensible, would not be disguised under the appearance of a branch of excise or customs, and would not be shared by any other order of the state, who are already supposed to be taxed to the utmost. There are instances, in some republics, of a hundredth penny, and sometimes of the fiftieth, being given to the support of the state; but this is always an extraordinary exertion of power, and can never become the foundation of a constant national defence. We have always found, where a government has mortgaged all its revenues, that it necessarily sinks into a state of languor, inactivity, and impotence.[35]

Such are the inconveniencies, which may reasonably be foreseen, of this situation, to which GREAT BRITAIN is visibly tending. Not to mention, the numberless inconveniencies, which cannot be foreseen, and which must result from so monstrous a situation as that of making the public the chief or sole proprietor of land, besides investing it with every branch of customs and excise, which the fertile imagination of ministers and projectors have been able to invent.

I must confess, that there is a strange supineness,[36] from long custom, creeped into all ranks of men, with regard to public debts, not unlike what divines so vehemently complain of with regard to their religious doctrines. We all own, that the most sanguine imagination cannot hope, either that this or any future ministry will be possessed of such rigid and steady frugality, as to make a considerable progress in the payment of our debts; or that the situation of foreign affairs will, for any long time, allow them leisure and tranquillity for such an undertaking. *What then is to become of us?*[37] Were we ever so good Christians, and ever so resigned to Providence; this, methinks, were a curious question, even considered as a speculative one, and what it might not be altogether impossible to form some conjectural solution of. The events here will depend little upon the contingencies of battles, negociations, intrigues, and factions. There seems to be a natural progress of things, which may guide our reasoning. As it would have required but a moderate share of prudence, when we first began this practice of mortgaging, to have foretold, from the nature of men and of ministers, that things would necessarily be carried to the length we see; so now, that they have at last happily reached it, it may not be difficult to guess at the consequences. It must, indeed, be one of these two events; either the nation must destroy public credit, or public credit will destroy the nation. It is impossible that they can both subsist, after the manner they have been hitherto managed, in this, as well as in some other countries.

There was, indeed, a scheme for the payment of our debts, which was proposed by an excellent citizen, Mr. HUTCHINSON,[38] above thirty years ago, and which was much approved of by some men of sense, but never was likely to take effect. He asserted, that there was a fallacy in imagining that the public owed this debt; for that really every individual owed a proportional share of it, and paid, in his taxes, a proportional share of the interest, beside the expence of levying these taxes. Had we not better, then, says he, make a distribution of the debt among ourselves, and each of us contribute a sum suitable to his property, and by that means discharge at once all our funds and public mortgages? He seems not to have considered, that the laborious poor pay a considerable part of the taxes by their annual consumptions,[39] though they could not advance, at once, a proportional part of the sum required. Not to mention, that property in money and stock in trade might easily be concealed or disguised; and that visible property in lands and houses would really at last answer for the whole: An inequality and oppression, which never would be submitted to. But though this project is not likely to take place; it is not altogether improbable, that, when the nation becomes heartily sick of their debts, and is cruelly oppressed by them, some daring projector may arise with visionary schemes for their discharge.[40] And as public credit will begin, by that time, to be a little frail, the least touch will destroy it, as happened in FRANCE during the regency;[41] and in this manner it will *die of the doctor.*

But it is more probable, that the breach of national faith will be the necessary effect of wars, defeats, misfortunes, and public calamities, or even perhaps of victories and conquests. I must confess, when I see princes and states fighting and quarrelling, amidst their debts, funds, and public mortgages, it always brings to my mind a match of cudgel-playing fought in a *China* shop. How can it be expected, that sovereigns will spare a species of property, which is pernicious to themselves and to the public, when they have so little compassion on lives and properties, that are useful to both? Let the time come (and surely it will come) when the new funds, created for the exigencies of the year, are not subscribed to, and raise not the money projected. Suppose, either that the cash of the nation is exhausted; or that our faith, which has hitherto been so ample, begins to fail us. Suppose, that, in this distress, the nation is threatened with an invasion; a rebellion is suspected or broken out at home; a squadron cannot be equipped for want of pay, victuals, or repairs; or even a foreign subsidy cannot be advanced. What must a prince or minister do in such an emergence? The right of self-preservation is unalienable[42] in every individual, much more in every community. And the folly of our statesmen must then be greater than the folly of those who first contracted debt, or, what is more, than that of those who trusted, or continue to trust this security, if these statesmen have the means of safety in their hands, and do not employ them. The funds, created and mortgaged, will, by that time, bring in a large yearly revenue, sufficient for the defence and security of the nation: Money is perhaps lying in the exchequer, ready for the discharge of the quarterly interest: Necessity calls, fear urges, reason exhorts, compassion alone exclaims: The money will immediately be seized for the current service, under the most solemn protestations, perhaps, of being immediately replaced. But no more is requisite. The whole fabric, already tottering, falls to the ground, and buries thousands in its ruins. And this, I think, may be called the *natural death* of public credit: For to this period it tends as naturally as an animal body to its dissolution and destruction.

So great dupes are the generality of mankind, that, notwithstanding such a violent shock to public credit, as a voluntary bankruptcy in ENGLAND would occasion, it would not probably be long ere credit would again revive in as flourishing a condition as before. The present king of FRANCE, during the late war,[43] borrowed money at lower interest than ever his grandfather[44] did; and as low as the BRITISH parliament, comparing the natural rate of interest[45] in both kingdoms. And though men are commonly more governed by what they have seen, than by what they foresee, with whatever certainty; yet promises, protestations, fair appearances, with the allurements of present interest, have such powerful influence as few are able to resist. Mankind are, in all ages, caught by the same baits: The same tricks, played over and over again, still trepan[46] them. The heights of popularity and patriotism are still the beaten road to power and tyranny; flattery to treachery; standing armies to arbitrary government;[47] and the glory of God to the temporal interest of the clergy. The fear of an everlasting destruction of credit, allowing it to be an evil, is a needless bugbear. A prudent man, in reality, would rather lend to the public immediately after we had taken a spunge to our debts,[48] than at present; as much as an opulent knave, even though one could not force him to pay, is a preferable debtor to an honest bankrupt: For the former, in order to carry on business, may find it his interest to discharge his debts, where they are not exorbitant: The latter has it not in his power. The reasoning of TACITUS,* as it is eternally true, is very applicable to our present case. *Sed vulgus ad magnitudinem beneficiorum aderat: Stultissimus quisque pecuniis mercabatur: Apud sapientes cassa habebantur, quæ neque dari neque accipi, salva republica, poterant.*[49] The public is a debtor, whom no man can oblige to pay. The only check which the creditors have upon her, is the interest of preserving credit; an interest, which may easily be overbalanced by a great debt, and by a difficult and extraordinary emergence, even supposing that credit irrecoverable. Not to mention, that a present necessity often forces states into measures, which are, strictly speaking, against their interest.

These two events, supposed above, are calamitous, but not the most calamitous. Thousands are thereby sacrificed to the safety of millions.

---

* *Hist. lib.* iii.

But we are not without danger, that the contrary event may take place, and that millions maybe sacrificed for ever to the temporary safety of thousands.* Our popular government, perhaps, will render it difficult or dangerous for a minister to venture on so desperate an expedient, as that of a voluntary bankruptcy. And though the house of Lords be altogether composed of proprietors of land, and the house of Commons chiefly; and consequently neither of them can be supposed to have great property in the funds. Yet the connections of the members may be so great with the proprietors, as to render them more tenacious of public faith, than prudence, policy, or even justice, strictly speaking, requires. And perhaps too, our foreign enemies may be so politic as to discover, that our safety lies in despair, and may not, therefore, show the danger, open and barefaced, till it be inevitable. The balance of power in EUROPE, our grandfathers, our fathers, and we, have all deemed too unequal to be preserved without our attention and assistance. But our children, weary of the struggle, and fettered with incumbrances, may sit down secure, and see their neighbours oppressed and conquered; till, at last, they themselves and their creditors lie both at the mercy of the conqueror. And this may properly enough be denominated the *violent death* of our public credit.

These seem to be the events, which are not very remote, and which reason foresees as clearly almost as she can do any thing that lies in the womb of time. And though the ancients maintained, that in order to reach the gift of prophecy, a certain divine fury or madness was requisite, one may safely affirm, that, in order to deliver such prophecies as these, no more is necessary, than merely to be in one's senses, free from the influence of popular madness and delusion.

# NOTE

## Note [S]

I have heard it has been computed, that all the creditors of the public, natives and foreigners, amount only to 17,000. These make a figure at present on their income; but in case of a public bankruptcy, would, in an instant, become the lowest, as well as the most wretched of the people. The dignity and authority of the landed gentry and nobility is much better rooted; and would render

---

* See NOTE [S].

the contention very unequal, if ever we come to that extremity. One would incline to assign to this event a very near period, such as half a century, had not our fathers' prophecies of this kind been already found fallacious, by the duration of our public credit so much beyond all reasonable expectation. When the astrologers in FRANCE were every year foretelling the death of HENRY IV. *These fellows*, says he, *must be right at last.*[50] We shall, therefore, be more cautious than to assign any precise date; and shall content ourselves with pointing out the event in general.

# Essay X

## *Of Some Remarkable Customs*

I shall observe three remarkable customs in three celebrated governments; and shall conclude from the whole, that all general maxims in politics ought to be established with great caution;[1] and that irregular and extraordinary appearances are frequently discovered in the moral, as well as in the physical world. The former, perhaps, we can better account for, after they happen, from springs and principles, of which every one has, within himself, or from observation, the strongest assurance and conviction: But it is often fully as impossible for human prudence, before-hand, to foresee and foretel them.

I. One would think it essential to every supreme council or assembly, which debates, that entire liberty of speech should be granted to every member, and that all motions or reasonings should be received, which can any wise tend to illustrate the point under deliberation. One would conclude, with still greater assurance, that, after a motion was made, which was voted and approved by that assembly in which the legislative power is lodged, the member who made the motion must for ever be exempted from future trial or enquiry. But no political maxim can, at first sight, appear more undisputable, than that he must, at least, be secured from all inferior jurisdiction; and that nothing less than the same supreme legislative assembly, in their subsequent meetings, could make him accountable for those motions and harangues, to which they had before given their approbation. But these axioms, however irrefragable they may appear, have all failed in the ATHENIAN government, from causes and principles too, which appear almost inevitable.

By the γραφὴ παρανόμων, or *indictment of illegality*, (though it has not been remarked by antiquaries or commentators) any man was tried and punished in a common court of judicature, for any law which had passed upon his motion, in the assembly of the people, if that law appeared to the court unjust, or prejudicial to the public. Thus DEMOS-THENES, finding that ship-money was levied irregularly, and that the poor bore the same burden as the rich in equipping the gallies, corrected this inequality by a very useful law,[2] which proportioned the expence to the revenue and income of each individual. He moved for this law in the assembly: he proved its advantages;* he convinced the people, the only legislature in ATHENS; the law passed, and was carried into execution: Yet was he tried in a criminal court for that law, upon the complaint of the rich, who resented the alteration that he had introduced into the finances.† He was indeed acquitted, upon proving anew the usefulness of his law.[3]

CTESIPHON moved in the assembly of the people, that particular honours should be conferred on DEMOSTHENES, as on a citizen affectionate and useful to the commonwealth: The people, convinced of this truth, voted those honours: Yet was CTESIPHON tried by the γραφὴ παρανόμων. It was asserted, among other topics, that DEMOSTHENES was not a good citizen, nor affectionate to the commonwealth: And the orator was called upon to defend his friend, and consequently himself; which he executed by that sublime piece of eloquence, that has ever since been the admiration of mankind.[4]

After the battle of CHÆRONEA,[5] a law was passed upon the motion of HYPERIDES, giving liberty to slaves, and inrolling them in the troops.‡ On account of this law, the orator was afterwards tried by the indictment above-mentioned, and defended himself, among other topics, by that stroke celebrated by PLUTARCH and LONGINUS.[6] *It was not I,* said he, *that moved for this law: It was the necessities of war; it was the battle of* CHÆRONEA. The orations of DEMOSTHENES abound with many instances of trials of this nature, and prove clearly, that nothing was more commonly practised.

The ATHENIAN Democracy was such a tumultuous government as we can scarcely form a notion of in the present age of the world. The whole collective body of the people voted in every law, without any limitation

---

* His harangue for it is still extant; περὶ Συμμορίας.
† Pro CTESIPHONTE.
‡ PLUTARCHUS *in vita decem oratorum.* DEMOSTHENES gives a different account of this law. *Contra* ARISTOGITON. *orat.* II. He says, that its purport was, to render the ἄτιμοι ἐπίτιμοι, or to restore the privilege of bearing offices to those who had been declared incapable. Perhaps these were both clauses of the same law.[7]

of property, without any distinction of rank, without controul from any magistracy or senate;* and consequently without regard to order, justice, or prudence. The ATHENIANS soon became sensible of the mischiefs attending this constitution: But being averse to checking themselves by any rule or restriction, they resolved, at least, to check their demagogues or counsellors, by the fear of future punishment and enquiry. They accordingly instituted this remarkable law; a law esteemed so essential to their form of government, that ÆSCHINES insists on it as a known truth, that, were it abolished or neglected, it were impossible for the Democracy to subsist.†

The people feared not any ill consequence to liberty from the authority of the criminal courts; because these were nothing but very numerous juries, chosen by lot from among the people. And they justly considered themselves as in a state of perpetual pupillage;⁸ where they had an authority, after they came to the use of reason, not only to retract and controul whatever had been determined, but to punish any guardian for measures which they had embraced by his persuasion. The same law had place in THEBES;‡ and for the same reason.

It appears to have been a usual practice in ATHENS, on the establishment of any law esteemed very useful or popular, to prohibit for ever its abrogation and repeal. Thus the demagogue,⁹ who diverted all the public revenues to the support of shows and spectacles, made it criminal so much as to move for a repeal of this law.§ Thus LEPTINES moved for a law, not only to recal all the immunities formerly granted, but to deprive the people for the future of the power of granting any more.¶ Thus all bills of attainder**¹⁰ were forbid, or laws that affected one ATHENIAN, without extending to the whole commonwealth. These absurd clauses, by which the legislature vainly attempted to bind itself

---

* The senate of the Bean was only a less numerous mob, chosen by lot from among the people; and their authority was not great.

† *In* CTESIPHONTEM. It is remarkable, that the first step after the dissolution of the Democracy by CRITIAS and the Thirty, was to annul the γραφὴ παρανόμων, as we learn from DEMOSTHENES κατα Τιμοκ. The orator in this oration gives us the words of the law, establishing the γραφὴ παρανόμων, pag. 297. *ex edit.* ALDI. And he accounts for it, from the same principles we here reason upon.¹¹

‡ PLUT. *in vita* PELOP.¹²

§ DEMOST. *Olynth*, 1. 2.¹³

¶ DEMOST. *contra* LEPT.¹⁴

** DEMOST. *contra* ARISTOCRATEM.¹⁵

for ever, proceeded from an universal sense in the people of their own levity and inconstancy.

II. A wheel within a wheel, such as we observe in the GERMAN empire,[16] is considered by Lord SHAFTESBURY* as an absurdity in politics: But what must we say to two equal wheels, which govern the same political machine, without any mutual check, controul, or subordination; and yet preserve the greatest harmony and concord? To establish two distinct legislatures, each of which possesses full and absolute authority within itself, and stands in no need of the other's assistance, in order to give validity to its acts; this may appear, before-hand, altogether impracticable, as long as men are actuated by the passions of ambition, emulation, and avarice, which have hitherto been their chief governing principles. And should I assert, that the state I have in my eye was divided into two distinct factions, each of which predominated in a distinct legislature, and yet produced no clashing in these independent powers; the supposition may appear incredible. And if, to augment the paradox, I should affirm, that this disjointed, irregular government, was the most active, triumphant, and illustrious commonwealth, that ever yet appeared; I should certainly be told, that such a political chimera was as absurd as any vision of priests or poets. But there is no need for searching long, in order to prove the reality of the foregoing suppositions: For this was actually the case with the ROMAN republic.[17]

The legislative power was there lodged in the *comitia centuriata* and *comitia tributa*.[18] In the former, it is well known, the people voted according to their *census*; so that when the first class was unanimous, though it contained not, perhaps, the hundredth part of the commonwealth, it determined the whole; and, with the authority of the senate, established a law. In the latter, every vote was equal; and as the authority of the senate was not there requisite, the lower people entirely prevailed, and gave law to the whole state. In all party-divisions, at first between the PATRICIANS and PLEBEIANS,[19] afterwards between the nobles and the people, the interest of the Aristocracy was predominant in the first legislature; that of the Democracy in the second: The one could always destroy what the other had established: Nay, the one, by a sudden and unforeseen motion, might take the start of the other, and totally annihilate its rival, by a vote, which, from the nature of the constitution,

---

* Essay on the freedom of wit and humour, part 3. § 2.[20]

had the full authority of a law. But no such contest is observed in the history of ROME: No instance of a quarrel between these two legislatures; though many between the parties that governed in each. Whence arose this concord, which may seem so extraordinary?

The legislature established in ROME, by the authority of SERVIUS TULLIUS, was the *comitia centuriata*, which, after the expulsion of the kings, rendered the government, for some time, very aristocratical. But the people, having numbers and force on their side, and being elated with frequent conquests and victories in their foreign wars, always prevailed when pushed to extremity, and first extorted from the senate the magistracy of the tribunes,[21] and next the legislative power of the *comitia tributa*. It then behoved the nobles to be more careful than ever not to provoke the people. For beside the force which the latter were always possessed of,[22] they had now got possession of legal authority, and could instantly break in pieces any order or institution which directly opposed them. By intrigue, by influence, by money, by combination, and by the respect paid to their character, the nobles might often prevail, and direct the whole machine of government: But had they openly set their *comitia centuriata* in opposition to the *tributa*, they had soon lost the advantage of that institution, together with their consuls, prætors, ediles,[23] and all the magistrates elected by it. But the *comitia tributa*, not having the same reason for respecting the *centuriata*, frequently repealed laws favourable to the Aristocracy: They limited the authority of the nobles, protected the people from oppression, and controuled the actions of the senate and magistracy. The *centuriata* found it convenient always to submit; and though equal in authority, yet being inferior in power, durst never directly give any shock to the other legislature, either by repealing its laws, or establishing laws, which, it foresaw, would soon be repealed by it.

No instance is found of any opposition or struggle between these *comitia*; except one slight attempt of this kind, mentioned by APPIAN in the third book of his civil wars.[24] MARK ANTHONY, resolving to deprive DECIMUS BRUTUS of the government of CISALPINE GAUL,[25] railed in the *Forum*, and called one of the *comitia*, in order to prevent the meeting of the other, which had been ordered by the senate. But affairs were then fallen into such confusion, and the ROMAN constitution was so near its final dissolution, that no inference can be drawn from such an expedient. This contest, besides, was founded more on form than party. It was the senate who ordered the *comitia tributa*, that they might obstruct the meeting of the *centuriata*, which, by the constitution, or at least forms of the government, could alone dispose of provinces.

Cicero was recalled by the *comitia centuriata*, though banished by the *tributa*, that is, by a *plebiscitum*.[26] But his banishment, we may observe, never was considered as a legal deed, arising from the free choice and inclination of the people. It was always ascribed to the violence alone of Clodius, and to the disorders introduced by him into the government.

III. The *third* custom, which we purpose to remark, regards England; and though it be not so important as those which we have pointed out in Athens and Rome, is no less singular and unexpected. It is a maxim in politics, which we readily admit as undisputed and universal, that a power, however great, when granted by law to an eminent magistrate, is not so dangerous to liberty, as an authority, however inconsiderable, which he acquires from violence and usurpation.[27] For, besides that the law always limits every power which it bestows, the very receiving it as a concession establishes the authority whence it is derived, and preserves the harmony of the constitution. By the same right that one prerogative is assumed without law, another may also be claimed, and another, with still greater facility; while the first usurpations both serve as precedents to the following, and give force to maintain them. Hence the heroism of Hampden's conduct,[28] who sustained the whole violence of royal prosecution, rather than pay a tax of twenty shillings, not imposed by parliament; hence the care of all English patriots[29] to guard against the first encroachments of the crown; and hence alone the existence, at this day, of English liberty.[30]

There is, however, one occasion, where the parliament has departed from this maxim; and that is, in the *pressing of seamen*.[31] The exercise of an irregular power is here tacitly permitted in the crown; and though it has frequently been under deliberation, how that power might be rendered legal, and granted, under proper restrictions, to the sovereign, no safe expedient could ever be proposed for that purpose; and the danger to liberty always appeared greater from law than from usurpation. While this power is exercised to no other end than to man the navy, men willingly submit to it, from a sense of its use and necessity; and the sailors, who are alone affected by it, find no body to support them, in claiming the rights and privileges, which the law grants, without distinction, to all ENGLISH subjects. But were this power, on any occasion, made an instrument of faction, or ministerial tyranny, the opposite faction, and indeed all lovers of their country, would immediately take the alarm, and support the injured party; the liberty of ENGLISHMEN would be asserted; juries would be implacable; and the tools of tyranny, acting both against law and equity, would meet with the severest vengeance. On the other hand, were the parliament to grant such an authority, they would probably fall into one of these two inconveniencies: They would either bestow it under so many restrictions as would make it lose its effect, by cramping the authority of the crown; or they would render it so large and comprehensive, as might give occasion to great abuses, for which we could, in that case, have no remedy. The very irregularity of the practice, at present, prevents its abuses, by affording so easy a remedy against them.

I pretend not, by this reasoning, to exclude all possibility of contriving a register for seamen, which might man the navy, without being dangerous to liberty. I only observe, that no satisfactory scheme of that nature has yet been proposed. Rather than adopt any project hitherto invented, we continue a practice seemingly the most absurd and unaccountable. Authority, in times of full internal peace and concord, is armed against law. A continued violence is permitted in the crown, amidst the greatest jealousy and watchfulness in the people; nay proceeding from those very principles: Liberty, in a country of the highest liberty, is left entirely to its own defence, without any countenance or protection: The wild state of nature[32] is renewed, in one of the most civilized societies of mankind: And great violence and disorder are committed, with impunity; while the one party pleads obedience to the supreme magistrate, the other the sanction of fundamental laws.[33]

# Essay XI

## Of the Populousness of Ancient Nations

There is very little ground, either from reason or observation, to conclude the world eternal or incorruptible.[1] The continual and rapid motion of matter, the violent revolutions with which every part is agitated, the changes remarked in the heavens,[2] the plain traces as well as tradition of an universal deluge,[3] or general convulsion of the elements; all these prove strongly the mortality of this fabric of the world, and its passage, by corruption or dissolution, from one state or order to another. It must therefore, as well as each individual form which it contains, have its infancy, youth, manhood, and old age; and it is probable, that, in all these variations, man, equally with every animal and vegetable, will partake. In the flourishing age of the world, it may be expected, that the human species should possess greater vigour both of mind and body, more prosperous health, higher spirits, longer life, and a stronger inclination and power of generation. But if the general system of things, and human society of course, have any such gradual revolutions, they are too slow to be discernible in that short period which is comprehended by history and tradition. Stature and force of body, length of life, even courage and extent of genius, seem hitherto to have been naturally, in all ages, pretty much the same. The arts and sciences, indeed, have flourished in one period, and have decayed in another:[4] But we may observe, that, at the time when they rose to greatest perfection among one people, they were perhaps totally unknown to all the neighbouring nations; and though they universally decayed in one age, yet in a succeeding generation they again revived, and diffused themselves over the world. As far, therefore, as observation reaches, there is no universal difference discernible in the human species; and though it were allowed, that the universe, like an animal body, had a natural progress from infancy to old age;[5] yet as it must still be uncertain, whether, at present, it be advancing to its point of perfection, or declining from it, we cannot thence presuppose any decay in human nature.* To prove, therefore, or account for that superior populousness of antiquity, which is commonly supposed, by the imaginary youth or vigour of the world, will scarcely be admitted by any just reasoner. These *general physical* causes[6] ought entirely to be excluded from this question.

There are indeed some more *particular physical* causes of import-ance. Diseases are mentioned in antiquity, which are almost unknown to modern medicine;[7] and new diseases[8] have arisen and propagated themselves, of which there are no traces in ancient history. In this particular we may observe, upon comparison, that the disadvantage is much on the side of the moderns. Not to mention some others of less moment; the small-pox commits such ravages,[9] as would almost alone account for the great superiority ascribed to ancient times. The tenth or the twelfth part of mankind, destroyed every generation, should make a vast difference, it may be thought, in the numbers of the people; and when joined to venereal distempers,[10] a new plague diffused every where, this disease is perhaps equivalent, by its constant operation, to the three great scourges of mankind, war, pestilence, and famine.[11] Were it certain, therefore, that ancient times were more populous than the present, and could no moral causes be assigned for so great a change; these physical causes alone, in the opinion of many, would be sufficient to give us satisfaction on that head.

But is it certain, that antiquity was so much more populous, as is pretended? The extravagancies of VOSSIUS, with regard to this subject, are well known.[12] But an author of much greater genius[13] and discern-ment has ventured to affirm, that, according to the best computations which these subjects will admit of, there are not now, on the face of the earth, the fiftieth part of mankind, which existed in the time of JULIUS CÆSAR.† It may easily be observed, that the comparison, in this case, must be imperfect, even though we confine ourselves to the scene of ancient history; EUROPE, and the nations round the MEDITERRANEAN. We know not exactly the numbers of any EUROPEAN kingdom, or even city, at present:[14] How can we pretend to calculate those of ancient cities and states, where historians have left us such imperfect traces? For my

* See NOTE [T].
† *Lettres* PERSANES. See also *L'Esprit des Loix*, liv. xxiii. cap. 17, 18, 19.

part, the matter appears to me so uncertain, that, as I intend to throw together some reflections on that head, I shall intermingle the enquiry concerning *causes* with that concerning *facts*; which ought never to be admitted, where the facts can be ascertained with any tolerable assurance. We shall, *first*, consider whether it be probable, from what we know of the situation of society in both periods, that antiquity must have been more populous; *secondly*, whether in reality it was so. If I can make it appear, that the conclusion is not so certain as is pretended, in favour of antiquity, it is all I aspire to.[15]

In general, we may observe, that the question, with regard to the comparative populousness of ages or kingdoms, implies important consequences, and commonly determines concerning the preference of their whole police,[16] their manners, and the constitution of their government. For as there is in all men, both male and female, a desire and power of generation, more active than is ever universally exerted, the restraints, which they lie under, must proceed from some difficulties in their situation, which it belongs to a wise legislature carefully to observe and remove. Almost every man who thinks he can maintain a family will have one; and the human species, at this rate of propagation, would more than double every generation.[17] How fast do mankind multiply in every colony or new settlement; where it is an easy matter to provide for a family; and where men are nowise straitened or confined, as in long established governments? History tells us frequently of plagues, which have swept away the third or fourth part of a people:[18] Yet in a generation or two, the destruction was not perceived; and the society had again acquired their former number. The lands which were cultivated, the houses built, the commodities raised, the riches acquired, enabled the people, who escaped, immediately to marry, and to rear families, which supplied the place of those who had perished.* And for a like reason, every wise, just, and mild government, by rendering the condition of its subjects easy and secure, will always abound most in people, as well as in commodities and riches. A country, indeed, whose climate and soil are fitted for vines, will naturally be more populous than one

* This too is a good reason why the small-pox does not depopulate countries so much as may at first sight be imagined. Where there is room for more people, they will always arise, even without the assistance of naturalization bills. It is remarked by DON GERONIMO DE USTARIZ, that the provinces of SPAIN, which send most people to the INDIES, are most populous; which proceeds from their superior riches.[19]

which produces corn only, and that more populous than one which is only fitted for pasturage. In general, warm climates, as the necessities of the inhabitants are there fewer, and vegetation more powerful, are likely to be most populous:[20] But if every thing else be equal, it seems natural to expect, that, wherever there are most happiness and virtue, and the wisest institutions, there will also be most people.[21]

The question, therefore, concerning the populousness of ancient and modern times, being allowed of great importance, it will be requisite, if we would bring it to some determination, to compare both the *domestic* and *political* situation of these two periods, in order to judge of the facts by their moral causes; which is the *first* view in which we proposed to consider them.

The chief difference between the *domestic* œconomy of the ancients and that of the moderns consists in the practice of slavery, which prevailed among the former, and which has been abolished for some centuries throughout the greater part of EUROPE. Some passionate admirers of the ancients, and zealous partizans of civil liberty, (for these sentiments, as they are, both of them, in the main, extremely just, are found to be almost inseparable) cannot forbear regretting the loss of this institution; and whilst they brand all submission to the government of a single person with the harsh denomination of slavery, they would gladly reduce the greater part of mankind to real slavery and subjection.[22] But to one who considers coolly on the subject it will appear, that human nature, in general, really enjoys more liberty at present, in the most arbitrary government of EUROPE, than it ever did during the most flourishing period of ancient times. As much as submission to a petty prince, whose dominions extend not beyond a single city, is more grievous than obedience to a great monarch; so much is domestic slavery more cruel and oppressive than any civil subjection whatsoever. The more the master is removed from us in place and rank, the greater liberty we enjoy; the less are our actions inspected and controled; and the fainter that cruel comparison becomes between our own subjection, and the freedom, and even dominion of another. The remains which are found of domestic slavery, in the AMERICAN colonies, and among some EUROPEAN nations, would never surely create a desire of rendering it more universal. The little humanity, commonly observed in persons, accustomed, from their infancy, to exercise so great authority over their fellow-creatures, and to trample upon human nature, were sufficient alone to disgust us with that unbounded dominion. Nor can a more probable reason be assigned for the severe, I might say, barbarous manners of ancient times, than the practice of domestic slavery; by which every man of rank was rendered a petty tyrant, and educated amidst the flattery, submission, and low debasement of his slaves.

According to ancient practice, all checks were on the inferior, to restrain him to the duty of submission; none on the superior, to engage him to the reciprocal duties of gentleness and humanity. In modern times, a bad servant finds not easily a good master, nor a bad master a good servant; and the checks are mutual, suitably to the inviolable and eternal laws of reason and equity.

The custom of exposing old, useless, or sick slaves in an island of the TYBER, there to starve, seems to have been pretty common in ROME; and whoever recovered, after having been so exposed, had his liberty given him, by an edict of the emperor CLAUDIUS; in which it was likewise forbidden to kill any slave merely for old age or sickness.* But supposing that this edict was strictly obeyed, would it better the domestic treatment of slaves, or render their lives much more comfortable? We may imagine what others would practise, when it was the professed maxim of the elder CATO, to sell his superannuated slaves for any price, rather than maintain what he esteemed a useless burden.†

The *ergastula*, or dungeons, where slaves in chains were forced to work, were very common all over ITALY. COLUMELLA‡ advises, that they be always built under ground; and recommends§ it as the duty of a careful overseer, to call over every day the names of these slaves, like the mustering of a regiment or ship's company, in order to know presently when any of them had deserted. A proof of the frequency of these *ergastula*, and of the great number of slaves usually confined in them.

A chained slave for a porter, was usual in ROME, as appears from OVID,¶ and other authors.** Had not these people shaken off all sense of compassion towards that unhappy part of their species, would they

---

* SUETONIUS in vita CLAUDII.[23]
† PLUT. in vita CATONIS.[24]
‡ Lib. i. cap. 6.[25]
§ Id. lib. xi. cap. 1.[26]
¶ Amor. lib. i. eleg. 6.[27]
** SUETON. *de claris rhetor.*[28] So also the ancient poet, *Janitoris tintinnire impedimenta audio.*[29]

have presented their friends, at the first entrance, with such an image of the severity of the master, and misery of the slave?

Nothing so common in all trials, even of civil causes, as to call for the evidence of slaves; which was always extorted by the most exquisite torments. DEMOSTHENES says,* that, where it was possible to produce, for the same fact, either freemen or slaves, as witnesses, the judges always preferred the torturing of slaves, as a more certain evidence.†

SENECA draws a picture of that disorderly luxury, which changes day into night, and night into day, and inverts every stated hour of every office in life. Among other circumstances, such as displacing the meals and times of bathing, he mentions, that, regularly about the third hour of the night, the neighbours of one, who indulges this false refinement, hear the noise of whips and lashes; and, upon enquiry, find that he is then taking an account of the conduct of his servants, and giving them due correction and discipline. This is not remarked as an instance of cruelty, but only of disorder, which, even in actions the most usual and methodical, changes the fixed hours that an established custom had assigned for them.‡

But our present business is only to consider the influence of slavery on the populousness of a state. It is pretended,[30] that, in this particular, the ancient practice had infinitely the advantage, and was the chief cause of that extreme populousness, which is supposed in those times. At present, all masters discourage the marrying of their male servants, and admit not by any means the marriage of the female, who are then supposed altogether incapacitated for their service. But where the property of the servants is lodged in the master, their marriage forms his riches, and brings him a succession of slaves that supply the place of those whom age and infirmity have disabled. He encourages, therefore, their propagation as much as that of his cattle; rears the young with the same care; and educates them to some art or calling, which may render them more useful or valuable to him. The opulent are, by this policy, interested in the being at least, though not in the well-being of the poor; and enrich themselves, by encreasing the number and industry

* In *Oniterem orat.* 1.[31]
† The same practice was very common in ROME; but CICERO seems not to think this evidence so certain as the testimony of free-citizens. *Pro Cælio.*[32]
‡ See NOTE [U].

of those who are subjected to them. Each man, being a sovereign in his own family, has the same interest with regard to it, as the prince with regard to the state; and has not, like the prince, any opposite motives of ambition or vain-glory, which may lead him to depopulate his little sovereignty. All of it is, at all times, under his eye; and he has leisure to inspect the most minute detail of the marriage and education of his subjects.*

Such are the consequences of domestic slavery, according to the first aspect and appearance of things: But if we enter more deeply into the subject, we shall perhaps find reason to retract our hasty determinations.[33] The comparison is shocking between the management of human creatures and that of cattle;[34] but being extremely just, when applied to the present subject, it may be proper to trace the consequences of it. At the capital, near all great cities, in all populous, rich, industrious provinces, few cattle are bred. Provisions, lodging, attendance, labour are there dear; and men find their account better in buying the cattle, after they come to a certain age, from the remoter and cheaper countries. These are consequently the only breeding countries for cattle; and by a parity of reason, for men too, when the latter are put on the same footing with the former. To rear a child in LONDON, till he could be serviceable would cost much dearer, than to buy one of the same age from SCOTLAND or IRELAND; where he had been bred in a cottage, covered with rags, and fed on oatmeal or potatoes.[35] Those who had slaves, therefore, in all the richer and more populous countries, would discourage the pregnancy of the females, and either prevent or destroy the birth. The human species would perish in those places where it ought to encrease the fastest; and a perpetual recruit be wanted from the poorer and more desert provinces. Such a continued drain would tend mightily to depopulate the state, and render great cities ten times more destructive than with us; where every man is master of himself, and provides for his children from the powerful instinct of nature, not the calculations of sordid interest. If LONDON, at present, without much encreasing, needs a yearly recruit from the country, of 5000 people, as is usually

---

* We may here observe, that if domestic slavery really encreased populousness, it would be an exception to the general rule, that the happiness of any society and its populousness are necessary attendants. A master, from humour or interest, may make his slaves very unhappy, yet be careful, from interest, to encrease their number. Their marriage is not a matter of choice with them, more than any other action of their life.

computed,[36] what must it require, if the greater part of the tradesmen and common people were slaves, and were hindered from breeding by their avaricious masters?

All ancient authors tell us, that there was a perpetual flux of slaves to ITALY from the remoter provinces, particularly SYRIA, CILICIA,* CAPPADOCIA, and the Lesser ASIA, THRACE, and ÆGYPT: Yet the number of people did not encrease in ITALY; and writers complain of the continual decay of industry and agriculture.† Where then is that extreme fertility of the ROMAN slaves, which is commonly supposed? So far from multiplying, they could not, it seems, so much as keep up the stock, without immense recruits. And though great numbers were continually manumitted[37] and converted into ROMAN citizens, the numbers even of these did not encrease,‡ till the freedom of the city was communicated to foreign provinces.[38]

The term for a slave, born and bred in the family, was *verna*;§ and these slaves seem to have been entitled by custom to privileges and indulgences beyond others; a sufficient reason why the masters would not be fond of rearing many of that kind.¶ Whoever is acquainted with the maxims of our planters,[39] will acknowledge the justness of this observation.**

ATTICUS is much praised by his historian for the care, which he took

---

* Ten thousand slaves in a day have often been sold for the use of the ROMANS, at DELUS in CILICIA. STRABO, lib. xiv.[40]

† COLUMELLA, lib. i. *proœm.* et cap. 2. et 7. VARRO, lib. iii. cap. 1. HORAT. lib. ii. od. 15. TACIT. *annal.* lib. iii. cap. 54. SUETON. *in vita* AUG. cap. xlii. PLIN. lib. xviii. cap. 13.[41]

‡ *Minore indies plebe ingenua*, says TACITUS, *ann.* lib. xxiv. cap. 7.[42]

§ See NOTE [X].

¶ *Verna* is used by ROMAN writers as a word equivalent to *scurra*, on account of the petulance and impudence of those slaves. MART. lib. i. ep. 42. HORACE also mentions the *vernæ procaces*; and PETRONIUS, cap. 24. *vernula urbanitas.* SENECA, *de provid.* cap. 1, *vernularum licentia.*[43]

** It is computed in the WEST INDIES, that a stock of slaves grow worse five *per cent.* every year, unless new slaves be bought to recruit them.[44] They are not able to keep up their number, even in those warm countries, where cloaths and provisions are so easily got. How much more must this happen in EUROPEAN countries, and in or near great cities? I shall add, that, from the experience of our planters, slavery is as little advantageous to the master as to the slave, wherever hired servants can be procured. A man is obliged to cloath and feed his slave; and he does no more for his servant: The price of the first purchase is, therefore, so much loss to him: not to mention, that the fear of punishment will never draw so much labour from a slave, as the dread of being turned off and not getting another service, will from a freeman.[45]

in recruiting his family from the slaves born in it:* May we not thence infer, that this practice was not then very common?

The names of slaves in the GREEK comedies, SYRUS, MYSUS, GETA, THRAX, DAVUS, LYDUS, PHRYX, &c. afford a presumption, that, at ATHENS at least, most of the slaves were imported from foreign countries.[46] The ATHENIANS, says STRABO,† gave to their slaves, either the names of the nations whence they were bought, as LYDUS, SYRUS; or the names that were most common among those nations, as MANES or MIDAS to a PHRYGIAN, TIBIAS to a PAPHLAGONIAN.

DEMOSTHENES, having mentioned a law which forbad any man to strike the slave of another, praises the humanity of this law; and adds, that, if the barbarians from whom the slaves were bought, had information, that their countrymen met with such gentle treatment, they would entertain a great esteem for the ATHENIANS.‡ ISOCRATES§ too insinuates, that the slaves of the GREEKS were generally or very commonly barbarians. ARISTOTLE in his Politics¶ plainly supposes, that a slave is always a foreigner. The ancient comic writers represented the slaves as speaking a barbarous language.** This was an imitation of nature.

It is well known that DEMOSTHENES, in his nonage, had been defrauded of a large fortune by his tutors, and that afterwards he recovered, by a prosecution at law, the value of his patrimony. His orations, on that occasion, still remain, and contain an exact detail of the whole substance left by his father,†† in money, merchandise, houses, and slaves, together with the value of each particular. Among the rest were 52 slaves, handicraftsmen, namely, 32 sword-cutlers, and 20 cabinet-makers;‡‡ all males; not a word of any wives, children or family, which they certainly would have had, had it been a common practice at ATHENS to breed from the slaves: And the value of the whole must have much depended on that circumstance. No female slaves are even

---

* CORN. NEPOS in vita ATTICI. We may remark, that ATTICUS's estate lay chiefly in EPIRUS, which, being a remote, desolate place, would render it profitable for him to rear slaves there.[47]
† Lib. vii.[48]
‡ In MIDIAM, p. 221. ex edit. ALDI.[49]
§ Panegyr.[50]
¶ Lib. vii. cap.10. sub fin.[51]
** ARISTOPH. Equites, l. 17. The ancient scholiast remarks on this passage βαρβαρίζει ως δοῦλος.[52]
†† In *Amphobum orat.* 1.[53]
‡‡ κλινοποιοὶ, makers of those beds which the ancients lay upon at meals.

so much as mentioned, except some house-maids, who belonged to his mother. This argument has great force, if it be not altogether conclusive.

Consider this passage of PLUTARCH,* speaking of the Elder CATO. "He had a great number of slaves, whom he took care to buy at the sales of prisoners of war; and he chose them young, that they might easily be accustomed to any diet or manner of life, and be instructed in any business or labour, as men teach any thing to young dogs or horses. ——And esteeming love the chief source of all disorders, he allowed the male slaves to have a commerce with the female in his family, upon paying a certain sum for this privilege: But he strictly prohibited all intrigues out of his family." Are there any symptoms in this narration of that care which is supposed in the ancients, of the marriage and propagation of their slaves? If that was a common practice, founded on general interest, it would surely have been embraced by Cato, who was a great œconomist, and lived in times when the ancient frugality and simplicity of manners were still in credit and reputation.

It is expressly remarked by the writers of the ROMAN law, that scarcely any ever purchase slaves with a view of breeding from them.†

Our lackeys and house-maids, I own, do not serve much to multiply their species: But the ancients, besides those who attended on their person, had almost all their labour performed, and even manufactures executed, by slaves, who lived, many of them, in their family; and some great men possessed to the number of 10,000. If there be any suspicion, therefore, that this institution was unfavourable to propagation, (and the same reason, at least in part, holds with regard to ancient slaves as modern servants) how destructive must slavery have proved?

History mentions a ROMAN nobleman, who had 400 slaves under the same roof with him: And having been assassinated at home by the furious revenge of one of them, the law was executed with rigour, and all without exception were put to death.‡ Many other ROMAN noblemen had families equally, or more numerous; and I believe every one will allow, that this would scarcely be practicable, were we to suppose all the slaves married, and the females to be breeders.§

* In vita CATONIS.[54]
† See NOTE [Y].
‡ TACIT. *ann.* lib. xiv. cap. 43.[55]
§ The slaves in the great houses had little rooms assigned them, called *cellæ*. Whence the name of cell was transferred to the monks room in a convent. See farther on this head,

So early as the poet HESIOD,* married slaves, whether male or female, were esteemed inconvenient. How much more, where families had encreased to such an enormous size as in ROME, and where the ancient simplicity of manners was banished from all ranks of people?

XENOPHON in his Oeconomics, where he gives directions for the management of a farm, recommends a strict care and attention of laying the male and the female slaves at a distance from each other. He seems not to suppose that they are ever married.[56] The only slaves among the GREEKS that appear to have continued their own race, were the HELOTES,[57] who had houses apart, and were more the slaves of the public than of individuals.†

The same author‡ tells us, that NICIAS's overseer, by agreement with his master, was obliged to pay him an obolus[58] a day for each slave; besides maintaining them, and keeping up the number. Had the ancient slaves been all breeders, this last circumstance of the contract had been superfluous.

The ancients talk so frequently of a fixed, stated portion of provisions assigned to each slave,§ that we are naturally led to conclude, that slaves lived almost all single, and received that portion as a kind of board-wages.

The practice, indeed, of marrying slaves seems not to have been very common, even among the country-labourers, where it is more naturally to be expected. CATO,¶ enumerating the slaves requisite to labour a vineyard of a hundred acres, makes them amount to 15; the overseer and his wife, *villicus* and *villica*, and 13 male slaves; for an olive plantation of 240 acres, the overseer and his wife, and 11 male slaves; and so in proportion to a greater or less plantation or vineyard.

VARRO,** quoting this passage of CATO, allows his computation to be just in every respect, except the last. For as it is requisite, says he, to have an overseer and his wife, whether the vineyard or plantation be great

---

JUST. LIPSIUS, Saturn. i. cap. 14. These form strong presumptions against the marriage and propagation of the family slaves.[59]
* Opera et Dies, lib. ii. l. 24. also l. 220.[60]
† STRABO, lib. viii.[61]
‡ De ratione redituum.[62]
§ See CATO de re rustica, cap. 56. Donatus in Phormion, I. 1. 9. SENECAE epist. 80.[63]
¶ De re rust. cap. 10, 11.[64]
** Lib. i. cap. 18.[65]

or small, this must alter the exactness of the proportion. Had CATO's computation been erroneous in any other respect, it had certainly been corrected by VARRO, who seems fond of discovering so trivial an error.

The same author,* as well as COLUMELLA,† recommends it as requisite to give a wife to the overseer, in order to attach him the more strongly to his master's service. This was therefore a peculiar indulgence granted to a slave, in whom so great confidence was reposed.

In the same place, VARRO mentions it as an useful precaution, not to buy too many slaves from the same nation, lest they beget factions and seditions in the family:[66] A presumption, that in ITALY, the greater part, even of the country labouring slaves, (for he speaks of no other) were bought from the remoter provinces. All the world knows, that the family slaves in ROME, who were instruments of show and luxury, were commonly imported from the east. *Hoc profecere*, says PLINY, speaking of the jealous care of masters, *mancipiorum legiones, et in domo turba externa, ac servorum quoque causa nomenclator adhibendus.*‡

It is indeed recommended by VARRO,§ to propagate young shepherds in the family from the old ones. For as grasing farms were commonly in remote and cheap places, and each shepherd lived in a cottage apart, his marriage and encrease were not liable to the same inconveniencies as in dearer places, and where many servants lived in the family; which was universally the case in such of the ROMAN farms as produced wine or corn. If we consider this exception with regard to shepherds, and weigh the reasons of it, it will serve for a strong confirmation of all our foregoing suspicions.¶

COLUMELLA,** I own, advises the master to give a reward, and even liberty to a female slave, that had reared him above three children: A proof, that sometimes the ancients propagated from their slaves; which, indeed, cannot be denied. Were it otherwise, the practice of slavery, being so common in antiquity, must have been destructive to a degree which no expedient could repair. All I pretend to infer from these reasonings is, that slavery is in general disadvantageous both to the happiness and

---

* Lib. i. cap. 17.[67]
† Lib. i. cap. 18.[68]
‡ Lib. xxxiii. cap. 1. So likewise TACITUS, *annal.* lib. xiv. cap. 44.[69]
§ Lib. ii. cap. 10.[70]
¶ Pastoris duri est hic filius, ille bubulci. JUVEN. sat. 11. 151.[71]
** Lib. i. cap. 8.[72]

populousness of mankind, and that its place is much better supplied by the practice of hired servants.

The laws, or, as some writers call them, the seditions of the GRAC-CHI,[73] were occasioned by their observing the encrease of slaves all over ITALY, and the diminution of free citizens. APPIAN* ascribes this encrease to the propagation of the slaves: PLUTARCH† to the purchasing of barbarians, who were chained and imprisoned, βαρβαρικα δεσμωτηρια.‡ It is to be presumed that both causes concurred.

SICILY, says FLORUS,§ was full of *ergastula*, and was cultivated by labourers in chains. EUNUS and ATHENIO excited the servile war,[74] by breaking up these monstrous prisons, and giving liberty to 60,000 slaves. The younger POMPEY augmented his army in SPAIN by the same expedient.¶ If the country labourers, throughout the ROMAN empire, were so generally in this situation, and if it was difficult or impossible to find separate lodgings for the families of the city servants, how unfavourable to propagation, as well as to humanity, must the institution of domestic slavery be esteemed?

CONSTANTINOPLE, at present, requires the same recruits of slaves from all the provinces, that ROME did of old; and these provinces are of consequence far from being populous.[75]

EGYPT, according to Mons. MAILLET,[76] sends continual colonies of black slaves to the other parts of the TURKISH empire; and receives annually an equal return of white: The one brought from the inland parts of AFRICA; the other from MINGRELIA, CIRCASSIA, and TARTARY.

Our modern convents are, no doubt, bad institutions: But there is

---

* De bel. civ. lib. i.[77]

† In vita TIB. & C. GRACCHI.[78]

‡ To the same purpose is that passage of the elder SENECA, ex controversia 5. lib. v. "Arata quondam populis rura, singulorum ergastulorum sunt; latiusque nunc villici, quam olim reges, imperant." "At nunc eadem," says PLINY, "vincti pedes, damnatae manus, inscripti vultus exercent." Lib. xviii. cap. 3. So also MARTIAL.

"Et sonet innumera compede Thuscus ager."     Lib. ix. ep. 23.

And LUCAN. "Tum longos jungere fines

    Agrorum, et quondam duro sulcata Camilli,

    Vomere et antiquas Curiorum passa ligones,

    Longa sub ignotis extendere rura colonis."     Lib. i.

       "Vincto fossore coluntur

    Hesperiae segetes.——"     Lib. vii.[79]

§ Lib. iii. cap. 19.[80]

¶ Id. lib. iv. cap. 8.[81]

reason to suspect, that anciently every great family in ITALY, and probably in other parts of the world, was a species of convent. And though we have reason to condemn all those popish institutions, as nurseries of superstition, burthensome to the public, and oppressive to the poor prisoners, male as well as female; yet may it be questioned whether they be so destructive to the populousness of a state, as is commonly imagined.[82] Were the land, which belongs to a convent, bestowed on a nobleman, he would spend its revenue on dogs, horses, grooms, footmen, cooks, and house-maids; and his family would not furnish many more citizens than the convent.[83]

The common reason, why any parent thrusts his daughters into nunneries, is, that he may not be overburthened with too numerous a family; but the ancients had a method almost as innocent, and more effectual to that purpose, to wit, exposing their children in early infancy. This practice was very common; and is not spoken of by any author of those times with the horror it deserves, or scarcely* even with disapprobation.[84] PLUTARCH, the humane, good-natured PLUTARCH,† mentions it as a merit in ATTALUS, king of PERGAMUS, that he murdered, or, if you will, exposed all his own children, in order to leave his crown to the son of his brother, EUMENES; signalizing in this manner his gratitude and affection to EUMENES, who had left him his heir preferably to that son. It was SOLON, the most celebrated of the sages of GREECE, that gave parents permission by law to kill their children.‡

Shall we then allow these two circumstances to compensate each other, to wit, monastic vows and the exposing of children, and to be unfavourable, in equal degrees, to the propagation of mankind? I doubt the advantage is here on the side of antiquity. Perhaps, by an odd connexion of causes, the barbarous practice of the ancients might rather render those times more populous. By removing the terrors of too numerous a family it would engage many people in marriage; and such is the force of natural affection, that very few, in comparison, would have resolution enough, when it came to the push, to carry into execution their former intentions.

CHINA, the only country where this practice of exposing children

---

* TACITUS blames it. De morib. Germ.[85]

† De fraterno amore. SENECA also approves of the exposing of sickly infirm children. De ira, lib. i. cap. 15.[86]

‡ SEXT. EMP. lib. iii. cap. 24.[87]

prevails at present, is the most populous country we know of; and every man is married before he is twenty.[88] Such early marriages could scarcely be general, had not men the prospect of so easy a method of getting rid of their children. I own, that* PLUTARCH speaks of it as a very general maxim of the poor to expose their children; and as the rich were then averse to marriage, on account of the courtship they met with from those who expected legacies from them, the public must have been in a bad situation between them.†

Of all sciences there is none, where first appearances are more deceitful than in politics. Hospitals for foundlings[89] seem favourable to the encrease of numbers; and perhaps, may be so, when kept under proper restrictions. But when they open the door to every one, without distinction, they have probably a contrary effect, and are pernicious to the state. It is computed, that every ninth child born at PARIS, is sent to the hospital; though it seems certain, according to the common course of human affairs, that it is not a hundredth child whose parents are altogether incapacitated to rear and educate him.[90] The great difference, for health, industry, and morals, between an education in an hospital and that in a private family, should induce us not to make the entrance into the former too easy and engaging. To kill one's own child is shocking to nature, and must therefore be somewhat unusual; but to turn over the care of him upon others, is very tempting to the natural indolence of mankind.

Having considered the domestic life and manners of the ancients, compared to those of the moderns; where, in the main, we seem rather superior, so far as the present question is concerned; we shall now examine the *political* customs and institutions of both ages, and weigh their influence in retarding or forwarding the propagation of mankind.

Before the encrease of the ROMAN power,[91] or rather till its full establishment, almost all the nations, which are the scene of ancient history, were divided into small territories or petty commonwealths, where of course a great equality of fortune prevailed, and the center of the government was always very near its frontiers.

This was the situation of affairs not only in GREECE and ITALY, but also in SPAIN, GAUL, GERMANY, AFRIC, and a great part of the Lesser

---

* De amore prolis.[92]
† See NOTE [Z].

ASIA: And it must be owned, that no institution could be more favourable to the propagation of mankind. For, though a man of an overgrown fortune, not being able to consume more than another, must share it with those who serve and attend him; yet their possession being precarious, they have not the same encouragement to marry, as if each had a small fortune, secure and independent. Enormous cities are, besides, destructive to society, beget vice and disorder of all kinds, starve the remoter provinces, and even starve themselves, by the prices to which they raise all provisions.[93] Where each man had his little house and field to himself, and each county had its capital, free and independent; what a happy situation of mankind![94] How favourable to industry and agriculture; to marriage and propagation! The prolific virtue of men, were it to act in its full extent, without that restraint which poverty and necessity imposes on it, would double the number every generation:[95] And nothing surely can give it more liberty, than such small commonwealths, and such an equality of fortune among the citizens. All small states naturally produce equality of fortune, because they afford no opportunities of great encrease; but small commonwealths much more, by that division of power and authority which is essential to them.

When XENOPHON* returned after the famous expedition with CYRUS, he hired himself and 6000 of the GREEKS into the service of SEUTHES, a prince of THRACE; and the articles of his agreement were, that each soldier should receive a *daric* a month, each captain two *darics*, and he himself, as general, four:[96] A regulation of pay which would not a little surprise our modern officers.

DEMOSTHENES and ÆSCHINES, with eight more, were sent ambassadors to PHILIP of MACEDON, and their appointments for above four months were a thousand *drachmas*, which is less than a *drachma* a day for each ambassador.†[97] But a *drachma* a day, nay sometimes two,‡[98] was the pay of a common foot-soldier.[99]

A centurion among the ROMANS had only double pay to a private man, in POLYBIUS's time,§ and we accordingly find the gratuities after a triumph regulated by that proportion.¶ But MARK ANTHONY and

---

* *De exp.* CYR. lib. vii.[100]
† DEMOST. *de falsa leg.* He calls it a considerable sum.[101]
‡ THUCYD. lib. iii.[102]
§ Lib. vi. cap. 37.[103]
¶ TIT. LIV. lib. xli. cap. 7. 13. *& alibi passim.*[104]

the triumvirate gave the centurions five times the reward of the other.*
So much had the encrease of the commonwealth encreased the inequality among the citizens.†

It must be owned, that the situation of affairs in modern times,
with regard to civil liberty, as well as equality of fortune, is not near so
favourable, either to the propagation or happiness of mankind. EUROPE
is shared out mostly into great monarchies;[105] and such parts of it as
are divided into small territories, are commonly governed by absolute
princes, who ruin their people by a mimicry of the greater monarchs,
in the splendor of their court and number of their forces.[106] SWISSER-
LAND alone and HOLLAND resemble the ancient republics; and though
the former is far from possessing any advantage either of soil, climate,
or commerce, yet the numbers of people, with which it abounds, notwithstanding their enlisting themselves[107] into every service in EUROPE,
prove sufficiently the advantages of their political institutions.[108]

The ancient republics derived their chief or only security from the
numbers of their citizens. The TRACHINIANS having lost great numbers
of their people, the remainder, instead of enriching themselves by the
inheritance of their fellow-citizens, applied to SPARTA, their metropolis,
for a new stock of inhabitants. The SPARTANS immediately collected
ten thousand men; among whom the old citizens divided the lands of
which the former proprietors had perished.‡

After TIMOLEON had banished DIONYSIUS from SYRACUSE, and
had settled the affairs of SICILY, finding the cities of SYRACUSE and
SELLINUNTIUM extremely depopulated by tyranny, war, and faction, he
invited over from GREECE some new inhabitants to repeople them.§
Immediately forty thousand men (PLUTARCH¶ says sixty thousand)
offered themselves; and he distributed so many lots of land among
them, to the great satisfaction of the ancient inhabitants: A proof at
once of the maxims of ancient policy, which affected populousness
more than riches; and of the good effects of these maxims, in the

---

* APPIAN. *De bell. civ.* lib. iv.[109]
† CÆSAR gave the centurions ten times the gratuity of the common soldiers, *De bello Gal-
lico*, lib. viii. In the RHODIAN cartel, mentioned afterwards, no distinction in the ransom
was made on account of ranks in the army.[110]
‡ DIOD. SIC. lib. xii. THUCYD. lib. iii.[111]
§ DIOD. SIC. lib. xvi.[112]
¶ *In vita* TIMOL.[113]

extreme populousness of that small country, GREECE, which could at once supply so great a colony. The case was not much different with the ROMANS in early times. He is a pernicious citizen, said M. CURIUS, who cannot be content with seven acres.* Such ideas of equality could not fail of producing great numbers of people.

We must now consider what disadvantages[114] the ancients lay under with regard to populousness, and what checks they received from their political maxims and institutions. There are commonly compensations in every human condition: and though these compensations be not always perfectly equal, yet they serve, at least, to restrain the prevailing principle. To compare them and estimate their influence, is indeed difficult, even where they take place in the same age, and in neighbouring countries: But where several ages have intervened, and only scattered lights are afforded us by ancient authors; what can we do but amuse ourselves by talking *pro* and *con,* on an interesting subject, and thereby correcting all hasty and violent determinations?[115]

*First*, We may observe, that the ancient republics were almost in perpetual war,[116] a natural effect of their martial spirit, their love of liberty, their mutual emulation, and that hatred which generally prevails among nations that live in close neighbourhood. Now, war in a small state is much more destructive than in a great one; both because all the inhabitants, in the former case, must serve in the armies; and because the whole state is frontier, and is all exposed to the inroads of the enemy.

The maxims of ancient war were much more destructive than those of modern; chiefly by that distribution of plunder, in which the soldiers were indulged. The private men in our armies are such a low set of people, that we find any abundance, beyond their simple pay, breeds confusion and disorder among them, and a total dissolution of discipline. The very wretchedness and meanness of those, who fill the modern armies, render them less destructive to the countries which they invade:[117] One instance, among many of the deceitfulness of first appearances in all political reasonings.†[118]

Ancient battles were much more bloody, by the very nature of the

* See NOTE [AA].

† The ancient soldiers, being free citizens, above the lowest rank, were all married. Our modern soldiers are either forced to live unmarried, or their marriages turn to small account towards the encrease of mankind. A circumstance which ought, perhaps, to be taken into consideration, as of some consequence in favour of the ancients.

weapons employed in them. The ancients drew up their men 16 or 20, sometimes 50 men deep, which made a narrow front; and it was not difficult to find a field, in which both armies might be marshalled, and might engage with each other. Even where any body of the troops was kept off by hedges, hillocks, woods, or hollow ways, the battle was not so soon decided between the contending parties, but that the others had time to overcome the difficulties which opposed them, and take part in the engagement. And as the whole army was thus engaged, and each man closely buckled to his antagonist, the battles were commonly very bloody, and great slaughter was made on both sides, especially on the vanquished. The long thin lines, required by fire-arms, and the quick decision of the fray, render our modern engagements but partial rencounters,[119] and enable the general, who is foiled in the beginning of the day, to draw off the greater part of his army, sound and entire.[120]

The battles of antiquity, both by their duration, and their resemblance to single combats, were wrought up to a degree of fury quite unknown to later ages. Nothing could then engage the combatants to give quarter, but the hopes of profit, by making slaves of their prisoners. In civil wars, as we learn from TACITUS,* the battles were the most bloody, because the prisoners were not slaves.

What a stout resistance must be made, where the vanquished expected so hard a fate! How inveterate the rage, where the maxims of war were, in every respect, so bloody and severe!

Instances are frequent, in ancient history, of cities besieged, whose inhabitants, rather than open their gates, murdered their wives and children, and rushed themselves on a voluntary death, sweetened perhaps by a little prospect of revenge upon the enemy.[121] GREEKS,† as well as BARBARIANS, have often been wrought up to this degree of fury. And the same determined spirit and cruelty must, in other instances less remarkable, have been destructive to human society, in those petty commonwealths, which lived in close neighbourhood, and were engaged in perpetual wars and contentions.

Sometimes the wars in GREECE, says PLUTARCH,‡ were carried on

* Hist. lib. ii. cap. 44.[122]
† As ABYDUS, mentioned by LIVY, lib. xxxi. cap. 17, 18. and POLYB. lib. xvi. As also the XANTHIANS, APPIAN. *de bell. civil.* lib. iv.[123]
‡ *In vita* ARATI.[124]

entirely by inroads, and robberies, and piracies. Such a method of war must be more destructive in small states, than the bloodiest battles and sieges.

By the laws of the twelve tables,[125] possession during two years formed a prescription for land; one year for moveables:* An indication, that there was not in ITALY, at that time, much more order, tranquillity, and settled police,[126] than there is at present among the TARTARS.[127]

The only cartel[128] I remember in ancient history, is that between DEMETRIUS POLIORCETES and the RHODIANS; when it was agreed, that a free citizen should be restored for 1000 *drachmas*, a slave bearing arms for 500.†

But, *secondly*, it appears that ancient manners were more unfavourable than the modern, not only in times of war, but also in those of peace; and that too in every respect, except the love of civil liberty and of equality, which is, I own, of considerable importance. To exclude faction from a free government, is very difficult, if not altogether impracticable; but such inveterate rage between the factions, and such bloody maxims, are found, in modern times amongst religious parties alone.[129] In ancient history, we may always observe, where one party prevailed, whether the nobles or people (for I can observe no difference in this respect‡) that they immediately butchered all of the opposite party who fell into their hands, and banished such as had been so fortunate as to escape their fury. No form of process, no law, no trial, no pardon. A fourth, a third, perhaps near half of the city was slaughtered, or expelled, every revolution; and the exiles always joined foreign enemies, and did all the mischief possible to their fellow-citizens; till fortune put it in their power to take full revenge by a new revolution. And as these were frequent in such violent governments, the disorder, diffidence, jealousy, enmity, which must prevail, are not easy for us to imagine in this age of the world.

There are only two revolutions I can recollect in ancient history, which passed without great severity, and great effusion of blood in massacres and assassinations, namely, the restoration of the ATHENIAN

* INST. lib ii. cap. 6.[130]
† DIOD. SICUL. lib. xx.[131]
‡ LYSIAS, who was himself of the popular faction, and very narrowly escaped from the thirty tyrants, says, that the Democracy was as violent a government as the Oligarchy. *Orat.* 24. *de statu popul.*[132]

Democracy by THRASYBULUS, and the subduing of the ROMAN republic by CÆSAR.[133] We learn from ancient history, that THRASYBULUS passed a general amnesty for all past offences; and first introduced that word, as well as practice, into GREECE.* It appears, however, from many orations of LYSIAS,† that the chief, and even some of the subaltern offenders, in the preceding tyranny, were tried, and capitally punished. And as to CÆSAR's clemency, though much celebrated, it would not gain great applause in the present age. He butchered, for instance, all CATO's senate, when he became master of UTICA;‡ and these, we may readily believe, were not the most worthless of the party. All those who had borne arms against that usurper, were attainted; and, by HIRTIUS's law, declared incapable of all public offices.

These people were extremely fond of liberty; but seem not to have understood it very well. When the thirty tyrants[134] first established their dominion at ATHENS, they began with seizing all the sycophants[135] and informers, who had been so troublesome during the Democracy, and putting them to death by an arbitrary sentence and execution. *Every man*, says SALLUST§ and LYSIAS,¶ *was rejoiced at these punishments*; not considering, that liberty was from that moment annihilated.

The utmost energy of the nervous style of THUCYDIDES, and the copiousness and expression of the GREEK language, seem to sink under that historian, when he attempts to describe the disorders, which arose from faction throughout all the GRECIAN commonwealths. You would imagine, that he still labours with a thought greater than he can find words to communicate. And he concludes his pathetic description with an observation, which is at once refined and solid. "In these contests," says he, "those who were the dullest, and most stupid, and had the least foresight, commonly prevailed. For being conscious of this weakness, and dreading to be over-reached by those of greater penetration, they went to work hastily, without premeditation, by the sword and poinard,[136]

---

* CICERO, PHILIP. I.[137]
† As *orat.* 11. *contra* ERATOST. *orat.* 12. *contra.* AGORAT. *orat.* 15. pro MANTITH.[138]
‡ APPIAN. *de bell. civ.* lib. ii.[139]
§ See CÆSAR's speech *de bell. Catil.*[140]
¶ *Orat.* 24.[141] And in *orat.* 29. he mentions the factious spirit of the popular assemblies as the only cause why these illegal punishments should displease.[142]

and thereby got the start of their antagonists, who were forming fine schemes and projects for their destruction."*

Not to mention DIONYSIUS† the elder, who is computed to have butchered in cool blood above 10,000 of his fellow-citizens; or AGATHOCLES,‡ NABIS,§ and others, still more bloody than he; the transactions, even in free governments, were extremely violent and destructive. At ATHENS, the thirty tyrants and the nobles, in a twelve-month, murdered, without trial, about 1200 of the people, and banished above the half of the citizens that remained.¶ In ARGOS, near the same time, the people killed 1200 of the nobles; and afterwards their own demagogues, because they had refused to carry their prosecutions farther.** The people also in CORCYRA killed 1500 of the nobles, and banished a thousand.†† These numbers will appear the more surprising, if we consider the extreme smallness of these states. But all ancient history is full of such instances.‡‡

When ALEXANDER ordered all the exiles to be restored throughout all the cities; it was found, that the whole amounted to 20,000 men;§§ the remains probably of still greater slaughters and massacres. What an astonishing multitude in so narrow a country as ancient GREECE! And what domestic confusion, jealousy, partiality, revenge, heart-burnings, must tear those cities, where factions were wrought up to such a degree of fury and despair.

It would be easier, says ISOCRATES to PHILIP, to raise an army in GREECE at present from the vagabonds than from the cities.[143]

Even when affairs came not to such extremities (which they failed not to do almost in every city twice or thrice every century) property was rendered very precarious by the maxims of ancient government. XENOPHON, in the Banquet of SOCRATES, gives us a natural unaffected

---

* Lib. iii.[144]
† PLUT. *de virt. & fort.* ALEX.[145]
‡ DIOD. SIC. lib. xviii, xix.[146]
§ TIT. LIV. xxxi, xxxiii, xxxiv.[147]
¶ DIOD. SIC. lib. xiv. ISOCRATES says there were only 5000 banished. He makes the number of those killed amount to 1500. AREOP. ÆSCHINES *contra* CTESIPH. assigns precisely the same number. SENECA (*de tranq. anim.* cap. 5.) says 1300.[148]
** DIOD. SIC. lib. xv.[149]
†† DIOD. SIC. lib. xiii.[150]
‡‡ See NOTE [BB].
§§ DIOD. SIC. lib. xviii.[151]

description of the tyranny of the ATHENIAN people. "In my poverty," says CHARMIDES, "I am much more happy than I ever was while possessed of riches: as much as it is happier to be in security than in terrors, free than a slave, to receive than to pay court, to be trusted than suspected. Formerly I was obliged to caress every informer; some imposition was continually laid upon me; and it was never allowed me to travel, or be absent from the city. At present, when I am poor I look big, and threaten others. The rich are afraid of me, and show me every kind of civility and respect; and I am become a kind of tyrant in the city." *[152]

In one of the pleadings of LYSIAS,† the orator very coolly speaks of it, by the by, as a maxim of the ATHENIAN people, that, whenever they wanted money, they put to death some of the rich citizens as well as strangers, for the sake of the forfeiture. In mentioning this, he seems not to have any intention of blaming them; still less of provoking them, who were his audience and judges.

Whether a man was a citizen or a stranger among that people, it seems indeed requisite, either that he should impoverish himself, or that the people would impoverish him, and perhaps kill him into the bargain. The orator last mentioned gives a pleasant account of an estate laid out in the public service;‡ that is, above the third of it in raree-shows[153] and figured dances.

I need not insist on the GREEK tyrannies, which were altogether horrible. Even the mixed monarchies, by which most of the ancient states of GREECE were governed, before the introduction of republics, were very unsettled. Scarcely any city, but ATHENS, says ISOCRATES, could show a succession of kings for four or five generations.§

Besides many other obvious reasons for the instability of ancient monarchies, the equal division of property among the brothers in private families, must, by a necessary consequence, contribute to unsettle and disturb the state. The universal preference given to the elder by modern laws, though it encreases the inequality of fortunes, has, however, this good effect, that it accustoms men to the same idea in public succession, and cuts off all claim and pretension of the younger.[154]

* Pag. 885. *ex edit.* LEUNCLAV.[155]
† *Orat.* 29. in NICOM.[156]
‡ See NOTE [CC].
§ Panath.[157]

The new settled colony of HERACLEA, falling immediately into faction applied to SPARTA, who sent HERIPIDAS with full authority to quiet their dissentions. This man, not provoked by any opposition, not inflamed by party rage, knew no better expedient than immediately putting to death about 500 of the citizens.* A strong proof how deeply rooted these violent maxims of government were throughout all GREECE.[158]

If such was the disposition of men's minds among that refined people, what may be expected in the commonwealths of ITALY, AFRIC, SPAIN, and GAUL, which were denominated barbarous? Why otherwise did the GREEKS so much value themselves on their humanity, gentleness, and moderation, above all other nations? This reasoning seems very natural. But unluckily the history of the ROMAN commonwealth, in its earlier times, if we give credit to the received accounts, presents an opposite conclusion. No blood was ever shed in any sedition at ROME, till the murder of the GRACCHI. DIONYSIUS HALICARNASSÆUS,† observing the singular humanity[159] of the ROMAN people in this particular, makes use of it as an argument that they were originally of GRECIAN extraction: Whence we may conclude, that the factions and revolutions in the barbarous republics were usually more violent than even those of GREECE above-mentioned.

If the ROMANS were so late in coming to blows, they made ample compensation, after they had once entered upon the bloody scene; and APPIAN's history[160] of their civil wars contains the most frightful picture of massacres, proscriptions, and forfeitures, that ever was presented to the world. What pleases most, in that historian, is, that he seems to feel a proper resentment of these barbarous proceedings; and talks not with that provoking coolness and indifference, which custom had produced in many of the GREEK historians.‡

The maxims of ancient politics contain, in general, so little humanity and moderation, that it seems superfluous to give any particular reason for the acts of violence committed at any particular period. Yet I cannot forbear observing, that the laws, in the later period of the ROMAN commonwealth, were so absurdly contrived, that they obliged

* DIOD. SIC. lib. xiv.[161]
† Lib. i.[162]
‡ See NOTE [DD].

the heads of parties to have recourse to these extremities. All capital punishments were abolished: However criminal, or, what is more, however dangerous any citizen might be, he could not regularly be punished otherwise than by banishment: And it became necessary, in the revolutions of party, to draw the sword of private vengeance; nor was it easy, when laws were once violated, to set bounds to these sanguinary proceedings. Had BRUTUS himself prevailed over the *triumvirate*, could he, in common prudence, have allowed OCTAVIUS and ANTHONY, to live, and have contented himself with banishing them to RHODES or MARSEILLES,[163] where they might still have plotted new commotions and rebellions? His executing C. ANTONIUS, brother to the *triumvir*, shows evidently his sense of the matter. Did not CICERO, with the approbation of all the wise and virtuous of ROME, arbitrarily put to death CATILINE's accomplices, contrary to law, and without any trial or form of process? And if he moderated his executions, did it not proceed, either from the clemency of his temper, or the conjunctures of the times? A wretched security in a government which pretends to laws and liberty![164]

Thus, one extreme produces another. In the same manner as excessive severity in the laws is apt to beget great relaxation in their execution; so their excessive lenity naturally produces cruelty and barbarity. It is dangerous to force us, in any case, to pass their sacred boundaries.

One general cause of the disorders, so frequent in all ancient governments, seems to have consisted in the great difficulty of establishing any Aristocracy in those ages, and the perpetual discontents and seditions of the people, whenever even the meanest and most beggarly were excluded from the legislature and from public offices.[165] The very quality of *freemen* gave such a rank, being opposed to that of slave, that it seemed to entitle the possessor to every power and privilege of the commonwealth. SOLON's* laws excluded no freeman from votes or elections, but confined some magistracies to a particular *census*;[166] yet were the people never satisfied till those laws were repealed. By the treaty with ANTIPATER,† no ATHENIAN was allowed a vote whose *census* was less than 2000 *drachmas* (about 60 *l. Sterling*). And though such a government would to us appear sufficiently democratical, it was so disagreeable to that people, that above two-thirds of them

* PLUTARCHUS *in vita* SOLON.[167]
† DIOD. SIC. lib. xviii.[168]

immediately left their country.\* CASSANDER reduced that *census* to the half;† yet still the government was considered as an oligarchical tyranny, and the effect of foreign violence.

SERVIUS TULLIUS's‡ laws seem equal and reasonable, by fixing the power in proportion to the property:[169] Yet the ROMAN people could never be brought quietly to submit to them.

In those days there was no medium between a severe, jealous Aristocracy, ruling over discontented subjects; and a turbulent, factious, tyrannical Democracy. At present, there is not one republic in EUROPE, from one extremity of it to the other, that is not remarkable for justice, lenity, and stability, equal to, or even beyond MARSEILLES, RHODES,[170] or the most celebrated in antiquity. Almost all of them are well-tempered Aristocracies.

But *thirdly*, there are many other circumstances, in which ancient nations seem inferior to the modern, both for the happiness and encrease of mankind. Trade, manufactures, industry, were no where, in former ages, so flourishing as they are at present in EUROPE. The only garb of the ancients, both for males and females, seems to have been a kind of flannel, which they wore commonly white or grey, and which they scoured as often as it became dirty.[171] TYRE, which carried on, after CARTHAGE, the greatest commerce of any city in the MEDITERRANEAN, before it was destroyed by ALEXANDER, was no mighty city, if we credit ARRIAN's account of its inhabitants.§ ATHENS is commonly supposed to have been a trading city: But it was as populous before the MEDIAN war[172] as at any time after it, according to HERODOTUS;¶ yet its commerce, at that time, was so inconsiderable, that, as the same historian observes,\*\* even the neighbouring coasts of ASIA were as little frequented by the GREEKS as the pillars of HERCULES:[173] For beyond these he conceived nothing.[174]

Great interest of money, and great profits of trade, are an infallible

---

\* Id. ibid.[175]

† Id. ibid.[176]

‡ TIT. LIV. lib. i. cap. 43.

§ Lib. ii. There were 8000 killed during the siege; and the captives amounted to 30,000. DIODORUS SICULUS, lib. xvii. says only 13,000: But he accounts for this small number, by saying that the TYRIANS had sent away before-hand part of their wives and children to CARTHAGE.[177]

¶ Lib. v. he makes the number of the citizens amount to 30,000.[178]

\*\* Ib. v.[179]

indication, that industry and commerce are but in their infancy.[180] We read in LYSIAS* of 100 *per cent.* profit made on a cargo of two talents, sent to no greater distance than from ATHENS to the ADRIATIC: Nor is this mentioned as an instance of extraordinary profit. ANTIDORUS, says DEMOSTHENES,† paid three talents and a half for a house which he let at a talent a year: And the orator blames his own tutors for not employing his money to like advantage. My fortune, says he, in eleven years minority, ought to have been tripled.[181] The value of 20 of the slaves left by his father,[182] he computes at 40 minas, and the yearly profit of their labour at 12.‡ The most moderate interest at ATHENS, (for there was higher§ often paid)[183] was 12 *per cent.*,¶ and that paid monthly.[184] Not to insist upon the high interest, to which the vast sums distributed in elections had raised money** at ROME, we find, that VERRES, before that factious period, stated 24 *per cent.* for money which he left in the hands of the publicans: And though CICERO exclaims against this article, it is not on account of the extravagant usury; but because it had never been customary to state any interest on such occasions.†† Interest, indeed, sunk at ROME, after the settlement of the empire:[185] But it never remained any considerable time so low, as in the commercial states of modern times.‡‡

Among the other inconveniencies, which the ATHENIANS felt from the fortifying of DECELIA by the LACEDEMONIANS, it is represented by THUCYDIDES,§§ as one of the most considerable, that they could not bring over their corn from EUBEA by land, passing by OROPUS; but were obliged to embark it, and to sail round the promontory of SUNIUM. A surprising instance of the imperfection of ancient navigation! For the water-carriage is not here above double the land.[186]

I do not remember a passage in any ancient author, where the growth of a city is ascribed to the establishment of a manufacture. The commerce, which is said to flourish, is chiefly the exchange of those commodities, for

* *Orat. 33. advers.* DIAGIT.[187]
† *Contra* APHOB. p. 25. *ex edit.* ALDI.[188]
‡ Id. p. 19.[189]
§ Id. ibid.
¶ Id. ibid. and ÆSCHINES *contra* CTESIPH.[190]
** *Epist. ad* ATTIC. lib. iv. epist.15.[191]
†† *Contra* VERR. *orat.* 3.[192]
‡‡ See Essay IV.[193]
§§ Lib. vii.[194]

which different soils and climates were suited. The sale of wine and oil into AFRICA, according to DIODORUS SICULUS,* was the foundation of the riches of AGRIGENTUM.[195] The situation of the city of SYBARIS, according to the same author† was the cause of its immense populousness; being built near the two rivers CRATHYS and SYBARIS.[196] But these two rivers, we may observe, are not navigable; and could only produce some fertile vallies, for agriculture and tillage; an advantage so inconsiderable, that a modern writer would scarcely have taken notice of it.

The barbarity of the ancient tyrants, together with the extreme love of liberty, which animated those ages, must have banished every merchant and manufacturer, and have quite depopulated the state, had it subsisted upon industry and commerce. While the cruel and suspicious DIONYSIUS was carrying on his butcheries, who, that was not detained by his landed property, and could have carried with him any art or skill to procure a subsistence in other countries, would have remained exposed to such implacable barbarity? The persecutions of PHILIP II. and LEWIS XIV. filled all EUROPE with the manufacturers of FLANDERS and of FRANCE.[197]

I grant, that agriculture is the species of industry chiefly requisite to the subsistence of multitudes; and it is possible, that this industry may flourish, even where manufactures and other arts are unknown and neglected. SWISSERLAND is at present a remarkable instance; where we find, at once, the most skilful husbandmen, and the most bungling tradesmen, that are to be met with in EUROPE.[198] That agriculture flourished in GREECE and ITALY, at least in some parts of them, and at some periods, we have reason to presume; And whether the mechanical arts had reached the same degree of perfection, may not be esteemed so material; especially, if we consider the great equality of riches in the ancient republics, where each family was obliged to cultivate, with the greatest care and industry, its own little field,[199] in order to its subsistence.

But is it just reasoning, because agriculture may, in some instances, flourish without trade or manufactures, to conclude, that, in any great extent of country, and for any great tract of time, it would subsist alone? The most natural way, surely, of encouraging husbandry, is, first, to excite other kinds of industry, and thereby afford the labourer a ready

* Lib. xiii.[200]
† Lib. xii.[201]

market for his commodities, and a return of such goods as may contribute to his pleasure and enjoyment. This method is infallible and universal; and, as it prevails more in modern government than in the ancient, it affords a presumption of the superior populousness of the former.[202]

Every man, says XENOPHON,* may be a farmer: No art or skill is requisite: All consists in industry, and in attention to the execution. A strong proof, as COLUMELLA hints,[203] that agriculture was but little known in the age of XENOPHON.

All our later improvements and refinements, have they done nothing towards the easy subsistence of men, and consequently towards their propagation and encrease? Our superior skill in mechanics; the discovery of new worlds, by which commerce has been so much enlarged; the establishment of posts; and the use of bills of exchange:[204] These seem all extremely useful to the encouragement of art, industry, and populousness. Were we to strike off these, what a check should we give to every kind of business and labour, and what multitudes of families would immediately perish from want and hunger? And it seems not probable, that we could supply the place of these new inventions by any other regulation or institution.

Have we reason to think, that the police[205] of ancient states was any wise comparable to that of modern, or that men had then equal security, either at home, or in their journies by land or water? I question not, but every impartial examiner would give us the preference in this particular.†

Thus, upon comparing the whole, it seems impossible to assign any just reason, why the world should have been more populous in ancient than in modern times. The equality of property among the ancients, liberty, and the small divisions of their states, were indeed circumstances favourable to the propagation of mankind: But their wars were more bloody and destructive, their governments more factious and unsettled, commerce and manufactures more feeble and languishing, and the general police more loose and irregular. These latter disadvantages seem to form a sufficient counterbalance to the former advantages; and rather

* Oecon.[206]
† See Part I. Essay XI.[207]

favour the opposite opinion to that which commonly prevails with regard to this subject.

But there is no reasoning, it may be said, against matter of fact. If it appear, that the world was then more populous than at present, we may be assured, that our conjectures are false, and that we have overlooked some material circumstance in the comparison. This I readily own: All our preceding reasonings, I acknowledge to be mere trifling, or, at least, small skirmishes and frivolous rencounters, which decide nothing. But unluckily the main combat, where we compare facts, cannot be rendered much more decisive. The facts, delivered by ancient authors, are either so uncertain or so imperfect as to afford us nothing positive in this matter. How indeed could it be otherwise? The very facts, which we must oppose to them, in computing the populousness of modern states, are far from being either certain or complete. Many grounds of calculation proceeded on by celebrated writers, are little better than those of the Emperor HELIOGABALUS, who formed an estimate of the immense greatness of ROME, from ten thousand pound weight of cobwebs which had been found in that city.*

It is to be remarked, that all kinds of numbers are uncertain in ancient manuscripts, and have been subject to much greater corruptions than any other part of the text; and that for an obvious reason. Any alteration, in other places, commonly affects the sense or grammar, and is more readily perceived by the reader and transcriber.

Few enumerations of inhabitants have been made of any tract of country by any ancient author of good authority, so as to afford us a large enough view for comparison.

It is probable, that there was formerly a good foundation for the number of citizens assigned to any free city; because they entered for a share in the government, and there were exact registers kept of them. But as the number of slaves is seldom mentioned, this leaves us in as great uncertainty as ever, with regard to the populousness even of single cities.

The first page of THUCYDIDES is, in my opinion, the commencement of real history. All preceding narrations are so intermixed with fable, that philosophers ought to abandon them, in a great measure, to the embellishment of poets and orators.†

---

* ÆLII LAMPRID. *in vita* HELIOGAB. cap. 26.[208]
† See NOTE [EE].

With regard to remote times, the numbers of people assigned[209] are often ridiculous, and lose all credit and authority. The free citizens of SYBARIS, able to bear arms, and actually drawn out in battle, were 300,000. They encountered at SIAGRA with 100,000 citizens of CROTONA, another GREEK city contiguous to them; and were defeated. This is DIODORUS SICULUS's* account; and is very seriously insisted on by that historian. STRABO† also mentions the same number of SYBARITES.[210]

DIODORUS SICULUS,‡ enumerating the inhabitants of AGRIGEN-TUM, when it was destroyed by the CARTHAGINIANS, says, that they amounted to 20,000 citizens, 200,000 strangers, besides slaves, who, in so opulent a city as he represents it, would probably be, at least, as numerous. We must remark, that the women and the children are not included; and that, therefore, upon the whole, this city must have con-tained near two millions of inhabitants.§ And what was the reason of so immense an encrease! They were industrious in cultivating the neigh-bouring fields, not exceeding a small ENGLISH county; and they traded with their wine and oil to AFRICA, which, at that time, produced none of these commodities.[211]

PTOLEMY, says THEOCRITUS,¶ commands 33,339 cities. I suppose the singularity of the number was the reason of assigning it. DIODORUS SICULUS** assigns three millions of inhabitants to ÆGYPT, a small number: But then he makes the number of cities amount to 18,000: An evident contradiction.

He says,†† the people were formerly seven millions.[212] Thus remote times are always most envied and admired.[213]

That XERXES's army was extremely numerous, I can readily believe; both, from the great extent of his empire, and from the practice among the eastern nations, of encumbering their camp with a superfluous multitude: But will any rational man cite HERODOTUS's wonderful narrations[214] as an authority? There is something very rational, I own,

---

* Lib. xii.[215]
† Lib. vi.[216]
‡ Lib. xiii.[217]
§ DIOGENES LAERTIUS (*in vita* EMPEDOCLIS) says, that AGRIGENTUM contained only 800,000 inhabitants.[218]
¶ Idyll. 17.[219]
** Lib. i.[220]
†† Idyll. 17.

in LYSIAS's* argument upon this subject. Had not XERXES's army been incredibly numerous, says he, he had never made a bridge over the HELLESPONT: It had been much easier to have transported his men over so short a passage, with the numerous shipping of which he was master.

POLYBIUS† says, that the ROMANS, between the first and second PUNIC wars,[221] being threatened with an invasion from the GAULS, mustered all their own forces, and those of their allies, and found them amount to seven hundred thousand men able to bear arms: A great number surely, and which, when joined to the slaves, is probably not less, if not rather more, than that extent of country affords at present.‡ The enumeration too seems to have been made with some exactness; and POLYBIUS gives us the detail of the particulars. But might not the number be magnified, in order to encourage the people?

DIODORUS SICULUS§ makes the same enumeration amount to near a million. These variations are suspicious. He plainly too supposes, that ITALY in his time was not so populous: Another suspicious circumstance. For who can believe, that the inhabitants of that country diminished from the time of the first PUNIC war to that of the *triumvirates?*[222]

JULIUS CÆSAR according to APPIAN,¶ encountered four millions of GAULS, killed one million, and made another million prisoners.** Supposing the number of the enemy's army and that of the slain could be exactly assigned, which never is possible; how could it be known how often the same man returned into the armies, or how distinguish the new from the old levied soldiers? No attention ought ever to be given to such loose, exaggerated calculations; especially where the author does not tell us the mediums, upon which the calculations were founded.

PATERCULUS†† makes the number of GAULS killed by CÆSAR amount only to 400,000: A more probable account, and more easily reconciled to the history of these wars given by that conqueror himself in his

---

* *Orat. funebris.*[223]

† Lib. ii.[224]

‡ The country that supplied this number, was not above a third of ITALY *viz.* the Pope's dominions, TUSCANY, and a part of the kingdom of NAPLES: But perhaps in those early times there were very few slaves, except in ROME, or the great cities.

§ Lib. ii.[225]

¶ CELTICA.[226]

** PLUTARCH (*in vita* CÆS.) makes the number that CÆSAR fought with amount to three millions; JULIAN (*in* CÆSARIBUS) to two.[227]

†† Lib. ii. cap. 47.[228]

Commentaries.* The most bloody of his battles were fought against the HELVETII and the GERMANS.

One would imagine, that every circumstance of the life and actions of DIONYSIUS the elder might be regarded as authentic, and free from all fabulous exaggeration; both because he lived at a time when letters flourished most in GREECE, and because his chief historian was PHIL- ISTUS, a man allowed to be of great genius, and who was a courtier and minister of that prince. But can we admit, that he had a standing army of 100,000 foot, 10,000 horse, and a fleet of 400 gallies?† These, we may observe, were mercenary forces, and subsisted upon pay, like our armies in EUROPE. For the citizens were all disarmed; and when DION after- wards invaded SICILY, and called on his countrymen to vindicate their liberty, he was obliged to bring arms along with him, which he distrib- uted among those who joined him.‡ In a state where agriculture alone flourishes, there may be many inhabitants; and if these be all armed and disciplined, a great force may be called out upon occasion: But great bodies of mercenary troops can never be maintained, without either great trade and numerous manufactures, or extensive dominions. The United Provinces never were masters of such a force by sea and land, as that which is said to belong to DIONYSIUS; yet they possess as large a territory, perfectly well cultivated, and have much more resources from their commerce and industry. DIODORUS SICULUS allows, that, even in his time, the army of DIONYSIUS appeared incredible;[229] that is, as I interpret it, was entirely a fiction, and the opinion arose from the exag- gerated flattery of the courtiers, and perhaps from the vanity and policy of the tyrant himself.

It is a usual fallacy, to consider all the ages of antiquity as one period, and to compute the numbers contained in the great cities mentioned by ancient authors, as if these cities had been all cotemporary. The GREEK colonies flourished extremely in SICILY during the age of ALEXANDER: But in AUGUSTUS's time they were so decayed, that almost all the prod- uce of that fertile island was consumed in ITALY.§[230]

Let us now examine the numbers of inhabitants assigned to particular

* See NOTE [FF].
† DIOD. SIC. lib. ii.[231]
‡ PLUTARCH *in vita* DIONIS.[232]
§ STRABO, lib. vi.[233]

cities in antiquity; and omitting the numbers of NINEVEH, BABYLON, and the EGYPTIAN THEBES, let us confine ourselves to the sphere of real history, to the GRECIAN and ROMAN states. I must own, the more I consider this subject, the more am I inclined to scepticism, with regard to the great populousness ascribed to ancient times.

ATHENS is said by PLATO* to be a very great city; and it was surely the greatest of all the GREEK† cities, except SYRACUSE, which was nearly about the same size in THUCYDIDES's‡ time, and afterwards encreased beyond it. For CICERO§ mentions it as the greatest of all the GREEK cities in his time; not comprehending, I suppose, either ANTIOCH or ALEXANDRIA under that denomination. ATHENÆUS¶ says, that, by the enumeration of DEMETRIUS PHALEREUS, there were in ATHENS 21,000 citizens, 10,000 strangers, and 400,000 slaves. This number is much insisted on by those whose opinion I call in question, and is esteemed a fundamental fact to their purpose: But, in my opinion, there is no point of criticism more certain, than that ATHENÆUS and CTESICLES, whom he quotes, are here mistaken, and that the number of slaves is, at least, augmented by a whole cypher, and ought not to be regarded as more than 40,000.[234]

*First*, When the number of citizens is said to be 21,000 by ATHENÆUS,** men of full age are only understood. For, (1.) HERODOTUS says,†† that ARISTAGORAS, ambassador from the IONIANS, found it harder to deceive one SPARTAN than 30,000 ATHENIANS; meaning, in a loose way, the whole state, supposed to be met in one popular assembly, excluding the women and children. (2.) THUCYDIDES‡‡ says, that, making allowance for all the absentees in the fleet, army, garrisons, and for people employed in their private affairs, the ATHENIAN assembly never rose to five thousand. (3.) The forces, enumerated by the same

---

* *Apolog.* SOCR.[235]

† ARGOS seems also to have been a great city; for LYCIAS contents himself with saying that it did not exceed ATHENS. Orat. 34.[236]

‡ Lib. vi. See also PLUTARCH *in vita* NICIÆ.[237]

§ *Orat. contra* VERREM, lib. iv. cap. 52. STRABO, lib. vi. says, it was twenty-two miles in compass. But then we are to consider, that it contained two harbours within it; one of which was a very large one, and might be regarded as a kind of bay.[238]

¶ Lib. vi. cap. 20.[239]

** DEMOSTHENES assigns 20,000; *contra* ARISTAG.[240]

†† Lib. v.[241]

‡‡ Lib. viii.[242]

historian,* being all citizens, and amounting to 13,000 heavy-armed infantry, prove the same method of calculation; as also the whole tenor of the GREEK historians, who always understand men of full age, when they assign the number of citizens in any republic. Now, these being but the fourth of the inhabitants, the free ATHENIANS were by this account 84,000; the strangers 40,000; and the slaves, calculating by the smaller number, and allowing that they married and propagated at the same rate with freemen, were 160,000; and the whole of the inhabitants 284,000: A number surely large enough. The other number, 1,720,000, makes ATHENS larger than LONDON and PARIS united.

*Secondly*, There were but 10,000 houses[243] in ATHENS.†

*Thirdly*, Though the extent of the walls, as given us by THUCYDIDES,‡ be great, (to wit, eighteen miles, beside the sea-coast): Yet XENOPHON § says, there was much waste ground[244] within the walls. They seem indeed to have joined four distinct and separate cities.¶

*Fourthly*, No insurrection of the slaves,[245] or suspicion of insurrection, is ever mentioned by historians; except one commotion of the miners.**

*Fifthly*, The treatment of slaves by the ATHENIANS is said by XENOPHON,†† and DEMOSTHENES,‡‡ and PLAUTUS,§§ to have been extremely gentle and indulgent: Which could never have been the case, had the disproportion been twenty to one. The disproportion is not so great in any of our colonies; yet are we obliged to exercise a rigorous military government over the negroes.[246]

*Sixthly*, No man is ever esteemed rich for possessing what may be reckoned an equal distribution of property in any country, or even triple or quadruple that wealth. Thus every person in ENGLAND is computed by some to spend six-pence a day: Yet is he esteemed but poor who has five times that sum. Now TIMARCHUS is said by ÆSCHINES ¶¶ to have been left in easy circumstances; but he was master only of ten slaves

* Lib. ii. DIODORUS SICULUS's account perfectly agrees, lib. xii.[247]
† XENOPHON. *Mem.* lib. ii.[248]
‡ Lib. ii.[249]
§ *De ratione red.*[250]
¶ See NOTE [GG].
** ATHEN. lib. vi.[251]
†† *De rep.* ATHEN.[252]
‡‡ PHILIP. 3.[253]
§§ STICHO.[254]
¶¶ *Contra* TIMARCH.[255]

employed in manufactures.[256] LYSIAS and his brother, two strangers, were proscribed by the thirty for their great riches; though they had but sixty a-piece.* DEMOSTHENES was left very rich by his father; yet he had no more than fifty-two slaves.† His workhouse, of twenty cabinet-makers, is said to be a very considerable manufactory.‡[257]

*Seventhly,* During the DECELIAN war, as the GREEK historians call it, 20,000 slaves deserted,[258] and brought the ATHENIANS to great distress, as we learn from THUCYDIDES.§ This could not have happened, had they been only the twentieth part. The best slaves would not desert.

*Eighthly,* XENOPHON¶ proposes a scheme for maintaining by the public 10,000 slaves: And that so great a number may possibly be supported, any one will be convinced, says he, who considers the numbers we possessed before the DECELIAN war. A way of speaking altogether incompatible with the larger number of ATHENÆUS.

*Ninthly,* The whole *census* of the state of ATHENS was less than 6000 talents.[259] And though numbers in ancient manuscripts be often suspected by critics, yet this is unexceptionable; both because DEMOSTHENES,** who gives it, gives also the detail, which checks him; and because POLYBIUS†† assigns the same number, and reasons upon it. Now, the most vulgar slave could yield by his labour an *obolus* a day, over and above his maintenance, as we learn from XENOPHON,‡‡ who says, that NICIAS's overseer paid his master so much for slaves, whom he employed in mines. If you will take the pains to estimate an *obolus* a day, and the slaves at 400,000, computing only at four years purchase, you will find the sum above 12,000 talents; even though allowance be made for the great number of holidays in ATHENS.[260] Besides, many of the slaves would have a much greater value from their art. The lowest that DEMOSTHENES estimates any of his§§ father's slaves is two minas a head. And upon this supposition, it is a little difficult, I confess, to reconcile even the number of 40,000 slaves with the *census* of 6000 talents.

* *Orat.* 11.[261]
† *Contra* APHOB.[262]
‡ Ibid.
§ Lib. vii.[263]
¶ *De rat. red.*[264]
** *De classibus.*[265]
†† Lib. ii. cap. 62.[266]
‡‡ *De rat. red.*[267]
§§ *Contra* APHOBUM.[268]

*Tenthly*, CHIOS is said by THUCYDIDES,* to contain more slaves than any GREEK city, except SPARTA. SPARTA then had more than ATHENS, in proportion to the number of citizens. The SPARTANS were 9000 in the town, 30,000 in the country.† The male slaves, therefore, of full age, must have been more than 780,000;[269] the whole more than 3,120,000. A number impossible to be maintained in a narrow barren country, such as LACONIA, which had no trade. Had the HELOTES been so very numerous, the murder of 2000 mentioned by THUCYDIDES,‡ would have irritated them, without weakening them.

Besides, we are to consider, that the number assigned by ATHENÆUS,§ whatever it is, comprehends all the inhabitants of ATTICA, as well as those of ATHENS. The ATHENIANS affected much a country life, as we learn from THUCYDIDES;¶ and when they were all chased into town, by the invasion of their territory during the PELO-PONNESIAN war, the city was not able to contain them; and they were obliged to lie in the porticoes, temples, and even streets, for want of lodging.**

The same remark is to be extended to all the other GREEK cities; and when the number of citizens is assigned, we must always under-stand it to comprehend the inhabitants of the neighbouring country, as well as of the city. Yet, even with this allowance, it must be con-fessed, that GREECE was a populous country, and exceeded what we could imagine concerning so narrow a territory, naturally not very fertile, and which drew no supplies of corn from other places. For, excepting ATHENS, which traded to PONTUS for that commodity, the other cities seem to have subsisted chiefly from their neighbouring territory.††

RHODES is well known to have been a city of extensive commerce,

---

* Lib. viii.[270]
† PLUTARCH. *in vita* LYCURG.[271]
‡ Lib. iv.[272]
§ The same author affirms, that CORINTH had once 460,000 slaves, ÆGINA 470,000. But the foregoing arguments hold stronger against these facts, which are indeed entirely absurd and impossible. It is however remarkable, that ATHENÆUS cites so great an authority as ARISTOTLE for this last fact: And the scholiast on PINDAR mentions the same number of slaves in ÆGINA.[273]
¶ Lib. ii.[274]
** THUCYD. lib. ii.[275]
†† See NOTE [HH].

and of great fame and splendor; yet it contained only 6000 citizens able to bear arms, when it was besieged by DEMETRIUS.*

THEBES was always one of the capital cities of GREECE:† But the number of its citizens exceeded not those of RHODES.‡ PHLIASIA is said to be a small city by XENOPHON,§ yet we find, that it contained 6000 citizens.¶ I pretend not to reconcile these two facts. Perhaps, XENOPHON calls PHLIASIA a small town, because it made but a small figure in GREECE, and maintained only a subordinate alliance with SPARTA; or perhaps the country, belonging to it, was extensive, and most of the citizens were employed in the cultivation of it, and dwelt in the neighbouring villages.

MANTINEA was equal to any city in ARCADIA:** Consequently it was equal to MEGALOPOLIS, which was fifty stadia, or six miles and a quarter in circumference.†† But MANTINEA had only 3000 citizens.‡‡ The GREEK cities, therefore, contained often fields and gardens, together with the houses; and we cannot judge of them by the extent of their walls. ATHENS contained no more than 10,000 houses;[276] yet its walls, with the sea-coast, were above twenty miles in extent.[277] SYRACUSE was twenty-two miles in circumference; yet was scarcely ever spoken of by the ancients as more populous than ATHENS. BABYLON was a square of fifteen miles, or sixty miles in circuit; but it contained large cultivated fields and inclosures, as we learn from PLINY.[278] Though AURELIAN's wall was fifty miles in circumference;§§ the circuit of all the thirteen divisions of ROME, taken apart, according to PUBLIUS VICTOR,[279] was only about forty-three miles. When an enemy invaded the country, all the inhabitants retired within the walls of the ancient cities, with their cattle and furniture, and instruments of husbandry: and the great height, to which the walls were raised, enabled a small number to defend them with facility.

---

* DIOD. SIC. lib. xx.[280]
† ISOCR. *paneg.*[281]
‡ See NOTE [II].
§ Hist. GRÆC. lib. vii.[282]
¶ Id. lib. vii.[283]
** POLYB. lib. ii.[284]
†† POLYC. lib. ix. cap. 20.[285]
‡‡ LYSIAS, orat. 34.[286]
§§ VOPISCUS *in vita* AUREL.[287]

SPARTA, says XENOPHON,* is one of the cities of GREECE that has the fewest inhabitants. Yet POLYBIUS† says, that it was forty-eight stadia in circumference, and was round.

All the ÆTOLIANS able to bear arms in ANTIPATER's time, deducting some few garrisons, were but ten thousand men.‡

POLYBIUS§ tells us, that the ACHÆAN league might, without any inconvenience, march 30 or 40,000 men: And this account seems probable: For that league comprehended the greater part of PELOPONNESUS. Yet PAUSANIAS,¶ speaking of the same period, says, that all the ACHÆANS able to bear arms, even when several manumitted slaves were joined to them, did not amount to fifteen thousand.

The THESSALIANS, till their final conquest by the ROMANS, were, in all ages, turbulent, factious, seditious, disorderly.** It is not therefore natural to suppose, that this part of GREECE abounded much in people.

We are told by THUCYDIDES,†† that the part of PELOPONNESUS, adjoining to PYLOS, was desart and uncultivated. HERODOTUS says,‡‡ that MACEDONIA was full of lions and wild bulls; animals which can only inhabit vast unpeopled forests. These were the two extremities of GREECE.

All the inhabitants of EPIRUS, of all ages, sexes and conditions, who were sold by PAULUS ÆMILIUS, amounted only to 150,000.§§ Yet EPIRUS might be double the extent of YORKSHIRE.

JUSTIN ¶¶ tells us, that, when PHILIP of MACEDON was declared head of the GREEK confederacy, he called a congress of all the states, except the LACEDEMONIANS, who refused to concur; and he found the force of the whole, upon computation, to amount to 200,000 infantry, and 15,000 cavalry. This must be understood to be all the citizens capable of bearing arms. For as the GREEK republics maintained no mercenary

---

* *De rep.* LACED. This passage is not easily reconciled with that of PLUTARCH above, who says, that SPARTA had 9000 citizens.[288]
† POLYB. lib. ix. cap. 20.[289]
‡ DIOD. SIC. lib. xviii.[290]
§ LEGAT.[291]
¶ *In* ACHAICIS.[292]
** TIT. LIV. lib. xxiv. cap. 51. PLATO *in* CRITONE.[293]
†† Lib. vii.[294]
‡‡ Lib. vii.[295]
§§ TIT. LIV. lib. xlv. cap. 34.[296]
¶¶ Lib. ix. cap. 5.[297]

forces, and had no militia distinct from the whole body of the citizens, it is not conceivable what other medium there could be of computation. That such an army could ever, by GREECE, be brought into the field, and be maintained there, is contrary to all history. Upon this supposition, therefore, we may thus reason. The free GREEKS of all ages and sexes were 860,000. The slaves, estimating them by the number of ATHEN-IAN slaves as above, who seldom married or had families, were double the male citizens of full age, to wit, 430,000. And all the inhabitants of ancient GREECE, excepting LACONIA, were about one million two hundred and ninety thousand: No mighty number, nor exceeding what may be found at present in SCOTLAND, a country of not much greater extent, and very indifferently peopled.

We may now consider the numbers of people in ROME and ITALY, and collect all the lights afforded us by scattered passages in ancient authors. We shall find, upon the whole, a great difficulty, in fixing any opinion on that head; and no reason to support those exaggerated calculations, so much insisted on by modern writers.[298]

DIONYSIUS HALICARNASSÆUS* says, that the ancient walls of ROME were nearly of the same compass with those of ATHENS, but that the suburbs ran out to a great extent; and it was difficult to tell, where the town ended or the country began. In some places of ROME, it appears, from the same author,† from JUVENAL,‡ and from other ancient writers,§ that the houses were high, and families lived in separate storeys, one above another: But it is probable, that these were only the poorer citizens, and only in some few streets. If we may judge from the younger PLINY's¶ account of his own house, and from BARTOLI's plans[299] of ancient buildings, the men of quality had very spacious palaces; and their buildings were like the CHINESE houses at this day, where each apartment is separated from the rest, and rises no higher than a single storey.[300] To which if we add, that the ROMAN nobility much affected extensive porticoes, and even woods** in town; we may perhaps allow VOSSIUS (though there is no manner of reason for it) to read

* Lib. iv.[301]
† Lib. x.[302]
‡ Satyr. iii. l. 269, 270.[303]
§ See NOTE [KK].
¶ See NOTE [LL].
** VITRUV. lib. v. cap. 11. TACIT. annal. lib. xi. cap. 3. SUETON. *in vita* OCTAV. cap. 72, &c.[304]

the famous passage of the elder PLINY* his own way, without admitting the extravagant consequences which he draws from it.

The number of citizens who received corn by the public distribution in the time of AUGUSTUS, were two hundred thousand.† This one would esteem a pretty certain ground of calculation: Yet is it attended with such circumstances as throw us back into doubt and uncertainty.

Did the poorer citizens only receive the distribution? It was calculated, to be sure, chiefly for their benefit. But it appears from a passage in CICERO‡ that the rich might also take their portion, and that it was esteemed no reproach in them to apply for it.

To whom was the corn given; whether only to heads of families, or to every man, woman, and child? The portion every month was five *modii* to each§ (about ⅚ of a bushel). This was too little for a family, and too much for an individual. A very accurate antiquary,¶ therefore, infers, that it was given to every man of full age: But he allows the matter to be uncertain.

Was it strictly enquired, whether the claimant lived within the precincts of Rome; or was it sufficient, that he presented himself at the monthly distribution? This last seems more probable.**

Were there no false claimants? We are told,†† that CÆSAR struck off at once 170,000, who had creeped in without a just title; and it is very little probable, that he remedied all abuses.

But, lastly, what proportion of slaves must we assign to these citizens? This is the most material question; and the most uncertain. It is very doubtful, whether ATHENS can be established as a rule for ROME. Perhaps the ATHENIANS had more slaves, because they employed them in manufactures, for which a capital city, like ROME, seems not so proper.

---

* See NOTE [MM].
† *Ex monument. Ancyr.*[305]
‡ *Tusc. Quæst. lib. iii. cap. 48.*[306]
§ *Licinius apud Sallust. hist. frag. lib. iii.*[307]
¶ *Nicolaus Hortensius de re frumentaria Roman.*[308]
** Not to take the people too much from their business, AUGUSTUS ordained the distribution of corn to be made only thrice a-year: But the people finding the monthly distributions more convenient, (as preserving, I suppose, a more regular œconomy in their family) desired to have them restored. SUETON. AUGUST. cap. 40.[309] Had not some of the people come from some distance for their corn, AUGUSTUS's precaution seems superfluous.
†† *Sueton. in Jul. cap. 41.*[310]

Perhaps, on the other hand, the ROMANS had more slaves, on account of their superior luxury and riches.

There were exact bills of mortality kept at ROME; but no ancient author has given us the number of burials, except SUETONIUS,* who tells us, that in one season, there were 30,000 names carried to the temple of LIBITINA: But this was during a plague;[311] which can afford no certain foundation for any inference.

The public corn, though distributed only to 200,000 citizens, affected very considerably the whole agriculture of ITALY:† a fact no wise reconcileable to some modern exaggerations with regard to the inhabitants of that country.

The best ground of conjecture I can find concerning the greatness of ancient ROME, is this: We are told by HERODIAN,‡ that ANTIOCH and ALEXANDRIA were very little inferior to ROME. It appears from DIODORUS SICULUS,§ that one straight street of ALEXANDRIA reaching from gate to gate, was five miles long; and as ALEXANDRIA was much more extended in length than breadth, it seems to have been a city nearly of the bulk of PARIS;¶ and ROME might be about the size of LONDON.

There lived in ALEXANDRIA, in DIODORUS SICULUS's time,** 300,000 free people, comprehending, I suppose, women and children.†† But what number of slaves? Had we any just ground to fix these at an equal number with the free inhabitants, it would favour the foregoing computation.

There is a passage in HERODIAN, which is a little surprising. He says positively, that the palace of the Emperor was as large as all the rest of the city.‡‡ This was NERO's golden house,[312] which is indeed represented by SUETONIUS §§ and PLINY as of an enormous extent;¶¶ but no power

---

* *In vita Neronis.*[313]
† *Sueton. Aug.* cap. 42.[314]
‡ Lib. iv. cap. 5.[315]
§ Lib. xvii.[316]
¶ See NOTE [NN].
** Lib. xvii.
†† He says ελευθεροι, not πολιται,[317] which last expression must have been understood of citizens alone, and grown men.
‡‡ Lib. iv. cap. 1. πασης πολεως. POLITIAN interprets it "ædibus majoribus etiam reliqua urbe."[318]
§§ See NOTE [OO].
¶¶ PLINIUS, lib. xxxvi. cap. 15. "Bis vidimus urbem totam cingi domibus principum, CAII ac NERONIS."[319]

of imagination can make us conceive it to bear any proportion to such a city as LONDON.

We may observe, had the historian been relating NERO's extravagance, and had he made use of such an expression, it would have had much less weight; these rhetorical exaggerations being so apt to creep into an author's style, even when the most chaste and correct. But it is mentioned by HERODIAN only by the by, in relating the quarrels between GETA and CARACALLA.

It appears from the same historian,* that there was then much land uncultivated, and put to no manner of use; and he ascribes it as a great praise to PERTINAX, that he allowed every one to take such land either in ITALY or elsewhere, and cultivate it as he pleased, without paying any taxes.[320] *Lands uncultivated, and put to no manner of use!* This is not heard of in any part of CHRISTENDOM; except in some remote parts of HUNGARY; as I have been informed.[321] And it surely corresponds very ill with that idea of the extreme populousness of antiquity, so much insisted on.

We learn from VOPISCUS,† that there was even in ETRURIA much fertile land uncultivated, which the Emperor AURELIAN intended to convert into vineyards, in order to furnish the ROMAN people with a gratuitous distribution of wine; a very proper expedient for depopulating still farther that capital and all the neighbouring territories.

It may not be amiss to take notice of the account which POLYBIUS‡ gives of the great herds of swine to be met with in TUSCANY and LOMBARDY, as well as in GREECE, and of the method of feeding them which was then practised. "There are great herds of swine," says he, "throughout all ITALY, particularly in former times, through ETRURIA and CISALPINE GAUL. And a herd frequently consists of a thousand or more swine. When one of these herds in feeding meets with another, they mix together; and the swine-herds have no other expedient for separating them than to go to different quarters, where they sound their horn; and these animals, being accustomed to that signal, run immediately each to the horn of his own keeper. Whereas in GREECE, if the herds of swine happen to mix in the forests, he who has the greater flock, takes

* Lib. ii. cap. 15.[322]
† In AURELIAN. cap. 48.[323]
‡ Lib. xii. cap. 2.[324]

cunningly the opportunity of driving all away. And thieves are very apt to purloin the straggling hogs, which have wandered to a great distance from their keeper in search of food."

May we not infer from this account, that the north of ITALY, as well as GREECE, was then much less peopled, and worse cultivated, than at present? How could these vast herds be fed in a country so full of inclosures, so improved by agriculture, so divided by farms, so planted with vines and corn intermingled together? I must confess, that POL-YBIUS's relation has more the air of that œconomy which is to be met with in our AMERICAN colonies, than the management of a EUROPEAN country.

We meet with a reflection in ARISTOTLE's* Ethics, which seems unaccountable on any supposition, and by proving too much in favour of our present reasoning, may be thought really to prove nothing. That philosopher, treating of friendship, and observing, that this rela-tion ought neither to be contracted to a very few, nor extended over a great multitude, illustrates his opinion by the following argument. "In like manner," says he, "as a city cannot subsist, if it either have so few inhabitants as ten, or so many as a hundred thousand; so is there a mediocrity required in the number of friends; and you destroy the essence of friendship by running into either extreme." What! impossible that a city can contain a hundred thousand inhabitants! Had ARIS-TOTLE never seen nor heard of a city so populous? This, I must own, passes my comprehension.

PLINY† tells us that SELEUCIA, the seat of the GREEK empire in the East, was reported to contain 600,000 people. CARTHAGE is said by STRABO‡ to have contained 700,000. The inhabitants of PEKIN[325] are not much more numerous. LONDON, PARIS, and CONSTANTINOPLE, may admit of nearly the same computation; at least, the two latter cities do not exceed it. ROME, ALEXANDRIA, ANTIOCH, we have already spoken of. From the experience of past and present ages, one might con-jecture that there is a kind of impossibility, that any city could ever rise much beyond this proportion. Whether the grandeur of a city be founded on commerce or on empire, there seem to be invincible obstacles, which

* Lib. ix. cap. 10. His expression is ανθρωπος, not πολιτης; inhabitant, not citizen.[326]
† Lib. vi. cap. 28.[327]
‡ Lib. xvii.[328]

prevent its farther progress. The seats of vast monarchies, by introducing extravagant luxury, irregular expence, idleness, dependence, and false ideas of rank and superiority, are improper for commerce. Extensive commerce checks itself, by raising the price of all labour and commodities.[329] When a great court engages the attendance of a numerous nobility, possessed of overgrown fortunes, the middling gentry remain in their provincial towns, where they can make a figure on a moderate income. And if the dominions of a state arrive at an enormous size, there necessarily arise many capitals, in the remoter provinces, whither all the inhabitants, except a few courtiers, repair for education, fortune, and amusement.* LONDON, by uniting extensive commerce and middling empire, has, perhaps, arrived at a greatness, which no city will ever be able to exceed.

Chuse DOVER or CALAIS for a center: Draw a circle of two hundred miles radius: You comprehend LONDON, PARIS, the NETHERLANDS, the UNITED PROVINCES, and some of the best cultivated parts of FRANCE and ENGLAND. It may safely, I think, be affirmed, that no spot of ground can be found, in antiquity, of equal extent, which contained near so many great and populous cities, and was so stocked with riches and inhabitants. To balance, in both periods, the states, which possessed most art, knowledge, civility, and the best police,[330] seems the truest method of comparison.

It is an observation of L'ABBE DU BOS,† that ITALY is warmer at present than it was in ancient times. "The annals of ROME tell us," says he, "that in the year 480 *ab U. C.* the winter was so severe that it destroyed the trees. The TYBER froze in ROME, and the ground was covered with snow for forty days. When JUVENAL‡ describes a superstitious woman, he represents her as breaking the ice of the TYBER, that she might perform her ablutions:

> *Hybernum fracta glacie descendet in amnem,*
> *Ter matutino Tyberi mergetur.*

---

* Such were ALEXANDRIA, ANTIOCH, CARTHAGE, EPHESUS, LYONS, &c. in the ROMAN empire. Such are even BOURDEAUX, THOLOUSE, DIJON, RENNES, ROUEN, AIX, &c. in FRANCE; DUBLIN, EDINBURGH, YORK, in the BRITISH dominions.
† Vol. ii. sect. 16.[331]
‡ Sat. 6.[332]

He speaks of that river's freezing as a common event. Many passages of HORACE suppose the streets of ROME full of snow and ice. We should have more certainty with regard to this point, had the ancients known the use of thermometers:[333] But their writers, without intending it, give us information, sufficient to convince us, that the winters are now much more temperate at ROME than formerly. At present the TYBER no more freezes at ROME than the NILE at CAIRO. The ROMANS esteem the winters very rigorous, if the snow lie two days, and if one see for eight and forty hours a few icicles hang from a fountain that has a north exposure."

The observation of this ingenious critic may be extended to other EUROPEAN climates. Who could discover the mild climate of FRANCE in DIODORUS SICULUS's* description of that of GAUL? "As it is a northern climate," says he, "it is infested with cold to an extreme degree. In cloudy weather, instead of rain there fall great snows; and in clear weather it there freezes so excessive hard, that the rivers acquire bridges of their own substance, over which, not only single travellers may pass, but large armies, accompanied with all their baggage and loaded waggons. And there being many rivers in GAUL, the RHONE, the RHINE, &c. almost all of them are frozen over; and it is usual, in order to prevent falling, to cover the ice with chaff and straw at the places where the road passes." *Colder than a* GALLIC *Winter,* is used by PETRONIUS as a proverbial expression.[334] ARISTOTLE says, that GAUL is so cold a climate that an ass could not live in it.†

North of the CEVENNES, says STRABO,‡ GAUL produces not figs and olives: And the vines, which have been planted, bear not grapes, that will ripen.

OVID positively maintains, with all the serious affirmation of prose, that the EUXINE sea was frozen over every winter in his time; and he appeals to ROMAN governours, whom he names, for the truth of his assertion.§ This seldom or never happens at present in the latitude of TOMI, whither OVID was banished. All the complaints of the same poet seem to mark a rigour of the seasons, which is scarcely experienced at present in PETERSBURGH or STOCKHOLM.

---

* Lib. iv.[335]
† De generat. anim. lib. ii.[336]
‡ Lib. iv.[337]
§ *Trist.* lib. iii. eleg. 9. *De Ponto*, lib. iv. eleg. 7, 9, 10.[338]

TOURNEFORT, a *Provençal*,[339] who had travelled into the same country, observes, that there is not a finer climate in the world: And he asserts, that nothing but OVID's melancholy could have given him such dismal ideas of it.[340] But the facts, mentioned by that poet, are too circumstantial to bear any such interpretation.

POLYBIUS* says, that the climate in ARCADIA was very cold, and the air moist.

"ITALY," says VARRO,† "is the most temperate climate in EUROPE. The inland parts" (GAUL, GERMANY, and PANNONIA, no doubt) "have almost perpetual winter."

The northern parts of SPAIN, according to STRABO,‡ are but ill inhabited, because of the great cold.

Allowing, therefore, this remark to be just, that EUROPE is become warmer than formerly; how can we account for it? Plainly, by no other method, than by supposing, that the land is at present much better cultivated, and that the woods are cleared, which formerly threw a shade upon the earth, and kept the rays of the sun from penetrating to it. Our northern colonies in AMERICA become more temperate, in proportion as the woods are felled;§[341] but in general, every one may remark, that cold is still much more severely felt, both in North and South AMERICA, than in places under the same latitude in EUROPE.

SASERNA, quoted by COLUMELLA,¶ affirmed, that the disposition of the heavens was altered before his time, and that the air had become much milder and warmer; as appears hence, says he, that many places now abound with vineyards and olive plantations, which formerly, by reason of the rigour of the climate, could raise none of these productions. Such a change, if real, will be allowed an evident sign of the better cultivation and peopling of countries before the age of SASERNA;** and if it be continued to the present times, is a proof, that these advantages have been continually encreasing throughout this part of the world.

---

* Lib. iv. cap. 21.[342]

† Lib. i. cap. 2.[343]

‡ Lib. iii.[344]

§ The warm southern colonies also become more healthful: And it is remarkable, that in the SPANISH histories of the first discovery and conquest of these countries, they appear to have been very healthful; being then well peopled and cultivated. No account of the sickness or decay of CORTES's or PIZARRO's small armies.

¶ Lib. i. cap. 1.[345]

** He seems to have lived about the time of the younger AFRICANUS; lib. i. cap. 1.[346]

Let us now cast our eye over all the countries which are the scene of ancient and modern history, and compare their past and present situation: We shall not, perhaps, find such foundation for the complaint of the present emptiness and desolation of the world. ÆGYPT is represented by MAILLET, to whom we owe the best account of it,[347] as extremely populous; though he esteems the number of its inhabitants to be diminished. SYRIA, and the Lesser ASIA, as well as the coast of BARBARY, I can readily own, to be desart in comparison of their ancient condition. The depopulation of GREECE is also obvious. But whether the country now called TURKY in EUROPE may not, in general, contain more inhabitants than during the flourishing period of GREECE, may be a little doubtful. The THRACIANS seem then to have lived like the TARTARS at present, by pasturage and plunder:* The GETES were still more uncivilized:† And the ILLYRIANS were no better.‡ These occupy nine-tenths of that country: And though the government of the TURKS be not very favourable to industry and propagation;[348] yet it preserves at least peace and order among the inhabitants; and is preferable to that barbarous, unsettled condition, in which they anciently lived.

POLAND and MUSCOVY in EUROPE are not populous; but are certainly much more so than the ancient SARMATIA and SCYTHIA; where no husbandry or tillage was ever heard of, and pasturage was the sole art by which the people were maintained. The like observation may be extended to DENMARK and SWEDEN. No one ought to esteem the immense swarms of people, which formerly came from the North, and over-ran all EUROPE, to be any objection to this opinion. Where a whole nation, or even half of it remove their seat; it is easy to imagine, what a prodigious multitude they must form; with what desperate valour they must make their attacks; and how the terror they strike into the invaded nations will make these magnify, in their imagination, both the courage and multitude of the invaders. SCOTLAND is neither extensive nor populous; but were the half of its inhabitants to seek new seats, they would form a colony as numerous as the TEUTONS and CIMBRI;[349] and would shake all EUROPE, supposing it in no better condition for defence than formerly.[350]

---

* *Xenoph. Exp.* lib. vii. *Polyb.* lib. iv. cap. 45.[351]
† *Ovid. passim, &c. Strabo*, lib. vii.[352]
‡ *Polyb.* lib. ii. cap. 12.[353]

GERMANY has surely at present[354] twenty times more inhabitants than in ancient times, when they cultivated no ground, and each tribe valued itself on the extensive desolation which it spread around; as we learn from CÆSAR,* and TACITUS,† and STRABO.‡ A proof, that the division into small republics will not alone render a nation populous, unless attended with the spirit of peace, order, and industry.[355]

The barbarous condition of BRITAIN in former times is well known, and the thinness of its inhabitants may easily be conjectured, both from their barbarity, and from a circumstance mentioned by HERODIAN,§ that all BRITAIN was marshy, even in SEVERUS's time, after the ROMANS had been fully settled in it above a century.

It is not easily imagined, that the GAULS were anciently much more advanced in the arts of life than their northern neighbours; since they travelled to this island for their education in the mysteries of the religion and philosophy of the DRUIDS.¶ I cannot, therefore, think, that GAUL was then near so populous as FRANCE is at present.

Were we to believe, indeed, and join together the testimony of APPIAN, and that of DIODORUS SICULUS, we must admit of an incredible populousness in GAUL. The former historian** says, that there were 400 nations in that country; the latter†† affirms, that the largest of the GALLIC nations consisted of 200,000 men, besides women and children, and the least of 50,000. Calculating, therefore, at a medium, we must admit of near 200 millions of people, in a country, which we esteem populous at present, though supposed to contain little more than twenty.‡‡ Such calculations, therefore, by their extravagance, lose all manner of authority. We may observe, that the equality of property, to which the populousness of antiquity may be ascribed,[356] had no place among the GAULS.§§ Their intestine wars also, before CÆSAR's

---

* *De Bello Gallico*, lib. vi.[357]
† *De Moribus Germ.*[358]
‡ Lib. vii.[359]
§ Lib. iii. cap. 47.[360]
¶ CÆSAR *de Bello Gallico*, lib. xvi. STRABO, lib. vii. says, the GAULS were not much more improved than the GERMANS.[361]
** Celt. pars 1.[362]
†† Lib. v.[363]
‡‡ Ancient GAUL was more extensive than modern FRANCE.
§§ CÆSAR *de Bello Gallico*, lib. vi.[364]

time, were almost perpetual.* And STRABO† observes, that, though all GAUL was cultivated, yet was it not cultivated with any skill or care; the genius of the inhabitants leading them less to arts than arms, till their slavery under ROME produced peace among themselves.

CÆSAR‡ enumerates very particularly the great forces which were levied in BELGIUM to oppose his conquests; and makes them amount to 208,000. These were not the whole people able to bear arms: For the same historian tells us, that the BELLOVACI could have brought a hundred thousand men into the field, though they engaged only for sixty. Taking the whole, therefore, in this proportion of ten to six, the sum of fighting men in all the states of BELGIUM was about 350,000; all the inhabitants a million and a half. And BELGIUM being about a fourth of GAUL, that country might contain six millions, which is not near the third of its present inhabitants.§ We are informed by CÆSAR, that the GAULS had no fixed property in land; but that the chieftains, when any death happened in a family, made a new division of all the lands among the several members of the family. This is the custom of *Tanistry*,[365] which so long prevailed in IRELAND, and which retained that country in a state of misery, barbarism, and desolation.

The ancient HELVETIA was 250 miles in length, and 180 in breadth, according to the same author;¶ yet contained only 360,000 inhabitants. The canton of BERNE alone has, at present, as many people.[366]

After this computation of APPIAN and DIODORUS SICULUS, I know not, whether I dare affirm, that the modern DUTCH are more numerous than the ancient BATAVI.

SPAIN is, perhaps, decayed from what it was three centuries ago; but if we step backward two thousand years, and consider the restless, turbulent, unsettled condition of its inhabitants, we may probably be inclined to think, that it is now much more populous. Many SPANIARDS killed themselves, when deprived of their arms by the ROMANS.** It appears from PLUTARCH,†† that robbery and plunder were esteemed honour-

---

* *Id. ibid.*[367]
† Lib. iv.[368]
‡ *De Bello Gallico*, lib. ii.[369]
§ See NOTE [PP].
¶ *De Bello Gallico*, lib. i.[370]
** *Titi Livii*, lib. xxxiv. cap. 17.[371]
†† *In vita Marii.*[372]

able among the SPANIARDS. HIRTIUS* represents in the same light the situation of that country in CÆSAR's time; and he says, that every man was obliged to live in castles and walled towns for his security. It was not till its final conquest under AUGUSTUS, that these disorders were repressed.† The account which STRABO‡ and JUSTIN§ give of SPAIN, corresponds exactly with those above mentioned. How much, therefore, must it diminish from our idea of the populousness of antiquity, when we find, that TULLY, comparing ITALY, AFRIC, GAUL, GREECE, and SPAIN, mentions the great number of inhabitants, as the peculiar circumstance, which rendered this latter country formidable?¶

ITALY, however, it is probable, has decayed:[373] But how many great cities does it still contain? VENICE, GENOA, PAVIA, TURIN, MILAN, NAPLES, FLORENCE, LEGHORN, which either subsisted not in ancient times, or were then very inconsiderable? If we reflect on this, we shall not be apt to carry matters to so great an extreme as is usual, with regard to this subject.

When the ROMAN authors complain, that ITALY, which formerly exported corn, became dependent on all the provinces for its daily bread, they never ascribe this alteration to the encrease of its inhabitants, but to the neglect of tillage and agriculture.** A natural effect of that pernicious practice of importing corn, in order to distribute it *gratis* among the ROMAN citizens, and a very bad means of multiplying the inhabitants of any country.†† The *sportula*,[374] so much talked of by MARTIAL and JUVENAL, being presents regularly made by the great lords to their smaller clients, must have had a like tendency to produce idleness,

---

* *De Bello Hisp.*[375]

† *Vell. Paterc.* lib. ii. § 90.[376]

‡ *Lib.* iii.[377]

§ *Lib.* xliv.[378]

¶ "Nec numero Hispanos, nec robore Gallos, nec calliditate Pœnos, nec artibus Græcos, nec denique hoc ipso hujus gentis, ac terræ domestico nativoque sensu, Italos ipsos ac Latinos——superavimus." *De harusp. resp.* cap. 9. The disorders of SPAIN seem to have been almost proverbial: "Nec impacatos a tergo horrebis Iberos." *Virg. Georg.* lib. iii. The IBERI are here plainly taken, by a poetical figure, for robbers in general.[379]

** VARRO *de re rustica*, lib. ii. præf. COLUMELLA præf. SUETON. AUGUST. cap. 42.[380]

†† Though the observations of L'Abbé du Bos should be admitted, that ITALY is now warmer than in former times, the consequence may not be necessary, that it is more populous or better cultivated. If the other countries of Europe were more savage and woody, the cold winds that blew from them, might affect the climate of Italy.

debauchery, and a continual decay among the people. The parish-rates have at present the same bad consequences in ENGLAND.[381]

Were I to assign a period, when I imagine this part of the world might possibly contain more inhabitants than at present, I should pitch upon the age of TRAJAN and the ANTONINES; the great extent of the ROMAN empire being then civilized and cultivated, settled almost in a profound peace both foreign and domestic, and living under the same regular police and government.*[382] But we are told, that all extensive governments, especially absolute monarchies, are pernicious to population, and contain a secret vice and poison, which destroy the effect of all these promising appearances.† To confirm this, there is a passage cited from PLUTARCH,‡ which being somewhat singular, we shall here examine it.

That author, endeavouring to account for the silence of many of the oracles, says, that it may be ascribed to the present desolation of the world, proceeding from former wars and factions; which common calamity, he adds, has fallen heavier upon GREECE than on any other country; insomuch, that the whole could scarcely at present furnish three thousand warriors; a number which, in the time of the MEDIAN war, were supplied by the single city of MEGARA. The gods, therefore, who affect works of dignity and importance, have suppressed many of their oracles, and deign not to use so many interpreters of their will to so diminutive a people.

I must confess, that this passage contains so many difficulties, that I know not what to make of it. You may observe, that PLUTARCH assigns, for a cause of the decay of mankind, not the extensive dominion of the ROMANS,[383] but the former wars and factions of the several states; all which were quieted by the ROMAN arms. PLUTARCH's reasoning, therefore, is directly contrary to the inference, which is drawn from the fact he advances.

POLYBIUS supposes, that GREECE had become more prosperous and flourishing after the establishment of the ROMAN yoke;§ and though that historian wrote before these conquerors had degenerated, from being the patrons, to be the plunderers of mankind; yet as we find from

---

* See NOTE [QQ].
† *L'Esprit de Loix*, liv. xxiii. chap.19.[384]
‡ *De Orac. Defectus.*[385]
§ See NOTE [RR].

TACITUS,* that the severity of the emperors afterwards corrected the licence of the governors, we have no reason to think that extensive monarchy so destructive as it is often represented.[386]

We learn from STRABO,† that the ROMANS, from their regard to the GREEKS, maintained, to his time, most of the privileges and liberties of that celebrated nation; and NERO afterwards rather encreased them.‡ How therefore can we imagine, that the ROMAN yoke was so burdensome over that part of the world? The oppression of the proconsuls was checked; and the magistracies in GREECE being all bestowed, in the several cities, by the free votes of the people, there was no necessity for the competitors to attend the emperor's court. If great numbers went to seek their fortunes in ROME, and advance themselves by learning or eloquence, the commodities of their native country, many of them would return with the fortunes which they had acquired, and thereby enrich the GRECIAN commonwealths.

But PLUTARCH says, that the general depopulation had been more sensibly felt in GREECE than in any other country. How is this reconcileable to its superior privileges and advantages?

Besides, this passage, by proving too much, really proves nothing. *Only three thousand men able to bear arms in all* GREECE! Who can admit so strange a proposition, especially if we consider the great number of GREEK cities, whose names still remain in history, and which are mentioned by writers long after the age of PLUTARCH? There are there surely ten times more people at present, when there scarcely remains a city in all the bounds of ancient GREECE. That country is still tolerably cultivated, and furnishes a sure supply of corn, in case of any scarcity in SPAIN, ITALY, or the south of FRANCE.

We may observe, that the ancient frugality of the GREEKS, and their equality of property, still subsisted during the age of PLUTARCH; as appears from LUCIAN.§ Nor is there any ground to imagine, that that country was possessed by a few masters, and a great number of slaves.

It is probable, indeed, that military discipline, being entirely useless, was extremely neglected in GREECE after the establishment of the

---

* *Annal.* lib i. cap. 2.[387]
† Lib. viii. and ix.[388]
‡ PLUTARCH. *De his qui sero a Numine puniuntur.*[389]
§ *De mercede conductis.*[390]

ROMAN empire; and if these commonwealths, formerly so warlike and ambitious, maintained each of them a small city-guard, to prevent mobbish disorders, it is all they had occasion for: And these, perhaps, did not amount to 3000 men, throughout all GREECE. I own, that, if PLUTARCH had this fact in his eye, he is here guilty of a gross paralogism,[391] and assigns causes no wise proportioned to the effects.[392] But is it so great a prodigy, that an author should fall into a mistake of this nature?*

But whatever force may remain in this passage of PLUTARCH, we shall endeavour to counterbalance it by as remarkable a passage in DIODORUS SICULUS, where the historian, after mentioning NINUS's army of 1,700,000 foot and 200,000 horse, endeavours to support the credibility of this account by some posterior facts; and adds, that we must not form a notion of the ancient populousness of mankind from the present emptiness and depopulation[393] which is spread over the world.† Thus an author, who lived at that very period of antiquity which is represented as most populous,‡ complains of the desolation which then prevailed, gives the preference to former times, and has recourse to ancient fables as a foundation for his opinion. The humour of blaming the present, and admiring the past, is strongly rooted in human nature, and has an influence even on persons endued with the profoundest judgment and most extensive learning.[394]

# NOTES

## Note [T]

COLUMELLA says, lib. iii. cap. 8. that in ÆGYPT and AFRICA the bearing of twins was frequent, and even customary; *gemini partus familiares, ac pæne solennes sunt.* If this was true, there is a physical difference both in countries and ages. For travellers make no such remarks on these countries at present. On the contrary, we are apt to suppose the northern nations more prolific. As those two countries were provinces of the ROMAN empire, it is difficult, though not altogether absurd, to suppose that such a man as COLUMELLA might be mistaken with regard to them.[395]

---

* See NOTE [SS].
† Lib. ii.[396]
‡ He was cotemporary with CÆSAR and AUGUSTUS.

## Note [U]

*Epist.* 122. The inhuman sports exhibited at ROME, may justly be considered too as an effect of the people's contempt for slaves, and was also a great cause of the general inhumanity of their princes and rulers. Who can read the accounts of the amphitheatrical entertainments without horror? Or who is surprised, that the emperors should treat that people in the same way the people treated their inferiors? One's humanity is apt to renew the barbarous wish of CALIG-ULA, that the people had but one neck: A man could almost be pleased, by a single blow, to put an end to such a race of monsters. You may thank God, says the author above cited, (*epist.* 7.) addressing himself to the ROMAN people, that you have a master (to wit the mild and merciful NERO) who is incapable of learning cruelty from your example. This was spoke in the beginning of his reign: But he fitted them very well afterwards; and, no doubt, was consider-ably improved by the sight of the barbarous objects, to which he had, from his infancy, been accustomed.[397]

## Note [X]

As *servus* was the name of the genus, and *verna* of the species, without any cor-relative, this forms a strong presumption, that the latter were by far the least numerous. It is an universal observation which we may form upon language, that where two related parts of a whole bear any proportion to each other, in numbers, rank or consideration, there are always correlative terms invented, which answer to both the parts, and express their mutual relation. If they bear no proportion to each other, the term is only invented for the less, and marks its distinction from the whole. Thus *man* and *woman, master* and *servant, father* and *son, prince* and *subject, stranger* and *citizen,* are correlative terms. But the words *seaman, carpenter, smith, tailor,* &c. have no correspondent terms, which express those who are no seamen, no carpenters, *&c.* Languages differ very much with regard to the particular words where this distinction obtains; and may thence afford very strong inferences, concerning the manners and cus-toms of different nations. The military government of the ROMAN emperors had exalted the soldiery so high, that they balanced all the other orders of the state: Hence *miles* and *paganus* became relative terms; a thing, till then, unknown to ancient, and still so to modern languages. Modern superstition exalted the clergy so high, that they overbalanced the whole state: Hence *clergy* and *laity* are terms opposed in all modern languages; and in these alone. And from the same principles I infer, that if the number of slaves bought by the ROMANS from foreign countries, had not extremely exceeded those which were bred at home, *verna* would have had a correlative, which would have expressed the former species of slaves. But these, it would seem, composed the main body of the ancient slaves, and the latter were but a few exceptions.

# Note [Y]

"Non temere ancillæ ejus rei causa comparantur ut pariant." *Digest.* lib. v. tit. 3. *de hæred. petit. lex* 27. The following texts are to the same purpose, "Spadonem morbosum non esse, neque vitiosum, verius mihi videtur; sed sanum esse, sicuti illum qui unum testiculum habet, qui etiam generare potest." *Digest.* lib. ii. tit. 1. *de ædilitio edicto, lex* 6. § 2. "Sin autem quis ita spado sit, ut tam necessaria pars corporis penitus absit, morbosus est." *Id. lex* 7. His impotence, it seems, was only regarded so far as his health or life might be affected by it. In other respects, he was full as valuable. The same reasoning is employed with regard to female slaves. "Quæritur de ea muliere quæ semper mortuos parit, an morbosa sit? et ait Sabinus, si vulvæ vitio hoc contingit, morbosam esse." *Id. lex* 14. It had even been doubted, whether a woman pregnant was morbid or vitiated; and it is determined, that she is sound, not on account of the value of her offspring, but because it is the natural part or office of women to bear children. "Si mulier prægnans venerit, inter omnes convenit sanam eam esse. Maximum enim ac præcipuum munus fœminarum accipere ac tueri conceptum. Puerperam quoque sanam esse; si modo nihil extrinsecus accedit, quod corpus ejus in aliquam valetudinem immitteret. De sterili Cœlius distinguere Trebatium dicit, ut si natura sterilis sit, sana sit; si vitio corporis, contra." *Id.*[398]

# Note [Z]

The practice of leaving great sums of money to friends, though one had near relations, was common in GREECE as well as ROME; as we may gather from LUCIAN.[399] This practice prevails much less in modern times; and BEN. JOHNSON's VOLPONE[400] is therefore almost entirely extracted from ancient authors, and suits better the manners of those times.

It may justly be thought, that the liberty of divorces in ROME[401] was another discouragement to marriage. Such a practice prevents not quarrels from *humour*, but rather encreases them; and occasions also those from *interest*, which are much more dangerous and destructive. See farther on this head, Part I. Essay XVIII.[402] Perhaps too the unnatural lusts of the ancients ought to be taken into consideration, as of some moment.[403]

# Note [AA]

PLIN. lib. xviii. cap. 3. The same author, in cap. 6. says, *Verumque fatentibus latifundia perdidere* ITALIAM; *jam vero et provincias. Sex domi semissem* AFRICÆ *possidebant, cum interfecit eos* NERO *princeps.* In this view the barbarous butchery committed by the first ROMAN emperors, was not, perhaps, so destructive to the public as we may imagine. These never ceased till they had extinguished all the illustrious families, which had enjoyed the plunder of the world, during the latter ages of the republic. The new nobles who arose in their place, were less splendid, as we learn from TACIT. *Ann.* lib. iii. cap. 55.[404]

# Note [BB]

We shall mention from DIODORUS SICULUS alone a few massacres, which passed in the course of sixty years, during the most shining age of GREECE. There were banished from SYBARIS 500 of the nobles and their partizans; lib. xii. p. 77. *ex edit.* RHODOMANNI. Of CHIANS, 600 citizens banished; lib. xiii. p. 189. At EPHESUS, 340 killed, 1000 banished; lib. xiii. p. 223. Of CYRENIANS, 500 nobles killed, all the rest banished; lib. xiv. p. 263. The CORINTHIANS killed 120, banished 500; lib. xiv. p. 304. PHÆBIDAS the SPARTAN banished 300 BÆOTIANS; lib. xv. p. 342. Upon the fall of the LACEDÆMONIANS, Democracies were restored in many cities, and severe vengeance taken of the nobles, after the GREEK manner. But matters did not end there. For the banished nobles, returning in many places, butchered their adversaries at PHIALÆ, in CORINTH, in MEGARA, in PHLIASIA. In this last place they killed 300 of the people; but these again revolting, killed above 600 of the nobles, and banished the rest; lib. xv. p. 357. In ARCADIA 1400 banished, besides many killed. The banished retired to SPARTA and to PALLANTIUM: The latter were delivered up to their countrymen, and all killed; lib. xv. p. 373. Of the banished from ARGOS and THEBES, there were 509 in the SPARTAN army; *id.* p. 374. Here is a detail of the most remarkable of AGATHOCLES's cruelties from the same author. The people before his usurpation had banished 600 nobles; lib. xix. p. 655. Afterwards that tyrant, in concurrence with the people, killed 4000 nobles, and banished 6000; *id.* p. 647. He killed 4000 people at GELA; *id.* p. 741. By AGATHOCLES's brother 8000 banished from SYRACUSE; lib. xx. p. 757. The inhabitants of ÆGESTA, to the number of 40,000, were killed, man, woman, and child; and with tortures, for the sake of their money; *id.* p. 802. All the relations, to wit, father, brother, children, grandfather, of his LIBYAN army, killed; *id.* p. 803. He killed 7000 exiles after capitulation; *id.* p. 816. It is to be remarked, that AGATHOCLES was a man of great sense and courage, and is not to be suspected of wanton cruelty, contrary to the maxims of his age.

# Note [CC]

In order to recommend his client to the favour of the people, he enumerates all the sums he had expended. When χωρηγὸς, 30 minas: Upon a chorus of men 20 minas; εἰς πυρριχισὰις, 8 minas; ἀνδράσι χορηγῶν, 50 minas; κυκλικῷ χωρῷ, 3 minas; Seven times trierarch, where he spent 6 talents: Taxes, once 30 minas, another time 40; γυμνασιαρχῶν, 12 minas; χορηγὸς παιδικῷ χωρῷ, 15 minas; κομοδοῖς χορηγῶν, 18 minas; πυρριχισαῖς, ἀγενείοις, 7 minas; τριήρει ἀμιλλομενος, 15 minas; ἀρχθέωρος, 30 minas: In the whole ten talents 38 minas.

An immense sum for an ATHENIAN fortune, and what alone would be esteemed great riches, *Orat.* 20. It is true, he says, the law did not oblige him absolutely to be at so much expence, not above a fourth. But without the favour of the people, no body was so much as safe; and this was the only way to gain it. See farther, *orat.* 24. *de pop. statu.* In another place, he introduces a speaker, who says that he had spent his whole fortune, and an immense one, eighty talents, for the people. *Orat.* 25. *de prob.* EVANDRI. The μέτοικοι, or strangers, find, says he, if they do not contribute largely enough to the people's fancy, that they have reason to repent it. *Orat.* 30. *contra* PHIL. You may see with what care DEMOSTHENES displays his expences of this nature, when he pleads for himself *de corona*; and how he exaggerates MIDIAS's stinginess in this particular, in his accusation of that criminal. All this, by the by, is a mark of a very iniquitous judicature: And yet the ATHENIANS valued themselves on having the most legal and regular administration of any people in GREECE.[405]

# Note [DD]

The authorities cited above, are all historians, orators, and philosophers, whose testimony is unquestioned. It is dangerous to rely upon writers who deal in ridicule and satyr. What will posterity, for instance, infer from this passage of Dr. SWIFT: "I told him, that in the kingdom of TRIBNIA (BRITAIN) by the natives called LANGDON (LONDON) where I had sojourned some time in my travels, the bulk of the people consist, in a manner, wholly of discoverers, witnesses, informers, accusers, prosecutors, evidences, swearers, together with their several subservient and subaltern instruments, all under the colours, the conduct, and pay of ministers of state and their deputies. The plots in that kingdom are usually the workmanship of those persons," *&c.* GULLIVERS *travels.* Such a representation might suit the government of ATHENS; not that of ENGLAND, which is remarkable even in modern times, for humanity, justice, and liberty. Yet the Doctor's satyr, though carried to extremes, as is usual with him, even beyond other satyrical writers, did not altogether want an object. The Bishop of ROCHESTER, who was his friend, and of the same party, had been banished a little before by bill of attainder, with great justice, but without such a proof as was legal, or according to the strict forms of common law.[406]

# Note [EE]

In general, there is more candour and sincerity in ancient historians, but less exactness and care, than in the moderns. Our speculative factions, especially those of religion, throw such an illusion over our minds, that men seem to regard impartiality to their adversaries and to heretics, as a vice or weakness: But the commonness of books, by means of printing, has obliged modern historians to be more careful in avoiding contradictions and incongruities. DIODORUS

SICULUS is a good writer, but it is with pain I see his narration contradict, in so many particulars, the two most authentic pieces of all GREEK history, to wit, XENOPHON's expedition, and DEMOSTHENES's orations. PLUTARCH and APPIAN seem scarce ever to have read CICERO's epistles.

## Note [FF]

PLINY, lib. vii. cap. 25. says, that CÆSAR used to boast, that there had fallen in battle against him one million one hundred and ninety-two thousand men, besides those who perished in the civil wars. It is not probable, that that conqueror could ever pretend to be so exact in his computation. But allowing the fact, it is likely, that the HELVETII, GERMANS, and BRITONS, whom he slaughtered, would amount to near a half of the number.[407]

## Note [GG]

We are to observe, that when DIONYSIUS HALYCARNASSÆUS says, that if we regard the ancient walls of ROME, the extent of that city will not appear greater than that of ATHENS; he must mean the ACROPOLIS and high town only. No ancient author ever speaks of the PYRÆUM, PHALERUS, and MUNYCHIA, as the same with ATHENS. Much less can it be supposed, that DIONYSIUS would consider the matter in that light, after the walls of CIMON and PERICLES were destroyed, and ATHENS was entirely separated from these other towns. This observation destroys all VOSSIUS's reasonings, and introduces common sense into these calculations.[408]

## Note [HH]

DEMOST. *contra* LEPT. The ATHENIANS brought yearly from PONTUS 400,000 medimni or bushels of corn, as appeared from the custom-house books. And this was the greater part of their importation of corn. This by the by is a strong proof that there is some great mistake in the foregoing passage of ATHENÆUS. For ATTICA itself was so barren of corn, that it produced not enough even to maintain the peasants. TIT. LIV. lib. xliii. cap. 6. And 400,000 medimni would scarcely feed 100,000 men during a twelvemonth. LUCIAN, in his *navigium sive vota*, says, that a ship, which, by the dimensions he gives, seems to have been about the size of our third rates,[409] carried as much corn as would maintain all ATTICA for a twelvemonth. But perhaps ATHENS was decayed at that time; and besides, it is not safe to trust to such loose rhetorical calculations.[410]

# Note [II]

DIOD. SIC. lib. xvii. When ALEXANDER attacked THEBES, we may safely conclude, that almost all the inhabitants were present. Whoever is acquainted with the spirit of the GREEKS, especially of the THEBANS, will never suspect, that any of them would desert their country, when it was reduced to such extreme peril and distress. As ALEXANDER took the town by storm, all those who bore arms were put to the sword without mercy; and they amounted only to 6000 men. Among these were some strangers and manumitted slaves. The captives, consisting of old men, women, children, and slaves, were sold, and they amounted to 30,000. We may therefore conclude that the free citizens in THEBES, of both sexes and all ages, were near 24,000; the strangers and slaves about 12,000. These last, we may observe, were somewhat fewer in proportion than at ATHENS; as is reasonable to imagine from this circumstance, that ATHENS was a town of more trade to support slaves, and of more entertainment to allure strangers. It is also to be remarked, that thirty-six thousand was the whole number of people, both in the city of THEBES, and the neighbouring territory: A very moderate number, it must be confessed; and this computation, being founded on facts which appear indisputable, must have great weight in the present controversy. The above-mentioned number of RHODIANS too were all the inhabitants of the island, who were free, and able to bear arms.[411]

# Note [KK]

STRABO, lib. v. says, that the emperor AUGUSTUS prohibited the raising houses higher than seventy feet.[412] In another passage, lib. xvi. he speaks of the houses of ROME as remarkably high. See also to the same purpose VITRUVIUS, lib. ii. cap. 8. ARISTIDES the sophist, in his oration εἰς Ῥώμην, says, that ROME consisted of cities on the top of cities;[413] and that if one were to spread it out, and unfold it, it would cover the whole surface of ITALY. Where an author indulges himself in such extravagant declamations, and gives so much into the hyperbolical style, one knows not how far he must be reduced. But this reasoning seems natural: If ROME was built in so scattered a manner as DIONYSIUS says, and ran so much into the country, there must have been very few streets where the houses were raised so high. It is only for want of room, that any body builds in that inconvenient manner.[414]

# Note[LL]

Lib. ii. epist. 16. lib. v. epist. 6. It is true, PLINY there describes a country-house: But since that was the idea which the ancients formed of a magnificent and convenient building, the great men would certainly build the same way in town. "In laxitatem ruris excurrunt," says SENECA of the rich and voluptuous, epist. 114.

VALERIUS MAXIMUS, lib. iv. cap. 4. speaking of CINCINNATUS's field of four acres, says, "Anguste se habitare nunc putat, cujus domus tantum patet quantum CINCINNATI rura patuerant." To the same purpose see lib. xxxvi. cap. 15. also lib. xviii. cap. 2.[415]

# Note [MM]

"Moenia ejus (ROMÆ) collegere ambitu imperatoribus, censoribusque VESP-ASIANIS, A. U. C. 828. pass. xiii. MCC. complexa montes septem, ipsa dividitur in regiones quatuordecim, compita earum 265. Ejusdem spatii mensura, currente a milliario in capite ROM. Fori statuto, ad singulas portas, quæ sunt hodie numero 37, ita ut duodecim portæ semel numerentur, prætereanturque ex veteribus septem, quæ esse desierunt, efficit passuum per directum 30,775. Ad extrema vero tectorum cum castris prætoriis ab eodem Milliario, per vicos omnium viarum, mensura collegit paulo amplius septuaginta millia passuum. Quo si quis altitudinem tectorum addat, dignam profecto, æstimationem concipiat, fateaturque nullius urbis magnitudinem in toto orbe potuisse ei comparari." PLIN. lib. iii. cap 5.[416]

All the best manuscripts of PLINY read the passage as here cited, and fix the compass of the walls of ROME to be thirteen miles. The question is, What PLINY means by 30,775 paces, and how that number was formed? The manner in which I conceive it, is this. ROME was a semicircular area of thirteen miles circumference. The Forum, and consequently the Milliarium, we know, was situated on the banks of the TYBER, and near the center of the circle, or upon the diameter of the semicircular area. Though there were thirty-seven gates to ROME, yet only twelve of them had straight streets, leading from them to the Milliarium. PLINY, therefore, having assigned the circumference of ROME, and knowing that that alone was not sufficient to give us a just notion of its surface, uses this farther method. He supposes all the streets, leading from the Milliarium to the twelve gates, to be laid together into one straight line, and supposes we run along that line, so as to count each gate once: In which case, he says, that the whole line is 30,775 paces: Or, in other words, that each street or radius of the semicircular area is upon an average two miles and a half; and the whole length of ROME is five miles, and its breadth about half as much, besides the scattered suburbs.

PERE HARDOUIN understands this passage in the same manner; with regard to the laying together the several streets of ROME into one line, in order to compose 30,775 paces: But then he supposes, that streets led from the Milliarium to every gate, and that no street exceeded 800 paces in length. But (1.) a semicircular area, whose radius was only 800 paces, could never have a circumference near thirteen miles, the compass of ROME as assigned by PLINY. A radius of two miles and a half forms very nearly that circumference. (2.) There is an absurdity in supposing a city so built as to have streets running to its center from every gate in its circumference. These streets must interfere as they approach. (3.) This diminishes too much from the greatness of ancient ROME, and reduces that city below even BRISTOL or ROTTERDAM.

The sense which VOSSIUS in his *Observationes variæ* puts on this passage of PLINY, errs widely in the other extreme. One manuscript of no authority, instead of thirteen miles, has assigned thirty miles for the compass of the walls of ROME. And VOSSIUS understands this only of the curvilinear part of the circumference; supposing, that as the TYBER formed the diameter, there were no walls built on that side. But (1.) this reading is allowed to be contrary to almost all the manuscripts. (2.) Why should PLINY, a concise writer, repeat the compass of the walls of ROME in two successive sentences? (3.) Why repeat it with so sensible a variation? (4.) What is the meaning of PLINY's mentioning twice the MILLIARIUM, if a line was measured that had no dependence on the MILLIARIUM? (5.) AURELIAN's wall is said by VOPISCUS to have been drawn *laxiore ambitu*,[417] and to have comprehended all the buildings and suburbs on the north side of the TYBER; yet its compass was only fifty miles; and even here critics suspect some mistake or corruption in the text; since the walls, which remain, and which are supposed to be the same with Aurelian's, exceed not twelve miles. It is not probable, that ROME would diminish from AUGUSTUS to AURELIAN.[418] It remained still the capital of the same empire; and none of the civil wars in that long period, except the tumults on the death of MAXIMUS and BALBINUS, ever affected the city. CARACALLA is said by AURELIUS VICTOR[419] to have encreased ROME. (6.) There are no remains of ancient buildings, which mark any such greatness of ROME. VOSSIUS's reply to this objection seems absurd, that the rubbish would sink sixty or seventy feet under ground. [420] It appears from SPARTIAN[421] (*in vita Severi*) that the five-mile stone *in via Lavicana* was out of the city. (7.) OLYMPIODORUS[422] and PUBLIUS VICTOR[423] fix the number of houses in ROME to be betwixt forty and fifty thousand. (8.) The very extravagance of the consequences drawn by this critic, as well as LIPSIUS,[424] if they be necessary, destroys the foundation on which they are grounded: That ROME contained fourteen millions of inhabitants; while the whole kingdom of FRANCE contains only five, according to his computation, &c.

The only objection to the sense which we have affixed above to the passage of PLINY, seems to lie in this, That PLINY, after mentioning the thirty-seven gates of ROME, assigns only a reason for suppressing the seven old ones, and says nothing of the eighteen gates, the streets leading from which terminated, according to my opinion, before they reached the Forum. But as PLINY was writing to the ROMANS, who perfectly knew the disposition of the streets, it is not strange he should take a circumstance for granted, which was so familiar to every body. Perhaps too, many of these gates led to wharfs upon the river.

# Note [NN]

QUINTUS CURTIUS says, its walls were ten miles in circumference, when founded by ALEXANDER; lib. iv. cap. 8. STRABO, who had travelled to ALEXANDRIA, as well as DIODORUS SICULUS, says it was scarce four miles long, and in most places about a mile broad; lib. 17. PLINY says it resembled a MACEDO-NIAN cassock, stretching out in the corners; lib. v. cap. 10. Notwithstanding this bulk of ALEXANDRIA, which seems but moderate, DIODORUS SICULUS, speaking of its circuit as drawn by ALEXANDER (which it never exceeded, as we learn from AMMIANUS MARCELLINUS, lib. xxii. cap. 16.), says it was μηγέθει διαφέροντα, *extremely great*, ibid. The reason which he assigns for its surpassing all cities in the world (for he excepts not ROME) is, that it contained 300,000 free inhabitants. He also mentions the revenues of the kings, to wit, 6000 talents, as another circumstance to the same purpose: No such mighty sum in our eyes, even though we make allowance for the different value of money. What STRABO says of the neighbouring country, means only that it was well peopled, οἰκούμενα καλῶς. Might not one affirm, without any great hyperbole, that the whole banks of the river from GRAVESEND to WINDSOR[425] are one city? This is even more than STRABO says of the banks of the lake MAREOTIS, and of the canal to CANOPUS. It is a vulgar saying in ITALY, that the king of SARDINIA has but one town in PIEDMONT; for it is all a town.[426] AGRIPPA in JOSEPHUS *de bello* JUDAIC. lib. ii. cap. 16. to make his audience comprehend the excessive greatness of ALEXANDRIA, which he endeavours to magnify, describes only the compass of the city as drawn by ALEXANDER: A clear proof that the bulk of the inhabitants were lodged there, and that the neighbouring country was no more than what might be expected about all great towns, very well cultivated, and well peopled.[427]

# Note [OO]

He says (in NERONE, cap. 30.) that a portico or piazza of it was 3000 feet long; "tanta laxitas ut porticus triplices milliarias haberet." He cannot mean three miles. For the whole extent of the house from the PALATINE to the ESQUILINE was not near so great. So when VOPISC. in AURELIANO mentions a portico in SALLUST's gardens, which he calls *porticus milliarensis*, it must be understood of a thousand feet. So also HORACE:

> "Nulla decempedis
> Metata privatis opacam
> Porticus excipiebat Arcton."     Lib. ii. ode 15.

So also in lib. i. satyr. 8.

> "Mille pedes in fronte, trecentos cippus in agrum
> Hic dabat."[428]

# Note [PP]

It appears from CÆSAR's account, that the GAULS had no domestic slaves, who formed a different order from the *Plebes*. The whole common people were indeed a kind of slaves to the nobility, as the people of POLAND are at this day: And a nobleman of GAUL had sometimes ten thousand dependents of this kind. Nor can we doubt, that the armies were composed of the people as well as of the nobility. The fighting men amongst the HELVETII were the fourth part of the inhabitants; a clear proof that all the males of military age bore arms. See CÆSAR *de bello Gall.* lib. i.

We may remark, that the numbers in CÆSAR's commentaries can be more depended on than those of any other ancient author, because of the GREEK translation, which still remains, and which checks the LATIN original.[429]

# Note [QQ]

The inhabitants of MARSEILLES lost not their superiority over the GAULS in commerce and the mechanic arts, till the ROMAN dominion turned the latter from arms to agriculture and civil life. See STRABO, lib. iv. That author, in several places, repeats the observation concerning the improvement arising from the ROMAN arts and civility: And he lived at the time when the change was new, and would be more sensible. So also PLINY: "Quis enim non, communicato orbe terrarum, majestate ROMANI imperii, profecisse vitam putet, commercio rerum ac societate festæ pacis, omniaque etiam, quæ occulta antea fuerant, in promiscuo usu facta." Lib. xiv. procem. "Numine deûm electa (speaking of ITALY) quæ cœlum ipsum clarius faceret, sparsa congregaret imperia, ritusque molliret, & tot populorum discordes, ferasque linguas sermonis commercio contraheret ad colloquia, & humanitatem homini daret; breviterque, una cunctarum gentium in toto orbe patria fieret"; lib. ii. cap. 5. Nothing can be stronger to this purpose than the following passage from TERTULLIAN, who lived about the age of SEVERUS. "Certe quidem ipse orbis in promptu est, cultior de die & instructior pristino. Omnia jam pervia, omnia nota, omnia negotiosa. Solitudines famosas retro fundi amœnissimi obliteraverunt, silvas arva domuerunt, feras pecora fugaverunt; arenæ seruntur, saxa panguntur, paludes eliquantur, tantæ urbes, quantæ non casæ quondam. Jam nec insulæ horrent, nec scopuli terrent; ubique domus, ubique populus, ubique respublica, ubique vita. Summum testimonium frequentiæ humanæ, onerosi sumus mundo, vix nobis elementa sufficiunt; & necessitates arctiores, et querelæ apud omnes, dum jam nos natura non sustinet." De anima, cap. 30. The air of rhetoric and declamation which appears in this passage, diminishes somewhat from its authority, but does not entirely destroy it. The same remark may be extended to the following passage of ARISTIDES the sophist, who lived in the age of ADRIAN. "The whole world," says he, addressing himself to the ROMANS, "seems to keep one holiday; and mankind, laying aside the sword which they formerly wore, now betake themselves to feasting and to joy. The cities, forgetting their ancient animosities, preserve only one emulation, which shall embellish itself most by every art and ornament; Theatres every where arise, amphitheatres, porticoes, aqueducts, temples, schools, academies; and one may safely pronounce, that the sinking world has been again raised by your auspicious empire. Nor have cities alone received an encrease of ornament and beauty; but the whole earth, like a garden or paradise, is cultivated and adorned: Insomuch, that such of mankind as are placed out of the limits of your empire (who are but few) seem to merit our sympathy and compassion."

It is remarkable, that though DIODORUS SICULUS makes the inhabitants of Æ GYPT, when conquered by the ROMANS, amount only to three millions; yet JOSEPH. *de bello Jud.* lib. ii. cap. 16. says, that its inhabitants, excluding those of ALEXANDRIA, were seven millions and a half, in the reign of NERO: And he expressly says, that he drew this account from the books of the ROMAN publicans, who levied the poll-tax. STRABO, lib. xvii. praises the superior police of the ROMANS with regard to the finances of Æ GYPT, above that of its former monarchs: And no part of administration is more essential to the happiness of a people. Yet we read in ATHENÆUS, (lib. i. cap. 25.) who flourished during the reign of the ANTONINES, that the town MAREIA, near ALEXANDRIA, which was formerly a large city, had dwindled into a village. This is not, properly speaking, a contradiction. SUIDAS (AUGUST.) says, that the Emperor AUGUSTUS, having numbered the whole ROMAN empire, found it contained only 4,101,017 men (ανδρες). There is here surely some great mistake, either in the author or transcriber. But this authority, feeble as it is, may be sufficient to counterbalance the exaggerated accounts of HERODOTUS and DIODORUS SICULUS with regard to more early times.[430]

# Note [RR]

Lib. ii. cap. 62. It may perhaps be imagined, that POLYBIUS, being dependent on ROME, would naturally extol the ROMAN dominion. But, in the *first* place, POLYBIUS, though one sees sometimes instances of his caution, discovers no symptoms of flattery. *Secondly*, This opinion is only delivered in a single stroke, by the by, while he is intent upon another subject; and it is allowed, if there be any suspicion of an author's insincerity, that these oblique propositions discover his real opinion better than his more formal and direct assertions.[431]

# Note [SS]

I must confess that that discourse of PLUTARCH, concerning the silence of the oracles, is in general of so odd a texture, and so unlike his other productions, that one is at a loss what judgment to form of it. It is written in dialogue, which is a method of composition that PLUTARCH commonly but little affects. The personages he introduces advance very wild, absurd, and contradictory opinions, more like the visionary systems or ravings of PLATO than the plain sense of PLUTARCH. There runs also through the whole an air of superstition and credulity, which resembles very little the spirit that appears in other philosophical compositions of that author. For it is remarkable, that, though PLUTARCH be an historian as superstitious as HERODOTUS or LIVY, yet there is scarcely, in all antiquity, a philosopher less superstitious, excepting CICERO and LUCIAN. I must therefore confess, that a passage of PLUTARCH, cited from this discourse, has much less authority with me, than if it had been found in most of his other compositions.

There is only one other discourse of PLUTARCH liable to like objections, to wit, that *concerning those whose punishment is delayed by the Deity*. It is also writ in dialogue, contains like superstitious, wild visions, and seems to have been chiefly composed in rivalship to PLATO, particularly his last book *de republica*.[432]

And here I cannot but observe, that Mons. FONTENELLE, a writer eminent for candor, seems to have departed a little from his usual character, when he endeavours to throw a ridicule upon PLUTARCH on account of passages to be met with in this dialogue concerning oracles. The absurdities here put into the mouths of the several personages are not to be ascribed to PLUTARCH. He makes them refute each other; and, in general, he seems to intend the ridiculing of those very opinions, which FONTENELLE would ridicule him for maintaining.[433] See *Histoire des oracles*.[434]

# Essay XII

## *Of the Original Contract*

As no party, in the present age, can well support itself, without a philo-sophical or speculative system of principles, annexed to its political or practical one; we accordingly find, that each of the factions, into which this nation is divided, has reared up a fabric of the former kind, in order to protect and cover that scheme of actions, which it pursues. The people being commonly very rude builders, especially in this speculative way, and more especially still, when actuated by party-zeal; it is natural to imagine, that their workmanship must be a little unshapely, and dis-cover evident marks of that violence and hurry, in which it was raised.[1] The one party, by tracing up government to the DEITY, endeavour to render it so sacred and inviolate, that it must be little less than sacrilege, however tyrannical it may become, to touch or invade it, in the small-est article.[2] The other party, by founding government altogether on the consent of the PEOPLE, suppose that there is a kind of *original contract*, by which the subjects have tacitly reserved the power of resisting their sovereign, whenever they find themselves aggrieved by that authority, with which they have, for certain purposes, voluntarily entrusted him.[3] These are the speculative principles of the two parties; and these too are the practical consequences deduced from them.

I shall venture to affirm, *That both these* systems *of speculative prin-ciples are just; though not in the sense, intended by the parties*: And, *That both the* schemes *of practical consequences are prudent; though not in the extremes, to which each party, in opposition to the other, has commonly endeavoured to carry them.*

That the DEITY is the ultimate author of all government, will never be denied by any, who admit a general providence, and allow, that all events in the universe are conducted by an uniform plan, and directed to wise purposes. As it is impossible for the human race to subsist, at least in any comfortable or secure state, without the protection of government; this institution must certainly have been intended by that beneficent Being, who means the good of all his creatures:[4] And as it has universally, in fact, taken place, in all countries, and all ages; we may conclude, with still greater certainty, that it was intended by that omniscient Being, who can never be deceived by any event or operation. But since he gave rise to it, not by any particular or miraculous interposition, but by his concealed and universal efficacy; a sovereign cannot, properly speaking, be called his vicegerent, in any other sense than every power or force, being derived from him, may be said to act by his commission. Whatever actually happens is comprehended in the general plan or intention of providence; nor has the greatest and most lawful prince any more reason, upon that account, to plead a peculiar sacredness or inviolable authority, than an inferior magistrate, or even an usurper, or even a robber and a pyrate. The same divine superintendant, who, for wise purposes, invested a TITUS or a TRAJAN with authority, did also, for purposes, no doubt, equally wise, though unknown, bestow power on a BORGIA or an ANGRIA.[5] The same causes, which gave rise to the sovereign power in every state, established likewise every petty jurisdiction in it, and every limited authority. A constable, therefore, no less than a king, acts by a divine commission, and possesses an indefeasible right.

When we consider how nearly equal all men are in their bodily force, and even in their mental powers and faculties, till cultivated by education; we must necessarily allow, that nothing but their own consent could, at first, associate them together, and subject them to any authority. The people, if we trace government to its first origin in the woods and desarts, are the source of all power and jurisdiction, and voluntarily, for the sake of peace and order, abandoned their native liberty, and received laws from their equal and companion. The conditions, upon which they were willing to submit, were either expressed, or were so clear and obvious, that it might well be esteemed superfluous to express them. If this, then, be meant by the *original contract*, it cannot be denied, that all government is, at first, founded on a contract, and that the most ancient rude combinations of mankind were formed chiefly by that principle. In vain, are we asked in what records this charter of our liberties is registered. It was not written on parchment, nor yet on leaves or barks of trees. It preceded the use of writing and all the other civilized arts of life. But we trace it plainly in the nature of man, and in the equality, or something approaching equality, which we find in all the individuals of that species. The force, which now prevails, and which is founded on fleets and armies, is plainly political, and derived from authority, the effect of established government. A man's natural force consists only in the vigour of his limbs, and the firmness of his courage; which could never subject multitudes to the command of one. Nothing but their own consent, and their sense of the advantages resulting from peace and order, could have had that influence.[6]

Yet even this consent was long very imperfect, and could not be the basis of a regular administration. The chieftain, who had probably acquired his influence during the continuance of war, ruled more by persuasion than command; and till he could employ force to reduce the refractory and disobedient, the society could scarcely be said to have attained a state of civil government.[7] No compact or agreement, it is evident, was expressly formed for general submission; an idea far beyond the comprehension of savages: Each exertion of authority in the chieftain must have been particular, and called forth by the present exigencies of the case: The sensible utility, resulting from his interposition, made these exertions become daily more frequent; and their frequency gradually produced an habitual, and, if you please to call it so, a voluntary, and therefore precarious, acquiescence in the people.

But philosophers, who have embraced a party (if that be not a contradiction in terms) are not contented with these concessions. They assert, not only that government in its earliest infancy arose from consent or rather the voluntary acquiescence of the people; but also, that, even at present, when it has attained its full maturity, it rests on no other foundation.[8] They affirm, that all men are still born equal, and owe allegiance to no prince or government, unless bound by the obligation and sanction of a *promise*. And as no man, without some equivalent, would forego the advantages of his native liberty, and subject himself to the will of another; this promise is always understood to be conditional, and imposes on him no obligation, unless he meet with justice and protection from his sovereign. These advantages the sovereign promises him in return; and if he fail in the execution, he has broken, on his part, the articles of engagement, and has thereby freed his subject from all obligations to allegiance. Such, according to these philosophers, is the foundation of authority in every government; and such the right of resistance, possessed by every subject.

But would these reasoners look abroad into the world, they would meet with nothing that, in the least, corresponds to their ideas,[9] or can warrant so refined and philosophical a system. On the contrary, we find, every where, princes, who claim their subjects as their property,[10] and assert their independent right of sovereignty, from conquest or succession. We find also, every where, subjects, who acknowledge this right in their prince, and suppose themselves born under obligations of obedience to a certain sovereign, as much as under the ties of reverence and duty to certain parents. These connexions are always conceived to be equally independent of our consent, in PERSIA and CHINA; in FRANCE and SPAIN; and even in HOLLAND and ENGLAND, wherever the doctrines above-mentioned have not been carefully inculcated. Obedience or subjection becomes so familiar, that most men never make any enquiry about its origin or cause, more than about the principle of gravity, resistance, or the most universal laws of nature. Or if curiosity ever move them; as soon as they learn, that they themselves and their ancestors have, for several ages, or from time immemorial, been subject to such a form of government or such a family; they immediately acquiesce, and acknowledge their obligation to allegiance.[11] Were you to preach, in most parts of the world, that political connexions are founded altogether on voluntary consent or a mutual promise, the magistrate would soon imprison you, as seditious, for loosening the ties of obedience; if your friends did not before shut you up as delirious, for advancing such absurdities. It is strange, that an act of the mind, which every individual is supposed to have formed, and after he came to the use of reason too, otherwise it could have no authority; that this act, I say, should be so much unknown to all of them, that, over the face of the whole earth, there scarcely remain any traces or memory of it.

But the contract, on which government is founded, is said to be the *original contract*; and consequently may be supposed too old to fall under the knowledge of the present generation. If the agreement, by which savage men first associated and conjoined their force, be here meant, this is acknowledged to be real; but being so ancient, and being obliterated by a thousand changes of government and princes, it cannot now be supposed to retain any authority.[12] If we would say any thing to the purpose, we must assert, that every particular government, which is lawful, and which imposes any duty of allegiance on the subject, was, at first, founded on consent and a voluntary compact. But besides that this supposes the consent of the fathers to bind the children, even to the most remote generations, (which republican writers will never allow)[13] besides this, I say, it is not justified by history or experience, in any age or country of the world.

Almost all the governments, which exist at present, or of which there remains any record in story, have been founded originally, either on usurpation or conquest, or both, without any pretence of a fair consent, or voluntary subjection of the people.[14] When an artful and bold man is placed at the head of an army or faction, it is often easy for him, by employing, sometimes violence, sometimes false pretences, to establish his dominion over a people a hundred times more numerous than his partizans.[15] He allows no such open communication, that his enemies can know, with certainty, their number or force. He gives them no leisure to assemble together in a body to oppose him. Even all those, who are the instruments of his usurpation, may wish his fall; but their ignorance of each other's intention keeps them in awe, and is the sole cause of his security. By such arts as these, many governments have been established; and this is all the *original contract,* which they have to boast of.

The face of the earth is continually changing, by the encrease of small kingdoms into great empires, by the dissolution of great empires into smaller kingdoms, by the planting of colonies, by the migration of tribes. Is there any thing discoverable in all these events, but force and violence? Where is the mutual agreement or voluntary association so much talked of?

Even the smoothest way, by which a nation may receive a foreign master, by marriage or a will, is not extremely honourable for the people; but supposes them to be disposed of, like a dowry or a legacy, according to the pleasure or interest of their rulers.[16]

But where no force interposes, and election takes place; what is this election so highly vaunted? It is either the combination of a few great men, who decide for the whole, and will allow of no opposition: Or it is the fury of a multitude, that follow a seditious ringleader, who is not known, perhaps, to a dozen among them, and who owes his advancement merely to his own impudence, or to the momentary caprice of his fellows.

Are these disorderly elections, which are rare too, of such mighty authority, as to be the only lawful foundation of all government and allegiance?

In reality, there is not a more terrible event, than a total dissolution of government, which gives liberty to the multitude, and makes the determination or choice of a new establishment depend upon a number, which nearly approaches to that of the body of the people: For it never comes entirely to the whole body of them. Every wise man, then, wishes to see, at the head of a powerful and obedient army, a general, who may speedily seize the prize, and give to the people a master, which they are so unfit to chuse for themselves. So little correspondent is fact and reality to those philosophical notions.

Let not the establishment at the *Revolution*[17] deceive us, or make us so much in love with a philosophical origin to government, as to imagine all others monstrous and irregular. Even that event was far from corresponding to these refined ideas. It was only the succession, and that only in the regal part of the government, which was then changed: And it was only the majority of seven hundred,[18] who determined that change for near ten millions.[19] I doubt not, indeed, but the bulk of those ten millions acquiesced willingly in the determination: But was the matter left, in the least, to their choice? Was it not justly supposed to be, from that moment, decided, and every man punished, who refused to submit to the new sovereign? How otherwise could the matter have ever been brought to any issue or conclusion?

The republic of ATHENS was, I believe, the most extensive democracy, that we read of in history: Yet if we make the requisite allowances for the women, the slaves, and the strangers, we shall find, that that establishment was not, at first, made, nor any law ever voted, by a tenth part of those who were bound to pay obedience to it: Not to mention the islands and foreign dominions, which the ATHENIANS claimed as theirs by right of conquest.[20] And as it is well known, that popular assemblies in that city were always full of licence and disorder, notwithstanding the institutions and laws by which they were checked: How much more disorderly must they prove, where they form not the established constitution, but meet tumultuously on the dissolution of the ancient government, in order to give rise to a new one? How chimerical must it be to talk of a choice in such circumstances?

The ACHÆANS enjoyed the freest and most perfect democracy of all antiquity; yet they employed force to oblige some cities to enter into their league, as we learn from POLYBIUS.*

* Lib. ii. cap. 38.[21]

HARRY the IVth and HARRY the VIIth of ENGLAND, had really no title to the throne but a parliamentary election; yet they never would acknowledge it, lest they should thereby weaken their authority.[22] Strange, if the only real foundation of all authority be consent and promise![23]

It is in vain to say, that all governments are or should be, at first, founded on popular consent, as much as the necessity of human affairs will admit. This favours entirely my pretension. I maintain, that human affairs will never admit of this consent; seldom of the appearance of it. But that conquest or usurpation,[24] that is, in plain terms, force, by dissolving the ancient governments, is the origin of almost all the new ones, which were ever established in the world. And that in the few cases, where consent may seem to have taken place, it was commonly so irregular, so confined, or so much intermixed either with fraud or violence, that it cannot have any great authority.

My intention here is not to exclude the consent of the people from being one just foundation of government where it has place. It is surely the best and most sacred of any. I only pretend, that it has very seldom had place in any degree, and never almost in its full extent. And that therefore some other foundation of government must also be admitted.

Were all men possessed of so inflexible a regard to justice, that, of themselves, they would totally abstain from the properties of others; they had for ever remained in a state of absolute liberty, without subjection to any magistrate or political society: But this is a state of perfection, of which human nature is justly deemed incapable. Again; were all men possessed of so perfect an understanding, as always to know their own interests, no form of government had ever been submitted to, but what was established on consent, and was fully canvassed by every member of the society: But this state of perfection is likewise much superior to human nature. Reason, history, and experience shew us, that all political societies have had an origin much less accurate and regular; and were one to choose a period of time, when the people's consent was the least regarded in public transactions, it would be precisely on the establish-ment of a new government. In a settled constitution, their inclinations are often consulted; but during the fury of revolutions, conquests, and public convulsions, military force or political craft usually decides the controversy.

When a new government is established, by whatever means, the people are commonly dissatisfied with it, and pay obedience more from fear and necessity, than from any idea of allegiance or of moral obligation. The prince is watchful and jealous, and must carefully guard against every beginning or appearance of insurrection. Time, by degrees, removes all these difficulties, and accustoms the nation to regard, as their lawful or native princes, that family, which, at first, they considered as usurpers or foreign conquerors. In order to found this opinion, they have no recourse to any notion of voluntary consent or promise, which, they know, never was, in this case, either expected or demanded. The original establishment was formed by violence, and submitted to from necessity. The subsequent administration is also supported by power, and acquiesced in by the people, not as a matter of choice, but of obligation. They imagine not, that their consent gives their prince a title: But they willingly consent, because they think, that, from long possession, he has acquired a title, independent of their choice or inclination.

Should it be said, that, by living under the dominion of a prince, which one might leave, every individual has given a *tacit* consent[25] to his authority, and promised him obedience; it may be answered, that such an implied consent can only have place, where a man imagines, that the matter depends on his choice. But where he thinks (as all mankind do who are born under established governments) that by his birth he owes allegiance to a certain prince or certain form of government; it would be absurd to infer a consent or choice, which he expressly, in this case, renounces and disclaims.

Can we seriously say, that a poor peasant or artizan has a free choice to leave his country, when he knows no foreign language or manners, and lives from day to day, by the small wages which he acquires? We may as well assert, that a man, by remaining in a vessel, freely consents to the dominion of the master; though he was carried on board while asleep,[26] and must leap into the ocean, and perish, the moment he leaves her.

What if the prince forbid his subjects to quit his dominions; as in TIBERIUS's time, it was regarded as a crime in a ROMAN knight that he had attempted to fly to the PARTHIANS, in order to escape the tyranny of that emperor?*[27] Or as the ancient MUSCOVITES[28] prohibited all travelling under pain of death? And did a prince observe, that many of his subjects were seized with the frenzy of migrating to foreign countries, he

* TACIT. Ann. vi. cap. 14.[29]

would doubtless, with great reason and justice, restrain them, in order to prevent the depopulation of his own kingdom. Would he forfeit the allegiance of all his subjects, by so wise and reasonable a law? Yet the freedom of their choice is surely, in that case, ravished from them.

A company of men, who should leave their native country, in order to people some uninhabited region, might dream of recovering their native freedom;[30] but they would soon find, that their prince still laid claim to them, and called them his subjects, even in their new settlement.[31] And in this he would but act conformably to the common ideas of mankind.

The truest *tacit* consent of this kind, that is ever observed, is when a foreigner settles in any country, and is beforehand acquainted with the prince, and government, and laws, to which he must submit: Yet is his allegiance, though more voluntary, much less expected or depended on, than that of a natural born subject. On the contrary, his native prince still asserts a claim to him. And if he punish not the renegade, when he seizes him in war with his new prince's commission; this clemency is not founded on the municipal law, which in all countries condemns the prisoner; but on the consent of princes, who have agreed to this indulgence, in order to prevent reprisals.

Did one generation of men go off the stage at once, and another succeed, as is the case with silk-worms and butterflies,[32] the new race, if they had sense enough to choose their government, which surely is never the case with men, might voluntarily, and by general consent, establish their own form of civil polity, without any regard to the laws or precedents, which prevailed among their ancestors. But as human society is in perpetual flux, one man every hour going out of the world, another coming into it, it is necessary, in order to preserve stability in government, that the new brood should conform themselves to the established constitution, and nearly follow the path which their fathers, treading in the footsteps of theirs, had marked out to them. Some innovations must necessarily have place in every human institution, and it is happy where the enlightened genius of the age give these a direction to the side of reason, liberty, and justice: but violent innovations no individual is entitled to make: they are even dangerous to be attempted by the legislature: more ill than good is ever to be expected from them: and if history affords examples to the contrary, they are not to be drawn into precedent, and are only to be regarded as proofs, that the science of politics affords few rules, which will not admit of some exception, and which may not sometimes be controuled by fortune and accident.[33] The violent innovations in the reign of HENRY VIII. proceeded from an imperious monarch, seconded by the appearance of legislative authority:[34] Those in the reign of CHARLES I. were derived from faction and fanaticism;[35] and both of them have proved happy in the issue: But even the former were long the source of many disorders, and still more dangers; and if the measures of allegiance were to be taken from the latter, a total anarchy must have place in human society, and a final period at once be put to every government.

Suppose, that an usurper, after having banished his lawful prince and royal family, should establish his dominion for ten or a dozen years in any country, and should preserve so exact a discipline in his troops, and so regular a disposition in his garrisons, that no insurrection had ever been raised, or even murmur heard, against his administration: Can it be asserted, that the people, who in their hearts abhor his treason, have tacitly consented to his authority, and promised him allegiance, merely because, from necessity, they live under his dominion? Suppose again their native prince restored, by means of an army, which he levies in foreign countries: They receive him with joy and exultation, and shew plainly with what reluctance they had submitted to any other yoke. I may now ask, upon what foundation the prince's title stands? Not on popular consent surely: For though the people willingly acquiesce in his authority, they never imagine, that their consent made him sovereign. They consent; because they apprehend him to be already, by birth, their lawful sovereign. And as to that tacit consent, which may now be inferred from their living under his dominion, this is no more than what they formerly gave to the tyrant and usurper.[36]

When we assert, that all lawful government arises from the consent of the people, we certainly do them a great deal more honour than they deserve, or even expect and desire from us. After the ROMAN dominions became too unwieldy for the republic to govern them, the people, over the whole known world, were extremely grateful to AUGUSTUS for that authority, which, by violence, he had established over them; and they shewed an equal disposition to submit to the successor, whom he left them, by his last will and testament. It was afterwards their misfortune, that there never was, in one family, any long regular succession; but that their line of princes was continually broken, either by private assassinations or public rebellions. The *prætorian* bands, on the failure of every family, set up one emperor; the legions in the East a second; those in GERMANY, perhaps, a third: And the sword alone could decide the controversy.[37] The condition of the people, in that mighty monarchy, was to be lamented, not because the choice of the emperor was never left to them; for that was impracticable: But because they never fell under any succession of masters, who might regularly follow each other. As to the violence and wars and bloodshed, occasioned by every new settlement; these were not blameable, because they were inevitable.[38]

The house of LANCASTER ruled in this island about sixty years;[39] yet the partizans of the white rose[40] seemed daily to multiply in ENG-LAND. The present establishment[41] has taken place during a still longer period. Have all views of right in another family been utterly extinguished; even though scarce any man now alive had arrived at years of discretion, when it was expelled, or could have consented to its dominion, or have promised it allegiance? A sufficient indication surely of the general sentiment of mankind on this head. For we blame not the partizans of the abdicated family,[42] merely on account of the long time, during which they have preserved their imaginary loyalty.[43] We blame them for adhering to a family, which, we affirm, has been justly expelled, and which, from the moment the new settlement took place, had forfeited all title to authority.

But would we have a more regular, at least a more philosophical, refutation of this principle of an original contract or popular consent; perhaps, the following observations may suffice.

All *moral* duties may be divided into two kinds.[44] The *first* are those, to which men are impelled by a natural instinct or immediate propensity, which operates on them, independent of all ideas of obligation, and of all views, either to public or private utility. Of this nature are, love of children, gratitude to benefactors, pity to the unfortunate. When we reflect on the advantage, which results to society from such humane instincts, we pay them the just tribute of moral approbation and esteem: But the person, actuated by them, feels their power and influence, antecedent to any such reflection.

The *second* kind of moral duties are such as are not supported by any original instinct of nature, but are performed entirely from a sense of obligation, when we consider the necessities of human society, and the impossibility of supporting it, if these duties were neglected. It is thus *justice* or a regard to the property of others, *fidelity* or the observance of promises, become obligatory, and acquire an authority over mankind. For as it is evident, that every man loves himself better than any other person, he is naturally impelled to extend his acquisitions as much as possible; and nothing can restrain him in this propensity, but reflection and experience, by which he learns the pernicious effects of that licence, and the total dissolution of society which must ensue from it. His original inclination, therefore, or instinct, is here checked and restrained by a subsequent judgment or observation.

The case is precisely the same with the political or civil duty of *allegiance*, as with the natural duties of justice and fidelity.[45] Our primary instincts lead us, either to indulge ourselves in unlimited freedom, or to seek dominion over others: And it is reflection only, which engages us to sacrifice such strong passions to the interests of peace and public order. A small degree of experience and observation suffices to teach us, that society cannot possibly be maintained without the authority of magistrates, and that this authority must soon fall into contempt, where exact obedience is not payed to it. The observation of these general and obvious interests is the source of all allegiance, and of that moral obligation, which we attribute to it.

What necessity, therefore, is there to found the duty of *allegiance* or obedience to magistrates on that of *fidelity* or a regard to promises, and to suppose, that it is the consent of each individual, which subjects him to government; when it appears, that both allegiance and fidelity stand precisely on the same foundation, and are both submitted to by mankind, on account of the apparent interests and necessities of human society? We are bound to obey our sovereign, it is said; because we have given a tacit promise to that purpose. But why are we bound to observe our promise? It must here be asserted, that the commerce and intercourse of mankind, which are of such mighty advantage, can have no security where men pay no regard to their engagements. In like manner, may it be said, that men could not live at all in society, at least in a civilized society, without laws and magistrates and judges, to prevent the encroachments of the strong upon the weak, of the violent upon the just and equitable. The obligation to allegiance being of like force and authority with the obligation to fidelity, we gain nothing by resolving the one into the other. The general interests or necessities of society are sufficient to establish both.

If the reason be asked of that obedience, which we are bound to pay to government, I readily answer, *because society could not otherwise subsist*: And this answer is clear and intelligible to all mankind. Your answer is, *because we should keep our word*. But besides, that no body, till trained in a philosophical system, can either comprehend or relish this answer: Besides this, I say, you find yourself embarrassed, when it is asked, *why we are bound to keep our word?* Nor can you give any answer, but what would, immediately, without any circuit, have accounted for our obligation to allegiance.

But *to whom is allegiance due? And who is our lawful sovereign?* This question is often the most difficult of any, and liable to infinite discussions.[46] When people are so happy, that they can answer, *Our present sovereign, who inherits, in a direct line, from ancestors, that have governed us for many ages*; this answer admits of no reply; even though historians, in tracing up to the remotest antiquity, the origin of that royal family, may find, as commonly happens, that its first authority was derived from usurpation and violence.[47] It is confessed, that private justice, or the abstinence from the properties of others, is a most cardinal virtue: Yet reason tells us, that there is no property in durable objects, such as lands or houses, when carefully examined in passing from hand to hand, but must, in some period, have been founded on fraud and injustice. The necessities of human society, neither in private nor public life, will allow of such an accurate enquiry: And there is no virtue or moral duty, but what may, with facility, be refined away, if we indulge a false philosophy, in sifting and scrutinizing it, by every captious rule of logic, in every light or position, in which it may be placed.

The questions with regard to private property have filled infinite volumes of law and philosophy, if in both we add the commentators to the original text; and in the end, we may safely pronounce, that many of the rules, there established, are uncertain, ambiguous, and arbitrary.[48] The like opinion may be formed with regard to the succession and rights of princes and forms of government. Several cases, no doubt, occur, especially in the infancy of any constitution, which admit of no determination from the laws of justice and equity: And our historian RAPIN pretends, that the controversy between EDWARD the Third and PHILIP DE VALOIS was of this nature, and could be decided only by an appeal to heaven, that is, by war and violence.[49]

Who shall tell me, whether GERMANICUS or DRUSUS ought to have succeeded to TIBERIUS, had he died, while they were both alive, without naming any of them for his successor? Ought the right of adoption to be received as equivalent to that of blood, in a nation, where it had the same effect in private families, and had already, in two instances, taken place in the public? Ought GERMANICUS to be esteemed the elder son because he was born before DRUSUS; or the younger, because he was adopted after the birth of his brother? Ought the right of the elder to be regarded in a nation, where he had no advantage in the succession of private families? Ought the ROMAN empire at that time to be deemed hereditary, because of two examples; or ought it, even so early, to be regarded as belonging to the stronger or to the present possessor, as being founded on so recent an usurpation?[50]

COMMODUS mounted the throne after a pretty long succession of excellent emperors,[51] who had acquired their title, not by birth, or public election, but by the fictitious rite of adoption. That bloody debauchee being murdered by a conspiracy suddenly formed between his wench and her gallant,[52] who happened at that time to be *Prætorian Præfect*;[53] these immediately deliberated about choosing a master to human kind, to speak in the style of those ages; and they cast their eyes on PERTINAX. Before the tyrant's death was known, the *Præfect* went secretly to that senator, who, on the appearance of the soldiers, imagined that his execution had been ordered by COMMODUS. He was immediately saluted emperor by the officer and his attendants; chearfully proclaimed by the populace; unwillingly submitted to by the guards; formally recognized by the senate; and passively received by the provinces and armies of the empire.

The discontent of the *Prætorian* bands broke out in a sudden sedition, which occasioned the murder of that excellent prince: And the world being now without a master and without government, the guards thought proper to set the empire formally to sale. JULIAN, the purchaser, was proclaimed by the soldiers, recognized by the senate, and submitted to by the people; and must also have been submitted to by the provinces, had not the envy of the legions begotten opposition and resistance. PESCENNIUS NIGER in SYRIA elected himself emperor, gained the tumultuary consent of his army, and was attended with the secret goodwill of the senate and people of ROME. ALBINUS in BRITAIN found an equal right to set up his claim; but SEVERUS, who governed PANNONIA, prevailed in the end above both of them. That able politician and warrior, finding his own birth and dignity too much inferior to the imperial crown,[54] professed, at first, an intention only of revenging the death of PERTINAX. He marched as general into ITALY; defeated JULIAN; and without our being able to fix any precise commencement even of the soldiers' consent, he was from necessity acknowledged emperor by the senate and people; and fully established in his violent authority by subduing NIGER and ALBINUS.*

*Inter hæc Gordianus* CÆSAR (says CAPITOLINUS, speaking of another period) *sublatus a militibus.* Imperator *est appellatus, quia non erat alius in præsenti.*[55] It is to be remarked, that GORDIAN was a boy of fourteen years of age.

Frequent instances of a like nature occur in the history of the emperors; in that of ALEXANDER's successors;[56] and of many other countries: Nor can any thing be more unhappy than a despotic government of this kind; where the succession is disjointed and irregular, and must be determined, on every vacancy, by force or election. In a free government, the matter is often unavoidable, and is also much less dangerous. The interests of liberty may there frequently lead the people, in their own defence, to alter the succession of the crown. And the constitution, being compounded of parts, may still maintain a sufficient stability, by resting on the aristocratical or democratical members, though the monarchical be altered, from time to time, in order to accommodate it to the former.

In an absolute government, when there is no legal prince, who has a title to the throne, it may safely be determined to belong to the first occupant. Instances of this kind are but too frequent, especially in the eastern monarchies. When any race of princes expires, the will or destination of the last sovereign will be regarded as a title. Thus the edict of LEWIS the XIVth,[57] who called the bastard princes to the succession in case of the failure of all the legitimate princes, would, in such an event, have some authority.† Thus the will of CHARLES the Second disposed of the whole SPANISH monarchy.[58] The cession of the ancient proprietor, especially when joined to conquest, is likewise deemed a good title. The general obligation, which binds us to government, is the interest and necessities of society; and this obligation is very strong. The

---

* HERODIAN, lib. ii.[59]
† See NOTE [TT].

determination of it to this or that particular prince or form of government is frequently more uncertain and dubious. Present possession has considerable authority in these cases, and greater than in private property; because of the disorders which attend all revolutions and changes of government.

We shall only observe, before we conclude, that, though an appeal to general opinion may justly, in the speculative sciences of metaphysics, natural philosophy, or astronomy, be deemed unfair and inconclusive, yet in all questions with regard to morals, as well as criticism, there is really no other standard, by which any controversy can ever be decided. And nothing is a clearer proof, that a theory of this kind is erroneous, than to find, that it leads to paradoxes, repugnant to the common sentiments of mankind, and to the practice and opinion of all nations and all ages. The doctrine, which founds all lawful government on an *original contract*, or consent of the people, is plainly of this kind; nor has the most noted of its partizans, in prosecution of it, scrupled to affirm, *that absolute monarchy is inconsistent with civil society, and so can be no form of civil government at all;** and *that the supreme power in a state cannot take from any man, by taxes and impositions, any part of his property, without his own consent or that of his representatives.*† What authority any moral reasoning can have, which leads into opinions so wide of the general practice of mankind, in every place but this single kingdom, it is easy to determine.

The only passage I meet with in antiquity, where the obligation of obedience to government is ascribed to a promise, is in PLATO's *Crito*: where SOCRATES refuses to escape from prison, because he had tacitly promised to obey the laws.[60] Thus he builds a *tory* consequence of passive obedience, on a *whig* foundation of the original contract.

New discoveries are not to be expected in these matters. If scarce any man, till very lately, ever imagined that government was founded on compact, it is certain, that it cannot, in general, have any such foundation.

The crime of rebellion among the ancients was commonly expressed by the terms νεωτερίζειν, *novas res moliri*.[61]

---

* See LOCKE on Government, chap. vii. § 90.[62]
† Id. chap. xi. § 138, 139, 140.[63]

# NOTES

# Note [TT]

It is remarkable, that, in the remonstrance of the duke of BOURBON and the legitimate princes, against this destination of LOUIS the XIVth, the doctrine of the *original contract* is insisted on, even in that absolute government. The FRENCH nation, say they, chusing HUGH CAPET and his posterity to rule over them and their posterity, where the former line fails, there is a tacit right reserved to choose a new royal family; and this right is invaded by calling the bastard princes to the throne, without the consent of the nation. But the Comte de BOULAINVILLIERS, who wrote in defence of the bastard princes, ridicules this notion of an original contract, especially when applied to HUGH CAPET; who mounted the throne, says he, by the same arts, which have ever been employed by all conquerors and usurpers. He got his title, indeed, recognized by the states after he had put himself in possession: But is this a choice or contract? The Comte de BOULAINVILLIERS, we may observe, was a noted republican; but being a man of learning, and very conversant in history, he knew that the people were never almost consulted in these revolutions and new establishments, and that time alone bestowed right and authority on what was commonly at first founded on force and violence.[64] See *Etat de la France*, Vol. III.

# Essay XIII

## Of Passive Obedience

In the former essay, we endeavoured to refute the *speculative* systems of politics advanced in this nation; as well the religious system of the one party, as the philosophical of the other. We come now to examine the *practical* consequences, deduced by each party, with regard to the measures of submission due to sovereigns.

As the obligation to justice is founded entirely on the interests of society, which require mutual abstinence from property, in order to preserve peace among mankind; it is evident, that, when the execution of justice would be attended with very pernicious consequences, that virtue must be suspended, and give place to public utility, in such extraordinary and such pressing emergencies. The maxim, *fiat Justitia & ruat Cœlum,*[1] let justice be performed, though the universe be destroyed, is apparently false, and by sacrificing the end to the means, shews a preposterous idea of the subordination of duties. What governor of a town makes any scruple of burning the suburbs, when they facilitate the approaches of the enemy? Or what general abstains from plundering a neutral country, when the necessities of war require it, and he cannot otherwise subsist his army? The case is the same with the duty of allegiance; and common sense teaches us, that, as government binds us to obedience only on account of its tendency to public utility,[2] that duty must always, in extraordinary cases, when public ruin would evidently attend obedience, yield to the primary and original obligation. *Salus populi suprema Lex,*[3] the safety of the people is the supreme law. This maxim is agreeable to the sentiments of mankind in all ages: Nor is any one, when he reads of the insurrections against NERO or PHILIP the Second, so infatuated with party systems, as not to wish success to the enterprize, and praise the undertakers.[4] Even our high monarchical party,[5] in spite of their sublime theory, are forced, in such cases, to judge, and feel, and approve, in conformity to the rest of mankind.

Resistance, therefore, being admitted in extraordinary emergencies, the question can only be among good reasoners, with regard to the degree of necessity, which can justify resistance, and render it lawful or commendable. And here I must confess, that I shall always incline to their side, who draw the bond of allegiance very close, and consider an infringement of it, as the last refuge[6] in desperate cases, when the public is in the highest danger, from violence and tyranny. For besides the mischiefs of a civil war, which commonly attends insurrection; it is certain, that, where a disposition to rebellion appears among any people, it is one chief cause of tyranny in the rulers, and forces them into many violent measures which they never would have embraced, had every one been inclined to submission and obedience. Thus the *tyrannicide* or assassination, approved of by ancient maxims, instead of keeping tyrants and usurpers in awe, made them ten times more fierce and unrelenting; and is now justly, upon that account, abolished by the laws of nations, and universally condemned as a base and treacherous method of bringing to justice these disturbers of society.[7]

Besides we must consider, that, as obedience is our duty in the common course of things, it ought chiefly to be inculcated; nor can any thing be more preposterous than an anxious care and solicitude in stating all the cases, in which resistance may be allowed.[8] In like manner, though a philosopher reasonably acknowledges, in the course of an argument, that the rules of justice may be dispensed with in cases of urgent necessity; what should we think of a preacher or casuist, who should make it his chief study to find out such cases, and enforce them with all the vehemence of argument and eloquence? Would he not be better employed in inculcating the general doctrine, than in displaying the particular exceptions, which we are, perhaps, but too much inclined, of ourselves, to embrace and to extend?

There are, however, two reasons, which may be pleaded in defence of that party among us,[9] who have, with so much industry, propagated the maxims of resistance; maxims, which, it must be confessed, are, in general, so pernicious, and so destructive of civil society. The *first* is, that their antagonists carrying the doctrine of obedience to such an extravagant height, as not only never to mention the exceptions in extraordinary cases (which might, perhaps, be excusable) but even positively to exclude them; it became necessary to insist on these exceptions, and defend the rights of injured truth and liberty. The *second*, and, perhaps, better reason, is founded on the nature of the BRITISH constitution and form of government.

It is almost peculiar to our constitution to establish a first magistrate with such high pre-eminence and dignity, that, though limited by the laws, he is, in a manner, so far as regards his own person, above the laws, and can neither be questioned nor punished for any injury or wrong, which may be committed by him.[10] His ministers alone, or those who act by his commission, are obnoxious to justice; and while the prince is thus allured, by the prospect of personal safety, to give the laws their free course, an equal security is, in effect, obtained by the punishment of lesser offenders, and at the same time a civil war is avoided, which would be the infallible consequence, were an attack, at every turn, made directly upon the sovereign. But though the constitution pays this salutary compliment to the prince, it can never reasonably be understood, by that maxim, to have determined its own destruction, or to have established a tame submission, where he protects his ministers, perseveres in injustice, and usurps the whole power of the commonwealth. This case, indeed, is never expressly put by the laws; because it is impossible for them, in their ordinary course, to provide a remedy for it, or establish any magistrate, with superior authority, to chastise the exorbitancies of the prince. But as a right without a remedy would be an absurdity; the remedy in this case, is the extraordinary one of resistance, when affairs come to that extremity, that the constitution can be defended by it alone. Resistance therefore must, of course, become more frequent in the BRITISH government, than in others, which are simpler, and consist of fewer parts and movements. Where the king is an absolute sovereign, he has little temptation to commit such enormous tyranny as may justly provoke rebellion: But where he is limited, his imprudent ambition, without any great vices, may run him into that perilous situation. This is frequently supposed to have been the case with CHARLES the First; and if we may now speak truth, after animosities are ceased, this was also the case with JAMES the Second. These were harmless, if not, in their private character, good men; but mistaking the nature of our constitution, and engrossing the whole legislative power, it became necessary to oppose them with some vehemence; and even to deprive the latter formally of that authority, which he had used with such imprudence and indiscretion.[11]

# Essay XIV

## Of the Coalition of Parties

To abolish all distinctions of party may not be practicable, perhaps not desirable, in a free government. The only dangerous parties are such as entertain opposite views with regard to the essentials of government, the succession of the crown, or the more considerable privileges belonging to the several members of the constitution; where there is no room for any compromise or accommodation, and where the controversy may appear so momentous as to justify even an opposition by arms to the pretensions of antagonists. Of this nature was the animosity, continued for above a century past,[1] between the parties in ENGLAND; an animosity which broke out sometimes into civil war, which occasioned violent revolutions, and which continually endangered the peace and tranquillity of the nation. But as there have appeared of late the strongest symptoms of an universal desire to abolish these party distinctions;[2] this tendency to a coalition affords the most agreeable prospect of future happiness, and ought to be carefully cherished and promoted by every lover of his country.

There is not a more effectual method of promoting so good an end, than to prevent all unreasonable insult and triumph of the one party over the other, to encourage moderate opinions, to find the proper medium in all disputes, to persuade each that its antagonist may possibly be sometimes in the right, and to keep a balance in the praise and blame, which we bestow on either side. The two former Essays, concerning the *original contract* and *passive obedience*, are calculated for this purpose with regard to the *philosophical* and *practical* controversies between the parties, and tend to show that neither side are in these respects so fully supported by reason as they endeavour to flatter themselves. We shall proceed to exercise the same moderation with regard to the *historical* disputes between the parties, by proving that each of them was justified by plausible topics; that there were on both sides wise men, who meant well to their country; and that the past animosity between the factions had no better foundation than narrow prejudice or interested passion.

The popular party, who afterwards acquired the name of whigs,[3] might justify, by very specious[4] arguments, that opposition to the crown, from which our present free constitution is derived. Though obliged to acknowledge, that precedents in favour of prerogative[5] had uniformly taken place during many reigns before CHARLES the First, they thought, that there was no reason for submitting any longer to so dangerous an authority. Such might have been their reasoning: As the rights of mankind are for ever to be deemed sacred, no prescription of tyranny or arbitrary power can have authority sufficient to abolish them. Liberty is a blessing so inestimable, that, wherever there appears any probability of recovering it, a nation may willingly run many hazards, and ought not even to repine at the greatest effusion of blood or dissipation of treasure. All human institutions, and none more than government, are in continual fluctuation. Kings are sure to embrace every opportunity of extending their prerogatives: And if favourable incidents be not also laid hold of for extending and securing the privileges of the people, an universal despotism must for ever prevail amongst mankind. The example of all the neighbouring nations proves, that it is no longer safe to entrust with the crown the same high prerogatives, which had formerly been exercised during rude and simple ages. And though the example of many late reigns may be pleaded in favour of a power in the prince somewhat arbitrary, more remote reigns afford instances of stricter limitations imposed on the crown; and those pretensions of the parliament, now branded with the title of innovations, are only a recovery of the just rights of the people.

These views, far from being odious, are surely large, and generous, and noble: To their prevalence and success the kingdom owes its liberty; perhaps its learning, its industry, commerce, and naval power: By them chiefly the ENGLISH name is distinguished among the society of nations, and aspires to a rivalship with that of the freest and most illustrious commonwealths of antiquity. But as all these mighty consequences could not reasonably be foreseen at the time when the contest began, the royalists of that age wanted not specious arguments on their side, by which they could justify their defence of the then established prerogatives of the prince. We shall state the question, as it might have appeared to them at the assembling of that parliament, which, by its violent encroachments on the crown, began the civil wars.[6]

The only rule of government, they might have said, known and acknowledged among men, is use and practice: Reason is so uncertain a guide that it will always be exposed to doubt and controversy: Could it ever render itself prevalent over the people, men had always retained it as their sole rule of conduct: They had still continued in the primitive, unconnected, state of nature, without submitting to political government, whose sole basis is, not pure reason, but authority and precedent. Dissolve these ties, you break all the bonds of civil society, and leave every man at liberty to consult his private interest, by those expedients, which his appetite, disguised under the appearance of reason, shall dictate to him. The spirit of innovation is in itself pernicious,[7] however favourable its particular object may sometimes appear: A truth so obvious, that the popular party themselves are sensible of it; and therefore cover their encroachments on the crown by the plausible pretence of their recovering the ancient liberties of the people.[8]

But the present prerogatives of the crown, allowing all the suppositions of that party, have been incontestably established ever since the accession of the House of TUDOR;[9] a period, which, as it now comprehends a hundred and sixty years, may be allowed sufficient to give stability to any constitution. Would it not have appeared ridiculous, in the reign of the Emperor ADRIAN,[10] to have talked of the republican constitution as the rule of government; or to have supposed, that the former rights of the senate, and consuls, and tribunes were still subsisting?[11]

But the present claims of the ENGLISH monarchs are much more favourable than those of the ROMAN emperors during that age. The authority of AUGUSTUS was a plain usurpation, grounded only on military violence, and forms such an epoch in the ROMAN history, as is obvious to every reader. But if HENRY VII. really, as some pretend, enlarged the power of the crown, it was only by insensible acquisitions, which escaped the apprehension of the people, and have scarcely been remarked even by historians and politicians.[12] The new government, if it deserve the epithet, is an imperceptible transition from the former; is entirely engrafted on it; derives its title fully from that root; and is to be considered only as one of those gradual revolutions, to which human affairs, in every nation, will be for ever subject.

The House of TUDOR, and after them that of STUART, exercised no prerogatives, but what had been claimed and exercised by the PLAN-TAGENETS.[13] Not a single branch of their authority can be said to be an innovation. The only difference is, that, perhaps, former kings exerted these powers only by intervals, and were not able, by reason of the opposition of their barons, to render them so steady a rule of adminis-tration. But the sole inference from this fact is, that those ancient times were more turbulent and seditious; and that royal authority, the consti-tution, and the laws have happily of late gained the ascendant.

Under what pretence can the popular party now speak of recovering the ancient constitution?[14] The former controul over the kings was not placed in the commons, but in the barons: The people had no authority, and even little or no liberty; till the crown, by suppressing these factious tyrants, enforced the execution of the laws, and obliged all the subjects equally to respect each others rights, privileges, and properties. If we must return to the ancient barbarous and feudal constitution; let those gentlemen, who now behave themselves with so much insolence to their sovereign, set the first example. Let them make court to be admitted as retainers to a neighbouring baron; and by submitting to slavery under him, acquire some protection to themselves; together with the power of exercising rapine and oppression over their inferior slaves and villains. This was the condition of the commons among their remote ancestors.

But how far back must we go, in having recourse to ancient constitu-tions and governments? There was a constitution still more ancient than that to which these innovators affect so much to appeal. During that period there was no *magna charta:*[15] The barons themselves possessed few regular, stated privileges: And the house of commons probably had not an existence.[16]

It is ridiculous to hear the commons, while they are assuming, by usurpation, the whole power of government, talk of reviving ancient institutions. Is it not known, that, though representatives received wages from their constituents; to be a member of the lower house was always considered as a burden, and an exemption from it as a privilege? Will they persuade us, that power, which, of all human acquisitions, is the most coveted, and in comparison of which even reputation and pleasure and riches are slighted, could ever be regarded as a burden by any man?

The property, acquired of late by the commons, it is said, entitles them to more power than their ancestors enjoyed.[17] But to what is this encrease of their property owing, but to an encrease of their liberty and their security? Let them therefore acknowledge, that their ancestors, while the crown was restrained by the seditious barons, really enjoyed less liberty than they themselves have attained, after the sovereign acquired the ascendant: And let them enjoy that liberty with moderation; and not forfeit it by new exorbitant claims, and by rendering it a pretence for endless innovations.

The true rule of government is the present established practice of the age.[18] That has most authority, because it is recent: It is also best known, for the same reason. Who has assured those tribunes, that the PLAN-TAGENETS did not exercise as high acts of authority as the TUDORS? Historians, they say, do not mention them. But historians are also silent with regard to the chief exertions of prerogative by the TUDORS. Where any power or prerogative is fully and undoubtedly established, the exercise of it passes for a thing of course, and readily escapes the notice of history and annals. Had we no other monuments of ELIZABETH's reign, than what are preserved even by CAMDEN, the most copious, judicious, and exact of our historians, we should be entirely ignorant of the most important maxims of her government.[19]

Was not the present monarchical government, in its full extent, authorized by lawyers, recommended by divines, acknowledged by politicians, acquiesced in, nay passionately cherished, by the people in general; and all this during a period of at least a hundred and sixty years, and till of late, without the smallest murmur or controversy? This general consent surely, during so long a time, must be sufficient to render a constitution legal and valid. If the origin of all power be derived, as is pretended, from the people;[20] here is their consent in the fullest and most ample terms that can be desired or imagined.

But the people must not pretend, because they can, by their consent, lay the foundations of government, that therefore they are to be permitted, at their pleasure, to overthrow and subvert them. There is no end of these seditious and arrogant claims. The power of the crown is now openly struck at:[21] The nobility are also in visible peril: The gentry will soon follow: The popular leaders, who will then assume the name of gentry, will next be exposed to danger: And the people themselves, having become incapable of civil government, and lying under the restraint of no authority, must, for the sake of peace, admit, instead of their legal and mild monarchs, a succession of military and despotic tyrants.[22]

These consequences are the more to be dreaded, as the present fury of the people, though glossed over by pretensions to civil liberty, is in reality incited by the fanaticism of religion;[23] a principle the most blind, headstrong, and ungovernable, by which human nature can possibly be actuated. Popular rage is dreadful, from whatever motive derived: But must be attended with the most pernicious consequences, when it arises from a principle, which disclaims all controul by human law, reason, or authority.[24]

These are the arguments, which each party may make use of to justify the conduct of their predecessors, during that great crisis. The event, if that can be admitted as a reason, has shown, that the arguments of the popular party were better founded; but perhaps, according to the established maxims of lawyers and politicians, the views of the royalists ought, before-hand, to have appeared more solid, more safe, and more legal. But this is certain, that the greater moderation we now employ in representing past events; the nearer shall we be to produce a full coalition of the parties, and an entire acquiescence in our present establishment. Moderation is of advantage to every establishment: Nothing but zeal can overturn a settled power: And an over-active zeal in friends is apt to beget a like spirit in antagonists. The transition from a moderate opposition against an establishment, to an entire acquiescence in it, is easy and insensible.

There are many invincible arguments, which should induce the malcontent party[25] to acquiesce entirely in the present settlement of the constitution. They now find, that the spirit of civil liberty, though at first connected with religious fanaticism, could purge itself from that pollution, and appear under a more genuine and engaging aspect; a friend to toleration, and an encourager of all the enlarged and generous sentiments that do honour to human nature.[26] They may observe, that the popular claims could stop at a proper period; and after retrenching the high claims of prerogative, could still maintain a due respect to monarchy, to nobility, and to all ancient institutions. Above all, they must be sensible, that the very principle, which made the strength of their party, and from which it derived its chief authority, has now deserted them, and gone over to their antagonists. The plan of liberty is settled; its happy effects are proved by experience; a long tract of time has given it stability; and whoever would attempt to overturn it, and to recall the past government or abdicated family,[27] would, besides other more criminal imputations, be exposed, in their turn, to the reproach of faction and innovation.[28] While they peruse the history of past events, they ought to reflect, both that those rights of the crown are long since annihilated, and that the tyranny, and violence, and oppression, to which they often gave rise, are ills, from which the established liberty of the constitution has now at last happily protected the people. These reflections will prove a better security to our freedom and privileges, than to deny, contrary to the clearest evidence of facts, that such regal powers ever had an existence. There is not a more effectual method of betraying a cause, than to lay the stress of the argument on a wrong place, and by disputing an untenable post, enure[29] the adversaries to success and victory.

# Essay XV

## *Of the Protestant Succession*

I suppose, that a member of parliament, in the reign of King WILLIAM or Queen ANNE, while the establishment of the *Protestant Succession* was yet uncertain, were deliberating concerning the party he would chuse in that important question, and weighing, with impartiality, the advantages and disadvantages on each side. I believe the following particulars would have entered into his consideration.[1]

He would easily perceive the great advantage resulting from the restoration of the STUART family; by which we should preserve the succession clear and undisputed, free from a pretender, with such a specious[2] title as that of blood, which, with the multitude, is always the claim, the strongest and most easily comprehended. It is in vain to say, as many have done, that the question with regard to *governors*, independent of *government*, is frivolous, and little worth disputing, much less fighting about.[3] The generality of mankind never will enter into these sentiments; and it is much happier, I believe, for society, that they do not, but rather continue in their natural prepossessions. How could stability be preserved in any monarchical government, (which, though, perhaps, not the best, is, and always has been, the most common of any) unless men had so passionate a regard for the true heir of their royal family; and even though he be weak in understanding, or infirm in years, gave him so sensible a preference above persons the most accomplished in shining talents, or celebrated for great achievements? Would not every popular leader put in his claim at every vacancy, or even without any vacancy; and the kingdom become the theatre of perpetual wars and convulsions?[4] The condition of the ROMAN empire, surely, was not, in this respect, much to be envied;[5] nor is that of the *Eastern* nations, who pay little regard to the titles of their sovereign, but sacrifice them, every day, to the caprice or momentary humour of the populace or soldiery.[6]

It is but a foolish wisdom, which is so carefully displayed, in undervaluing princes, and placing them on a level with the meanest of mankind.[7] To be sure, an anatomist finds no more in the greatest monarch than in the lowest peasant or day-labourer; and a moralist may, perhaps, frequently find less. But what do all these reflections tend to? We, all of us, still retain these prejudices in favour of birth and family; and neither in our serious occupations, nor most careless amusements, can we ever get entirely rid of them. A tragedy, that should represent the adventures of sailors, or porters, or even of private gentlemen, would presently disgust us; but one that introduces kings and princes, acquires in our eyes an air of importance and dignity. Or should a man be able, by his superior wisdom, to get entirely above such prepossessions, he would soon, by means of the same wisdom, again bring himself down to them, for the sake of society, whose welfare he would perceive to be intimately connected with them. Far from endeavouring to undeceive the people in this particular, he would cherish such sentiments of reverence to their princes; as requisite to preserve a due subordination in society. And though the lives of twenty thousand men be often sacrificed to maintain a king in possession of his throne, or preserve the right of succession undisturbed, he entertains no indignation at the loss, on pretence that every individual of these was, perhaps, in himself, as valuable as the prince he served. He considers the consequences of violating the hereditary right of kings: Consequences, which may be felt for many centuries; while the loss of several thousand men brings so little prejudice to a large kingdom, that it may not be perceived a few years after.

The advantages of the HANOVER succession are of an opposite nature, and arise from this very circumstance, that it violates hereditary right; and places on the throne a prince, to whom birth gave no title to that dignity.[8] It is evident, from the history of this island, that the privileges of the people have, during near two centuries, been continually upon the encrease, by the division of the church-lands, by the alienations of the barons' estates, by the progress of trade, and above all, by the happiness of our situation, which, for a long time, gave us sufficient security, without any standing army or military establishment.[9] On the contrary, public liberty has, almost in every other nation of EUROPE, been, during the same period, extremely upon the decline; while the people were disgusted at the hardships of the old feudal militia, and rather chose to entrust their prince with mercenary armies,[10] which he

easily turned against themselves. It was nothing extraordinary, therefore, that some of our BRITISH sovereigns[11] mistook the nature of the
constitution, at least, the genius of the people; and as they embraced all
the favourable precedents left them by their ancestors, they overlooked
all those which were contrary, and which supposed a limitation in our
government. They were encouraged in this mistake, by the example of
all the neighbouring princes, who bearing the same title or appellation,
and being adorned with the same ensigns of authority, naturally led
them to claim the same powers and prerogatives. It appears from the
speeches, and proclamations of JAMES I. and the whole train of that
prince's actions, as well as his son's, that he regarded the ENGLISH
government as a simple monarchy, and never imagined that any considerable part of his subjects entertained a contrary idea.[12] This opinion
made those monarchs discover their pretensions, without preparing
any force to support them; and even without reserve or disguise, which
are always employed by those, who enter upon any new project, or
endeavour to innovate in any government. The flattery of courtiers farther confirmed their prejudices; and above all, that of the clergy, who
from several passages of *scripture*, and these wrested too, had erected
a regular and avowed system of arbitrary power.[13] The only method of
destroying, at once, all these high claims and pretensions, was to depart
from the true hereditary line, and choose a prince, who, being plainly a
creature of the public, and receiving the crown on conditions, expressed
and avowed, found his authority established on the same bottom with
the privileges of the people.[14] By electing him in the royal line, we cut
off all hopes of ambitious subjects, who might, in future emergencies,
disturb the government by their cabals and pretensions: By rendering
the crown hereditary in his family, we avoided all the inconveniencies of
elective monarchy: And by excluding the lineal heir,[15] we secured all our
constitutional limitations, and rendered our government uniform and
of a piece. The people cherish monarchy, because protected by it: The
monarch favours liberty, because created by it. And thus every advantage is obtained by the new establishment, as far as human skill and
wisdom can extend itself.

These are the separate advantages of fixing the succession, either in
the house of STUART, or in that of HANOVER. There are also disadvantages in each establishment, which an impartial patriot would ponder
and examine, in order to form a just judgment upon the whole.

The disadvantages of the protestant succession consist in the foreign dominions,[16] which are possessed by the princes of the HANOVER line, and which, it might be supposed, would engage us in the intrigues and wars of the continent, and lose us, in some measure, the inestimable advantage we possess, of being surrounded and guarded by the sea, which we command. The disadvantages of recalling the abdicated family consist chiefly in their religion, which is more prejudicial to society than that established amongst us, is contrary to it, and affords no toleration, or peace, or security to any other communion.

It appears to me, that these advantages and disadvantages are allowed on both sides; at least, by every one who is at all susceptible of argument or reasoning. No subject, however loyal, pretends to deny, that the disputed title and foreign dominions of the present royal family are a loss. Nor is there any partizan of the STUARTS, but will confess, that the claim of hereditary, indefeasible right, and the Roman Catholic religion, are also disadvantages in that family. It belongs, therefore, to a philosopher alone, who is of neither party,[17] to put all the circumstances in the scale, and assign to each of them its proper poise and influence. Such a one will readily, at first, acknowledge that all political questions are infinitely complicated, and that there scarcely ever occurs, in any deliberation, a choice, which is either purely good, or purely ill. Consequences, mixed and varied, may be foreseen to flow from every measure: And many consequences, unforeseen, do always, in fact, result from every one. Hesitation, and reserve, and suspence, are, therefore, the only sentiments he brings to this essay or trial. Or if he indulges any passion, it is that of derision against the ignorant multitude, who are always clamorous and dogmatical, even in the nicest questions, of which, from want of temper, perhaps still more than of understanding, they are altogether unfit judges.[18]

But to say something more determinate on this head, the following reflections will, I hope, show the temper, if not the understanding of a philosopher.

Were we to judge merely by first appearances, and by past experience, we must allow that the advantages of a parliamentary title in the house of HANOVER are greater than those of an undisputed hereditary title in the house of STUART; and that our fathers acted wisely in preferring the former to the latter. So long as the house of STUART ruled in GREAT BRITAIN, which, with some interruption, was above eighty years,[19] the government was kept in a continual fever, by the contention between the privileges of the people and the prerogatives of the crown. If arms were dropped, the noise of disputes continued: Or if these were silenced, jealousy still corroded the heart, and threw the nation into an unnatural ferment and disorder. And while we were thus occupied in domestic disputes, a foreign power,[20] dangerous to public liberty, erected itself in EUROPE, without any opposition from us, and even sometimes with our assistance.[21]

But during these last sixty years,[22] when a parliamentary establishment has taken place; whatever factions may have prevailed either among the people or in public assemblies, the whole force of our constitution has always fallen to one side, and an uninterrupted harmony has been preserved between our princes and our parliaments. Public liberty, with internal peace and order, has flourished almost without interruption: Trade and manufactures, and agriculture, have encreased: The arts, and sciences, and philosophy, have been cultivated. Even religious parties have been necessitated to lay aside their mutual rancour: And the glory of the nation has spread itself all over EUROPE; derived equally from our progress in the arts of peace, and from valour and success in war. So long and so glorious a period no nation almost can boast of: Nor is there another instance in the whole history of mankind, that so many millions of people have, during such a space of time, been held together, in a manner so free, so rational, and so suitable to the dignity of human nature.

But though this recent experience seems clearly to decide in favour of the present establishment, there are some circumstances to be thrown into the other scale; and it is dangerous to regulate our judgment by one event or example.

We have had two rebellions[23] during the flourishing period above mentioned, besides plots and conspiracies without number.[24] And if none of these have produced any very fatal event, we may ascribe our escape chiefly to the narrow genius of those princes who disputed our establishment;[25] and we may esteem ourselves so far fortunate. But the claims of the banished family, I fear, are not yet antiquated;[26] and who can foretel, that their future attempts will produce no greater disorder?

The disputes between privilege and prerogative may easily be composed by laws, and votes, and conferences, and concessions; where there is tolerable temper or prudence on both sides, or on either side. Among contending titles, the question can only be determined by the sword, and by devastation, and by civil war.

A prince, who fills the throne with a disputed title, dares not arm his subjects; the only method of securing a people fully, both against domestic oppression and foreign conquest.

Notwithstanding our riches and renown, what a critical escape did we make, by the late peace,[27] from dangers, which were owing not so much to bad conduct and ill success in war, as to the pernicious practice of mortgaging our finances, and the still more pernicious maxim of never paying off our incumbrances?[28] Such fatal measures would not probably have been embraced, had it not been to secure a precarious establishment.

But to convince us, that an hereditary title is to be embraced rather than a parliamentary one, which is not supported by any other views or motives; a man needs only transport himself back to the æra of the restoration, and suppose, that he had a seat in that parliament which recalled the royal family,[29] and put a period to the greatest disorders that ever arose from the opposite pretensions of prince and people. What would have been thought of one, that had proposed, at that time, to set aside CHARLES II. and settle the crown on the Duke of YORK[30] or GLOUCESTER,[31] merely in order to exclude all high claims, like those of their father and grandfather? Would not such a one have been regarded as an extravagant projector, who loved dangerous remedies, and could tamper and play with a government and national constitution like a quack with a sickly patient?[32]

In reality, the reason assigned by the nation for excluding the race of STUART, and so many other branches of the royal family, is not on account of their hereditary title (a reason, which would, to vulgar apprehensions, have appeared altogether absurd), but on account of their religion.[33] Which leads us to compare the disadvantages above mentioned in each establishment.

I confess, that, considering the matter in general, it were much to be wished, that our prince had no foreign dominions,[34] and could confine all his attention to the government of this island. For not to mention some real inconveniencies that may result from territories on the continent, they afford such a handle for calumny and defamation, as is greedily seized by the people, always disposed to think ill of their superiors. It must, however, be acknowledged, that HANOVER, is, perhaps, the spot of ground in EUROPE the least inconvenient for a King of ENGLAND. It lies in the heart of GERMANY, at a distance from the great powers, which are our natural rivals: It is protected by the laws of the empire,[35] as well as by the arms of its own sovereign: And it serves only to connect us more closely with the house of AUSTRIA, our natural ally.[36]

The religious persuasion of the house of STUART is an inconvenience of a much deeper dye, and would threaten us with much more dismal consequences. The Roman Catholic religion, with its train of priests and friers, is more expensive than ours: Even though unaccompanied with its natural attendants of inquisitors, and stakes, and gibbets, it is less tolerating: And not content with dividing the sacerdotal from the regal office (which must be prejudicial to any state), it bestows the former on a foreigner,[37] who has always a separate interest from that of the public, and may often have an opposite one.

But were this religion ever so advantageous to society, it is contrary to that which is established among us, and which is likely to keep possession, for a long time, of the minds of the people. And though it is much to be hoped, that the progress of reason will, by degrees, abate the acrimony of opposite religions all over EUROPE; yet the spirit of moderation has, as yet, made too slow advances to be entirely trusted.

Thus, upon the whole, the advantages of the settlement in the family of STUART, which frees us from a disputed title, seem to bear some proportion with those of the settlement in the family of HANOVER, which frees us from the claims of prerogative: But at the same time, its disadvantages, by placing on the throne a Roman Catholic, are greater than those of the other establishment, in settling the crown on a foreign prince. What party an impartial patriot, in the reign of K. WILLIAM or Q. ANNE, would have chosen amidst these opposite views, may, perhaps, to some appear hard to determine.

But the settlement in the house of HANOVER has actually taken place.[38] The princes of that family, without intrigue, without cabal, without solicitation on their part, have been called to mount our throne,[39] by the united voice of the whole legislative body. They have, since their accession, displayed, in all their actions, the utmost mildness, equity, and regard to the laws and constitution.[40] Our own ministers, our own parliaments, ourselves have governed us; and if aught ill has befallen us, we can only blame fortune or ourselves. What a reproach must we become among nations, if, disgusted with a settlement so deliberately made, and whose conditions have been so religiously observed, we should throw every thing again into confusion; and by our levity and rebellious disposition, prove ourselves totally unfit for any state but that of absolute slavery and subjection?

The greatest inconvenience, attending a disputed title, is, that it brings us in danger of civil wars and rebellions. What wise man, to avoid this inconvenience, would run directly into a civil war and rebellion? Not to mention, that so long possession, secured by so many laws, must, ere this time, in the apprehension of a great part of the nation, have begotten a title in the house of HANOVER, independent of their present possession: So that now we should not, even by a revolution, obtain the end of avoiding a disputed title.[41]

No revolution made by national forces, will ever be able, without some other great necessity, to abolish our debts and incumbrances, in which the interest of so many persons is concerned. And a revolution made by foreign forces, is a conquest: A calamity, with which the precarious balance of power threatens us, and which our civil dissentions are likely, above all other circumstances, to bring upon us.[42]

# Essay XVI

## *Idea of a Perfect Commonwealth*

It is not with forms of government, as with other artificial contrivances; where an old engine[1] may be rejected, if we can discover another more accurate and commodious, or where trials may safely be made, even though the success be doubtful. An established government has an infinite advantage, by that very circumstance of its being established;[2] the bulk of mankind being governed by authority, not reason, and never attributing authority to any thing that has not the recommendation of antiquity. To tamper, therefore, in this affair, or try experiments merely upon the credit of supposed argument and philosophy, can never be the part of a wise magistrate, who will bear a reverence to what carries the marks of age; and though he may attempt some improvements for the public good, yet will he adjust his innovations, as much as possible, to the ancient fabric, and preserve entire the chief pillars and supports of the constitution.

The mathematicians in EUROPE have been much divided concerning that figure of a ship, which is the most commodious for sailing; and HUYGENS, who at last determined the controversy, is justly thought to have obliged the learned, as well as commercial world; though COLUMBUS had sailed to AMERICA, and Sir FRANCIS DRAKE made the tour of the world, without any such discovery.[3] As one form of government must be allowed more perfect than another, independent of the manners and humours of particular men; why may we not enquire what is the most perfect of all, though the common botched and inaccurate governments seem to serve the purposes of society, and though it be not so easy to establish a new system of government, as to build a vessel upon a new construction? The subject is surely the most worthy curiosity of any the wit of man can possibly devise. And who knows, if this controversy were fixed by the universal consent of the wise and learned, but, in some future age, an opportunity might be afforded of reducing the theory to practice, either by a dissolution of some old government, or by the combination of men to form a new one, in some distant part of the world? In all cases, it must be advantageous to know what is most perfect in the kind, that we may be able to bring any real constitution or form of government as near it as possible, by such gentle alterations and innovations as may not give too great disturbance to society.

All I pretend to in the present essay is to revive this subject of speculation; and therefore I shall deliver my sentiments in as few words as possible. A long dissertation on that head would not, I apprehend, be very acceptable to the public, who will be apt to regard such disquisitions both as useless and chimerical.[4]

All plans of government, which suppose great reformation in the manners of mankind, are plainly imaginary.[5] Of this nature, are the *Republic* of PLATO, and the *Utopia* of Sir THOMAS MORE. The OCEANA is the only valuable model of a commonwealth, that has yet been offered to the public.

The chief defects of the OCEANA seem to be these. *First,* Its rotation[6] is inconvenient, by throwing men, of whatever abilities, by intervals, out of public employments. *Secondly,* Its *Agrarian*[7] is impracticable. Men will soon learn the art, which was practised in ancient ROME, of concealing their possessions under other people's name; till at last, the abuse will become so common, that they will throw off even the appearance of restraint. *Thirdly,* The OCEANA provides not a sufficient security for liberty, or the redress of grievances. The senate must propose, and the people consent; by which means, the senate have not only a negative upon the people, but, what is of much greater consequence, their negative goes before the votes of the people. Were the King's negative of the same nature in the ENGLISH constitution, and could he prevent any bill from coming into parliament, he would be an absolute monarch. As his negative follows the votes of the houses, it is of little consequence:[8] Such a difference is there in the manner of placing the same thing. When a popular bill has been debated in parliament, is brought to maturity, all its conveniencies and inconveniencies, weighed and balanced; if afterwards it be presented for the royal assent, few princes will venture to reject the unanimous desire of the people. But could the King crush a disagreeable bill in embryo (as was the case, for some time, in the SCOT-TISH parliament, by means of the lords of the articles),[9] the BRITISH government would have no balance, nor would grievances ever be redressed: And it is certain, that exorbitant power proceeds not, in any government, from new laws, so much as from neglecting to remedy the abuses, which frequently rise from the old ones. A government, says MACHIAVEL, must often be brought back to its original principles.[10] It appears then, that, in the OCEANA, the whole legislature may be said to rest in the senate; which HARRINGTON would own to be an inconvenient form of government, especially after the *Agrarian* is abolished.

Here is a form of government, to which I cannot, in theory, discover any considerable objection.

Let GREAT BRITAIN and IRELAND, or any territory of equal extent, be divided into 100 counties, and each county into 100 parishes, making in all 10,000. If the country, proposed to be erected into a commonwealth be of more narrow extent, we may diminish the number of counties; but never bring them below thirty. If it be of greater extent, it were better to enlarge the parishes, or throw more parishes into a county, than encrease the number of counties.

Let all the freeholders of twenty pounds[11] a-year in the county, and all the householders worth 500 pounds in the town parishes, meet annually in the parish church, and chuse, by ballot, some freeholder of the county for their member, whom we shall call the county *representative*.

Let the 100 county representatives, two days after their election, meet in the county town, and chuse by ballot, from their own body, ten county *magistrates*, and one *senator*. There are, therefore, in the whole commonwealth, 100 senators, 1100 county magistrates, and 10,000 county representatives.[12] For we shall bestow on all senators the authority of county magistrates, and on all county magistrates the authority of county representatives.

Let the senators meet in the capital, and be endowed with the whole executive power of the commonwealth; the power of peace and war, of giving orders to generals, admirals, and ambassadors, and, in short, all the prerogatives of a BRITISH King, except his negative.

Let the county representatives meet in their particular counties, and possess the whole legislative power of the commonwealth; the greater number of counties deciding the question; and where these are equal, let the senate have the casting vote.

Every new law must first be debated in the senate; and though rejected by it, if ten senators insist and protest, it must be sent down to the counties. The senate, if they please, may join to the copy of the law their reasons for receiving or rejecting it.

Because it would be troublesome to assemble all the county representatives for every trivial law, that may be requisite, the senate have their choice of sending down the law either to the county magistrates or county representatives.

The magistrates, though the law be referred to them, may, if they please, call the representatives, and submit the affair to their determination.

Whether the law be referred by the senate to the county magistrates or representatives, a copy of it, and of the senate's reasons, must be sent to every representative eight days before the day appointed for the assembling, in order to deliberate concerning it. And though the determination be, by the senate, referred to the magistrates, if five representatives of the county order the magistrates to assemble the whole court of representatives, and submit the affair to their determination, they must obey.

Either the county magistrates or representatives may give, to the senator of the county, the copy of a law to be proposed to the senate; and if five counties concur in the same order, the law, though refused by the senate, must come either to the county magistrates or representatives, as is contained in the order of the five counties.

Any twenty counties, by a vote either of their magistrates or representatives, may throw any man out of all public offices for a year. Thirty counties for three years.

The senate has a power of throwing out any member or number of members of its own body, not to be re-elected for that year. The senate cannot throw out twice in a year the senator of the same county.

The power of the old senate continues for three weeks after the annual election of the county representatives. Then all the new senators are shut up in a conclave, like the cardinals;[13] and by an intricate ballot, such as that of VENICE or MALTA,[14] they chuse the following magistrates; a protector,[15] who represents the dignity of the commonwealth, and presides in the senate; two secretaries of state;[16] these six councils, a council of state, a council of religion and learning, a council of trade, a council of laws, a council of war, a council of the admiralty, each council consisting of five persons; together with six commissioners of the treasury and a first commissioner. All these must be senators. The senate also names all the ambassadors to foreign courts, who may either be senators or not.

The senate may continue any or all of these, but must re-elect them every year.

The protector and two secretaries have session and suffrage[17] in the council of state. The business of that council is all foreign politics. The council of state has session and suffrage in all the other councils.

The council of religion and learning inspects the universities and clergy. That of trade inspects every thing that may affect commerce. That of laws inspects all the abuses of law by the inferior magistrates, and examines what improvements may be made of the municipal law. That of war inspects the militia and its discipline, magazines, stores, &c. and when the republic is in war, examines into the proper orders for generals. The council of admiralty has the same power with regard to the navy, together with the nomination of the captains and all inferior officers.

None of these councils can give orders themselves, except where they receive such powers from the senate. In other cases, they must communicate every thing to the senate.

When the senate is under adjournment, any of the councils may assemble it before the day appointed for its meeting.

Besides these councils or courts, there is another called the court of *competitors*; which is thus constituted. If any candidates for the office of senator have more votes than a third of the representatives, that candidate, who has most votes, next to the senator elected, becomes incapable for one year of all public offices, even of being a magistrate or representative: But he takes his seat in the court of competitors. Here then is a court which may sometimes consist of a hundred members, sometimes have no members at all; and by that means, be for a year abolished.

The court of competitors has no power in the commonwealth. It has only the inspection of public accounts, and the accusing of any man before the senate. If the senate acquit him, the court of competitors may, if they please, appeal to the people, either magistrates or representatives. Upon that appeal, the magistrates or representatives meet on the day appointed by the court of competitors, and chuse in each county three persons; from which number every senator is excluded. These, to the number of 300, meet in the capital, and bring the person accused to a new trial.

The court of competitors may propose any law to the senate; and if refused, may appeal to the people, that is, to the magistrates or representatives, who examine it in their counties. Every senator, who is thrown out of the senate by a vote of the court, takes his seat in the court of competitors.

The senate possesses all the judicative authority of the house of Lords, that is, all the appeals from the inferior courts. It likewise appoints the Lord Chancellor, and all the officers of the law.

Every county is a kind of republic within itself, and the representatives may make bye-laws; which have no authority 'till three months after they are voted. A copy of the law is sent to the senate, and to every other county. The senate, or any single county, may, at any time, annul any bye-law of another county.

The representatives have all the authority of the BRITISH justices of peace in trials, commitments, &c.

The magistrates have the appointment of all the officers of the revenue in each county. All causes with regard to the revenue are carried ultimately by appeal before the magistrates. They pass the accompts of all the officers; but must have their own accompts examined and passed at the end of the year by the representatives.

The magistrates name rectors or ministers to all the parishes.

The Presbyterian government is established; and the highest ecclesiastical court is an assembly or synod of all the presbyters of the county. The magistrates may take any cause from this court, and determine it themselves.

The magistrates may try, and depose or suspend any presbyter.[18]

The militia is established in imitation of that of SWISSERLAND, which being well known, we shall not insist upon it.[19] It will only be proper to make this addition, that an army of 20,000 men be annually drawn out by rotation, paid and encamped during six weeks in summer; that the duty of a camp may not be altogether unknown.

The magistrates appoint all the colonels and downwards. The senate all upwards. During war, the general appoints the colonel and downwards, and his commission is good for a twelvemonth. But after that, it must be confirmed by the magistrates of the county, to which the regiment belongs. The magistrates may break any officer in the county regiment. And the senate may do the same to any officer in the service. If the magistrates do not think proper to confirm the general's choice, they may appoint another officer in the place of him they reject.

All crimes are tried within the county by the magistrates and a jury. But the senate can stop any trial, and bring it before themselves.

Any county may indict any man before the senate for any crime.

The protector, the two secretaries, the council of state, with any five or more that the senate appoints, are possessed, on extraordinary emergencies, of *dictatorial* power for six months.

The protector may pardon any person condemned by the inferior courts.

In time of war, no officer of the army that is in the field can have any civil office in the commonwealth.

The capital, which we shall call LONDON, may be allowed four members in the senate. It may therefore be divided into four counties. The representatives of each of these chuse one senator, and ten magistrates. There are therefore in the city four senators, forty-four magistrates, and four hundred representatives. The magistrates have the same authority as in the counties. The representatives also have the same authority; but they never meet in one general court: They give their votes in their particular county, or division of hundreds.

When they enact any bye-law, the greater number of counties or divisions determines the matter. And where these are equal, the magistrates have the casting vote.

The magistrates chuse the mayor, sheriff, recorder, and other officers of the city.

In the commonwealth, no representative, magistrate, or senator, as such, has any salary. The protector, secretaries, councils, and ambassadors, have salaries.

The first year in every century is set apart for correcting all inequalities,[20] which time may have produced in the representative. This must be done by the legislature.

The following political aphorisms may explain the reason of these orders.

The lower sort of people and small proprietors are good judges enough of one not very distant from them in rank or habitation; and therefore, in their parochial meetings, will probably chuse the best, or nearly the best representative: But they are wholly unfit for county-meetings, and for electing into the higher offices of the republic. Their ignorance gives the grandees an opportunity of deceiving them.

Ten thousand, even though they were not annually elected, are a basis large enough for any free government. It is true, the nobles in POLAND[21] are more than 10,000, and yet these oppress the people. But as power always continues there in the same persons and families, this makes them, in a manner, a different nation from the people. Besides the nobles are there united under a few heads of families.

All free governments must consist of two councils, a lesser and greater; or, in other words, of a senate and people. The people, as HARRINGTON observes,[22] would want wisdom, without the senate: The senate, without the people, would want honesty.

A large assembly of 1000, for instance, to represent the people, if allowed to debate, would fall into disorder. If not allowed to debate, the senate has a negative upon them, and the worst kind of negative, that before resolution.

Here therefore is an inconvenience, which no government has yet fully remedied, but which is the easiest to be remedied in the world. If the people debate, all is confusion: If they do not debate, they can only resolve; and then the senate carves[23] for them. Divide the people into many separate bodies; and then they may debate with safety, and every inconvenience seems to be prevented.

Cardinal de RETZ says, that all numerous assemblies, however composed, are mere mob, and swayed in their debates by the least motive.[24] This we find confirmed by daily experience. When an absurdity strikes a member, he conveys it to his neighbour, and so on, till the whole be infected. Separate this great body; and though every member be only of middling sense, it is not probable, that any thing but reason can prevail over the whole. Influence and example being removed, good sense will always get the better of bad among a number of people.

There are two things to be guarded against in every *senate:* Its combination, and its division. Its combination is most dangerous. And against this inconvenience we have provided the following remedies. 1. The great dependence of the senators on the people by annual elections; and that not by an undistinguishing rabble, like the ENGLISH electors,[25] but by men of fortune and education.[26] 2. The small power they are allowed. They have few offices to dispose of. Almost all are given by the magistrates in the counties. 3. The court of competitors, which being composed of men that are their rivals, next to them in interest, and uneasy in their present situation, will be sure to take all advantages against them.

The division of the senate is prevented, 1. By the smallness of their number. 2. As faction supposes a combination in a separate interest, it is prevented by their dependence on the people. 3. They have a power of expelling any factious member. It is true, when another member of the same spirit comes from the county, they have no power of expelling him: Nor is it fit they should; for that shows the humour to be in the people, and may possibly arise from some ill conduct in public affairs. 4. Almost any man, in a senate so regularly chosen by the people, may be supposed fit for any civil office. It would be proper, therefore, for the senate to form some *general* resolutions with regard to the disposing of offices among the members: Which resolutions would not confine them in critical times, when extraordinary parts on the one hand, or extra-ordinary stupidity on the other, appears in any senator; but they would be sufficient to prevent intrigue and faction, by making the disposal of the offices a thing of course. For instance, let it be a resolution, That no man shall enjoy any office, till he has sat four years in the senate: That, except ambassadors, no man shall be in office two years following: That no man shall attain the higher offices but through the lower: That no man shall be protector twice, &c. The senate of VENICE govern them-selves by such resolutions.[27]

In foreign politics the interest of the senate can scarcely ever be div-ided from that of the people; and therefore it is fit to make the senate absolute with regard to them; otherwise there could be no secrecy or refined policy. Besides, without money no alliance can be executed; and the senate is still sufficiently dependant. Not to mention, that the legis-lative power being always superior to the executive, the magistrates or representatives may interpose whenever they think proper.

The chief support of the BRITISH government is the opposition of interests; but that, though in the main serviceable, breeds endless fac-tions. In the foregoing plan, it does all the good without any of the harm. The *competitors* have no power of controlling the senate: They have only the power of accusing, and appealing to the people.

It is necessary, likewise, to prevent both combination and division in the thousand magistrates. This is done sufficiently by the separation of places and interests.

But lest that should not be sufficient, their dependence on the 10,000 for their elections, serves to the same purpose.

Nor is that all: For the 10,000 may resume the power whenever they please; and not only when they all please, but when any five of a hundred please, which will happen upon the very first suspicion of a separate interest.

The 10,000 are too large a body either to unite or divide, except when they meet in one place, and fall under the guidance of ambitious leaders. Not to mention their annual election, by the whole body of the people, that are of any consideration.

A small commonwealth is the happiest government in the world within itself, because every thing lies under the eye of the rulers: But it may be subdued by great force from without. This scheme seems to have all the advantages both of a great and a little commonwealth.[28]

Every county-law may be annulled either by the senate or another county; because that shows an opposition of interest: In which case no part ought to decide for itself. The matter must be referred to the whole, which will best determine what agrees with general interest.

As to the clergy and militia, the reasons of these orders are obvious. Without the dependence of the clergy on the civil magistrates, and without a militia, it is in vain to think that any free government will ever have security or stability.

In many governments, the inferior magistrates have no rewards but what arise from their ambition, vanity, or public spirit. The salaries of the FRENCH judges amount not to the interest of the sums they pay for their offices. The DUTCH burgo-masters have little more immediate profit than the ENGLISH justices of peace, or the members of the house of commons formerly.[29] But lest any should suspect, that this would beget negligence in the administration (which is little to be feared, considering the natural ambition of mankind),[30] let the magistrates have competent salaries. The senators have access to so many honourable and lucrative offices, that their attendance needs not be bought. There is little attendance required of the representatives.

That the foregoing plan of government is practicable, no one can doubt, who considers the resemblance that it bears to the commonwealth of the United Provinces,[31] a wise and renowned government. The alterations in the present scheme seem all evidently for the better. 1. The representation is more equal. 2. The unlimited power of the burgo-masters in the towns, which forms a perfect aristocracy in the DUTCH commonwealth, is corrected by a well-tempered democracy, in giving to the people the annual election of the county representatives. 3. The negative, which every province and town has upon the whole body of the DUTCH republic, with regard to alliances, peace and war, and the imposition of taxes, is here removed. 4. The counties, in the present plan, are not so independent of each other, nor do they form separate bodies so much as the seven provinces; where the jealousy and envy of the smaller provinces and towns against the greater, particularly HOLLAND and AMSTERDAM, have frequently disturbed the government. 5. Larger powers, though of the safest kind, are intrusted to the senate than the States-General possess; by which means, the former may become more expeditious, and secret in their resolutions, than it is possible for the latter.

The chief alterations that could be made on the BRITISH government, in order to bring it to the most perfect model of limited monarchy, seem to be the following. *First*, The plan of CROMWELL's parliament[32] ought to be restored, by making the representation equal, and by allowing none to vote in the county elections who possess not a property of 200 pounds value. *Secondly*, As such a house of Commons would be too weighty for a frail house of Lords, like the present, the Bishops and SCOTCH Peers ought to be removed:[33] The number of the upper house ought to be raised to three or four hundred: Their seats not hereditary, but during life: They ought to have the election of their own members; and no commoner should be allowed to refuse a seat that was offered him. By this means the house of Lords would consist entirely of the men of chief credit, abilities, and interest in the nation; and every turbulent leader in the house of Commons might be taken off, and connected by interest with the house of Peers. Such an aristocracy would be an excellent barrier both to the monarchy and against it.[34] At present, the balance of our government depends in some measure on the abilities and behaviour of the sovereign; which are variable and uncertain circumstances.

This plan of limited monarchy, however corrected, seems still liable to three great inconveniences. *First*, It removes not entirely, though it may soften, the parties of *court* and *country*. *Secondly*, The king's personal character must still have great influence on the government. *Thirdly*, The sword is in the hands of a single person, who will always neglect to discipline the militia, in order to have a pretence for keeping up a standing army.[35]

We shall conclude this subject, with observing the falsehood of the common opinion, that no large state, such as FRANCE or GREAT BRITAIN, could ever be modelled into a commonwealth, but that such a form of government can only take place in a city or small territory.[36] The contrary seems probable. Though it is more difficult to form a republican government in an extensive country than in a city; there is more facility, when once it is formed, of preserving it steady and uniform, without tumult and faction. It is not easy, for the distant parts of a large state to combine in any plan of free government; but they easily conspire in the esteem and reverence for a single person, who, by means of this popular favour, may seize the power, and forcing the more obstinate to submit, may establish a monarchical government. On the other hand, a city readily concurs in the same notions of government, the natural equality of property favours liberty, and the nearness of habitation enables the citizens mutually to assist each other. Even under absolute princes, the subordinate government of cities is commonly republican; while that of counties and provinces is monarchical. But these same circumstances, which facilitate the erection of commonwealths in cities, render their constitution more frail and uncertain. Democracies are turbulent. For however the people may be separated or divided into small parties, either in their votes or elections; their near habitation in a city will always make the force of popular tides and currents very sensible. Aristocracies are better adapted for peace and order, and accordingly were most admired by ancient writers; but they are jealous and oppressive. In a large government, which is modelled with masterly skill, there is compass and room enough to refine the democracy, from the lower people, who may be admitted into the first elections or first concoction[37] of the commonwealth, to the higher magistrates, who direct all the movements. At the same time, the parts are so distant and remote, that it is very difficult, either by intrigue, prejudice, or passion, to hurry them into any measures against the public interest.

It is needless to enquire, whether such a government would be immortal. I allow the justness of the poet's exclamation on the endless projects of human race, *Man and for ever!*[38] The world itself probably is not immortal.[39] Such consuming plagues[40] may arise as would leave even a perfect government a weak prey to its neighbours. We know not to what length enthusiasm, or other extraordinary movements of the human mind, may transport men, to the neglect of all order and public good. Where difference of interest is removed, whimsical and unaccountable factions often arise, from personal favour or enmity. Perhaps, rust may grow to the springs of the most accurate political machine, and disorder its motions. Lastly, extensive conquests, when pursued, must be the ruin of every free government;[41] and of the more perfect governments sooner than of the imperfect; because of the very advantages which the former possess above the latter. And though such a state ought to establish a fundamental law against conquests; yet republics have ambition as well as individuals, and present interest makes men forgetful of their posterity. It is a sufficient incitement to human endeavours, that such a government would flourish for many ages; without pretending to bestow, on any work of man, that immortality, which the Almighty seems to have refused to his own productions.

# Withdrawn Essays

# Essay I

## Of Essay-Writing

The elegant Part of Mankind, who are not immers'd in the animal Life, but employ themselves in the Operations of the Mind, may be divided into the *learned* and *conversible*. The Learned are such as have chosen for their Portion the higher and more difficult Operations of the Mind, which require Leisure and Solitude, and cannot be brought to Perfection, without long Preparation and severe Labour. The conversible World join to a sociable Disposition, and a Taste of Pleasure, an Inclination to the easier and more gentle Exercises of the Understanding, to obvious Reflections on human Affairs, and the Duties of common Life, and to the Observation of the Blemishes or Perfections of the particular Objects, that surround them. Such Subjects of Thought furnish not sufficient Employment in Solitude, but require the Company and Conversation of our Fellow-Creatures, to render them a proper Exercise for the Mind: And this brings Mankind together in Society, where every one displays his Thoughts and Observations in the best Manner he is able, and mutually gives and receives Information, as well as Pleasure.

The Separation of the Learned from the conversible World seems to have been the great Defect of the last Age, and must have had a very bad Influence both on Books and Company:[1] For what Possibility is there of finding Topics of Conversation fit for the Entertainment of rational Creatures, without having Recourse sometimes to History, Poetry, Politics, and the more obvious Principles, at least, of Philosophy? Must our whole Discourse be a continued Series of gossipping Stories and idle Remarks? Must the Mind never rise higher, but be perpetually

> *Stun'd and worn out with endless Chat*
> *Of WILL did this, and NAN said that.*[2]

This wou'd be to render the Time spent in Company the most un-entertaining, as well as the most unprofitable Part of our Lives.

On the other Hand, Learning has been as great a Loser by being shut up in Colleges and Cells, and secluded from the World and good Company. By that Means, every Thing of what we call *Belles Lettres* became totally barbarous, being cultivated by Men without any Taste of Life or Manners, and without that Liberty and Facility of Thought and Expression, which can only be acquir'd by Conversation. Even Philosophy went to Wrack by this moaping recluse Method of Study, and became as chimerical in her Conclusions as she was unintelligible in her Stile and Manner of Delivery. And indeed, what cou'd be expected from Men who never consulted Experience in any of their Reasonings, or who never search'd for that Experience, where alone it is to be found, in common Life and Conversation?

'Tis with great Pleasure I observe, That Men of Letters, in this Age, have lost, in a great Measure, that Shyness and Bashfulness of Temper, which kept them at a Distance from Mankind; and, at the same Time, That Men of the World are proud of borrowing from Books their most agreeable Topics of Conversation. 'Tis to be hop'd, that this League betwixt the learned and conversible Worlds, which is so happily begun, will be still farther improv'd to their mutual Advantage; and to that End, I know nothing more advantageous than such *Essays* as these with which I endeavour to entertain the Public. In this View, I cannot but consider myself as a Kind of Resident or Ambassador[3] from the Dominions of Learning to those of Conversation; and shall think it my constant Duty to promote a good Correspondence betwixt these two States, which have so great a Dependence on each other. I shall give Intelligence to the Learned of whatever passes in Company, and shall endeavour to import into Company whatever Commodities I find in my native Country proper for their Use and Entertainment. The Balance of Trade we need not be jealous of, nor will there be any Difficulty to preserve it on both Sides.[4] The Materials of this Commerce must chiefly be furnish'd by Conversation and common Life: The manufacturing of them alone belongs to Learning.

As 'twou'd be an unpardonable Negligence in an Ambassador not to pay his Respects to the Sovereign of the State where he is commission'd to reside; so it wou'd be altogether inexcusable in me not to address myself, with a particular Respect, to the Fair Sex, who are the Sovereigns of the Empire of Conversation. I approach them with Reverence; and were not my Countrymen, the Learned, a stubborn independent Race of Mortals, extremely jealous of their Liberty, and unaccustom'd to Subjection, I shou'd resign into their fair Hands the sovereign Authority over the Republic of Letters. As the Case stands, my Commission extends no farther, than to desire a League, offensive and defensive, against our common Enemies, against the Enemies of Reason and Beauty, People of dull Heads and cold Hearts. From this Moment let us pursue them with the severest Vengeance: Let no Quarter be given, but to those of sound Understandings and delicate Affections;[5] and these Characters, 'tis to be presum'd, we shall always find inseparable.

To be serious, and to quit the Allusion before it be worn thread-bare, I am of Opinion, that Women, that is, Women of Sense and Education (for to such alone I address myself) are much better Judges of all polite Writing than Men of the same Degree of Understanding; and that 'tis a vain Pannic, if they be so far terrify'd with the common Ridicule that is levell'd against learned Ladies, as utterly to abandon every Kind of Books and Study to our Sex. Let the Dread of that Ridicule have no other Effect, than to make them conceal their Knowledge before Fools, who are not worthy of it, nor of them. Such will still presume upon the vain Title of the Male Sex to affect a Superiority above them: But my fair Readers may be assur'd, that all Men of Sense, who know the World, have a great Deference for their Judgment of such Books as ly within the Compass of their Knowledge, and repose more Confidence in the Delicacy of their Taste, tho' unguided by Rules, than in all the dull Labours of Pedants and Commentators. In a neighbouring Nation,[6] equally famous for good Taste, and for Gallantry, the Ladies are, in a Manner, the Sovereigns of the *learned* World, as well as of the *conversible*; and no polite Writer pretends to venture upon the Public, without the Approbation of some celebrated Judges of that Sex. Their Verdict is, indeed, sometimes complain'd of; and, in particular, I find, that the Admirers of *Corneille*, to save that great Poet's Honour upon the Ascendant that *Racine* began to take over him, always said, That it was not to be expected, that so old a Man could dispute the Prize, before such Judges, with so young a Man as his Rival. But this Observation has been found unjust, since Posterity seems to have ratify'd the Verdict of that Tribunal: And *Racine*, tho' dead, is still the Favourite of the Fair Sex, as well as of the best Judges among the Men.

There is only one Subject, on which I am apt to distrust the Judgment of Females, and that is, concerning Books of Gallantry and Devotion, which they commonly affect as high flown as possible; and most of them seem more delighted with the Warmth, than with the justness of the Passion. I mention Gallantry and Devotion as the same Subject, because, in Reality, they become the same when treated in this Manner; and we may observe, that they both depend upon the very same Complexion. As the Fair Sex have a great Share of the tender and amorous Disposition, it perverts their Judgment on this Occasion, and makes them be easily affected, even by what has no Propriety in the Expression nor Nature in the Sentiment. Mr. *Addison*'s elegant Discourses of Religion have no Relish with them, in Comparison of Books of mystic Devotion:[7] And *Otway*'s Tragedies[8] are rejected for the Rants of Mr. *Dryden*.[9]

Wou'd the Ladies correct their false Taste in this Particular; Let them accustom themselves a little more to Books of all Kinds: Let them give Encouragement to Men of Sense and Knowledge to frequent their Company: And finally, let them concur heartily in that Union I have projected betwixt the learned and conversible Worlds. They may, perhaps, meet with more Complaisance from their usual Followers than from Men of Learning; but they cannot reasonably expect so sincere an Affection: And, I hope, they will never be guilty of so wrong a Choice, as to sacrifice the Substance to the Shadow.[10]

# Essay II

## *Of Moral Prejudices*

There is a Set of Men lately sprung up amongst us, who endeavour to distinguish themselves by ridiculing every Thing, that has hitherto appear'd sacred and venerable in the Eyes of Mankind. Reason, Sobriety, Honour, Friendship, Marriage, are the perpetual Subjects of their insipid Raillery:[1] And even public Spirit, and a Regard to our Country, are treated as chimerical and romantic.[2] Were the Schemes of these Anti-reformers to take Place, all the Bonds of Society must be broke, to make Way for the Indulgence of a licentious Mirth and Gaiety: The Companion of our drunken Frollics must be prefer'd to a Friend or Brother: Dissolute Prodigality must be supply'd at the Expence of every Thing valuable, either in public or private: And Men shall have so little Regard to any Thing beyond themselves, that, at last, a free Constitution of Government must become a Scheme perfectly impracticable among Mankind, and must degenerate into one universal System of Fraud and Corruption.[3]

There is another Humour, which may be observ'd in some Pretenders to Wisdom, and which, if not so pernicious as the idle petulant Humour above-mention'd, must, however, have a very bad Effect on those, who indulge it. I mean that grave philosophic Endeavour after Perfection,[4] which, under Pretext of reforming Prejudices and Errors, strikes at all the most endearing Sentiments of the Heart, and all the most useful Byasses[5] and Instincts, which can govern a human Creature. The *Stoics* were remarkable for this Folly among the Antients; and I wish some of more venerable Characters in latter Times had not copy'd them too faithfully in this Particular.[6] The virtuous and tender Sentiments, or Prejudices, if you will, have suffer'd mightily by these Reflections; while a certain sullen Pride or Contempt of Mankind has prevail'd in their Stead, and has been esteem'd the greatest Wisdom; tho', in Reality, it be the most egregious Folly of all others. *Statilius* being sollicited by *Brutus* to make one of that noble Band, who struck the GOD-like Stroke[7] for the Liberty of *Rome*, refus'd to accompany them, saying, *That all Men were Fools or Mad, and did not deserve that a wise Man should trouble his Head about them.*[8]

My learned Reader will here easily recollect the Reason, which an antient Philosopher[9] gave, why he wou'd not be reconcil'd to his Brother, who sollicited his Friendship. He was too much a Philosopher to think, that the Connexion of having sprung from the same Parent, ought to have any Influence on a reasonable Mind, and exprest his Sentiment after such a Manner as I think not proper to repeat. When your Friend is in Affliction, says *Epictetus*, you may counterfeit a Sympathy with him, if it give him Relief; but take Care not to allow any Compassion to sink into your Heart, or disturb that Tranquillity, which is the Perfection of Wisdom.[10] *Diogenes* being askt by his Friends in his Sickness, What should be done with him after his Death? *Why*, says he, *throw me out into the Fields.* "What!" reply'd they, "to the Birds or Beasts." No: *Place a Cudgel by me, to defend myself withal.* "To what Purpose," say they, "you will not have any Sense, nor any Power of making Use of it." *Then if the Beasts shou'd devour me*, cries he, *shall I be any more sensible of it?* I know none of the Sayings of that Philosopher, which shews more evidently both the Liveliness and Ferocity of his Temper.[11]

How different from these are the Maxims by which *Eugenius*[12] conducts himself! In his Youth he apply'd himself, with the most unwearied Labour, to the Study of Philosophy; and nothing was ever able to draw him from it, except when an Opportunity offer'd of serving his Friends, or doing a Pleasure to some Man of Merit. When he was about thirty Years of Age, he was determin'd to quit the free Life of a Batchelor (in which otherwise he wou'd have been inclin'd to remain) by considering, that he was the last Branch of an antient Family, which must have been extinguish'd had he died without Children. He made Choice of the virtuous and beautiful *Emira* for his Consort, who, after being the Solace of his Life for many Years, and having made him the Father of several Children, paid at last the general Debt to Nature.[13] Nothing cou'd have supported him under so severe an Affliction, but the Consolation he receiv'd from his young Family, who were now become dearer to him on account of their deceast Mother. One Daughter in particular is his Darling, and the secret Joy of his Soul; because her Features, her Air, her Voice recal every Moment the tender Memory of his Spouse, and fill his Eyes with Tears. He conceals this Partiality as much as possible; and none but his intimate Friends are acquainted with it. To them he reveals all his Tenderness; nor is he so affectedly Philosophical, as even to call it by the Name of *Weakness*. They know, that he still keeps the Birth-day of *Emira* with Tears, and a more fond and tender Recollection of past Pleasures; in like Manner as it was celebrated in her Lifetime with Joy and Festivity. They know, that he preserves her Picture with the utmost Care, and has one Picture in Minature, which he always wears next to his Bosom: That he has left Orders in his last Will, that, in whatever Part of the World he shall happen to die, his Body shall be transported, and laid in the same Grave with her's: And that a Monument shall be erected over them, and their mutual Love and Happiness celebrated in an Epitaph, which he himself has compos'd for that Purpose.

A few Years ago I receiv'd a Letter from a Friend,[14] who was abroad on his Travels, and shall here communicate it to the Public. It contains such an Instance of a Philosophic Spirit, as I think pretty extraordinary, and may serve as an Example, not to depart too far from the receiv'd Maxims of Conduct and Behaviour, by a refin'd Search after Happiness or Perfection. The Story I have been since assur'd of as Matter of Fact.[15]

*Paris Aug. 2. 1737.*

Sir,

I know you are more curious of Accounts of Men than of Buildings, and are more desirous of being inform'd of private History than of public Transactions; for which Reason, I thought the following Story, which is the common Topic of Conversation in this City, wou'd be no unacceptable Entertainment to you.

A young Lady of Birth and Fortune, being left intirely at her own Disposal, persisted long in a Resolution of leading a single Life, notwithstanding several advantageous Offers that had been made to her. She had been determin'd to embrace this Resolution, by observing the many unhappy Marriages among her Acquaintance, and by hearing the Complaints, which her Female Friends made of the Tyranny, Inconstancy, Jealousy or Indifference of their Husbands. Being a Woman of strong Spirit and an uncommon Way of thinking, she found no Difficulty either in forming or maintaining this Resolution, and cou'd not suspect herself of such Weakness, as ever to be induc'd, by any Temptation, to depart from it. She had, however, entertain'd a strong Desire of having a Son, whose Education she was resolv'd to make the principal Concern of her Life, and by that Means supply the Place of those other Passions, which she was resolv'd for ever to renounce. She push'd her Philosophy to such an uncommon Length, as to find no Contradiction betwixt such a Desire and her former Resolution; and accordingly look'd about, with great Deliberation, to find, among all her Male-Acquaintance, one whose Character and Person were agreeable to her, without being able to satisfy herself on that Head. At Length, being in the Play-house one Evening, she sees in the *Parterre*,[16] a young Man of a most engaging Countenance and modest Deportment; and feels such a Pre-possession in his Favour, that she had Hopes this must be the Person she had long sought for in vain. She immediately dispatches a Servant to him; desiring his Company, at her Lodgings, next Morning. The young Man was over-joy'd at the Message, and cou'd not command his Satisfaction, upon receiving such an Advance from a Lady of so great Beauty, Reputation and Quality. He was, therefore, much disappointed, when he found a Woman, who wou'd allow him no Freedoms; and amidst all her obliging Behaviour, confin'd and over-aw'd him to the Bounds of rational Discourse and Conversation. She seem'd, however, willing to commence a Friendship with him; and told him, that his Company wou'd always be acceptable to her, whenever he had a leisure Hour to bestow. He needed not much Entreaty to renew his Visits, being so struck with her Wit and Beauty, that he must have been unhappy, had he been debarr'd her Company. Every Conversation serv'd only the more to inflame his Passion, and gave him more Occasion to admire her Person and Understanding, as well as to rejoice in his own Good-fortune. He was not, however, without Anxiety, when he consider'd the Disproportion of their Birth and Fortune; nor was his Uneasiness allay'd even when he reflected on the extraordinary Manner in which their Acquaintance had commenc'd. Our Philosophical Heroine, in the mean Time, discover'd, that her Lover's personal Qualities did not belye his Phisiognomy; so that, judging there was no Occasion for any farther Trial, she takes a proper Opportunity of communicating to him her whole Intention. Their Intercourse continu'd for sometime, till at last her Wishes were crown'd, and she was now Mother of a Boy, who was to be the Object of her future Care and Concern. Gladly wou'd she have continu'd her Friendship with the Father; but finding him too passionate a Lover to remain within the Bounds of Friendship, she was oblig'd to put a Violence upon herself. She sends him a Letter, in which she had inclos'd a Bond of Annuity for a Thousand Crowns; desiring him, at the same Time, never to see her more, and to forget, if possible, all past Favours and Familiarities. He was Thunder-struck at receiving this Message; and, having tried, in vain, all the Arts that might win upon the Resolution of a Woman, resolv'd at last to attack her by her *Foible*. He commences a Law-suit against her before the Parliament of *Paris*; and claims his Son, whom he pretends a Right to educate as he pleas'd, according to the usual Maxims of the Law in such Cases. She pleads, on the other Hand, their express Agreement before their Commerce, and pretends, that he had renounc'd all Claim to any Offspring that might arise from their Embraces. It is not yet known, how the Parliament will determine in this extraordinary Case, which puzzles all the Lawyers, as much as it does the Philosophers. As soon as they come to any Issue, I shall inform you of it, and shall embrace any Opportunity of subscribing myself, as I do at present.

SIR,

*Your most humble Servant.*

# Essay III

## Of the Middle Station of Life

The Moral of the following Fable[1] will easily discover itself, without my explaining it. One Rivulet meeting another, with whom he had been long united in strictest Amity, with noisy Haughtiness and Disdain thus bespoke him, "What, Brother! Still in the same State! Still low and creeping! Are you not asham'd, when you behold me, who, tho' lately in a like Condition with you, am now become a great River, and shall shortly be able to rival the *Danube* or the *Rhine*,[2] provided those friendly Rains continue, which have favour'd my Banks, but neglected yours." Very true, replies the humble Rivulet; "You are now, indeed, swoln to great Size: But methinks you are become, withal, somewhat turbulent and muddy. I am contented with my low Condition and my Purity."

Instead of commenting upon this Fable, I shall take Occasion, from it, to compare the different Stations of Life, and to perswade such of my Readers as are plac'd in the Middle Station to be satisfy'd with it, as the most eligible of all others.[3] These form the most numerous Rank of Men, that can be suppos'd susceptible of Philosophy; and therefore, all Discourses of Morality ought principally to be address'd to them. The Great are too much immers'd in Pleasure;[4] and the Poor too much occupy'd in providing for the Necessities of Life, to hearken to the calm Voice of Reason. The Middle Station, as it is most happy in many Respects, so particularly in this, that a Man, plac'd in it, can, with the greatest Leisure, consider his own Happiness, and reap a new Enjoyment, from comparing his Situation with that of Persons above or below him.

*AGUR*'s Prayer[5] is sufficiently noted. *Two Things have I requir'd of thee, deny me them not before I die, Remove far from me Vanity and Lies; Give me neither Poverty nor Riches, feed me with Food convenient for me: Lest I be full and deny thee, and say, Who is the Lord? Or lest I be poor, and steal, and take the Name of my GOD in vain.* The middle Station is here justly recommended, as affording the fullest *Security* for Virtue; and I may also add, that it gives Opportunity for the most ample *Exercise* of it, and furnishes Employment for every good Quality, which we can possibly be possest of. Those, who are plac'd among the lower Rank of Men, have little Opportunity of exerting any other Virtue, besides those of Patience, Resignation, Industry and Integrity. Those, who are advanc'd into the higher Stations, have full Employment for their Generosity, Humanity, Affability and Charity. When a Man lyes betwixt these two Extremes, he can exert the former Virtues towards his *Superiors*, and the latter towards his *Inferiors*. Every moral Quality, which the human Soul is susceptible of, may have its Turn, and be called up to Action: And a Man may, after this Manner, be much more certain of his Progress in Virtue, than where his good Qualities lye dormant, and without Employment.

But there is another Virtue, that seems principally to ly among *Equals*, and is, for that Reason, chiefly calculated for the middle Station of Life. This Virtue is FRIENDSHIP. I believe most Men of generous Tempers are apt to envy the Great, when they consider the large Opportunities such Persons have of doing Good to their Fellow-creatures, and of acquiring the Friendship and Esteem of Men of Merit. They make no Advances in vain, and are not oblig'd to associate with those whom they have little Kindness for; like People of inferior Stations, who are subject to have their Proffers of Friendship rejected, even where they wou'd be most fond of placing their Affections. But tho' the Great have more Facility in acquiring Friendships, they cannot be so certain of the Sincerity of them, as Men of a lower Rank; since the Favours, they bestow, may acquire them Flattery, instead of Goodwill and Kindness. It has been very judiciously remark'd, that we attach ourselves more by the Services we perform than by those we receive, and that a Man is in Danger of losing his Friends by obliging them too far.[6] I shou'd, therefore, chuse to ly in the middle Way, and to have my Commerce with my Friend varied both by Obligations given and receiv'd. I have too much Pride to be willing that all the Obligations should ly on my Side; and shou'd be afraid, that, if they all lay on his, he wou'd also have too much Pride to be entirely easy under them, or have a perfect Complacency in my Company.

We may also remark of the middle Station of Life, that it is more favourable to the acquiring of *Wisdom* and *Ability*,[7] as well as of *Virtue*, and that a Man so situate has a better Chance for attaining a Knowledge both of Men and Things, than those of a more elevated Station. He enters, with more Familiarity, into human Life: Every Thing appears in its natural Colours before him: He has more Leisure to form Observations; and has, beside, the Motive of Ambition to push him on in his Attainments; being certain, that he can never rise to any Distinction or Eminence in the World, without his own Industry. And here I cannot forbear communicating a Remark, which may appear somewhat extraordinary, *viz.* That 'tis wisely ordain'd by Providence, that the middle Station shou'd be the most favourable to the improving our natural Abilities, since there is really more Capacity requisite to perform the Duties of that Station, than is requisite to act in the higher Spheres of Life. There are more natural Parts, and a stronger Genius requisite to make a good Lawyer or Physician, than to make a great Monarch. For let us take any Race or Succession of Kings, where Birth alone gives a Title to the Crown: The *English* Kings, for Instance; who have not been esteemed the most shining in History. From the Conquest to the Succession of his present Majesty, we may reckon twenty eight Sovereigns, omitting those who died Minors. Of these, eight are esteem'd Princes of great Capacity, *viz.* the *Conqueror*, *Harry* II. *Edward* I. *Edward* III. *Harry* V. and VII. *Elisabeth*, and the late King *William*. Now, I believe every one will allow, that, in the common Run of Mankind, there are not eight out of twenty eight, who are fitted, by Nature, to make a Figure either on the Bench or at the Bar. Since *Charles* VII. ten Monarchs have reign'd in *France*, omitting *Francis* II. Five of these have been esteem'd Princes of Capacity, *viz. Loüis* XI. XII. and XIV. *Francis* I. and *Harry* IV. In short, the governing of Mankind well, requires a great deal of Virtue, Justice, and Humanity, but not a surprising Capacity. A certain Pope, whose Name I have forgot, us'd to say, *Let us divert ourselves, my Friends, the World governs itself.*[8] There are, indeed, some critical Times, such as those in which *Harry* IV.[9] liv'd, that call for the utmost Vigour; and a less Courage and Capacity, than what appear'd in that great Monarch, must have sunk under the Weight. But such Circumstances are rare; and even then, Fortune does, at least, one Half of the Business.

Since the common Professions, such as Law or Physic, require equal, if not superior Capacity, to what are exerted in the higher Spheres of

Life, 'tis evident, that the Soul must be made of still a finer Mold, to shine in Philosophy or Poetry, or in any of the higher Parts of Learning. Courage and Resolution are chiefly requisite in a Commander: Justice and Humanity in a Statesman: But Genius and Capacity in a Scholar. Great Generals, and great Politicians, are found in all Ages and Countries of the World, and frequently start out, at once, even amongst the greatest Barbarians. *Sweden* was sunk in Ignorance, when it produc'd *Gustavus Ericson*, and *Gustavus Adolphus*: *Muscovy*, when the *Czar* appear'd: And, perhaps, *Carthage*, when it gave Birth to *Hannibal*. But *England* must pass thro' a long Gradation of its *Spencers*, *Johnsons*, *Wallers*, *Drydens*, before it arrive at an *Addison* or a *Pope*. A happy Talent for the liberal Arts and Sciences, is a Kind of Prodigy among Men.[10] Nature must afford the richest Genius that comes from her Hands; Education and Example must cultivate it from the earliest Infancy; And Industry must concur to carry it to any Degree of Perfection. No Man needs be surprised to see *Kouli-Kan* among the *Persians*: But *Homer*, in so early an Age, among the *Greeks*, is certainly Matter of the highest Wonder.

A Man cannot show a Genius for War, who is not so fortunate as to be trusted with Command; and it seldom happens, in any State or Kingdom, that several, at once, are plac'd in that Situation. How many *Marlboroughs* were there in the confederate Army, who never rose so much as to the Command of a Regiment? But I am perswaded, there has been but one *Milton* in *England* within these hundred Years; because every one may exert the Talents for Poetry who is possest of them; and no one cou'd exert them under greater Disadvantages than that divine Poet. If no Man were allow'd to write Verses, but who was, before-hand, nam'd to be *laureat*, cou'd we expect a Poet in ten thousand Years?

Were we to distinguish the Ranks of Men by their Genius and Capacity more, than by their Virtue and Usefulness to the Public, great Philosophers wou'd certainly challenge the first Rank, and must be plac'd at the Top of human Kind. So rare is this Character, that, perhaps, there has not, as yet, been above two in the World, who can lay a just Claim to it. At least, *Galilæo* and *Newton* seem to me so far to excel all the rest, that I cannot admit any other into the same Class with them.

Great Poets may challenge the second Place; and this Species of Genius, tho' rare, is yet much more frequent than the former. Of the *Greek* Poets that remain, *Homer* alone seems to merit this Character: Of the *Romans*, *Virgil*, *Horace* and *Lucretius*: Of the *English*, *Milton* and *Pope*: *Corneille, Racine, Boileau* and *Voltaire* of the *French*: And *Tasso* and *Ariosto* of the *Italians*.

Great Orators and Historians are, perhaps, more rare than great Poets: But as the Opportunities for exerting the Talents requisite for Eloquence, or acquiring the Knowledge requisite for writing History, depend, in some Measure, upon Fortune, we cannot pronounce these Productions of Genius to be more extraordinary than the former.

I should now return from this Digression, and show, that the middle Station of Life is more favourable to *Happiness*, as well as to *Virtue* and *Wisdom*: But as the Arguments, that prove this, seem pretty obvious, I shall here forbear insisting on them.

# Essay IV

## Of Impudence and Modesty

I am of opinion, That the common complaints against Providence are ill-grounded, and that the good or bad qualities of men are the causes of their good or bad fortune, more than what is generally imagined.[1] There are, no doubt, instances to the contrary, and these too pretty numerous; but few, in comparison of the instances we have of a right distribution of prosperity and adversity: nor indeed could it be otherwise from the common course of human affairs. To be endowed with a benevolent disposition, and to love others, will almost infallibly procure love and esteem;[2] which is the chief circumstance in life, and facilitates every enterprize and undertaking; besides the satisfaction, which immediately results from it. The case is much the same with the other virtues. Prosperity is naturally, though not necessarily, attached to virtue and merit; and adversity, in like manner, to vice and folly.

I must, however, confess, that this rule admits of an exception, with regard to one moral quality; and that *modesty* has a natural tendency to conceal a man's talents, as *impudence* displays them to the utmost, and has been the only cause why many have risen in the world, under all the disadvantages of low birth and little merit. Such indolence and incapacity is there in the generality of mankind, that they are apt to receive a man for whatever he has a mind to put himself off for;[3] and admit his overbearing airs as proofs of that merit which he assumes to himself. A decent assurance seems to be the natural attendant of virtue;[4] and few men can distinguish impudence from it: As, on the other hand, diffidence, being the natural result of vice and folly, has drawn disgrace upon modesty, which in outward appearance so nearly resembles it.

As impudence, though really a vice, has the same effects upon a man's fortune, as if it were a virtue; so we may observe, that it is almost as difficult to be attained, and is, in that respect, distinguished from all the other vices, which are acquired with little pains, and continually encrease upon indulgence. Many a man, being sensible that modesty is extremely prejudicial to him in making his fortune, has resolved to be impudent, and to put a bold face upon the matter: But, it is observable, that such people have seldom succeeded in the attempt, but have been obliged to relapse into their primitive modesty. Nothing carries a man through the world like a true genuine natural impudence. Its counterfeit is good for nothing, nor can ever support itself. In any other attempt, whatever faults a man commits and is sensible of, he is so much the nearer his end. But when he endeavours at impudence, if he ever failed in the attempt, the remembrance of that failure will make him blush, and will infallibly disconcert him: After which every blush is a cause for new blushes, till he be found out to be an arrant cheat, and a vain pretender to impudence.

If any thing can give a modest man more assurance, it must be some advantages of fortune, which chance procures to him. Riches naturally gain a man a favourable reception in the world, and give merit a double lustre, when a person is endowed with it; and supply its place, in a great measure, when it is absent. It is wonderful to observe what airs of superiority fools and knaves, with large possessions, give themselves above men of the greatest merit in poverty. Nor do the men of merit make any strong opposition to these usurpations; or rather seem to favour them by the modesty of their behaviour.[5] Their good sense and experience make them diffident of their judgment, and cause them to examine every thing with the greatest accuracy: As, on the other hand, the delicacy of their sentiments makes them timorous lest they commit faults, and lose in the practice of the world that integrity of virtue, so to speak, of which they are so jealous. To make wisdom agree with confidence, is as difficult as to reconcile vice and modesty.

These are the reflections which have occurred upon this subject of impudence and modesty; and I hope the reader will not be displeased to see them wrought into the following allegory,[6]

JUPITER, in the beginning, joined VIRTUE, WISDOM, and CONFIDENCE together; and VICE, FOLLY, and DIFFIDENCE: And thus connected, sent them into the world. But though he thought he had matched them with great judgment, and said that *Confidence* was the natural companion of *Virtue*, and that *Vice* deserved to be attended with *Diffidence*, they had not gone far before dissension arose among them. *Wisdom*, who was the guide of the one company, was always accustomed before she ventured upon any road, however beaten, to examine it carefully; to enquire whither it led; what dangers, difficulties and hindrances might possibly or probably occur in it. In these deliberations she usually consumed some time; which delay was very displeasing to *Confidence*, who was always inclined to hurry on, without much forethought or deliberation, in the first road he met. *Wisdom* and *Virtue* were inseparable: But *Confidence* one day, following his impetuous nature, advanced a considerable way before his guides and companions; and not feeling any want of their company, he never enquired after them, nor ever met with them more. In like manner, the other society, though joined by JUPITER, disagreed and separated. As *Folly* saw very little way before her, she had nothing to determine concerning the goodness of roads, nor could give the preference to one above another; and this want of resolution was encreased by *Diffidence*, who, with her doubts and scruples, always retarded the journey. This was a great annoyance to *Vice*, who loved not to hear of difficulties and delays, and was never satisfied without his full career, in whatever his inclinations led him to. *Folly*, he knew, though she hearkened to *Diffidence*, would be easily managed when alone; and therefore, as a vicious horse throws his rider, he openly beat away this controller of all his pleasures, and proceeded in his journey with *Folly*, from whom he is inseparable. *Confidence* and *Diffidence* being, after this manner, both thrown loose from their respective companies, wandered for some time; till at last chance led them at the same time to one village. *Confidence* went directly up to the great house, which belonged to WEALTH, the lord of the village; and without staying for a porter, intruded himself immediately into the innermost apartments, where he found *Vice* and *Folly* well received before him. He joined the train; recommended himself very quickly to his landlord; and entered into such familiarity with *Vice*, that he was enlisted in the same company with *Folly*. They were frequent guests of *Wealth*, and from that moment inseparable. *Diffidence*, in the mean time, not daring to approach the great house, accepted of an invitation from POVERTY, one of the tenants; and entering the cottage, found *Wisdom* and *Virtue*, who being repulsed by the landlord, had retired thither. *Virtue* took compassion of her, and *Wisdom* found, from her temper, that she would easily improve: So they admitted her into their society. Accordingly, by their means, she altered in a little time somewhat of her manner, and becoming much more amiable and engaging, was now known by the name of *Modesty*. As ill company has a greater effect than good, *Confidence*, though more refractory to counsel and example, degenerated so far by the society of *Vice* and *Folly*, as to pass by the name of IMPUDENCE. Mankind, who saw these societies as JUPITER first joined them, and know nothing of these mutual desertions, are thereby led into strange mistakes; and wherever they see *Impudence*, make account of finding *Virtue* and *Wisdom*, and wherever they observe *Modesty*, call her attendants *Vice* and *Folly*.

# Essay V

## *Of Love and Marriage*

I know not whence it proceeds, that women are so apt to take amiss every thing which is said in disparagement of the married state; and always consider a satyr upon matrimony as a satyr upon themselves. Do they mean, that they are the parties principally concerned, and that if a backwardness to enter into that state should prevail in the world, they would be the greatest sufferers? Or, are they sensible, that the misfortunes and miscarriages of the married state are owing more to their sex than to ours? I hope they do not intend to confess either of these two particulars, or to give such an advantage to their adversaries, the men, as even to allow them to suspect it.

I have often had thoughts of complying with this humour of the fair sex, and of writing a panegyric upon marriage: But, in looking around for materials, they seemed to be of so mixed a nature, that at the conclusion of my reflections, I found that I was as much disposed to write a satyr, which might be placed on the opposite pages of the panegyric: And I am afraid, that as satyr is, on most occasions, thought to contain more truth than panegyric, I should have done their cause more harm than good by this expedient. To misrepresent facts is what, I know, they will not require of me. I must be more a friend to truth,[1] than even to them, where their interests are opposite.

I shall tell the women what it is our sex complains of most in the married state; and if they be disposed to satisfy us in this particular, all the other differences will easily be accommodated. If I be not mistaken, 'tis their love of dominion,[2] which is the ground of the quarrel; tho' 'tis very likely, that they will think it an unreasonable love of it in us, which makes us insist so much upon that point. However this may be, no passion seems to have more influence on female minds, than this for power; and there is a remarkable instance in history of its prevailing above

229

another passion, which is the only one that can be supposed a proper counterpoise for it. We are told that all the women in SCYTHIA once conspired against the men, and kept the secret so well, that they executed their design before they were suspected.[3] They surprised the men in drink, or asleep; bound them all fast in chains; and having called a solemn council of the whole sex, it was debated what expedient should be used to improve the present advantage, and prevent their falling again into slavery. To kill all the men did not seem to the relish of any part of the assembly, notwithstanding the injuries formerly received; and they were afterwards pleased to make a great merit of this lenity of theirs. It was, therefore, agreed to put out the eyes of the whole male sex, and thereby resign in all future time the vanity which they could draw from their beauty, in order to secure their authority. We must no longer pretend to dress and show, say they; but then we shall be free from slavery. We shall hear no more tender sighs; but in return we shall hear no more imperious commands. Love must for ever leave us; but he will carry subjection along with him.

'Tis regarded by some as an unlucky circumstance, since the women were resolved to maim the men, and deprive them of some of their senses, in order to render them humble and dependent, that the sense of hearing could not serve their purpose, since 'tis probable the females would rather have attacked that than the sight: And I think it is agreed among the learned, that, in a married state, 'tis not near so great an inconvenience to lose the former sense as the latter. However this may be, we are told by modern anecdotes, that some of the SCYTHIAN women did secretly spare their husband's eyes; presuming, I suppose, that they could govern them as well by means of that sense as without it. But so incorrigible and untractable were these men, that their wives were all obliged, in a few years, as their youth and beauty decayed, to imitate the example of their sisters; which it was no difficult matter to do in a state where the female sex had once got the superiority.

I know not if our SCOTTISH ladies derive any thing of this humour from their SCYTHIAN ancestors;[4] but, I must confess that I have often been surprized to see a woman very well pleased to take a fool for her mate, that she might govern with the less controul; and could not but think her sentiments, in this respect, still more barbarous than those of the SCYTHIAN women above-mentioned; as much as the eyes of the understanding are more valuable than those of the body.

But to be just, and to lay the blame more equally, I am afraid it is the fault of our sex, if the women be so fond of rule, and that if we did not abuse our authority, they would never think it worth while to dispute it. Tyrants, we know, produce rebels; and all history informs us, that rebels, when they prevail, are apt to become tyrants in their turn.[5] For this reason, I could wish there were no pretensions to authority on either side; but that every thing was carried on with perfect equality, as between two equal members of the same body. And to induce both parties to embrace those amicable sentiments, I shall deliver to them PLATO's account of the origin of love and marriage.[6]

Mankind, according to that fanciful philosopher, were not, in their original, divided into male and female, as at present; but each individual person was a compound of both sexes, and was in himself both husband and wife, melted down into one living creature. This union, no doubt, was very intire, and the parts very well adjusted together, since there resulted a perfect harmony betwixt the male and female, altho' they were obliged to be inseparable companions. And so great were the harmony and happiness flowing from it, that the ANDROGYNES[7] (for so PLATO calls them) or MEN-WOMEN, became insolent upon their prosperity, and rebelled against the Gods. To punish them for this temerity, JUPITER could contrive no better expedient, than to divorce the male part from the female, and make two imperfect beings of the compound, which was before so perfect. Hence the origin of men and women, as distinct creatures. But notwithstanding this division, so lively is our remembrance of the happiness which we enjoyed in our primæval state, that we are never at rest in this situation; but each of these halves is continually searching thro' the whole species to find the other half, which was broken from it: And when they meet, they join again with the greatest fondness and sympathy. But it often happens, that they are mistaken in this particular; that they take for their half what no way corresponds to them; and that the parts do not meet nor join in with each other, as is usual in fractures. In this case the union was soon dissolved, and each part is set loose again to hunt for its lost half, joining itself to every one whom it meets, by way of trial, and enjoying no rest till its perfect sympathy with its partner shews, that it has at last been successful in its endeavours.

Were I disposed to carry on this fiction of PLATO, which accounts for the mutual love betwixt the sexes in so agreeable a manner, I would do it by the following allegory.

When JUPITER had separated the male from the female, and had quelled their pride and ambition by so severe an operation, he could not but repent him of the cruelty of his vengeance, and take compassion on poor mortals, who were now become incapable of any repose or tranquillity. Such cravings, such anxieties, such necessities arose, as made them curse their creation, and think existence itself a punishment. In vain had they recourse to every other occupation and amusement. In vain did they seek after every pleasure of sense, and every refinement of reason. Nothing could fill that void, which they felt in their hearts, or supply the loss of their partner, who was so fatally separated from them. To remedy this disorder, and to bestow some comfort, at least, on the human race in their forlorn situation, JUPITER sent down LOVE and HYMEN[8] to collect the broken halves of human kind, and piece them together in the best manner possible. These two deities found such a prompt disposition in mankind to unite again in their primæval state, that they proceeded on their work with wonderful success for some time; till at last, from many unlucky accidents, dissension arose betwixt them. The chief counsellor and favourite of HYMEN was CARE, who was continually filling his patron's head with prospects of futurity; a settlement, family, children, servants; so that little else was regarded in all the matches *they* made. On the other hand, *Love* had chosen PLEASURE for his favourite, who was as pernicious a counsellor as the other, and would never allow *Love* to look beyond the present momentary gratification, or the satisfying of the prevailing inclination. These two favourites became, in a little time, irreconcileable enemies, and made it their chief business to undermine each other in all their undertakings. No sooner had *Love* fixed upon two halves, which he was cementing together, and forming to a close union, but *Care* insinuates himself, and bringing HYMEN along with him, dissolves the union produced by love, and joins each half to some other half, which he had provided for it. To be revenged of this, *Pleasure* creeps in upon a pair already joined by HYMEN; and calling *Love* to his assistance, they under hand contrive to join each half by secret links, to halves, which HYMEN was wholly unacquainted with. It was not long before this quarrel was felt in its pernicious consequences; and such complaints arose before the throne of JUPITER, that he was obliged to summon the offending parties to appear before him, in order to give an account of their proceedings. After hearing the pleadings on both sides, he ordered an immediate reconcilement betwixt *Love* and HYMEN, as the only expedient for giving happiness to mankind: And that he might be sure this reconcilement should be durable, he laid his strict injunctions on them never to join any halves without consulting their favourites *Care* and *Pleasure*, and obtaining the consent of both to the conjunction. Where this order is strictly observed, the *Androgyne* is perfectly restored, and the human race enjoy the same happiness as in their primæval state. The seam is scarce perceived that joins the two beings; but both of them combine to form one perfect and happy creature.

# Essay VI

## *Of the Study of History*

There is nothing which I would recommend more earnestly to my female readers than the study of history, as an occupation, of all others, the best suited both to their sex and education, much more instructive than their ordinary books of amusement, and more entertaining than those serious compositions, which are usually to be found in their closets. Among other important truths,[1] which they may learn from history, they may be informed of two particulars, the knowledge of which may contribute very much to their quiet and repose; *That* our sex, as well as theirs, are far from being such perfect creatures as they are apt to imagine, and, *That* Love is not the only passion, which governs the male-world, but is often overcome by avarice, ambition, vanity, and a thousand other passions. Whether they be the false representations of mankind in those two particulars, which endear romances and novels so much to the fair sex, I know not; but must confess that I am sorry to see them have such an aversion to matter of fact, and such an appetite for falshood. I remember I was once desired by a young beauty, for whom I had some passion, to send her some novels and romances for her amusement in the country; but was not so ungenerous as to take the advantage, which such a course of reading might have given me, being resolved not to make use of poisoned arms against her.[2] I therefore sent her PLUTARCH's lives, assuring her, at the same time, that there was not a word of truth in them from beginning to end. She perused them very attentively, 'till she came to the lives of ALEXANDER and CÆSAR, whose names she had heard of by accident; and then returned me the book, with many reproaches for deceiving her.

I may indeed be told, that the fair sex have no such aversion to history, as I have represented, provided it be *secret* history,[3] and contain some memorable transaction proper to excite their curiosity. But as I do not find that truth, which is the basis of history, is at all regarded in those anecdotes, I cannot admit of this as a proof of their passion for that study. However this may be, I see not why the same curiosity might not receive a more proper direction, and lead them to desire accounts of those who lived in past ages, as well as of their cotemporaries. What is it to CLEORA, whether FULVIA entertains a secret commerce of *Love* with PHILANDER, or not? Has she not equal reason to be pleased, when she is informed (what is whispered about among historians) that CATO's sister had an intrigue with CÆSAR, and palmed her son, MARCUS BRUTUS, upon her husband for his own, tho' in reality he was her gallant's? And are not the loves of MESSALINA or JULIA as proper subjects of discourse as any intrigue that this city has produced of late years?

But I know not whence it comes, that I have been thus seduced into a kind of raillery against the ladies: Unless, perhaps, it proceed from the same cause, which makes the person, who is the favourite of the company, be often the object of their good-natured jests and pleasantries. We are pleased to address ourselves after any manner, to one who is agreeable to us; and, at the same time, presume, that nothing will be taken amiss by a person, who is secure of the good opinion and affections of every one present. I shall now proceed to handle my subject more seriously,[4] and shall point out the many advantages, which flow from the study of history, and show how well suited it is to every one, but particularly to those who are debarred the severer studies, by the tenderness of their complexion, and the weakness of their education. The advantages found in history seem to be of three kinds, as it amuses the fancy, as it improves the understanding, and as it strengthens virtue.

In reality, what more agreeable entertainment to the mind, than to be transported into the remotest ages of the world, and to observe human society, in its infancy, making the first faint essays towards the arts and sciences:[5] To see the policy of government, and the civility of conversation refining by degrees, and every thing which is ornamental to human life advancing towards its perfection. To remark the rise, progress, declension, and final extinction of the most flourishing empires:[6] The virtues, which contributed to their greatness, and the vices, which drew on their ruin. In short, to see all human race, from the beginning of time, pass, as it were, in review before us; appearing in their true colours, without any of those disguises, which, during their life-time, so much perplexed the judgment of the beholders. What spectacle can be imagined, so magnificent, so various, so interesting? What amusement, either of the senses or imagination, can be compared with it? Shall those trifling pastimes, which engross so much of our time, be preferred as more satisfactory, and more fit to engage our attention? How perverse must that taste be, which is capable of so wrong a choice of pleasures?[7]

But history is a most improving part of knowledge, as well as an agreeable amusement; and a great part of what we commonly call *Erudition*, and value so highly, is nothing but an acquaintance with historical facts. An extensive knowledge of this kind belongs to men of letters; but I must think it an unpardonable ignorance in persons of whatever sex or condition, not to be acquainted with the history of their own country, together with the histories of ancient GREECE and ROME. A woman may behave herself with good manners, and have even some vivacity in her turn of wit; but where her mind is so unfurnished, 'tis impossible her conversation can afford any entertainment to men of sense and reflection.

I must add, that history is not only a valuable part of knowledge, but opens the door to many other parts, and affords materials to most of the sciences. And indeed, if we consider the shortness of human life, and our limited knowledge, even of what passes in our own time, we must be sensible that we should be for ever children[8] in understanding, were it not for this invention, which extends our experience to all past ages, and to the most distant nations; making them contribute as much to our improvement in wisdom, as if they had actually lain under our observation. A man acquainted with history may, in some respect, be said to have lived from the beginning of the world, and to have been making continual additions to his stock of knowledge in every century.

There is also an advantage in that experience which is acquired by history, above what is learned by the practice of the world, that it brings us acquainted with human affairs, without diminishing in the least from the most delicate sentiments of virtue. And, to tell the truth, I know not any study or occupation so unexceptionable as history in this particular. Poets can paint virtue in the most charming colours; but, as they address themselves entirely to the passions, they often become advocates for vice. Even philosophers are apt to bewilder themselves in the subtilty of their speculations; and we have seen some go so far as to deny the reality of all moral distinctions.[9] But I think it a remark worthy the attention of the speculative, that the historians have been, almost without exception, the true friends of virtue, and have always represented it in its proper colours, however they may have erred in their judgments of particular persons. MACHIAVEL himself discovers a true sentiment of virtue in his history of FLORENCE. When he talks as a *Politician*, in his general reasonings, he considers poisoning, assassination and perjury, as lawful arts of power; but when he speaks as an *Historian*, in his particular narrations, he shows so keen an indignation against vice, and so warm an approbation of virtue, in many passages, that I could not forbear applying to him that remark of HORACE, That if you chace away nature, tho' with ever so great indignity, she will always return upon you.[10] Nor is this combination of historians in favour of virtue at all difficult to be accounted for. When a man of business enters into life and action, he is more apt to consider the characters of men, as they have relation to his interest, than as they stand in themselves; and has his judgment warped on every occasion by the violence of his passion. When a philosopher contemplates characters and manners in his closet, the general abstract view of the objects leaves the mind so cold and unmoved, that the sentiments of nature have no room to play, and he scarce feels the difference between vice and virtue. History keeps in a just medium[11] betwixt these extremes, and places the objects in their true point of view. The writers of history, as well as the readers, are sufficiently interested in the characters and events, to have a lively sentiment of blame or praise; and, at the same time, have no particular interest or concern to pervert their judgment.

> *Veræ voces tum demum pectore ab imo*
> *Eliciuntur.*          LUCRET.[12]

# Essay VII

*Of Avarice*

'Tis easy to observe, that comic writers exaggerate every character, and draw their fop, or coward with stronger features than are any where to be met with in nature. This moral kind of painting for the stage has been often compared[1] to the painting for cupolas and cielings, where the colours are over-charged, and every part is drawn excessively large, and beyond nature. The figures seem monstrous and disproportioned, when seen too nigh; but become natural and regular, when set at a distance, and placed in that point of view, in which they are intended to be surveyed. For a like reason, when characters are exhibited in theatrical representations, the want of reality removes, in a manner, the personages; and rendering them more cold and unentertaining, makes it necessary to compensate, by the force of colouring, what they want in substance. Thus we find in common life, that when a man once allows himself to depart from truth in his narrations, he never can keep within the bounds of probability; but adds still some new circumstance to render his stories more marvellous, and to satisfy his imagination. Two men in buckram suits became eleven to Sir JOHN FALSTAFF before the end of his story.[2]

There is only one vice, which may be found in life with as strong features, and as high a colouring as needs be employed by any satyrist or comic poet; and that is AVARICE. Every day we meet with men of immense fortunes, without heirs, and on the very brink of the grave, who refuse themselves the most common necessaries of life, and go on heaping possessions on possessions, under all the real pressures of the severest poverty. An old usurer, says the story, lying in his last agonies was presented by the priest with the crucifix to worship. He opens his eyes a moment before he expires, considers the crucifix, and cries, *These jewels are not true; I can only lend ten pistoles upon such a pledge.* This was probably the invention of some epigrammatist; and yet every one, from his own experience, may be able to recollect almost as strong instances of perseverance in avarice. 'Tis commonly reported of a famous miser in this city, that finding himself near death, he sent for some of the magistrates, and gave them a bill of an hundred pounds, payable after his decease; which sum he intended should be disposed of in charitable uses; but scarce were they gone, when he orders them to be called back, and offers them ready money, if they would abate five pounds of the sum. Another noted miser in the north, intending to defraud his heirs, and leave his fortune to the building an hospital, protracted the drawing of his will from day to day; and 'tis thought, that if those interested in it had not paid for the drawing it, he had died intestate. In short, none of the most furious excesses of love and ambition are in any respect to be compared to the extremes of avarice.

The best excuse that can be made for avarice is, that it generally prevails in old men, or in men of cold tempers, where all the other affections are extinct; and the mind being incapable of remaining without some passion or pursuit, at last finds out this monstrously absurd one, which suits the coldness and inactivity of its temper. At the same time, it seems very extraordinary, that so frosty, spiritless a passion should be able to carry us farther than all the warmth of youth and pleasure. But if we look more narrowly into the matter, we shall find, that this very circumstance renders the explication of the case more easy. When the temper is warm and full of vigour, it naturally shoots out more ways than one, and produces inferior passions to counter-balance, in some degree, its predominant inclination. 'Tis impossible for a person of that temper, however bent on any pursuit, to be deprived of all sense of shame, or all regard to the sentiments of mankind. His friends must have some influence over him: And other considerations are apt to have their weight. All this serves to restrain him within some bounds. But 'tis no wonder that the avaritious man, being, from the coldness of his temper, without regard to reputation, to friendship, or to pleasure, should be carried so far by his prevailing inclination, and should display his passion in such surprising instances.

Accordingly we find no vice so irreclaimable as avarice: And though there scarcely has been a moralist or philosopher, from the beginning of the world to this day, who has not levelled a stroke at it, we hardly find a single instance of any person's being cured of it. For this reason, I am more apt to approve of those, who attack it with wit and humour, than of those who treat it in a serious manner. There being so little hopes of doing good to the people infected with this vice, I would have the rest of mankind, at least, diverted by our manner of exposing it: As indeed there is no kind of diversion, of which they seem so willing to partake.

Among the fables of *Monsieur de la* MOTTE, there is one levelled against avarice, which seems to me more natural and easy, than most of the fables of that ingenious author.[3] A miser, says he, being dead, and fairly interred, came to the banks of the STYX, desiring to be ferried over along with the other ghosts. CHARON[4] demands his fare, and is surprized to see the miser, rather than pay it, throw himself into the river, and swim over to the other side, notwithstanding all the clamour and opposition that could be made to him. All hell was in an uproar; and each of the judges was meditating some punishment, suitable to a crime of such dangerous consequence to the infernal revenues. Shall he be chained to the rock with PROMETHEUS?[5] Or tremble below the precipice in company with the DANAIDES?[6] Or assist SISYPHUS[7] in rolling his stone? No, says MINOS,[8] none of these. We must invent some severer punishment. Let him be sent back to the earth, to see the use his heirs are making of his riches.

I hope it will not be interpreted as a design of setting myself in opposition to this celebrated author, if I proceed to deliver a fable of my own, which is intended to expose the same vice of avarice. The hint of it was taken from these lines of Mr. POPE.

> *Damn'd to the mines, an equal fate betides*
> *The slave that digs it, and the slave that hides.*[9]

Our old mother Earth once lodged an indictment against AVARICE before the courts of heaven, for her wicked and malicious council and advice, in tempting, inducing, persuading, and traiterously seducing the children of the plaintiff to commit the detestable crime of parricide upon her, and, mangling her body, ransack her very bowels for hidden treasure.[10] The indictment was very long and verbose; but we must omit a great part of the repetitions and synonymous terms, not to tire our readers too much with our tale. AVARICE, being called before JUPITER to answer to this charge, had not much to say in her own defence. The injustice was clearly proved upon her. The fact, indeed, was notorious, and the injury had been frequently repeated. When therefore the plaintiff demanded justice, JUPITER very readily gave sentence in her favour; and his decree was to this purpose, That since dame *Avarice*, the defendant, had thus grievously injured dame *Earth*, the plaintiff, she was hereby ordered to take that treasure, of which she had feloniously robbed the said plaintiff, by ransacking her bosom, and in the same manner, as before, opening her bosom, restore it back to her, without diminution or retention. From this sentence, it shall follow, says JUPITER to the by-standers, That, in all future ages, the retainers of *Avarice* shall bury and conceal their riches,[11] and thereby restore to the earth what they took from her.

# Essay VIII

## A Character of Sir Robert Walpole

There never was a Man, whose Actions and Character have been more earnestly and openly canvassed,[1] than those of the present Minister, who, having govern'd a learn'd and free Nation for so long a Time, amidst such mighty Opposition, may make a large Library of what has been wrote for and against him, and is the Subject of above Half the Paper that has been blotted in this Nation within these Twenty Years.[2] I wish, for the Honour of our Country, that any one Character of him had been drawn with such *Judgment* and *Impartiality*, as to have some Credit with Posterity, and to show, that our Liberty has, once at least, been imploy'd to good Purpose. I am only afraid of failing in the former Quality of Judgment: But if it shou'd be so, 'tis but one Page more thrown away, after an hundred Thousand, upon the same Subject, that have perish'd, and become useless. In the mean Time, I shall flatter myself with the pleasing Imagination, that the following Character will be adopted by future Historians.

Sir *ROBERT WALPOLE*, Prime Minister of *Great Britain*, is a Man of Ability, not a Genius; good natur'd, not virtuous;[3] constant, not magnanimous; moderate, not equitable.* His Virtues, in some Instances, are free from the Allay of those Vices, which usually accompany such Virtues: He is a generous Friend, without being a bitter Enemy. His Vices, in other Instances, are not compensated by those Virtues which are nearly ally'd to them: His Want of Enterprise is not attended with Frugality.[4] The private Character of the Man is better than the public: His Virtues more than his Vices: His Fortune greater than his Fame. With many good Qualities he has incurr'd the public Hatred: With good Capacity he has not escap'd Ridicule. He would have been esteem'd more worthy

---

* Moderate in the Exercise of Power, not equitable in engrossing it.

of his high Station, had he never possest it;[5] and is better qualify'd for the second than for the first Place in any Government. His Ministry has been more advantageous to his Family than to the Public, better for this Age than for Posterity, and more pernicious by bad Precedents than by real Grievances. During his Time Trade has flourish'd, Liberty declin'd, and Learning gone to Ruin.[6] As I am a Man, I love him; as I am a Scholar, I hate him; as I am a *Briton*, I calmly wish his Fall. And were I a Member of either House, I wou'd give my Vote for removing him from *St. James*'s;[7] but shou'd be glad to see him retire to *Houghton-Hall*,[8] to pass the Remainder of his Days in Ease and Pleasure.

# Posthumously Published
Essays

## Of Suicide[1]

One considerable advantage, that arises from philosophy, consists in the sovereign antidote, which it affords to superstition and false religion. All other remedies against that pestilent distemper are vain, or, at least, uncertain. Plain good-sense, and the practice of the world, which alone serve most purposes of life, are here found ineffectual: History, as well as daily experience, affords instances of men, endowed with the strongest capacity for business and affairs, who have all their lives crouched under slavery to the grossest superstition. Even gaiety and sweetness of temper, which infuse a balm into every other wound, afford no remedy to so virulent a poison; as we may particularly observe of the fair sex, who, tho' commonly possessed of these rich presents of nature, feel many of their joys blasted by this importunate intruder. But when sound philosophy has once gained possession of the mind, superstition is effectually excluded; and one may safely affirm, that her triumph over this enemy is more compleat than over most of the vices and imperfections, incident to human nature. Love or anger, ambition or avarice, have their root in the temper and affections, which the soundest reason is scarce ever able fully to correct. But superstition, being founded on false opinion, must immediately vanish, when true philosophy has inspired juster sentiments of superior powers. The contest is here more equal between the distemper and the medicine: And nothing can hinder the latter from proving effectual, but its being false and sophisticated.

It will here be superfluous to magnify the merits of philosophy, by displaying the pernicious tendency of that vice, of which it cures the human mind. The superstitious man, says Tully,* is miserable in every scene, in every incident of life. Even sleep itself, which banishes all other

* *De Divin.* lib. ii.[2]

cares of unhappy mortals, affords to him matter of new terror; while he examines his dreams, and finds in those visions of the night, prognostications of future calamities.[3] I may add, that, tho' death alone can put a full period to his misery, he dares not fly to this refuge, but still prolongs a miserable existence, from a vain fear, lest he offend his maker, by using the power, with which that beneficent being has endowed him. The presents of God and Nature are ravished from us by this cruel enemy; and notwithstanding that one step would remove us from the regions of pain and sorrow, her menaces still chain us down to a hated being, which she herself chiefly contributes to render miserable.

It is observed of such as have been reduced by the calamities of life to the necessity of employing this fatal remedy, that, if the unseasonable care of their friends deprive them of that species of death, which they proposed to themselves, they seldom venture upon any other, or can summon up so much resolution, a second time, as to execute their purpose. So great is our horror of death, that when it presents itself under any form, besides that to which a man has endeavoured to reconcile his imagination, it acquires new terrors, and overcomes his feeble courage. But when the menaces of superstition are joined to this natural timidity, no wonder it quite deprives men of all power over their lives; since even many pleasures and enjoyments, to which we are carried by a strong propensity, are torn from us by this inhuman tyrant. Let us here endeavour to restore men to their native liberty, by examining all the common arguments against Suicide, and shewing, that That action may be free from every imputation of guilt or blame; according to the sentiments of all the antient philosophers.[4]

If Suicide be criminal, it must be a transgression of our duty, either to God, our neighbour, or ourselves.

To prove, that Suicide is no transgression of our duty to God, the following considerations may perhaps suffice. In order to govern the material world, the almighty creator has established general and immutable laws, by which all bodies, from the greatest planet to the smallest particle of matter, are maintained in their proper sphere and function. To govern the animal world, he has endowed all living creatures with bodily and mental powers; with senses, passions, appetites, memory, and judgment; by which they are impelled or regulated in that course of life, to which they are destined. These two distinct principles of the material and animal world continually encroach upon each other, and mutually retard or forward each other's operation. The powers of men and of all other animals are restrained and directed by the nature and qualities of the surrounding bodies; and the modifications and actions of these bodies are incessantly altered by the operation of all animals. Man is stopped by rivers in his passage over the surface of the earth; and rivers, when properly directed, lend their force to the motion of machines, which serve to the use of man. But tho' the provinces of the material and animal powers are not kept entirely separate, there result from thence no discord or disorder in the creation: On the contrary, from the mixture, union, and contrast of all the various powers of inanimate bodies and living creatures, arises that surprizing harmony and proportion, which affords the surest argument of supreme wisdom.

The providence of the deity appears not immediately in any operation, but governs every thing by those general and immutable laws, which have been established from the beginning of time. All events, in one sense, may be pronounced the action of the almighty: They all proceed from those powers, with which he has endowed his creatures. A house, which falls by its own weight, is not brought to ruin by his providence more than one destroyed by the hands of men; nor are the human faculties less his workmanship than the laws of motion and gravitation. When the passions play, when the judgment dictates, when the limbs obey; this is all the operation of God; and upon these animate principles, as well as upon the inanimate, has he established the government of the universe.[5]

Every event is alike important in the eyes of that infinite being, who takes in, at one glance, the most distant regions of space and remotest periods of time. There is no one event, however important to us, which he has exempted from the general laws that govern the universe, or which he has peculiarly reserved for his own immediate action and operation. The revolutions of states and empires depend upon the smallest caprice or passion of single men; and the lives of men are shortened or extended by the smallest accident of air or diet, sunshine or tempest.[6] Nature still continues her progress and operation; and if general laws be ever broken by particular volitions of the deity, 'tis after a manner which entirely escapes human observation. As on the one hand, the elements and other inanimate parts of the creation carry on their action without regard to the particular interest and situation of men; so men are entrusted to their own judgment and discretion in the various shocks of matter, and may employ every faculty, with which they are endowed, in order to provide for their ease, happiness, or preservation.

What is the meaning, then, of that principle, that a man, who, tired of life, and hunted by pain and misery, bravely overcomes all the natural terrors of death, and makes his escape from this cruel scene; that such a man, I say, has incurred the indignation of his creator, by encroaching on the office of divine providence, and disturbing the order of the universe? Shall we assert, that the Almighty has reserved to himself, in any peculiar manner, the disposal of the lives of men, and has not submitted that event, in common with others, to the general laws, by which the universe is governed? This is plainly false. The lives of men depend upon the same laws as the lives of all other animals; and these are subjected to the general laws of matter and motion. The fall of a tower or the infusion of a poison will destroy a man equally with the meanest creature: An inundation sweeps away every thing, without distinction, that comes within the reach of its fury. Since therefore the lives of men are for ever dependent on the general laws of matter and motion; is a man's disposing of his life criminal, because, in every case, it is criminal to encroach upon these laws, or disturb their operation? But this seems absurd. All animals are entrusted to their own prudence and skill for their conduct in the world, and have full authority, as far as their power extends, to alter all the operations of nature. Without the exercise of this authority, they could not subsist a moment. Every action, every motion of a man innovates in the order of some parts of matter, and diverts, from their ordinary course, the general laws of motion. Putting together, therefore, these conclusions, we find, *that* human life depends upon the general laws of matter and motion, and *that* 'tis no encroachment on the office of providence to disturb or alter these general laws. Has not every one, of consequence, the free disposal of his own life?[7] And may he not lawfully employ that power with which nature has endowed him?

In order to destroy the evidence of this conclusion, we must shew a reason, why this particular case is excepted. Is it because human life is of so great importance, that it is a presumption for human prudence to dispose of it? But the life of man is of no greater importance to the universe than that of an oyster.[8] And were it of ever so great importance, the order of nature has actually submitted it to human prudence, and reduced us to a necessity, in every incident, of determining concerning it.

Were the disposal of human life so much reserved as the peculiar province of the almighty that it were an encroachment on his right for men to dispose of their own lives; it would be equally criminal to act for the preservation of life as for its destruction.[9] If I turn aside a stone, which is falling upon my head, I disturb the course of nature, and I invade the peculiar province of the almighty, by lengthening out my life, beyond the period, which, by the general laws of matter and motion, he had assigned to it.[10]

A hair, a fly, an insect[11] is able to destroy this mighty being, whose life is of such importance. Is it an absurdity to suppose, that human prudence may lawfully dispose of what depends on such insignificant causes?

It would be no crime in me to divert the *Nile* or *Danube* from its course, were I able to effect such purposes. Where then is the crime of turning a few ounces of blood[12] from their natural chanels!

Do you imagine that I repine at providence or curse my creation, because I go out of life, and put a period to a being, which, were it to continue, would render me miserable? Far be such sentiments from me. I am only convinced of a matter of fact, which you yourself acknowledge possible, that human life may be unhappy, and that my existence, if farther prolonged, would become ineligible. But I thank providence, both for the good, which I have already enjoyed, and for the power, with which I am endowed, of escaping the ill that threatens me.* To you it belongs to repine at providence, who foolishly imagine that you have no such power, and who must still prolong a hated being, tho' loaded with pain and sickness, with shame and poverty.[13]

Do you not teach, that when any ill befalls me, tho' by the malice of my enemies, I ought to be resigned to providence; and that the actions of men are the operations of the almighty as much as the actions of inanimate beings? When I fall upon my own sword, therefore, I receive my death equally from the hands of the deity, as if it had proceeded from a lion, a precipice, or a fever.

The submission, which you require to providence, in every calamity, that befalls me, excludes not human skill and industry; if possibly, by their means, I can avoid or escape the calamity. And why may I not employ one remedy as well as another?

If my life be not my own, it were criminal for me to put it in danger,

---

* *Agamus Deo gratias, quod nemo in vita teneri potest.* Seneca, *Epist.* xii.[14]

as well as to dispose of it: Nor could one man deserve the appellation of *Hero*, whom glory or friendship transports into the greatest dangers, and another merit the reproach of *Wretch* or *Miscreant*, who puts a period to his life, from the same or like motives.[15]

There is no being, which possesses any power or faculty, that it receives not from its creator; nor is there any one, which, by ever so irregular an action, can encroach upon the plan of his providence, or disorder the universe. Its operations are his work equally with that chain of events, which it invades; and which ever principle prevails, we may, for that very reason, conclude it to be most favoured by him. Be it animate or inanimate, rational or irrational, 'tis all a case: It's power is still derived from the supreme creator, and is alike comprehended in the order of his providence. When the horror of pain prevails over the love of life: When a voluntary action anticipates the effect of blind causes; it is only in consequence of those powers and principles, which he has implanted in his creatures. Divine providence is still inviolate, and placed far beyond the reach of human injuries.

It is impious, says the old *Roman* superstition,* to divert rivers from their course, or invade the prerogatives of nature. 'Tis impious, says the *French* superstition, to inoculate for the small-pox, or usurp the business of providence, by voluntarily producing distempers and maladies. 'Tis impious, says the modern *European* superstition, to put a period to our own life, and thereby rebel against our creator. And why not impious, say I, to build houses, cultivate the ground, and sail upon the ocean? In all these actions, we employ our powers of mind and body to produce some innovation in the course of nature; and in none of them do we any more. They are all of them, therefore, equally innocent or equally criminal.

*But you are placed by providence, like a sentinel, in a particular station; and when you desert it, without being recalled, you are guilty of rebellion against your almighty sovereign, and have incurred his displeasure.*[16] I ask, why do you conclude, that Providence has placed me in this station? For my part, I find, that I owe my birth to a long chain of causes, of which many, and even the principal, depended upon voluntary actions of men.[17] *But Providence guided all these causes, and nothing happens in the universe without its consent and co-operation.* If so, then

* *Tacit. Ann.* lib. i.[18]

neither does my death, however voluntary, happen without it's consent; and whenever pain and sorrow so far overcome my patience as to make me tired of life, I may conclude, that I am recalled from my station, in the clearest and most express terms.

It is providence, surely, that has placed me at present in this chamber: But may I not leave it, when I think proper, without being liable to the imputation of having deserted my post or station? When I shall be dead, the principles, of which I am composed, will still perform their part in the universe, and will be equally useful in the grand fabric, as when they composed this individual creature.[19] The difference to the whole will be no greater than between my being in a chamber and in the open air. The one change is of more importance to me than the other; but not more so to the universe.

It is a kind of blasphemy to imagine, that any created being can disturb the order of the world, or invade the business of providence. It supposes, that that being possesses powers and faculties, which it received not from its creator, and which are not subordinate to his government and authority. A man may disturb society, no doubt; and thereby incur the displeasure of the almighty: But the government of the world is placed far beyond his reach and violence. And how does it appear, that the almighty is displeased with those actions, that disturb society? By the principles which he has implanted in human nature, and which inspire us with a sentiment of remorse, if we ourselves have been guilty of such actions, and with that of blame and disapprobation, if we ever observe them in others. Let us now examine, according to the method proposed, whether Suicide be of this kind of actions, and be a breach of our duty to our *neighbour* and to society.[20]

A man, who retires from life, does no harm to society. He only ceases to do good; which, if it be an injury, is of the lowest kind.

All our obligations to do good to society seem to imply something reciprocal. I receive the benefits of society, and therefore ought to promote it's interest. But when I withdraw myself altogether from society, can I be bound any longer?[21]

But allowing, that our obligations to do good were perpetual, they have certainly some bounds. I am not obliged to do a small good to society, at the expence of a great harm to myself. Why then should I prolong a miserable existence, because of some frivolous advantage, which the public may, perhaps, receive from me? If upon account of age and infirmities, I may lawfully resign any office, and employ my time altogether in fencing against these calamities, and alleviating, as much as possible, the miseries of my future life: Why may I not cut short these miseries at once by an action, which is no more prejudicial to society?[22]

But suppose, that it is no longer in my power to promote the interest of the public: Suppose, that I am a burden to it: Suppose, that my life hinders some person from being much more useful to the public. In such cases my resignation of life must not only be innocent but laudable. And most people, who lie under any temptation to abandon existence, are in some such situation. Those, who have health, or power, or authority, have commonly better reason to be in humour with the world.

A man is engaged in a conspiracy for the public interest; is seized upon suspicion; is threatened with the rack; and knows, from his own weakness, that the secret will be extorted from him: Could such a one consult the public interest better than by putting a quick period to a miserable life? This was the case of the famous and brave *Strozzi* of *Florence*.[23]

Again, suppose a malefactor justly condemned to a shameful death; can any reason be imagined, why he may not anticipate his punishment, and save himself all the anguish of thinking on its dreadful approaches? He invades the business of providence no more than the magistrate did, who ordered his execution; and his voluntary death is equally advantageous to society, by ridding it of a pernicious member.

That Suicide may often be consistent with interest and with our duty to *ourselves*, no one can question, who allows, that age, sickness, or misfortune may render life a burthen, and make it worse even than annihilation. I believe that no man ever threw away life, while it was worth keeping.[24] For such is our natural horror of death, that small motives will never be able to reconcile us to it. And tho' perhaps the situation of a man's health or fortune did not seem to require this remedy, we may at least be assured, that any one, who, without apparent reason, has had recourse to it, was curst with such an incurable depravity or gloominess of temper, as must poison all enjoyment, and render him equally miserable as if he had been loaded with the most grievous misfortunes.

If suicide be supposed a crime, 'tis only cowardice can impel us to it. If it be no crime, both prudence and courage should engage us to rid ourselves at once of existence, when it becomes a burthen. 'Tis the only way, that we can then be useful to society, by setting an example, which, if imitated, would preserve to every one his chance for happiness in life, and would effectually free him from all danger of misery.*

* It would be easy to prove, that Suicide is as lawful under the *christian* dispensation as it was to the heathens. There is not a single text of scripture,[25] which prohibits it. That great and infallible rule of faith and practice, which must controul all philosophy and human reasoning, has left us, in this particular, to our natural liberty. Resignation to providence is, indeed, recommended in scripture; but that implies only submission to ills, which are unavoidable, not to such as may be remedied by prudence or courage. *Thou shalt not kill* is evidently meant to exclude only the killing of others, over whose life we have no authority.[26] That this precept like most of the scripture precepts, must be modified by reason and common sense, is plain from the practice of magistrates, who punish criminals capitally, notwithstanding the letter of this law.[27] But were this commandment ever so express against Suicide, it could now have no authority. For all the law of *Moses* is abolished,[28] except so far as it is established by the law of nature; and we have already endeavoured to prove, that Suicide is not prohibited by that law. In all cases, *Christians* and *Heathens* are precisely upon the same footing; and if *Cato* and *Brutus*, *Arria* and *Portia* acted heroically, those who now imitate their example ought to receive the same praises from posterity. The power of committing Suicide is regarded by Pliny as an advantage which men possess even above the deity himself. *Deus non sibi potest mortem consciscere, si velit, quod homini dedit optimum in tantis vitæ pœnis.* Lib. ii. Cap. 7.[29]

# Of the Immortality of the Soul

By the mere light of reason it seems difficult to prove the Immortality of the Soul. The arguments for it are commonly derived either from *metaphysical* topics, or *moral* or *physical*. But in reality, it is the gospel, and the gospel alone,[1] that has brought life and immortality to light.

I. METAPHYSICAL topics are founded on the supposition that the soul is immaterial,[2] and that it is impossible for thought to belong to material substance.[3]

But just metaphysics teach us, that the notion of substance is wholly confused and imperfect, and that we have no other idea of any substance than as an aggregate of particular qualities, inhering in an unknown something.[4] Matter, therefore, and spirit are at bottom equally unknown; and we cannot determine what qualities may inhere in the one or in the other.

They likewise teach us, that nothing can be decided *a priori* concerning any cause or effect; and that experience being the only source of our judgments of this nature, we cannot know from any other principle, whether matter, by its structure or arrangement, may not be the cause of thought. Abstract reasonings cannot decide any question of fact or existence.

But admitting a spiritual substance to be dispersed throughout the universe, like the etherial fire of the *Stoics*,[5] and to be the only inherent subject of thought; we have reason to conclude from *analogy*, that nature uses it after the same manner she does the other substance, matter. She employs it as a kind of paste or clay; modifies it into a variety of forms and existences; dissolves after a time each modification; and from it's substance erects a new form.[6] As the same material substance may successively compose the body of all animals, the same spiritual substance may compose their minds:[7] Their consciousness, or that system of thought, which they formed during life, may be continually dissolved by death; and nothing interest them in the new modification. The most positive asserters of the mortality of the soul, never denied the immortality of its substance. And that an immaterial substance, as well as a material, may lose its memory or consciousness appears, in part, from experience, if the soul be immaterial.

Reasoning from the common course of nature, and without supposing any *new* interposition of the supreme cause, which ought always to be excluded from philosophy; what is incorruptible must also be ingenerable. The soul, therefore, if immortal, existed before our birth: And if the former state of existence no wise concerned us, neither will the latter.

Animals undoubtedly feel, think, love, hate, will, and even reason, tho' in a more imperfect manner than man. Are their souls also immaterial and immortal?

II. Let us now consider the *moral* arguments, chiefly those arguments derived from the justice of God, which is supposed to be farther interested in the farther punishment of the vicious, and reward of the virtuous.

But these arguments are grounded on the supposition, that God has attributes beyond what he has exerted in this universe, with which alone we are acquainted. Whence do we infer the existence of these attributes?

It is very safe for us to affirm, that, whatever we know the deity to have actually done, is best; but it is very dangerous to affirm, that he must always do what to us seems best. In how many instances would this reasoning fail us with regard to the present world?

But if any purpose of nature be clear, we may affirm, that the whole scope and intention of man's creation, so far as we can judge by natural reason, is limited to the present life. With how weak a concern, from the original, inherent structure of the mind and passions, does he ever look farther? What comparison, either for steddiness or efficacy, between so floating an idea, and the most doubtful persuasion of any matter of fact, that occurs in common life.

There arise, indeed, in some minds, some unaccountable terrors with regard to futurity: But these would quickly vanish, were they not artificially fostered by precept and education. And those, who foster them; what is their motive? Only to gain a livelihood, and to acquire power and riches in this world.[8] Their very zeal and industry, therefore, are an argument against them.

What cruelty, what iniquity, what injustice in nature, to confine thus all our concern, as well as all our knowledge, to the present life, if there be another scene still awaiting us, of infinitely greater consequence? Ought this barbarous deceit to be ascribed to a beneficent and wise being?

Observe with what exact proportion the task to be performed and the performing powers are adjusted throughout all nature. If the reason of man gives him a great superiority above other animals, his necessities are proportionably multiplied upon him. His whole time, his whole capacity, activity, courage, passion, find sufficient employment, in fencing against the miseries of his present condition. And frequently, nay almost always, are too slender for the business assigned them.

A pair of shoes, perhaps, was never yet wrought to the highest degree of perfection, which that commodity is capable of attaining. Yet is it necessary, at least very useful, that there should be some politicians and moralists, even some geometers, historians, poets, and philosophers among mankind.

The powers of men are no more superior to their wants, considered merely in this life, than those of foxes and hares are, compared to *their* wants and to *their* period of existence. The inference from parity of reason is therefore obvious.

On the theory of the soul's mortality, the inferiority of women's capacity is easily accounted for: Their domestic life requires no higher faculties of mind or body. This circumstance vanishes and becomes absolutely insignificant, on the religious theory: The one sex has an equal task to perform with the other: Their powers of reason and resolution ought also to have been equal, and both of them infinitely greater than at present.

As every effect implies a cause, and that another, till we reach the first cause of all, which is the Deity; every thing, that happens, is ordained by him;[9] and nothing can be the object of his punishment or vengeance.

By what rule are punishments and rewards distributed? What is the divine standard of merit and demerit? Shall we suppose, that human sentiments have place in the deity? However bold that hypothesis, we have no conception of any other sentiments.

According to human sentiments, sense, courage, good manners, industry, prudence, genius, &c. are essential parts of personal merit. Shall we therefore erect an elysium for poets and heroes, like that of the antient mythology? Why confine all rewards to one species of virtue?

Punishment, without any proper end or purpose, is inconsistent with *our* ideas of goodness and justice; and no end can be served by it after the whole scene is closed.

Punishment, according to *our* conceptions, should bear some proportion to the offence. Why then eternal punishment for the temporary offences of so frail a creature as man? Can any one approve of *Alexander's* rage, who intended to exterminate a whole nation, because they had seized his favourite horse, *Bucephalus?*\*

Heaven and hell suppose two distinct species of men, the good and the bad. But the greatest part of mankind float between vice and virtue.

Were one to go round the world with an intention of giving a good supper to the righteous and a sound drubbing to the wicked, he would frequently be embarrassed in his choice, and would find, that the merits and demerits of most men and women scarcely amount to the value of either.

To suppose measures of approbation and blame, different from the human, confounds every thing. Whence do we learn, that there is such a thing as moral distinctions but from our own sentiments?

What man, who has not met with personal provocation (or what good natur'd man who has) could inflict on crimes, from the sense of blame alone, even the common, legal, frivolous punishments? And does any thing steel the breast of judges and juries against the sentiments of humanity but reflections on necessity and public interest?

By the Roman law, those who had been guilty of parricide and confessed their crime, were put into a sack, along with an ape, a dog, and a serpent; and thrown into the river: Death alone was the punishment of those, who denied their guilt, however fully proved. A criminal was tryed before *Augustus*, and condemned after full conviction: But the humane emperor, when he put the last interrogatory, gave it such a turn as to lead the wretch into a denial of his guilt. *You surely*, said the prince, *did not kill your father.*† This lenity suits our natural ideas of

---

\* Quint. Curtius, lib. vi. cap. 5.[10]
† Sueton. August. cap. 3.[11]

RIGHT, even towards the greatest of all criminals, and even tho' it prevents so inconsiderable a sufferance. Nay, even the most bigotted priest would naturally, without reflection, approve of it; provided the crime was not heresy or infidelity. For as these crimes hurt himself in his *temporal* interests and advantages; perhaps he may not be altogether so indulgent to them.

The chief source of moral ideas is the reflection on the interests of human society.[12] Ought these interests, so short, so frivolous, to be guarded by punishments, eternal and infinite? The damnation of one man is an infinitely greater evil in the universe, than the subversion of a thousand million of kingdoms.

Nature has rendered human infancy peculiarly frail and mortal; as it were on purpose to refute the notion of a probationary state.[13] The half of mankind dye before they are rational creatures.

III. The *physical* arguments from the analogy of nature are strong for the mortality of the soul; and these are really the only philosophical arguments, which ought to be admitted with regard to this question, or indeed any question of fact.

Where any two objects are so closely connected, that all alterations, which we have ever seen in the one, are attended with proportionable alterations in the other; we ought to conclude, by all rules of analogy, that, when there are still greater alterations produced in the former, and it is totally dissolved, there follows a total dissolution of the latter.

Sleep, a very small effect on the body, is attended with a temporary extinction; at least, a great confusion in the soul.

The weakness of the body and that of the mind in infancy are exactly proportioned; their vigor in manhood; their sympathetic disorder in sickness; their common gradual decay in old age. The step farther seems unavoidable; their common dissolution in death.

The last symptoms, which the mind discovers, are disorder, weakness, insensibility, stupidity, the forerunners of its annihilation. The farther progress of the same causes, encreasing the same effects, totally extinguish it.

Judging by the usual analogy of nature, no form can continue, when transferred to a condition of life very different from the original one, in which it was placed. Trees perish in the water; fishes in the air; animals in the earth. Even so small a difference as that of climate is often fatal. What reason then to imagine, that an immense alteration, such as is made on the soul by the dissolution of its body and all its organs of thought and sensation, can be effected without the dissolution of the whole?

Every thing is in common between soul and body. The organs of the one are all of them the organs of the other. The existence therefore of the one must be dependent on that of the other.

The souls of animals are allowed to be mortal; and these bear so near a resemblance to the souls of men, that the analogy from one to the other forms a very strong argument. Their bodies are not more resembling; yet no one rejects the arguments drawn from comparative anatomy. The *Metempsychosis*[14] is therefore the only system of this kind, that philosophy can so much as hearken to.

Nothing in this world is perpetual. Every being, however seemingly firm, is in continual flux and change: The world itself gives symptoms of frailty and dissolution: How contrary to analogy, therefore, to imagine, that one single form, seemingly the frailest of any, and, from the slightest causes, subject to the greatest disorders, is immortal and indissoluble?[15] What a daring theory is that! How lightly, not to say, how rashly entertained!

How to dispose of the infinite number of posthumous existences ought also to embarrass the religious theory. Every planet, in every solar system, we are at liberty to imagine peopled with intelligent, mortal beings: At least, we can fix on no other supposition. For these, then, a new universe must, every generation, be created, beyond the bounds of the present universe; or one must have been created at first so prodigiously wide as to admit of this continual influx of beings. Ought such bold suppositions to be received by any philosophy; and that merely on pretence of a bare possibility?

When it is asked, whether *Agamemnon, Thersites, Hannibal, Nero*, and every stupid clown, that ever existed in *Italy, Scythia, Bactria*, or *Guinea*, are now alive; can any man think, that a scrutiny of nature will furnish arguments strong enough to answer so strange a question in the affirmative? The want of arguments, without revelation, sufficiently establishes the negative.

*Quanto facilius*, says *Pliny*,* *certiusque sibi quemque credere, ac specimen securitatis antigenitali sumere experimento.* Our insensibility,

* Lib. vii. cap. 55.[16]

before the composition of the body, seems to natural reason a proof of a like state after its dissolution.

Were our horror of annihilation an original passion, not the effect of our general love of happiness, it would rather prove the mortality of the soul. For as nature does nothing in vain, she would never give us a horror against an impossible event. She may give us a horror against an unavoidable event, provided our endeavours, as in the present case, may often remove it to some distance. Death is in the end unavoidable; yet the human species could not be preserved, had not nature inspired us with an aversion towards it.

All doctrines are to be suspected, which are favoured by our passions. And the hopes and fears which give rise to this doctrine, are very obvious.

It is an infinite advantage in every controversy, to defend the negative.[17] If the question be out of the common experienced course of nature, this circumstance is almost, if not altogether, decisive. By what arguments or analogies can we prove any state of existence, which no one ever saw, and which no wise resembles any that ever was seen? Who will repose such trust in any pretended philosophy, as to admit upon its testimony the reality of so marvellous a scene? Some new species of logic is requisite for that purpose; and some new faculties of the mind, which may enable us to comprehend that logic.

Nothing could set in a fuller light the infinite obligations, which mankind have to divine revelation; since we find, that no other medium could ascertain this great and important truth.[18]

# Unpublished Essays

## An Historical Essay on Chivalry and modern Honour

After the Tyranny of the Roman Empire over the World & of the Roman Emperors over the Romans themselves, had banish'd all Virtue, Wit & Reason from the Earth, & nothing but their faint Graces & Footsteps remain'd among Mankind, that Nation, which had risen by Virtue, must of necessity suffer an Alteration in their Empire, since they had made so great a one in their manners. But as without some such Revolution in public Affairs, 'tis impossible for a polite Nation, by slow Degrees, & by an ill constituted Government alone to become altogether barbarous, their Change, however great, cou'd never extend to the entire banishment of all Arts, but in common Life at least, there must remain near the same Perfection in Handicrafts Arts, & in Conversation a Tincture of their former Civility. But these, however great Ornaments they may be esteemd are merely Ornaments, serving nothing to Defence, but rather like fine Cloaths & rich Embroideries in Soldiers, draw on the Attacks of Enemies. 'Tis certain that the great Allurement of these Barbarians, who overspread the Roman Empire,[1] was the Riches & Plenty of it, & the Effects of these Arts in which themselves were defective; to which we may add, the Softness of the Inhabitants, a further Effect of them. But as in War, these polite & luxurious Arts made them more easily conquerd, they must in peace give them a kind of Conquest over their Conquerors,[2] & produce a Conformity of Manners betwixt the Victors & the Vanquish'd. This went so far, & these Barbarians Imitation of the Romans was carryd to such a length, that they even consented to reject their own Religion,[3] & tho' every Nation in its Conquest over another is apt to call it a Prevalency of its own Gods over those of the Vanquish'd, they scrupled not to exchange their victorious ones for these they had overcome.

Nor wou'd they only imitate the antient manners, but woud naturally invent at first any other, which was suitable to that Twilight of Reason, by which their Minds were bewilder'd. The antient Inhabitants were sunk into an irrecoverable Indolence & Inactivity, & having stupidly lost the perfection of these Arts transmitted to them from their Fore-fathers, cannot be suppos'd in a Condition of inventing new ones.[4] Their Conquerors on the contrary came with Freshness & Alacrity to the Busyness, & being encourag'd both by the Novelty of these Subjects & by the Success of their Arms, woud naturally engraft some new kind of Fruit on the antient Stock. Had their Invasion & Conquest happen'd while the Grecian Philosophy was yet in any tolerable Condition, they wou'd probably have engrafted on this Stock; but as that was disgrac'd, & even purposely render'd odious, by the Christian Religion,[5] which then prevaild, & which they embrac'd, they were reduc'd to work upon some other, that lay more in common Life. There they wou'd embellish after a Method of their own, & study Excellencys & Beautys beyond the Original, from which they drew, their first Notions.

Tis observable of the humane Mind, that when it is smit with any Idea of Merit or Perfection, beyond what its Faculties can attain, & in the pursuit of which, it uses not Reason & Experience for its Guide, it knows no Mean, but as it gives the Rein & even adds the Spur to every florid Conceit or Fancy, runs in a moment quite wide of Nature. Thus we find, when, without Discretion, it indulges its devote Fervors, that, working in such fairy-ground,[6] it quickly burys itself in its own Whim-sies & Chimera's, & raises up to itself a new set of Passions, Affections, Desires, Objects, & in short a perfectly new World of its own, inhabited by different Beings, & regulated by different Laws, from this of ours. In this new World 'tis so possest that it can endure no Interruption from the old; but as Nature is apt still on every Occasion to recall it thither it must undermine it by Art, & retiring altogether from the Commerce of Mankind, if it be so bent upon its religious Exercise, from the Mystic by an easy transition degenerate into the Hermite. The same thing is observable in Philosophy, which tho it cannot produce a different World in which we may wander, makes us act in this as if we were different Beings from the rest of Mankind; at least makes us frame to ourselves, tho' we cannot execute them, Rules of Conduct different from those which are set to us by Nature.[7] No Engine can supply the place of Wings, & make us fly, tho' the Imagination of such a one may make us stretch & strain & elevate our selves upon our Tip-toes.[8] And in this Case of an imagin'd Merit, the farther our Chimera's hurry us from Nature, & the Practice of the World, the better pleas'd we are, as valuing ourselves upon the Singularity of our Notions, & thinking we depart from the rest of mankind only by flying above them. Where there is none we excell, we are apt to think we have no excellency, & Self-conceit makes us take every Singularity for an Excellency.

When therefore these Barbarians came first to the Relish of some degree of Virtue & Politeness beyond what they had ever before been acquainted with, their Minds wou'd necessarily stretch themselves into some vast Conceptions of things which not being corrected by sufficient Judgement & Experience must be empty & unsolid. These who had first bred these Conceptions in them could not assist them in their Birth, as the Grecians did the Romans,[9] but being themselves scarce half-civiliz'd would be rather apt to entertain any extravagant mishapen Conceit of their Conquerors, than able to lick it into any Form.[10]

'Twas thus that that Monster of Romantick Chivalry or Knight-Errantry, by the necessary Operation of the Principles of Human Nature, was brought into the World; & 'tis remarkable that it descended from the Moors & Arabians,[11] who learning somewhat of the Roman Civil-ity from the Provinces they conquer'd, & being themselves a Southern People, which are commonly observed to be more quick & inventive than the Northern, were the first who fell upon this Vein of Atchieve-ment. When it was once broken upon it run like Wildfire over all the Nations of Europe, who being in the same Situation with these Nations kindled with the least Spark

What kind of monstrous Birth this of Chivalry must prove we may learn from considering the different Revolutions in the Arts, particularly in Architecture, & comparing the Gothic with the Grecian[12] Models of it. The one are plain, simple, & regular, but withal majestic & beautyful, which when these Barbarians unskillfully imitated, they run into a wild Profusion of Ornaments, & by these rude Embellishments departed far from Nature & a just Simplicity. They were struck with the Beauties of the antient Buildings, but ignorant how to preserve a just Mean; & giving an unbounded Liberty to their Fancy in heaping Ornament upon Ornament, they made the whole a heap of Confusion, & Irregularity. For the same Reason, when they wou'd rear up a new Scheme of Man-ners or Heroism, it must be strangely overcharged with Ornaments, & no part exempt from their unskillful refinements. And this we find to have been actually the Case, as may be proven by running over the several parts of it.

The first & most conspicuous part must infallibly be Courage or Warlike Bravery. 'Tis observable that in all rude Ages, & in the Infancy of every State, this is alwise the most admir'd Virtue. All Ideas of Merit naturally descend from the Governors of the Nation,[13] & from these who by their very Office, have a kind of Merit in our Eyes & are set in the fairest point of View to recommend any other Merit of which they are possest. The Accomplishments these alwise principally aspire to are such as capacitate them for Government, & enable them to acquire Autority & use it when acquir'd. Of these Courage is the chief. The only Virtue that can contest with it is Conduct or Policy, which is a Virtue that is never apprehended, until the Age has from long Experience become considerably refin'd. Simple & untaught Nature betakes itself alwise to Force to obtain its Ends, & even admires more bodily Force, & that mental Force of Courage, which resembles it, than an Ability of a different kind, which may teach the right Use of both. Nor wou'd it only be the Example of Rulers that woud make Courage celebrated, but their Precept likewise. Courage is a more suitable Virtue for Subjects than Conduct, & is absolutely necessary in Wars, the chief Business & Source of Greatness, in all unciviliz'd Nations: For which reason, 'twould be sure of the Approbation of all Politicians they being the persons, who principally reap Advantage by it.

Hence in Rome about its earliest Time we find this Virtue in so great Repute that the general Name of Virtue was deriv'd from it,[14] & indeed it so far swallowd up all the others, that 'twas alone sufficient to bring a man into Credit, & without it all his other Virtues were of no avail. Hence likewise this was the reigning Quality of the first Grecian Heroes, as they are celebrated by Homer, who on all Occasions makes it the distinguishing Mark of Merit, & in advancing one Man above another thinks it sufficient to advance his Courage, conjoining along with it bodily Strength, which is its Instrument.

This therefore woud likewise become the chief Virtue of these Cavaliers or Romantic Heroes, & the Virtue which of all others, they wou'd most affect. 'Tis a property very conspicuous in this Virtue, that it naturally exerts itself on the View of any superior Strength or Prowess, & endeavors to overcome every possibility of Opposition, tho' not immediatly directed against it. This goes so far that Courage where it is not regulated by Discretion, but keeps itself ready for any Call rises at every thing which can exercise it, & courts all Dangers, & every Opportunity of exerting itself. 'Tis an aspiring Quality & hews down whatever seems to overshadow it.

'Tis upon this Property that these Fables are founded of Hercules Pirithous, Theseus, Jason, & others of that Breed, who, as the Grecian Poets tell us, whenever they heard of a Dragon or Monster stronger than themselves, immediatly lookt on it as their Antagonist, & to run from one Adventure of this kind to another was their constant Business. 'Tis indeed true that these are nothing but Fables; yet notwithstanding, like the Romance of Amadis de Gaul, & Lancelot de Lake, & others of that kind, show'd the Nations [*sic*] of Bravery in the Age, when they were devisd. Besides tis commonly thought that there was some Foundation[15] for the Stories of Hercules & Theseus, & other Fables of the Heathen Mythology, tho' strangely disguis'd by the Fictions of the Poets & of Tradition.

So far of Resemblance is there betwixt the Heroes of Poetry & of Romance. But this could not remain any time. On the first Growth of Heroism, & when Men, by forming themselves into larger Societies, began to conceive different Notions of things from what are bred in these ungovernd & lesser Societys or Tribes, they woud naturally, from the Novelty of the Subject, exceed Nature, & overcharge their Courage with something excessive & monstrous. But as in this Case, the Idea of Heroism is form'd only from Men's own Imaginations, it cou'd not very much exceed their Abilities, but a little Practice, Experience, & Reflection must soon reduce it to Nature, & instead of an empty Shadow make it a solid Substance. On the contrary the Moorish & Gothic Heroes had their Fancy prompted by the Foot-steps of something great & gallant, beyond what of themselves they cou'd ever have conceiv'd, & far beyond what they had any light or Example to guide them in the Attainment of. No Wonder so great a grasp & so small a reach; so great an Endeavor & so small Abilities, produc'd very fantastical Effects on their manners, & such as were difficult to moderate & reduce to Nature & a just Simplicity.

Upon this is founded, that first & most remarkable Difference, betwixt the poetic & Romantic Heroes, & indeed betwixt the great Men of the first antient History & first modern, that tho' they both valued themselves upon their Bravery above all other Virtues, in the first it bore that Air, which naturally attends it when not corrected by Reason or better Example, of Savageness & Barbarity, which converted them in a manner into Pirates & Robbers; whereas the second, from an affectation of Civility, endeavor'd to throw into all their Behavior, the most courteous & humane Air imaginable & that sublime Generosity, which alwise attends the most elevate and refin'd Courage.[16] This indeed display'd in a thousand fantastic forms; so that one cannot but prefer the plain roughness of the one to the chimerical & affected Politeness of the other: But however if it be not better 'tis at least an Endeavor to be so.

The method by which these courteous Knights acquir'd this extreme Civility of theirs, was by mixing Love with their Courage. Love is a very generous Passion, & well fitted both to that Humanity & Courage they wou'd reconcile. The only one that can contest with it is Friendship, which, besides that 'tis too refin'd a Passion for common Use is not by many degrees so natural as Love, to which almost every one has a great Propensity, & which 'tis impossible to see a beautyful Woman, without feeling some Touches of. Besides, as Love is a capricious Passion 'tis the more susceptible of these fantastic Forms, which it must take when it mixes with Chivalry. Friendship is a solid & serious thing, & like the Love of their Countrey in the Roman Heroes, woud dispell & put to Flight all the Chimera's inseparable from this Spirit of Adventure.

So that a Mistress is as necessary to a Cavalier or Knight-Errant as a God or Saint to a Devotee.[17] Nor wou'd he stop here, or be contented with a submiss[18] Reverence & Adoration to one of the Sex, but wou'd extend in some degree the same Civility to the whole, & by a curious Reversement of the Order of Nature, make them the superior. This is no more than what is suitable to that infinite Generosity of which he makes Profession. Every thing below him he treats with Submission, & every thing above him, with Contumacy. Thus he carries these double Symptoms of Generosity which Virgil makes mention of into Extravagance

Parcere subjectis & debellare superbos.[19]

Hence arises the Knight-Errants strong & irreconciliable Aversion to all Giants with his most humble & respectful Submission to all Damsels. These two Affections of his, he unites in all his Adventures, which are alwise design'd to relieve distrest Damsels from the Captivity & Violence of Giants.[20]

As a Cavalier is compos'd of the greatest Warmth of Love, temperd with the most humble submission & Respect, his Mistresses Behavior is in every point, the Reverse of this, & what is conspicuous in her Temper is the utmost Coldness along with the greatest Haughtyness & Disdain; untill at last Gratitude for the many Deliverances she has met with, & the Giants & Monsters without Number that he has destroy'd for her Sake, reduces her tho' unwilling to the Necessity of commencing a Bride. Here the Chastity of Women, which, from the Necessity of human Affairs, has been in all Ages & Countreys an extravagant Point of Honour with them is run into still greater Extravagance, that none of the Sexes may be exempt from this fantastic Ornament.

Such were the Notions of Bravery in that Age & such the Fictions by which they form'd Models of it. The Effects these had on their ordinary Life & Conversation was, First an extravagant Gallantry & Adoration of the whole Female Sex, & Romantic Notions of extraordinary Constancy, Fidelity & refin'd Passion for one Mistress. Secondly the Introduction of the Practice of single Combat. How naturally this sprung up from Chivalry may easily be understood. A Knight-Errant fights not like another Man full of Passion & Resentment, but with the utmost Civility mixt with his undaunted Courage. He salutes you before he cuts your Throat, & a plain Man who understood nothing of the Mystery wou'd take him for a treacherous Ruffian, & think that like Judas he was betraying with a Kiss,[21] while he is showing his generous Calmness & amicable Courage.[22] In consequence of this every thing is performed with the greatest Ceremony & Order; & whenever either Chance or his superior Bravery makes either of them victorious, he generously gives his Antagonist his Life & again embraces him as his Friend. When these fantastic Practices have come in Use the amaz'd World, who merely because there is nothing real in all this must certainly imagine there is a great deal, cou'd not but look upon such a courteous Enmity as the most heroic & sublime thing in Nature, & instead of punishing any Murder that might ensue, as the Law directs in such Cases, wou'd praise & applaud the Murderer. Thus Tilts & Tournaments became the reigning

Entertainments

## Of the Poems of Ossian

I think the fate of this Production the most curious Effect of Prejudice, where superstition had no share, that ever was in the World. A tiresome, insipid, Performance,[1] which, if it had been presented in its real Form, as the work of a contemporary, an obscure Highlander,[2] no-man cou'd ever have had the Patience to have once perus'd has, by passing for the Poetry of a royal Bard[3] who flourished fifteen Centuries ago, been universally read, has been pretty generally admired, and has been translated in Prose and Verse, into several languages of Europe.[4] Even the Style of the suppos'd English Translation has been admired, tho harsh and absurd in the highest degree; jumping perpetually from Verse to Prose, and from Prose to Verse, and running most of it in the light Cadence and Measure of Molly Mog.[5] Such is the Erse Epic, which has been puff'd, with a Zeal and Enthusiasm, that has drawn a Ridicule on my Countreymen.

But to cut off at once the whole Source of its Reputation, I shall collect a few very obvious Arguments against the Notion of its great Antiquity, with which so many people have been intoxicated, and which alone made it worthy of any Attention.

(1) The very manner in which it was presented to the public forms a strong Presumption against its Authenticity. The pretended Translator goes on a Mission[6] to the Highlands to recover and collect a Work, which, he affirmed, was dispersed in Fragments among the Natives. He returns and gives a Quarto Volume, and then another Quarto, with the same unsupported Assurance, as if it were a Translation of the Orlando Furioso[7] or Lusiade[8] or any Poem the best known in Europe. It might have been expected, at least, that he woud have told the Public and the Subscribers to his Mission, and the Purchasers of his Book; <u>this Part I got from such a Person in such a Place; that other part from</u>

such another Person; I was enabled to correct my first Copy of such a Passage by the Recital of such another Person; a fourth supplys such a defect in my first Copy. By such a History of his gradual Discoveries, he wou'd have given some face of Probability to them: Any man of common Sense, who was in earnest, must in this Case have seen the peculiar Necessity of that Precaution. Any man, that had a Regard to his own Character woud have anxiously follow'd that obvious and easy Method: All the Friends of the pretended Translator exhorted and entreated him to give them and the public that Satisfaction. No! those who cou'd doubt his Veracity were Fools, whom it was not worth while to satisfy. The most incredible of all Facts was to be taken on his word, whom no-body knew: and an Experiment was to be made, I suppose in jest, how far the Credulity of the public woud give way to Assurance and dogmatical Affirmation.

(2) But to show the utter Incredibility of the Fact, let these following Considerations be weigh'd, or rather simply reflected on: For it seems ridiculous to weigh them. Consider the Size of these Poems. What is given us is asserted to be only a Part of a much greater Collection; yet even these Pieces amount to two Quartos. And they were compos'd, you say, in the Highlands about 15 Centuries ago; and have been faithfully transmitted ever since by oral Tradition thro Ages totally ignorant of Letters, by the rudest perhaps of all the European Nations, the most necessitous, the most turbulent, the most ferocious, and the most unsettled.[9] Did ever any Event happen, that approached within a hundred Degrees of this mighty wonder, even to the Nations the most fortunate in their Climate and Situation? Can a Ballad be shown, that has pass'd uncorrupted by oral Tradition thro three Generations among the Greeks or Italians or Phenicians or Egyptians or even among the Natives of such Countries, as Otaheitee or Malacca, who seem exempted by Nature from all Attention but to Amusement, to Poetry and Music?[10]

But the Celtic Nations, it is said, had peculiar Advantages[11] for preserving their traditional Poetry. The Irish, the Welsh, the Bretons are all Celtic Nations, much better entitled than the Highlanders, from their Soil, and Climate, and Situation, to have Leizure for these Amusements: They accordingly present us, not with compleat Epic and Historical Poems (for they never had the Assurance to go that Length) but with very copious and circumstantial Traditions which are allowd by all Men of Sense to be scandalous and ridiculous Impostures.

(3) The Style and Genius of these pretended Poems are another sufficient Proof of the Imposition. The Lapland and Runic Odes,[12] convey'd
to us, besides their small Compass, have a savage Rudeness and sometimes Grandeur, suited to those Ages. But this Erse Poetry has an insipid
Correctness, and Regularity and Uniformity, which betrays a man without Genius, that has been acquainted with the Productions of civiliz'd
Nations, and had his Imagination so limited to that Tract, that it was
impossible for him even to mimic the Character, which he pretended to
assume.[13]

The manners are still a more striking Proof of their want of Authenticity.[14] We see nothing but the affected Generosity and Gallantry of
Chivalry, which are quite unknown not only to all savage People but
to every Nation not trained in these artificial Modes of thinking.[15] In
Homer for Instance and Virgil and Ariosto, the Heroes are represented
as making a nocturnal Incursion into the Camp of the Enemy. Homer
and Virgil, who certainly were educated in much more civilizd Ages
than those of Ossian, make no Scruple of representing their Heroes
as committing undistinguished Slaughter on the sleeping Foe:[16] But
Orlando walks quietly thro the Camp of the Saracens, and scorns to
kill even an Infidel who cannot defend himself.[17] Gaul & Oscar are
Knight Errants still more romantic: They make a Noise in the midst
of the Enemies Camp that they may waken them, and thereby have
a Right to fight with them and to kill them.[18] Nay, Fingal carries his
Ideas of Chivalry still farther, much beyond what was ever dreamt of by
Amadis de Gaul or Lancelot du Lake.[19] When his Territory is invaded,
he scorns to repulse the Enemy with his whole Force: He sends only
an equal Number against them under an inferior Captain: When these
are repuls'd, he sends a second Detachment: And it is not till after a
double Defeat, that he deigns himself to descend from the Hill where
he had remained all the while an idle Spectator, and to attack the
Enemy.[20] Fingal and Swaran combat each other all day with the greatest
Fury: When Darkness suspends the Fight, they feast together with the
greatest Amity: And then renew the Combat with the Return of Light.[21]
Are these the manners of barbarous Nations or even of people, that have
common sense? We may remark, that all this narrative is suppos'd to be
given us by a contemporary Poet: The Facts therefore must be supposd
entirely or nearly conformable to Truth. The Gallantry and extreme
delicacy towards the women, which is found in these productions, is, if

possible, still more contrary to the manners of Barbarians. Among all rude Nations, Force and Courage are the predominant Virtues; and the Inferiority of the females in these particulars renders them an object of Contempt, not of Deference and Regard.[22]

(4) But I derive a new Argument against the Antiquity of these Poems from the general Tenor of the Narrative. Where Manners are represented in them, probability or even possibility are totally disregarded: But in all other respects the Events are within the Course of Nature, no Giants, no Monsters, no Magic, no incredible Feats of Strength or Activity.[23] Every Transaction is conformable to familiar Experience, and scarcely even deserves the Name of wonderful. Did this ever happen in antient and barbarous Poetry? Why is this characteristic wanting so essential to rude and ignorant Ages? Ossian, you say, was singing the Exploits of his Contemporaries and therefore cou'd not falsify them in any great Degree. But if this had been a Restraint, your pretended Ossian had never sung the Exploits of his Contemporaries: He had gone back a Generation or two, which woud have been sufficient to thrown an entire Obscurity on the Events; and he wou'd thereby have attaind the Marvellous, which is alone striking to Barbarians. I desire it may [be] observ'd, that Manners are the only Circumstances, which a rude People cannot falsify; because they have no Notion of any Manners beside their own: But it is easy for them to let loose their Imagination, and violate the Course of Nature in every other particular; and indeed they take no Pleasure in any other kind of Narrative. In Ossian Nature is violated, where alone she ought to have been preserv'd: Is preserv'd where alone she ought to have been violated.

(5) But there is another Species of the Marvellous wanting in Ossian, which is inseparable from all Nations, civiliz'd as well as barbarous, but still more, if possible, from the barbarous; And that is Religion: No religious Sentiment in this Erse Poetry: All those Celtic Heroes are more compleat Atheists than ever were bred in the School of Epicurus.[24] To account for this Singularity, we are told, that, a few Generations before Ossian the People quarrelled with their Druidical Priests, and having expelled them, never afterwards adopted any other Species of Religion.[25] It is not quite unnatural, I own, for the People to quarrel with their Priests; as we did with ours at the Reformation: But we attached Ourselves with fresh Zeal to our new Preachers & new System; and this Passion encreas'd in proportion to our Hatred of the Old.[26] But I

suppose the Reason of this strange Absurdity in our new Erse Poetry, is, that the Author, finding by the assumed Age of his Heroes, that he must have given them the Druidical Religion, and not trusting to his Literature[27] (which seems indeed to be very slender) for making the Representations consistent with Antiquity; thought it safest to give them no Religion at all: A Circumstance so wonderfully unnatural that it is sufficient alone, if Men had Eyes, to detect the Imposition.

(6) The State of the Arts, as represented in those poems, is totally incompatible with the Age, assignd to them. We know, that the Houses even of the Southern Britons, till conquerd by the Romans, were nothing but Huts erected in the Woods:[28] But a stately stone Building is mention'd by Ossian, of which the Walls remain, after it is consumd with fire:[29] The melancholy Circumstance of a Fox is describd, who looks out at the Windows; an Image, if I be not mistaken, borrowd from the Scripture.[30] The Caledonians, as well as the Irish, had no Shipping but Currochs,[31] or wicker Boats cover'd with Hydes: Yet are they represented as passing, in great military Expeditions, from the Hebrides, to Denmark, Norway, & Sweden: A most glaring Absurdity. They live entirely by Hunting,[32] yet muster Armies, which make Incursions to these Countries as well as to Ireland: Though, it is certain from the Experience of America,[33] that the whole Highlands woud scarce subsist a hundred Persons by Hunting. They are totally unacquainted with Fishing;[34] though that Occupation first tempts all rude Nations to venture on the Sea. Ossian alludes to a Wind or Water Mill,[35] a Machine then unknown to the Greeks & Romans, according to the Opinion of the best Antiquaries.[36] His Barbarians, though ignorant of Tillage, are well acquainted with the Method of working all kinds of Metals.[37] The Harp is the musical Instrument of Ossian; but the Bag-pipe, from time immemorial, has been the Instrument of the Highlanders. If ever the Harp had been known among them, it never had given place to the other barbarous Discord. Stridenti stipula miserum disperdere carmen.[38]

(7) All the historical Facts of this Poem are oppos'd by Traditions, which, if all these Tales be not equally contemptible, seem to merit much more Attention. The Irish Scoti are the undoubted Ancestors of the present Highlanders, who are but a small Colony of that antient people.[39] But the Irish Traditions make Fingal, Ossian, Oscar all Irish Men, and place them some Centuries distant from the Erse Heroes. They represent

them as Giants and Monsters and Enchanters, a sure Mark of a considerable Antiquity of these Traditions.[40] I ask the Partisans of Erse Poetry, since the Names of these Heroes have crept over to Ireland and have become quite familiar to the Natives of that Country; how it happens, that not a Line of this Poetry, in which they are all celebrated, which alone, it is pretended, preserves their Memory, with our Highlanders, and which is composd by one of these Heroes themselves in the Irish Language, ever found its way thither? The Songs and Traditions of the Senachees, the genuine Poetry of the Irish, carry in their Rudeness & Absurdity, the inseparable Attendants of Barbarism, a very different Aspect from the insipid Correctness of Ossian; where the Incidents, if you will pardon the Antithesis, are the most unnatural, merely because they are natural.[41] The same Observation extends to the Welsh, another Celtic Nation.[42]

(8) The Fiction of these Poems is, if possible, still more palpably detected, by the great Numbers of other Traditions, which, the Author pretends, are still fresh in the Highlands, with regard to all these Personages. The Poems, compos'd in the Age of Trathal, and Cormac, Ancestors of Ossian, are, he says, full of Complaints against the Roguery and Tyranny of the Druids. He talks as familiarly of the Poetry of that Period as Lucian or Longinus woud of the Greek Poetry of the Socratic Age.[43] I suppose here is a new rich Mine of Poetry ready to break out upon us, if the Author thinks it can turn to account. For probably, he does not mind the Danger of Detection, which he has little Reason to apprehend from his Experience of the public Credulity. But I shall venture to assert, without any Reserve or farther Enquiry, that there is no Highlander, who is not, in some degree, a man of Letters, that ever so much as heard there was a Druid in the World.

The Margin of every Page almost of this wonderful Production is supported, as he pretends, by minute oral Traditions with regard to the Personages. To the Poem of Darthula there is prefixed a long account of the Pedigree Marriages and Adventures of three Brothers, Nathos, Althos, and Ardan, Heroes that livd 1500 Years ago in Argyleshire, and whose Memory it seems is still celebrated there and in every part of the Highlands.[44] How ridiculous to advance such a Pretension to the Learned, who know that there is no Tradition of Alexander the Great all over the East; that the Turks, who have heard of him from their communication with the Greeks, believe him to have been the Captain of Solomon's

Guard;[45] that the Greek and Roman Story, the moment it departs from the historical Ages, becomes a heap of Fiction & Absurdity,[46] that Cyrus himself, the Conqueror of the East, became so much unknown even in little more than half a Century, that Herodotus himself, born & bred in Asia, within the Limits of the Persian Empire, coud tell nothing of him, more than of Crœsus, the contemporary of Cyrus, and who reigned in the neighbourhood of the Historian, but the most ridiculous Fables; and that the Grand-father of Hengist & Horsa, the first Saxon Conquerors, was conceivd to be a Divinity. I suppose, it is sufficiently evident, that without the help of Books & History, the very Name of Julius Cæsar woud at present be totally unknown in Europe. A Gentleman, who travell'd into Italy, told me, that in visiting Frascati or Tusculum, his Cicerone[47] show'd him the Foundation & Ruins of Cicero's Country house. He asked the Fellow who this Cicero might be <u>Un grandissimo Gigante</u>, said he.

(9) I ask, since the Memory of Fingal and his Ancestors and Descendants is still so fresh in the Highlands, how it happens, that none of the Compilers of the Scotch fabulous History[48] ever laid hold of them, and inserted them in the List of our antient Monarchs, but were oblig'd to have recourse to direct Fiction and Lying to make out their Genealogies. It is to be remarked, that the Highlanders, who are now but an inferior part of the Nation, antiently compos'd the whole; so that no Tradition of theirs coud be unknown to the Court, the Nobility, and the whole Kingdom. Where then have these wonderful Traditions skulked during so many Centuries, that they have never come to light till yesterday; and the very Names of our antient Kings are unknown, though it is pretended, that a very particular Narrative of their Transactions was still preserved, and universally diffused among a numerous Tribe, who are the original Stem of the Nation. Father Innes, the only judicious Writer, that ever touchd our antient History, finds in monastic Records, the Names and little more than the Names of Kings from Fergus, whom we call Fergus the second,[49] who liv'd long after the suppos'd Fingal; and he thence begins the true History of the Nation.[50] He had too good Sense to give any Attention to pretended Traditions even of Kings; much less woud he have believ'd that the Memory and Adventures of every Leader of Banditti in every Valley of the Highlands coud be circumstantially preserv'd by oral Tradition thro' more than fifteen Centuries.

(10) I shall observe, that the Character of the Author, from all his

Publications (for I shall mention nothing else) gives us the greatest Reason to suspect him of such a ludicrous Imposition on the public: For to be sure it is only ludicrous; or at most a Trial of Wit, like that of the Sophist, who gave us Phalaris's Epistles;[51] or of him that counterfeited Cicero's Consolation,[52] or supply'd the Fragments of Petronius.[53] These literary Amusements have been very common; and unless supported by too violent Asseverations, or persisted in too long, never drew the opprobrious Appellation of Impostor on the Author.

He writes an antient History of Britain,[54] which is plainly ludicrous: He gives us a long circumstantial History of the Emigrations of the Belgæ, Cimbri, and Sarmatæ,[55] so unsupported by any Author of Antiquity that nothing but a particular Revelation coud warrant it, and yet it is deliverd with such seeming Confidence (for we must not think he was in earnest) that the History of the Punic Wars is not related with greater Seriousness by Livy.[56] He has even left palpable Contradictions in his Narrative, in order to try the Faith of his Reader. He tells us, for Instance, that the present Inhabitants of Germany have no more Connexion with the Germans mention'd by Tacitus[57] than with the antient Inhabitants of Peloponnesus: The Saxons and Angles in particular were all Sarmatians, a quite different Tribe from the Germans, in manners, laws, language, and customs. Yet a few Pages after, when he pretends to deliver the Origin of the Anglo-Saxon Constitution, he professedly derives the whole Account from Tacitus. All this was only an Experiment, to see how far the Force of Affirmation could impose on the Credulity of the public: But it did not succeed: He was here in the open day-light of Greek and Roman Erudition, not in the Obscurity of his Erse Poetry and Tradition.

Finding the Style of his Ossian admired by some, he attempts a Translation of Homer[58] in the very same Style. He begins and finishes in six Weeks a Work, that was for ever to eclipse the Translation of Pope,[59] whom he does not even deign to mention in his Preface: But this Joke was still more unsuccessful. He made a Shift, however, to bring the work to a second Edition, where he says, that, notwithstanding all the Envy of his malignant Opponents, his Name alone will preserve the Work to a more equitable Posterity.

In short, let him now take off the Mask, and fairly and openly laugh at the Credulity of the Public, who coud believe, that long Erse Epics had been secretly preserv'd in the Highlands of Scotland from the Age of Severus[60] till his time. The Imposition is so gross, that he may well ask the world how they coud ever possibly believe him to be in earnest.

But it may reasonably be expected that I shoud mention the external positive Evidence,[61] which is brought by D[r] Blair to support the Authenticity of these Poems. I own, that this Evidence, considerd in itself, is very respectable, and sufficient to support any Fact, that both lies within the bounds of Credibility, and has not become a Matter of Party. But will any man pretend to bring human Testimony to prove, that above twenty thousand Verses have been transmitted, by Tradition & Memory during more than 1500 Years, that is, above fifty Generations, according to the ordinary Course of Nature? Verses too, which have not in their Subject any thing alluring or inviting to the People, no Miracles, no wonders, no Superstition, no useful Instruction: A People too, who during twelve Centuries at least of that Period had no writing, no Alphabet; and who, even in the other three Centuries made very little Use of that imperfect Alphabet for any purpose: A People, who, from the miserable Disadvantages of their Soil and Climate, were perpetually struling with the greatest Necessities of Nature; who, from the Imperfections of Government, livd in a continual State of internal Hostility, ever harass'd with the Incursions of neighbouring Tribes, or meditating Revenge and Retaliation on their Neighbours. Have such a People Leizure to think of any Poetry, except perhaps a miserable Song or Ballad in Praise of their own Chieftain or to the Disparagement of his Rivals?

I shoud be sorry to be suspected of saying any thing against the Manners of the present Highlanders.[62] I really believe, that, besides their signal Bravery, there is not any People in Europe, not even excepting the Swiss,[63] who have more plain honesty and fidelity, are more capable of Gratitude and Attachment than that Race of Men. Yet it was, no doubt, a great Surprize to them to hear, that over and above their known good Qualities, they were also possessed of an Excellence, which they never dreamt of, an elegant Taste in Poetry, and inherited, from the most remote Antiquity, the finest Compositions of that kind, far surpassing the popular traditional Poems of any other Language. No wonder they crowded to give Testimony in favour of their Authenticity. Most of them, no doubt, were sincere in the Delusion. The same Names, that were to be found in their popular Ballads were carefully preserved in the new publication: Some Incidents too were perhaps transferr'd from the one to the other: Some Sentiments also might be copy'd: And on the whole they were willing to believe, and still more willing to perswade others, that the whole was genuine. On such Occasions, the greatest Cloud of witnesses makes no manner of Evidence. What Jansenist was there in Paris, which contains several thousands, that woud not have given Evidence for the Miracles of Abbé Paris? The Miracle is greater, but not the Evidence, with regard to the Authenticity of Ossian.[64]

The late President Forbes was a great Believer in the second Sight;[65] and I make no question, but he coud, on a month's warning, have over-powerd you with Evidence in its favour. But as finite added to finite never approaches a hair's breadth nearer to Infinite; so a fact, incredible in itself, acquires not the smallest Accession of Probability, by the Accumulation of Testimony.[66]

The only real wonder in this whole Affair is that a Person of so fine a Taste as D^r Blair shoud be so great an Admirer of these Productions; and one of so clear and cool a Judgement collect Evidence of their Authenticity.

# Appendices

# *Appendix 1*

## 1. Advertisement to *1741*

### ADVERTISEMENT

Most of these ESSAYS were wrote with a View of being publish'd as WEEKLY-PAPERS, and were intended to comprehend the Designs both of the SPECTATORS and CRAFTSMEN. But having dropt that Undertaking, partly from LAZINESS, partly from WANT of LEISURE, and being willing to make Trial of my Talents for Writing, before I ventur'd upon any more serious Compositions, I was induced to commit these Trifles to the Judgment of the Public. Like most new Authors, I must confess, I feel some Anxiety concerning the Success of my Work: But one Thing makes me more secure; That the READER may condemn my Abilities, but must approve of my Moderation and Impartiality in my Method of handling POLITICAL SUBJECTS: And as long as my Moral Character is in Safety, I can, with less Anxiety, abandon my Learning and Capacity to the most severe Censure and Examination. Public Spirit, methinks, shou'd engage us to love the Public, and to bear an equal Affection to all our Country-Men; not to hate one Half of them, under Pretext of loving the Whole. This PARTY-RAGE I have endeavour'd to repress, as far as possible; and I hope this Design will be acceptable to the moderate of both Parties; at the same Time, that, perhaps, it may displease the Bigots of both.

The READER must not look for any Connexion among these ESSAYS, but must consider each of them as a Work apart. This is an Indulgence that is given to all ESSAY-WRITERS, and is an equal Ease both to

WRITER and READER, by freeing them from any tiresome Stretch of Attention or Application.

## 2. Advertisement to *1742a*

### ADVERTISEMENT

'Tis proper to inform the READER, that, in those ESSAYS, intitled, *The Epicurean*, *Stoic*, &c. a certain Character is personated; and therefore, no Offence ought to be taken at any Sentiments contain'd in them.

The Character of Sir ROBERT WALPOLE was drawn some Months ago, when that Great MAN was in the Zenith of his Power. I must confess, that, at present, when he seems to be upon the Decline, I am inclin'd to think more favourably of him, and to suspect, that the Antipathy, which every true born *Briton* naturally bears to Ministers of State, inspir'd me with some Prejudice against him. The impartial READER, if any such there be; or Posterity, if such a Trifle can reach them, will best be able to correct my Mistakes in this Particular.

# *Appendix 2*

## HUME ON WILKIE'S *EPIGONIAD*

In May 1757 the clergyman William Wilkie (1721–1772) published at Edinburgh an Homeric epic poem in heroic couplets, *The Epigoniad*. The poem took for its subject the siege of Thebes by Theseus and the *epigones*, i.e. the descendants of those heroes who had earlier besieged Thebes. Wilkie prefaced his poem with an extensive essay on modern epic poetry, which addressed *inter alia* the problems created for this poetic form by the supersession of paganism by Christianity.

Hume had been acquainted with Wilkie since at least 1755, and they were both members of the Select Society (of which Hume was Treasurer).[1] When *The Epigoniad* was about to be published Hume had recommended it warmly to his London publisher William Strahan:

> I have wrote to Mr Millar of a new Epic Poem that is to be publishd this Week in Edinburgh: It is calld the Epigoniad, & is wrote by one Mr Wilkie, a Minister. It is a Production of great Genius. I recommend it to you to read it when it comes to London. If you like it you will naturally speak of it among your Acquaintance.[2]

And in the month following publication Hume had also praised the poem to Gilbert Elliot, calling it 'the wonderful Production of the Epigoniad', expressing his hope that Elliot, who had 'so much Love for Arts, & for your native Country', would be 'very industrious in propagating the Fame' of this 'most singular Production, full of Sublimity & Genius, adorn'd by a noble, harmonious, forcible, & even correct versification', and passing on some anecdotes about the author.[3]

Two months later Hume was clearly anxious about the silence from London concerning his friend's poem, as he wrote again to Andrew

Millar inquiring 'what the Connoisseurs with you say of that singular Piece the Epigoniad'.[4] But by August he was bitterly aware that Wilkie's efforts had not found favour even with some of his own countrymen, as he sighed to Gilbert Elliot: 'I find the Public, with you, have rejected the Epigoniad, for the present. They may do so if they please: But it has a great deal of Merit, much more than any one of them is capable of throwing into a Work.'[5]

For in the meantime *The Epigoniad* had been reviewed negatively by Tobias Smollett in *The Critical Review*.[6] Smollett had struck a note of dismissive scorn at the outset by means of an allusion to Pope's *Essay on Criticism*: 'the piece before us, which resembles an epic poem in very little else but the outward form, and extent of it, dragging its slow length along through nine tedious books'.[7] He went on to deplore *The Epigoniad* as 'a poor and servile imitation of the great Homer, whose defects our author hath faithfully copied, whilst the beauties of that divine writer have unluckily escaped him', before concluding that 'in our opinion, the author of the Epigoniad, though apparently a man of learning and taste, is by no means equal to the great task which he has undertaken'.[8]

In September, Hume tried to rescue the situation by means of a further appeal to Millar:

> Nothing surprizes me more than the Ill Usage which the Epigoniad has receiv'd. Every body here likes it extremely. The Plan & Story is not so much admired; as the Poetry & Versification: But your Critics seem willing to allow it no Merit at all. I fancy it has not been enough dispers'd; and that your engaging in it, wou'd extremely forward its Success. The whole Edition is out: There were 550 disposd of here: 200 sent to London. As the Author is my very good Friend & Acquaintance, I shoud be much pleasd to bring you to an understanding together; If the bad success on the first Edition has not discouragd you, I wou'd engage him to make you Proposals for that Purpose. He will correct all the Blemishes remark'd.[9]

This was followed by a similar appeal later the same month to a friend in Ireland, James Edmonstoune.[10] But clearly stronger and more direct measures were called for.

A second edition of *The Epigoniad* was published in 1759, and on this occasion Hume wrote (anonymously) to *The Critical Review* in Wilkie's defence.[11] Although this letter is not strictly speaking an essay, it is included here for three reasons: 1) it sheds light on Hume's literary aesthetics; 2) Hume's defence of Wilkie illustrates his understanding of the peculiar predicament of Scottish authors writing for predominantly English readerships; and 3) Hume's extenuation of the fable of Wilkie's poem makes an interesting comparison with his much later essay on Ossian, which also touches on the subject of the manners and morals of the heroes of antiquity, and their remoteness from modern manners.

## To the Authors of the CRITICAL REVIEW.

GENTLEMEN,

The great advantages which result from literary journals have recommended the use of them all over Europe; but as nothing is free from abuse, it must be confessed, that some inconveniencies have also attended these undertakings. The works of the learned multiply in such a surprising manner, that a journalist, in order to give an account to the public of all new performances, is obliged to peruse a small library every month; and as it is impossible for him to bestow equal attention on every piece which he criticizes, he may readily be surprised into mistakes, and give to a book such a character as, on a more careful perusal, he would willingly retract. Even performances of the greatest merit are not secure against this injury, and, perhaps, are sometimes the most exposed to it. An author of genius scorns the vulgar arts of catching applause; he pays no court to the great; gives no adulation to those celebrated for learning; takes no care to provide himself of partizans, or *proneurs*, as the French call them; and by that means his work steals unobserved into the world; and it is some time before the public, and even men of penetration, are sensible of its merit. We take up the book with prepossession, peruse it carelessly, are feebly affected by its beauties, and lay it down with neglect, perhaps with disapprobation.

The public has done so much justice to the gentlemen engaged in the Critical Review, as to acknowledge that no literary journal was ever carried on in this country with equal spirit and impartiality; yet I must confess, that an article published in your Review of 1757, gave me great surprize, and not a little uneasiness. It regarded a book called the Epigoniad, a poem of the Epic kind, which was at that time published with great applause at Edinburgh, and of which a few copies had been sent up to London. The author of that article had surely been lying under strong prepossessions, when he spoke so negligently of a work which abounds in such sublime beauties, and could endeavour to discredit a poem, consisting of near six thousand lines, on account of a few mistakes in expression and prosody, proceeding entirely from the author's being a Scotchman, who had never been out of his own country. As there is a new edition published of this poem, wherein all or most of these trivial mistakes are

corrected, I flatter myself that you will gladly lay hold of this opportunity of retracting your oversight, and doing justice to a performance,
which may, perhaps, be regarded as one of the ornaments of our language. I appeal from your sentence, as an old woman did from a sentence
pronounced by Philip of Macedon: I appeal from Philip, ill-counselled
and in a hurry, to Philip well-advised, and judging with deliberation. The
authority which you possess with the public makes your censure fall with
weight; and I question not but you will be the more ready on that account
to redress any injury, into which either negligence, prejudice, or mistake,
may have betrayed you. As I profess myself to be an admirer of this performance, it will afford me pleasure to give you a short analysis of it, and
to collect a few specimens of those great beauties in which it abounds.

The author, who appears throughout his whole work to be a great
admirer and imitator of Homer, drew the subject of this poem from the
fourth Iliad, where Sthenelus gives Agamemnon a short account of the
sacking [of] Thebes. After the fall of those heroes, celebrated by Statius,
their sons, and among the rest Diomede, undertook the siege of that city,
and were so fortunate as to succeed in their enterprize, and to revenge
on the Thebans and the tyrant Creon, the death of their fathers. These
young heroes were known to the Greeks under the title of the Epigoni,
or the Descendants; and for this reason the author has given to his poem
the title of Epigoniad; a name, it must be confessed, somewhat unfort-
unately chosen: for as this particular was known only to a very few of the
learned, the public were not able to conjecture what could be the subject
of the poem, and were apt to neglect what it was impossible for them to
understand.

There remained a tradition among the Greeks, that Homer had taken
this second siege of Thebes for the subject of a poem, which is lost; and
our author seems to have pleased himself with the thoughts of reviving
the work, as well as of treading in the footsteps of his favourite author.
The actors are mostly the same with those of the Iliad; Diomede is the
hero; Ulysses, Agamemnon, Menelaus, Nestor, Idomeneus, Merion, even
Thersites, all appear in different passages of the poem; and act parts suitable to the lively characters drawn of them by that great master. The
whole turn of this new poem would almost lead us to imagine, that the
Scottish bard had found the lost manuscript of that father of poetry, and
had made a faithful translation of it into English. Longinus imagines,
that the Odyssey was executed by Homer in his old age: we shall allow

the Iliad to be the work of his middle age; and we shall suppose, that the Epigoniad was the essay of his youth, where his noble and sublime genius breaks forth by frequent intervals, and gives strong symptoms of that constant flame which distinguished its meridian.

The poem consists of nine books. We shall open up the subject of it in the author's own words.

> 'Ye pow'rs of song! with whose immortal fire
> Your bard inraptur'd sung Pelides' ire,
> To Greece so fatal, when in evil hour,
> He brav'd, in stern debate, the sov'reign pow'r,
> By like example, teach me now to show
> From love, no less, what dire disasters flow.
> For when the youth of Greece, by Theseus led,
> Return'd to conquer where their fathers bled,
> And punish guilty Thebes, by heav'n ordain'd
> For perfidy to fall, and oaths profan'd;
> Venus, still partial to the Theban arms,
> Tydeus' son seduc'd by female charms;
> Who, from his plighted faith by passion sway'd,
> The chiefs, the army, and himself betray'd.
>
> 'This theme did once your fav'rite bard employ,
> Whose verse immortaliz'd the fall of Troy:
> But time's oblivious gulf, whose circle draws
> All mortal things by fate's eternal laws,
> In whose wide vortex worlds themselves are tost,
> And rounding swift successively are lost,
> This song hath snatch'd. I now resume the strain,
> Not from proud hope and emulation vain,
> By this attempt to merit equal praise
> With worth heroic, born in happier days.
> Sooner the weed, that with the Spring appears,
> And in the Summer's heat its blossom bears,
> But, shriv'ling at the touch of Winter hoar,
> Sinks to its native earth, and is no more;
> Might match the lofty oak, which long hath stood,
> From age to age, the monarch of the wood.
> But love excites me, and desire to trace

His glorious steps, tho' with unequal pace.
Before me still I see his awful shade,
With garlands crown'd of leaves which never fade;
He points the path to fame, and bids me scale
Parnassus' slipp'ry height, where thousands fail:
I follow trembling; for the cliffs are high,
And hov'ring round them watchful harpies fly,
To snatch the poet's wreath with envious claws,
And hiss contempt for merited applause.'

The poet supposes that Cassandra, the daughter of the king of Pelignium in Italy, was pursued by the love of Echetus, a barbarous tyrant in the neighbourhood; and as her father rejected his addresses, he drew on himself the resentment of the tyrant, who made war upon him, and forced him to retire into Etolia, where Diomede gave him protection. This hero falls himself in love with Cassandra, and is so fortunate as to make equal impressions on her heart; but before the completion of his marriage, he is called to the siege of Thebes, and leaves, as he supposes, Cassandra in Etolia with her father. But Cassandra, anxious for her lover's safety, and unwilling to part from the object of her affections, had secretly put on a man's habit, had attended him in the camp, and had fought by his side in all his battles. Mean while the siege of Thebes is drawn out to some length; and Venus, who favours that city, in opposition to Juno and Pallas, who seek its destruction, deliberates concerning the proper method of raising the siege. The fittest expedient seems to be the exciting in Diomede a jealousy of Cassandra, and persuading him, that her affections were secretly engaged to Echetus, and that the tyrant had invaded Etolia in pursuit of his mistress: for this purpose Venus sends down Jealousy, whom the author personifies under the name of Zelotypé. Her person and flight are painted in the most splendid colours that poetry affords.

'First to her feet the winged shoes she binds,
Which tread the air, and mount the rapid winds;
Aloft they bear her thro' th'ethereal plain,
Above the solid earth and liquid main;
Her arrows next she takes of pointed steel,
For sight too small, but terrible to feel;
Rous'd by their smart, the savage lion roars,
And mad to combat rush the tusky boars,

Of wounds secure; for where their venom lights,
What feels their power all other torment slights,
A figur'd zone, mysteriously design'd,
Around her waist her yellow robe confin'd:
There dark Suspicion lurk'd, of sable hue;
There hasty Rage his deadly dagger drew;
Pale Envy inly pin'd; and by her side
Stood Phrenzy, raging with his chains unty'd;
Affronted Pride with thirst of vengeance burn'd,
And Love's excess to deepest hatred turn'd.
All these the artist's curious hand express'd,
The work divine his matchless skill confess'd.
The virgin last, around her shoulders slung
The bow; and by her side the quiver hung:
Then, springing up, her airy course she bends
For Thebes; and lightly o'er the tents descends.
The son of Tydeus, 'midst his bands, she found
In arms compleat, reposing on the ground;
And, as he slept, the hero thus address'd,
Her form to fancy's waking eye express'd.'

Diomede, moved by the instigations of jealousy, and eager to defend his
mistress and his country, calls an assembly of the princes, and proposes
to raise the siege of Thebes, on account of the difficulty of the enterprize
and dangers which surround the army. Theseus, the general, breaks out
into a passion at this proposal; but is pacified by Nestor. Idomeneus rises,
and reproaches Diomede for his dishonourable counsel; and among other
topics upbraids him with his degeneracy from his father's bravery.

'Should now, from hence arriv'd, some warrior's ghost
Greet valiant Tydeus on the Stygian coast,
And tell, when danger or distress is near,
That Diomed persuades the rest to fear;
He'd shun the synod of the mighty dead,
And hide his anguish in the deepest shade:
Nature in all an equal course maintains;
The lion's whelp succeeds to awe the plains;
Pards gender pards; from tygers tygers spring;

No doves are hatch'd beneath a vultur's wing:
Each parent's image in his offspring lives;
But nought of Tydeus in his son survives.'

The debate is closed by Ulysses, who informs the princes that the
Thebans are preparing to march out in order to attack them; and that
it is vain for them to deliberate any longer concerning the continuance
of the war.

We have next the description of a battle between the Thebans under
Creon, and the confederate Greeks under Theseus. This battle is full of
the spirit of Homer. We shall not trouble our reader with particulars,
which would appear insipid in prose, especially if compared to the lively
poetry of our author. We shall only transcribe one passage, as a specimen
of his happy choice of circumstances.

'Next Arcas, Cleon, valiant Chromius, dy'd;
With Dares, to the Spartan chiefs ally'd.
And Phœmius, whom the Gods in early youth
Had form'd for virtue and the love of truth;
His gen'rous soul to noble deeds they turn'd,
And love to mankind in his bosom burn'd:
Cold thro' his throat the hissing weapon glides,
And on his neck the waving locks divides.
His fate the Graces mourn'd. The Gods above,
Who sit around the starry throne of Jove,
On high Olympus bending from the skies,
His fate beheld with sorrow-streaming eyes.
Pallas alone, unalter'd and serene,
With secret triumph saw the mournful scene:
Not hard of heart; for none of all the pow'rs,
In earth or ocean, or th'Olympian tow'rs,
Holds equal sympathy with human grief,
Or with a freer hand bestows relief;
But conscious that a mind by virtue steel'd,
To no impression of distress will yield;
That, still unconquer'd, in its awful hour
O'er death it triumphs with immortal pow'r.'

The battle ends with advantage to the confederate Greeks; but the approach of night prevents their total victory.

Creon, king of Thebes, sends next an embassy to the confederate Greeks, desiring a truce of seven days, in order to bury the dead. Diomede, impatient to return home, and stimulated by jealousy, violently opposes this overture, but is over-ruled by the other princes; and the truce is concluded. The author, in imitation of Homer, and the other antient poets, takes here an opportunity of describing games celebrated for honouring the dead. The games he has chosen are different from those which are to be found among the antients, and the incidents are new and curious.

Diomede took no share in these games: his impatient spirit could not brook the delay which arose from the truce: he pretends that he consented not to it, and is not included in it: he therefore proposes to his troops to attack the Thebans, while they are employed in performing the funeral rites of the dead; but is opposed in this design by Deiphobus, his tutor, who represents to him in the severest terms the rashness and iniquity of his proposal. After some altercation Diomede, impatient of contradiction in his favourite object, and stung by the free reproaches of his tutor, breaks out into a violent passion, and throws his spear at Deiphobus, which pierced him to the heart.

This incident, which is apt to surprise us, seems to have been copied by our author, from that circumstance in the life of Alexander, where this heroic conqueror, moved by a sudden passion, stabs Clytus, his antient friend, by whom his life had been formerly saved in battle. The repentance of Diomede is equal to that of Alexander. No sooner had he struck the fatal blow than his eyes are opened: he is sensible of his guilt and shame: he refuses all consolation: abstains even from food; and shuts himself up alone in his tent. His followers, amazed at the violence of his passion, keep at a distance from him; all but Cassandra, who enters his tent with a potion, which she had prepared for him. While she stands before him alone, her timidity and passion betray her sex; and Diomede immediately perceives her to be Cassandra, who had followed him to the camp under a warlike disguise. As his repentance for the murder of Deiphobus was now the ruling passion in his breast, he is not moved by tenderness for Cassandra: on the contrary, he considers her as the cause, however innocent, of the murder of his friend and of his own guilt; and he treats her with such coldness that she retires in confusion. She even leaves the camp, and resolves to return to her father in Etolia; but is taken on the road by a party of Thebans, who carry her to Creon. That tyrant determines to make the most political use of this incident: he sends privately a message to Diomede, threatening to put Cassandra to death, if that hero would not agree to a separate truce with Thebes. This proposal is at first rejected by Diomede, who threatens immediate destruction to Creon and all his race. Nothing can be more artfully managed by the poet than this incident. We shall hear him in his own words.

> 'Sternly the hero ended, and resign'd,
> To fierce disorder, all his mighty mind.
> Already in his thoughts, with vengeful hands,
> He dealt destruction 'midst the Theban bands,
> In fancy saw the tott'ring turrets fall,
> And led his warriors o'er the level'd wall.
> Rous'd with the thought, from his high seat he sprung;
> And grasp'd the sword, which on a column hung;
> The shining blade he balanc'd thrice in air;
> His launces next he view'd, and armor fair.
> When, hanging 'midst the costly panoply,
> A scarf embroider'd met the hero's eye,
> Which fair Cassandra's skilful hands had wrought;
> A present for her lord, in secret brought,
> That day, when first he led his martial train
> In arms, to combat on the Theban plain.
> As some strong charm, which magic sounds compose,
> Suspends a downward torrent as it flows;
> Checks in the precipice its headlong course,
> And calls it trembling upwards to its source:
> Such seem'd the robe, which, to the hero's eyes,
> Made the fair artist in her charms to rise.
> His rage, suspended in its full career,
> To love resigns, to grief and tender fear.
> Glad would he now his former words revoke,
> And change the purpose which in wrath he spoke;
> From hostile hands his captive fair to gain,
> From fate to save her, or the servile chain:
> But pride, and shame, the fond design supprest;

Silent he stood, and lock'd it in his breast.
Yet had the wary Theban well divin'd,
By symptoms sure, each motion of his mind:
With joy he saw the heat of rage suppress'd;
And thus again his artful words address'd.'

The truce is concluded for twenty days; but the perfidious Creon, hoping that Diomede would be over-awed by the danger of his mistress, resolves to surprise the Greeks; and accordingly makes a sudden attack upon them, breaks into their camp, and carries every thing before him. Diomede at first stands neuter; but when Ulysses suggests to him, that, after the defeat of the confederate Greeks he has no security; and that so treacherous a prince as Creon will not spare, much less restore, Cassandra, he takes to arms, assaults the Thebans, and obliges them to seek shelter within their walls. Creon, in revenge, puts Cassandra to death, and shows her head over the walls. The sight so inflames Diomede, that he attacks Thebes with double fury, takes the town by scalade, and gratifies his vengeance by the death of Creon.

This is a short abstract of the story, on which this new poem is founded. The reader may perhaps conjecture (what I am not very anxious to conceal) that the execution of the Epigoniad is better than the design, the poetry superior to the fable, and the colouring of the particular parts more excellent than the general plan of the whole. Of all the great Epic poems which have been the admiration of mankind, the Jerusalem of Tasso alone would make a tolerable novel, if reduced to prose, and related without that splendor of versification and imagery by which it is supported: yet in the opinion of many great judges, the Jerusalem is the least perfect of all these productions; chiefly, because it has least nature and simplicity in the sentiments, and is most liable to the objection of affectation and conceit. The story of a poem, whatever may be imagined, is the least essential part of it: the force of the versification, the vivacity of the images, the justness of the descriptions, the natural play of the passions, are the chief circumstances which distinguish the great poet from the prosaic novelist, and give him so high a rank among the heroes in literature: and I will venture to affirm, that all these advantages, especially the three former, are to be found in an eminent degree in the Epigoniad. The author, inspired with the true genius of Greece, and smit with the most profound veneration for Homer, disdains all frivolous ornaments; and relying entirely on his sublime imagination, and his nervous and harmonious expression, has ventured to present to his reader the naked beauties of nature, and challenges for his partizans all the admirers of genuine antiquity.

There is one circumstance in which the poet has carried his boldness of copying antiquity beyond the practice of many, even judicious moderns. He has drawn his personages, not only with all the simplicity of the Grecian heroes, but also with some degree of their roughness, and even of their ferocity. This is a circumstance which a mere modern is apt to find fault with in Homer, and which, perhaps, he will not easily excuse in his imitator. It is certain, that the ideas of manners are so much changed since the age of Homer, that though the Iliad was always among the antients conceived to be a panegyric on the Greeks, yet the reader is now almost always on the side of the Trojans, and is much more interested for the humane and soft manners of Priam, Hector, Andromache, Sarpedon, Æneas, Glaucus, nay, even of Paris and Helen, than for the severe and cruel bravery of Achilles, Agamemnon, and the other Grecian heroes. Sensible of this inconvenience, Fenelon, in his elegant romance, has softened extremely the harsh manners of the heroic ages, and has contented himself with retaining that amiable simplicity by which these ages were distinguished. If the reader be displeased, that the British poet has not followed the example of the French writer, he must, at least, allow, that he has drawn a more exact and faithful copy of antiquity, and has made fewer sacrifices of truth to ornament.

There is another circumstance of our author's choice which will be liable to dispute. It may be thought, that by introducing the heroes of Homer, he has lost all the charms of novelty, and leads us into fictions, which are somewhat stale and thread-bare. Boileau, the greatest critic of the French nation, was of a very different opinion.

> 'La fable offre a l'esprit mille agréments divers
> Là tous les noms heureux semblent nez pour les vers:
> Ulysse, Agamemnon, Oreste, Idomenée,
> Helene, Menelas, Paris, Hector, Enee.'

It is certain that there is in that poetic ground a kind of enchantment which allures every person of a tender and lively imagination: nor is this impression diminished, but rather much encreased, by our early introduction to the knowledge of it in our perusal of the Greek and Latin classics.

The same great French critic makes the apology of our poet in his use of the antient mythology.

> 'Ainsi dans cet amas de nobles fictions,
> Le poete s'egaye en mille inventions,
> Orne, eleve, embellit, agrandit toutes choses,
> Et trouve sous sa main des fleurs toujours ecloses.'

It would seem, indeed, that if the machinery of the heathen gods be not admitted, Epic poetry, at least all the marvellous part of it, must be entirely abandoned. The christian religion, for many reasons, is unfit for the fabulous ornaments of poetry: the introduction of allegory, after the manner of Voltaire, is liable to many objections: and though a mere historical Epic poem, like Leonidas, may have its beauties, it will always be inferior to the force and pathetic of tragedy, and must resign to that species of poetry the precedency which the former composition has always challenged among the productions of human genius. But with regard to these particulars, the author has himself made a sufficient apology in the judicious and spirited preface, which accompanies his poem.

But though our poet has, in general, followed so successfully the footsteps of Homer, he has, in particular passages, chosen other antient poets for his model. His seventh book contains an episode, very artfully inserted, concerning the death of Hercules; where he has plainly had Sophocles in his view, and has ventured to engage in a rivalship with that great master of the tragic scene. If the sublimity of our poet's imagination, and the energy of his stile appears any where conspicuous, it is in this episode, which we shall not scruple to compare with any poetry in the English language. Nothing can be more pathetic than the complaints of Hercules, when the poison of the centaur's robe begins first to prey upon him.

> 'Sov'reign of heav'n and earth! whose boundless sway
> The fates of men and mortal things obey!
> If e'er delighted from the courts above,
> In human form, you sought Alcmena's love;
> If fame's unchanging voice to all the earth,
> With truth, proclaims you author of my birth;

Whence, from a course of spotless glory run,
Successful toils and wreaths of triumph won,
Am I thus wretched? better, that before
Some monster fierce had drunk my streaming gore;
Or crush'd by Cacus, foe to gods and men,
My batter'd brains had strew'd his rocky den:
Than, from my glorious toils and triumphs past,
To fall subdu'd by female arts, at last.
O cool my boiling blood, ye winds, that blow
From mountains loaded with eternal snow,
And crack the icy cliffs: in vain! in vain!
Your rigor cannot quench my raging pain!
For round this heart the furies wave their brands,
And wring my entrails with their burning hands.
Now bending from the skies, O wife of Jove!
Enjoy the vengeance of thy injur'd love:
For fate, by me, the Thund'rer's guilt atones;
And, punish'd in her son, Alcmena groans:
The object of your hate shall soon expire;
Fix'd on my shoulders preys a net of fire:
Whom nor the toils nor dangers could subdue,
By false Eurystheus dictated from you;
Nor tyrants lawless, nor the monstrous brood,
Which haunts the desert or infests the flood,
Nor Greece, nor all the barb'rous climes that lie
Where Phœbus ever points his golden eye;
A woman hath o'erthrown! ye gods! I yield
To female arts, unconquer'd in the field.
My arms—alas! are these the same that bow'd
Antæus, and his giant force subdu'd?
That dragg'd Nemea's monster from his den;
And slew the dragon in his native fen?
Alas, alas! their mighty muscles fail,
While pains infernal ev'ry nerve assail:
Alas, alas! I feel in streams of woe
These eyes dissolv'd, before untaught to flow.
Awake my virtue, oft in dangers try'd,
Patient in toils, in deaths unterrify'd,

Rouse to my aid; nor let my labors past,
With fame atchiev'd, be blotted by the last:
Firm and unmov'd, the present shock endure;
Once triumph, and for ever rest secure.'

Our poet, though his genius be in many respects very original, has not disdained to imitate even modern poets. He has added to his heroic poem a dream, in the manner of Spenser, where the poet supposes himself to be introduced to Homer, who censures his poem in some particulars, and excuses it in others. This poem is indeed a species of apology for the Epigoniad, wrote in a very lively and elegant manner: it may be compared to a well-polished gem, of the purest water, and cut into the most beautiful form. Those who would judge of our author's talents for poetry, without perusing his larger work, may satisfy their curiosity, by running over this short poem. They will see the same force of imagination and harmony of numbers, which distinguish his longer performance; and may thence, with small application, receive a favourable impression of our author's genius.

# Appendix 3

## Hume's Essays: Dates of Composition and First Publication

| Essay | Composed | Published |
|---|---|---|
| Historical Essay on Chivalry and modern Honour | early 1730s | – |
| Of Essay-Writing | pre-July 1739? | 1742 |
| Of Moral Prejudices | pre-July 1739 | 1742 |
| Of Love and Marriage | pre-July 1739 | 1741 |
| Of the Middle Station of Life | pre-July 1739? | 1742 |
| The Epicurean | pre-Oct. 1739 | 1742 |
| The Stoic | pre-Oct. 1739 | 1742 |
| The Platonist | pre-Oct. 1739 | 1742 |
| The Sceptic | pre-Oct. 1739 | 1742 |
| Of the Delicacy of Taste and Passion | pre-1741 | 1741 |
| Of the Liberty of the Press | pre-1741 | 1741 |
| That Politics may be reduced to a Science | pre-1741 | 1741 |
| Of the First Principles of Government | pre-1741 | 1741 |
| Of the Independency of Parliament | pre-1741 | 1741 |
| Whether the British Government inclines more to Absolute Monarchy, or to a Republic | pre-1741 | 1741 |
| Of Parties in General | pre-1741 | 1741 |
| Of the Parties of Great Britain | pre-1741 | 1741 |
| Of Superstition and Enthusiasm | pre-1741 | 1741 |
| Of the Dignity or Meanness of Human Nature | pre-1741 | 1741 |

| | | |
|---|---|---|
| Of Civil Liberty | pre-1741 | 1741 |
| Of Impudence and Modesty | pre-1741 | 1741 |
| Of the Study of History | pre-1741 | 1741 |
| Of Avarice | pre-1741 | 1741 |
| Of Eloquence | post-Feb. 1741 | 1742 |
| A Character of Sir Robert Walpole | post-Feb. 1741 | 1742 |
| Of the Rise and Progress of the Arts and Sciences | pre-1742 | 1742 |
| Of Polygamy and Divorces | pre-1742 | 1742 |
| Of Simplicity and Refinement in Writing | pre-1742 | 1742 |
| Of the Original Contract | summer 1747 to Jan. 1748 | 1748 |
| Of Passive Obedience | summer 1747 | 1748 |
| Of the Protestant Succession | late 1747 to Jan. 1748 | 1752 |
| Of National Characters | 1747–1748 | 1748 |
| Of Tragedy | 1749–1751 | 1757 |
| Of the Populousness of Ancient Nations | pre-April 1750 to March 1751 | 1752 |
| Of the Balance of Trade | drafted by Oct. 1750 | 1752 |
| Of Refinement in the Arts | post-1750 | 1752 |
| Of Commerce | 1749–1751 | 1752 |
| Of Money | 1749–1751 | 1752 |
| Of Interest | 1749–1751 | 1752 |
| Of the Balance of Power | 1749–1751 | 1752 |
| Of Taxes | 1749–1751 | 1752 |
| Of Public Credit | 1749–1751 | 1752 |
| Of Some Remarkable Customs | 1749–1751 | 1752 |
| Idea of a Perfect Commonwealth | 1749–1751 | 1752 |
| Of Suicide | pre-1755 | 1777 |

| | | |
|---|---|---|
| Of the Immortality of the Soul | pre-1755 | 1777 |
| Of the Standard of Taste | 1756–1757 | 1757 |
| Of the Jealousy of Trade | spring–autumn, 1758 | 1760 |
| Of the Coalition of Parties | summer 1759 | 1760 |
| Of the Origin of Government | pre-1 March 1774 | 1777 |
| Of the Poems of Ossian | April 1773–November 1775 | – |

# Notes

# Essays, Moral, Political, and Literary:
## Part II

### I. OF COMMERCE

Published in: *1752a, 1752b, 1753, 1754, 1758, 1760, 1764, 1767, 1768, 1770, 1772, 1777a*
Significant revisions:
There is only one substantive revision of importance:
1) *1752a–1758* omit *'balance of trade'* (above, p. 4).
Copy text: *1777a*
Headnote:

In the 'Early Memoranda' Hume had commented on the surprising lack of interest in the history of trade and the economic principles of commerce – a lack of interest which he believed had lasted until at least the early sixteenth century: 'There is not a Word of Trade in all Matchiavel, which is strange considering that Florence rose only by Trade' (NLS MS 23159, item 14, p. 16; cf. Mossner, 'Memoranda', p. 508). Hume must later have realized that he had oversimplified in saying this, since in 'Of Refinement in the Arts' he summarizes a chapter of Machiavelli's *History of Florence* (I.xxxix) in which Machiavelli argues that the Florentine concentration on trade had undermined its military capacity (above, p. 20; cf. Machiavelli, *Works*, pp. 20–21).

The seventeenth century had seen an awakening interest in commerce, in the work for instance of Pufendorf (Hont, *Jealousy of Trade*, pp. 159–84); and in the following century Colbert had commissioned Pierre Huet to write his *Histoire du commerce et de la navigation des anciens* (1716). But, as Istvan Hont has shown, this interest in commerce was impure, particularly in France during the reign of Louis XIV, since it was stimulated by a desire to conscript the energies of commerce to state-building and the enhancement of the state's capacity to wage war: 'France was the worst offender in the corrupt application of reason of state to trade. Louis' absolutist regime welded war and trade into a single new policy. Colbert understood its logic well and gave it a pristinely clear expression. "Commerce," he wrote in a famous memorandum to the King in 1669, "is a perpetual and peaceable war of wit and energy (*d'esprit et d'industrie*) among all nations"' (Hont, *Jealousy of Trade*, p. 23). Presumably it was these contextual pressures which led Hume (in a move that may otherwise surprise the modern reader of an essay on commerce) to spend so much time towards the beginning of the essay discussing the apparent trade-off between a state's employing its manpower as 'tradesmen and manufacturers', rather than in 'fleets and armies' (above, p. 5).

Hume's argument was that this opposition between flourishing commerce and the physical power of the state was illusory, for 'according to the most natural course of things, industry and arts and trade encrease the power of the sovereign as well as the happiness of the subjects' (above, p. 8). He also noted that commerce was nourished in liberal or republican regimes, and then tended in its turn (and contrary to the ancient prejudice about prosperity undermining liberty) to reinforce and extend public freedom. Adam Smith would be particularly impressed by this insight: 'commerce and manufactures gradually introduced order and good government, and with them, the liberty and security of individuals ... This, though it has been the least observed, is by far the most important of all their effects. Mr. Hume is the only writer who, so far as I know, has hitherto taken notice of it' (Smith, *Wealth*, III.iv.4, vol. I, p. 412). This effect of commercial activity in strengthening and making more precise men's sense of justice had, however, been noted a few years beforehand by Montesquieu, in the *Esprit des Lois*, book XX, chapter 2: 'L'esprit de commerce produit dans les hommes un certain sentiment de justice exacte, opposé d'un coté au brigandage, & de l'autre à ces vertus morales qui font qu'on ne discute pas toûjours ses intérêts avec rigidité, & qu'on peut les négliger pour ceux des autres' (Montesquieu, *Esprit*, vol. II, p. 3).

This more humane and sociable conception of commerce had also been discussed by Montesquieu in books XX and XXI of the *Esprit des Lois*; and these new accounts of commerce were underpinned by the fuller and more accurate data on the flows of trade that had begun to be built up in Europe at the end of the seventeenth century. Rousseau had, with characteristic acuity, noted this change in the intellectual climate: 'Les anciens Politiques parloient sans cesse de mœurs & de vertu; les nôtres ne parlent que de commerce & d'argent' (Rousseau, *Discours*, p. 38). For comment, see Robertson, *Enlightenment*, pp. 521–8.

1. *every coffee-house conversation*] Note that in the withdrawn essay 'Of Essay-Writing' Hume had expressed the wish to be 'a Kind of Resident or Ambassador from the Dominions of Learning to those of Conversation' (above, p. 212): a comment that nods towards Addison's similar ambition, placed in the mouth of Mr. Spectator, 'to have it said of me, that I have brought Philosophy out of Closets and Libraries, Schools and Colleges, to

dwell in Clubs and Assemblies, at Tea-Tables and in Coffee-Houses' (Addison, *Spectator*, no. 10, 12 March 1711, vol. I, p. 44). This comment by Hume therefore signals a change of direction in the later essays, away from the Addisonian ease that he had initially imitated and towards longer, more demanding essays on difficult, sometimes quite technical, subjects that are (as Hume says) 'out of the common road', and which aim at instruction rather than mere entertainment (above, p. 4).

2. *the chief business of philosophers ... also the chief business of politicians*] This alignment of the political and the philosophical characters is striking given what Hume says in other essays about their incompatibility: for example, the remark in 'Of the Protestant Succession' that 'a philosopher ... is of neither party' (above, p. 191).

3. *a very variable being*] Possibly an echo of Montesquieu's description of man in the 'Preface' to the *Esprit des Lois* as 'cet Etre flexible, se pliant dans la Société aux pensées & aux impressions des autres' (Montesquieu, *Esprit*, vol. I, pp. ii–iii).

4. *The bulk ... so employed*] Hume here alludes broadly to what has become known as 'stadial theory', namely a natural history of the development of human society which posited four stages of development, each marked by a different mode of subsistence: 1) hunter-gathering; 2) pastoral nomadism; 3) agriculture; 4) commercial society. The classic study remains that of R. L. Meek, *Social Science and the Ignoble Savage* (Cambridge: Cambridge University Press, 1976).

5. *above a third*] Hume refers to a passage in chapter 22 of Jean-François Melon's *Essai politique sur le commerce*: 'Sur vingt parties d'habitans, il y en a environ seize de Laboureurs (*a*), deux d'Artisans, une d'Eglise, de Justice & de Militaire, & une de Négocians, de Financiers & de Bourgeois' (Melon, *Essai politique*, p. 289). Note (*a*) glosses 'Laboureurs' as 'Vignerons ou Cultivateurs'. Melon advances this statistic as part of his argument that the agricultural labourer should be the principal object of the legislator's concern: 'C'est ici où le Législateur doit prendre la Balance des hommes, car il est fait pour les rendre tous heureux, chacun selon sa profession, & le Laboureur mérite plus d'attention que les autres, parce qu'il est plus nombreux, & que son travail est plus essentiel; ... Négliger cette portion d'hommes à cause de leur prétenduë bassesse, est une injustice grossiere & dangereuse; car alors l'équilibre de cette Balance fondamentale des Hommes & du Commerce seroit rompue' (pp. 289–90); and therefore that, eventually, 'l'Agriculture doit être chez nous le premier objet du Commerce' (p. 343). Hume is committed to a different view, in which the progress of society eventually allows agriculture to recede in importance.

6. *chimerical*] i.e. fanciful or visionary.

7. *one to a hundred*] Hume gives no source, but the proportion is roughly deducible from the passage in Melon's *Essai politique* to which he has just

referred. It was an arresting statistic that would later catch Gibbon's eye: 'It has been calculated by the ablest politicians, that no state, without being soon exhausted, can maintain above the hundredth part of its members in arms and idleness' (Gibbon, *Decline and Fall*, vol. I, p. 127).

8. *against the LATINS*] 'Undique, non urbana tantum sed etiam agresti iuventute, decem legiones scriptae dicuntur quaternum milium et ducenorum peditum equitumque trecenorum, quem nunc novum exercitum, si qua externa vis ingruat, hae vires populi Romani, quas vix terrarum capit orbis, contractae in unum haud facile efficiant; adeo in quae laboramus sola crevimus, divitias luxuriamque'; 'They say that soldiers were enlisted everywhere, not in the City alone but in the country, and ten legions were embodied, each of four thousand two hundred foot and three hundred horse. The raising of a new army of this size to-day, in case of any aggression from abroad, could not easily be compassed by the concentration on one object of the existing resources of the Roman People, though the world hardly contains them; so strictly has our growth been limited to the only things for which we strive, – wealth and luxury' (Livy, *Ab Urbe Condita*, VII.xxv.8–9).

9. *ILLYRICUM*] The eastern shore of the Adriatic, comprising modern-day Croatia and Montenegro.

10. *lib. vii*] 'οὐδὲν γὰρ ἄλλο ἢ πόλει ἐκπεπολιορκημένη ἐῴκεσαν ὑποφευγούσῃ, καὶ ταύτῃ οὐ σμικρᾷ· μυριάδες γὰρ τοῦ ξύμπαντος ὄχλου οὐκ ἐλάσσους τεσσάρων ἅμα ἐπορεύοντο'; 'For indeed they looked like nothing else than a city in secret flight after a siege, and that no small city; for in the entire throng no fewer than four myriads were on the march together' (Thucydides, VII. lxxv.5).

11. *lib. vii*] 'κατὰ μὲν οὖν τὴν Σικελίαν ὁ Διονύσιος ἐκ μιᾶς τῆς τῶν Συρακοσίων πόλεως ἐξήγαγεν ἐπὶ τὰς στρατείας πεζῶν μὲν δώδεκα μυριάδας, ἱππεῖς δὲ μυρίους καὶ δισχιλίους, ναῦς δὲ μακρὰς ἐξ ἑνὸς λιμένος τετρακοσίας, ὧν ἦσαν ἔνιαι τετρήρεις καὶ πεντήρεις'; 'In Sicily, for instance, Dionysius led forth on his campaigns from the single city of the Syracusans one hundred and twenty thousand foot-soldiers and twelve thousand cavalry, and from a single harbour four hundred warships, some of which were quadriremes and quinqueremes' (Diodorus Siculus, II.v.6). Cf. 'Of the Populousness of Ancient Nations', above, p. 127.

12. *what peculiar laws*] The principal sources for the Lycurgan constitution of Sparta are Plutarch's *Life of Lycurgus*, his *Sayings of Spartans* and *Sayings of Spartan Women*, and Xenophon, *Constitution of the Lacedaimonians*.

13. *amor patriæ*] i.e. love of the fatherland.

14. *luxuriemque*] 'so strictly has our growth been limited to the only things for which we strive, – wealth and luxury' (Livy, *Ab Urbe Condita*, VII.xxv.9).

15. *A habit of indolence*] Hume makes a similar point in 'Of Taxes' (above, p. 72).

16. *He imposes . . . retrench . . . subsistence*] In 'Of Taxes' (above, p. 71) Hume will repeat the point that one of the natural responses to the imposition of

a tax on consumption is retrenchment (the other is to work harder). He thereby takes issue with an opposed argument, used by those such as Locke who held that all taxes ultimately resolve into a tax on land, because the imposition of taxes on consumption led to increases in wages, which were ultimately borne by the landowner. Hume is aware that, although the point of incidence of a tax is rarely where the burden of the tax will ultimately settle (at least in its entirety), nevertheless it is only in rare cases that the full impact of a tax can be passed on elsewhere. The more normal occurrence is that everybody accepts a measure of financial pain, while at the same time transferring what they can of it on to others.

17. *manufactures . . . store up so much labour*] cf. the entry in the 'Early Memoranda': 'A Pound of Steel when manufactur'd may become of 10.000 £ Value.' (NLS MS 23159, item 14, p. 9; cf. Mossner, 'Memoranda', p. 503).

18. *It would then . . . arts and luxury*] By showing that luxury was harmful to ancient societies because of their lack of manufactures, but is beneficial to modern societies because of the store of labour it represents, Hume offers an argument against the civic humanist assumption that luxury is, at all times and in all places, a solvent of virtue and prosperity.

19. *the advantage of foreign commerce*] Having addressed prejudices against luxury, Hume now moves on to offer arguments against the prevailing mercantilist doctrine of trade; see Harris, *Hume*, pp. 267–9.

20. *rests contented with its native commodities*] As Mandeville had argued in *The Fable of the Bees* when he depicted the economically depressing effects of frugality: 'As Pride and Luxury decrease, / So by degrees they leave the Seas. / Not Merchants now, but Companies / Remove whole Manufactories. / All Arts and Crafts neglected lie; / Content, the Bane of Industry, / Makes 'em admire their homely Store, / And neither seek nor covet more' (Mandeville, *Fable*, vol. I, pp. 34–5).

21. *richer and happier*] In the *Esprit des Lois*, book XX, chapter 4, Montesquieu had also noted the different kinds of commercial activity characteristic of monarchies and republics: 'Le Commerce a du repport avec la Constitution. Dans le Gouvernement d'un seul il est fondé sur le Luxe, & son objet unique est de procurer à la Nation qui le fait, tout ce qui peut servir à son orgueil, à ses délices & à ses fantaisies. Dans le Gouvernement de plusieurs, il est ordinairement fondé sur l'économie' (Montesquieu, *Esprit*, vol. II, pp. 4–5).

22. *If we consult history . . . domestic luxury*] In *Wealth of Nations*, III.iii.20, Adam Smith would echo this observation: 'In the modern history of Europe, their [manufactures'] extension and improvement have generally been posterior to those which were the offspring of foreign commerce' (Smith, *Wealth*, vol. I, p. 410). Hume would repeat the point in 'Of the Jealousy of Trade', where improvements in manufactures are traced to 'our imitation of foreigners' (above, p. 60).

23. *CHINA ... territories*] European estimates of the aptitude for commerce among the Chinese had declined during the early eighteenth century. Louis le Comte, writing towards the end of the seventeenth century, had depicted a nation addicted to trade: 'Enfin, leur dixiéme maxime est de donner un grand cours au commerce par tout l'Empire ... Ce grand commerce unit entre eux tous ces peuples, & porte l'abondance dans toutes les villes' (Le Comte, *Memoires*, vol. II, pp. 73 and 75). At the same time, Le Comte had noted a disposition towards sharp practice among the Chinese, which contaminated their commercial practice: 'L'injustice & la tromperie sont à la Chine si ordinaires ... qu'il y en a peu qui se soient enrichis par une autre voye. Un marchand vend toûjours tout le plus cher qu'il luy est possible, & il ne donne de bonnes marchandises que quand il ne peut se défaire des mauvaises. L'adresse, qui est particuliere à cette nation, semble luy donner droit de falsifier toutes choses' (ibid., pp. 249–50). Jean-Baptiste du Halde, writing in Paris early during the next century and compiling his *Description* from the reports of those who had travelled to China, devoted a chapter to the 'Commerce des Chinois' (Du Halde, *Description*, vol. II, pp. 169–73). He had praised Chinese commerce as 'très-florissant' (ibid., p. 169), but he had also noted (drawing silently on Le Comte) that it was almost entirely internal: 'Le commerce qui se fait dans l'intérieur de la Chine est si grand, que celui de l'Europe entiere ne doit pas lui être comparé. Les Provinces sont comme autant de Roïaumes, qui se communiquent les unes aux autres ce qu'elles ont de propre; & c'est ce qui unit entr'eux tous ces peuples, & qui porte l'abondance dans toutes les Villes' (ibid., p. 169); however, 'Le commerce étant aussi abondant, ... dans toutes les Provinces de la Chine; il n'est pas surprenant que ses Habitans se mettent si peu en peine de commercer au dehors, sur-tout quand on fait attention au mépris naturel qu'ils ont pour toutes les Nations Etrangeres' (ibid., p. 170). More recently, Jean-François Melon had noted the insignificance and backwardness of Chinese commerce: 'Très ignorans dans le Commerce, ils y sont fripons par principe' (Melon, *Essai politique*, p. 389). Cf. also Ferguson, *Civil Society*, p. 138, and esp. p. 206: 'After a history of some thousand years employed in manufacture and commerce, the inhabitants of China are still the most laborious and industrious of any people on the surface of the earth.'

24. *Lord BACON ... alike*] 'Let States that aime at *Greatnesse*, take heed how their *Nobility* and *Gentlemen*, doe multiply too fast. For that maketh the Common Subject, grow to be a Peasant, and Base Swaine, driven out of Heart, and in effect but the *Gentlemans* Labourer. Even as you may see in Coppice Woods; *If you leaue your staddles too thick, you shall neuer haue cleane Underwood, but Shrubs and Bushes.* So in Countries, if the *Gentlemen* be too many, the *Commons* will be base; And you will bring it to that, that not the hundred poll, will be fit for an Helmet: Especially as to the *Infantery*, which is the Nerve of an Army: And so there will be Great

Population, and Little Strength. This, which I speake of, hath been no where better seen, then by comparing of *England* and *France*; whereof *England*, though farre lesse in Territory and Population, hath been (neverthelesse) an Overmatch; In regard, the *Middle People* of *England*, make good Souldiers, which the *Peasants* of *France* doe not. And herein, the device of King *Henry* the Seventh, (whereof I have spoken largely in the *History of his Life*) was Profound, and Admirable; In making Farmes, and houses of Husbandry, of a Standard; That is, maintained with such a Proportion of Land unto them, as may breed a Subject, to live in Convenient Plenty, and no Servile Condition; And to keepe the Plough in the Hands of the Owners, and not meere Hirelings' (Bacon, *Essayes*, 'Of the True Greatnesse of Kingdomes and Estates', pp. 92–3).

25. *It may seem ... this paradox*] cf. the entry in the 'Early Memoranda': 'The People commonly live poorest in Countrys, which have the richest natural Soil' (NLS MS 23159, item 14, p. 19; cf. Mossner, 'Memoranda', p. 510). Hume will make a similar observation in 'Of Taxes', using a quotation from Sir William Temple about Ireland to corroborate the point (above, p. 72).

26. *any police*] See above, vol. 1, p. 285, n. 36

27. *Curis ... corda*] 'sharpening men's wits by cares' (Virgil, *Georgics*, I.123). Montesquieu had made a similar point about the beneficial effect that natural hardship can have on men's commercial activity: 'Il y a deux sortes de Peuples pauvres; ceux que la dureté du Gouvernement a rendu tels, & ces gens-là sont incapables de presqu'aucune vertu, parce que leur pauvreté fait une partie de leur servitude; les autres ne sont pauvres que parce qu'ils ont dédaigné, ou parce qu'ils n'ont pas connu les commodités de la vie; & ceux-ci peuvent faire de grandes choses, parce que cette pauvreté fait une partie de leur liberté' (*Esprit des Lois*, XX.iii; Montesquieu, *Esprit*, vol. II, p. 4: cf. also ibid., XX.v; vol. II, p. 7).

28. *lib. ii*] 'Equidem etiam illud animadverto, quod, qui proprio nomine perduellis esset, is hostis vocaretur, lenitate verbi rei tristitiam mitigatam. Hostis enim apud maiores nostros is dicebatur, quem nunc peregrinum dicimus'; 'This also I observe – that he who would properly have been called "a fighting enemy" (*perduellis*) was called "a guest" (*hostis*), thus relieving the ugliness of the fact by a softened expression; for "enemy" (*hostis*) meant to our ancestors what we now call "stranger" (*peregrinus*)' (Cicero, *De Officiis*, I.xii).

29. *POLYBIUS, lib. iii*] Polybius devotes a section of Book III (xxii–xxv) to a detailed consideration of the early treaties between Rome and Carthage, so that 'ἀλλ' ἦ τις ὁμολογουμένη θεωρία τῶν ἀπὸ τῆς ἀρχῆς ὑπαρξάντων δικαίων Ῥωμαίοις καὶ Καρχηδονίοις πρὸς ἀλλήλους ἕως εἰς τοὺς καθ' ἡμᾶς καιρούς', 'there may be some survey generally recognized as accurate of the treaties between Rome and Carthage up to our own time' (Polybius, III.xxi).

30. *SALLEE and ALGERINE rovers*] Pirates who infested the Barbary coast of North Africa in the seventeenth and eighteenth centuries.

## 2. OF REFINEMENT IN THE ARTS

Published in: *1752a, 1752b, 1753, 1754, 1758, 1760, 1764, 1767, 1768, 1770, 1772, 1777a*

Significant revisions:

1) In *1752a–1758* this essay is entitled 'Of Luxury'.

2) *1752a–1753* read 'the *Grecian* and *Asiatic* luxury' (*1752a*, p. 32), not 'the ASIATIC luxury' (above, p. 20).

3) *1752a–1758* read 'Luxury or refinement on pleasure has . . .' (*1752a*, p. 33; cf. above, p. 20).

4) *1752a–1760* read 'the *Gothic* barons' (*1752a*, p. 35; cf. above, p. 21).

5) *1768* inserts the following additional paragraph, immediately preceding that beginning 'I thought this reasoning . . .' (above, p. 24):

'Prodigality is not to be confounded with a refinement in the arts. It even appears, that that vice is much less frequent in the cultivated ages. Industry and gain beget this frugality, among the lower and middle ranks of men; and in all the busy professions. Men of high rank, indeed, it may be pretended, are more allured by the pleasures, which become more frequent. But idleness is the great source of prodigality at all times; and there are pleasures and vanities in every age, which allure men equally when they are unacquainted with better enjoyments. Not to mention, that the high interest, payed in rude times, quickly consumes the fortunes of the landed gentry, and multiplies their necessities.' (*1768*, p. 315).

This paragraph was withdrawn in *1770* and subsequent editions.

Copy text: *1777a*

Headnote:

Ever since Sallust had composed his analyses of the decline of the Roman republic during the first century BC, analyses in which the agent of moral and political corruption had been identified as the wealth that had flowed into Rome as a result of her conquests, luxury had been condemned as the solvent of both the health of a state and the virtue of her citizens. As Hume says in the *Enquiry Concerning the Principles of Morals*, II, 'Of Benevolence': 'Luxury, or a refinement on the pleasures and conveniencies of life, had long been supposed the source of every corruption in government, and the immediate cause of faction, sedition, civil wars, and the total loss of liberty. It was, therefore, universally regarded as a vice, and was an object of declamation to all satirists, and severe moralists. Those, who prove, or attempt to prove, that such refinements rather tend to the encrease of industry, civility, and arts, regulate anew our *moral* as well as *political* sentiments, and represent, as laudable and innocent, what had formerly been regarded as pernicious or blameable' (*ECPM*, pp. 11–12). Once peoples and societies had progressed, luxury (or, to use the less vulnerable term Hume eventually preferred, 'refinement') was no longer harmful, though it might remain so to more primitive peoples, as Hume's proxy in 'A Dialogue', Palamedes, read-ily admits: 'A degree of luxury may be ruinous and pernicious in a native of SWITZERLAND, which only fosters the arts, and encourages industry in a FRENCHMAN or ENGLISHMAN. We are not, therefore, to expect, either the same sentiments, or the same laws in BERNE, which prevail in LONDON or PARIS' (*ECPM*, p. 119).

The most direct overturning of the traditional association between luxury, political decline and moral corruption had been attempted by Ber-nard Mandeville. In *The Fable of the Bees* (first published as a poem, 'The Grumbling Hive', in 1704; subsequently expanded with an extensive com-mentary in 1714 as *The Fable of the Bees*) Mandeville had advanced the view that the prosperity of society depended on the indulgence of human vices, including the appetite for luxury: hence the book's famous subtitle, 'Private Vices, Publick Benefits'. In remark 'L', Mandeville noted the trad-itional view about the perniciousness of luxury: 'It is a receiv'd Notion, that Luxury is as destructive to the Wealth of the whole Body Politic, as it is to that of every individual Person who is guilty of it, and that a National Fru-gality enriches a Country in the same manner as that which is less general increases the Estates of private Families. I confess, that tho' I have found Men of much better Understanding than my self of this Opinion, I cannot help dissenting from them in this Point' (Mandeville, *Fable*, vol. I, pp. 108–9). Mandeville's resistance to this customary view had two elements. The first, economic, element was a denial that a taste for luxury necessarily led to a ruinous balance of trade (although there was a strong mercantilist cast to Mandeville's economic thought: he urged politicians to 'keep a watchful Eye over the Balance of Trade in general, and never suffer that all the For-eign Commodities together, that are imported in one Year, shall exceed in Value what of their own Growth or Manufacture is in the same exported to others' [Mandeville, *Fable*, vol. I, p. 116]). The second, moral, element was a denial that a taste for luxury, which must of necessity be confined to a small fraction of society, posed any grave threat to society as a whole: 'since I have seen something of the World, the Consequences of Luxury to a Nation seem not so dreadful to me as they did. As long as Men have the same Appetites, the same Vices will remain. In all large Societies, some will love Whoring and others Drinking. The Lustful that can get no handsome clean Women, will content themselves with dirty Drabs; and those that cannot purchase true *Hermitage* or *Pontack*, will be glad of more ordinary *French* Claret' (Mandeville, *Fable*, vol. I, p. 118). The upshot was Mandeville's advice that men should abandon their hypocritical denunciations of luxury unless they were also willing to live in primitive austerity: 'Pride and Luxury are the great Promoters of Trade', and if they were to be suppressed, 'Trade would in a great Measure decay'; and 'Great Wealth and Foreign Treasure will ever scorn to come among Men, unless you'll admit their inseparable

Companions, Avarice and Luxury' (Mandeville, *Fable*, vol. I, pp. 124 and 185). This frank encouragement on Mandeville's part to accept the reality of human nature, with all its disorderly appetites and vices, and furthermore to recognize that the well-being of society in fact to a large degree depended on the indulgence of those appetites and vices, led to the widespread denunciation of *The Fable of the Bees* as an encouragement to immorality. Hume's view of luxury is as positive as was that of Mandeville; but he seeks to pare away from the defence of luxury that outspoken embracing of personal vice which had made *The Fable of the Bees* so notorious. (On the significance of Mandeville for Hume's early intellectual development, see Harris, *Hume*, pp. 53–63.) A withdrawal from the automatic censure of luxury was accordingly present in the advanced opinion of Hume's day, although it was far from ubiquitous. For example, Jean-François Melon had included in his *Essai politique sur le commerce* (Paris, 1736) a lengthy chapter defending luxury from what he called 'un esprit chagrin & envieux' (Melon, *Essai politique*, pp. 105–29; quotation on pp. 105–6); albeit Melon's defence of luxury rested on grounds more Mandevillean than Hume would have found comfortable.

However, this whole subject had been electrified in the years immediately preceding the publication of Hume's essay by Rousseau's *Discours* (Geneva, 1750), composed in response to the prize question posed by the Académie de Dijon, 'Si le rétablissement des Sciences & des Arts a contribué à épurer les Mœurs'. Rousseau's answer had been resoundingly negative. According to Rousseau, the arts and sciences were what reconciled men to the disguised slavery of modern society: 'Tandis que le Gouvernement & les Loix pourvoient à la sûreté & au bien-être des hommes assembles; les Sciences, les Lettres & les Arts, moins despotiques & plus puissans peut-être, étendent des guirlandes de fleurs sur les chaînes de fer dont ils sont chargés, étouffent en eux le sentiment de cette liberté originelle pour laquelle ils sembloient être nés, leur font aimer leur esclavage & en forment ce qu'on appelle des Peuples policés. Le besoin éleva les Trônes; les Sciences & les Arts les ont affermis. Puissances de la Terre, aimez les talens, & protégez ceux qui les cultivent. Peuples policés, cultivez-les: Heureux esclaves, vous leur devez ce goût délicat & fin dont vous vous piquez; cette douceur de caractere & cette urbanité de mœurs qui rendent parmi vous le commerce si liant & si facile; en un mot, les apparences de toutes les vertus sans en avoir aucune' (pp. 5–7). The outcome, according to Rousseau, had been predictable and dire: 'nos ames se sont corrompuës à mesure que nos Sciences & nos Arts se sont avancés à la perfection' (p. 13). Hume's essay, however, does not engage directly and explicitly with Rousseau's *Discours*, but follows a diametrically opposite tack.

Duncan Forbes described this essay as 'an abridged version' of what Hume would explore in greater detail in his *History of England*, namely the connected development of law and liberty, and the rise of commerce, arts, and a middling order of society (Forbes, *Politics*, pp. 296–7).

For commentary on the general topic of luxury, see John Sekora, *Luxury: The Concept in Western Thought, Eden to Smollett* (Baltimore, MD: The Johns Hopkins University Press, 1977).

1. *bounds between the virtue and the vice*] Hume here recapitulates an observation in the *Treatise of Human Nature*, III.ii.6: 'all kinds of vice and virtue run insensibly into each other, and may approach by such imperceptible degrees as will make it very difficult, if not absolutely impossible, to determine when the one ends, and the other begins' (*THN*, p. 339).

2. *I have, indeed . . . a gratification*] Bernard of Clairvaux is supposed out of a misplaced asceticism to have refrained from looking at the beauty of Lake Geneva from the window of his cell (*Opera S. Bernardi*, ed. Mabillon, 6 vols [Venice, 1750], vol. VI, pp. 1232 and 1383). Gibbon would also be struck by this instance of pointless mortification (Gibbon, *Decline and Fall*, vol. III, p. 625, n. 30). The italicized phrase '*covenant with his eyes*' is biblical: see Job 31:1.

3. *subject*] Something affording matter for action of a specified kind; here, a synonym for wealth (*OED*, 'subject', *n.*, 14 a, citing this passage).

4. *men of libertine principles . . . to society*] An allusion to the provocative theories of Mandeville. Adam Smith would take a similar view: see 'Of licentious Systems', *Theory of Moral Sentiments*, VII.ii.4 (Smith, *Theory*, pp. 306–14).

5. *We cannot reasonably expect . . . are neglected*] An insight which would make a great impression on the Venetian historian of trade Francesco Mengotti (1749–1830) (Mengotti, *Commerce*, p. 18 and fn. 'n'). Woollen cloth had been one of the principal manufactures of England since the late medieval period.

6. *One may safely . . . of cookery*] The Tartars are the nomads of the Eurasian steppes. Their diet was at this time the object of much puzzled Western attention. Jean-Baptiste du Halde had deplored its exclusively carnal nature: 'These *Mongols* live on Milk and the Flesh of their Cattle, which they eat almost raw' (Jean-Baptiste du Halde, *A Description of the Empire of China and Chinese-Tartary*, 2 vols [London, 1738], vol. II, p. 277). John Bell, recalling travels across Eurasia between 1715 and 1721, recorded the following: 'There are still here [in Kassimova] a few MAHOMETAN TARTARS who are allowed the free exercise of their religion, and have a small oratory. I accompanied our interpreter to visit one of them, an old acquaintance of his. He was a very decent man; we saw a horse newly killed, which they intended to eat. They prefer this kind of food to beef, and invited us to share their repast, which we declined, pretending we had not time' (Bell, *Travels*, vol. I, p. 15; cf. p. 217). Gibbon would remark that the Tartars or Scythians (terms he regarded as synonymous) 'indifferently feed on the flesh of those

animals that have been killed for the table, or have died of disease. Horse-flesh, which in every age and country has been proscribed by the civilised nations of Europe and Asia, they devour with peculiar greediness; and this singular taste facilitates the success of their military operations' (Gibbon, *Decline and Fall*, vol. I, p. 1027). The French practice of eating horse meat would begin only in the next century. The first *boucherie chevaline* opened in Nancy in 1866, at the joint instigation of the zoologist and teratologist Isidore Geoffroy Saint-Hilaire (1805–1861) and the hippophagist Émile Decroix (1821–1901).

7. *reproached him*] 'Εἰ δὲ δεῖ μηδὲ τὰ μικρὰ τῶν ἠθῶν σημεῖα παραλιπεῖν ὥσπερ εἰκόνα ψυχῆς ὑπογραφομένους, λέγεται, τότε πολλὴν ἅμιλλαν καὶ μέγαν ἀγῶνα πρὸς τὸν Κάτωνα τοῦ Καίσαρος ἔχοντος καὶ τῆς βουλῆς εἰς ἐκείνους ἀνηρτημένης, δελτάριόν τι μικρὸν ἔξωθεν εἰσκομισθῆναι τῷ Καίσαρι. τοῦ δὲ Κάτωνος εἰς ὑποψίαν ἄγοντος τὸ πρᾶγμα καὶ διαβάλλοντος εἶναί τινας τοὺς κινουμένους, καὶ κελεύοντος ἀναγινώσκειν τὰ γεγραμμένα, τὸν Καίσαρα τῷ Κάτωνι προσδοῦναι τὸ δελτάριον ἐγγὺς ἑστῶτι. τὸν δὲ ἀναγνόντα Σερβιλίας τῆς ἀδελφῆς ἐπιστόλιον ἀκόλαστον πρὸς τὸν Καίσαρα γεγραμμένον, ἐρώσης καὶ διεφθαρμένης ὑπ᾽ αὐτοῦ, προσρῖψαί τε τῷ Καίσαρι καὶ εἰπεῖν, "Κράτει, μέθυσε", καὶ πάλιν οὕτως ἐπὶ τὸν ἐξ ἀρχῆς λόγον τραπέσθαι'; 'Now, since we must not pass over even the slight tokens of character when we are delineating as it were a likeness of the soul, the story goes that on this occasion, when Caesar was eagerly engaged in a great struggle with Cato and the attention of the senate was fixed upon the two men, a little note was brought in from outside to Caesar. Cato tried to fix suspicion upon the matter and alleged that it had something to do with the conspiracy, and bade him read the writing aloud. Then Caesar handed the note to Cato, who stood near him. But when Cato had read the note, which was an unchaste letter from his sister Servilia to Caesar, with whom she was passionately and guiltily in love, he threw it to Caesar, saying, "Take it, thou sot", and then resumed his speech' (Plutarch, *Cato the Younger*, XXIV.1–2).

8. *storehouse of labour . . . public service*] An echo of an observation Hume has already made in 'Of Commerce': 'Trade and industry are really nothing but a stock of labour, which, in times of peace and tranquillity, is employed to the ease and satisfaction of individuals; but in the exigencies of state, may, in part, be turned to public advantage' (above, p. 10).

9. GUICCIARDIN . . . *so great an effort*] Guicciardini emphasizes the financial overreach of Charles's expedition into Italy: 'For *Charles* . . . could neither be dissuaded from going personally into *Italy* by the Intreaties of his whole Kingdom, nor retarded by the Want of Money; there not being, at that Time, a Sufficiency for the present Exigencies, without pawning, and that for no considerable Sum, certain Jewels he had borrowed of the Duke of *Savoy*, the Marchioness of *Montferrato*, and some other Noblemen of his own King-dom. All the Money of the Finances, and what *Lodovico* had left him, had partly been expended in fitting out his Fleet, on which great Dependance had

been laid, and the rest inconsiderately dissipated at *Lyons* among his Favourites. Nor could he, easily, procure a fresh Supply: For, in those Days, Princes were not accustomed to extort Money from their Subjects, as they have since been taught to do, by immoderate Avarice and Ambition, without any Regard to human and divine Laws' (Guicciardini, *History*, vol. I, pp. 133–4).

10. *late king of FRANCE*] i.e. Louis XIV, who had died in 1715.

11. *400,000 men*] cf. the entry in the 'Early Memoranda': 'Every French Seaman and Soldier costs 15 Sous a day upon [an *inserted above the line*] Averrage; every ~~English~~ Soldier in English Pay costs a Shilling. ~~The~~ In ~~Kings~~ Williams War the French had 600.000 Men in Pay by Sea & Land' (NLS MS 23159, item 14, p. 11; cf. Mossner, 'Memoranda', p. 504). The inscription was on the pedestal of the equestrian statue of Louis XIV that was taken down in 1792. Gibbon was perhaps recalling this passage when he wrote, referring to the military exertions of the reign of Louis XIV, that 'France still feels that extraordinary effort' (Gibbon, *Decline and Fall*, vol. I, p. 47, n. 69). In chapter 27 of the *Siècle de Louis XIV* Voltaire had estimated the eventual size of Louis's army at four hundred and fifty thousand (Voltaire, *Siècle*, vol. II, pp. 128–9).

12. *MAZARINE's death*] Cardinal Mazarin had died in March 1661. Thereafter Louis XIV ruled without any designated 'first minister', launching France on the course of territorial expansion which would lead her neighbours to conclude that the king aimed at universal monarchy. These fears led to three major continental wars: the Franco-Dutch War (1672–8), the War of the Grand Alliance (1689–97), and the War of the Spanish Succession (1701–14). Hume's 'near thirty years' is accurate, since the total duration of these three wars comes to twenty-seven years.

13. *police*] See above, vol. 1, p. 285, n. 36.

14. *bias*] set course or inclination (*OED*, 'bias', *n.*, 4, citing this passage). Cf. Hume's earlier use of this term in a political context in the concluding sentence of 'Of the Parties of Great Britain' (above, vol. 1, p. 65).

15. *anger . . . whetstone of courage*] Proverbial since classical times, when Cicero characterized it as a maxim of the Peripatetics: 'Primum multis verbis iracundiam laudant: cotem fortitudinis esse dicunt'; 'In the first place they praise irascibility at great length; they name it the whetstone of bravery' (*Tusculan Disputations*, IV.xix). It was common in English literature of the earlier seventeenth century: 'Be this the whetstone of your sword. Let grief / Convert to anger; blunt not the heart, enrage it' (*Macbeth*, IV.iii.228–9). Cf. also George Hakewill, *King Davids Vow for Reformation of Himselfe* (1621), p. 125: 'just anger being the whetstone of courage'. The phrase endured as current into the earlier eighteenth century, but is found less frequently: e.g. Isaac Mauduit, *A Sermon on the Coronation of . . . Queen Anna* (1702), p. 40: 'Anger is the Whetstone of Strength'; cf. also William Sheridan, *Several Discourses* (1706), p. 237, and John Mackqueen, *Two Essays* (1711), p. 13. The phrase also now began to be burlesqued: see Thomas Randolph, *The*

*Muses Looking Glass; (or, The Stage Re-View'd.) A Comedy* (1706), p. 42. By the time Hume was writing the proverb was in danger of becoming a ludicrous piece of rodomontade.

16. *DATAMES*] In his life of Datames, Cornelius Nepos had paid tribute to his strategic intelligence: 'Quo neque acutius ullius imperatoris cogitatum neque celerius factum usquam legimus'; 'Never have I read anywhere of a cleverer stratagem of any commander, or one which was more speedily executed' ('Datames', VI.viii). Cf. Frontinus, *Stratagems*, II.ix.

17. *PYRRHUS*] According to Plutarch, Pyrrhus made this remark before the battle of Heraclea: 'πυθόμενος δὲ τοὺς Ῥωμαίους ἐγγὺς εἶναι καὶ πέραν τοῦ Σίριος ποταμοῦ καταστρατοπεδεύειν, προσίππευσε τῷ ποταμῷ θέας ἕνεκα· καὶ κατιδὼν τάξιν τε καὶ φυλακὰς καὶ κόσμον αὐτῶν καὶ τὸ σχῆμα τῆς στρατοπεδείας ἐθαύμασε, καὶ τῶν φίλων προσαγορεύσας τὸν ἐγγυτάτω, "Τάξις μέν," εἶπεν, "ὦ Μεγάκλεις, αὕτη τῶν βαρβάρων οὐ βάρβαρος, τὸ δὲ ἔργον εἰσόμεθα"'; 'When he learned that the Romans were near and lay encamped on the further side of the river Siris, he rode up to the river to get a view of them; and when he had observed their discipline, the appointment of their watches, their order, and the general arrangement of their camp, he was amazed, and said to the friend who was nearest him: "The discipline of these Barbarians is not barbarous; but the result will show us what it amounts to"' (Plutarch, *Life of Pyrrhus*, XVI.iv–v). This anecdote had also caught the attention of Montaigne: 'Quand le Roy Pyrrhus passa en Italie, après qu'il eut reconnu l'ordonnance de l'armée que les Romains luy envoyoient au devant: "Je ne sçay, dit-il, quels barbares sont ceux-ci (car les Grecs appelloyent ainsi toutes les nations estrangieres), mais la disposition de cette armée que je voy n'est aucunement barbare"' (Montaigne, 'Des Cannibales', in Montaigne, *Œuvres*, p. 200).

18. *the modern ITALIANS … martial spirit*] Machiavelli had attributed the loss of martial vigour among the modern Italians to the ruinous practice of employing mercenaries (*The Prince*, chapter 12). In *Liberty*, Thomson had contrasted the heroism of the ancient Romans with the depravity of their modern descendants: 'The People mark, / Matchless, while fir'd by me; to Public Good / Inexorably firm, just, generous, brave, / Afraid of nothing but unworthy Life, / Elate with Glory, an Heroic Soul / Known to the Vulgar Breast: behold them now / A thin despairing Number, all-subdu'd, / The Slaves of Slaves, by Superstition fool'd, / By Vice unman'd and a licentious Rule, / In Guile ingenious, and in Murder brave' (Part I, ll. 216–25).

19. *The ITALIAN historians*] Hume here is summarizing the final chapter of book I of Machiavelli's *History of Florence*: 'Among the principal States, Queen *Giovanna* held the Kingdom of *Naples*, *La Marca*, the *Patrimony*, and *Romagna*. Part of their Towns belong'd to the Church, part to their particular Governours, or others which had Usurp'd them: as *Ferrara*, *Modeno*, *Reggio*, to the Family of the *Esti*, *Faenzi* to the *Manfredi*, *Imola* to the *Alidosi*, *Furli* to the *Ordelassi*, *Rimini* and *Pesaro* to the *Malatesti*, and *Camerino* to the

House *Varana*. *Lombardy* was divided, part under Duke *Philip*, and part under the *Venetian*. All the rest who had any soveraignty or principality in those parts, being extinct, except only the House of *Gonzagua*, which govern'd in *Mantua* at that time. Of *Tuscany* the greatest part was under the Dominion of the *Florentine*; *Lucca* only, and *Siena* liv'd free under their own Laws: *Lucca* under the *Guinigi*, and *Siena* of it self. The *Genoueses*, being free sometimes, sometimes under the authority of the *French*, and sometimes of the *Visconti*; they lived without any great reputation, and were reckon'd among the meaner and most inconsiderable states of that Countrey. Their principal Potentates were not themselves in Command, but their Armies managed by their Generals. Duke *Philip* confin'd himself to his Chamber, and not being to be seen, his Wars were manag'd by Commissioners. The *Venetians* altering their Scene, and making War by Land, they disbarqued that Army which had made them so glorious by Sea; and according to the Custom of their Countrey, gave the Command of it to other people. The Pope, being a Religious person, and *Giovanna* Queen of *Naples* a Woman, were not so proper to Command in person, and therefore did that by necessity which others did by indiscretion. The *Florentines* were under the same necessity, for their frequent divisions having exhausted their Nobility, and the Government of the City remaining in the hands of such as were bred up to Merchandize; in their Wars they were forc'd to follow the fortune and direction of strangers: So that the Armies all *Italy* over, were in the hands of the smaller Princes, or such as had no Soveraignty at all. Those smaller Princes embracing those Commands, not from any impulse or stimulation of Glory, but to live plentifully and safe ... By this means, the Art of War became so mean and unserviceable, every little Officer that had but the least spark of Experience could have easily corrected it' (Machiavelli, *Works*, pp. 20–21).

20. *War then ... least bloodshed*] The bloodlessness of battles fought by mercenaries was noted with contempt by Machiavelli in chapter 12 of *The Prince*: 'they [the Condottieri, or mercenary commanders] endeavour'd with all possible industry to prevent trouble or fear either to themselves or their Souldiers, and their way was by killing no body in fight, only taking one another Prisoners, and dismissing them afterwards without either prejudice or ransom. When they were in Leaguer before a Town, they shot not rudely amongst them in the night, nor did they in the Town disturb them with any sallies in their Camp; no approaches or intrenchments were made at unseasonable hours, and nothing of lying in the field when Winter came on; and all these things did not happen by negligence in their Officers, but were part of their discipline, and introduc'd (as is said before) to ease the poor Souldier both of labour and danger, by which practices they have brought *Italy* both into slavery, and contempt' (Machiavelli, *Works*, p. 216).

21. *All the LATIN classics*] An interesting point of limited convergence between Hume and Hobbes, who had also deplored the influence exerted by classical

republican texts over the political opinions of the English youth who had studied them. According to Hobbes, in the colleges of Oxford and Cambridge the gentry had been made to read the republican political theory of ancient Greece and Rome, 'the democratical principles of Aristotle and Cicero'; and from them they had derived mistaken ideas of liberty and government (Hobbes, *Behemoth*, p. 43: cf. pp. 155 and 158). The result was that a frequent cause of rebellion had been 'the Reading of the books of Policy, and Histories of the antient Greeks, and Romans': 'And by reading of these Greek, and Latine Authors, men from their childhood have gotten a habit (under a false shew of Liberty,) of favouring tumults, and of licentious controlling the actions of their Soveraigns; and again of controlling those controllers, with the effusion of so much blood; as I think I may truly say, there was never any thing so deerly bought, as these Western parts have bought the learning of the Greek and Latine tongues' (Hobbes, *Leviathan*, chapters 29 and 21, pp. 225 and 150).

22. *taste for painting . . . drinking*] 'Ibi primum insuevit exercitus populi Romani amare, potare; signa, tabulas pictas, vasa caelata mirari; ea privatim et publice rapere, delubra spoliare, sacra profanaque omnia polluere'; 'There [in Asia under Lucius Sulla] it was that an army of the Roman people first became accustomed to indulge in women and wine; to admire statues, paintings, and chased vessels; to steal them from private houses and public places; to pillage shrines, and to desecrate everything, both sacred and profane' (Sallust, *Bellum Catilinam*, XI.vi).

23. *And so popular . . . correctness*] Hume here summarizes the hostile verdicts on Sallust that have come down to us from antiquity. Asinius Pollio mocked Sallust for his affected diction; Quintilian criticized him for his exordiums and digressions (*Institutio Oratoria*, III.viii.9); Cicero (although now the attribution is considered uncertain) composed a speech *In Sallustium*, which attacks Sallust for corruption. More recently Gerardus Vossius had renewed the charge of corruption in his *De Historicis Latinis* (1627).

24. *what really proceeded from an ill modelled government*] A further expression of Hume's distancing of himself from the virtue politics of Renaissance republicanism, and of his conviction that political institutions are of far greater influence over the health or disorder of a society than the morality of its citizens.

25. *champagne and ortolans*] Ortolans are a kind of bunting, formerly regarded as a delicacy, and hence a byword for luxury. Hume may be recalling Mandeville, who in 'The Grumbling Hive', the poem prefacing his *Fable of the Bees*, notes how, once the bees have abandoned their vices, 'No Vintner's Jilt in all the Hive / Could wear now Cloth of Gold, and thrive; / Nor *Torcol* such vast Sums advance, / For *Burgundy* and *Ortelans*' (Mandeville, *Fable*, vol. I, p. 33). Cf. also John Locke's fantasy of the son of a rich farmer, 'a fashionable

young Gentleman, that cannot Dine without *Champane* and *Burgundy*, nor Sleep but in a Damask Bed' (Locke, *Considerations*, p. 26).

26. *What has chiefly ... knowledge and refinement*] The preceding two paragraphs amount to an important statement of Hume's dissociation of himself from republican or civic humanist analyses of decline, and are expressive of the distance he wishes to put between himself and the 'virtue politics' associated typically with Machiavelli (notwithstanding the extensive use he has just made of Machiavelli). Furthermore, in the phrase 'ill modelled government', Hume expresses his conviction that political institutions and constitutional design are of much greater importance than the moral health of individual citizens.

27. *Of all ... acquainted*] cf. Montesquieu's comments on the economic plight of Poland: 'La Pologne ... n'a presqu'aucune des choses que nous appellons les effets mobiliers de l'univers, si-ce-n'est le bled de ses terres. Quelques Seigneurs possèdent des provinces entières; ils pressent le laboureur pour avoir une plus grande quantité de bled qu'ils puissent envoyer aux étrangers, & se procurer les choses que demande leur luxe. Si la Pologne ne commerçoit avec aucune Nation, ses peuples seroient plus heureux. Ses Grands qui n'auroient que leur bled, le donneroient à leurs païsans pour vivre; de trop grands Domaines leur seroient à charge, ils les partageroient à leurs païsans; tout le monde trouvant des peaux ou des laines dans ses troupeaux, il n'y auroit plus une dépense immense à faire pour les habits; les Grands qui aiment toûjours le luxe, & qui ne le pourroient trouver que dans leur païs, encourageroient les pauvres au travail. Je dis que cette Nation seroit plus florissante, à moins qu'elle ne devint barbare, chose que les Loix pourroient prévenir' (*Esprit des Lois*, book XX, chapter 21; Montesquieu, *Esprit*, vol. II, p. 23). See also the annotation for 'That Politics may be reduced to a Science' (above, vol. 1, pp. 216–17, n. 6).

28. *corruption may seem ... established liberty*] cf. the note on '*private bribery*' to 'Of the Independency of Parliament' (above, vol. 1, p. 240, n. 11).

29. *governing without parliaments*] Before 1689 Parliament did not sit continuously, and quite long periods might naturally occur in which there was no Parliament in existence. For instance, during the reign of James I there was no Parliament between 1610 and 1621 (aside from the 'Addled Parliament' of 1614), and also between 1622 and 1624. These vacancies of Parliament should however be distinguished from a declared intention by the Crown to govern without Parliament (which entailed on the part of the Crown a resolve to do without the grants and supplies which only a Parliament could provide). Charles I had made the attempt in the so-called 'Personal Rule', which lasted from March 1629 to April 1640. For comment, see Kevin Sharpe, *The Personal Rule of Charles I* (New Haven, CT, and London: Yale University Press, 1992).

30. *the phantom of prerogative*] The royal prerogative refers to the special right or privilege exercised by a monarch over all other persons (*OED*, 'prerogative', *n.*, 2 a). In England the royal prerogative included: the right of sending and receiving ambassadors, making treaties, making war and concluding peace, conferring honours, nominating to bishoprics, choosing ministers of state, summoning Parliament, refusing assent to a bill and pardoning those under legal sentence; with many other political, ecclesiastical, and judicial privileges. The origin, scope, and exercise of the prerogative had been a point of friction between the Crown and Parliament in the later seventeenth century. The defenders of Stuart monarchy had tended to think of the royal prerogative as above or outside the law. Others, such as Andrew Marvell in *An Account of the Growth of Popery and Arbitrary Government* (1677), had insisted that the king's 'very Prerogative is no more then what the Law has determined' (Marvell, *Prose Works*, vol. II, p. 225) – in other words, that the prerogative was subsequent, not antecedent, to law, and hence did not stand above it.

31. *If we consider . . . free government*] Adam Smith would later admire Hume's acuity in observing how commerce served to reinforce the political liberty and security of property on which it depended for its first flourishing (Smith, *Wealth*, p. 412, III.iv.4). However, there may be a tension between what Hume says here and what he has said in 'Of the Rise and Progress of the Arts and Sciences', that although free governments are the 'only proper *nursery* for the arts and sciences', once established '*these noble plants . . . may . . . be transplanted into any government*' (above, vol. 1, pp. 98 and 102).

32. *In rude . . . vassals or tenants*] Another recapitulation of a point made in 'Of Commerce': 'Where manufactures and mechanic arts are not cultivated, the bulk of the people must apply themselves to agriculture . . .' (above, p. 8).

33. *the encrease . . . hands of the commons*] An echo of the analysis of changing distributions of wealth and property in England since the accession of Henry VII (1485) that had been first advanced by James Harrington in *Oceana* (1656). Bolingbroke had subscribed to the same point in letter 11 of *A Dissertation upon Parties*, where he drew attention to 'that great change in the balance of property, which began in the reigns of Henry the Seventh, and Henry the Eighth, and carried a great part of that weight into the scale of the commons, which had lain before in the scale of the peers and clergy' (Bolingbroke, *Political Writings*, p. 98).

34. *To declaim . . . human nature*] The essay 'Of the Populousness of Ancient Nations' (above, pp. 95–160) is another attack on this distorting principle of the human mind. It concludes: 'The humour of blaming the present, and admiring the past, is strongly rooted in human nature, and has an influence even on persons endued with the profoundest judgment and most extensive learning' (above, p. 148). Hume had considered, and offered an explanation of, the distorting effect on our judgement exerted by distance in time in

the *Treatise of Human Nature*, II.iii.7–8 (*THN*, pp. 274–80). William Wilkie had echoed this opinion of Hume's in the prefatory essay to his epic poem *The Epigoniad* (Edinburgh, 1757), pp. vii–viii: 'there is in our minds a principle which leads us to admire past times, especially those which are most remote from our own'. In classical literature, the same thought is expressed by Marcus Aper, one of the speakers in Tacitus's *Dialogus de Oratoribus*, who deplores 'vitio autem malignitatis humanae vetera semper in laude, praesentia in fastidio esse'; 'the carping spirit of mankind that whereas what is old is always held in high esteem, anything modern is viewed with disdain' (XVIII.iii–iv).

35. *peas at CHRISTMAS*] A notable extravagance, because so out of season. Hume is again recalling Mandeville, *The Fable of the Bees*: 'The Courtier's gone, that with his Miss / Sup'd at his house on *Christmas* Peas; / Spending as much in two Hours' Stay, / As keeps a Troop of Horse a Day' (Mandeville, *Fable*, vol. I, p. 33). Cf. Anon., *The True Meaning of the Fable of the Bees* (1726), p. 20. There is a similar observation in Jean-François Melon's *Essai politique sur le commerce*: 'L'exemple du Luxe au plus haut point, & même au ridicule, est dans la cherté excessive de quelques denrees frivoles, que l'homme somptueux étale avec profusion dans un repas, dont il veut faire consister le mérite dans la cherté. Pourquoi se récrier sur cette folle dépense? Cet argent gardé, dans son coffre, seroit mort pour la société. Le Jardinier le reçoit, il l'a mérité par son travail excité de nouveau; ses enfans presque nuds en sont habillés, ils mangent du pain abondamment, se portent mieux, & travaillent avec une esperance gaye . . .' (Melon, *Essay politique*, pp. 123–4).

36. *a contradiction in terms*] Because, for Hume, questions of vice and virtue can always ultimately be resolved into questions of public utility, as he states in the *Enquiry Concerning the Principles of Morals*: 'It appears to be matter of fact, that the circumstance of *utility*, in all subjects, is a source of praise and approbation: That it is constantly appealed to in all moral decisions concerning the merit and demerit of actions: That it is the *sole* source of that high regard paid to justice, fidelity, honour, allegiance, and chastity: That it is inseparable from all the other social virtues, humanity, generosity, charity, affability, lenity, mercy, and moderation: And, in a word, that it is a foundation of the chief part of morals, which has a reference to mankind and our fellow-creatures' (*ECPM*, V.ii, p. 45).

37. *let us never pronounce . . . society*] Here Hume separates himself from the doctrine of Mandeville, whose writings he has been shadowing at a number of points in the final section of this essay.

38. *Fable of the Bees*] In 'An Enquiry into the Origin of Moral Virtue' Mandeville had presented our ideas of vice and virtue as fictions imposed on the people by self-interested legislators: 'The Chief Thing, therefore, which Lawgivers and other wise Men, that have laboured for the Establishment of Society, have endeavour'd, has been to make the People they were to govern,

believe, that it was more beneficial for every Body to conquer than indulge his Appetites, and much better to mind the Publick than what seem'd his private Interest . . . It being the Interest then of the very worst of them, more than any, to preach up Publick-spiritedness, that they might reap the Fruits of the Labour and Self-denial of others, and at the same time indulge their own Appetites with less disturbance, they agreed with the rest, to call every thing, which, without Regard to the Publick, Man should commit to gratify any of his Appetites, VICE; if in that Action there cou'd be observed the least prospect, that it might either be injurious to any of the Society, or ever render himself less serviceable to others: And to give the Name of VIRTUE to every Performance, by which Man, contrary to the impulse of Nature, should endeavour the Benefit of others, or the Conquest of his own Passions out of a Rational Ambition of being good' (Mandeville, *Fable*, vol. I, pp. 42 and 48–9).

### III. OF MONEY

Published in: *1752a, 1752b, 1753, 1754, 1758, 1760, 1764, 1767, 1768, 1770, 1772, 1777a*

Significant revisions:

Hume made eight, quite limited, revisions to the text of this essay:

1) *1752a–1768* read 'thrice as numerous' (*1752a*, p. 42; cf. above, p. 25).

2) *1753* inserts the note 'This is . . . AMSTERDAM.' (above, p. 27).

3) *1752a–1768* add two sentences to the paragraph ending '. . . speculative politicians.' (above, p. 27): 'For to these only I all along address myself. 'Tis enough that I submit to the ridicule sometimes, in this age, attach'd to the character of a philosopher, without adding to it that which belongs to a projector.' (*1752a*, p. 45).

4) *1752b* adds the final sentence 'And as . . . old standard.' to note * (above, p. 35, NOTE [Q]). (This had been included in the 'Errata' printed in *1752a*.)

5) *1752a–1768* read 'hoarded in granaries' (*1752a*, p. 53; cf. above, p. 31).

6) *1752a–1770* read 'reserve for the maintenance' (*1752a*, p. 53; cf. above, p. 31).

7) *1752a–1752b* read 'about seven millions a year, of which not above a tenth part goes' (*1752a*, p. 56; cf. above, p. 32).

8) *1752a–1768* read 'the stated club in the inns' (*1752a*, p. 59; cf. above, p. 34).

Copy text: *1777a*

Headnote:

Locke had said that the subject of money was 'artificially perplexed, rather than in it self mysterious' (*Further Considerations Concerning Raising the Value of Money*, second edition [1696], sig. A4ᵛ). Nevertheless, the consequences of the invention and use of money had been profound, as Locke himself had recognized in the 'Second Treatise', § 36 ff., where he had explained how the invention of money had shifted men's ideas about natural property, facilitating both larger possessions and creating a legitimate right to such larger possessions (Locke, *Two Treatises*, pp. 293 ff.). In 'Of Money' Hume sought to clear away many of the natural and intuitive, but in fact deeply misleading, ideas men held on this subject. At the same time, here and in 'Of Interest', he also focused on a particular pitfall in philosophical explanation, namely the tendency to confuse mere correlations with real causes.

Hume's later thoughts on money, which were more hospitable to its conventional nature, can be found in his long letter to the Abbé Morellet of 10 July 1769 (*Letters*, vol. II, 203–6).

1. *Money is not . . . smooth and easy*] cf. Jean-François Melon, *Essai politique sur le commerce*: 'L'Or & l'Argent sont, de convention genérale, le gage, l'équivalent, ou la mesure commune de tout ce qui sert à l'usage des hommes' (Melon, *Essai politique*, p. 166). Locke had used the metaphor of money driving the wheels of trade (Locke, *Considerations*, pp. 17, 29 and 40). Daniel Defoe had presented credit as the '*Oil* of the Wheel' of trade (*Essay upon Publick Credit* [1710], p. 9). Cf. also Berkeley, *Querist*, topic 461, p. 62.

2. *the greater or less . . . no consequence*] Similar opinions against what Berkeley called 'the prejudiced and narrow way of thinking about gold and silver' had been expressed by Berkeley himself in *The Querist*, e.g. topic 562: 'Whether there can be a greater mistake in politics, than to measure the wealth of a nation by its gold and silver?' (Berkeley, *Querist*, pp. 75 and 77). The point had been echoed by Vanderlint: 'it is of no Consequence, whether any Nation hath a vast deal of Gold and Silver, or but very little Money amongst them, if sufficient Care be taken to make the Plenty of every thing great enough, to make the Money they have, amply extend to circulate their Trade in every Branch, so as fully to employ and support all their People' (Vanderlint, *Money*, p. 55). Cf. also Locke: 'Riches do not consist in having more Gold and Silver, but in having more in proportion, than the rest of the World, or than our Neighbours' (Locke, *Some Considerations of the Consequences of the Lowering of Interest, and Raising the Value of Money*, second edition [1696], p. 14). Adam Smith would also discuss money and the common error which confused plenty of money with genuine wealth (Smith, *Wealth*, IV.i, vol. I, pp. 429–51).

3. *HARRY VII.'s*] Henry VII (1457–1509), king of England. His reign had been regarded as a crucial economic and political turning point by James Harrington in *Oceana* (1656). There were four crowns in a pound sterling.

4. *mercenary troops*] In this anti-Machiavellian *obiter dictum* Hume takes aim at another popular belief of the time which he nevertheless regarded as unfounded, namely the prejudice in favour of militias as friendly to liberty,

and against standing armies and mercenaries as the instruments of despotism. For a selection of texts and discussion of the underlying issues, see
David Womersley (ed.), *Writings on Standing Armies* (Indianapolis, IN: Liberty Fund, 2020). Adam Smith would follow Hume in this line of argument
(Smith, *Wealth*, V.i.a.23; V.i.a.28; V.i.a.39; pp. 699–700, 701 and 705–6).

5. *Our small army ... twice as numerous*] Several entries in the 'Early
Memoranda' relate to the comparative size and expense of the military
establishments of modern European nations. Two are especially relevant:
'Every French Seaman and Soldier costs 15 Sous a day upon [an *inserted
above the line*] Averrage; every ~~English~~ Soldier in English Pay costs a Shilling.
~~The~~ In Kings Williams War the French had 600.000 Men in Pay by Sea &
Land.'; '100.000 £ sufficient to maintain 10.000 French or German Forces.
Pulteney' (NLS MS 23159, item 14, pp. 11 and 12; cf. Mossner, 'Memo-
randa', pp. 504–5).

6. *the late war*] i.e. the War of the Austrian Succession (1740–48). Hume had
been involved in this conflict, serving in the expeditionary force under General James St Clair (see above, vol. 1, p. 364, n. 41). See Mossner, *Life*, pp.
187–204.

7. *There seems ... established commerce*] Hume would repeat this insight
concerning the naturalness of growth and decay in artificial as well as natural entities in a letter to Lord Kames of 4 March 1758: 'Great empires,
great cities, great commerce, all of them receive a check, not from accidental events, but necessary principles' (*Letters*, vol. I, p. 272). Hume may be
recalling Francis Hutcheson, who in his *A System of Moral Philosophy* (composed before 1738; published posthumously in 1755) had held that 'States
themselves have within them the seeds of death and destruction' (Hutcheson,
*System*, vol. II, p. 377); but the idea is almost a commonplace, and reaches
back to antiquity. Shaftesbury had commented on the awkwardness of
empire in 'Sensus Communis', III.ii: 'Vast Empires are in many respects
unnatural: but particularly in this, That be they ever so well constituted,
the Affairs of many must, in such Governments, turn upon a very few; and
the Relation be less sensible, and in a manner lost, between the Magistrate
and the People, in a Body so unweildy in its Limbs, and whose Members
lie so remote from one another, and distant from the Head' (Shaftesbury,
*Characteristicks*, vol. I, p. 63). Adam Ferguson would moralize on the fatal
hunger of imperial acquisition, particularly if facilitated by a misapplication of the benefits of commerce: 'What may not the fleets and armies of
Europe, with the access they have by commerce to every part of the world,
and the facility of their conveyance, effect, if that ruinous maxim should prevail, That the grandeur of a nation is to be estimated from the extent of its
territory; or, That the interest of any particular people consists in reducing
their neighbours to servitude'; 'That which the despotical *master has sown,
cannot quicken unless it die*; it must languish and expire by the effect of its

own abuse, before the human spirit can spring up anew, or bear those fruits which constitute the honour and the felicity of human nature' (Ferguson, *Civil Society*, pp. 148 and 262). Adam Smith would later estimate the usual 'course of human prosperity' at approximately two hundred years (Smith, *Wealth*, p. 425, III.iv.20). Cf. the note in the 'Early Memoranda' on the natural history of empire: 'There seems to be a natural Course of Things, which brings on the Destruction of great Empires. They push their Conquests till they come to barbarous Nations, which stop their Progress, by the Difficulty of subsisting great Armies. After that, the Nobility & considerable Men of the conquering Nation & best Provinces withdraw gradually from the [frontier *inserted above the line*] Army, by reason of its Distance from the Capital & barbarity of the Country, in which they quarter: They forget the Use of War. Their barbarous Soldiers become their Masters. These have no Law but their Sword, both from their bad Education, & from their Distance from the Sovereign [to whom they bear no Affection *inserted above the line*]. Hence Disorder, Violence, Anarchy, & Tyranny, & a Dissolution of Empire.' (NLS MS 23159, item 14, p. 27; cf. Mossner, 'Memoranda', pp. 517–18). Cf. also Rousseau, *Contrat*, book II, chapter 9 (pp. 62–6).

8. *This has made me . . . every nation*] In his letter to Montesquieu of 10 April 1749 Hume had also doubted the economic utility of banks and the paper credit they make possible: 'Les banques sont commodes, mais on peut mettre en doute si elles sont fort utiles. Avant 1706, il y avoit une quantité suffisante d'or et d'argent dans toutes nos colonies pour les usages communs; on y introduisit un papier de crédit ou papier courant, qui fit sortir tout l'argent et a eu de si pernicieuses conséquences que le Parlement est résolu de l'abolir cette session' (*Letters*, vol. I, p. 136). Hume therefore diverges from Berkeley, who repeatedly in *The Querist* had suggested that, since money was purely conventional, there was no true difference between *specie* and paper money: topic 23, 'Whether money is to be considered as having an intrinsic value, or as being a commodity, a standard, a measure, or a pledge, as is variously suggested by writers? and whether the true idea of money, as such, be not altogether that of a ticket or counter?'; topic 33, 'Whether current Bank notes may not be deemed money? and whether they are not actually the greater part of the money of this kingdom?'; topic 40, 'Whether a fertile land, and the industry of its inhabitants, would not prove inexhaustible funds of real wealth, be the counters for conveying and recording thereof what you will, paper, gold, or silver?' (Berkeley, *Querist*, pp. 3, 5 and 6). Locke, however, had been adamant that the value of money was not purely conventional, but rather was related to the amount of pure silver in the coin: see his *Further Considerations Concerning Raising the Value of Money*, second edition (1696).

9. *would prefer paper . . . safe custody*] cf. Berkeley, *The Querist*, topic 226: 'Whether it be not agreed that paper hath, in many respects, the advantage

above coin, as being of more dispatch in payments, more easily transferred, preserved and recovered when lost?' (Berkeley, *Querist*, p. 31).

10. *more largely hereafter*] In 'Of the Balance of Trade' and 'Of Public Credit' (above, pp. 46–59 and 75–87).

11. *It is indeed ... estimating them*] cf. Hobbes, *Leviathan*, chapter 24: 'For Gold and Silver, being (as it happens) almost in all Countries of the world highly valued, is a commodious measure of the value of all things else between Nations; and Mony (of what matter soever coyned by the Soveraign of a Common-wealth,) is a sufficient measure of the value of all things else, between the Subjects of that Common-wealth' (Hobbes, *Leviathan*, p. 174). Berkeley had made a similar point in *The Querist*, topic 23: 'Whether money is to be considered as having an intrinsic value, or as being a commodity, a standard, a measure, or a pledge, as is variously suggested by writers? and whether the true idea of money, as such, be not altogether that of a ticket or counter?' (Berkeley, *Querist*, p. 3).

12. *the bank of AMSTERDAM*] Hume may be recalling Jean-François Melon, who in his *Essai politique* had dwelt on the wisdom of the policy of the bank of Amsterdam, which 'ne paye point, parce qu'elle a un emploi avantageux' (Melon, *Essai politique*, pp. 301–4; quotation on p. 301); or possibly Berkeley, who in many topics of *The Querist* had drawn attention to the bank of Amsterdam (Berkeley, *Querist*, p. 6; cf. also pp. 30, 31, 33, 34, 40, 41, 42, 60). However, the bank of Amsterdam had been also discussed by Davenant, Sir William Temple, Ricard and Megens (Steuart, *Principles*, vol. II, p. 292). Adam Smith would include a digression on 'Banks of Deposit, particularly ... that of Amsterdam' in *The Wealth of Nations* (IV.iii.b) (Smith, *Wealth*, pp. 479–88, esp. pp. 486–8, in which the principles and mode of operation of the Bank of Amsterdam are described in some detail; cf. also Smith, *Wealth*, p. 818, V.ii.a.4). In the advertisement to the fourth edition of that work Smith would acknowledge the guidance on this subject he had received from 'Mr. Henry Hope of Amsterdam'. Smith's opinion that 'no printed account' of the Bank of Amsterdam 'had ever appeared to me satisfactory, or even intelligible' (Smith, *Wealth*, vol. I, p. 9), perhaps overlooks the earlier accounts of it given by Sir James Steuart (Steuart, *Principles*, vol. II, pp. 292–309) and by Nicolas Magens, in *The Universal Merchant* (1753), pp. 32–8. Cf. the entry in the 'Early Memoranda': 'There is computed to be 3000 Tun of Gold in the Bank of Amsterdam at 100.000 Florins a Tun Id.' (NLS MS 23159, item 14, p. 18; cf. Mossner, 'Memoranda', p. 510).

13. *sentire possit*] 'ὥσπερ Ἀνάχαρσις ἔλεγε τῷ νομίσματι τοὺς Ἕλληνας πρὸς οὐδὲν ἕτερον ἢ τὸ ἀριθμεῖν χρωμένους ὁρᾶν'; 'but, as Anacharsis said of the Greeks that he never saw them put their money to any use save to count it ...' (Plutarch, *Moralia*, 'How a Man May Become Aware of His Progress in Virtue', VII).

14. *since the discovery ... gold and silver*] cf. two notes in the 'Early Memoranda': 'There is commonly coin'd in England 500.000 Pound [in Gold

*inserted above the line*]; every year; & brought into Europe three Millions. Id.'; 'In 1721. The English & Dutch drew more Money from Spain than France did' (NLS MS 23159, item 14, pp. 12 and 18; cf. Mossner, 'Memoranda', pp. 505 and 510). The ruinous effect of the exploitation of the gold and silver mines of South America on the Spanish economy had been noted by many writers. Locke had suspected the moral character of the Spanish, as much as the laws of economics: ''Tis Death in *Spain* to export Money: And yet they, who furnish all the World with Gold and Silver, have least of it amongst themselves. *Trade* fetches it away from that lazy and indigent People, notwithstanding all their artificial and forced contrivances to keep it there. It follows *Trade* against the rigour of their Laws; and their want of Foreign Commodities makes it openly be carried out at Noon-Day' (Locke, *Considerations*, p. 116). Jean-François Melon, in his *Essai politique sur le commerce*, wrote: 'Les Espagnols ont fait la découverte de l'Amerique, & leur cruelle politique a crû ne pouvoir se l'assujettir & se l'assurer, qu'en exterminant les naturels du païs. Il fallut les remplacer par des Espagnols qui accoururent avec avidité, & dépeuplerent le païs de la domination, pour aller peupler le riche païs des mines: c'est l'époque & la cause de la décadence de la puissance Espagnole, qui depuis a langui avec les titres pompeux des païs qui reconnoissoient ses loix' (Melon, *Essai politique*, p. 38; see also pp. 203–4). Berkeley had concurred in *The Querist*, topic 43: 'Whether even gold, or silver, if they should lessen the industry of its inhabitants, would not be ruinous to a country? and whether Spain be not an instance of this?' (Berkeley, *Querist*, p. 6). More recently, it had also been remarked on by Montesquieu: 'Si l'Europe a trouvé tant d'avantage dans le Commerce de l'Amérique, il seroit naturel de croire que l'Espagne en auroit reçu de plus grands. Elle tira du Monde nouvellement découvert une quantité d'or & d'argent si prodigieuse, que ce que l'on en avoit eu jusqu'alors ne pouvoit y être comparé. Mais (ce qu'on n'auroit jamais soupçonné) la misére la fit échouer presque par-tout' (*Esprit des Lois*, book XXI, chapter 18, and cf. also chapter 22; Montesquieu, *Esprit*, vol. II, pp. 75–80, quotation on p. 75). In 1776 Adam Smith would note that the 'discovery of the mines of America diminished the value of gold and silver in Europe. This diminution . . . is still going on gradually, and is likely to continue to do so for a long time' (Smith, *Wealth*, vol. I, p. 52; I.v.12; cf. pp. 210–11; I.xi.f.3, where Smith notes the universal acceptance of this opinion, which is 'accounted for accordingly in the same manner by every body; and there never has been any dispute either about the fact, or about the cause of it', but also says that the inflationary effect of this discovery 'appears to have been compleated' by 1636: p. 211, I.xi.g.1; see also p. 437, IV.i.14, and p. 447, IV.i.32, for further comments on the impact of the American mines on Europe). See also Cantillon, *Essai*, p. 212. Francesco Mengotti would repeatedly cite the effect of South American gold and silver on the Spanish economy to illustrate the similar precariousness of the economy of the Roman republic, reliant as it had been on the influx of pillage and booty rather than on commerce (Mengotti, *Commerce*, pp. 71, 118, 138–9, 161, 172–3).

15. *though the high price ... that encrease*] As Cantillon had pointed out: 'J'estime en général qu'une augmentation d'argent effectif cause dans un Etat une augmentation proportionnée de consommation, qui produit par degrés l'augmentation des prix' (Cantillon, *Essai*, p. 215).

16. *specie*] coined money (*OED*, 'specie', *n.*, 3 b).

17. *CADIZ*] A seaport on the south-west coast of Spain into which bullion from the Spanish possessions in America was imported.

18. *From the whole ... less quantity*] Vanderlint also argued that to focus on the quantity of gold and silver in a nation, rather than the application and circulation of it, was a mistake: 'It is of no Consequence, whether any Nation hath a vast deal of Gold and Silver, or but very little Money amongst them, if sufficient Care be taken to make the Plenty of every thing great enough, to make the Money they have, amply extend to circulate their Trade in every Branch, so as fully to employ and support all their People' (Vanderlint, *Money*, p. 55).

19. *the force of GERMANY ... manufactures*] Hume had travelled through Germany in 1748 when he was secretary to General St Clair in his embassy to the courts of Vienna and Turin in the diplomatic aftermath of the War of the Austrian Succession; and he wrote a very detailed account of what he observed as he passed through Germany in the form of a journal addressed to his brother John Home of Ninewells. Hume was greatly impressed by the prosperity of Germany: 'Germany is undoubtedly a very fine Country, full of industrious honest People, & were it united it woud be the greatest Power that ever was in the World ... There are great Advantages, in travelling, & nothing serves more to remove Prejudices: For I confess I had entertain'd no such advantageous Idea of Germany: And it gives a Man of Humanity Pleasure to see that so considerable a Part of Mankind as the Germans are in so tolerable a Condition' (*Letters*, vol. I, pp. 114–33; quotation on p. 126).

20. *POCCI-DANARI*] i.e. 'little money'.

21. *If the coin ... annihilated*] Hume here recalls Locke: 'For that [money] which is not let loose into *Trade*, is all one whil'st hoarded up, as if it were not in Being' (Locke, *Considerations*, p. 120).

22. *the WEST INDIES*] Hume refers to Central and South America, which under Spanish dominion had supplied large amounts of silver and gold to Europe, thereby greatly increasing the amount of precious metal in circulation. See above, p. 332–4, n. 14. Hume would revert to this subject in the *History of England*: 'After the discovery and conquest of the West-Indies, gold and silver became every day more plentiful in England, as well as in the rest of Europe; and the price of all commodities and provisions rose to a height beyond what had been known, since the declension of the Roman

empire. As the revenue of the crown rose not in proportion, the prince was insensibly reduced to poverty amidst the general riches of his subjects, and required additional funds, in order to support the same magnificence and force, which had been maintained by former monarchs. But while money thus flowed into England, we may observe, that, at the same time, and probably from that very cause, arts and industry of all kinds received a mighty encrease; and elegance in every enjoyment of life became better known, and more cultivated among all ranks of people' (*History of England*, vol. V, p. 39).

23. *their AFRICAN trade*] i.e. in slaves.

24. *Were the question proposed . . . manufactures*] A glance perhaps at the argument of Rousseau's notorious *Discours* of 1750, in which he had denied that the rise of arts and industry had contributed to improving human happiness and virtue.

25. *often to be met with in historians*] A mercantilist fallacy.

26. *digest it into every vein, so to speak*] A metaphor perhaps derived from Hobbes, who in chapter 24 of *Leviathan* had also compared the circulation of money in a state to the circulation of nourishing blood through the body: 'this Concoction [money], is as it were the Sanguification of the Commonwealth: For naturall Bloud is in like manner made of the fruits of the Earth; and circulating, nourisheth by the way, every Member of the Body of Man' (Hobbes, *Leviathan*, p. 174).

27. *We may . . . maintained by it*] cf. Du Halde on the great size of the Chinese state machine: 'Dans une aussi vaste étenduë qu'est celle de la Chine, les soins d'entretenir les ouvrages publics, le gouvernement des troupes, le réglement des Finances, le maintien de la Justice, & sur-tout le choix des Magistrats, toutes ces diverses fonctions, si elles étoient réünies deans un seul Tribunal, produiroient sans doute une grande confusion dans les résolutions, & une lenteur dans l'action qui ruineroit les affaires. Ainsi il a été nécessaire de multiplier les Mandarins, & à la Cour, & dans les Provinces' (Du Halde, *Description*, vol. I, p. 119).

28. *little more than a farthing!*] cf. the entry in the 'Early Memoranda': 'The common Reckoning in the ~~Italian~~ Inns [in Lombardy *inserted above the line*] only ~~a Semis a head~~, about a ½ ~~pence~~ [farthing *inserted above the line*]. Id. Lib. 2. C. 15. They bargaind only for the head, not for particular Provisions as in Greece, w^ch Polybius reckons a great Proof of Plenty in ~~Italy~~ that Country.' (NLS MS 23159, item 14, p. 28; cf. Mossner, 'Memoranda', p. 518).

29. *concoction*] Part of the vocabulary of the somatic metaphor for the way money operates in an economy; used also by Hobbes (above, p. 335, n. 26).

30. *lib. iv*] Hume refers to Tacitus's review of the military capabilities of the Roman Empire on land during the reign of Tiberius: 'Sed praecipuum robur Rhenum iuxta, commune in Germanos Gallosque subsidium, octo legiones erant. Hispaniae recens perdomitae tribus habebantur. Mauros Iuba rex

acceperat donum populi Romani. Cetera Africae per duas legiones parique numero Aegyptus, dehinc initio ab Suriae usque ad flumen Euphraten, quantum ingenti terrarum sinu ambitur, quattuor legionibus coercita, accolis Hibero Albanoque et aliis regibus, qui magnitudine nostra proteguntur adversum externa imperia. Et Thraeciam Rhoemetalces ac liberi Cotyis, ripamque Danuvii legionum duae in Pannonia, duae in Moesia attinebant, totidem apud Delmatiam locatis, quae positu regionis a tergo illis, ac si repentinum auxilium Italia posceret, haud procul accirentur, quamquam insideret urbem proprius miles, tres urbanae, novem praetoriae cohortes, Etruria ferme Umbriaque delectae aut vetere Latio et coloniis antiquitus Romanis. At apud idonea provinciarum sociae triremes alaeque et auxilia cohortium, neque multo secus in iis virium: sed persequi incertum fuit, cum ex usu temporis huc illuc mearent, gliscerent numero et aliquando minuerentur'; 'Our main strength, however, lay on the Rhine – eight legions ready to cope indifferently with the German or the Gaul. The Spains, finally subdued not long before, were kept by three. Mauretania, by the national gift, had been transferred to King Juba. Two legions held down the remainder of Africa; a similar number, Egypt: then, from the Syrian marches right up to the Euphrates, four sufficed for the territories enclosed in that enormous reach of ground; while, on the borders, the Iberian, the Albanian, and other monarchs, were secured against alien power by the might of Rome. Thrace was held by Rhoemetalces and the sons of Cotys; the Danube bank by two legions in Pannonia and two in Moesia; two more being posted in Dalmatia, geographically to the rear of the other four, and within easy call, should Italy claim sudden assistance – though, in any case, the capital possessed a standing army of its own: three urban and nine praetorian cohorts, recruited in the main from Etruria and Umbria or Old Latium and the earlier Roman colonies. Again, at suitable points of the provinces, there were the federate warships, cavalry divisions and auxiliary cohorts in not much inferior strength: but to trace them was dubious, as they shifted from station to station, and, according to the exigency of the moment, increased in number or were occasionally diminished' (Tacitus, *Annals*, IV.v).

31. *cap. 15*] 'περὶ δὲ τῆς κατὰ μέρος εὐωνίας καὶ δαψιλείας τῶν πρὸς τὴν τροφὴν ἀνηκόντων οὕτως ἄν τις ἀκριβέστατα κατανοήσειε· ποιοῦνται γὰρ τὰς καταλύσεις οἱ διοδεύοντες τὴν χώραν ἐν τοῖς πανδοκείοις, οὐ συμφωνοῦντες περὶ τῶν κατὰ μέρος ἐπιτηδείων, ἀλλ᾽ ἐρωτῶντες πόσου τὸν ἄνδρα δέχεται. ὡς μὲν οὖν ἐπὶ τὸ πολὺ παρίενται τοὺς καταλύτας οἱ πανδοκεῖς, ὡς ἱκανὰ πάντ᾽ ἔχειν τὰ πρὸς τὴν χρείαν, ἡμιασσαρίου· τοῦτο δ᾽ ἔστι τέταρτον μέρος ὀβολοῦ· σπανίως δὲ τοῦθ᾽ ὑπερβαίνουσι'; 'The cheapness and abundance of all articles of food will be most clearly understood from the following fact. Travellers in this country who put up in inns do not bargain for each separate article they require, but ask what is the charge *per diem* for one person. The innkeepers, as a rule, agree to receive guests, providing them with enough of all they require for

half an *as* per diem, i.e. the fourth part of an obol, the charge being very seldom higher' (Polybius, II.xv.4–6).

32. *cap. 11*] 'invenimus legatos Carthaginiensium dixisse nullos hominum inter sese benignius vivere quam Romanos. eodem enim argento apud omnes cenitavisse ipsos'; 'We read that the Carthaginian ambassadors declared that no race of mankind lived on more amicable terms with one another than the Romans, inasmuch as in a round of banquets they had found the same service of plate in use at every house!' (Pliny the Elder, *Natural History*, XXXIII.l).

33. *lib. i*] Hume refers to some details of the rabble-rousing speech given by the mutineer, Percennius, when his fellow soldiers had learned of the death of Augustus: 'Enimvero militiam ipsam gravem, infructuosam: denis in diem assibus animam et corpus aestimari; hinc vestem, arma, tentoria; hinc saevitiam centurionum et vacationes munerum redimi'; 'In fact, the whole trade of war was comfortless and profitless: ten asses a day was the assessment of body and soul: with that they had to buy clothes, weapons and tents, bribe the bullying centurion and purchase a respite from duty!' (Tacitus, *Annals*, I.xvii).

34. *So little expensive*] Gibbon, perhaps mindful of this passage, would also contrast the comparative lightness of the Roman military establishment with those of modern Europe: 'If we review this general state of the Imperial forces; of the cavalry as well as infantry; of the legions, the auxiliaries, the guards, and the navy; the most liberal computation will not allow us to fix the entire establishment by sea and by land at more than four hundred and fifty thousand men: a military power, which, however formidable it may seem, was equalled by a monarch of the last century, whose kingdom was confined within a single province of the Roman empire [i.e. Louis XIV]' (Gibbon, *Decline and Fall*, vol. I, p. 47).

35. *For money . . . EUROPEAN kingdoms*] cf. the entry in the 'Early Memoranda': 'After the Conquest of Ægypt by Augustus the Prices of every thing doubl'd in Rome' (NLS MS 23159, item 14, p. 17; cf. Mossner, 'Memoranda', p. 509).

36. *Mons. du TOT*] Du Tot's *Réflexions politiques sur les finances et le commerce* (1738) had been translated as *Political Reflections upon the Finances and Commerce of France* (1739).

37. *MELON*] A translation of Melon's *Essai politique sur le commerce* (Paris, 1734; a second, enlarged edition, Paris, 1736) had been published in Dublin in 1739.

38. *PARIS de VERNEY*] See Joseph Paris-Duverney, *Examen du livre intitulé Réflexions politiques sur les finances et le commerce, par de Tott* (1740).

39. *the example . . . the old standard*] Hume refers to the 'Great Re-Coinage' of 1696, which had attempted to address the erosion of value in the English coinage as a result of clipping and forgery.

## IV. OF INTEREST

Published in: *1752a, 1752b, 1753, 1754, 1758, 1760, 1764, 1767, 1768, 1770, 1772, 1777a*
Significant revisions:

Hume made only two substantive changes to the text of this essay:

1) *1752a–1768* read 'merely a fictitious value, arising from the agreement and convention of men, the greater' (*1752a*, p. 63; cf. above, p. 37).

2) *1752a–1760* include an additional footnote, deleted in *1764* and all subsequent editions, appended to 'demand for borrowing.' (above, p. 37):

'*I HAVE been inform'd by a very eminent lawyer and a man of great knowledge and observation, that it appears from antient papers and records, that, about four centuries ago, money, in *Scotland*, and probably in other parts of *Europe*, was only at five *per cent.* and afterwards rose to ten before the discovery of the *West Indies*. This fact is curious; but might easily be reconcil'd to the foregoing reasoning. Men, in that age, liv'd so much at home, and in so very simple and frugal a manner, that they had no occasion for money; and tho' the lenders were then few, the borrowers were still fewer. The high rate of interest among the early *Romans* is accounted for by historians from the frequent losses sustain'd by the inroads of the enemy.' (*1752a*, pp. 65–6, n. *).

Copy text: *1777a*
Headnote:

Prior to the later seventeenth century, and in a moral climate where the negative connotations of usury had not been entirely erased, it was widely assumed that permissible interest rates could and should be set by legislative fiat. In England interest rates had been reduced by law from 10% to 8% in 1623, and again from 8% to 6% in 1660 (Massie, *Interest*, p. 6, n. *). In the 'Early Memoranda' Hume had noted that the ancient Romans had fixed rates of interest by law: 'The Romans were able to force Interest by Law. For they once limited the Interest to 12 p$^r$ Cent as an Ease to the People: And 4 or 5 Years after reduc'd it to six. Livy. Lib. 7.' (NLS MS 23159, item 14, p. 19; cf. Mossner, 'Memoranda', p. 511).

In such a setting the concept of a 'natural' rate of interest could hardly arise, since the charging of interest itself was, although acknowledged to be occasionally necessary, also unnatural and unlawful, as God himself had told Moses: 'If thou lend money to any of my people that is poor by thee, thou shalt not be to him as an usurer, neither shalt thou lay upon him usury' (Exodus 22:25).

However, after the Restoration, as state governance and finances in Europe were modernized and remodelled, the stigma attaching to both borrowing and lending declined, and the development of public credit as an instrument of government moved forward. The nature of interest thus became freshly salient, and attracted the attention of acute thinkers such as Sir William Petty and Locke, whose 'position paper' on interest, written for Shaftesbury in the early 1670s, had (according to Peter Laslett) 'results of considerable consequence to the future of the British economy' (Locke, *Two Treatises*, p. 29). For both Petty and Locke, the interest rate was a purely fiscal matter relating to supply and demand: scarcity of money led to high rates of interest, abundance of money led to low rates of interest.

The earliest published use of the phrase 'natural rate of interest', at least in England, confirms this tentative periodization, as it appears to have been coined in John Locke's *Some Considerations of the Consequences of the Lowering of Interest, and Raising the Value of Money* (1692); this is presumably the eventually published version of the essay he had written for Shaftesbury in the 1670s. The earliest use of the simpler phrase 'natural interest', in a purely economic sense, occurs in Petty's *A Treatise of Taxes and Contributions* (1662), chapter 5, 'Of Usury', p. 29.

From an early date Hume was deeply interested in the question of interest, as the many entries on the subject in the 'Early Memoranda' indicate. Moreover, the subsequent use in 'Of the Populousness of Ancient Nations' of many of these details of rates of interest gleaned from the writings of antiquity shows that for Hume rates of interest were more than a narrowly fiscal matter. Properly considered, they might shed light on apparently remote questions of social organization, human psychology and motivation, and the conditions of human flourishing.

In 1750 Joseph Massie had published *An Essay on the Governing Causes of the Natural Rate of Interest*, and he had respectfully crossed swords with Petty and Locke. For Massie, the natural rate of interest was not a product of the plenty or scarcity of money, but rather was related to the circumstantial profitability of trade. When trade is flourishing, competition will in the long run drive down profits, and with suppressed profits from trade the natural rate of interest will also fall. James Harris explains the linkage clearly: 'interest is seen as a price paid for the opportunity to make a profit with someone else's money. People will allow others to make a profit with their money when they cannot make more from their money by investing it themselves. So the rate at which they will lend is bound to be at least equal to the profitability of trade in general' (Harris, *Hume*, p. 274). In Massie's words: 'the natural Rate of Interest is governed by the Profits of Trade to Particulars' (Massie, *Interest*, p. 61). Hume's essay adheres very closely to Massie's ultimately psychological argument concerning how and why people are induced to lend and to borrow.

1. *plenty of money*] The prevailing and 'natural' assumption, as articulated, e.g., by Sir William Petty: 'the natural Fall of Interest, is the Effect of the Increase of Money' (Massie, *Interest*, p. 6); by Locke: 'the natural Interest of Money is raised ... When the Money of a Country is but little' (Locke, *Considerations*, p. 10); and more recently by Jean-François Melon, in his

*Essai politique sur le commerce*: 'L'interêt a diminué à mesure que la quantité d'argent a augmenté en Europe' (Melon, *Essai politique*, p. 273).

2. *BATAVIA*] The capital of the Dutch East Indies, corresponding to modern-day Jakarta.

3. *An effect . . . cause*] Hume would invoke this general principle of causal proportionality once more in 'Of the Populousness of Ancient Nations' (above, p. 148).

4. *Prices have . . . precious metals*] cf. the similar comment in 'Of Money' (above, p. 26). Hume here is correcting, among others, John Locke, the Scottish financial projector John Law (1671–1729) and Montesquieu, all of whom had assumed that the cause of the lowering of interest rates since the discovery of the Spanish West Indies was the enlargement of the quantity of gold and silver in Europe which had ensued: see Locke, *Considerations*, p. 72; Law, *Money and Trade*, pp. 71–2; and Montesquieu, *Esprit*, vol. II, pp. 89–90, book XXII, chapter 6. Adam Smith would later praise Hume's acuity on this point (Smith, *Wealth*, p. 354, II.iv.9). In 1755 Richard Cantillon, too, would follow Hume's lead here (Cantillon, *Essai*, pp. 282–3).

5. *specie*] See above, p. 334, n. 16.

6. *great profits arising from commerce*] In 1776 Adam Smith would declare it a maxim 'that wherever a great deal can be made by the use of money, a great deal will commonly be given for the use of it; and that wherever little can be made by it, less will commonly be given for it' (Smith, *Wealth*, p. 105, I.ix.4).

7. *small advance of commerce and industry*] A point to which Hume would revert in 'Of the Populousness of Ancient Nations': 'Great interest of money, and great profits of trade, are an infallible indication, that industry and commerce are but in their infancy' (above, pp. 120–21).

8. *the principle . . . concomitant effect*] In the *Treatise of Human Nature*, I. iii.15, Hume had specified eight conditions which must be satisfied before we can say that *x* is a cause of *y* (*THN*, pp. 116–17). Mistaking 'a collateral effect for a cause' (above, p. 30) was also a failure in reasoning on which Hume had focused in 'Of Money'.

9. *GARCILASSO DE LA VEGA*] The economic consequences of the Spanish conquest of Peru are discussed in Garcilaso de la Vega's *Comentarios Reales* (1608–17), translated by Sir Paul Rycaut as *The Royal Commentaries of Peru* (1688), part II, book I, chapters 2–7, pp. 419–26.

10. *lib. li*] 'τοσοῦτον γὰρ τὸ πλῆθος τῶν χρημάτων διὰ πάσης ὁμοίως τῆς πόλεως ἐχώρησεν ὥστε τὰ μὲν κτήματα ἐπιτιμηθῆναι, τὰ δὲ δανείσματα ἀγαπητῶς ἐπὶ δραχμῇ πρότερον ὄντα τότε ἐπὶ τῷ τριτημορίῳ αὐτῆς γενέσθαι'; 'So vast an amount of money, in fact, circulated through all parts of the city alike, that the price of goods rose and loans for which the borrower had been glad to pay twelve per cent, could now be had for one third that rate' (Dio Cassius, LI.xxi.5). Dio is describing the economic consequences at Rome of

Augustus's victories in 29 BC. Noted also by Mengotti, *Commerce*, p. 167 and n. *p.*

11. *cap. 3*] 'Huc accedunt semisses usurarum sestertia tria milia et quadringenti octoginta nummi biennii temporis, quo velut infantia vinearum cessat a fructu'; 'Added to this is interest at six per cent, per annum, amounting to 3480 sesterces for the two-year period when the vineyards, in their infancy as it were, are delayed in bearing' (Columella, *On Agriculture*, III.iii.9). Columella is discussing the economics of planting a vineyard.

12. *ep. 18*] 'Nam pro quingentis milibus nummum, quae in alimenta ingenuorum ingenuarumque promiseram, agrum ex meis longe pluris actori publico mancipavi; eundem vectigali imposito recepi, tricena milia annua daturus'; 'I had promised a capital sum of 500,000 sesterces for the maintenance of free-born boys and girls, but instead of paying this over I transferred some of my landed property (which was worth considerably more) to the municipal agent, and then had it reconveyed back to me charged with an annual rent payable of 30,000 sesterces' (Pliny the Younger, *Letters*, VII.xviii.2–3). Pliny is writing to his friend Caninius Rufus and advising him as to the best way to endow a municipal feast in perpetuity.

13. *ep. 62*] 'Pecuniae publicae, domine, providentia tua et ministerio nostro et iam exactae sunt et exiguntur; quae vereor ne otiosae iaceant. Nam et praediorum comparandorum aut nulla aut rarissima occasio est, nec inveniuntur qui velint debere rei publicae, praesertim duodenis assibus, quanti a privatis mutuantur'; 'Thanks to your foresight, Sir, the sums owed to public funds have been paid in under my administration, or are in process of being so; but I am afraid the money may remain uninvested. There is no opportunity, or practically none, of purchasing landed property, and people cannot be found who will borrow from public funds, especially at the rate of twelve per cent, the same rate as for private loans' (Pliny the Younger, *Letters*, X.liv.1). Pliny is writing to the emperor Trajan to encourage him to lower the rate of interest, which he says the provincials find onerous. Hume had made several notes on Roman rates of interest in his 'Early Memoranda': 'The Romans pay'd 12 per Cent Interest for money'; 'The Interest in Rome reducd to 6 per Cent under Tiberius. Tacit.'; 'The Romans were able to force Interest by Law. For they once limited the Interest to 12 per Cent, as an Ease to the People: And 4 or 5 Years after reducd it to six. Livy. Lib. 7.' (NLS MS 23159, item 14, pp. 13, 17 and 19; cf. Mossner, 'Memoranda', pp. 506, 508 and 511).

## V. OF THE BALANCE OF TRADE

Published in: *1752a, 1752b, 1753, 1754, 1758, 1760, 1764, 1767, 1768, 1770, 1772, 1777a*. A French translation was published in the *Journal œconomique* in 1754.

Significant revisions:

> Of the revisions made to the text of this essay, perhaps the most interesting and thought-provoking is that which relates to the character of Jonathan Swift (below, no. 2).
>
> 1) *1752a–1758* read 'I have been told, that many old acts of parliament show the same ignorance in the nature of commerce. And to this day, in a neighbouring kingdom, the exportation' (*1752a*, p. 79), and *1760* reads 'There are proofs in many old acts of the SCOTCH parliament of the same ignorance in the nature of commerce. And to this day, in FRANCE, the exportation' (*1760*, vol. II, p. 82); not 'There are proofs . . . the exportation' (above, p. 46).
>
> 2) *1752a–1752b* read 'an author, who has more humour than knowledge, more taste than judgment, and more spleen, prejudice, and passion than any of these qualities.' (*1752a*, p. 81; cf. above, p. 47).
>
> 3) *1752a–1760* read 'with which we are in this kingdom so much infatuated.' (*1752a*, p. 89; cf. above, p. 51).
>
> 4) *1752a–1760* omit the two paragraphs 'It must, however . . . third of that sum.' (above, pp. 53–5).
>
> 5) *1752a–1760* read 'But as our darling projects of paper credit are pernicious, being almost the only expedient' (*1752a*, p. 92; cf. above, p. 55).
>
> 6) *1752a–1768* read '1,700,000' (*1752a*, p. 94), not '2,700,000' (above, p. 55).
>
> 7) *1752a–1768* read 'amass'd a sum greater than that of *Harry* the VII?*' and append the following note: '*There were about eight ounces of silver in a pound *Sterling* in *Harry* the VII.'s time.' (*1752a*, p. 94; cf. above, p. 55).
>
> 8) *1752a–1752b* omit 'For above . . . all ITALY.' (above, p. 59).

Copy text: *1777a*

Headnote:

> A draft of this essay had been composed by October 1750, when James Oswald of Dunnikier had written to Hume to criticize it (*Letters*, vol. I, p. 142, n. 6). Hume had replied to Oswald and defended the argument of this essay in a letter of 1 November 1750 (*Letters*, vol. I, pp. 142–4). But he also clarified the expression of his argument in response to Oswald's criticisms: 'My expression in the Essay needs correction, which has occasioned you to mistake it' (*Letters*, vol. I, p. 143). For an example of such clarification, see below, p. 357, n. 56.
>
> The balance of trade was one of the principal pillars of the mercantilist economics that Hume was determined to undermine and, if possible, to discredit. The radical error in mercantilism had been to confuse national wealth with the accumulation of bullion in gold and silver (rather than, as the enlightened economics explored and championed by Hume and Adam Smith would have it, population and the capacity to produce manufactured goods). Captured by this confusion of wealth with bullion, mercantilist economics had focused, at the level of economic policy, on the importance of

achieving and defending a positive balance of payments. This mercantilist principle had been given crude but clear expression in 1664 by Thomas Mun: 'The ordinary means … to encrease our wealth and treasure is by *Forraign Trade*, wherein wee must ever observe this rule; to sell more to strangers yearly than wee consume of theirs in value' (*England's Treasure by Forraign Trade. Or, The Ballance of our Forraign Trade is The Rule of our Treasure* [1664], p. 11). Sir Josiah Child had restated the same principle with slightly more sophistication in 1692: '*if the Exports exceeds the Imports*, it is concluded the *Nation* gets by the general course of its *Trade*, it being supposed that the over-plush is Imported in *Bulloin* [*sic*], and so adds to the Treasure of the Kingdom; *Gold and Silver being taken for the measure and standard of Riches*' (Child, *New Discourse*, p. 136). In 1714, in remark 'L' to *The Fable of the Bees*, Mandeville would recommend close attention to this issue to 'Good Politicians': 'above all, they'll keep a watchful Eye over the Balance of Trade in general, and never suffer that all the Foreign Commodities together, that are imported in one Year, shall exceed in Value what of their own Growth or Manufacture is in the same exported to others' (Mandeville, *Fable*, vol. I, p. 116). In 1729 Joshua Gee had concluded his work on *The Trade and Navigation of Great-Britain Considered* (1729) by urging policies that would turn 'the Balance of Trade in our Favour … [and] greatly contribute to the Encrease of the Wealth of the Nation' ('Conclusion', p. 5). And as late as 1755 Richard Cantillon would still adhere to this principle: 'Il faut pour relever un Etat, s'attacher à y faire rentrer annuellement & constamment une balance réelle de commerce' (Cantillon, *Essai*, p. 256). Even as enlightened and subtle a thinker as Montesquieu might be mesmerized by the balance of trade, as his comments in book XX, chapter 21 of the *Esprit des Lois* show: 'Un païs qui envoye toujours moins de marchandises ou de denrées qu'il n'en reçoit, se met lui-même en équilibre en s'appauvrissant: il recevra toujours moins, jusqu'à ce que dans une pauvreté extrême il ne reçoive plus rien' (Montesquieu, *Esprit*, vol. II, p. 22).

Against this view, Hume argued that it was finally impossible to prevent accumulated money from flowing from a rich nation to a poorer neighbour. The mercantilist pursuit of a permanent positive balance of trade committed nations to a Sisyphean labour that was pointless, misanthropic and even self-harming – for how will your poor neighbours be able to purchase the goods you wish to sell them except with money? Such is the message, both shrewd and humane, behind the conclusion of 'Of the Jealousy of Trade', that 'not only as a man, but as a BRITISH subject, I pray for the flourishing commerce of GERMANY, SPAIN, ITALY, and even FRANCE itself' (above, p. 63).

Hume's challenge to this intuitive but misleading economic doctrine would be taken further by Adam Smith, whose analysis of the flows of money and goods between nations follows that of Hume at points quite closely, and who in the *Wealth of Nations* would repeatedly dismiss the fetishizing of the balance of trade as an absurdity that had perverted the economic life of Europe (Smith, *Wealth*, III.i.1, p. 377; IV.i.8–10, pp. 432–4; and IV.iii.c.2, p. 488).

On the connotations of the language of 'balance', see Robertson, *Enlightenment*, p. 62. Cf. the entry in the 'Early Memoranda': 'The Ballance of Exchange to Germany was always to our Advantage except in 1720.' (NLS MS 23159, item 14, p. 11; cf. Mossner, 'Memoranda', p. 504).

1. *two GREEK words ... discoverer*] 'ὁμοίως δὲ καὶ συκοφάντῃ τοὔνομα γενέσθαι κεκωλυμένου γὰρ ἐκφέρειν τὰ σῦκα, μηνύοντες καὶ φαίνοντες τοὺς ἐξάγοντας ἐκλήθησαν "συκοφάνται"'; 'It was in the same way, they say, that the sycophant won his name. Since the export of figs was prohibited, men who revealed and gave information against those who did export them were called "sycophants"' (Plutarch, *Moralia*, 'On Being a Busybody', XVI). The two Greek words are 'σῦκον' (a fig) and 'φάντης' (one who shows or reveals).

2. *EDWARD III*] Hume also comments on the economics of this reign in the *History of England*: 'Commerce and industry were certainly at a very low ebb during this period [the reign of Edward III]. The bad police of the country alone affords a sufficient reason. The only exports were wool, skins, hydes, leather, butter, tin, lead, and such unmanufactured goods, of which wool was by far the most considerable.... Edward endeavoured to introduce and promote the woollen manufacture by giving protection and encouragement to foreign weavers, and by enacting a law, which prohibited every one from wearing any cloth but of English fabric. The parliament prohibited the exportation of woollen goods, which was not so well judged, especially while the exportation of unwrought wool was so much allowed and encouraged. A like injudicious law was made against the exportation of manufactured iron' (*History of England*, vol. II, pp. 279–80). The statutes in question are 11 Edw. III. cap. 2, and 28 Edw. III. cap. 5.

3. *The same jealous ... exportation*] Jean-François Melon had also mocked this irrational fear concerning the export of specie: 'Disons encore un mot, sur le transport de l'argent à l'Etranger, que la plûpart ont regardé comme pernicieux. Pensent-ils que c'est un present qu'on fait? Si la balance du commerce est inégale, nous ne pouvons solder que par là: si elle est égale, l'Etranger devient notre débiteur, notre tributaire; & le Change nous sera toujours avantageux' (Melon, *Essai politique*, pp. 257–8).

4. *custom-house books*] The earliest, and very imperfect, attempt to capture statistically the flows of imports and exports. Hume had long been aware of their inaccuracy, as an entry in the 'Early Memoranda' shows: 'Our Exports no Rule to judge of our Trade. Men [Masters *entered above the line*] enter more than they export to perswade others that their Ship is near full.' (NLS MS 23159, item 14, p. 32; cf. Mossner, 'Memoranda', p. 505).

5. *Mr. GEE*] Hume refers to Gee's *The Trade and Navigation of Great-Britain Considered* (1729), a work of which the subtitle, 'That the surest Way for a Nation to increase in Riches, is to prevent the Importation of such Foreign Commodities as may be rais'd at Home', reveals its autarchist principles. In his *Lectures on Jurisprudence* delivered in 1762–3, Adam Smith would echo his friend: 'No nation can be ruined by the ballance of trade being against them. If we look into Gees book we find that trade to all the nations of Europe had a ballance against us excepting Spain, Portugall, and Ireland, besides the American plantations, for the West Indian islands had a vast ballance against us. This he represents as threatening us with immediate ruin; and as Swift imagined that in six or seven years there would not be a shill. or a guinea left in Ireland, notwithstanding of which Ireland is improving very fast, so he seems to have imagined that England would be utterly ruined in a short time if some stop was not put to this destructive and ruinous forreign trade. This indeed has been the cry, that the forreign trade would be the ruin of England, ever since the time of Ch. 2ᵈ, and notwithstanding of this the nation has continually improved in riches, in strength, and opulence; and money when wanted is raised in greater abundance and with greater facility now than ever . . . No nation can ever be ruind by this. The same thing ruins nations as individualls, viz their consumption being greater than their produce' (Smith, *Jurisprudence*, pp. 392–3: cf. pp. 506–7 and 513).

6. *an expensive foreign war*] Presumably the War of the Austrian Succession (1740–48).

7. *Dr. SWIFT*] Hume refers to Swift's *A Short View of the State of Ireland* (1727–8). Note the important variant above, no. 2 in the list of variants.

8. *specie*] i.e. coined money.

9. *the HARRYS and EDWARDS*] i.e. the medieval and early-modern period, from 1100 (the accession of Henry I) to 1553 (the death of Edward VI).

10. *naturalists*] i.e. students of natural science.

11. *from the INDIES*] On the importation of precious metals from South America, and its impact on the economies of Europe, see above, p. 49.

12. *But as any body of water . . . latter*] The hydraulic metaphor Hume uses to illustrate the natural principle of the flow of money between countries was perhaps coloured by his recent observations of the canals and dykes of the Low Countries, through which he had travelled in 1748: 'Holland [is] . . . an unbounded Plain divided by Canals, & Ditches & Rivers. The Sea higher than the Country: The Towns higher than the Sea: And the Ramparts higher than the Towns' (*Letters*, vol. I, p. 114). He had employed the same hydraulic metaphor in his letter of 10 April 1749 to Montesquieu, and there too he had applied it to the question of the balance of trade in a passage which is in general close to the wording and argument of this essay: 'Il paroît que nous avons en Angleterre une trop grande jalousie de la balance du commerce. Il est difficile que l'équilibre se rompe au point de faire un tort considérable

à une nation. Si la moitié de l'argent qui est en Angleterre étoit subitement anéantie, le travail et les marchandises deviendroient subitement à si bon marché qu'il s'en suivroit subitement une grande exportation qui attireroit chez nous l'argent de tous nos voisins. Si la moitié de l'argent qui est en Angleterre étoit subitement doublée, les marchandises deviendroient subitement beaucoup plus chères, l'importation croîtroit au préjudice de l'exportation et notre argent, se repandroit chez tous nos voisins. Il semble que l'argent, non plus que l'eau, ne peut être élevé ni abaissé aucune part beaucoup au delà du niveau auquel il est dans les endroits où la communication est ouverte, mais qu'il doit toujours s'élever ou s'abaisser en proportion des marchandises et du travail qui sont dans chaque Etat' (*Letters*, vol. I, pp. 136–7). Cf. also the similar point Hume makes to James Oswald of Dunnikier (*Letters*, vol. I, p. 143). Smith would follow Hume in the use of hydraulic metaphors to illustrate economic processes (see, e.g., Smith, *Wealth*, pp. 511–13, IV.v.a.19).

13. *the Heptarchy*] The Anglo-Saxon kingdoms of England from the fifth to the ninth centuries. See *History of England*, vol. I, pp. 23–54.

14. *Since the union . . . art and industry?*] The Union between Scotland and England had occurred in 1707, in the teeth of strong opposition from some Scots, who feared the economic and political consequences of being absorbed into their larger and richer southern neighbour. Hume here writes as an enlightened defender of the Union.

15. *L'ABBE DU BOS*] Hume refers to Dubos's *Les Interets de l'Angleterre malentendus dans la guerre presente* (Amsterdam, 1703), a pretended translation of a fictitious English book by a member of the House of Commons, mischievously intended to persuade the English to abandon the War of the Spanish Succession (Hume does not appear to be aware of Dubos's disingenuousness). Dubos reviews England's economic relations with Scotland on pp. 45–8, speaking in his assumed *persona* of an English MP: 'Si nous voulons engager l'Ecosse à souscrire à l'acte que nous passâmes il y a deux ans en faveur de ce Prince [the Act of Succession of 1701, which transferred the English throne to the House of Hanover in the event that there was no heir born of Queen Anne], il faut lui accorder *l'incorporation*, ou cette union entière des deux Roiaumes tant de fois demandée par les Ecossois, & toûjours refusée par les Anglois . . . Cette union ne se peut faire sans que la richesse de l'Angleterre diminuë de moitié. Les Ecossois sont plus sobres, plus souples & plus actifs que les Anglois. Les vivres sont à meilleur marché dans leur pays que dans le nôtre. En voilà trop pour faire passer toutes nos manufactures de laine en Ecosse dez que l'on y pourra transporter nos laines écrues avec la même liberté que l'on les transporte d'une Comté d'Angleterre dans une autre . . . Les Ecossois connoissent la situation où nous nous sommes mis, & ils en veulent profiter' (pp. 45–8).

16. *the TWEED*] A river forming part of the border between Scotland and England.

17. *any man . . . at this day*] In 1748 Hume himself had travelled across Europe while serving in the diplomatic mission of General St Clair to Vienna and Turin, and had recorded his observations, many of which address details of prosperity and industry, in a long letter to John Home of Ninewells (*Letters*, vol. I, pp. 114–33).

18. *Our jealousy . . . commodity*] The irrationality of English jealousy of French prosperity would also strike Adam Smith in part VI of *The Theory of Moral Sentiments*, included for the first time in the sixth edition of 1790: 'France and England may each of them have some reason to dread the increase of the naval and military power of the other; but for either of them to envy the internal happiness and prosperity of the other, the cultivation of its lands, the advancement of its manufactures, the increase of its commerce, the security and number of its ports and harbours, its proficiency in all the liberal arts and sciences, is surely beneath the dignity of two such great nations. These are all real improvements of the world we live in. Mankind are benefited, human nature is ennobled by them. In such improvements each nation ought, not only to endeavour to excel, but from the love of mankind, to promote, instead of obstructing the excellence of its neighbours. These are all proper objects of national emulation, not of national prejudice or envy' (Smith, *Theory*, VI.ii.2.4, p. 229: cf. also Smith, *Wealth*, pp. 467–8, IV.ii.38).

19. *There are many . . . grubbed up*] For examples drawn from the first half of the eighteenth century of this anxiety about the amount of land being converted to viticulture in France, see Hugh Johnson, *The Story of Wine: From Noah to Now*, new edition (Académie du Vin Library, 2020), pp. 259–61. Cf. also Smith, *Wealth*, I.xi, pp. 170–71.

20. *So sensible . . . every other product*] Jean-François Melon had esteemed wheat as the basic commercial commodity: 'le bled est la base du Commerce, parce qu'il est le soutien necessaire de la vie, & sa provision doit être le premier objet du Legislateur' (Melon, *Essai politique*, p. 4).

21. *VAUBAN*] Hume refers to Vauban's *Projet d'une dixme royale* (1707), which had been translated into English as *A Project for a Royal Tythe* (1708). One of Vauban's targets in this project were the abuses arising from the 'Doüanes Provinciales' (Vauban, *Projet*, p. 3), of which those applied to the wines of the south were frequently in the forefront of his mind (e.g. Vauban, *Projet*, pp. 9 and 31–2). Vauban's *Projet* had been mentioned (and cursorily described) by Jean-François Melon (Melon, *Essai politique*, pp. 358, 368–9 and 393).

22. *paper-credit*] A foreshadowing of the gloomy prognostications of the essay 'Of Public Credit' (above, pp. 75–87); and an interesting indication of Hume's preference for money to take the form of precious metal, and hence of his (perhaps surprisingly un-modern) suspicion of paper money.

23. *banish a great part of those precious metals*] Adam Smith will later endorse this deduction: 'But the paper cannot go abroad; because at a distance from

the banks which issue it, and from the country in which payment of it can be exacted by law, it will not be received in common payments. Gold and silver, therefore, to the amount of eight hundred thousand pounds will be sent abroad, and the channel of home circulation will remain filled with a million of paper, instead of the million of those metals which filled it before' (Smith, *Wealth*, II.ii, p. 294).

24. *chequer-notes*] i.e. exchequer bills.

25. *The FRENCH have no banks*] The Banque Générale (later the Banque Royale) created by John Law in 1716 had collapsed in 1720, and this had led to a suspicion of banks among the French which would endure until the creation of the Banque de France by Napoléon in 1800. Hume had noted the unusualness of the arrangements for public credit in France in his 'Early Memoranda': 'Bills of Exchange in France dont pass like Money or bank Notes' (NLS MS 23159, item 14, p. 15; cf. Mossner, 'Memoranda', p. 507).

26. *Essay III*] i.e. 'Of Money'.

27. *The same fashion . . . unlimited*] In the aftermath of the War of the Austrian Succession (1740–48), Genoa had suffered a financial crisis as a result of its being under Austrian control since 1746.

28. *Our tax on plate . . . impolitic*] In the mid-eighteenth century a tax was levied on those owning more than 100 ounces of silver plate. This tax would be abolished only in 1851.

29. *Before the introduction . . . colonies*] Hume had discussed this situation in the American colonies in a letter of 10 April 1749 to Montesquieu: 'Avant 1706, il y avoit une quantité suffisante d'or et d'argent dans toutes nos colonies pour les usages communs; on y introduisit un papier de crédit ou papier courant, qui fit sortir tout l'argent et a eu de si pernicieuses conséquences que le Parlement est résolu de l'abolir cette session' (*Letters*, vol. I, p. 136). In 1769 he would revert to the topic of the currency arrangements of the colonies in a letter to the Abbé Morellet (*Letters*, vol. II, pp. 204–5). In 1751 Parliament had enacted legislation that restricted the power of the colonial governments to issue paper money (24 George II, c. 53).

30. *LYCURGUS*] 'πρῶτον μὲν γὰρ ἀκυρώσας πᾶν νόμισμα χρυσοῦν καὶ ἀργυροῦν μόνῳ χρῆσθαι τῷ σιδηρῷ προσέταξε· καὶ τούτῳ δὲ ἀπὸ πολλοῦ σταθμοῦ καὶ ὄγκου δύναμιν ὀλίγην ἔδωκε, ὥστε δέκα μνῶν ἀμοιβὴν ἀποθήκης τε μεγάλης ἐν οἰκίᾳ δεῖσθαι καὶ ζεύγους ἄγοντος. τούτου δὲ κυρωθέντος ἐξέπεσεν ἀδικημάτων γένη πολλὰ τῆς Λακεδαίμονος. τίς γὰρ ἢ κλέπτειν ἔμελλεν ἢ δωροδοκεῖν ἢ ἀποστερεῖν ἢ ἁρπάζειν ὃ μήτε κατακρύψαι δυνατὸν ἦν μήτε κεκτῆσθαι ζηλωτόν, ἀλλὰ μηδὲ κατακόψαι λυσιτελές· ὀξεῖ γάρ, ὡς λέγεται, διαπύρου σιδήρου τὸ στόμωμα κατασβέσας ἀφείλετο τὴν εἰς τἆλλα χρείαν καὶ δύναμιν, ἀδρανοῦς καὶ δυσέργου γενομένου . . . ἀλλὰ οὕτως ἀπερημωθεῖσα κατὰ μικρὸν ἡ τρυφὴ τῶν ζωπυρούντων καὶ τρεφόντων αὐτὴ δι᾿ αὑτῆς ἐμαραίνετο· καὶ πλεῖον οὐδὲν ἦν τοῖς πολλὰ κεκτημένοις, ὁδὸν οὐκ ἐχούσης εἰς μέσον τῆς εὐπορίας, ἀλλ᾿ ἐγκατῳκοδομημένης καὶ ἀργούσης'; 'In the first place, he withdrew all gold and silver money from

currency, and ordained the use of iron money only. Then to a great weight and mass of this he gave a trifling value, so that ten minas' worth required a large storeroom in the house, and a yoke of cattle to transport it. When this money obtained currency, many sorts of iniquity went into exile from Lacedaemon. For who would steal, or receive as a bribe, or rob, or plunder that which could neither be concealed, nor possessed with satisfaction, nay, nor even cut to pieces with any profit? For vinegar was used, as we are told, to quench the red-hot iron, robbing it of its temper and making it worthless for any other purpose, when once it had become brittle and hard to work ... But luxury, thus gradually deprived of that which stimulated and supported it, died away of itself, and men of large possessions had no advantage over the poor, because their wealth found no public outlet, but had to be stored up at home in idleness' (Plutarch, *Lycurgus*, IX.1–2 and 4).

31. *specie*] see above, p. 334, n. 16.

32. *There was an invention ... of this nature*] This system of credit had been introduced by the Royal Bank of Scotland in 1728. Adam Smith would describe at some length the recent Scottish innovations in the financing of trade in *The Wealth of Nations*, book II, chapter 2 (Smith, *Wealth*, pp. 297–320, II.ii.41–84). Note, however, the entry in the 'Early Memoranda': 'The Origin of Bills of Exchange from the Jews being banish'd France' (NLS MS 23159, item 14, p. 13; cf. Mossner, 'Memoranda', p. 506). In chapter 16 of Book XXI of the *Esprit des Lois* Montesquieu would agree: 'Ils [the Jews] inventérent les Lettres de change; & par ce moyen le Commerce pût éluder la violence & se maintenir par-tout; le négociant le plus riche n'ayant que des biens invisibles qui pouvoient être envoyés partout & ne laissoient de trace nulle-part' (Montesquieu, *Esprit*, vol. II, p. 68).

33. *so small as twenty pounds*] cf. Adam Smith: 'Whoever has a credit of this kind with one of those companies, and borrows a thousand pounds upon it, for example, may repay this sum piecemeal, by twenty and thirty pounds at a time ...' (Smith, *Wealth*, p. 299, II.ii.45).

34. *After this practice ... farther*] Two private banks had recently been established in Glasgow: the Ship Bank (1749) and the Glasgow Arms Bank (1750). Adam Smith would later report the popular belief that these innovations had doubled the trade of Glasgow and quadrupled that of Scotland as a whole, without however wholly subscribing to those estimates himself: 'Whether the trade, either of Scotland in general, or of the city of Glasgow in particular, has really increased in so great a proportion, during so short a period, I do not pretend to know. If either of them has increased in this proportion, it seems to be an effect too great to be accounted for by the sole operation of this cause. That the trade and industry of Scotland, however, have increased very considerably during this period, and that the banks have contributed a good deal to this increase, cannot be doubted' (Smith, *Wealth*, p. 297, II.ii.41). Patrick O'Brien has underlined the importance of

decentralized initiatives in developing the credit system of Britain after the Glorious Revolution: 'The whole credit system evolved, moreover, without serious hindrance from central government and the courts. Punishments for those who could not meet their debts remained severe and probably deterred many would-be entrepreneurs from taking more than carefully calculated risks. Nevertheless, rules for the extension of credit could be left to the prudence and honour of businessmen. The law confined itself to the protection of creditors from fraud but recognised bills of exchange as assignable and negotiable instruments of credit, that is, as paper promises that could circulate as money. No legal restrictions were placed on the foundation and activities of city and country banks' (O'Brien, 'Connections', p. 62).

35. *the recoinage made after the union*] cf. above, p. 337, n. 39. The Scots recoinage took place between 1707 and 1710.

36. *near a million of specie*] Adam Smith would concur: 'The whole value of the gold and silver, therefore, which circulated in Scotland before the union, cannot be estimated at less than a million sterling' (Smith, *Wealth*, p. 298, II.ii.42).

37. *a third of that sum*] Adam Smith estimated that 'In the present times the whole circulation of Scotland cannot be estimated at less than two millions, of which that part which consists in gold and silver, more probably does not amount to half a million' (Smith, *Wealth*, p. 298, II.ii.42).

38. *the immense treasure . . . HARRY VII.*] Hume would supply more detail in the *History of England*: 'so insatiable was his [Henry VII's] avarice, that . . . [by] all these arts of accumulation, joined to a rigid frugality in his expence, he so filled his coffers, that he is said to have possessed in ready money the sum of 1,800,000 pounds: A treasure almost incredible, if we consider the scarcity of money in those times'. In a footnote, Hume translated that fortune into contemporary values: 'Silver was during this reign 37 shillings and sixpence a pound, which makes Henry's treasure near three millions of our present money' (*History of England*, vol. III, p. 68 and n. t).

39. *MEDIAN and PELOPONNESIAN wars*] The Median War, between the Hellenes and the Persians, lasted from 492 to 449 BC, and resulted in a check to Persian ambitions for westward expansion. The Peloponnesian War, between the Delian League led by Athens and the Peloponnesian League led by Sparta, lasted from 431 to 404 BC, and ended with the defeat of Athens at the sea battle of Aegospotami (405 BC) and her surrender the following year. It was the subject of Thucydides's great history.

40. *STANIAN*] Hume refers to Stanyan's *An Account of Switzerland* (1714): 'Berne in particular, has at this time 300000 Pounds Sterling at Interest; yet that Sum, as I am credibly inform'd, makes not a Sixth Part of what remains in the Treasury' (Stanyan, *Switzerland*, p. 187): and on this point of the sterling holdings of the Bernese, see also Berkeley, *Querist*, p. 56. Stanyan suggests that the appearance of poverty in some of the Swiss cantons was deceptive:

'This Country, considered in general, being naturally barren, and the Inhabitants ill supplying that Defect by their Commerce, the Publick Revenues cannot be very considerable ... However, if the Wealth of a State is to be computed, like that of a single Person, by the Income in Proportion to the Issues, some of these Common-wealths ought not to be called Poor. For tho' their yearly Incomes be small, yet they are greater than their Expences; so that they can afford to lay up a little Sum every Year, which in a long Course of Time amounts to a considerable Treasure' (p. 182); 'When I say, Some of the Common-wealths of *Switzerland* ought not to be called Poor, I mean those with Cities; for the Petty or Popular Cantons have scarce any publick Revenues, but tax themselves by Voluntary Contributions, according as the present Occasion requires' (p. 183).

41. *lib. xii*] Hume refers to Pericles's speech to the Athenians, reassuring them that they possessed the wherewithal to guarantee victory: 'παρῄνει δὲ καὶ περὶ τῶν παρόντων ἅπερ καὶ πρότερον, παρασκευάζεσθαί τε ἐς τὸν πόλεμον καὶ τὰ ἐκ τῶν ἀγρῶν ἐσκομίζεσθαι, ἔς τε μάχην μὴ ἐπεξιέναι, ἀλλὰ τὴν πόλιν ἐσελθόντας φυλάσσειν, καὶ τὸ ναυτικόν, ἧπερ ἰσχύουσιν, ἐξαρτύεσθαι, τά τε τῶν ξυμμάχων διὰ χειρὸς ἔχειν, λέγων τὴν ἰσχὺν αὐτοῖς ἀπὸ τούτων εἶναι τῶν χρημάτων τῆς προσόδου, τὰ δὲ πολλὰ τοῦ πολέμου γνώμῃ καὶ χρημάτων περιουσίᾳ κρατεῖσθαι. θαρσεῖν τε ἐκέλευε προσιόντων μὲν ἑξακοσίων ταλάντων ὡς ἐπὶ τὸ πολὺ φόρου κατ᾽ ἐνιαυτὸν ἀπὸ τῶν ξυμμάχων τῇ πόλει ἄνευ τῆς ἄλλης προσόδου, ὑπαρχόντων δὲ ἐν τῇ ἀκροπόλει ἔτι τότε ἀργυρίου ἐπισήμου ἑξακισχιλίων ταλάντων (τὰ γὰρ πλεῖστα τριακοσίων ἀποδέοντα μύρια ἐγένετο, ἀφ᾽ ὧν ἔς τε τὰ προπύλαια τῆς ἀκροπόλεως καὶ τἆλλα οἰκοδομήματα καὶ ἐς Ποτείδαιαν ἀπανηλώθη), χωρὶς δὲ χρυσίου ἀσήμου καὶ ἀργυρίου ἔν τε ἀναθήμασιν ἰδίοις καὶ δημοσίοις καὶ ὅσα ἱερὰ σκεύη περί τε τὰς πομπὰς καὶ τοὺς ἀγῶνας καὶ σκῦλα Μηδικὰ καὶ εἴ τι τοιουτότροπον, οὐκ ἐλάσσονος ἢ πεντακοσίων ταλάντων'; 'And he gave them the same advice as before about the present situation: that they should prepare for the war, should bring in their property from the fields, and should not go out to meet the enemy in battle, but should come into the city and there act on the defensive; that they should equip their fleet, in which their strength lay, and keep a firm hand upon their allies, explaining that the Athenian power depended on revenue of money received from the allies, and that, as a general rule, victories in war were won by abundance of money as well as by wise policy. And he bade them be of good courage, as on an average six hundred talents of tribute were coming in yearly from the allies to the city, not counting the other sources of revenue, and there were at this time still on hand in the Acropolis six thousand talents of coined silver (the maximum amount had been nine thousand seven hundred talents, from which expenditures had been made for the construction of the Propylaea of the Acropolis and other buildings, as well as for the operations at Potidaea). Besides, there was uncoined gold and silver in public and private dedications, and all the sacred vessels used in the processions and

games, and the Persian spoils and other treasures of like nature, worth not less than five hundred talents' (Thucydides, II.xiii.2–4). Περὶ δὲ τοῦ πολέμου πεφροντισμένως ἀπολογισάμενος ἐξηριθμήσατο μὲν τὸ πλῆθος τῶν συμμάχων τῇ πόλει καὶ τὴν ὑπεροχὴν τῆς ναυτικῆς δυνάμεως, πρὸς δὲ τούτοις τὸ πλῆθος τῶν μετακεκομισμένων ἐκ Δήλου χρημάτων εἰς τὰς Ἀθήνας, ἃ συνέβαινεν ἐκ τῶν φόρων ταῖς πόλεσι κοινῇ συνηθροῖσθαι κοινῶν δ᾽ ὄντων τῶν μυρίων ταλάντων ἀπανήλωτο πρὸς τὴν κατασκευὴν τῶν προπυλαίων καὶ τὴν Ποτιδαίας πολιορκίαν τετρακισχίλια τάλαντα· καὶ καθ᾽ ἕκαστον ἐνιαυτὸν ἐκ τοῦ φόρου τῶν συμμάχων ἀνεφέρετο τάλαντα τετρακόσια ἑξήκοντα. χωρὶς δὲ τούτων τά τε πομπεῖα καὶ τὰ Μηδικὰ σκῦλα πεντακοσίων ἄξια ταλάντων ἀπεφήνατο, ἔν τε τοῖς ἱεροῖς ἀπεδείκνυεν ἀναθημάτων τε πλῆθος καὶ τὸ τῆς Ἀθηνᾶς ἄγαλμα ἔχειν χρυσίου πεντήκοντα τάλαντα, ὡς περιαιρετῆς οὔσης τῆς περὶ τὸν κόσμον κατασκευῆς· καὶ ταῦτα, ἀναγκαῖα εἰ καταλάβοι χρεία, χρησαμένους παρὰ τῶν θεῶν πάλιν ἀποκαταστήσειν ἐν εἰρήνῃ· τούς τε τῶν πολιτῶν βίους διὰ τὴν πολυχρόνιον εἰρήνην πολλὴν ἐπίδοσιν εἰληφέναι πρὸς εὐδαιμονίαν'; 'Speaking of the war, Pericles, after defending his course in well-considered words, enumerated first the multitude of allies Athens possessed and the superiority of its naval strength, and then the large sum of money which had been removed from Delos to Athens and which had in fact been gathered from the tribute into one fund for the common use of the cities; from the ten thousand talents in the common fund four thousand had been expended on the building of the Propylaea and the siege of Potidaea; and each year there was an income from the tribute paid by the allies of four hundred and sixty talents. Beside this he declared that the vessels employed in solemn processions and the booty taken from the Medes were worth five hundred talents, and he pointed to the multitude of votive offerings in the various sanctuaries and to the fact that the fifty talents of gold on the statue of Athena for its embellishment was so constructed as to be removable; and he showed that all these, if dire need befell them, they could borrow from the gods and return to them again when peace came, and that also by reason of the long peace the manner of life of the citizens had made great strides toward prosperity' (Diodorus Siculus, XII.xl.1–3). In the 'Early Memoranda' Hume had taken note of this passage in Thucydides, and of the topic of Athenian wealth in general: 'The Athenians stord up three Myriads of Silver Talents & 3000 of unwrought Gold before the Peloponnesian War. Æsch. Epist. Only 10000. Dem. περι συν. Only a thousand Æsch. περι παραπρες: sub fine. 7000 afterwards. I. in whole 8000. They had 1200 talents a year Id. They had 6000 Talents in bank, 600 a year says Thuc: L. 2 § 13 4000 Talents were spent before. Page. 108.' (NLS MS 23159, item 14, p. 27; cf. Mossner, 'Memoranda', p. 517).

42. *Epist.*] 'Πάλιν δὲ εἰς πόλεμον διὰ Μεγαρέας πεισθέντες καταστῆναι, καὶ τὴν χώραν τμηθῆναι προέμενοι καὶ πολλῶν ἀγαθῶν στερηθέντες, εἰρήνης ἐδεήθημεν, καὶ ἐποιησάμεθα διὰ Νικίου τοῦ Νικηράτου. καὶ πάλιν ἐν τῷ χρόνῳ τούτῳ ἑπτακισχίλια τάλαντα ἀνηνέγκαμεν εἰς τὴν ἀκρόπολιν διὰ τὴν εἰρήνην ταύτην,

τριήρεις δ᾽ ἐκτησάμεθα πλωίμους καὶ ἐντελεῖς οὐκ ἐλάττους ἢ τριακοσίας, φόρος δ᾽ ἡμῖν κατ᾽ ἐνιαυτὸν προσήει πλέον ἢ χίλια καὶ διακόσια τάλαντα, καὶ Χερρόνησον καὶ Νάξον καὶ Εὔβοιαν εἴχομεν, πλείστας δ᾽ ἀποικίας ἐν τοῖς χρόνοις τούτοις ἀπεστείλαμεν᾽; 'But again we were persuaded to go to war, now because of the Megarians. Having given up our land to be ravaged, and suffering great privations, we longed for peace, and finally concluded it through Nicias, the son of Niceratus. In the period that followed we again deposited treasure in the Acropolis, seven thousand talents, thanks to this peace, and we acquired triremes, seaworthy and fully equipped, no fewer than three hundred in number; a yearly tribute of more than twelve hundred talents came in to us; we held the Chersonese, Naxos, and Euboea, and in these years we sent out a host of colonies' (Aeschines, *On the Embassy*, CLXXV). 'ἐξ οὗ δ᾽ οἱ διερωτῶντες ὑμᾶς οὗτοι πεφήνασι ῥήτορες "τί βούλεσθε; τί γράψω; τί ὑμῖν χαρίσωμαι;" προπέποται τῆς παραυτίκα χάριτος τὰ τῆς πόλεως πράγματα, καὶ τοιαυτὶ συμβαίνει, καὶ τὰ μὲν τούτων πάντα καλῶς ἔχει, τὰ δ᾽ ὑμέτερ᾽ αἰσχρῶς᾽; 'But ever since this breed of orators appeared who ply you with such questions as "What would you like? What shall I propose? How can I oblige you?" the interests of the state have been frittered away for a momentary popularity. The natural consequences follow, and the orators profit by your disgrace' (Demosthenes, *Third Olynthiac*, XXII).

43. *Συμμορίας*] 'ἐπειδὰν δὲ ταῦθ᾽ οὕτως ἔχονθ᾽ ὑπάρχῃ, κελεύω, ἐπειδὴ τὸ τίμημ᾽ ἐστὶ τῆς χώρας ἑξακισχιλίων ταλάντων, ἵν᾽ ὑμῖν καὶ τὰ χρήματ᾽ ᾖ συντεταγμένα, διελεῖν τοῦτο καὶ ποιῆσαι καθ᾽ ἑξήκοντα τάλανθ᾽ ἑκατὸν μέρη, εἶτα πένθ᾽ ἑξηκονταταλαντίας εἰς ἑκάστην τῶν μεγάλων τῶν εἴκοσι συμμοριῶν ἐπικληρῶσαι, τὴν δὲ συμμορίαν ἑκάστῳ τῶν μερῶν μίαν ἑξηκονταταλαντίαν ἀποδοῦναι, ὅπως, ἂν μὲν ὑμῖν ἑκατὸν δέῃ τριήρων, τὴν μὲν δαπάνην ἑξήκοντα τάλαντα συντελῇ, τριήραρχοι δ᾽ ὦσι δώδεκα, ἂν δὲ διακοσίων, τριάκοντα μὲν ᾖ τάλαντα τὴν δαπάνην συντελοῦντα, ἓξ δὲ σώματα τριηραρχοῦντα, ἐὰν δὲ τριακοσίων, εἴκοσι μὲν ᾖ τάλαντα τὴν δαπάνην διαλύοντα, τέτταρα δὲ σώματα τριηραρχοῦντα᾽; 'When these preliminaries are settled, I propose that your wealth also should be organized, and that as the ratable value of the country is six thousand talents, this sum should be divided into a hundred parts of sixty talents each, and that then five of these parts should be allotted to each of the twenty full boards, and that the board itself should assign one part, consisting of sixty talents, to each of its own five groups. Thus, if you want a hundred war-galleys the cost of each will be covered by the sixty talents and there will be twelve trierarchs for each; if you want two hundred, there will be thirty talents to cover the cost and six persons to serve as trierarchs; if you want three hundred, there will be twenty talents for the cost and four persons to serve' (Demosthenes, *On the Navy-Boards*, XIX–XX). The 'Early Memoranda' again provides a parallel: 'The Census of the Athenians was 6000 Talents. περι συμμοριας. Qu Whether was this annual or the whole Stock. If the latter, their Forces must have been vastly high; since the twelfth Part was

sometimes exacted. Id. [It was the whole Stock as Polybius says expressly Lib. 2 C 63 *inserted below the line*]' (NLS MS 23159, item 14, pp. 24–5; cf. Mossner, 'Memoranda', p. 515).

44. *cap.* 62] Ὀ μὴν ἀλλὰ τούτοις ἐξῆς φησιν ἀπὸ τῶν ἐκ τῆς Μεγάλης πόλεως λαφύρων ἑξακισχίλια τάλαντα τοῖς Λακεδαιμονίοις πεσεῖν, ὧν τὰ δισχίλια Κλεομένει δοθῆναι κατὰ τοὺς ἐθισμούς. ἐν δὲ τούτοις πρῶτον μὲν τίς οὐκ ἂν θαυμάσειε τὴν ἀπειρίαν καὶ τὴν ἄγνοιαν τῆς κοινῆς ἐννοίας ὑπὲρ τῆς τῶν Ἑλληνικῶν πραγμάτων χορηγίας καὶ δυνάμεως; ἣν μάλιστα δεῖ παρὰ τοῖς ἱστοριογράφοις ὑπάρχειν. ἐγὼ γὰρ οὐ λέγω κατ' ἐκείνους τοὺς χρόνους, ἐν οἷς ὑπό τε τῶν ἐν Μακεδονίᾳ βασιλέων, ἔτι δὲ μᾶλλον ὑπὸ τῆς συνεχείας τῶν πρὸς ἀλλήλους πολέμων ἄρδην κατέφθαρτο τὰ Πελοποννησίων, ἀλλ' ἐν τοῖς καθ' ἡμᾶς καιροῖς, ἐν οἷς πάντες ἐν καὶ ταὐτὸ λέγοντες μεγίστην καρποῦσθαι δοκοῦσιν εὐδαιμονίαν, ὅμως ἐκ Πελοποννήσου πάσης ἐξ αὐτῶν τῶν ἐπίπλων χωρὶς σωμάτων οὐχ οἷόν τε συναχθῆναι τοσοῦτο πλῆθος χρημάτων. καὶ διότι τοῦτο νῦν οὐκ εἰκῇ, λόγῳ δέ τινι μᾶλλον ἀποφαινόμεθα, δῆλον ἐκ τούτων. τίς γὰρ ὑπὲρ Ἀθηναίων οὐχ ἱστόρηκε διότι καθ' οὓς καιροὺς μετὰ Θηβαίων εἰς τὸν πρὸς Λακεδαιμονίους ἐνέβαινον πόλεμον, καὶ μυρίους μὲν ἐξέπεμπον στρατιώτας, ἑκατὸν δ' ἐπλήρουν τριήρεις, ὅτι τότε κρίναντες ἀπὸ τῆς ἀξίας ποιεῖσθαι τὰς εἰς τὸν πόλεμον εἰσφορὰς ἐτιμήσαντο τήν τε χώραν τὴν Ἀττικὴν ἅπασαν καὶ τὰς οἰκίας, ὁμοίως δὲ καὶ τὴν λοιπὴν οὐσίαν· ἀλλ' ὅμως τὸ σύμπαν τίμημα τῆς ἀξίας ἐνέλιπε τῶν ἑξακισχιλίων διακοσίοις καὶ πεντήκοντα ταλάντοις. ἐξ οὐκ ἀπεοικὸς ἂν φανείη τὸ περὶ Πελοποννησίων ἄρτι ῥηθὲν ὑπ' ἐμοῦ. κατὰ δ' ἐκείνους τοὺς καιροὺς ἐξ αὐτῆς τῆς Μεγάλης πόλεως ὑπερβολικῶς ἀποφαινόμενος οὐκ ἄν τις εἰπεῖν τολμήσειε πλείω γενέσθαι τριακοσίων, ἐπειδήπερ ὁμολογούμενόν ἐστι διότι καὶ τῶν ἐλευθέρων καὶ τῶν δουλικῶν σωμάτων τὰ πλεῖστα συνέβη διαφυγεῖν εἰς τὴν Μεσσήνην. μέγιστον δὲ τῶν προειρημένων τεκμήριον· οὐδενὸς γὰρ ὄντες δεύτεροι τῶν Ἀρκάδων Μαντινεῖς οὔτε κατὰ τὴν δύναμιν οὔτε κατὰ τὴν περιουσίαν, ὡς αὐτὸς οὗτός φησιν, ἐκ πολιορκίας δὲ καὶ παραδόσεως ἁλόντες, ὥστε μήτε διαφυγεῖν μηδένα μήτε διακλαπῆναι ῥᾳδίως μηδέν, ὅμως τὸ πᾶν λάφυρον ἐποίησαν μετὰ τῶν σωμάτων κατὰ τοὺς αὐτοὺς καιροὺς τάλαντα τριακόσια'; 'Further he tells us that from the booty of Megalopolis six thousand talents fell to the Lacedaemonians, of which two thousand were given to Cleomenes according to usage. Now in this statement one marvels first at his lack of practical experience and of that general notion of the wealth and power of Greece so essential to a historian. For, not speaking of those times, when the Peloponnese had been utterly ruined by the Macedonian kings and still more by continued intestinal wars, but in our own times, when all are in complete unison and enjoy, it is thought, very great prosperity, I assert that a sale of all the goods and chattels, apart from slaves, in the whole Peloponnese would not bring in such a sum. That I do not make this assertion lightly but after due estimate will be evident from the following consideration. Who has not read that when the Athenians, in conjunction with the Thebans, entered on the war against the Lacedaemonians, sending out a force of ten thousand

men and manning a hundred triremes, they decided to meet the war expenses by a property tax and made a valuation for this purpose of the whole of Attica including the houses and other property. This estimate, however, fell short of 6,000 talents by 250, from which it would seem that my assertion about the Peloponnese at the present day is not far wide of the mark. But as regards the times of which we are dealing, no one, even if he were exaggerating, would venture to say that more than three hundred talents could be got out of Megalopolis, since it is an acknowledged fact that most of the free population and the slaves had escaped to Messene. But the best proof of what I say is the following: Mantinea, both in wealth and power, was second to no city in Arcadia, as Phylarchus himself says, and it surrendered after a siege, so that it was not easy for anyone to escape or for anything to be stolen, but yet the value of the whole booty together with slaves amounted at this very period to but three hundred talents' (Polybius, II.lxii).

45. *cap. 40*] 'Summam omnis captivi auri argentique translati sestertium milliens ducenties fuisse Valerius Antias tradit; qua haud dubie maior aliquanto summa ex numero plaustrorum ponderibusque auri, argenti generatim ab ipso scriptis absumptum efficitur. Alterum tantum aut in bellum proximum aut in fuga, cum Samothracen peteret, dissipatum tradunt; eoque id mirabilius erat, quod tantum pecuniae intra triginta annos post bellum Philippi cum Romanis partim ex fructu metallorum, partim ex vectigalibus aliis coacervatum fuerat. Itaque admodum inops pecuniae Philippus, Perseus contra praedives bellare cum Romanis coepit'; 'The total of all the captured gold and silver which was carried in the procession was one hundred and twenty million sesterces, according to the account of Valerius Antias; no doubt a somewhat larger total than this is made up from the number of wagons and the weights of gold and silver in various forms which are mentioned by this same author. As much again was either expended in the late war, or scattered during the flight, when Perseus was making for Samothrace, according to the historians; and this fact is the more marvellous, because this huge sum of money was accumulated within thirty years after Philip's war with the Romans, partly from the output of the mines, and partly from other revenues. Philip therefore began his war against Rome when he was rather ill-supplied with funds, but Perseus, when he was very rich' (Livy, XLV.xl.1–3).

46. *cap. 9*] 'Quo anno et Octavii praetoris navalis et Anicii regem Illyriorum Gentium ante currum agentis triumphi fuere celebres. Quam sit adsidua eminentis fortunae comes invidia altissimisque adhaereat, etiam hoc colligi potest, quod cum Anicii Octaviique triumphum nemo interpellaret, fuere, qui Pauli impedire obniterentur. Cuius tantum priores excessit vel magnitudine regis Persei vel specie simulacrorum vel modo pecuniae, ut bis miliens centiens sestertium aerario intulerit is, et omnium ante actorum comparationem amplitudine vicerit'; 'In this year two other triumphs were celebrated:

that of Octavius, the praetor in charge of the fleet, and that of Anicius, who drove before his triumphal chariot Gentius, King of the Illyrians. How inseparable a companion of great success is jealousy, and how she attaches herself to the most eminent, may be gathered from this fact: although no one raised objections to the triumphs of Octavius and Anicius, there were those who tried to place obstacles in the way of that of Paulus. His triumph so far exceeded all former ones, whether in the greatness of King Perseus himself, or in the display of statues and the amount of money borne in the procession, that Paulus contributed to the treasury two hundred million sesterces, and by reason of this vast sum eclipsed all previous triumphs by comparison' (Velleius Paterculus, I.ix.5–6).

47. *cap. 3*] 'intulit et Aemilius Paulus Perseo rege victo e Macedonica praeda |M̄M̄M̄|, a quo tempore populus Romanus tributum pendere desiit'; 'Aemilius Paulus also after the defeat of King Perseus paid in to the treasury from the booty won in Macedonia 300 million sesterces; and from that date onward the Roman nation left off paying the citizens' property-tax' (Pliny the Elder, *Natural History*, XXXIII.xvii).

48. *ibid.*] See above, p. 355, n. 45.

49. *PTOLEMIES*] i.e. the ruling dynasty in Egypt from 305 to 30 BC.

50. *ARBUTHNOT's computation*] Hume has misread Arbuthnot's tables. Arbuthnot specifies an equivalent of £193.15s per Attic talent (and even this rate of exchange yields only £143,375,000, not Hume's even larger figure). But the Ptolemaic talent (which must be what Appian is referring to) was much less valuable, at only £20. This equivalent yields a more reasonable (but still considerable) total of £14,800,000 (Arbuthnot, *Tables*, pp. 23 and 24).

51. *which the Author of the world has intended*] For the sceptical scrutiny that Hume elsewhere applies to such appeals to providential design, see above, vol. 1, p. 333, n. 18. In 'Of the Jealousy of Trade' Hume would make nature, rather than a deity, the designer of this beneficial distribution of benefits: 'Nature, by giving a diversity of geniuses, climates, and soils, to different nations, has secured their mutual intercourse and commerce, as long as they all remain industrious and civilized' (above, p. 61). Montesquieu had made a similar point in the *Esprit des Lois*, book XXI, chapter 4: 'Le commerce ancien que nous connoissons se faisant d'un port de la Méditerranée à l'autre, étoit presque tout dans le Midi. Or les peuples du même climat ayant chez eux à peu près les mêmes choses, n'ont pas tant de besoin de commercer entr'eux que ceux d'un climat différent. Le Commerce en Europe étoit donc autrefois moins étendu, qu'il ne l'est aprésent' (Montesquieu, *Esprit*, vol. II, pp. 28–9).

52. *Proem.*] 'χρημάτων δ' ἐν τοῖς θησαυροῖς τέσσαρες καὶ ἑβδομήκοντα μυριάδες ταλάντων Αἰγυπτίων'; 'They also had in their treasury seven hundred and forty thousand Egyptian talents' (Appian, *Roman History*, 'Preface', X).

53. *We ought . . . only one*] A reference to a passage in Swift's *An Answer to a Paper called A Memorial of the Poor Inhabitants, Tradesmen and Labourers*

*of the Kingdom of Ireland* (1728): 'But I will tell you a *Secret*, which I learned many Years ago from the Commissioners of the *Customs* in *London*: They said, when any *Commodity* appeared to be taxed above a *moderate Rate*, the Consequence was to lessen that Branch of the Revenue by one Half; and one of those Gentlemen pleasantly told me, that the Mistake of Parliaments, on such Occasions, was owing to an Error of computing Two and Two to make Four; whereas, in the Business of laying *heavy Impositions*, Two and Two never made more than One; which happens by lessening the Import, and the strong Temptation of running such Goods as paid high Duties' (Swift, *Prose Writings*, vol. XII, p. 21). Adam Smith would also refer to this passage (Smith, *Wealth*, p. 882, V.ii.k.27).

54. *What immense ... three long wars?*] Flanders corresponds approximately to modern-day Belgium. In the period 1688–1750 (the period from the Glorious Revolution to the composition of the essay) this region was the scene of repeated military action involving principally England, the United Provinces, France and Spain. The 'three long wars' to which Hume refers are the War of the Grand Alliance (1689–97), the War of the Spanish Succession (1701–14) and the War of the Austrian Succession (1740–48).

55. *flowing to ROME*] As a result of fiscal transfers from Catholic countries to the Papal See. Note that Hume added this sentence in 1753 (see list of substantive revisions above, no. 8): an interesting indication of his increasing disapproval of the economic consequences of sacerdotalism.

56. *It must carefully be remarked ... imperfect*] This clarificatory footnote was added after November 1750 because, as a result of correspondence with James Oswald of Dunnikier, Hume had realized that he had not made his thinking entirely clear on this point: 'I never meant to say that money, in all countries which communicate, must necessarily be on a level, but only on a level proportioned to their people, industry, and commodities' (*Letters*, vol. I, pp. 142–3 and n. 1; see also headnote).

## VI. OF THE JEALOUSY OF TRADE

Published in: *1760, 1764, 1767, 1768, 1770, 1772, 1777a*
Significant revisions:
    None.
Copy text: *1777a*
Headnote:
    For the composition and publication of this essay, see Harris, *Hume*, pp. 423–5, and *Letters*, vol. I, p. 317 and n. 3. Hume wrote the essay probably in late 1758. In a letter of 4 March 1758 to Lord Kames, who had sent Hume some MSS by Josiah Tucker on questions of trade, Hume replied: 'There is a hint thrown out in the papers, which gave me great satisfaction, because

it concurs with a principle which I have thrown out to your Lordship, and which you seemed not to disapprove of. I was indeed so pleased with it, that, as I told you, I intended to make it the subject of a political discourse, as soon as I should have occasion to give a new edition of that work. My principle is levelled against the narrow malignity and envy of nations, which can never bear to see their neighbours thriving, but continually repine at any new efforts towards industry made by any other nation. We desire, and seem by our absurd politics to endeavour to repress trade in all our neighbours, and would be glad that all Europe were reduced to the same state of desolation as Turkey: the consequence of which must be, that we would have little more than domestic trade, and would have nobody either to sell or buy from us' (*Letters*, vol. I, p. 272).

This essay indirectly expresses Hume's dismay at England's motives for engaging in the Seven Years' War (1756–63). It was a view with which Josiah Tucker concurred: 'But is this Spell, this Witchcraft, of the Jealousy of Trade never to be dissolved? . . . For of all Absurdities, that of going to War for the Sake of getting Trade is the most absurd; and nothing in Nature can be so extravagantly foolish' (Tucker, *Securing Trade*, p. 40). For commentary, see Hont, *Jealousy of Trade*, pp. 5–37; in particular his insight that 'jealousy of trade was a mongrel idiom, describing a process of corruption. It implied that in modern politics the logic of trade was bent to the logic of war' (ibid., p. 6). Hont also draws attention to the relevance for Hume's essay of Johann Justi's contemporary pamphlet, *Die Chimäre des Gleichgewichts der Handlung und Schiffahrt* (Altona, 1759); see Hont, *Jealousy of Trade*, pp. 34–7.

1. *one species of ill-founded jealousy*] Namely the fallacy, exploded in 'Of the Balance of Trade', that a nation might find that its supply of money is depleted by trade.
2. *this narrow and malignant opinion*] cf. 'narrow malignity' (*Letters*, vol. I, p. 272).
3. *continue still to repine*] cf. 'continually repine' (*Letters*, vol. I, p. 272).
4. *Nature . . . civilized*] cf. the rather different phrasing of essentially the same thought in 'Of the Balance of Trade', where Hume admires 'that free communication and exchange which the Author of the world has intended, by giving them soils, climates, and geniuses, so different from each other' (above, p. 57).
5. *The DUTCH . . . formerly*] Another observation in which we can see a foreshadowing of the argument of 'Of Public Credit' (above, pp. 75–87).
6. *narrow and malignant politics*] See above, p. 358, n. 2.
7. *I shall therefore . . . even FRANCE itself*] For Smith's echoing of this opinion about the foolishness of English jealousy of the French, see 'Of the Balance of Trade', above, p. 347, n. 18.

## VII. OF THE BALANCE OF POWER

Published in: *1752a, 1752b, 1753, 1754, 1758, 1760, 1764, 1767, 1768, 1770, 1772, 1777a*
Significant revisions:

Hume made four adjustments to the text of this essay, two of which are very substantial:

1) *1752a* appends a long note to 'their Italic wars' (above, p. 66):

'\*THERE have strong suspicions, of late, arisen amongst critics, and, in my opinion, not without reason, concerning the first ages of the *Roman* history; as if they were almost entirely fabulous, 'till after the sacking of the city by the *Gauls*; and were even doubtful for some time afterwards, 'till the *Greeks* began to give attention to *Roman* affairs, and commit them to writing. This scepticism, however, seems to me scarcely defensible in its full extent, with regard to the domestic history of *Rome*, which has some air of truth and probability, and cou'd scarce be the invention of an historian, who had so little morals or judgment as to indulge himself in fiction and romance. The revolutions seem so well proportion'd to their causes: The progress of the factions is so conformable to political experience: The manners and maxims of the age are so uniform and natural, that scarce any real history affords more just reflection and improvement. Is not *Machiavel*'s comment on *Livy* (a work surely of great judgment and genius) founded entirely on this period, which is represented as fabulous. I wou'd willingly, therefore, in my private sentiments, divide the matter with these critics; and allow, that the battles and victories and triumphs of those ages had been extremely falsify'd by family memoirs, as *Cicero* says they were: But as in the accounts of domestic factions, there were two opposite relations transmitted to posterity, this both serv'd as a check upon fiction, and enabled latter historians to gather some truth from comparison and reasoning. Half of the slaughter, which *Livy* commits on the *Æqui* and the *Volsci*, wou'd depopulate *France* and *Germany*; and that historian, tho' perhaps he may justly be charg'd as superficial, is at last shock'd himself with the incredibility of his narration. The same love of exaggeration seems to have magnify'd the numbers of the *Romans* in their armies, and *census*.' (*1752a*, pp. 105–6)

2) *1752a–1768* insert an additional paragraph immediately following '. . . so much infatuated.' (above, p. 68):

'*Europe* has now, for above a century, remain'd on the defensive against the greatest force, that ever, perhaps, was form'd by the civil or political combination of mankind. And such is the influence of the maxim here treated of, that tho' that ambitious nation, in the five last general wars, have been victorious in four\*, and unsuccessful only in one†, they have not much enlarg'd their dominions, nor acquir'd a total ascendant over *Europe*. On the contrary, there remain still some hopes of maintaining the resistance so long, that the natural revolutions of human affairs, together with unforeseen events and accidents, may guard us against universal monarchy, and preserve the world from so great an evil.

'*THOSE concluded by the peace of the *Pyrenees, Nimeguen, Ryswick* and *Aix-la-Chapelle.*

'† THAT concluded by the peace of *Utrecht.*' (*1752a*, pp. 109–10).

3) *1752a–1768* read 'IN the three last of these general wars, *Britain* has stood foremost in the glorious struggle; and she still maintains her station, as guardian of the general liberties of *Europe*, and patron of mankind.' (*1752a*, p. 110; cf. above, p. 68).

4) *1752a–1764* read 'ENORMOUS monarchies, such as *Europe*, at present, is in danger of falling into, are, probably' (*1752a*, p. 112; cf. above, p. 69).

Copy text: *1777a*

Headnote:

Compare the later essay by Johann Justi, *Die Chimäre des Gleichgewichts von Europa* (Altona, 1758). For comment, see Hont, *Jealousy of Trade*, pp. 34–7. As Hont says, this essay, 'which could equally have merited the title "Of Universal Empire", was a scathing indictment of all non-defensive warfare' (Hont, *Jealousy of Trade*, p. 333). On the general subject, see Herbert Butterfield, 'The Balance of Power', in *Diplomatic Investigations: Essays in the Theory of International Politics*, ed. Herbert Butterfield and M. Wight (Cambridge, MA: Harvard University Press, 1966), pp. 132–48. Note what Hume had said in 'Of Civil Liberty': 'The *balance of power* is a secret in politics, fully known only to the present age' (above, vol. 1, p. 80). This seems (depending on how much emphasis is placed on 'fully') at variance with the tendency of this later essay; as well as with certain entries in the 'Early Memoranda' (e.g. below, p. 363, n. 17).

1. *LEUCTRA*] At the battle of Leuctra in 371 BC a Theban army under the command of Epaminondas defeated an invading Spartan army. In 369 BC, to restore the balance of power in Greece and to counter the growing ascendancy of Thebes, Athens had entered into an alliance with her traditional enemy, Sparta.

2. *Whoever ... speculatist*] This text had caught Hume's eye in the 'Early Memoranda': 'The Notion of the Ballance of Power seems to be contain'd in Demosthenes Oration υπερ Μεγαλοπολ: more clearly than in any antient Author' (NLS MS 23159, item 14, p. 25; cf. Mossner, 'Memoranda', p. 515). The yoking of English and Venetian here indicates that, for the time being, Hume is associating himself (albeit doubtless only temporarily) with the neo-Machiavellian thought of Harrington and Henry Neville, for both of whom Venice embodied a republican model that England might and should follow.

3. *Lib. i*] 'Προϊόντος δὲ τοῦ χρόνου ὁ μὲν Ἀστυάγης ἐν τοῖς Μήδοις ἀποθνήσκει, ὁ δὲ Κυαξάρης ὁ τοῦ Ἀστυάγους παῖς, τῆς δὲ Κύρου μητρὸς ἀδελφός, τὴν βασιλείαν ἔσχε τὴν Μήδων. Ὁ δὲ τῶν Ἀσσυρίων βασιλεὺς κατεστραμμένος μὲν πάντας Σύρους, φῦλον πάμπολυ, ὑπήκοον δὲ πεποιημένος τὸν ΑΡΑΒίΩΝ βασιλέα, ὑπηκόους δὲ ἔχων ἤδη καὶ Ὑρκανίους, πολιορκῶν δὲ καὶ Βακτρίους, ἐνόμιζεν, εἰ τοὺς Μήδους ἀσθενεῖς ποιήσειε, πάντων γε τῶν πέριξ ῥαδίως ἄρξειν· ἰσχυρότατον γὰρ τῶν ἐγγὺς φύλων τοῦτο ἐδόκει εἶναι. οὕτω δὴ διαπέμπει πρός τε τοὺς ὑπ' αὐτὸν πάντας καὶ πρὸς Κροῖσον τὸν Λυδῶν βασιλέα καὶ πρὸς τὸν Καππαδοκῶν καὶ πρὸς Φρύγας ἀμφοτέρους καὶ πρὸς Παφλαγόνας καὶ Ἰνδοὺς καὶ πρὸς Κᾶρας καὶ Κίλικας, τὰ μὲν καὶ διαβάλλων τοὺς Μήδους καὶ Πέρσας, λέγων ὡς μεγάλα τ' εἴη ταῦτα ἔθνη καὶ ἰσχυρὰ καὶ συνεστηκότα εἰς ταὐτό, καὶ ἐπιγαμίας ἀλλήλοις πεποιημένοι εἶεν, καὶ κινδυνεύσοιεν, εἰ μή τις αὐτοὺς φθάσας ἀσθενώσοι, ἐπὶ ἓν ἕκαστον τῶν ἐθνῶν ἰόντες καταστρέψασθαι. οἱ μὲν δὴ καὶ τοῖς λόγοις τούτοις πειθόμενοι συμμαχίαν αὐτῷ ἐποιοῦντο, οἱ δὲ καὶ δώροις καὶ χρήμασιν ἀναπειθόμενοι· πολλὰ γὰρ καὶ τοιαῦτα ἦν αὐτῷ'; 'In the course of time Astyages died in Media, and Cyaxares, the son of Astyages and brother of Cyrus's mother, succeeded to the Median throne. At that time the king of Assyria had subjugated all Syria, a very large nation, and had made the king of Arabia his vassal; he already had Hyrcania under his dominion and was closely besetting Bactria. So he thought that if he should break the power of the Medes, he should easily obtain dominion over all the nations round about; for he considered the Medes the strongest of the neighbouring tribes. Accordingly, he sent around to all those under his sway and to Croesus, the king of Lydia, to the king of Cappadocia; to both Phrygias, to Paphlagonia, India, Caria, and Cilicia; and to a certain extent also he misrepresented the Medes and Persians, for he said that they were great, powerful nations, that they had intermarried with each other, and were united in common interests, and that unless some one attacked them first and broke their power, they would be likely to make war upon each one of the nations singly and subjugate them. Some, then, entered into an alliance with him because they actually believed what he said; others, because they were bribed with gifts and money, for he had great wealth' (Xenophon, *Cyropaedia*, I.v.2–3).

4. *Lib. i*] 'ἤρξαντο δὲ αὐτοῦ Ἀθηναῖοι καὶ Πελοποννήσιοι λύσαντες τὰς τριακοντούτεις σπονδὰς αἳ αὐτοῖς ἐγένοντο μετὰ Εὐβοίας ἅλωσιν. δι' ὅ τι δ' ἔλυσαν, τὰς αἰτίας προύγραψα πρῶτον καὶ τὰς διαφοράς, τοῦ μή τινα ζητῆσαί ποτε ἐξ ὅτου τοσοῦτος πόλεμος τοῖς Ἕλλησι κατέστη. τὴν μὲν γὰρ ἀληθεστάτην πρόφασιν, ἀφανεστάτην δὲ λόγῳ τοὺς Ἀθηναίους ἡγοῦμαι μεγάλους γιγνομένους καὶ φόβον παρέχοντας τοῖς Λακεδαιμονίοις ἀναγκάσαι ἐς τὸ πολεμεῖν'; 'And the war began when the Athenians and Peloponnesians broke the thirty years' truce, concluded between them after the capture of Euboea. The reasons why they broke it and the grounds of their quarrel I have first set forth, that no one may ever have to inquire for what cause the Hellenes became involved in so great a war. The truest explanation, although it has been the least often advanced, I believe to

have been the growth of the Athenians to greatness, which brought fear to the Lacedaemonians and forced them to war' (Thucydides, I.xxiii.4–6). See also I.cxviii.2: 'πρὶν δὴ ἡ δύναμις τῶν Ἀθηναίων σαφῶς ᾔρετο καὶ τῆς ξυμμαχίας αὐτῶν ἥπτοντο. τότε δὲ οὐκέτι ἀνασχετὸν ἐποιοῦντο, ἀλλ᾽ ἐπιχειρητέα ἐδόκει εἶναι πάσῃ προθυμίᾳ καὶ καθαιρετέα ἡ ἰσχύς, ἢν δύνωνται, ἀραμένοις δὴ τόνδε τὸν πόλεμον'; 'But at last the power of the Athenians began clearly to exalt itself and they were laying hands upon their allies. Then the Lacedaemonians could bear it no longer, but determined that they must attack the Athenian power with all zeal and overthrow it, if they could, by undertaking this war.' Cf., for passages with a similar import, I.cxxii.2 and I.cxxiv.3.

5. *And upon ... CHAERONEA*] At the battle of Chaeronea in 338 BC a Macedonian army defeated an allied Greek army and thereby established Macedonian hegemony in Greece.

6. *the Ostracism of ATHENS*] An Athenian institution introduced by Cleisthenes in the sixth century BC as a safeguard against tyranny, which provided that an assembly of the people could vote to exile an Athenian for ten years by writing the name of the intended exile on a piece of broken pottery (οστρακον). In chapter 21 of *Leviathan*, Hobbes had used the Athenian practice of ostracism as an illustration of the unlimited power of the sovereign (Hobbes, *Leviathan*, p. 148).

7. *the Petalism of SYRACUSE*] An institution similar to the ostracism of Athens, except that the name of the intended exile was written on olive leaves (πεταλον).

8. *PHILIP*] i.e. Philip II of Macedon.

9. *The successors of ALEXANDER*] i.e. the so-called 'Diadochi'. See below, p. 363, n. 11.

10. *lib. viii*] 'Παρῄνει δὲ καὶ τῷ Τισσαφέρνει μὴ ἄγαν ἐπείγεσθαι τὸν πόλεμον διαλῦσαι, μηδὲ βουληθῆναι ἢ κομίσαντα ναῦς Φοινίσσας ἅσπερ παρεσκευάζετο ἢ Ἕλλησι πλείοσι μισθὸν πορίζοντα τοῖς αὐτοῖς τῆς τε γῆς καὶ τῆς θαλάσσης τὸ κράτος δοῦναι, ἔχειν δ᾽ ἀμφοτέρους ἐᾶν δίχα τὴν ἀρχὴν καὶ βασιλεῖ ἐξεῖναι ἐπὶ τοὺς αὐτῷ λυπηροὺς τοὺς ἑτέρους ἐπάγειν. γενομένης δ᾽ ἂν καθ᾽ ἓν τῆς ἐς γῆν καὶ θάλασσαν ἀρχῆς, ἀπορεῖν ἂν αὐτὸν οἷς τοὺς κρατοῦντας ξυγκαθαιρήσει, ἢν μὴ αὐτὸς βούληται μεγάλῃ δαπάνῃ καὶ κινδύνῳ ἀναστάς ποτε διαγωνίσασθαι. εὐτελέστερα δὲ τάδ᾽ εἶναι, βραχεῖ μορίῳ τῆς δαπάνης καὶ ἅμα μετὰ τῆς ἑαυτοῦ ἀσφαλείας αὐτοὺς περὶ ἑαυτοὺς τοὺς Ἕλληνας κατατρῖψαι'; 'Alcibiades also urged Tissaphernes not to be too eager to bring the war to an end, nor to take such a course, either by bringing there the Phoenician fleet which he was equipping or by providing pay for a larger number of Hellenes, as would give the command of both the land and the sea to the same people, but to let the dominion be divided between the two sides, so that it would be possible for the King to lead the one party or the other against those that were troublesome to him. But if the dominion of both land and sea were united, the King himself would have no one with whom he could co-operate in destroying

the stronger, and would have no alternative but sooner or later to rise up himself and, at great expense and risk, fight a decisive struggle. The cheaper course was this – at a small fraction of the expense and at the same time with security to himself to wear the Hellenes out one upon the other' (Thucydides, VIII.xlvi.1–2).

11. *lib. xx*] In Book 20 of his history Diodorus Siculus relates the beginnings of the manoeuvring by Antigonus against his fellow Diadochi. Antigonus's downfall was related in Book 21, of which only fragments remain. However, some are pertinent to Hume's point: "Ὅτι Ἀντίγονος ὁ βασιλεὺς ἐξ ἰδιώτου γενόμενος δυνάστης καὶ πλεῖστον ἰσχύσας τῶν καθ᾽ αὑτὸν βασιλέων οὐκ ἠρκέσθη ταῖς παρὰ τῆς τύχης δωρεαῖς, ἀλλ᾽ ἐπιβαλόμενος τὰς τῶν ἄλλων βασιλείας εἰς αὑτὸν ἀδίκως περιστῆσαι τὴν ἰδίαν ἀπέβαλεν ἀρχὴν ἅμα καὶ τοῦ ζῆν ἐστερήθη'; 'King Antigonus, who rose from private station to high power and became the mightiest king of his day, was not content with the gifts of Fortune, but undertook to bring unjustly into his own hands the kingdoms of all the others; thus he lost his own dominion and was deprived of life as well' (Diodorus Siculus, XXI.i.4b).

12. *IPSUS*] A battle fought between some of the Diadochi, or successors of Alexander the Great, in 301 BC in Phrygia.

13. *PTOLEMIES*] See above, p. 356, n. 49.

14. *the fabulous history of their ITALIC wars*] These are contained in the first two books of Livy's history of Rome.

15. *HANNIBAL's invasion of the ROMAN state*] Hannibal entered Italy after crossing the Alps in 218 BC. After defeating the Romans in several battles on Italian soil he occupied most of southern Italy for fifteen years, before being defeated by Scipio Africanus at the battle of Zama in 202 BC.

16. *PHILIP of MACEDON*] i.e. Philip V.

17. *ancient historians . . . sound policy*] cf. Strabo, XIV.ii.5. See also two notes in the 'Early Memoranda': 'Perseus Ambassadors to the Rhodians spoke a Style like the Modern with regard to the Ballance of Power but are condemnd by Livy. Lib. 42. Cap. 46'; 'The Notion of the Ballance of Power seems to be contain'd in Demosthenes Oration υπερ Μεγαλοπολ: more clearly than in any antient Author' (NLS MS 23159, item 14, pp. 21 and 25; cf. Mossner, 'Memoranda', pp. 512 and 515).

18. *cap. 51*] 'ἐπεὶ δὲ Πτολεμαῖος ἀπογνοὺς μὲν τὸ ἔθνος Κλεομένει χορηγεῖν ἐπεβάλετο, βουλόμενος αὐτὸν ἐπαλείφειν ἐπὶ τὸν Ἀντίγονον διὰ τὸ πλείους ἐλπίδας ἔχειν ἐν τοῖς Λακεδαιμονίοις ἤπερ ἐν τοῖς Ἀχαιοῖς τοῦ δύνασθαι διακατέχειν τὰς τῶν ἐν Μακεδονίᾳ βασιλέων ἐπιβολάς'; 'In the first place Ptolemy threw over the League and began to give financial support to Cleomenes with a view of setting him on to attack Antigonus, as he hoped to be able to keep in check more effectually the projects of the Macedonian kings with the support of the Lacedaemonians than with that of the Achaeans' (Polybius, II.li.2–3).

19. *cap. 104*] 'δῆλον γὰρ εἶναι παντὶ τῷ καὶ μετρίως περὶ τὰ κοινὰ σπουδάζοντι καὶ νῦν, ὡς ἐάν τε Καρχηδόνιοι Ῥωμαίων ἐάν τε Ῥωμαῖοι Καρχηδονίων περιγένωνται τῷ πολέμῳ, διότι κατ' οὐδένα τρόπον εἰκός ἐστι τοὺς κρατήσαντας ἐπὶ ταῖς Ἰταλιωτῶν καὶ Σικελιωτῶν μεῖναι δυναστείαις, ἥξειν δὲ καὶ διατείνειν τὰς ἐπιβολὰς καὶ δυνάμεις αὐτῶν πέρα τοῦ δέοντος. διόπερ ἠξίου πάντας μὲν φυλάξασθαι τὸν καιρόν, μάλιστα δὲ Φίλιππον. εἶναι δὲ φυλακήν, ἐὰν ἀφέμενος τοῦ καταφθείρειν τοὺς Ἕλληνας καὶ ποιεῖν εὐχειρώτους τοῖς ἐπιβαλλομένοις κατὰ τοὐναντίον ὡς ὑπὲρ ἰδίου σώματος βουλεύηται, καὶ καθόλου πάντων. τῶν τῆς Ἑλλάδος μερῶν ὡς οἰκείων καὶ προσηκόντων αὐτῷ ποιῆται πρόνοιαν· τοῦτον γὰρ τὸν τρόπον χρωμένου τοῖς πράγμασι τοὺς μὲν Ἕλληνας εὔνους ὑπάρχειν αὐτῷ καὶ βεβαίους συναγωνιστὰς πρὸς τὰς ἐπιβολάς, τοὺς δ' ἔξωθεν ἧττον ἐπιβουλεύσειν αὐτοῦ τῇ δυναστείᾳ, καταπεπληγμένους τὴν τῶν Ἑλλήνων πρὸς αὐτὸν πίστιν. εἰ δὲ πραγμάτων ὀρέγεται, πρὸς τὰς δύσεις βλέπειν αὐτὸν ἠξίου καὶ τοῖς ἐν Ἰταλίᾳ συνεστῶσι πολέμοις προσέχειν τὸν νοῦν, ἵνα γενόμενος ἔφεδρος ἔμφρων πειραθῇ σὺν καιρῷ τῆς τῶν ὅλων ἀντιποιήσασθαι δυναστείας'; 'For it is now evident even to those of us who give but scanty attention to affairs of state, that whether the Carthaginians beat the Romans or the Romans the Carthaginians in this war, it is not in the least likely that the victors will be content with the sovereignty of Italy and Sicily, but they are sure to come here and extend their ambitions and their forces beyond the bounds of justice. Therefore I implore you all to secure yourselves against this danger, and I address myself especially to King Philip. For you, Sire, the best security is, instead of exhausting the Greeks and making them an easy prey to the invader, on the contrary to take thought for them as for your own body, and to attend to the safety of every province of Greece as if it were part and parcel of your own dominions. For if such be your policy the Greeks will bear you affection and render sure help to you in case of attack, while foreigners will be less disposed to plot against your throne, impressed as they will be by the loyalty of the Greeks to you. If you desire a field of action, turn to the west and keep your eyes on the war in Italy, so that, wisely biding your time, you may some day at the proper moment compete for the sovereignty of the world' (Polybius, V.civ.3–7).

20. *cap. 33*] 'Xenophanes per praesidia Romana in Campaniam, inde qua proximum fuit in castra Hannibalis pervenit foedusque cum eo atque amicitiam iungit legibus his: ut Philippus rex quam maxima classe – ducentas autem naves videbatur effecturus – in Italiam traiceret et vastaret maritimam oram, bellum pro parte sua terra marique gereret; ubi debellatum esset, Italia omnis cum ipsa urbe Roma Carthaginiensium atque Hannibalis esset praedaque omnis Hannibali cederet; perdomita Italia navigarent in Graeciam bellumque cum quibus regi placeret gererent; quae civitates continentis quaeque insulae ad Macedoniam vergunt, eae Philippi regnique eius essent'; 'Proceeding through the Roman posts into Campania, and from there to the camp of Hannibal by the shortest route, Xenophanes [Philip's ambassador] struck a

treaty of friendship with him, the terms being as follows: King Philip was to cross to Italy with the largest fleet he could muster – it seemed likely that he would bring it up to two hundred ships – and there lay waste the coast and conduct land and sea operations as best he could. At the war's end, all Italy together with the city of Rome itself was to belong to the Carthaginians and Hannibal, and all plunder would go to Hannibal. With Italy conquered, they would then sail to Greece and make war on any peoples of the king's choosing. City-states on the mainland and islands off Macedonia would belong to Philip and his realm' (Livy, XXIII.xxxiii.9–12).

21. *A simple treaty . . . mankind*] Or as we would say, being less inclined to use the subjunctive mood, 'would have barred'; since no such treaty between Masinissa and the Carthaginians was ever made. Although Masinissa, the king of Numidia, began the Second Punic War as an ally of Carthage, he defected from them in 206 BC, and provided vital assistance to Scipio Africanus in his invasion of Carthaginian territory in 204 BC. His cavalry, which he led personally, were decisive in the final defeat of Hannibal at the battle of Zama in 202 BC.

22. *the war of the auxiliaries*] More commonly known as the Mercenary, or Truceless, War, fought between Carthage and her disaffected mercenary troops from 241 to 237 BC. Our principal source for this war is Polybius, I.lxv–lxxxviii. It is also discussed by Diodorus Siculus and Dio Cassius, although with less authority. Gustave Flaubert would choose this war as the exotic and violent backdrop for his historical novel *Salammbô* (1862).

23. *cap. 83*] Ἱέρων δ᾽ ἀεὶ μέν ποτε κατὰ τὸν ἐνεστῶτα πόλεμον μεγάλην ἐποιεῖτο σπουδὴν εἰς πᾶν τὸ παρακαλούμενον ὑπ᾽ αὐτῶν, τότε δὲ καὶ μᾶλλον ἐφιλοτιμεῖτο, πεπεισμένος συμφέρειν ἑαυτῷ καὶ πρὸς τὴν ἐν Σικελίᾳ δυναστείαν καὶ πρὸς τὴν Ῥωμαίων φιλίαν τὸ σῴζεσθαι Καρχηδονίους, ἵνα μὴ παντάπασιν ἐξῇ τὸ προτεθὲν ἀκονιτὶ συντελεῖσθαι τοῖς ἰσχύουσι, πάνυ φρονίμως καὶ νουνεχῶς λογιζόμενος. οὐδέποτε γὰρ χρὴ τὰ τοιαῦτα παρορᾶν, οὐδὲ τηλικαύτην οὐδενὶ συγκατασκευάζειν δυναστείαν, πρὸς ἣν οὐδὲ περὶ τῶν ὁμολογουμένων ἐξέσται δικαίων ἀμφισβητεῖν᾽; 'Hiero during the whole of the present war had been most prompt in meeting their requests, and was now more complaisant than ever, being convinced that it was in his own interest for securing both his Sicilian dominions and his friendship with the Romans, that Carthage should be preserved, and that the stronger power should not be able to attain its ultimate object entirely without effort. In this he reasoned very wisely and sensibly, for such matters should never be neglected, and we should never contribute to the attainment by one state of a power so preponderant, that none dare dispute with it even for their acknowledged rights' (Polybius, I.lxxxiii.2–5).

24. *the emperor CHARLES*] i.e. Charles V.

25. *mines of gold and silver*] i.e. in America. Hume has discussed the paradoxical impact of the importing of bullion from these mines on the economies of both Spain and Europe more generally in 'Of Money' (above, pp. 27-8), 'Of

Interest' (above, p. 43) and 'Of the Balance of Trade' (above, p. 49). Many of Hume's insights into the counter-intuitive truths of economic life derive from his reflections on this accident of history, and what it reveals about the fallacious economic notions into which men tend naturally to fall. Cf. the note in the 'Early Memoranda': 'Above 40. Millions of Pieces of Eight comes into Europe every Year' (NLS MS 23159, item 14, p. 12; cf. Mossner, 'Memoranda', p. 505).

26. *A new power succeeded*] i.e. France, which under Louis XIV also aspired to universal monarchy.

27. *that spirit . . . infatuated*] In 1748 Hume had commented tartly on the ostentatious culture of Roman Catholicism he had observed during his travels through Austria. See in particular his remarks on the monks of Melk and on the court's observation of Easter Week (*Letters*, vol. I, pp. 125 and 126).

28. *general wars*] i.e. the War of the Grand Alliance (1689–97), the War of the Spanish Succession (1701–14), the War of the Austrian Succession (1740–48) and the Seven Years' War (1756–63).

29. *In the first place . . . obstinacy and passion*] Hume was a steady foe to English Francophobia, which he regarded as irrational. In his letter to the Abbé le Blanc of 12 September 1754 he declared that he abhorred 'that low Practice, so prevalent in England, of speaking with Malignity of France' (*Letters*, vol. I, p. 194). In the *Treatise of Human Nature*, I.iii.13, he had deplored prejudicial errors associated with nationality: 'An *Irishman* cannot have wit, and a *Frenchman* cannot have solidity; for which reason, tho' the conversation of the former in any instance be visibly very agreeable, and of the latter very judicious, we have entertain'd such a prejudice against them, that they must be dunces or fops in spite of sense and reason. Human nature is very subject to errors of this kind; and perhaps this nation as much as any other' (*THN*, p. 100). In Part VI of *The Theory of Moral Sentiments*, added to the sixth edition of 1790, Adam Smith would reflect on the paradox that statesmen pursuing the balance of power thereby secured the public benefit of peace but were generally motivated by narrow feelings of national advantage: 'The most extensive public benevolence which can commonly be exerted with any considerable effect, is that of the statesmen, who project and form alliances among neighbouring or not very distant nations, for the preservation either of, what is called, the balance of power, or of the general peace and tranquillity of the states within the circle of their negotiations. The statesmen, however, who plan and execute such treaties, have seldom any thing in view, but the interest of their respective countries' (Smith, *Theory*, VI.ii.2.6, p. 230).

30. *RYSWICK*] The Treaty of Ryswick (1697) concluded the War of the Grand Alliance.

31. *UTRECHT*] The Treaty of Utrecht (signed 1713; ratified 1714) concluded the War of the Spanish Succession.

32. *AIX-LA-CHAPELLE*] The Treaty of Aix-la-Chapelle (1748) concluded the War of the Austrian Succession.

33. *all our public debts … our neighbours*] cf. 'Of Public Credit' (above, pp. 75–87).

34. *Habent … alienos*] Tacitus, *Histories*, I.xxxvii. Hume was fond of this quotation, and had used it already in 'Of the Rise and Progress of the Arts and Sciences', above, vol. 1, p. 97 and n. 23.

35. *All the world … EUROPE*] Popular support for Maria Theresa, then merely queen of Hungary, had been building among the English people after Frederick II of Prussia's invasion of Silesia, and in April 1741 Walpole had been obliged to propose a subsidy of £300,000 to her, and a contingent of 12,000 Danish and Hessian troops, paid for by England. Further support was voted through in Parliament in December 1742. The resulting War of the Austrian Succession (1740–48) had launched a struggle for mastery in Europe which would be resolved for the time being only by the Seven Years' War (1756–63). Hume's persuasion of the futility of this conflict can only have been sharpened by the fact that, by the Treaty of Aix-la-Chapelle in 1748, Maria Theresa had been obliged to acquiesce in the Prussian annexation of Silesia. Hume had enjoyed a ringside seat at the diplomatic aftermath of the War of the Austrian Succession, travelling in 1748 to Turin and Vienna as aide-de-camp to General St Clair.

36. *That remedy of funding*] Hume refers to the system of deficit financing which England had adopted after 1688: see above, vol. 1, p. 249, n. 13. In 'Of Public Credit' (above, pp. 75–87) he attacked this system as 'ruinous, beyond all controversy' (above, p. 76). Adam Smith would also deplore the 'ruinous expedient of perpetual funding' (*Wealth of Nations*, V.iii.41; Smith, *Wealth*, vol. II, p. 921).

37. *If the ROMAN … before its establishment*] cf. the young Gibbon's similar judgement, while on the Grand Tour in October 1764, writing to his father from Rome: 'Whatever ideas books may have given us of the greatness of that people [the ancient Romans], Their accounts of the most flourishing state of Rome fall infinitely short of the picture of its ruins. I am convinced there never never [*sic*] existed such a nation and I hope for the happiness of mankind that there never will again' (Gibbon, *Letters*, vol. I, p. 184).

38. *Enormous monarchies … pay and plunder*] cf. the parallel note in the 'Early Memoranda': 'There seems to be a natural Course of Things, which brings on the Destruction of great Empires. They push their Conquests till they come to barbarous Nations, which stop their Progress, by the Difficulty of subsisting great Armies. After that, the Nobility & considerable Men of the conquering Nation & best Provinces withdraw gradually from the [frontier *inserted above the line*] Army, by reason of its Distance from the Capital & barbarity of the Country, in which they quarter: They forget the Use of War. Their barbarous Soldiers become their Masters. These have no Law but their Sword, both from their bad Education, & from their Distance from the Sovereign [to whom they bear no Affection *inserted above the line*]. Hence

Disorder, Violence, Anarchy, &-Tyranny, & a Dissolution of Empire' (NLS MS 23159, item 14, p. 27; cf. Mossner, 'Memoranda', pp. 517–18). Cf. Wallace: 'there seems to be fixed in nature a certain boundary, and just standard, by which every thing either is, or ought to be limited. Thus cities, by growing too large, become destructive; and empires, by being too extensive, become unweildy' (Wallace, *Dissertation*, p. 328). Hume would revert to the same thought in a letter of 4 March 1758 to Lord Kames: 'It was never surely the intention of Providence, that any one nation should be a monopolizer of wealth: and the growth of all bodies, artificial as well as natural, is stopped by internal causes, derived from their enormous size and greatness. Great empires, great cities, great commerce, all of them receive a check, not from accidental events, but necessary principles' (*Letters*, vol. I, pp. 271–2). Cf. also Francis Hutcheson on the unnaturalness and perniciousness of empire: 'The insisting on old claims and tacit conventions, to extend civil power of distant nations, and form grand unwieldly empires, without regard to the obvious maxims of humanity, has been one great source of human misery' (Hutcheson, *System*, vol. II, p. 309).

39. *CRAVATES . . . TARTARS . . . HUSSARS . . . COSSACS*] All light cavalry forces drawn from either on or beyond the northern and eastern borders of Europe. The Crabats or Croats had served under Wallenstein on the side of the Catholic League in the Thirty Years' War (1618–1648). The Tartars originated in northern and central Asia, and had begun to encroach on more westerly territories in the thirteenth century. The Hussars were originally Hungarian forces, whose name and distinctive uniform had been widely adopted by the cavalry of other nations in the seventeenth and eighteenth centuries. The Cossacks originated from north of the Black Sea, and had supplied military strength to the Tsar, although in the mid-eighteenth century they had repeatedly risen against the harsh rule of the Russian Empire and had suffered ruthless repression. In the eighteenth century these light auxiliary troops were feared because of their ill-discipline and their indulgence in atrocities, such as the torture and mutilation of prisoners (Robertson, *Enlightenment*, p. 11). However, in *The Wealth of Nations* Adam Smith would allude in passing to an economic incentive which also made these bodies of light cavalry particularly terrible to the populations of the countries in which they operated: 'It is with them [mendicant orders of the Roman Catholic Church], as with the hussars and light infantry of some armies; no plunder, no pay' (Smith, *Wealth*, p. 790, V.i.g.2).

## VIII. OF TAXES

Published in: *1752a, 1752b, 1753, 1754, 1758, 1760, 1764, 1767, 1768, 1770, 1772, 1777a*

Significant revisions:

Hume made several important and substantial revisions to the text of this essay:

1) *1752a–1768* read: 'There is a maxim, that prevails amongst those, whom, in this country, we call *ways and means men*, and who are denominated *Financiers* and *Maltotiers* in *France*;' (*1752a*, p. 115; cf. above, p. 71).

2) *1752a–1768* insert the following two additional paragraphs immediately following '. . . necessity for industry.' (above, p. 72):

''TIS always observ'd, in years of scarcity, if it be not extreme, that the poor labour more, and really live better, than in years of great plenty, when they indulge themselves in idleness and riot. I have been told, by a considerable manufacturer, that in the year 1740, when bread and provisions of all kinds were very dear, his workmen not only made a shift to live, but paid debts, which they had contracted in former years, that were much more favourable and abundant.*

'THIS doctrine, therefore, with regard to taxes, may be admitted in some degree: But beware of the abuse. Taxes, like necessity, when carry'd too far, destroy industry, by engendring despair; and even before they reach this pitch, they raise the wages of the labourer and manufacturer, and heighten the price of all commodities. An attentive, disinterested legislature will observe the point, when the emolument ceases, and the prejudice begins: But as the contrary character is much more common, 'tis to be fear'd, that taxes, all over *Europe*, are multiplying to such a degree, as will entirely crush all art and industry; tho', perhaps, their first increase, along with other circumstances, might contribute to the growth of these advantages.

'*To this purpose, see also discourse I, at the end.' (*1752a*, pp. 118–19).

3) *1770* introduces the phrase 'They naturally produce sobriety and frugality, if judiciously imposed:' (above, p. 72; cf. *1770*, vol. II, p. 128).

4) *1752a–1764* present a very different text of the paragraph 'It is an opinion . . . of his labour.' (above, pp. 73–4):

'THERE is a prevailing opinion, that all taxes, however levy'd, fall upon the land at last. Such an opinion may be useful in *Britain*, by checking the landed gentlemen, in whose hands our legislature is lodg'd, and making them preserve great regard for trade and industry. But I must confess, that this principle, tho' first advanc'd by a celebrated writer, has so little appearance of reason, that, were it not for his authority, it had never been receiv'd by any body. Every man, to be sure, is desirous of pushing off from himself the burthen of any tax, that is impos'd, and laying it upon others: But as every man has the same inclination, and is upon the defensive; no set of men can be suppos'd to prevail altogether in this contest. And why the landed gentleman shou'd be the victim of the whole, and shou'd not be able to defend himself, as well as others are, I cannot readily imagine. All tradesmen, indeed, wou'd willingly prey upon him, and divide him among them, if they cou'd: But this inclination they always have, tho' no taxes were levy'd; and the same methods, by which he guards against the imposition of tradesmen before taxes, will serve him afterwards, and make them share the burthen with him.' (*1752a*, pp. 120–21).

5) *1768* reads: 'No labour in any commodities, that are exported, can be very considerably raised in the price, without losing the foreign market; and as some part of almost every manufactory is exported, this circumstance keeps the price of most species of labour nearly the same after the imposition of taxes. I may add, that it has this effect upon the whole: For were any kind of labour paid beyond its proportion, all hands would flock to it, and would soon sink it to a level with the rest.' (*1768*, p. 390; cf. above, p. 74).

Copy text: *1777a*

Headnote:

On the general question of the principles and practices of taxation in ancient societies, see the recent collection of essays published as *Ancient Taxation: The Mechanics of Extraction in Comparative Perspective*, ed. Jonathan Valk and Irene Soto Marín (New York: New York University Press, 2021). As a young man Hume had been deeply interested in how, and at what rates, ancient societies had been taxed. Many entries in the 'Early Memoranda' relate to these questions, and a number of these entries would be put to work in constructing the argument of 'Of the Populousness of Ancient Nations'.

Until the 1690s the financial sinews of the English state had been comparatively weak. Before the Civil Wars the tax regime had been unsystematic but stable: 'much of the energy of government was devoted to designing, agreeing and imposing a variety of taxes and rates to support the activities of local and national government. This was a fruitful period for national initiatives aiming to fund areas of expenditure such as military expeditions or the supply of the household and court. In the localities elaborate rating systems were developed to cope with these charges, and those imposed directly by local government, such as rates for the poor, the gaols, the highways or the militia. In individual villages these ratings had to be harmonised with those for the church. Thus, at all levels of government raising money was a constant concern, but these efforts were simply the sharp end of governmental commitments on a number of fronts' (Braddick, *State Formation*, pp. 65–6).

However, during the Civil Wars both Parliamentarians and Royalists had encountered extraordinary problems of supply. Both sides had been reduced to expedients such as sequestrating money and valuables, and pawning jewels. Loans were to be had only at ruinous rates of interest. But the taxation-gathering abilities of the state had been strengthened by the fiscal pressures arising from the Civil Wars: 'The increase in the military capacity of the English state between 1642 and 1646 was a more dramatic change than anything achieved in the preceding three generations. It rested on reform of taxation, mainly undertaken between 1640 and 1643, which produced sums of money vastly greater than those available to earlier regimes. Reliable flows of money supported more effective borrowing, further increasing the military potential of the state' (Braddick, *State Formation*, p. 221). It had been this transformed tax-gathering potential that had allowed William III after 1690 to finance his continental campaigns by mortgaging a portion of the state's tax revenues. The Williamite apologist Sir Richard Blackmore would refer to these developments with deceptive mildness, calling them 'Ways and Means as were least Burdensom and uneasy to the People' (Blackmore, *History*, p. 6). Yet Blackmore clearly understood how the new system of deficit finance worked: 'The former Parliaments chose rather to Establish Funds for Publick Supplys, than to use any Methods of raising them within the year; divers Branches of the King's Revenue were by His Majestys own consent, subjected to great Anticipations, and the most easy and obvious Funds were already setled, and sufficiently loaded' (Blackmore, *History*, pp. 20–21). Therefore, after the accession of William III 'an effective and predictable tax regime was the asset against which, ultimately, the government was securing its credit' (Braddick, *State Formation*, p. 267). It was the propensity of European states to engage in ever more costly warfare that forced governments to find new sources of revenue, and to develop and (more difficult) justify new taxes: 'The financial setting of the tax problems of the time [the period from the Long Parliament to the Treaty of Utrecht] was the need for an enormously increased revenue' (Kennedy, *Taxation*, p. 23). In 'Of Public Credit' Hume would cast a cold eye on what he feared would be the ruinous consequences of these financial innovations.

As the principles and practice of taxation assumed greater prominence in affairs of state, so too the subject had attracted the attention of political philosophers. In chapter 30 of *Leviathan*, Hobbes had argued that taxes should fall on consumption, not on income or assets such as land: 'To Equall Justice, appertaineth also the Equall imposition of Taxes; the Equality whereof dependeth not on the Equality of riches, but on the Equality of the debt, that every man oweth to the Common-wealth for his defence . . . Seeing then the benefit that every one receiveth thereby, is the enjoyment of life, which is equally dear to poor, and rich; the debt which a poor man oweth them that defend his life, is the same which a rich man oweth for the defence of his; saving that the rich, who have the service of the poor, may be debtors not onely for their own persons, but for many more. Which considered, the Equality of Imposition, consisteth rather in the Equality of that which is consumed, than of the riches of the persons that consume the same. For what reason is there, that he which laboureth much, and sparing the fruits of his labour, consumeth little, should be more charged, then he that living idly, getteth little, and spendeth all he gets; seeing the one hath no more protection from the Common-wealth, then the other? But when the Impositions, are layd upon those things which men consume, every man payeth Equally for what he useth: Nor is the Common-wealth defrauded, by the luxurious waste of private men' (Hobbes, *Leviathan*, pp. 238–9). For Locke, the problem of taxation was not its point of impact, for he believed that ultimately all taxes resolved themselves into a tax on land (this being their point of incidence). In *Two Treatises*, accordingly, his concern had been directed, not so much towards the question of where taxation should fall, but rather on the legal and political process that must be followed before taxes can be raised at all: 'they [the legislative power] must not raise Taxes on the Property of the People, without the Consent of the People, given by themselves, or their Deputies' ('Second Treatise', § 142, *Two Treatises*, p. 363).

According to Kennedy, Walpole's administration 'marks the transition between seventeenth and eighteenth century views of taxation' (Kennedy, *Taxation*, p. 98), and this transition is the immediate context of Hume's essay. There are two contextual pressures that Hume wished to withstand in 'Of Taxes'. The first is the opposition to taxes on consumption that had in 1707 been one aspect of Scottish resistance to union with England. The second and more recent is the opposition to Walpole's Excise Bill, which had revived Locke's theory that all taxes fall ultimately on land (Seligman, *Taxation*, p. 106). In its support of taxes on consumption and its dissuasion from taxes on land, 'Of Taxes' is a pro-Walpolean text, and should be read alongside Hume's temperate assessment of Walpole's legacy.

Hume's letters to Turgot of 5 August 1766 and late September 1766 further reveal his views on taxation, and in particular his disagreement with Locke and with the school of Physiocrats (of which Turgot was a leading member) that ultimately all taxes fall on land (*Letters*, vol. II, pp. 74–7 and 88–95). A number of entries in the 'Early Memoranda' demonstrate that the subject of taxation was of interest to the younger Hume: see, e.g., the entries in NLS MS 23159, item 14, pp. 9–10; cf. Mossner, 'Memoranda', p. 503.

For further commentary on the topics of this essay and on the general history of taxation, see: J. R. McCulloch, 'Taxation', *Encyclopedia Britannica* (1824); Stephen Dowell, *A History of Taxation and Taxes in England: from the earliest times to the present day*, 4 vols (London: Longmans, 1884), esp. vol. II, books 1 and 2; E. R. A. Seligman, *The Shifting and Incidence of Taxation*, fourth edition (New York: Columbia University Press, 1921); W. Kennedy, *English Taxation, 1640–1799: An Essay on Policy and Opinion* (London: G. Bell, 1913); B. E. V. Sabine, *A Short History of Taxation* (London: Butterworths, 1980); Patrick O'Brien, 'The Political Economy of British Taxation, 1660–1815', *Economic History Review*, second series, vol. XLI (1988), pp. 1–32; J. V. Beckett and Michael Turner, 'Taxation and Economic Growth in Eighteenth-Century England', *Economic History Review*, second series, vol. XLIII (1990), pp. 377–403.

1. *a prevailing maxim . . . reasoners*] The counter-intuitive view that 'Impositions upon a People . . . make them thrive' and that in consequence '*Taxes
are no Charge* . . . but on the contrary a Gain to all' (Daniel Defoe, *Taxes
no Charge* [1690], pp. 5 and 9) was common in the late seventeenth century: cf. also William Waterhouse, *One Tale is Good, Until Another is Told*
(1662), pp. 29–30; Sir William Petty, *Several Essays in Political Arithmetick*
(1699), pp. 195–210 (i.e. chapter 2 of *Political Arithmetick*); and Pieter de
la Court, *The True Interest and Political Maxims of the Republick of Holland and West Friesland* (1702), p. 109. The twentieth-century historian of
taxation, Edwin Seligman, summarized the prevailing argument as follows:
'Most of the writers of the close of the seventeenth and the first half of
the eighteenth century imagined that taxes on the necessaries of life would
constitute a great stimulus toward an improvement in the condition of the
laborer, in sobriety, carefulness, and efficiency. A tax on labor would thus,
they thought, be a real spur to industry and commerce, and a benefit to the
community in general; for low wages mean low cost of production. When
the necessaries of life are taxed, runs the argument, not only will the laborer
have to work harder and longer to maintain himself, – which will be a benefit
to him, – but, on the other hand, there will be a reduction in the labor-cost
to the employer, which will be an advantage to the community' (Seligman,
*Taxation*, p. 46). The argument had been revived and restated in mid-century
by Josiah Tucker, who had asserted that 'the high Duties, Taxes and Excises
upon the Necessaries of Life are so far from being a Disadvantage to Trade
. . . that they are eventually the chief Support of it' (*A Brief Essay* [1750],
p. 54). Montesquieu had recently protested against the perverse inhumanity
of this doctrine: 'On a pourtant conclu de la pauvreté de ces petits païs, que
pour que le peuple fut industrieux il faloit des charges pesantes. On auroit
mieux fait d'en conclure qu'il n'en faut pas . . . L'effet des richesses d'un païs
c'est de mettre de l'ambition dans tous les cœurs. L'effet de la pauvreté est d'y
faire naître le désespoir. La première s'irrite par le travail, l'autre se console
par la paresse. La Nature est juste envers les hommes; elle les recompense de
leurs peines; elle les rend laborieux, parce qu'à de plus grands travaux elle
attache de plus grandes récompenses. Mais si un pouvoir arbitraire ôte les
récompenses de la Nature, on reprend le dégoût pour le travail, & l'inaction
paroît être le seul bien' (*Esprit des Lois*, book XIII, chapter 2; Montesquieu,
*Esprit*, vol. I, p. 338). Seligman is generally sceptical that taxes can stimulate
industry: 'the assertion [that taxes can act as a spur to industry] is indeed
open to grave doubt, for taxes on industry must indubitably be regarded on
the whole as a drag or burden on industry, rather than as a spur to industry.
But . . . it is none the less a fact that there have frequently been cases where
the attention of the producer was first directed to the possibility of improving
the productive process by some new burden which started a whole branch of

industry out of its comparative lethargy and caused it to forsake the old rut' (Seligman, *Taxation*, p. 6). The example he gives is the stimulating effect of the imposition of excise duties on the production of Scotch whisky.

2. *many natural disadvantages*] Montesquieu had made a similar observation on the benefits that can be produced by natural (as opposed to artificial) hardship: 'Il y a deux sortes de Peuples pauvres; ceux que la dureté du Gouvernement a rendu tels, & ces gens-là sont incapables de presqu'aucune vertu, parce que leur pauvreté fait une partie de leur servitude; les autres ne sont pauvres que parce qu'ils ont dédaigné, ou parce qu'ils n'ont pas connu les commodités de la vie; & ceux-ci peuvent faire de grandes choses, parce que cette pauvreté fait une partie de leur liberté' (*Esprit des Lois*, book XX, chapter 3; Montesquieu, *Esprit*, vol. II, p. 4: cf. also ibid., book XX, chapter 5; vol. II, p. 7).

3. *TYRE ... HOLLAND*] Montesquieu gives a very similar list of commercial republics that either have flourished or are at the present day flourishing (*Esprit des Lois*, book XX, chapter 4; Montesquieu, *Esprit*, vol. II, p. 5).

4. *trade has come late into that kingdom*] A reaction to the notable expansion in French commerce that had occurred during the reign of Louis XIV.

5. *After which ... industry*] 'This Account of the Original of Trade, agrees with the Experience of all Ages, and with the Constitutions of all Places, where it has most flourish'd in the World, as *Tyre*, *Carthage*, *Athens*, *Syracuse*, *Agrigentum*, *Rhodes*, *Venice*, *Holland*; and will be so obvious to every Man, that knows and considers the Situation, the Extent, and the Nature, of all those Countries, that it will need no Enlargement upon the Comparisons' (Temple, *Works*, vol. I, p. 61). Cf. the annotation to the quotation of Virgil, *Georgics*, I.123, in 'Of Commerce' (above, p. 315, n. 27).

6. *The best taxes ... consumptions*] Again, Hume follows the judgement of Montesquieu: 'Le tribut naturel au Gouvernement modéré, est l'impôt sur les marchandises. Cet impôt étant réellement payé par l'acheteur, quoique le Marchand l'advance, est un prêt que le Marchand a déja fait à l'acheteur: ainsi il faut regarder le Négociant, d'un côté, comme le débiteur général de l'Etat, & comme le créancier de tous les Particuliers. Il avance à l'Etat le Droit que l'acheteur lui payera quelque jour, & il a payé pour l'acheteur le droit qu'il a payé pour la marchandise. On sent donc que plus le Gouvernement est modéré, que plus l'esprit de liberté régne, que plus les fortunes ont de sureté, plus il est facile au Marchand d'avancer à l'Etat & de preter au particulier des Droits considérables. En Angleterre un marchand prête réellement à l'Etat cinquante ou soixante livres sterling à chaque tonneau de vin qu'il reçoit. Quel est le Marchand qui oseroit faire une chose ce cette espèce dans un païs gouverné comme la Turquie? Et quand il l'oseroit faire, comment le pourrait-il avec une fortune suspecte, incertaine, ruinée?' (*Esprit des Lois*, book XIII, chapter 14; Montesquieu, *Esprit*, vol. I, pp. 351–2). However, a preference for taxes on consumption as opposed to taxes on property

is present in the earliest, mid-seventeenth-century, English discussions of the theory of taxation, after they had been introduced in practice by Parliament in 1643 and laid at first on beer, ale, cider and perry; later also on soap, cloth and spirits (John Pym being known in consequence as the 'father of the excise'). In chapter 30 of *Leviathan* Hobbes had given the preference to taxes on consumption on grounds of equity: 'when the Impositions, are layd upon those things which men consume, every man payeth Equally for what he useth' (Hobbes, *Leviathan*, p. 239) – a judgement which echoed the eventual conclusion of Parliament in August 1649, that an excise was 'the most equal and indifferent levy that could be laid on the people' (Dowell, *Taxation*, vol. II, p. 11). It is worth noting, however, that excises, or taxes on consumption, had long been detested by the English as a badge of slavery (Dowell, *Taxation*, vol. II, pp. 8–9, 11 and 104–5); and were resisted as 'an innovation on the opinion and practice of centuries' (Kennedy, *Taxation*, p. 51). Furthermore, they had been denounced in Scotland in the early eighteenth century as an aspect of the debate on the benefits or otherwise of union with England (Seligman, *Taxation*, pp. 39–40). Hume may naturally have been aware of that strand of debate in his native country, and have wished to resist it. Francis Hutcheson had also thrown his weight behind taxes on consumption: 'these are most convenient which are laid on matters of luxury and splendour, rather than the necessaries of life; on foreign products and manufactures, rather than domestick; and such as can be easily raised without many expensive offices for collecting them' (Hutcheson, *System*, vol. II, p. 341). More recently, in the 1730s, Walpole's project for an excise had stirred up bitter resistance, which had flared up once more in the early 1750s, at just the moment when Hume was composing this essay. The anonymous author of *An Appeal to the Public* (1751) is characteristic of this recrudescence of anti-excise sentiment: 'This is the general Light in which *Excises* ought to be consider'd ... as they are of all Impositions the most injurious to *Liberty*, so they are the most *unequal* in their Nature, and fall the most *heavily* on *Property*' (p. 51). The definition of 'excise' supplied by Johnson in his *Dictionary* (1755) – 'A hateful tax levied upon commodities, and adjudged not by the common judges of property, but wretches hired by those to whom excise is paid' – was condemned by the law officers of the Crown as a libel on the commissioners of excise. In 1767, when the idea of an excise was on the point of being revived, Chesterfield advised a change of language: 'As for a general excise, it must change its name by act of parliament before it will go down with the people, who know names better than things' (Chesterfield, *Miscellaneous Works*, 4 vols [1779], vol. IV, p. 214).

7. *especially those of luxury*] A point made by, among others, the author (possibly Sir William Petty) of *Britannia Languens* (1680), who noted: 'such *Excises* as affect and over-burthen the *beneficial parts* of Trade, are of pernicious Consequence. Secondly, that an Universality of *Excise* is both

inconvenient and unnecessary; But that there may be *Excises* Imposed on many Superfluities, and Excesses, in Meats, Drinks, or Equipages, or upon some imported Goods *Consumed at home*, which would be no prejudice to any kind of Trade' (p. 294). The idea that taxes should not be levied on necessities but only on superfluities was deeply ingrained in the later seventeenth and earlier eighteenth centuries (Kennedy, *Taxation*, p. 77), Walpole asserting in 1733, as almost a commonplace, that 'All reasonable Men agree, that Taxes upon Luxury are the most just Taxes' (*Some General Considerations Concerning the Alteration and Improvement of Publick Revenues* [1733], p. 17). It is interesting, however, that Hume does not mention Walpole's Salt Tax, a tax on consumption but levied on a necessity rather than a luxury. Walpole's eventually unsuccessful pursuit of this tax marks the limit of Hume's endorsement of his taxation policy.

8. *least felt by the people*] The Bristol merchant John Cary had argued that the tax system should be so arranged that 'the Poor bear little or none of the Burthen, their Province being more properly to labour and fight than pay' (John Cary, *An Essay on the State of England* [Bristol, 1695], p. 173). In the same year Charles Davenant had urged that 'the proper Commodities to lay Excises upon, are those, which serve meerly to Luxury; because that way the Poor would be least affected' (*An Essay upon Ways and Means of Supplying the War* [1695], p. 130). Parliament had taken the same view: 'in 1694 the House of Commons agreed to a proposal to impose a wine duty rather than a suggested leather tax, on the principle, which it had embodied in a resolution, that it is better to impose taxes which fall on superfluities rather than necessaries, and on the rich rather than the common people' (Kennedy, *Taxation*, p. 30). Nevertheless, although many at this time argue that the poor should be lightly but proportionally taxed, very few argued in the manner of Cary that they should be *exempt* from tax: 'The acceptance in the seventeenth century of the doctrine that the poor man should pay taxation is one of the landmarks in English political opinion' (Kennedy, *Taxation*, p. 67).

9. *in some measure, voluntary*] This point had also been noted in the preceding century in relation to taxes on consumption: 'no Person can complain; who consumes little, will have but little to pay' (A. Burnaby, *Two Proposals* [1696], p. 2). The same observation had been made by Charles Davenant the previous year concerning the excise: 'every one, in a manner, Taxes himself, making Consumption according to his will or ability' (*An Essay upon Ways and Means* [1695], p. 124). Josiah Tucker, writing immediately before Hume, concurred on the voluntary nature of these taxes, praising them as 'a Tax, which no Man could complain of, as it would be his own voluntary Act and Deed' (*A Brief Essay . . . With Regard to Trade* [1750], p. 165). Adam Smith would later agree emphatically, in language close to that used by Hume: 'every act of payment is perfectly voluntary, and what he [the workman] can

avoid if he chuses to do so' (*Wealth of Nations*, V.ii.k.18; Smith, *Wealth*, p. 878). Cf. Patrick O'Brien: 'Most indirect taxes, customs certainly but also many excise duties, fell upon expenditures that ministers could present as luxurious or superfluous, so that the payment of taxes on consumption was perceived to be voluntary in their eyes' (O'Brien, 'Connections', p. 69).

10. *gradually and insensibly*] This virtue in taxes on consumption had been noted as early as the late seventeenth century: 'the People pay it insensibly in the Value of the Goods they buy; for we must not think that the *Merchants* or *Traders* pay all the Money of the *Customs* and *Excise*; they are but the Depositors of it, and the People paying it in a way so secret and insensible, it meeteth not with any Contradiction from them, as it would do, were they themselves to lay down the present money' ('W.C.', *A Discourse . . . Towards the Raising Moneys by an Excise* [1695], p. 4). Cf. Kennedy, *Taxation*, p. 61, and Smith, *Jurisprudence*, p. 533.

11. *sobriety and frugality*] An anticipation of the point Hume will shortly make, that the natural response of the poor man to the imposition of a tax on consumptions is either to retrench his use, or to increase his labour, and thus an aspect of Hume's resistance to the argument, deployed by those who contended that ultimately all taxes fell on land, that taxes on consumption led to increases in wages. The point that higher prices lead paradoxically to cheaper and better-performed labour would be made by William Temple: 'those who have closely attended to the disposition and conduct of a manufacturing populace, have always found, that labouring less, and not cheaper, has been the consequence of a low price of provisions, and that when provisions are dear, from whatever cause, labour is always plenty, always well performed, and, of course, is always cheap. This is a paradox which nothing but experience could teach us to explain. In order to do this, let us observe, first, That mankind in General are naturally inclined to ease and indolence, and that nothing but absolute necessity will enforce labour and industry. Secondly, That the poor, in general, work only for the bare necessaries of life, and for the means of a low debauch, which when obtained they cease to labour, till roused again by necessity. Thirdly, That it is best for themselves, as well as for society, that the poor should be constantly employed' (*Considerations on Taxes* [1765], pp. 6–7). See also Josiah Tucker, *A Brief Essay . . . With Regard to Trade* (1750), p. 54. Adam Smith would dismiss the idea, and argue instead that high wages encouraged the industry of the worker: 'The liberal reward of labour, as it encourages the propagation, so it increases the industry of the common people. The wages of labour are the encouragement of industry, which, like every other human quality, improves in proportion to the encouragement it receives. A plentiful subsistence increases the bodily strength of the labourer, and the comfortable hope of bettering his condition, and of ending his days perhaps in ease and plenty, animates him to exert that strength to the utmost. Where wages are high, accordingly, we shall always

find the workmen more active, diligent, and expeditious, than where they are low' (*Wealth of Nations*, I.viii.44; Smith, *Wealth*, p. 99).

12. *ep. 11*] Hume refers to a list Cicero provides, not actually of the cities with the greatest commerce, but of those which supplied grain to Rome, and the fleets of which in 49 BC the consuls were intending to blockade in order to produce famine in Rome and so put pressure on Caesar: 'nec vero dubito quin exitiosum bellum impendeat, cuius initium ducetur a fame. et me tamen doleo non interesse huic bello! in quo tanta vis sceleris futura est ut, cum parentis non alere nefarium sit, nostri principes antiquissimam et sanctissimam parentem, patriam, fame necandam putent. atque hoc non opinione timeo sed interfui sermonibus. omnis haec classis Alexandria, Colchis, Tyro, Sidone, Arado, Cypro, Pamphylia, Lycia, Rhodo, Chio, Byzantio, Lesbo, Smyrna, Mileto, Coo ad intercludendos commeatus Italiae et ad occupandas frumentarias provincias comparatur'; 'Nor have I any doubt that a destructive war is ahead, to be introduced by famine. And yet I grieve that I am not participating in such a war! The criminality of it! To refuse to maintain one's parents is wicked, but our leaders think it right and proper to starve that older, most venerable parent, their country, to death. And this is no conjectural fear of mine; I was present when it was discussed. All this fleet from Alexandria, Colchis, Tyre, Sidon, Aradus, Cyprus, Pamphylia, Lycia, Rhodes, Chios, Byzantium, Lesbos, Smyrna, Miletus, Cos, is being collected with the object of cutting Italy's lifelines and occupying the grain-exporting provinces' (Cicero, *Letters to Atticus*, 176 [IX.ix].2).

13. *chap. 6*] See Temple, *Works*, vol. I, p. 61. Hume slightly misquotes: Temple speaks of the 'plenty of the Food' in Ireland, not the 'plenty of the soil', as Hume writes.

14. *expensive in the levying*] An allusion to the necessity of employing excise officers, the cost and intrusiveness of whom were a recurrent source of resentment. Cf. the entry in the 'Early Memoranda': 'The Expence of levying the Customs in England computed at 27 p$^r$ Cent.' (NLS MS 23159, item 14, p. 14; cf. Mossner, 'Memoranda', p. 506).

15. *Taxes upon possessions ... deficiencies of the other*] A glancing reference to recent events. In 1747 Pelham had introduced a tax on coaches in order to cover the expenditure of suppressing the Jacobite rebellion of 1745: 'This was the first tax aimed at property, by taking an article of expenditure as primâ facie evidence of the possession of means' (Dowell, *Taxation*, vol. II, p. 120).

16. *the arbitrary*] Adam Smith would once again echo the judgement of his friend: 'The tax which each individual is bound to pay ought to be certain, and not arbitrary. The time of payment, the manner of payment, the quantity to be paid, ought all to be clear and plain to the contributor, and to every other person. Where it is otherwise, every person subject to the tax is put more or less in the power of the tax-gatherer, who can either aggravate

the tax upon any obnoxious contributor, or extort, by the terror of such aggravation, some present or perquisite to himself. The uncertainty of taxation encourages the insolence and favours the corruption of an order of men who are naturally unpopular, even where they are neither insolent nor corrupt. The certainty of what each individual ought to pay is, in taxation, a matter of so great importance, that a very considerable degree of inequality, it appears, I believe, from the experience of all nations, is not near so great an evil as a very small degree of uncertainty' (*Wealth of Nations*, V.ii.b.4: Smith, *Wealth*, vol. II, pp. 825–6). It may be that Hume has in mind the tax system of the Protectorate: 'The chief taxes in England, during the time of the commonwealth, were the monthly assessments, the excise, and the customs. The assessments were levied on personal estates as well as on land; and commissioners were appointed in each county for rating the individuals' (*History of England*, vol. VI, p. 146).

17. *poll-taxes*] i.e. capitation taxes levied equally on all members of a community without regard to their wealth or ability to pay. Montesquieu had characterized them as the form of taxation natural to despotism: 'L'Impôt par tête est plus naturel à la Servitude; l'impôt sur les marchandises est plus naturel à la Liberté, parce qu'il se rapporte d'une manière moins directe à la personne' (*Esprit des Lois*, book XIII, chapter 14; Montesquieu, *Esprit*, vol. I, p. 350). Sir William Petty had deplored the injustice of poll taxes: 'The evil of this way is, that it is very unequal; men of unequal abilities, all paying alike, and those who have greatest charges of Children paying most; that is, by how much the poorer they are, by so much the harder are they taxed' (Petty, *Taxes*, p. 42). The association between poll taxes and arbitrary government had been cemented by publications such as *The French King's Declaration for Settling the General Poll-Tax* (1695), which was intended to illustrate '*the difference betwixt a Legal and Tyrannical Government*' (sig. A2ʳ). Nevertheless, they had been resorted to by English governments in the later seventeenth century, particularly during the reign of William III, in order to meet the high costs of his European military campaigns (Dowell, *Taxation*, vol. II, pp. 31–2 and 48–9). For Adam Smith's critical analysis of the nature and operation of such taxes, see *Wealth of Nations*, V.ii.g.11 and V.ii.j (Smith, *Wealth*, pp. 857 and 867–9). After this penultimate experiment poll taxes were abandoned until 1989, when their ill-advised reintroduction eventually brought down a prime minister (Margaret Thatcher the following year): 'The poll tax of 1698 was the last; and henceforth this form of tax passed, together with the hearth money, into the list of taxes tried and never again to be imposed in England. "What minister," said Henry Fox in 1748, "would presume again to suggest the hated hearth-money of the Stuarts, or the poll taxes of the reign of William III?"' (Dowell, *Taxation*, vol. II, p. 49). Kennedy gives a useful list of poll taxes levied between the Long Parliament and 1698 (Kennedy, *Taxation*, p. 50).

18. *a duty upon commodities checks itself*] cf. 'Of the Balance of Trade', where Hume notes that 'if the duties on wine were lowered to a third, they would yield much more to the government than at present' (above, p. 58).

19. *Historians inform us ... empire*] Among the historians of antiquity, it is Zosimus who criticized the fiscal policy of Constantine most vigorously: '*Constantine* ... not onely perpetually wasted the Revenue of the Empire in unnecessary Expences, and Presents, which were bestow'd upon unworthy and vile Persons: but he likewise oppressed those that paid the Tribute, and enrich'd those that were of no use or service in the Government. For he mistook Prodigality for Magnificence. He also laid a Tax of Gold and Silver upon all Merchants, and Tradesmen even to the meanest of all: nor did he spare so much as the poorest Whore. Insomuch that upon the return of every fourth year, when the Tax was to be paid, a man could hear nothing but lamentation and complaints through all the whole City. And when the time came, there was nothing but Whips and Torments provided for them who by reason of their extream poverty could not pay the money. Nay, Mothers were fain to part with their Children, and Fathers to prostitute their Daughters, for money to satisfie the Collectors of this Gold and Silver exaction. And because he had a mind to invent some plague for the richer sort of People, he call'd 'em all forth and made 'em Prætors, for which Dignity he demanded of 'em a vast sum of money. For which reason, when they whose business it was to manage this Affair came into any of the Cities, you might see the People run all away into other Countreys, for fear of gaining that honour with the loss of all they had. Now he had a Particular of all the best Estates, and so imposed a Tribute upon each of 'em, which he called, *a Purse*. And with such Exactions he exhausted all the Towns: for they endur'd so long even after *Constantine*'s time, that the Money was all drain'd clear out of the Cities and many of 'em forsaken by the Inhabitants' (Zosimus, *History*, pp. 120–22). Gibbon would later comment on the malign consequences of Constantine's taxation policy in chapter 17 of *The Decline and Fall* (Gibbon, *Decline and Fall*, vol. I, pp. 632–41).

20. *publicans*] i.e. tax-farmers.

21. *It is an opinion ... consumptions*] The most influential English statement of this position is found in John Locke's *Some Considerations of the Consequences of the Lowering of Interest, and Raising the Value of Money*, second edition (1696): '*Taxes*, however contriv'd, and out of whose Hand soever immediately taken, do in a Country, where their great Fund is in Land, for the most part terminate upon Land' (p. 88). Locke concludes that therefore it would be better simply to tax land in the first place: 'It is in vain in a Country whose great Fund is Land, to hope to lay the publick charge of the Government on any thing else; there at last it will terminate. The Merchant (do what you can) will not bear it, the Labourer cannot, and therefore the Landholder must: And whether he were best do it, by laying it directly, where

it will at last settle, or by letting it come to him by the sinking of his Rents, which when they are once fallen every one knows are not easily raised again, let him consider' (ibid., pp. 96–7; cf. Dowell, *Taxation*, vol. II, p. 104). It was a view revived and echoed in the 1730s by Wayman Lee: 'The Truth is, if Land Owners, in this and other Instances, can and do prevent the Load of a Tax from falling directly and immediately on themselves, yet in the last Resort there it will fall, let them shift it seemingly as far off as they will in the first Imposition; and, perhaps, just so much farther off from them as 'tis laid in the first Instant, and according to common View and Estimation, just so much the more heavily it comes upon them at the last' (*An Essay to Ascertain the Value of Leases and Annuities* [1737], p. 109). Cf. Charles Davenant: 'All Taxes whatsoever, are in their last resort a Charge upon Land; and though Excises will affect Land in no degree like Taxes that Charge it directly, yet Excises will always lye so heavily upon the Landed Men, as to make them concern'd in Parliament, to continue such Duties no longer than the Necessity of the War continues' (*An Essay upon Ways and Means of Supplying the War* [1695], p. 153); John Asgill: 'whatever will buy Land will buy all Commodities. What we call Commodities is nothing but *Land severed from the Soil*: The Owners of the Soil in every Country have the sale of all Commodities of the Growth of that Country, and consequently have the power of giving Credit in that Country ... Man deals in nothing but Earth; the Merchants are the Factors of the World, to exchange one part of the Earth for another' (*Several Assertions* [1696], p. 21); and the anonymous author of *Some Thoughts on the Interest of Money* (1738?): 'though the many windings and turnings in Trade may make it longer e'er the Tax reaches the Landholder, and may prevent our discovering how it takes its Course, yet there it must and does come at last' (p. 95). It was a view that had been given new energy by attempts to resist Walpole's Excise scheme in the early 1730s (Seligman, *Taxation*, p. 106), of which William Pulteney's comments in *A Review of the Excise-Scheme* (1733) are typical: 'As for easing of *Land* by *Excises*, it hath been fully proved by unanswerable Authority that *all Taxes*, in this Kingdom, must ultimately affect *Land* ...' (p. 22). Jacob Vanderlint's *Money Answers All Things* (1734) was also influential: 'as I have now proved that the Land gives all we have, notwithstanding the Importation of any Quantity of foreign Goods, I will next shew that it must pay all the Taxes, levy them how we will' (p. 112). Expressions of it can be found as late as the 1760s; e.g. Vivant de Mezague, *A General View of England* (1766), pp. 17 and 200, and George Lowe, *Considerations on ... Bounties* (1768), p. 32. Moreover, in France the physiocrats, led by François Quesnay, would argue that, because land alone yielded a surplus, it alone should be the object of taxation (Robertson, *VSIE*, pp. 74–5): and in *The Wealth of Nations* Adam Smith would associate the physiocrats with this position (Smith, *Wealth*, p. 830, V.ii.c.7). However, in the decades preceding the composition of Hume's essay the appropriateness of a land tax had also been contested. Sir William Petty had concluded that 'a Land-taxe resolves into an irregular Excize upon Consumptions' (Petty, *Taxes*, p. 21). During the next century Daniel Defoe, in *Fair Payment No Spunge* (1717), preferred taxes on land to taxes on consumption, but on grounds of social equity, arguing that 'when Land is Tax'd, the Rich pay more than the Poor; but when the Product of Land is tax'd, *the Poor* pay more than *the Rich*,' because 'the Rich pay for their Land because they have it; the Poor pay for their daily Necessaries, because they have them not' (p. 61). At a practical level, it had been Walpole's settled policy to reduce the land tax to the lowest possible rate (Dowell, *Taxation*, vol. II, pp. 92, 96 and 99–103), denouncing it in 1732 as 'the most unequal, the most grievous and the most oppressive tax that ever was raised in this country' (Kennedy, *Taxation*, p. 103). Later in the century Adam Smith would agree that the Land Tax was inequitable, but would counter that this was mitigated by its virtues of being unintrusive to determine, cheap to collect and not a burden on industry (*Wealth of Nations*, V.ii.c; Smith, *Wealth*, pp. 828–36; Smith, *Jurisprudence*, pp. 531–3). It had been only the emergency of the war with Spain that had induced Walpole in November 1739 to raise the rate at which the land tax was assessed once more (Dowell, *Taxation*, vol. II, pp. 111–12). Nevertheless, a stereotyped land tax was thus in force, albeit at varying rates, throughout the first three-quarters of the eighteenth century, and public opinion remained broadly supportive of it, notwithstanding arguments such as those advanced here by Hume (Kennedy, *Taxation*, pp. 96 and 123). Attempts to reduce the Land Tax after the end of the War of the Austrian Succession in 1748 were resisted and ultimately unsuccessful (see, for arguments against reduction, Robert Nugent, *Considerations* [1749] and *Farther Considerations* [1751]; and for comment, see Kennedy, *Taxation*, pp. 127–8). These developments are an important part of the immediate context of Hume's essay. Note the significant variant in the text of the essay at this point (above, p. 369, variant no. 4).

22. *heightening his wages*] In this paragraph Hume takes issue with the arguments of those who had contended that all taxes ultimately fall on land, the mechanism of the shifting from the point of impact (the person who initially pays the tax) to the point of incidence (where the cost of the tax ultimately settles) being the raising of wages. Hume's perception of the 'stickiness' of wages in response to the imposition of taxation on consumption is consistent with his preference for such taxes to fall on luxuries. It was a logical consistency not observed by all commentators on tax, some of whom liked to argue both that taxes on necessities were grievous to the poor man, and that they induced him to raise his wages (in which case, of course, the burden of the tax was shifted to the person who paid those wages): see Kennedy, *Taxation*, pp. 109–10.

23. *gives him protection*] Hobbes too had rested the subject's duty to obey on the ability of the sovereign to protect him: 'The Obligation of Subjects to the Soveraign, is understood to last as long, and no longer, than the power lasteth, by which he is able to protect them. For the right men have by Nature to protect themselves, when none else can protect them, can by no Covenant be relinquished'; 'And thus I have brought to an end my Discourse of Civill and Ecclesiasticall Government, occasioned by the disorders of the present time, without partiality, without application, and without other designe, than to set before mens eyes the mutuall Relation between Protection and Obedience; of which the condition of Humane Nature, and the Laws Divine, (both Naturall and Positive) require an inviolable observation' (Hobbes, *Leviathan*, pp. 153 and 491).

24. *Grand Signior*] i.e. the Ottoman sultan. Hume would refer again to the alleged inability of the Ottoman sultan to impose taxation in 'Of the Origin of Government' (above, p. 233, n. 7). In the 'Early Memoranda' Hume had noted that taxation was a power of sovereignty among the ancient Romans (NLS MS 23159, item 14, p. 10; cf. Mossner, 'Memoranda', p. 503).

25. *It is regarded . . . perseverance*] 'It is impossible exactly to describe the Wealth and ways of Gains exercised by these Potent Governours to enrich themselves; for a *Turk* is ingenious to get Wealth, and hasty to grow rich; . . .'; 'one [Mufti] of late years, famous in *Turky*, for his knowledge and riches, called *Samozade*; one who had piled those heaps of all things that were rich and curious, as were too tedious and long to insert in a Catalogue in this place. It may suffice, that being executed in the time of the last Wars against the Emperour of *Germany* for some conspiracy against the Great Visier, such a Treasure was found appertaining to him (all which was confiscated to the Grand Signior) as was sufficient to have enriched and raised his Prince, had he been impoverished, and in a declining condition' (Rycaut, *Present State*, pp. 51 and 57).

## 9. OF PUBLIC CREDIT

Published in: *1752a, 1752b, 1753, 1754, 1758, 1760, 1764, 1767, 1768, 1770, 1772, 1777a*

Significant revisions:

This essay was heavily and repeatedly revised, in ways which reveal the trajectory of Hume's rapidly developing thought on the topic of public debt. In *1764* Hume, dismayed by the effect of the Seven Years' War – 'that . . . ruinous War; more pernicious to the Victors than to the Vanquished' (*New Letters*, p. 235) – on the size of the British public debt, added material to this essay that made his analysis of the consequences of public debt significantly more pessimistic (see Harris, *Hume*, p. 425, and item 9 in the list of significant variants below). Note, however, what Hont says concerning the misleading effect of these revisions: '[Hume's] intricate essay was originally divided into two parts linked by a difficult bridge, and this interstitial material was greatly expanded in a 1764 revision. It is this expanded section that today seizes our attention, that seems to bear the bulk of the argument, and has distorted our readings. Understanding Hume's argument requires reading "Of Public Credit" in reverse, against the order of Hume's own presentation, and initially ignoring the later insertion, thereby restoring Hume's sense of the political space available for his original analysis of the politics of public debt' (Hont, *Jealousy of Trade*, pp. 327–8).

1) *1752a–1768* read 'beyond the evidence of a hundred demonstrations;' (*1752a*, p. 124; cf. above, p. 76).

2) *1752a–1768* omit 'It is very . . . upon posterity.' (above, pp. 76–7).

3) *1752a–1768* append an additional sentence to the paragraph ending '. . . party among us.' (above, p. 77): 'And these puzzling arguments, (for they deserve not the name of specious) tho' they cou'd not be the foundation of lord *Orford*'s conduct; for he had more sense; serv'd at least to keep his partizans in countenance, and perplex the understanding of the nation.' (*1752a*, p. 126).

4) *1752a–1768* add the following two additional paragraphs immediately following '. . . wars and negociations.' (above, p. 77):

'THERE is a word, which is here in the mouth of every body, and which, I find, has also got abroad, and is much employ'd by foreign writers,* in imitation of the *English*; and that is CIRCULATION. This word serves as an account of every thing; and tho' I confess, that I have sought for its meaning in the present subject, ever since I was a school-boy, I have never yet been able to discover it. What possible advantage is there which the nation can reap by the easy transference of stock from hand to hand? Or is there any paralel to be drawn from the circulation of other commodities, to that of chequer notes and *India* bonds? Where a manufacturer has a quick sale of his goods to the merchant, the merchant to the shop-keeper, the shop-keeper to his customers; this enlivens industry, and gives new encouragement to the first dealer or the manufacturer and all his tradesmen, and makes them produce more and better commodities of the same species. A stagnation is here pernicious, wherever it happens; because it operates backwards, and stops or benumbs the industrious hand in its production of what is useful to human life. But what production we owe to *Change-alley*, or even what consumption, except that of coffee, and pen, ink and paper, I have not yet learn'd; nor can one foresee the loss or decay of any one beneficial commerce or commodity, tho' that place and all its inhabitants were for ever bury'd in the ocean.

'BUT tho' this term, circulation, has never been explain'd by those, who insist so much on the advantages that result from it, there seems, however, to be some benefit of a similar kind, arising from our incumbrances: As indeed, what human evil is there, which is not attended with some advantage? We shall endeavour to explain, that we may estimate the weight we ought to allow it. '*Melon, Du Tot, Law, in the pamphlets, publish'd in *France*.' (*1752a*, pp. 126–8).

5) *1752a–1764* append the following note to '. . . encouraging industry.' (above, p. 78):
'*On this head, I shall observe, without interrupting the thread of the argument, that the multiplicity of our public debts serves rather to sink the interest, and that the more the government borrows, the cheaper may they expect to borrow; contrary to first appearance, and contrary to common opinion. The profits of trade have an influence on interest. See discourse IV ['Of Interest'].' (*1752a*, pp. 129–30).

6) *1752a–1768* omit 'The immense greatness . . . democratical frenzy.' (above, p. 78).

7) *1768* adds the following passage (which was deleted in *1770* and subsequent editions) to the paragraph ending '. . . otherwise they would be.' (above, p. 79): 'We may also remark, that this increase of prices, derived from paper-credit, has a more durable and a more dangerous influence than when it arises from a great increase of gold and silver: Where an accidental overflow of money raises the price of labour and commodities, the evil remedies itself in a little time: The money soon flows out into all the neighbouring nations: The prices fall to a level: And industry may be continued as before; a relief, which cannot be expected, where the circulating specie consists chiefly of paper, and has no intrinsic value.' (*1768*, p. 398).

8) *1752a–1760* read 'these debts, are a check upon industry, heighten the price of labour, and are an oppression on the poorer sort.' (*1752a*, p. 131; cf. above, p. 79).

9) *1752a–1760* omit the six paragraphs 'Suppose the public . . . able to invent.' (above, pp. 80–82).

10) *1752a–1768* append a note to '. . . such an undertaking.' (above, p. 83):
'*IN times of peace and security, when alone it is possible to pay debt, the money'd interest are averse to receive partial payments, which they know not how to dispose of to advantage; and the landed interest are averse to continue the taxes requisite for that purpose. Why therefore shou'd a minister persevere in a measure so disagreeable to all parties? For the sake, I suppose, of a posterity, which he will never see, or of a few reasonable, reflecting people, whose united interest, perhaps, will not be able to secure him the smallest borough in *England*. 'Tis not likely we shall ever find any minister so bad a politician. With regard to these narrow, destructive maxims of politics, all ministers are expert enough.' (*1752a*, p. 134).

11) *1752a–1768* append a note to '. . . *die of the doctor*.' (above, p. 84):
'*SOME neighbouring states practise an easy expedient, by which they lighten their public debts. The *French* have a custom (as the *Romans*

formerly had) of augmenting their money; and this the nation has been so much familiariz'd to, that it hurts not public credit, tho' it be really cutting off at once, by an edict, so much of their debts. The *Dutch* diminish the interest without the consent of their creditors; or which is the same thing, they arbitrarily tax the funds as well as other property. Cou'd we practise either of these methods, we need never be opprest by the national debt; and 'tis not impossible but one of these, or some other method may, at all adventures, be try'd, on the augmentation of our encumbrances and difficulties. But people in this country are so good reasoners upon whatever regards their interest, that such a practice will deceive no body; and public credit will probably tumble at once by so dangerous a trial.' (*1752a*, pp. 136–7).

12) *1752a–1768* present 'So great dupes ... their interest.' (above, p. 85) as a footnote appended to '... dissolution and destruction.' (above, p. 85).

13) *1752a–1768* read 'our foreign enemies, or rather enemy (for we have but one to dread) may be so politic' (*1752a*, p. 140; cf. above, p. 86).

Copy text: *1777a*

Headnote:

The background to, and essential context for, this essay was the expansion of the national debt which had occurred in England since the Glorious Revolution of 1688, and the percentage of the tax revenues of the state that were required to service it. Patrick O'Brien has summarized how those statistics changed over the course of the eighteenth century, and their impact on the allocation of tax revenues to expenditure: 'Over the period 1688–1815, the proportions of tax revenues allocated to service government debt increased from less than 5 per cent before the Glorious Revolution, reached 56 per cent just after the War of American Independence, and remained in the 50 per cent range for the early decades of the nineteenth century' (O'Brien, 'Connections', p. 67).

Hume's concerns about the size of the national debt had taken root as early as 1741. In 'Of Civil Liberty' (then entitled 'Of Liberty and Despotism') he had identified the source of modern degeneracy in free governments as 'the practice of contracting debt, and mortgaging the public revenues, by which taxes may, in time, become altogether intolerable, and all the property of the state be brought into the hands of the public. This practice is of modern date' (above, vol. 1, p. 82; cf. *1741*, p. 186). In the final remarks he added to his character of Sir Robert Walpole when the essay had been demoted from being a separate, free-standing piece to being a footnote to the essay 'That Politics may be reduced to a Science', he observed that '*the not paying more of our public Debts was, as hinted in this Character, a great, and the only great, Error in that long Administration*' (*1748a*, p. 38). In the 'Early Memoranda' he had noted (without comment): 'The Interest of the public Debt above 45 Millions.' (NLS MS 23159, item 14, p. 15; cf. Mossner, 'Memoranda', p. 507).

These concerns strengthened markedly, as Britain's imperial ambitions involved her in a series of continental wars that Hume regarded as blunders. On 11 March 1771 he would write to his publisher William Strahan: 'I wish I coud have the same Idea with you of the Prosperity of our public Affairs. But when I reflect, that, from 1740 to 1761, during the Course of no more than 21 Years, while a most pacific Monarch sat on the Throne of France, the Nation ran in Debt about a hundred Millions; that the wise and virtuous Minister, Pitt, could contract more Incumbrances, in six months of an unnecessary War, than we have been able to discharge during eight Years of Peace; and that we persevere in the same frantic Maxims; I can forsee nothing but certain and speedy Ruin either to the Nation or to the public Creditors' (*Letters*, vol. II, p. 237). In the penultimate paragraph of 'Of the Jealousy of Trade' Hume had cited the Dutch as an illustration of the decline that awaited those nations addicted to public credit (above, p. 62). Notwithstanding his criticisms of Britain's system of public credit, however, Hume played that system profitably, as the letter to his brother of 1766 testifies: 'I have sold out my four per cents in the Stocks, at 1545 pounds. I keep only the long Annuities, which I coud sell for between 4 & 500 pounds; so that I am a Gainer near 500 Pounds by the Stockjobbing' (*Letters*, vol. II, p. 7).

Bolingbroke, too, had been dismayed – or, perhaps, had affected to be dismayed – by the prospect of ever-increasing public debt. In letter 19 of *A Dissertation upon Parties* he wrote: 'It is impossible to look forward, without horror, on the consequences that may still follow. The ordinary expenses of our government are defrayed, in great measure, by anticipation and mortgages. In time of peace, in days of prosperity, as we boast them to be, we contract new debts, and we create new funds. What must we do in war, and in national distress? What will happen, when we have mortgaged and funded all we have to mortgage and to fund; when we have mortgaged to new creditors that sinking fund which was mortgaged to other creditors not yet paid off; when we have mortgaged all the product of our land, and even our land itself? Who can answer, that the whole body of the people will suffer themselves to be treated, in favour of an handful of men (for they who monopolize the whole power, and may in time monopolize the whole property of the funds, are indeed but an handful), who can answer, that the whole body of the people will suffer themselves to be treated, in favour of such an handful, as the poor Indians are, in favour of the Spaniards; to be parcelled out in lots, as it were; and to be assigned, like these Indians to the Spanish planters, to toil and starve for the proprietors of the several funds? Who can answer, that a scheme, which oppresses the farmer, ruins the manufacturer, breaks the merchant, discourages industry, and reduces fraud into system; which beggars so often the fair adventurer and innocent proprietor; which drains continually a portion of our national wealth away to foreigners, and draws most perniciously the rest of that immense property that was diffused among thousands, into the pockets of a few; who can answer that such a scheme will always be endured?' (Bolingbroke, *Political Writings*, p. 181). For further comment, see: Hont, *Jealousy of Trade*, pp. 325–53, and John Pocock, 'Hume and the American Revolution: The Dying Thoughts of a North Briton', in his *Virtue, Commerce, and History* (Cambridge: Cambridge University Press, 1985), pp. 125–41.

In 1776 Adam Smith would recognize that 'the reasons and causes which have induced almost all modern governments to mortgage some part of this revenue [i.e. taxes], or to contract debts' was an important and emergent topic in contemporary economics; and he would attempt to gauge 'what have been the effects of those debts upon the real wealth, the annual produce of the land and labour of society' (Smith, *Wealth*, vol. I, p. 12).

Pamphlets on public credit were published frequently in the first half of the eighteenth century, and their dates of publication tended to cluster around certain crises: 1714 and the accession of the Hanoverians; 1720 and the South Sea Bubble; 1748 and the end of the War of the Austrian Succession. They divide fairly neatly into jeremiads foretelling imminent national bankruptcy and panegyrics on the wisdom of the administration. Dispassionate, patient economic insight is in short supply.

A final comparison is perhaps relevant. One of the most celebrated of all the *Spectator* papers was no. 3 (3 March 1711) on public credit. Addison's essay takes the form of a dream Mr. Spectator has after visiting the Bank of England. In this dream public credit is 'a beautiful Virgin seated on a Throne of Gold' behind which are 'a prodigious Heap of Bags of Mony' (Addison, *Spectator*, vol. I, pp. 15 and 16). The entry of a youth, representing the Old Pretender, followed by 'hideous Phantoms', causes Public Credit to sicken and her money bags to shrink, until the arrival of Liberty and Monarchy (representing the Hanoverian dynasty identified in the Act of Settlement as the presumptive heirs to the throne) restores her to health and replenishes her bags of money (Addison, *Spectator*, vol. I, pp. 16–17). Plainly this was principally an anti-Jacobite paper. But it is still worth noting that Addison's view of public credit seems to be along the lines of 'the more the merrier'. The proximate danger for Addison was that the practice of public credit should fail, rather than that it should flourish. Hume's gradual abandonment of Addisonianism in essay-writing, therefore, might be visible in his substantive political and economic judgements, as well as in his literary and stylistic mannerisms.

1. *hoard up treasures before-hand*] cf. two entries in the 'Early Memoranda': '60.000 Sterling amassd before hand for building the Capitol. Dᵒ. Lib. 1.'; 'The Romans never borrowd but in the last degree of Necessity as after the Battle of Cannae upon the new War with Macedon. Dᵒ. Lib. 23. Cap. 48' (NLS MS 23159, item 14, p. 20; cf. Mossner, 'Memoranda', p. 511); 'Dᵒ'

(for 'ditto') refers to Livy. Cf. also what Hume has said in 'Of Money' about the utility of an institution such as the Bank of Amsterdam, which simply hoarded its deposits: 'so large a sum, lying ready at command, would be a convenience in times of great public danger and distress; and what part of it was used might be replaced at leisure, when peace and tranquillity was restored to the nation' (above, p. 27).

2. *PTOLEMIES*] See above, p. 356, n. 49.

3. *If I remember ... JEWISH princes*] See 2 Kings 18:15 and 2 Chronicles 32:27–9.

4. *PHILIP ... PERSEUS ... MACEDON*] Hume has already commented on the size of this treasure in 'Of the Balance of Trade' (above, p. 56).

5. *Every one ... civil wars*] Plutarch relates how Caesar looted the state treasury (Plutarch, *Caesar*, XXXV.2–4), but does not put a value on what he took.

6. *discovered*] i.e. displayed or manifested (see *OED*, 'discover' *v*. I 5b).

7. *and we find ... exigency*] Augustus: Tacitus, *Annals*, I.xi, and Suetonius, *Deified Augustus*, CI.iv. Tiberius: Suetonius, *Tiberius*, XXXV and XLVI–XLIX. Vespasian: Suetonius, *Vespasianus*, XVI. Severus: Dio, *Roman History*, LXXVII.xvi.3–4.

8. *Essay V*] In 'Of the Balance of Trade', above, p. 56.

9. *ALCIB. I*] 'τοῦτο μὲν γὰρ εἰ ἐθέλεις τοὺς Λακεδαιμονίων πλούτους ἰδεῖν, γνώσῃ ὅτι πολὺ τἀνθάδε τῶν ἐκεῖ ἐλλείπει. γῆν μὲν γὰρ ὅσην ἔχουσι τῆς θ᾽ ἑαυτῶν καὶ Μεσσήνης, οὐδ᾽ ἂν εἷς ἀμφισβητήσειε τῶν τῇδε πλήθει οὐδὲ ἀρετῇ, οὐδ᾽ αὖ ἀνδραπόδων κτήσει τῶν τε ἄλλων καὶ τῶν εἱλωτικῶν, οὐδὲ μὴν ἵππων γε, οὐδ᾽ ὅσα ἄλλα βοσκήματα κατὰ Μεσσήνην νέμεται· ἀλλὰ ταῦτα μὲν πάντα ἐῶ χαίρειν, χρυσίον δὲ καὶ ἀργύριον οὐκ ἔστιν ἐν πᾶσιν Ἕλλησιν ὅσον ἐν Λακεδαίμονι ἰδίᾳ· πολλὰς γὰρ ἤδη γενεὰς εἰσέρχεται μὲν αὐτόσε ἐξ ἁπάντων τῶν Ἑλλήνων, πολλάκις δὲ καὶ ἐκ τῶν βαρβάρων, ἐξέρχεται δὲ οὐδαμόσε, ἀλλ᾽ ἀτεχνῶς κατὰ τὸν Αἰσώπου μῦθον, ὃν ἡ ἀλώπηξ πρὸς τὸν λέοντα εἶπε, καὶ τοῦ εἰς Λακεδαίμονα νομίσματος εἰσιόντος μὲν τὰ ἴχνη τὰ ἐκεῖσε τετραμμένα δῆλα, ἐξιόντος δὲ οὐδαμῇ ἄν τις ἴδοι· ὥστε εὖ χρὴ εἰδέναι ὅτι καὶ χρυσῷ καὶ ἀργύρῳ οἱ ἐκεῖ πλουσιώτατοί εἰσι τῶν Ἑλλήνων, καὶ αὐτῶν ἐκείνων ὁ βασιλεύς· ἔκ τε γὰρ τῶν τοιούτων μέγισται λήψεις καὶ πλεῖσταί εἰσι τοῖς Ββασιλεῦσιν, ἔτι δὲ καὶ ὁ βασιλικὸς φόρος οὐκ ὀλίγος γίγνεται, ὃν τελοῦσιν οἱ Λακεδαιμόνιοι τοῖς βασιλεῦσιν'; 'For in this respect you have only to look at the wealth of the Spartans, and you will perceive that our riches here are far inferior to theirs. Think of all the land that they have both in their own and in the Messenian country: not one of our estates could compete with theirs in extent and excellence, nor again in ownership of slaves, and especially of those of the helot class, nor yet of horses, nor of all the flocks and herds that graze in Messene. However, I pass over all these things: but there is more gold and silver privately held in Lacedaemon than in the whole of Greece; for during many generations treasure has been passing in to them from every part of Greece, and often from the barbarians

also, but not passing out to anyone; and just as in the fable of Aesop, where the fox remarked to the lion on the direction of the footmarks, the traces of the money going into Lacedaemon are clear enough, but nowhere are any to be seen of it coming out; so that one can be pretty sure that those people are the richest of the Greeks in gold and silver, and that among themselves the richest is the king; for the largest and most numerous receipts of the kind are those of the kings, and besides there is the levy of the royal tribute in no slight amount, which the Spartans pay to their kings' (Plato, *Alcibiades 1*, 122d–123b).

10. *Lib. iii*] A number of passages in Arrian refer to Alexander's seizures of Persian treasure: 'καὶ Δαρεῖον μὲν οὐ καταλαμβάνει ἐν Ἀρβήλοις, ἀλλὰ ἔφευγεν οὐδέν τι ἐλινύσας Δαρεῖος· τὰ χρήματα δὲ ἐγκατελήφθη καὶ ἡ κατασκευὴ πᾶσα, καὶ τὸ ἅρμα τὸ Δαρείου αὖθις ἐγκατελήφθη καὶ ἡ ἀσπὶς αὖθις καὶ τὰ τόξα ἑάλω'; 'However, he did not catch Darius at Arbela, as he continued his flight without pause, though his treasure and all his equipment was captured and his chariot was seized then a second time, and his shield was taken a second time, and his bow and arrows too' (III.xv.5); 'ἀφίκετο δὲ ἐς Σοῦσα Ἀλέξανδρος ἐκ Βαβυλῶνος ἐν ἡμέραις εἴκοσι· καὶ παρελθὼν ἐς τὴν πόλιν τά τε χρήματα παρέλαβεν ὄντα ἀργυρίου τάλαντα ἐς πεντακισμύρια καὶ τὴν ἄλλην κατασκευὴν τὴν βασιλικήν. πολλὰ δὲ καὶ ἄλλα κατελήφθη αὐτοῦ, ὅσα Ξέρξης ἀπὸ τῆς Ἑλλάδος ἄγων ἦλθε, τά τε ἄλλα καὶ Ἁρμοδίου καὶ Ἀριστογείτονος χαλκαῖ εἰκόνες. καὶ ταύτας Ἀθηναίοις ὀπίσω πέμπει Ἀλέξανδρος, καὶ νῦν κεῖνται Ἀθήνησιν ἐν Κεραμεικῷ αἱ εἰκόνες, ᾗ ἄνιμεν ἐς πόλιν, καταντικρὺ μάλιστα τοῦ Μητρῴου, <οὐ> μακρὰν τῶν Εὐδανέμων τοῦ βωμοῦ· ὅστις δὲ μεμύηται ταῖν θεαῖν ἐν Ἐλευσῖνι, οἶδε τοῦ Εὐδανέμου τὸν βωμὸν ἐπὶ τοῦ δαπέδου ὄντα'; 'Alexander reached Susa in twenty days from Babylon; he entered the city and took over the treasure, up to fifty thousand Talents of silver, and all the rest of the royal belongings. A good deal was captured there in addition, all that Xerxes brought back from Greece, notably bronze statues of Harmodius and Aristogeiton, which Alexander sent back to the Athenians; they are now set up at Athens in the Cerameicus, on the way by which we ascend the Acropolis, just opposite the Metroön, not far from the altar of the Eudanemoi. Anyone who has been initiated into the mysteries of the Two Goddesses at Eleusis is aware that the altar of Eudanemos is in the plain' (III.xvi.7–8); 'ἐντεῦθεν δὲ αὖθις σπουδῇ ἤλαυνεν ἐς Πέρσας, ὥ<σ>τε ἔφθη ἀφικέσθαι πρὶν τὰ χρήματα διαρπάσασθαι τοὺς φύλακας. ἔλαβε δὲ καὶ τὰ ἐν Πασαργάδαις χρήματα ἐν τοῖς Κύρου τοῦ πρώτου θησαυροῖς'; 'Thence he hurried on again towards Persia and arrived there before the garrison had plundered the treasure. He also captured the treasure which had been at Pasargadae in the treasury of Cyrus the First' (III.xviii.10).

11. *vita ALEX.*] 'Ἀλέξανδρος δὲ Σούσων κυριεύσας παρέλαβεν ἐν τοῖς βασιλείοις τετρακισμύρια τάλαντα νομίσματος, τὴν δὲ ἄλλην κατασκευὴν καὶ πολυτέλειαν ἀδιήγητον. ὅπου φασὶ καὶ πορφύρας Ἑρμιονικῆς εὑρεθῆναι τάλαντα πεντακισχίλια,

συγκειμένης μὲν ἐξ ἐτῶν δέκα δεόντων διακοσίων, πρόσφατον δὲ τὸ ἄνθος ἔτι καὶ νεαρὸν φυλαττούσης'; 'On making himself master of Susa, Alexander came into possession of forty thousand talents of coined money in the palace, and of untold furniture and wealth besides. Among this they say was found five thousand talents' weight of purple from Hermione, which, although it had been stored there for a hundred and ninety years, still kept its colours fresh and lively' (Plutarch, *Alexander*, XXXVI.1); 'ὅσον ἐν Σούσοις, τὴν δὲ ἄλλην κατασκευὴν καὶ τὸν πλοῦτον ἐκκομισθῆναί φασι μυρίοις ὀρικοῖς ζεύγεσι καὶ πεντακισχιλίαις καμήλοις'; 'and they say that as much coined money was found there as at Susa, and that it took ten thousand pairs of mules and five thousand camels to carry away the other furniture and wealth there' (Plutarch, *Alexander*, XXXVII.2).

12. *lib. iv*] 'πιθανώτερος δ' ἐστὶν ὁ Ποσειδωνίου λόγος· τὰ μὲν γὰρ εὑρεθέντα ἐν τῇ Τολώσσῃ χρήματα μυρίων που καὶ πεντακισχιλίων ταλάντων γενέσθαι φησί, τὰ μὲν ἐν σηκοῖς ἀποκείμενα, τὰ δ' ἐν λίμναις ἱεραῖς, οὐδεμίαν κατασκευὴν ἔχοντα, ἀλλ᾽ ἀργὸν χρυσίον καὶ ἄργυρον'; 'However, the account of Poseidonius is more plausible: for he says that the treasure that was found in Tolosa amounted to about fifteen thousand talents (part of it stored away in sacred enclosures, part of it in sacred lakes), un-wrought, that is, merely gold and silver bullion' (Strabo, IV.i.13).

13. *the ancient maxims . . . than the modern*] A rare moment in which Hume is prepared to admit that the moderns have fallen below the standard set by the ancients. Although Hume was aware that to 'declaim against present times, and magnify the virtue of remote ancestors, is a propensity almost inherent in human nature' ('Of Refinement in the Arts', above, p. 22), this was nevertheless a natural inclination which on most occasions he wished to resist: cf., e.g., 'Of the Populousness of Ancient Nations': 'The humour of blaming the present, and admiring the past, is strongly rooted in human nature, and has an influence even on persons endued with the profoundest judgment and most extensive learning' (above, p. 148). Cf. also the *Treatise of Human Nature*, II.iii.7–8 (*THN*, pp. 274–80).

14. *It would scarcely . . . upon posterity*] Hume failed to foresee that the development of a sophisticated bond market would operate naturally to curb the inevitable tendency of politicians to debauch the state finances; and this despite his alertness to the operation of natural self-regulating mechanisms in economic life. His comment later in this essay, that the 'only check which the creditors have upon her [the state], is the interest of preserving credit' (above, p. 85), perhaps marks a step towards that insight.

15. *What then . . . without limitation?*] One of the authors of this 'new paradox' was Jean-François Melon, who had argued (rather in the manner of Keynes *avant la lettre*) for the essential innocence of public debt: 'Les Dettes d'un Etat sont des Dettes de la main droite à la main gauche, dont le corps ne se

trouvera point affoibli, s'il a la quantité d'alimens nécessaires, & s'il sçait les distribuer' (Melon, *Essai politique*, p. 296). Melon cites as corroboration for his opinion 'un Memoire Anglois' of 1731 designed to 'prouver qu'un Etat devenoit plus florissant par ses Dettes' (ibid.). This was perhaps Erasmus Philips's *The State of the Nation* (1731), which had contended that the public debt stimulated consumption and circulation of money, and hence had beneficial economic consequences. Adam Smith would reject this way of viewing public debt as an expression of 'the sophistry of the mercantile system' (Smith, *Wealth*, pp. 926–7, V.iii.52).

16. *panegyrics . . . NERO*] Examples of the rhetorical exercise known as the paradoxical encomium, in which students were required to praise something or someone obviously undeserving of praise.

17. *great ministers, and by a whole party*] i.e. Sir Robert Walpole and the Court Whigs. Cf. the similar reproach levelled at Walpole by Adam Smith in his lectures on jurisprudence: 'To stop this clamour Sir Robert Walpole endeavoured to shew that the public debt was no inconvenience, tho' it is to be supposed that a man of his abilities saw the contrary himself' (Smith, *Jurisprudence*, p. 515).

18. *Bank-stock, or India-bonds*] i.e. bonds offered by the East India Company, which at this time were a proxy for public debt.

19. *scritoire*] A writing-desk, usually lockable, constructed to contain stationery and documents; in early use, often one of a portable size; more recently, chiefly applied to a larger piece of furniture, a bureau or secretary (*OED*, 'escritoire', *n.*).

20. *Public securities . . . whole society*] This paragraph recapitulates an insight which Hume seems first to have expressed to Montesquieu in his letter of 10 April 1749: 'L'énumeration que vous faites des inconvénients des dettes publiques est fort juste. Mais n'ont-elles aucun avantage? Les marchands qui ont des capitaux dans les fonds publics ne gardent que peu d'argent dans leurs coffres pour les besoins de leur commerce; ils peuvent disposer quand il leur plaît de ces capitaux pour reponde à quelque demande que ce soit. Par conséquent, ces capitaux servent à deux fins: premièrement, à leur produire un revenu fixe: secondement, à faire aller leur commerce; par conséquent le marchand peut soutenir le commerce avec de moindres profits sur les marchandises, ce qui est avantageux pour le commerce. En parlant de ceci à un homme qui a beaucoup de connoissances, Milord Lonsdale, il me fit remarquer un autre avantage, qui cependant me paroît plus douteux: les capitaux, dit-il, que l'on a dans les fonds publics sont dans une circulation continuelle et forment une espèce d'argent; l'abondance de l'argent diminue l'intérêt et favorise le commerce' (*Letters*, vol. I, p. 137; cf. also p. 144). Note, however, the more positive account Hume had given of these innovative financial instruments, especially as developed in Scotland, in 'Of the Balance of Trade' (above, pp. 53–5).

21. *LONDON ... enormous size*] But cf. Hume's much more relaxed comments on the size of the economy of London compared with that of the rest of the kingdom in 'Of the Balance of Trade' (above, p. 59, n. R).

22. *Jacobitish violence*] The Jacobites were supporters of the exiled house of Stuart. There had been Jacobite rebellions in 1715 and 1745.

23. *democratical frenzy*] i.e. a republican uprising. In Addison's *Spectator* paper on public credit two of the 'hideous Phantoms' which cause Public Credit to sicken and die are 'the Genius of a Common-Wealth' (i.e. republican principles) and 'a young Man of about twenty two Years of Age' (i.e. the Old Pretender, James Francis Edward Stuart, here representing the Jacobite threat) (Addison, *Spectator*, vol. I, p. 16).

24. *foreigners ... national funds*] The canton of Berne was particularly long in British public debt: '*Berne* in particular, has at this time 300000 Pounds Sterling at Interest' (Stanyan, *Switzerland*, p. 187): Hume had noted this long position in 'Of the Balance of Trade' (above, pp. 56–7). Adam Smith would also draw attention to the foreign deposits of the 'powerful canton of Berne', which had 'accumulated ... a very large sum, supposed to amount to several millions, part of which is deposited in a publick treasure, and part is placed at interest in what are called the publick funds of the different indebted nations of Europe, chiefly in those of France and Great Britain' (Smith, *Wealth*, pp. 812–13, V.i.g.41; cf. also pp. 819–20, V.ii.a.9).

25. *must support itself in the society of nations*] cf. the comment in 'Of the Jealousy of Trade' on the declining standing of the Dutch, which Hume attributes to their immoderate indulgence in public credit (above, p. 62).

26. *We have ... than before*] 'Les Dettes d'un Etat sont des Dettes de la main droite à la main gauche, dont le corps ne se trouvera point affoibli, s'il a la quantité d'alimens nécessaires, & s'il sçait les distribuer' (Melon, *Essai politique*, p. 296).

27. *Duties ... upon possessions*] cf. Hume's comments on the inconveniency of taxes on possessions in 'Of Taxes' (above, p. 73).

28. *who have no connexions with the state*] It is perhaps surprising to find Hume falling in with the old prejudice that possession of land was a form of property that should enjoy political advantages over monetary property. Only the strength of Hume's fear of the extent and tendency of public credit can explain that surprising association; and, in its turn, that unexpected association is an index to the strength of his fear. For an account of the origins and growth of this prejudice in eighteenth-century England, see John Barrell, *English Literature in History 1730–80: An Equal, Wide Survey* (London: Hutchinson, 1983).

29. *Adieu to all ideas of nobility, gentry, and family*] In 'Of Commerce', however, Hume had smiled on the mobility in social hierarchy that might result from trade: 'the few merchants, who possess the secret of this importation and exportation, make great profits; and becoming rivals in wealth to the

ancient nobility, tempt other adventurers to become their rivals in commerce' (above, p. 11). In the *Wealth of Nations*, III.iv.16, Adam Smith would depict the movement of riches between rather than within families as a consequence of commerce, not of recklessness over public debt: 'In commercial countries, therefore, riches, in spite of the most violent regulations of law to prevent their dissipation, very seldom remain long in the same family' (Smith, *Wealth*, vol. I, p. 422).

30. *and by this means . . . the sovereign*] The idea that the aristocracy of a nation might serve to moderate the influence of the sovereign is found in republican thinkers of the later seventeenth century such as Henry Neville (see, e.g., Neville, *Plato*, pp. 138–40). It finds its most rapturous expression in Edmund Burke's account of the function of a 'natural aristocracy' in his *An Appeal from the New to the Old Whigs* (1791), pp. 129–30; in that connection, note Hume's phrase, 'instituted by the hand of nature'. Cf. the congruent comment in 'Of the Populousness of Ancient Nations' on the constitutional importance of an aristocracy: 'One general cause of the disorders, so frequent in all ancient governments, seems to have consisted in the great difficulty of establishing any Aristocracy in those ages, and the perpetual discontents and seditions of the people, whenever even the meanest and most beggarly were excluded from the legislature and from public offices' (above, p. 119). In 'Idea of a Perfect Commonwealth' Hume would forge a role for the aristocracy intended to make it 'an excellent barrier both to the monarchy and against it' (above, p. 206).

31. *mercenary armies*] cf. the similar disparagement of standing armies below (p. 396 and n. 47).

32. *Elections . . . bribery and corruption alone*] cf. the note in the 'Early Memoranda' concerning the corruption of the House of Commons during the reign of Charles II by means of pensions: 'The sum of 252.467 £ given in Bribes to the Parliament in 3 years during the Reign of Char. 2' (NLS MS 23159, item 14, p. 22; cf. Mossner, 'Memoranda', p. 513). In letter 3 of his *A Dissertation upon Parties* Bolingbroke had defended this Parliament against the charge of corruption: 'I cannot hear it called the pensioner-Parliament, as it were by way of eminence, without a degree of honest indignation; especially in the age in which we live, and by some of those who affect the most to bestow upon it this ignominious appellation' (Bolingbroke, *Political Writings*, p. 27).

33. *our late wars*] Principally a reference to the War of the Austrian Succession (1740–48) and the Seven Years' War (1756–63).

34. *the consent of the annuitants*] Contrary to Hume's pessimistic forecast, this 'haircut' had in fact been recently obtained by Henry Pelham: see Dickson, *Revolution*, pp. 228–43.

35. *We have always . . . impotence*] cf. the comments on the Dutch in 'Of the Jealousy of Trade' (above, p. 62).

36. *a strange supineness*] Whereas Hume thought that, on questions of party politics, his contemporaries in Britain tended to be overexcited and needed to be calmed, in respect of certain economic questions he thought on the contrary that they were culpably relaxed and needed to be stirred up. This difference in Hume's perception of the emotional disposition of his readership goes some way towards explaining the very different tone of these two kinds of essay.

37. *What then ... of us?*] cf. Matthew 19:27. In the eighteenth century this question carried strong religious overtones, and addressed the concerns of believers about the afterlife and their personal fate within it: see, e.g., George Fothergill, *Sermons on Several Subjects and Occasions* (Oxford: Clarendon Press, 1761), p. 158; Thomas Bowman, *The Principles of Christianity* (1769), p. 93; George Whitefield, *A Select Collection of Letters*, 3 vols (1772), vol. III, p. 200; Alexander Mackenzie, *Frequent Communion* (1780), pp. 112–23; Thomas Forster, *Sermons upon Various Subjects*, 2 vols (1785?), vol. I, pp. 28–29 and 114; Thomas Bisset, *Sermons* (Edinburgh, 1788), p. 91; Adam Ferguson, *Principles of Moral and Political Science*, 2 vols (1792), vol. I, p. 339. Hume's application of the phrase to the subject of public credit therefore seems arch.

38. *HUTCHINSON*] In 1718 Archibald Hutcheson had published *Some Calculations and Remarks Relating to the Present State of the Publick Debts and Funds*, in which he argued that debt had increased greatly since the accession of George I in 1714. Hume, however, refers to an earlier publication by Hutcheson, *Some Considerations Relating to the Payment of the Publick Debts* (1717) in which, as Hume describes, Hutcheson proposed that the public debt could be cleared by dividing it among the population. In the 'Early Memoranda' Hume noted that a quarter of the national debt had in fact been repaid after the Treaty of Ryswick in 1697: 'Five Millions of Debt pay'd betwixt the Peace of Ryswick & the late War. Twenty millions reduc'd to fifteen [*correction for the Scotticism* fiveteen].' (NLS MS 23159, item 14, p. 17; cf. Mossner, 'Memoranda', p. 509). The 'late War' is presumably the War of the Spanish Succession (1701–14).

39. *by their annual consumptions*] On which subject, see Hume's comments in 'Of Taxes' (above, p. 72).

40. *But though ... discharge*] See above, n. 38.

41. *during the regency*] i.e. the period between 1715 and 1723, when Louis XV was a minor and Philippe II, Duc d'Orléans (1674–1723), ruled as regent. The Duc d'Orléans had supported the schemes of John Law, which had led in 1720 to a general financial collapse in France.

42. *self-preservation is unalienable*] In antiquity the natural rightness of the instinct to self-preservation was an opinion associated with the Stoics, Cicero placing it in the mouth of Cato in *De Finibus*: '"Placet his," inquit, "quorum ratio mihi probatur, simul atque natum sit animal (hinc enim est

ordiendum), ipsum sibi conciliari et commendari ad se conservandum et ad suum statum eaque quae conservantia sunt eius status diligenda, alienari autem ab interitu iisque rebus quae interitum videantur afferre'; 'He began: "It is the view of those whose system I adopt [i.e. the Stoics], that immediately upon birth (for that is the proper point to start from) a living creature feels an attachment for itself, and an impulse to preserve itself and to feel affection for its own constitution and for those things which tend to preserve that constitution; while on the other hand it conceives an antipathy to destruction and to those things which appear to threaten destruction"' (III.v). In seventeenth-century Europe, the principle of self-preservation had been made a cornerstone of natural-law theory. See, e.g., Hobbes: 'no Law can oblige a man to abandon his own preservation' (*Leviathan*, chapter 27; Hobbes, *Leviathan*, p. 208; cf. also p. 153 for another statement of the inalienability of this right). Locke would concur: 'The first and strongest desire God Planted in Men, and wrought into the very Principles of their Nature being that of Self-preservation, that is the Foundation of a right to the Creatures, for the particular support and use of each individual Person himself' ('First Treatise', § 88, in Locke, *Two Treatises*, p. 206). Cf. also Pufendorf, *Duty*, p. 53: 'self-preservation is valued so highly that it is held to exempt a man in many cases from the obligation of the common laws, if that is the only way it can be secured'; and Grotius, *Rights of War and Peace*, chapter II: "tis the first Duty of every one to preserve himself in his natural State, to see after those Things which are agreeable to Nature, and to avert those which are repugnant' (Grotius, *Rights*, vol. 1, p. 180).

43. *the late war*] Louis XV, during the War of the Austrian Succession (1740–48).

44. *his grandfather*] In fact, Louis XIV was Louis XV's great-grandfather.

45. *natural rate of interest*] i.e. the rate of interest that would obtain without legal restrictions.

46. *trepan*] deceive. A slightly old-fashioned word in 1752.

47. *standing armies to arbitrary government*] Contrast this with Hume's earlier dissociation of himself from this Whiggish doctrine in 'Of Money', where he had seemed to defend the reasonableness of the use of mercenary troops by rich trading nations such as Britain, Holland and Carthage (above, p. 25). This is another instance of Hume's late reversion towards positions he earlier would have condemned as vulgar Whiggism; cf. also his rejection of 'mercenary armies' (above, p. 81).

48. *taken a spunge to our debts*] i.e. brought about a voluntary bankruptcy by disowning public debt. In Addison's *Spectator* paper on public credit (see the headnote, above, p. 388), the 'young Man' (representing the Old Pretender, James Francis Edward Stuart) whose entry so afflicts Public Credit that she faints and dies away, carries 'a Spunge in his left Hand'; thus glancing at the Whiggish allegation that a Stuart restoration would precipitate the disowning of public debt and thus the destruction of public credit (Addison,

*Spectator*, vol. I, p. 16). (He is represented as carrying the spunge in his left hand, because in antiquity nothing auspicious could be performed with the left, or sinister, hand.) For other examples, see: Arthur Sykes, *A Letter to a Friend* (1717), p. 21; John Crookshanks, *Some Seasonable Remarks* (1718), p. 12; Henry Brooke and G. Berkeley, *Essays Against Popery, Slavery, and Arbitrary Power* (Manchester, 1750?), p. 63; Josiah Tucker, *Four Tracts* (1774), p. 128; Robert Peel, *The National Debt Productive of National Prosperity* (1787), p. 46. Note Sir John Sinclair's citation of this passage of Hume's essay in his *The History of the Public Revenue of the British Empire, Part III* (1790), p. 271, n. i.

49. *poterant*] 'But the mob attended in delight on the great indulgences that he [Vitellius] bestowed; the most foolish citizens bought them, while the wise regarded as worthless privileges which could neither be granted nor accepted if the state was to stand' (Tacitus, *Histories*, III.lv).

50. *When the astrologers ... at last*] A common anecdote, but cf., e.g., Pierre Bayle, *Pensées Diverses* (Rotterdam, 1683), §18, p. 45: 'Ce qui a été fort bien remarqué par Henri le Grand. Il ne se passoit point d'année, ni de mois où les Astrologues n'annonçeassent le terrible menaçe de sa mort. *Ils diront vrai enfin,* (dit un jour ce Prince) *& le public se souviendra mieux de la seule fois où leur prediction aura été vraye, que de tant d'autres où ils ont predit à faux.*'


## X. OF SOME REMARKABLE CUSTOMS

Published in: *1752a, 1752b, 1753, 1754, 1758, 1760, 1764, 1767, 1768, 1770, 1772, 1777a*

Significant revisions:

Hume made just one small revision to the final sentence of this essay.

1) *1752a–1768* read: 'And great violences and disorders, amongst the people, the most humane and best natur'd, are committed with impunity; ...' (*1752a*, p. 154; cf. above, p. 94).

Copy text: *1777a*

Headnote:

An essay which clearly contributes to Hume's general objective, when writing of politics and society, of introducing more hesitancy and less extreme dogmatism into the political opinions of his readers; as is stated in the very first sentence of the essay.

1. *I shall ... great caution*] Contrast the commitment to the investigation of 'general principles' announced at the beginning of 'Of Commerce', the essay which stood at the head of *Political Discourses* (1752) (above, p. 4).

2. *a very useful law*] cf. Demosthenes, *De Corona*, CII–CIX.

3. *By the ... usefulness of his law*] Demosthenes: see above, p. 397, n. 2. Cf. two notes in the 'Early Memoranda': 'The γραφη παρανομων a singular & a seemingly an absurd Law among the Athenians; by which a man coud be try'd & punish'd for promulgating a bad Law to the People, the only Legislators. This shows a remarkable Diffidence which the People had in their own Judgement. Demosthenes was try'd & acquitted for his Law περι συμμαρια. Περι ϛτεφ'; 'The first Law, on the Establishment of the Oligarchy in Athens was the Abolishing of the γραφη παρανομων' (NLS MS 23159, item 14, pp. 25 and 28; cf. Mossner, 'Memoranda', pp. 516 and 518).

4. *that sublime ... mankind*] Demosthenes's defence of Ctesiphon is now more usually referred to as the *De Corona*.

5. *CHÆRONEA*] See above, p. 362, n. 5.

6. *LONGINUS*] 'ὡς νὴ Δία καὶ ὁ Ὑπερείδης κατηγορούμενος, ἐπειδὴ τοὺς δούλους μετὰ τὴν ἧτταν ἐλευθέρους ἐψηφίσατο, "τοῦτο τὸ ψήφισμα," εἶπεν, "οὐχ ὁ ῥήτωρ ἔγραψεν ἀλλ᾽ ἡ ἐν Χαιρωνείᾳ μάχη"'; 'And then, to be sure, there is Hyperides on his trial, when he had moved the enfranchisement of the slaves after the Athenian reverse. "It was not the speaker that framed this measure, but the battle of Chaeronea"' (Longinus, *On the Sublime*, XV.x).

7. *same law*] 'ἀτίμοι ἐπιτίμοι'; 'the disenfranchised enfranchised'. 'κριθεὶς δ᾽ ὑπὸ τοῦ Ἀριστογείτονος παρανόμων ἐπὶ τῷ γράψαι μετὰ Χαιρώνειαν τοὺς μετοίκους πολίτας ποιήσασθαι τοὺς δὲ δούλους ἐλευθέρους, ἱερὰ δὲ καὶ παῖδας καὶ γυναῖκας εἰς τὸν Πειραιᾶ ἀποθέσθαι, ἀπέφυγεν. αἰτιωμένων δέ τινων αὐτὸν ὡς παριδόντα πολλοὺς νόμους ἐν τῷ ψηφίσματι, "ἐπεσκότει," ἔφη, "μοι τὰ Μακεδόνων ὅπλα" καὶ "οὐκ ἐγὼ τὸ ψήφισμα ἔγραψα ἡ δ᾽ ἐν Χαιρωνείᾳ μάχη"'; 'And when he was brought to trial by Aristogeiton for illegal conduct in proposing a decree after the battle of Chaeroneia to grant citizenship to the resident aliens, to set the slaves free, and to put the sacred objects, the children, and the women in Peiraeus for safekeeping, he was acquitted. And when certain persons blamed him for having disregarded many laws in his decree, he said, "The shields of the Macedonians cast a shadow over my eyes", and "It was not I, but the battle of Chaeroneia, that proposed the decree"' (Plutarch, *Moralia, Lives of the Ten Orators*, 'Hypereides', 849a). 'ὅτε γὰρ Ὑπερείδης ἔγραψε, τῶν περὶ Χαιρώνειαν ἀτυχημάτων τοῖς Ἕλλησι γενομένων, καὶ τῆς πόλεως ὑπὲρ αὐτῶν τῶν ἐδαφῶν εἰς κίνδυνον μέγιστον κατακεκλειμένης, εἶναι τοὺς ἀτίμους ἐπιτίμους, ἵν᾽ ὁμονοοῦντες ἅπαντες ὑπὲρ τῆς ἐλευθερίας προθύμως ἀγωνίζωνται, ἐάν τις κίνδυνος τηλικοῦτος καταλαμβάνῃ τὴν πόλιν, τούτου τοῦ ψηφίσματος γραφὴν παρανόμων ἀπενέγκας ἠγωνίζετ᾽ ἐν τῷ δικαστηρίῳ'; 'For after the disasters to the Greek forces at Chaeroneia, when the very foundations of our State were threatened with the utmost danger, when Hypereides proposed that the disfranchised citizens should be reinstated in order that, if any such danger should menace our State, all classes might unite wholeheartedly in the struggle for liberty, the defendant indicted this decree as unconstitutional and conducted his case in court' (Demosthenes, *Against Aristogeiton 2*, XI).

8. *pupillage*] state of wardship (*OED*, 'pupillage', *n.*, 1 a).

9. *the demagogue*] i.e. Eubulus (*fl.* 350–340 BC). The Theoric fund had been established by Pericles so that poorer citizens might attend the festivals. Eubulus had attempted to divert all the city's surplus revenue to this fund.

10. *bills of attainder*] i.e. the formal instruments of attainder, which is the legal consequences of judgement of death or outlawry, in respect of treason or felony, viz. forfeiture of estate real and personal, corruption of blood, so that the condemned could neither inherit nor transmit by descent, and generally, the extinction of all civil rights and capacities (*OED*, 'attainder', *n.*, 1 a).

11. *here reason upon*] 'Τούτων δ᾿ ἐχόντων οὕτως, καὶ τῶν καιρῶν ὄντων τῇ πόλει τοιούτων ὁποίους τινὰς αὐτοὺς ὑμεῖς ὑπολαμβάνετε εἶναι, ἓν ὑπολείπεται μέρος τῆς πολιτείας, εἴ τι κἀγὼ τυγχάνω γιγνώσκων, αἱ τῶν παρανόμων γραφαί. εἰ δὲ καὶ ταύτας καταλύσετε ἢ τοῖς καταλύουσιν ἐπιτρέψετε, προλέγω ὑμῖν, ὅτι λήσετε κατὰ μικρὸν τῆς πολιτείας τισὶ παραχωρήσαντες'; 'Under such circumstances, and in a political situation the gravity of which you yourselves understand, only one part of the constitution is left to us – if I too may lay claim to some discernment – the suits against illegal motions. But if you shall annul these also, or give way to those who are trying to annul them, I warn you that before you know it you will step by step have surrendered your rights to a faction' (Aeschines, Ag*ainst Ctesiphon*, V). 'ἀκούω δ᾿ ἔγωγε καὶ τὸ πρότερον οὕτω καταλυθῆναι τὴν δημοκρατίαν, παρανόμων πρῶτον γραφῶν καταλυθεισῶν καὶ τῶν δικαστηρίων ἀκύρων γενομένων'; 'I have been told that in time past popular government was overthrown in this way, when indictments for illegal legislation were abolished, and courts of justice were stripped of authority' (Demosthenes, *Against Timocrates*, CLIV). For the text of the law, see ibid., XXXIII.

12. *PELOP.*] 'τοῦτο τὸ ψήφισμα γράφεται Πελοπίδας παρανόμων, ἰσχυριζόμενος ὅτι Θηβαίοις οὐ πάτριον ἦν ἰδίᾳ κατ᾿ ἄνδρα τιμᾶν, ἀλλὰ τῇ πατρίδι κοινῶς τὸ τῆς νίκης ὄνομα σῴζειν'; 'This decree [to have a picture of a victory dedicated to Charon] was attacked as unconstitutional by Pelopidas, who insisted that it was not a custom with the Thebans to honour any one man individually, but for the whole country to have the glory of a victory' (Plutarch, *Life of Pelopidas*, XXV.vii).

13. *Olynth. 1.2*] Hume's reference is mistaken.

14. *contra LEPT.*] Demosthenes, *Against Leptines*, I–IV.

15. *contra ARISTOCRATEM*] 'ἔστι μὲν οὐκέτι τῶν φονικῶν ὅδ᾿ ὁ νῦν ἀνεγνωσμένος νόμος, ὦ ἄνδρες δικασταί, οὐδ᾿ ὁτιοῦν δ᾿ ἧττον ἔχει καλῶς, εἴπερ καὶ ἄλλος τις. ὥσπερ γὰρ τῆς ἄλλης πολιτείας ἴσον μέτεστιν ἑκάστῳ, οὕτως ᾤετο δεῖν καὶ τῶν νόμων ἴσον μετέχειν πάντας ὁ θεὶς αὐτόν, καὶ διὰ ταῦτ᾿ ἔγραψε "μηδὲ νόμον ἐπ᾿ ἀνδρὶ ἐξεῖναι θεῖναι, ἐὰν μὴ τὸν αὐτὸν ἐφ᾿ ἅπασιν Ἀθηναίοις"'; 'The statute just read is not, like the others, taken from the Laws of Homicide, but it is just as good, – as good as ever law was. The man who introduced it was of opinion that, as every citizen has an equal share in civil rights, so everybody should

have an equal share in the laws; and therefore he moved that it should not be lawful to propose a law affecting any individual, unless the same applied to all Athenians' (Demosthenes, *Against Aristocrates*, LXXXVI).

16. GERMAN *empire*] For Hume's observations on German politics during his travels across Europe in 1748, see *Letters*, vol. I, pp. 119–26.

17. *the* ROMAN *republic*] cf. the note in the 'Early Memoranda': 'Polybius says that all Money Matters belong'd to the Senate. The ~~Rom~~ Censors levyd all the Taxes, & farm'd them out to the Roman Knights. The Romans coud be no great Politicians; since the Senate coud not gain the Sovereignity nor the Censors the Supreme Magistracy notwithstanding these Advantages.' (NLS MS 23159, item 14, p. 10; cf. Mossner, 'Memoranda', pp. 503–4).

18. *comitia . . . tributa*] There were three types of *comitia*, or assembly, in the Roman republic, each of which had a distinctive composition and function. The *comitia centuriata* was the assembly of the Roman people in 'hundreds', a military division created by Servius Tullius. The *comitia curiata* was the assembly of the wards, or curiae, at Rome. The *comitia tributa* was the assembly of the Roman people collected in their tribes. They had often been discussed in the context of English politics. In 1565 Sir Thomas Smith had compared the *comitia centuriata* to the English Parliament (Smith, *Republica*, pp. 78–9). The functions of the Roman *comitia* had engaged the attention of earlier seventeenth-century theorists of popular sovereignty (both for and against) such as Sir Robert Filmer: see Lee, *Popular Sovereignty*, pp. 308–9. Harrington had described their operation in *Oceana* (Harrington, *Works*, pp. 211–12); as had Henry Neville in *Plato Redivivus* (Neville, *Plato*, p. 61). The general political issue raised by the competing jurisdictions of the various Roman *comitia* is that of co-ordinate powers: a problem which had loomed large in English politics of the later seventeenth century, and which was especially pressing during the Exclusion Crisis. As Neville had confidently said: 'This is certain, that where-ever any two Co-ordinate Powers do differ, and there be no Power on Earth to reconcile them otherwise, nor any Umpire, they will, *de facto*, fall together by the Ears' (Neville, *Plato*, p. 175). Pocock finds the problem of co-ordinate powers at the root of the constitutional perplexities of the 1640s: 'Two lawful authorities were competing for his [the Christian subject's] allegiance, and neither could destroy the legitimacy of the other; to decide that one or the other was not lawful was, in a traditionalist society, almost certainly to conclude that it had never been, and so to destroy tradition' (Harrington, *Works*, p. 22). Note the entries in the 'Early Memoranda': 'The Roman Senate were oblig'd / by Law / to give their Authority to the <u>Comitia Centuriata</u> before the Suffrages were call'd. Do. Lib. 8. Cap. 12'; 'Every Part of the Office of the Senate coud be brought before the People; even the Distribution of Provinces; an evident Part of the Executive. Do. Lib. 10. C. 24' (NLS MS 23159, item 14, pp. 19 and 20; cf. Mossner,

'Memoranda', p. 511). Hume's point is that Roman experience teaches that the problem of co-ordinate powers (notwithstanding the dogmatism of a Whig such as Neville) is not insurmountable, and does not inevitably lead to political chaos.

19. *PATRICIANS and PLEBEIANS*] i.e. the ruling class and the common people.

20. *part 3. § 2*] Shaftesbury is discussing the pleasure men take in what Burke would later call the 'small platoons': "'Tis in such Bodys as these [empires] that strong Factions are aptest to engender. The associating Spirits, for want of Exercise, form new Movements, and seek a narrower Sphere of Activity, when they want Action in a greater. Thus we have *Wheels within Wheels*. And in some National Constitutions (notwithstanding the Absurdity in Politicks) we have *one Empire within another*. Nothing is so delightful as to incorporate' (Shaftesbury, *Characteristicks*, vol. I, p. 63). Cf. Ezekiel 1:15–16 and 10:10.

21. *magistracy of the tribunes*] The office of the tribunes, or guardians of the interests of the people, had been founded in 494 BC.

22. *the force . . . possessed of*] cf. 'Of the First Principles of Government': 'FORCE is always on the side of the governed' (above, vol. 1, p. 36).

23. *consuls, prætors, ediles*] All political offices in republican Rome.

24. *APPIAN . . . civil wars*] 'ὅ τε νόμος ὁ περὶ τῆς Κελτικῆς προυγράφετο αὐτίκα, ὀρρωδούσης πάνυ τῆς βουλῆς καὶ ἐπινοούσης, εἰ μὲν ὁ Ἀντώνιος αὐτὸν προβουλεύοι, κωλύειν προβουλευόμενον, εἰ δὲ ἀπροβούλευτον ἐς τὸν δῆμον ἐσφέροι, τοὺς δημάρχους ἐς κώλυσιν ἐπιπέμπειν. ἦσαν δ᾽ οἳ καὶ τὸ ἔθνος ὅλως ἐλευθεροῦν ἡγεμονίας ἠξίουν· οὕτως ἐδεδοίκεσαν ἀγχοῦ τὴν Κελτικὴν οὖσαν. ὁ δὲ Ἀντώνιος αὐτοῖς ἀντενεκάλει, εἰ Δέκμῳ μὲν αὐτὴν πιστεύουσιν, ὅτι Καίσαρα ἀπέκτεινεν, αὑτῷ δ᾽ ἀπιστοῦσιν, ὅτι οὐκ ἀπέκτεινε τὸν καταστρεψάμενον αὐτὴν καὶ κλίναντα ἐς γόνυ, ἀπορρίπτων ἤδη ταῦτα φανερῶς ἐς ἅπαντας ὡς ἐφηδομένους τοῖς γεγονόσιν. ἐλθούσης δὲ τῆς κυρίας ἡμέρας ἡ μὲν βουλὴ τὴν λοχῖτιν ἐνόμιζεν ἐκκλησίαν συλλεγήσεσθαι, οἱ δὲ νυκτὸς ἔτι τὴν ἀγορὰν περισχοινισάμενοι τὴν φυλέτιν ἐκάλουν, ἀπὸ συνθήματος ἐληλυθυῖαν. καὶ ὁ δημότης λεώς, ἀχθόμενος τῷ Ἀντωνίῳ, συνέπρασσεν ὅμως διὰ τὸν Καίσαρα ἐφεστῶτα τοῖς περισχοινίσμασι καὶ δεόμενον. ἐδεῖτο δὲ μάλιστα μέν, ἵνα μὴ Δέκμος ἄρχοι χώρας τε ἐπικαίρου καὶ στρατιᾶς ἀνδροφόνος ὢν τοῦ πατρός, ἐπὶ δὲ τούτῳ καὶ ἐς χάριν Ἀντωνίου συνηλλαγμένον. προσεδόκα δὲ ἄρα τι καὶ αὐτὸς ἀντιλήψεσθαι παρὰ Ἀντωνίου. διαφθαρέντων δὲ χρήμασι τῶν δημάρχων ὑπ᾽ Ἀντωνίου καὶ κατασιωπώντων ὁ νόμος ἐκυροῦτο, καὶ ὁ στρατὸς Ἀντωνίῳ μετ᾽ αἰτίας εὐπρεποῦς ἤδη τὸν Ἰόνιον ἐπέρα'; 'The law concerning the province of Gaul was promulgated at once, to the utter dismay of the senators. They intended to block it in the senate, if Antony introduced it in the senate first, and, if he brought it to the people without consulting the senate first, to send in the tribunes to veto it. There were some who even recommended that the province be made free of Roman control altogether, so greatly had they come to fear the proximity of Gaul. But Antony levelled

a countercharge against them, saying that they trusted Decimus with the province because he had killed Caesar, and that they distrusted himself because he had not killed the man who had subdued Gaul and brought it to its knees. These claims he now hurled openly against everyone, accusing them all of being pleased at what had happened. When the day for the voting arrived the senate expected that the Centuriate Assembly would be convened, but while it was still night Antony's men roped off the Forum and summoned the Tribal Assembly, who had gathered by prearranged plan. Although the common people were annoyed at Antony, they nevertheless cooperated with him because Octavian stood by the ropes and asked them to do so. He asked this particularly to prevent Decimus, one of his father's murderers, from having command of an important territory and army and, in addition, to oblige Antony, with whom he was reconciled. To be sure, he also expected to get something from Antony in return. As the tribunes had been bribed by Antony and remained silent, the law was passed and now that Antony had a plausible reason, his army began to cross the Ionian gulf' (Appian, *Civil Wars*, III.xxx.115–19).

25. *CISALPINE GAUL*] A Roman province in modern-day northern Italy, south of the Alps.

26. *plebiscitum*] A resolution of the people.

27. *It is a maxim . . . and usurpation*] cf. the similar comment in 'Whether the British Government Inclines More to Absolute Monarchy, or to a Republic': 'an irregular authority, not avowed by the laws, is always more dangerous than a much greater authority, derived from them. A man, possessed of usurped power, can set no bounds to his pretensions . . . On the contrary, a legal authority, though great, has always some bounds, which terminate both the hopes and pretensions of the person possessed of it' (above, vol. 1, p. 50). The insight perhaps derives from Machiavelli, *Discourses*, book I, chapter 34, of which part of the subtitle is: '*how that Power which is usurp'd, and illegally assumed, is pernitious to a State, not that which is conferred legally by the suffrage of the people*'. At the beginning of the following chapter, Machiavelli summarizes the import of chapter 34 in terms close to those used by Hume: 'In the last Chapter we have shewn that a power legally conferred, and by the suffrage of the people, is not dangerous to the State; but that which is usurped, and gotten by force . . .' (Machiavelli, *Works*, pp. 303 and 304).

28. *the heroism of HAMPDEN's conduct*] Hume gives a fuller account in the *History of England*: 'This year [1638], John Hambden acquired, by his spirit and courage, universal popularity throughout the nation, and has merited great renown with posterity, for the bold stand which he made, in defence of the laws and liberties of his country. After the imposing of ship-money, Charles, in order to discourage all opposition, had proposed this question to the judges: "Whether, in a case of necessity, for the defence of

the kingdom, he might not impose this taxation? and whether he were not sole judge of the necessity?" These guardians of law and liberty replied, with great complaisance, "That in a case of necessity he might impose that taxation, and that he was sole judge of the necessity." Hambden had been rated at twenty shillings for an estate, which he possessed in the county of Buckingham. Yet notwithstanding this declared opinion of the judge[s], notwithstanding the great power, and sometimes rigorous maxims of the crown, notwithstanding the small prospect of relief from parliament; he resolved, rather than tamely submit to so illegal an imposition, to stand a legal prosecution, and expose himself to all the indignation of the court. The case was argued during twelve days, in the exchequer chamber, before all the judges of England; and the nation regarded, with the utmost anxiety, every circumstance of this celebrated trial. The event was easily foreseen: But the principles, and reasonings, and behaviour of the parties, engaged in the trial, were much canvassed and enquired into; and nothing could equal the favour paid to the one side, except the hatred which attended the other' (*History of England*, vol. V, pp. 245–6). Hampden lost his case, but this was a pyrrhic victory for the crown: 'Hambden . . . obtained by the trial the end, for which he had so generously sacrificed his safety and his quiet: The people were rouzed from their lethargy, and became sensible of the danger, to which their liberties were exposed' (*History of England*, vol. V, p. 248).

29. *all ENGLISH patriots*] Although we now take 'patriot' to mean simply someone who loves their homeland (*OED*, 'patriot', *n.* and *adj.*, A I 1 a), in the eighteenth century it had acquired a more particular and politically coloured meaning of 'a person who claims to be disinterestedly or self-sacrificingly devoted to his or her country, but whose actions or intentions are considered to be detrimental or hypocritical; a false or feigned patriot' (A I 1 b). Hence Johnson's definition of 'patriot' as, primarily, 'one whose ruling passion is the love of his country', but with the secondary meaning of a 'factious disturber of the government'. This is therefore a surprisingly Whiggish remark by Hume. Contrast the bitter remarks on 'patriotism' towards the end of 'Of Public Credit': 'Mankind are, in all ages, caught by the same baits: The same tricks, played over and over again, still trepan them. The heights of popularity and patriotism are still the beaten road to power and tyranny . . .' (above, p. 85). In a letter to William Strahan of 3 March 1772 Hume would confess to being 'disgusted with the Licentiousness of our odious Patriots' (*Letters*, vol. II, p. 261). However, in the early 1740s Hume might use the term with a lighter heart, as when he teases William Mure that his tendency to grumble 'is a good Prognostic of your being a Patriot' (*Letters*, vol. I, p. 45).

30. *hence alone . . . ENGLISH liberty*] Again, perhaps a surprising remark. In the *History of England* Hume attempted to shift the period when English liberty

was established from the 1640s to 1688, 'that great event, which . . . made a new settlement of the whole constitution' (*History of England*, vol. VI, p. 531).

31. *pressing of seamen*] The right claimed by the Crown forcibly to make men serve in the navy. Hume had noted popular disquiet at the operations of the press gang in the 'Early Memoranda': 'In K. William's Time the Press-Gang condemnd for Murder for killing a man in impressing him.' (NLS MS 23159, item 14, p. 12: cf. Mossner, 'Memoranda', p. 505).

32. *state of nature*] An important concept in seventeenth-century English political theory, salient in the work of both Hobbes (see, e.g., Hobbes, *Leviathan*, chapter 13, p. 88) and Locke (see, e.g., Locke, *Two Treatises*, 'Second Treatise', chapter 2, 'Of the State of Nature', § 6, p. 271); although conceptualized very differently by those two thinkers. In the *Treatise of Human Nature*, III. ii.2, Hume had viewed the concept of a state of nature sceptically, as 'a mere philosophical fiction, which never had, and never cou'd have any reality' (*THN*, p. 317; cf. *ECPM*, III, 'Of Justice', p. 17).

33. *fundamental laws*] Fundamental laws are those which underwrite a constitution or form of government, and to which subsequent laws should conform; a synonymous term, in Leveller writings, was 'law paramount' (Morton, *Freedom*, pp. 40–41; cf. also John Lilburne, *Legall Fundamentall Liberties* [1649]). For scholarly commentary in an English context, see J. W. Gough, *Fundamental Law in English Constitutional History* (Oxford: Clarendon Press, 1955). The concept of fundamental law had been embraced by common lawyers such as Coke, who had insisted that Magna Carta was simply declaratory of 'the fundamentall Laws of *England*' (Coke, *Selected Writings*, vol. II, p. 748; cf. Brady, *History*, 'Preface', sig. B1r and p. xliii for mocking commentaries on this). 'Fundamental law' was, however, a protean concept which might be deployed with equal ease by either side or any faction in the growing rift between Crown and Parliament in the mid-seventeenth century. John Pym had accused Thomas Wentworth, Earl of Strafford, of endeavouring by 'his words, actions and counsels to subvert the fundamental law of England and Ireland'; on 3 January 1642, King Charles would instruct the Lord Keeper to impeach Lord Kimbolton and the five members of the Commons on the grounds that 'they had endeavoured to subvert the fundamental laws and government of the kingdom' (Kenyon, *Stuart Constitution*, pp. 213 and 241); and in 1653 John Lilburne would claim that the purpose of resisting the king had been the 'restauration of the Fundamental Laws and Rights of the Nation' (Morton, *Freedom*, p. 334). The *Grand Remonstrance* of 1641 had deplored 'a malignant and pernicious design of subverting the fundamental laws and principles of government, upon which the religion and justice of this kingdom are firmly established' and had accused the senior clergy of making 'canons that contain in them many matters contrary to the King's prerogative, to the fundamental laws and statutes of the realm, to the right of Parliaments, to the property and liberty of the subject, and matters

tending to sedition and of dangerous consequence, thereby establishing their own usurpations, justifying their altar-worship, and those other superstitious innovations which they formerly introduced without warrant of law'. Harrington had included fundamental laws of the agrarian and the ballot in the constitution of *Oceana*, defining fundamental laws as 'such as state what it is that a man may call his own, that is to say property, and what the means be whereby a man may enjoy his own, that is to say protection; the first is also called dominion, and the second empire or sovereign power' (Harrington, *Works*, pp. 230–31; cf. also pp. 333–4). The language of fundamental law had been invoked in Parliament during the 1650s (see, e.g., Burton, *Diary*, vol. II, pp. 48 and 81). Bishop Burnet would recall how the idea of fundamental law had been reinvigorated during the Exclusion Crisis: 'All lawyers had great regard to fundamental laws. And it was a maxim among our lawyers, that even an Act of Parliament against *Magna Charta* was null of it self' (Burnet, *History*, vol. I, p. 458; cf. Grey, *Debates*, vol. VIII, pp. 60 and 240, and *Of the Fundamental Laws or Politick Constitution of this Kingdom*, in *State-Tracts*, vol. II, pp. 22–6). Moreover, the concept might be made legally operative in even the gravest crises of state: for example, in 1689 the Convention Parliament would cite as one of their reasons for declaring the throne vacant that James II had 'violated the fundamental Laws' (Grey, *Debates*, vol. IX, p. 25). Nevertheless, the concept was arguably incoherent and empty: 'The fundamental law or constitution was an ancient law or constitution; the concept had been built up by the search for precedents coupled with the common-law habit of mind that made it fatally easy to presume that anything which was in the common law, and which it was desired to emphasize, was immemorial' (Pocock, *Ancient Constitution*, p. 49). Accordingly the concept of fundamental law was one on which later royalist writers such as Robert Brady delighted to pour scorn: 'For here never was Pact between King and People, nor Fundamental Terms of Government agreed between them; nor indeed ever was there, or is it possible for any such thing to be in any Nation of the World: Matter of Fact so long as we have any Memorials of it in these Kingdoms, shews the contrary' (Brady, *History*, 'Preface', sig. B2r–v; cf. also *Antimonarchical Authors* [1699], sig. B2v). Hobbes is briskly sceptical about fundamental law: Hobbes, *Leviathan*, chapter 26; 'There is also another distinction of Laws, into *Fundamentall*, and *not Fundamentall*: but I could never see in any Author, what a Fundamentall Law signifieth' (Hobbes, *Leviathan*, p. 199). He goes on to give a mischievously innovative definition of it, which transforms it from a brake on the sovereign to a reinforcement of the obligation of the subject to obey: 'For a Fundamentall Law in every Common-wealth is that, which being taken away, the Common-wealth faileth, and is utterly dissolved; as a building whose Foundation is destroyed. And therefore a Fundamentall Law is that, by which Subjects are bound to uphold whatsoever power is given to the Soveraign, whether a Monarch, or a Soveraign Assembly, without which the Common-wealth cannot stand; such as is the power of War and Peace, of Judicature, of Election of Officers, and of doing whatsoever he shall think necessary for the Publique good' (Hobbes, *Leviathan*, p. 200). Hobbes, *Behemoth*, pp. 67–8, and esp. p. 158: 'The only fundamental law in every commonwealth is to obey the laws from time to time, which he shall make to whom the people have given the supreme power.' Equally, however, the concept of fundamental law might be discounted by a thinker of a much more populist character, such as John Warr, who coolly remarked in 1649 that it was 'no such idol as men make it' (Wootton, *Divine Right*, p. 153). For Thomas Goddard's mockery of this point, see Goddard, *Plato's Demon*, pp. 373–4. For Hume's sceptical, but not entirely dismissive, comments on fundamental law, see the *Treatise of Human Nature*, III.ii.10 (*THN*, p. 359).

## XI. OF THE POPULOUSNESS OF ANCIENT NATIONS

Published in: *1752a, 1752b, 1753, 1754, 1758, 1760, 1764, 1767, 1768, 1770, 1772, 1777a*

Significant revisions:

Given the comparative paucity of the revisions to this essay in relation to its great length, and the slightness of many of them, it is interesting to note Hume's polite (and, perhaps, merely polite) comment in a letter of 26 February 1753 to a fellow member of the Edinburgh Philosophical Society, Robert Wallace (1697–1771): 'Your Work has convinc'd me, that I must make a great many Alterations' (*New Letters*, p. 35). He explained himself more fully to Montesquieu on 26 June 1753: 'I could have made many more amendments, by correcting the errors remarked by my antagonist; but, as that would have injured his work, I shall abstain at present, in hopes that a new edition will give me an opportunity' (*Letters*, vol. I, p. 178). Nevertheless, the text of this essay does show signs of interesting and important revisal.

1) In *1752a* and *1752b*, the following footnote was appended to the title of the essay:

'*An eminent clergyman in *Edinburgh*, having wrote, some years ago, a discourse on the same question with this, of the populousness of antient nations, was pleas'd lately to communicate it to the author. It maintain'd the opposite side of the argument, to what is here insisted on, and contained much erudition and good reasoning. The author acknowledges to have borrow'd, with some variations, from that discourse, two computations, that with regard to the number of inhabitants in *Belgium*, and that with regard to those in *Epirus*. If this learned gentleman be prevail'd on to publish his dissertation, it will serve to give great light into the present question, the most curious and important of all questions of erudition.' (*1752a*, p. 155).

2) In *1753–1768* the following note was substituted for the above:
'"An ingenious writer has honour'd this discourse with an answer, full of politeness, erudition, and good sense. So learn'd a refutation would have made the author suspect, that his reasonings were entirely overthrown, had he not us'd the precaution, from the beginning, to keep himself on the sceptical side; and having taken this advantage of the ground, he was enabled, tho' with much inferior forces, to preserve himself from a total defeat. That Reverend gentleman will always find, where his antagonist is so entrench'd, that it will be very difficult to force him. *Varro*, in such a situation, could defend himself against *Hannibal*, *Pharnaces* against *Cæsar*. The author, however, very willingly acknowledges, that his antagonist has detected many mistakes both in his authorities and reasonings; and it was owing entirely to that gentleman's indulgence, that many more errors were not remark'd. In this edition, advantage has been taken of his learn'd animadversions, and the discourse has been render'd less imperfect than formerly.' (*1753*, vol. IV, p. 135).

3) *1752a–1758* read: 'Almost every man, who thinks he can maintain a family, will have one; and the human species, at this rate of propagation, wou'd more than double every generation, were every one coupled as soon as he comes to the age of puberty.' (*1752a*, p. 159; cf. above, p. 97).

4) *1770* adds 'In general, warm climates ... populous:' (above, p. 97).

5) *1752a–1752b* read: '... confin'd in them. *Partem Italiæ ergastula a solitudine vindicant*, says *Livy*.' (*1752a*, p. 163; cf. above, p. 99).

6) *1777a* inserts 'I shall add, that ... from a freeman.' (*1777a*, vol. I, p. 407, n. *; cf. above, p. 102, n. **).

7) *1758–1777a* insert 'ARISTOTLE ... of nature.' (*1758*, p. 214; cf. above, p. 103).

8) *1770–1777a* insert ', and even manufactures executed,' (*1770*, vol. II, p. 185; cf. above, p. 104).

9) *1752a–1752b* omit 'The same author ... superfluous.' (above, p. 105).

10) *1752a–1752b* omit 'So likewise TACITUS ... 44.' (above, p. 106, n. ‡).

11) *1752a–1768* read 'as nurseries of the most abject superstition' (*1752a*, p. 179; cf. above, p. 108).

12) *1752a–1768* read 'The infinite difference' (*1752a*, p. 182; cf. above, p. 109).

13) *1752a–1768* include the following additional sentence and note at the end of the paragraph ending '... sound and entire.' (above, p. 113):
'Cou'd *Folard*'s project of the column take place (which seems impracticable*) it wou'd render modern battles as destructive as the antient.
'*WHAT is the advantage of the column after it has broke the enemy's line? Only, that it then takes them in the flank, and dissipates whatever stands near it by a fire from all sides. But till it has broke them, does it not present a flank to the enemy, and that expos'd to their musquetry, and what is much worse, to their cannon?' (*1752a*, pp. 189–90).

14) *1752a–1768* add the following sentence to the footnote reference to Justinian's *Institutes* (above, p. 114, n. *):
''Tis true, the same law seems to have been continu'd, till the time of *Justinian*. But abuses, introduc'd by barbarism, are not always corrected by civility.' (*1752a*, p. 191, n. †).

15) *1752a–1768* read: '. . . religious parties alone, where bigotted priests are the accusers, judges, and executioners.' (*1752a*, p. 192; cf. above, p. 114).

16) *1752a–1770* insert the following additional sentence: '. . . capitally punish'd. This is a difficulty not clear'd up, and even not observ'd, by antiquarians and historians. And as to . . .' (*1752a*, p. 193; cf. above, p. 115).

17) *1752a–1768* add the following to the footnote reference to book III of Thucydides (above, p. 116, n. *):
'The country in *Europe*, wherein I have observ'd the factions to be most violent and party hatred the strongest, is *Ireland*. This goes so far as to cut off even the most common intercourse of civilities betwixt protestants and catholics. Their cruel insurrections, and the severe revenges which they have taken of each other, are the causes of this mutual ill-will, which is the chief source of disorder, poverty, and depopulation in that country. The *Greek* factions, I imagine, to have been inflam'd still to a higher degree of rage: The revolutions being commonly more frequent, and the maxims of assassination much more avow'd and acknowledg'd.' (*1752a*, pp. 194–95, n. ‡).

18) *1752a–1764* omit ', and is not to be suspected . . . of his age.' (above, p. 151, n. BB; cf. *1752a*, pp. 196–97, n. *). In *1768* the final sentence of this footnote reads: ''Tis to be remarked, that AGATHOCLES was a man of great sense and courage: His violent tyranny, therefore, is a stronger proof of the manners of the age.' (*1768*, pp. 456–57, n. ‖).

19) *1752a–1772* omit 'At present . . . Aristocracies.' (above, p. 120).

20) *1752a–1754* omit 'not less, if not rather' (above, p. 126).

21) *1752a–1752b* omit 'But perhaps . . . great cities.' (above, p. 126, n. ‡; cf. *1752a*, p. 215, n. †).

22) *1752a–1772* omit the footnote to Pliny's account of the casualties inflicted by Cæsar (above, p. 153, n. FF).

23) *1752a–1772* omit 'The most bloody . . . the GERMANS.' (above, p. 127).

24) *1752a–1758* insert the following additional paragraph following that ending '. . . the tyrant himself.' (above, p. 127):
'THE critical art may very justly be suspected of temerity, when it pretends to correct or dispute the plain testimony of antient historians by any probable or analogical reasonings: Yet the licence of authors upon all subjects, particularly with regard to numbers, is so great, that we ought still to retain a kind of doubt or reserve, whenever the facts advanc'd depart, in the least, from the common bounds of nature and experience. I shall give an instance with regard to modern history. Sir *William Temple* tells us, in his memoirs, that, having a free conversation with *Charles* the II, he took the opportunity

of representing to that monarch the impossibility of introducing into this island the religion and government of *France*, chiefly on account of the great force, requisite to subdue the spirit and liberty of so brave a people. "The *Romans*, says he, were forc'd to keep up 12 legions for that purpose" (a great absurdity*) "and *Cromwell* left an army of near eighty thousand men." Must not this last fact be regarded as unquestion'd by future critics, when they find it asserted by a wise and learned minister of state, contemporary to the fact, and who addrest his discourse, upon an ungrateful subject, to a great monarch, who was also contemporary, and who himself broke those very forces about fourteen years before. Yet by the most undoubted authority, we may insist, that *Cromwell's* army, when he died, did not amount to half the number here mention'd.

'*Strabo*, lib. 4. says that one legion would be sufficient, with a few cavalry; but the *Romans* commonly kept up somewhat a greater force in this island; which they never took pains entirely to subdue.' (*1752a*, pp. 218–19).

*1754–1758* include the following additional footnote, cued to 'here mention'd.':

'† It appears, that *Cromwel's* parliament in 1656 settled but 1,300,000 pound a year on him for the constant charges of government in all the three kingdoms. See *Scobel*, chap. 31. This was to supply fleet, army, and civil list. It appears from *Whitlocke*, that, in the year 1649, the sum of 80,000 pounds a-month was the estimate for 40,000 men. We must conclude, therefore, that *Cromwel* had much less than that number upon pay in 1656. In the very instrument of government, 20,000 foot and 10,000 horse are fix'd by *Cromwel* himself, and afterwards confirm'd by the parliament, as the regular standing army of the commonwealth. That number, indeed, seems not to have been much exceeded, during the whole time of the protectorship. See farther *Thurloe*, vol 2. p. 413. 499. 568. We may there see, that tho' the Protector had more considerable armies in *Ireland* and *Scotland*, he had not sometimes more than 4 or 5000 men in *England*.' (*1754*, vol. IV, p. 193, n. †).

25) *1752a* and *1752b* read: '. . . so much for slaves, whom he employ'd in digging of mines; and also kept up the number of slaves. If you will . . .' (*1752a*, p. 224; cf. above, p. 130).

*1753–1770* read: '. . . so much for slaves, whom he employ'd in digging of mines. If you will . . .' (*1753*, vol. IV, p. 198).

26) *1752a–1772* omit 'And 400,000 . . . a twelvemonth.' (above, p. 153, n. HH).

27) *1752a–1752b* omit 'When ALEXANDER . . . to bear arms.' (above, p. 154, n. II).

28) *1752a–1752b* omit 'Perhaps, XENOPHON . . . neighbouring villages.' (above, p. 132).

29) *1752a–1752b* omit ', deducting some few garrisons,' (above, p. 133).

30) *1752a–1752b* omit 'We are told ... of GREECE.' (above, p. 133).

31) *1752a–1752b* insert the following footnote, cued to 'the extent of *York-shire*.' (above, p. 133; cf. *1752a*, pp. 229–30):

'‖ A LATE *French* writer, in his *observations on the Greeks*, has remark'd, that *Philip* of *Macedon*, being declar'd captain general of the *Greeks*, wou'd have been back'd by the force of 230,000 of that nation in his intended expedition against *Persia*. This number comprehends, I suppose, all the free citizens, throughout all the cities; but the authority, on which that computation is founded, has, I own, escap'd either my memory or reading; and that writer, tho' otherwise very ingenious, has given into a bad practice, of delivering a great deal of erudition, without one citation. But supposing, that that enumeration cou'd be justify'd by good authority from antiquity, we may establish the following computation. The free *Greeks* of all ages and sexes were 920,000: The slaves, computing them by the number of *Athenian* slaves as above, who seldom marry'd or had families, were double the male citizens of full age, *viz.* 460,000. And the whole inhabitants of antient *Greece* about one million, three hundred and eighty thousand. No mighty number, nor much exceeding what may be found at present in *Scotland*, a country of nearly the same extent, and which is very indifferently peopled.' (*1752a*, pp. 229–30, n. ‖).

32) *1752a–1752b* omit the paragraph 'JUSTIN tells us ... indifferently peopled.' (above, pp. 133–4).

33) *1752a–1754* omit '*Colder than* ... live in it.' (above, p. 140).

34) *1758–1770* omit 'ARISTOTLE says ... live in it.' (above, p. 140).

35) *1752a–1752b* read: 'Taking the whole, therefore, in this proportion of ten to six, the sum of fighting men in all the states of *Belgium* was above half a million; the whole inhabitants two millions. And *Belgium* being about the fourth of *Gaul*, that country might contain eight millions, which is not above the third of its present inhabitants.*' (*1752a*, pp. 250–51; cf. above, p. 144).

36) *1753–1770* omit 'near' (above, p. 144).

37) *1752a–1752b* omit ', who formed a different order from the *Plebes*' (above, p. 158, n. PP).

38) *1752a–1758* omit 'We are informed ... desolation.' (above, p. 144).

39) *1752a–1752b* read: '... entirely destroy it. A man of violent imagination, such as *Tertullian*, augments every thing equally; and for that reason his comparative judgments are the most to be depended on. The same remark ...' (*1752a*, p. 255, n. *; cf. above, p. 158, n. QQ).

Copy text: *1777a*

Headnote:

Although the subject of the populousness of ancient nations had long been of interest to Hume, and lay behind a group of entries in his 'Early Memoranda' (see NLS MS 23159, item 14, pp. 23–8; cf. Mossner, 'Memoranda', pp. 514–18), the composition of the greater part of this essay was comparatively late, occupying as it did the early months of 1750 (and details in Hume's correspondence suggest that he may have been still embellishing his text in March 1751: *Letters*, vol. I, pp. 152–3, 157 and 159). On 18 April 1750 Hume wrote to John Clephane: 'The last thing I took my hand from was a very learned, elaborate discourse, concerning the populousness of antiquity; not altogether in opposition to *Vossius* and *Montesquieu*, who exaggerate that affair infinitely; but, starting some doubts, and scruples, and difficulties, sufficient to make us suspend our judgment on that head' (*Letters*, vol. I, p. 140). Writing on 18 February 1751 to Gilbert Elliot of Minto, Hume confirmed the date of composition: 'I have amus'd myself lately with an Essay or Dissertation on the Populousness of Antiquity, which led me into many Disquisitions concerning both the public & the domestic Life of the Antients' (*Letters*, vol. I, p. 152). In this letter Hume also asks to borrow a copy of Strabo, and confesses that 'He is an Author I never read' (ibid., p. 153). So we can infer that all the many references to Strabo in this essay were added in a subsequent process of enrichment and corroboration between 10 March 1751, when Elliot's copy of Strabo was ready to be sent to Hume, and later in March or April of the same year when Hume returned it (ibid., pp. 157 and 158). (Note, however, that there is a reference to Strabo in the 'Early Memoranda', so it cannot be true that Hume had not read Strabo at all before 1751: NLS MS 23159, item 14, p. 23; cf. Mossner, 'Memoranda', p. 514.)

In composing this text, which exceeds in respect of both length and erudition all Hume's other essays, Hume turned his mind to questions of the relation between antiquity and modernity which had struck wide and deep roots in European intellectual culture (although he had approached issues relevant to this broad subject much earlier: see the headnote to 'Of the Rise and Progress of the Arts and Sciences', and the connection discussed there with Locke's 'First Treatise' [see above, vol. 1, p. 308]). These general questions had become salient in the late seventeenth century with the eruption of the 'Querelle des anciens et des modernes' (although the question of population does not map very accurately on to the central point at issue in the 'Querelle', at least in its French form, which is about the relative cultural and intellectual achievements of modernity and antiquity).

Nevertheless, the view that the population of the world had contracted was widespread, and (in the absence of historical statistics) difficult to refute. It was an aspect of the almost immemorial conviction that the world was declining from an original golden age (on which belief, see *ECPM*, pp. 16–17); and it had the power to infect even strong minds that might instinctively resist such fables. In his *History of Florence*, Machiavelli had offered an account of late antiquity in Europe in which the overflowing populousness of the north had led to barbarian incursions on the Roman Empire, as a result of which 'the Times [grew] worse and worse' and were marked by declining populations (Machiavelli, *Works*, p. 2): this line of exposition would also later be followed by Juan de Mariana in his *General History of Spain*, book V, chapter 1. Nor did the philosophical enjoy any immunity to this fear of depopulation: 'Montesquieu claimed in the *Persian Letters* that the world's present population was only a tenth of what it had been in ancient times, and that the current rate of decline would make humanity extinct in another thousand years. Few censuses were even attempted. The first was held in Iceland in 1703 by the Danish government, because the country's extreme impoverishment made it necessary to calculate the need for economic assistance. When censuses were undertaken, the result might be treated as a state secret. Thus the results of the Austrian census of 1754 lay hidden in the archives until the twentieth century. In Britain, a bill proposing an annual census was presented to Parliament in 1753 but met with fierce opposition, partly as an attack on English liberty, partly because in the Old Testament David was punished for conducting a census at the prompting of Satan (1 Chr. 21:1). The bill reached the House of Lords but lapsed on procedural grounds, and nobody was interested enough to revive it. Only in 1801 was a national census held, under the pressures of worries about depopulation and the need to determine Britain's human resources at a time of war' (Robertson, *Enlightenment*, pp. 403–4; cf. *Lettres Persanes*, letter 112 in Montesquieu, *Œuvres*, p. 121; other examples might be found in the *Esprit des Lois*, book XXI, chapter 6 and the conclusion of chapter 7). In France there was widespread anxiety that luxury was leading to a decline in population (Robertson, *Enlightenment*, p. 549). Clearly, the belief in depopulation was one that Hume, an advocate of both material refinement and modernity, would wish to challenge.

In his letter to Clephane, Hume mentioned the Dutch scholar and collector of manuscripts Isaak Vossius (1618–1689) and the French *philosophe* Charles-Louis de Secondat, baron de Montesquieu (1689–1755) as earlier writers who had in his opinion exaggerated the populousness of antiquity; and their names duly recur as adversaries in the text of 'Of the Populousness of Ancient Nations' (see above, pp. 96). In the first section of *Variarum observationum liber* (1685), entitled 'De Antiquæ Romæ et Aliarum quarumdam Urbium magnitudine' ('Of the size of ancient Rome and certain other towns', pp. 1–68), Vossius had argued that at its peak ancient Rome had a population of fourteen million, and occupied a site much greater than that of seventeenth-century London and Paris (pp. 65–6). In Montesquieu's *Lettres Persanes* (1721), letters 112–22 argue that the population of the world had decreased since antiquity, and in Book XXIII of the *Esprit des Lois* (1748) Montesquieu had returned to the same theme, arguing that the growth of the Roman Empire had led to a decline in the population of Europe and the Near East. Adam Ferguson would take a more cautious line: 'The Romans became wealthy in pursuing their conquests; and probably, for a certain period, increased the numbers of mankind, while their disposition to war seemed to threaten the earth with desolation' (Ferguson, *Civil Society*, p. 132).

However, Hume was also addressing a much narrower question which had arisen in connection with Robert Wallace. Before 1745 Wallace had read a paper on the populousness of antiquity to the Edinburgh Philosophical Society (of which Hume would become Secretary in 1751); and he had allowed Hume to read an enlarged and revised version of that paper before 1751 (Luehrs, 'Population', p. 321; *New Letters*, pp. 28–9). Hume in return sent Wallace a copy of his own essay on the same topic (which would be first published as part of *Political Discourses* in 1752). Wallace's *Dissertation on the Numbers of Mankind* was published in 1753, and it included an explicit response to Hume's essay. Hume discussed his amiable exchanges with Wallace in a letter to Montesquieu of 26 June 1753 (*Letters*, vol. I, pp. 176–8). As he exclaimed in a letter of 29 September 1751 to Wallace himself, 'Why cannot all the World entertain different Opinions about any Subject, as amicably as we do?' (*New Letters*, p. 30). Hume's friendliness towards Wallace must be due in part to Wallace's protest against the campaign in 1745 by the Presbyterian clergy of Edinburgh opposing Hume's candidacy for the Edinburgh chair in philosophy (*London Chronicle*, vol. XL [1776], p. 444).

In a footnote printed in *1752a* and *1752b* (but then deleted) Hume called the scholarly debate on the populousness of antiquity 'the most curious and important of all questions of erudition' (*Political Discourses*, p. 155, n. *). Here he was in agreement with Wallace: 'the illustration of this subject is of very great importance, and is closely connected with the deepest policy and most intimate constitution of human society' (Wallace, *Dissertation*, p. 14). The debate on the populousness of ancient nations possessed this importance because it held implications for what, in the Enlightenment, was the momentous question of whether an agrarian or a commercial society better supported human flourishing (Luehrs, 'Population', p. 320). Locke had noted a correlation between absolute monarchy and the waning of population: 'He that doubts this, let him look into the Absolute Monarchies of the World, and see what becomes of the Conveniencies of Life, and the Multitudes of People' ('First Treatise', § 41, in Locke, *Two Treatises*, p. 170). (Hume would have agreed that free governments make for human flourishing; however, he would also have said that modern absolute monarchies were in fact more free governments than many earlier governments of which the constitutional design had seemed to be more aligned with the exercise of freedom on the part of the governed.) In the year preceding the composition of this essay, the naturalist Georges de Buffon had touched on this topic when he considered the influence of 'les mœurs' on the vigour and health of the human animal: 'un peuple policé qui vit dans une certaine aisance, qui est accoûtumé à une vie réglée, douce & tranquille, qui par les soins d'un bon gouvernement est à l'abri d'une certaine misère, & ne peut manquer des choses de première nécessité, sera par cette seule raison composé d'hommes plus forts, plus beaux & mieux faits qu'une nation sauvage & indépendante, où chaque individu ne tirant aucun secours de la société, est obligé de pourvoir à sa subsistance, de souffrir alternativement la faim ou les excès d'une nourriture souvent mauvaise, de s'épuiser de travaux ou de lassitude, d'éprouver les rigueurs du climat sans pouvoir s'en garantir, d'agir en un mot plus souvent comme animal que comme homme' (*Histoire Naturelle*, vol. III [Paris, 1749], pp. 446–7). As Hume put it: 'if every thing else be equal, it seems natural to expect, that, wherever there are most happiness and virtue, and the wisest institutions, there will also be most people' (above, p. 98; cf. Locke, 'First Treatise', § 59: 'the main intention of Nature, which willeth the increase of Mankind' [Locke, *Two Treatises*, p. 183]). This was a principle to which Wallace had also subscribed: 'The question concerning the number of mankind in antient and modern times, under antient or modern governments, is not to be considered as a matter of pure curiosity, but of the greatest importance; since it must be a strong presumption in favour of the customs or policy of any government, if, *cæteris paribus*, it is able to raise up and maintain a greater number of people' (Wallace, *Dissertation*, p. 14, n. *). However, Wallace sought to derive the opposite conclusion from the principle: 'if we shall find that antient policy, antient manners, and antient customs were better calculated, to make nations great and populous, than modern policy, modern manners, and modern customs; this will be an argument *a priori*, for the truth of that hypothesis, which we have endeavoured to establish *a posteriori*' (Wallace, *Dissertation*, pp. 79–80).

By subscribing to the 'general rule, that the happiness of any society and its populousness are necessary attendants' (above, p. 101, n. *), by arguing for the greater populousness of modern Europe, and by therefore implicitly contending for the superiority of modern commercial societies over the agrarian communities of antiquity, in 'Of the Populousness of Ancient Nations' Hume was developing, reinforcing and extending the arguments in favour of commercial modernity that he had set out in 'Of Commerce' and 'Of Refinement in the Arts' (in 1752, entitled 'Of Luxury'). Wallace, however, was emphatically on the other side of the question concerning the social consequences of material refinement and growing opulence: 'in the false refinements and extravagancies of such over-grown monarchies, we may see one considerable cause of the ruin of the world' (Wallace, *Dissertation*, p. 117; cf. also p. 160). Interestingly, both Wallace and Hume might have invoked the support of Rousseau. On the one hand, Rousseau had allowed that the growth of population was a reliable indicator of a mode of life that supported human flourishing: 'Mais supposons que les hommes eussent tellement multiplié, que les productions naturelles n'eussent pas suffi pour les nourrir; supposition qui, pour le dire en passant, montreroit un grand avantage pour l'Espéce humaine dans cette maniére de vivre …' (Rousseau, *Inegalité*, p. 41). Yet he had also maintained that the refinement of the arts and sciences had led to human degeneration: 'nos ames se sont corrompues à mesure que nos Sciences & nos Arts se sont avancés à la perfection' (Rousseau, *Discours*, p. 16). However, by the time of Hume's death the connection between population growth and human flourishing had become an orthodoxy, at least in enlightened Scottish circles. In 1776 Adam Smith would declare, emphatically and simply, that the 'most decisive mark of the prosperity of any country is the increase of the number of its inhabitants' (Smith, *Wealth*, pp. 87–8, I.viii.23).

Hume's interest in the question of population remained alive even after this essay had been published. In July 1757 he asked Andrew Millar to obtain for him a copy of Mirabeau's *L'Ami des hommes, ou Traité de la Population*, 5 parts (Avignon, 1756–60) (*Letters*, vol. I, pp. 257 and 259–60).

A final point of interest concerns the way Hume reads the literature of antiquity in this essay, which we might characterize as reading not for the intended sense of the author, but rather for what the author's words unintentionally reveal or disclose. This reading of literature not as authorial communication but rather as social symptom has affinities with the way Machiavelli had read Livy in the *Discourses*, as well as with the techniques of reading and interpretation developed by chronologists such as Sir Isaac Newton (on this last point, see Robertson, *Enlightenment*, p. 60).

For helpful commentary on this under-discussed but important essay, see M. A. Box and Michael Silverthorne, 'The "Most Curious & Important of All Questions of Erudition": Hume's Assessment of the Populousness of Ancient Nations', in Spencer, *David Hume*, pp. 225–54. Box and Silverthorne supply a useful outline of Hume's argument in this essay on pp. 228–30.

Note also the deletion of the long note from the text of 'Of the Balance of Power' as published in *1752a*, which has a bearing on the subject of 'Of the Populousness of Ancient Nations' (above, p. 359, variant no. 1).

1. *eternal or incorruptible*] Hume here follows closely the opening of Wallace's *Dissertation*: 'As there is nothing in the form and condition of this Earth, or in any of the appearances of Nature, to excite in us the idea of their necessary existence, or make us believe that this our globe was from eternity . . .' (Wallace, *Dissertation*, p. 1). In *Lettres Persanes*, letter 113, Montesquieu, too, had denied the eternity of the world, in terms that Hume followed closely: 'Le Monde, mon cher Rhedi, n'est point incorruptible' (Montesquieu, *Œuvres*, p. 121). The doctrine of the eternity of the world was regarded as an affront to biblical doctrine, as William Wotton stated: 'Among all the Hypotheses of those who would destroy our most holy Faith, none is so plausible as that of the *Eternity of the World* . . . Now the Notion of the Eternity of Mankind, through infinite successive Generations of Men, cannot be at once more effectually and more popularly confuted, than by shewing

how the World has gone on, from Age to Age, improving; and consequently, that it is at present much more knowing than it ever was since the earliest Times to which History can carry us' (Wotton, *Reflections*, 'Preface', A7$^{r-v}$). Hume's disavowal of this doctrine serves two purposes. It suavely disarms any suspicions of hostility to Christianity on his part; and it locates the essay broadly within the context of the various ramifications of the 'Querelle des anciens et des modernes', and on the side of the moderns.

2. *in the heavens*] cf. Hume's later reference to Saserna's observations on the heavens (above, p. 141). In *Lettres Persanes*, letter 113, Montesquieu had made a similar observation: 'les Cieux mêmes ne le sont pas [incorruptibles]: les astronomes sont des témoins oculaires de leurs changements, qui sont des effets bien naturels du mouvement universel de la matière' (Montesquieu, *Œuvres*, p. 121).

3. *an universal deluge*] Another blandly orthodox pronouncement. The tradition of a universal deluge had recently been defended in Patrick Cockburn's *Enquiry into the Truth . . . of the Mosaic Deluge* (1750). In Part VI of the *Dialogues Concerning Natural Religion*, the sceptic Philo speaks of 'Strong and almost incontestable Proofs . . . that every part of this Globe has continu'd for many Ages entirely cover'd with Water' (*Hume on Religion*, p. 200). In *Lettres Persanes*, letter 113, Montesquieu had also touched on these traditions: 'Mais pourquoi parler de la destruction qui aurait pu arriver au Genre humain? N'est-elle pas arrivée, en effet, et le Déluge ne le réduisit-il pas à une seule famille?' (Montesquieu, *Œuvres*, p. 122).

4. *The arts and sciences . . . in another*] A topic upon which Hume had written in 'Of the Rise and Progress of the Arts and Sciences' (above, vol. 1, pp. 93–112).

5. *the universe . . . to old age*] An Epicurean emphasis most readily found in Lucretius, *De Rerum Natura*, e.g. V.91–109: 'Quod superest, ne te in promissis plura moremur, / principio maria ac terras caelumque tuere: / quorum naturam triplicem, tria corpora, Memmi, / tris species tam dissimilis, tria talia texta, / una dies dabit exitio, multosque per annos / sustentata ruet moles et machina mundi. / nec me animi fallit quam res nova miraque menti / accidat exitium caeli terraeque futurum, / et quam difficile id mihi sit pervincere dictis; / ut fit ubi insolitam rem adportes auribus ante, / nec tamen hanc possis oculorum subdere visu / nec iacere indu manus, via qua munita fidei / proxima fert humanum in pectus templaque mentis. / sed tamen effabor. dictis dabit ipsa fidem res / forsitan, et graviter terrarum motibus ortis / omnia conquassari in parvo tempore cernes. / quod procul a nobis flectat fortuna gubernans, / et ratio potius quam res persuadeat ipsa / succidere horrisono posse omnia victa fragore'; 'To proceed then, and to make no more delay with promises, observe first of all sea and earth and sky: this threefold nature, these three masses, Memmius, these three forms so different, these three textures so interwoven, one day shall consign to destruction; the mighty and complex system of the world, upheld through many years, shall

crash into ruins. Yet I do not forget how novel and strange it strikes the mind that destruction awaits the heavens and the earth, and how difficult it is for me to prove this by argument; as happens when you invite a hearing for something hitherto unfamiliar, which you cannot bring within the scope of vision nor put into the hands, whereby the highway of belief leads straight to the heart of man and the precincts of his intelligence. Nevertheless I will speak out. My words will perhaps win credit by plain facts, and within some short time you will see violent earthquakes arise and all things convulsed with shocks. But may pilot fortune steer this far from us, and may pure reason rather than experience persuade that the whole world can collapse borne down with a frightful-sounding crash.' The mortality of the universe had also been touched on by Fontenelle, again in the context of the 'Querelle' (Fontenelle, *Poésies*, pp. 201–4). Cf. Montesquieu, *Lettres Persanes*, letter 112: 'Comment la Nature a-t-elle pu perdre cette prodigieuse fécondité des premiers temps? Serait-elle déjà dans sa vieillesse, et tomberait-elle de langueur?' (Montesquieu, *Œuvres*, p. 121).

6. *general physical causes*] cf. Wallace, *Dissertation*, p. 12: 'The causes of this paucity of inhabitants, and irregularity of increase, are manifold. Some of them may be called physical, as they depend entirely on the course of nature, and are independent on mankind. Others of them are moral, and depend on the affections, passions and institutions of men.' Wallace, however, also dismissed consideration of physical causes from his argument: 'Causes of this nature [i.e. physical causes] may be supposed to operate in the same climates in different ages, and in different climates in the same age. Mankind may be greatly wasted by plagues and famines, and a fruitful land may become a desart. Yet neither do causes of this kind seem sufficient for explaining the phænomenon of so great a decay of people. Nor indeed does it appear that there has been any such alteration in the state of nature as could make any considerable difference, either over all the earth, or in particular regions: we do not therefore build on natural causes of this sort' (Wallace, *Dissertation*, p. 80). Cf. *Lettres Persanes*, letters 113 and 114: 'Je te ferai voir, dans une lettre suivante, qu'indépendamment des causes physiques, il y en a de morales qui ont produit cet effet [of depopulation]'; 'Tu cherches la raison pourquoi la Terre est moins peuplée qu'elle ne l'était autrefois, et, si tu y fais bien attention, tu verras que la grande différence vient de celle qui est arrivée dans les mœurs' (Montesquieu, *Œuvres*, p. 122).

7. *unknown to modern medicine*] e.g. the plague of Athens, which Hume has mentioned in 'The Sceptic' (above, vol. 1, pp. 142–3).

8. *new diseases*] e.g. venereal disease, which was then believed to be an import from the Americas.

9. *small-pox commits such ravages*] Smallpox was a disease which showed no regard for social standing: Louis XIV had suffered from it as a child, and Louis XV would die of it in 1774. Inoculation had been introduced to

Europe from the Levant in the early eighteenth century, after being practised in China for many years.

10. *venereal distempers*] Here again Hume is shadowing Wallace: 'some diseases, unknown to antiquity, may have made great havock in modern times: among these, two are remarkable, the *Lues Venerea*, and the *Small Pox* ...' (Wallace, *Dissertation*, pp. 80–81). Cf. *Lettres Persanes*, letter 113: 'Il n'y a pas deux siècles que la plus honteuse de toutes les maladies se fit sentir en Europe, en Asie, et en Afrique; elle fit, dans très peu de temps, des effets prodigieux: c'était fait des hommes si elle avait continué ses progrès avec la même furie. Accablés de maux dès leur naissance, incapables de soutenir le poids des charges de la Société, ils auraient péri misérablement' (Montesquieu, *Œuvres*, p. 122).

11. *war, pestilence, and famine*] cf. Montesquieu, *Lettres Persanes*, letter 112: 'je parcours la Terre, et je n'y trouve que des délabrements: je crois la voir sortir des ravages de la peste et de la famine' (Montesquieu, *Œuvres*, p. 121). This triplet of the causes of mortality snagged on the memory of Gibbon, who would echo it when describing the consequences of the political turmoil in the Roman Empire in the middle of the third century: 'we might suspect, that war, pestilence, and famine, had consumed, in a few years, the moiety of the human species' (Gibbon, *Decline and Fall*, vol. I, p. 294). Cf. Revelation 6:1–8.

12. *extravagancies ... well known*] As set out in his *Variarum observationum liber* (1685). See above, headnote, pp. 412–13. Wallace had also distanced himself from Vossius: 'As an example of too great a prepossession in favour of antiquity, we may reckon the assertion of *Isaac Vossius*, who is not only of opinion that the earth was much more populous in antient than modern times, but even brings down the number of the inhabitants of *Europe* in his own age to 30 millions; a computation undoubtedly far below the just account' (Wallace, *Dissertation*, p. 34).

13. *an author of much greater genius*] i.e. Montesquieu. See above, headnote, pp. 412–13. Hume alludes to letters 112–22 of *Lettres Persanes* (Montesquieu, *Œuvres*, pp. 121–7) and also to Book XXIII of the *Esprit des Lois*, esp. chapter 19. In this opening section of his essay Hume has been touching on many of the topics on which Montesquieu had alighted in his own discussion of ancient populousness. Again, Wallace distances himself from the exposed and extreme position of Montesquieu: 'But, what is much more surprising in so great a man, we find the learned author of *Lettres Persanes*, published some years ago, giving it as his opinion, that there were 50 times as many people in the world, in the days of *Julius Cæsar* the first *Roman* Emperor, as at present; which is certainly too high a proportion' (Wallace, *Dissertation*, p. 35). Cf. Hume's praise of Montesquieu in 1751 as a 'late author of genius, as well as learning', who had proposed 'a system of political knowledge, which abounds in ingenious and brilliant thoughts, and is not wanting in solidity' (*ECPM*, III, 'Of Justice', p. 22).

14. *We know not ... at present*] Although rudimentary collections of statistics relating to population were compiled in antiquity (most famously the census ordered by Augustus: see Luke 2:1–3), and in Europe during the later Middle Ages (e.g. Villani's fourteenth-century *Nuova Cronica*, which reports data relating to Florence), in England the regular compilation of reliable if incomplete statistics concerning population and mortality began no earlier than 1662 with the work of John Graunt and Sir William Petty. National decennial censuses of the entire population of Great Britain would not begin until 1801. Cf. Wallace, *Dissertation*, pp. 14–15: 'nay, after the most accurate search, it will perhaps be found impossible to determine precisely at what rate mankind have either increased or decreased, in particular ages or countries; or from what particular causes such variations have happened. Exact registers of such things have never been kept, and indeed could never have been preserved in such an unsettled state of human affairs.'

15. *If I can make it appear ... aspire to*] Writing to Montesquieu on 26 June 1753, Hume explained the sceptical and tentative stance he had adopted in this essay: 'I should be much afraid that I am entirely refuted [by Wallace's *Dissertation*], had I not, all along, in my essay, kept on the sceptical and doubtful side, which, in most subjects, gives a man so much the advantage of the ground, that it is very difficult to force him' (*Letters*, vol. I, p. 177). Cf. 'where several ages have intervened, and only scattered lights are afforded us by ancient authors; what can we do but amuse ourselves by talking *pro* and *con*, on an interesting subject, and thereby correcting all hasty and violent determinations?'; 'It is an infinite advantage in every controversy, to defend the negative' (above, pp. 112 and 262). Although in those passages Hume laid the emphasis on the tactical advantage bestowed by philosophical hesitation, at other moments he would present that posture in a less instrumental light, as an aspect of philosophical honesty and good manners. In 'Of the Protestant Succession' Hume would characterize the general stance of the philosopher when considering political questions as one of 'Hesitation, and reserve, and suspence' (above, p. 191); in the 'Conclusion' of *ECPM* he would state that 'nothing can be more unphilosophical than to be positive or dogmatic on any subject' (p. 78); and in 1754 he would tell the physicist John Stewart that 'the positive Air, which prevails in that Book [the *Treatise of Human Nature*] ... so much displeases me, that I have not Patience to review it' (*Letters*, vol. I, p. 187). *The Natural History of Religion* (1757) would end on a similar note of suspended judgement: 'The whole is a riddle, an ænigma, an inexplicable mystery. Doubt, uncertainty, suspence of judgment appear the only result of our most accurate scrutiny, concerning this subject' (*NHR*, p. 87). Wallace, perhaps inadvertently acknowledging the success of Hume's sceptical strategy, would confess that his adversary's 'pompous arguments ... puzzled, but did not convince' him (Wallace, *Dissertation*, p. 163). But Hume had been aware that most philosophers had

not observed what he believed was the true philosophical temperament ever since he had opened the *Treatise of Human Nature* by observing that nothing had been 'more usual and natural for those, who pretend to discover any thing new to the world in philosophy and the sciences, than to insinuate the praises of their own systems, by decrying all those, which have been advanc'd before them' (*THN*, 'Introduction', p. 3; cf. ibid., I.iii.9, on the virtue of 'scrupulous hesitation' in philosophy, vol. I, p. 74).

16. *police*] See above, vol. 1, p. 285, n. 36.

17. *the human species . . . every generation*] An allusion to the opening section of Wallace's *Dissertation*, in which he calculates the natural rate of the increase of a human population, and asserts that mankind 'double themselves in each period of 33⅓ years' (Wallace, *Dissertation*, pp. 1–9, quotation on p. 5). Sir William Petty had noted that 'London *doubles in Forty Years, and all* England *in Three hundred and sixty Years*', and also that '*the Periods of doubling the People, are found to be in all Degrees, from between Ten, to Twelve hundred Years*' (Petty, *Essay*, p. 6). Adam Smith would introduce a further geographical variable into these calculations: 'Through the greater part of Europe, the number of inhabitants is not supposed to double in less than five hundred years. In several of our North American colonies, it is found to double in twenty or five-and-twenty years' (Smith, *Wealth*, p. 423, III.iv.19; cf. also I.viii.23).

18. *History . . . part of a people*] The Bible reports outbreaks of plague in Egypt (e.g. Exodus 11); and Thucydides famously describes the occurrence of plague in Athens in 430 BC (Thucydides, II.47–55). Cf. the note in the 'Early Memoranda': 'In Nero's time 30.000 buryd in one Autumn, while there was a Plague' (NLS MS 23159, item 14, p. 17; cf. Mossner, 'Memoranda', p. 509). Cf. also Montesquieu, *Lettres Persanes*, letter 113: 'Les histoires sont pleines de ces pestes universelles qui ont tour à tour désolé l'Univers' (Montesquieu, *Œuvres*, p. 121). In late antiquity a virulent and prolonged outbreak of plague in Constantinople from 542 to 594 decimated the population and spread across the empire. Gibbon would not agree with Hume as to the inevitable elasticity of population, since these losses had still not been made good: 'No facts have been preserved to sustain an account, or even a conjecture, of the numbers that perished in this extraordinary mortality. I only find, that during three months, five, and at length ten, thousand persons died each day at Constantinople; that many cities of the East were left vacant, and that in several districts of Italy the harvest and the vintage withered on the ground. The triple scourge of war, pestilence, and famine, afflicted the subjects of Justinian, and his reign is disgraced by a visible decrease of the human species, which has never been repaired in some of the fairest countries of the globe' (Gibbon, *Decline and Fall*, vol. II, p. 777). Cf. Hume's remarks in his *History of England* on the Black Death (1347–51): 'a destructive pestilence, which invaded that kingdom as well as the rest of

Europe; and is computed to have swept away near a third of the inhabitants in every country, which it attacked. It was probably more fatal in great cities than in the country; and above fifty thousand souls are said to have perished by it in London alone. This malady first discovered itself in the north of Asia, was spread over all that country, made its progress from one end of Europe to the other, and sensibly depopulated every state through which it passed' (*History of England*, vol. II, p. 243). Hume's comments on the plague year of 1666 are more concise: 'The plague had broken out in London; and that with such violence as to cut off, in a year, near 90,000 inhabitants' (*History of England*, vol. VI, p. 200). Cf. Wallace, *Dissertation*, p. 12: 'Other causes of this kind [physical] are more variable; such as, the inclemency of particular seasons, plagues, famines, earthquakes, and inundations of the sea; which sweep off great numbers of men, as well as other animals, and prevent the quicker replenishing of the earth.'

19. *superior riches*] 'their [emigrants from Spain] going over to America has not reduced, but rather augmented the number of people in Spain; and experience also confirms it: for those provinces most abound with inhabitants, when the greatest number of Spaniards have gone abroad' (Uztáriz, *Commerce*, vol. I, p. 46).

20. *A country . . . most populous*] cf. Wallace: 'For cold and barren heaths, rocky mountainous tracts, marshes which cannot be drained, inhospitable sands, and many other sorts of unfruitful soils, cannot produce equal quantities of food, and, by consequence, *cæteris paribus*, cannot be so well stored with people, as softer and more fertile climes' (Wallace, *Dissertation*, p. 16).

21. *But if . . . be most people*] A statement of the general principle of a correlation between populousness and wider human flourishing which bestows on the question of the populousness of antiquity a more than antiquarian importance. Wallace had agreed: 'it must be a strong presumption in favour of the customs or policy of any government, if, *cæteris paribus*, it is able to raise up and maintain a greater number of people' (Wallace, *Dissertation*, p. 14, n.*).

22. *Some passionate admirers . . . subjection*] Principally an allusion to Andrew Fletcher of Saltoun, who in the second of his *Two Discourses Concerning the Affairs of Scotland* (Edinburgh, 1698) had seriously proposed the reintroduction of slavery as a cure for the beggary and vagabondage which presently infested Scotland, and which he saw as arising from the misplaced idealism of the early Christians in pursuing the emancipation of the slave populations of antiquity: '*I doubt not, that what I have said will meet, not only with all the misconstruction and obloquy, but all the disdain, fury and outcries, of which either ignorant Magistrates, or proud, lazy and miserable people are capable. Would I bring back Slavery into the world? Shall men of immortal Souls, and by nature equal to any, be sold as Beasts? Shall they and their posterity be for ever subjected to the most miserable of all conditions;*

*the inhuman barbarity of Masters, who may beat, mutilate, torture, starve or kill so great a number of mankind at pleasure? Shall the far greater part of the Commonwealth be Slaves, not that the rest may be free, but Tyrants over them? With what face can we oppose the tyranny of Princes, and recommend such opposition as the highest Virtue, if we make our selves Tyrants over the greatest part of mankind? Can any man, from whom such a thing has once escaped, ever offer to speak for Liberty? But they must pardon me if I tell them, that I regard not names, but things; and that the misapplication of names has confounded every thing'* (Fletcher, *Discourses*, 'Second Discourse', pp. 10–11). In *Lettres Persanes*, letter 115, Montesquieu had discovered a source of populousness in the practices of ancient slavery among the Romans: 'Bien loin d'empêcher, par des voies forcées, la multiplication de ces esclaves, ils la favorisaient au contraire de tout leur pouvoir; ils les associaient le plus qu'ils pouvaient par des espèces de mariages. Par ce moyen, ils remplissaient leurs maisons de domestiques de tous les sexes, de tous les âges, et l'État d'un peuple innombrable' (Montesquieu, *Œuvres*, p. 123). Wallace, following Montesquieu, had suggested that the institution of slavery had contributed to the greater populousness of antiquity: 'GOD forbid! that I should ever be an advocate for slavery, ecclesiastic, civil, or domestic, on account of any accidental advantages which it may happen to produce; yet it must be confessed, that considering it only with respect to the phænomenon we are at present examining, it seems probable, that the antient condition of servants contributed something to the greater populousness of antiquity, and that the antient slaves were more serviceable in raising up people, than the inferior ranks of men in modern times' (Wallace, *Dissertation*, p. 91). Wallace retorted the phrase 'passionate admirers' on Hume (Wallace, *Dissertation*, p. 163). Hume here shows a sensitivity to the difference between metaphorical (or political) slavery and literal bodily slavery which many of his near contemporaries, such as Locke or Swift, did not share.

23. *vita CLAUDII*] 'Cum quidam aegra et adfecta mancipia in insulam Aesculapi taedio medendi exponerent, omnes qui exponerentur liberos esse sanxit, nec redire in dicionem domini, si convaluissent; quod si quis necare quem mallet quam exponere, caedis crimine teneri' (Suetonius, *Claudius*, XXV.2); 'When certain men were exposing their sick and worn-out slaves on the Island of Aesculapius because of the trouble of treating them, Claudius decreed that all such slaves were free, and that if they recovered, they should not return to the control of their master; but if anyone preferred to kill such a slave rather than to abandon him, he was liable to the charge of murder.'

24. *vita CATONIS*] 'οὐδένα δὲ πώποτε πρίασθαι δοῦλον ὑπὲρ τὰς χιλίας δραχμὰς καὶ πεντακοσίας, ὡς ἂν οὐ τρυφερῶν οὐδ᾽ ὡραίων, ἀλλ᾽ ἐργατικῶν καὶ στερεῶν, οἷον ἱπποκόμων καὶ βοηλατῶν, δεόμενος· καὶ τούτους δὲ πρεσβυτέρους γενομένους ᾤετο δεῖν ἀποδίδοσθαι καὶ μὴ βόσκειν ἀχρήστους' (Plutarch, *Life of Marcus Cato*, IV.4); 'he never paid more than fifteen hundred drachmas for a slave,

since he did not want them to be delicately beautiful, but sturdy workers, such as grooms and herdsmen, and these he thought it his duty to sell when they got oldish, instead of feeding them when they were useless.'

25. *Lib. i. cap. 6*] 'Optime solutis servis cellae meridiem aequinoctialem spectantes fient; vinctis quam saluberrimum subterraneum ergastulum plurimis, sitque id angustis inlustratum fenestris atque a terra sic editis, ne manu contingi possint' (Columella, *On Agriculture*, I.vi.3); 'It will be best that cubicles for unfettered slaves be built to admit the midday sun at the equinox; for those who are in chains there should be an underground prison, as wholesome as possible, receiving light through a number of narrow windows built so high from the ground that they cannot be reached with the hand.'

26. *lib. xi. cap. 1*] 'Itaque mancipia vincta, quae sunt ergastuli, per nomina quotidie citare debebit atque explorare, ut sint diligenter compedibus innexa: tum etiam custodiae sedes an tuta et recte munita sit: nec, si quem dominus aut ipse vinxerit, sine iussu patrisfamiliae resolvat' (Columella, *On Agriculture*, XI.i.22); 'And so he will have to call over the names of the slaves in the prison, who are in chains, every day and make sure that they are carefully fettered and also whether the place of confinement is well secured and properly fortified; and he should not release anyone whom his master or he himself has bound without an order from the lord of the house.'

27. *eleg. 6*] 'Ianitor – indignum! – dura religate catena, / difficilem moto cardine pande forem! / quod precor, exiguum est – aditu fac ianua parvo / obliquum capiat semiadaperta latus'; 'Janitor – unworthy fate! – bound with the hard chain, move on its hinge the surly portal, and open it! What I entreat is slight – see that the door stand but half ajar, enough to receive me sidewise through the small approach' (Ovid, *Amores*, I.vi.1–4).

28. *rhetor*] 'M. Otacilius Pitholaus servisse dicitur atque etiam ostiarius vetere more in catena fuisse, donec ob ingenium ac studium litterarum manumissus'; 'Manius Otacilius Pitholaus is said to have been a slave and even to have served as a doorkeeper in chains, according to the ancient custom, until he was set free because of his talent and interest in letters' (Suetonius, *Lives of Illustrious Men: Rhetoricians*, III).

29. *audio*] 'I hear the chains of the door-keeper rattle', Lucius Afranius (*fl.* 2nd century BC), *Vopiscus*; a fragment preserved in Nonius Marcellinus, *De compendiosa doctrina*, 40 M.

30. *It is pretended*] Hume here may again be thinking of Andrew Fletcher of Saltoun, who had argued for a reintroduction of slavery as a remedy for Scottish indigence and mendicancy in the second of his *Two Discourses Concerning the Affairs of Scotland* (Edinburgh, 1698). There he contended that: '*the condition of Slaves among the Antients, will upon serious consideration appear to be only a better provision in their Governments than any we have, that no man might want the necessities of life, nor any person*

*able to work be burdensom to the Commonwealth*' (p. 13; and see above, pp. 421–2, n.22).

31. *orat.* 1] Ὑμεῖς μὲν τοίνυν καὶ ἰδίᾳ καὶ δημοσίᾳ βάσανον ἀκριβεστάτην πασῶν πίστεων νομίζετε, καὶ ὁπόταν δοῦλοι καὶ ἐλεύθεροι παραγένωνται, δέῃ δ' εὑρεθῆναι τὸ ζητούμενον, οὐ χρῆσθε ταῖς τῶν ἐλευθέρων μαρτυρίαις, ἀλλὰ τοὺς δούλους βασανίζοντες, οὕτω ζητεῖτε τὴν ἀλήθειαν εὑρεῖν'; 'You on your part hold that in both private and public matters the torture is the most certain of all methods of proof, and when slaves and freemen are both available, and the truth of a matter is to be sought out, you make no use of the testimony of the freemen, but seek to ascertain the truth by torturing the slaves; and very properly, men of the jury' (Demosthenes, *Against Onetor*, I, xxxvii).

32. *Pro Cælio*] It is difficult to locate in Cicero's *Pro Cælio* a passage which makes precisely this point about the superiority of the testimony of free citizens compared with that of slaves, although the differing credibility of different kinds of testimony is certainly at the heart of Cicero's concern in this speech.

33. *retract our hasty determinations*] cf. the note in the 'Early Memoranda': ''Tis a presumption that the antient Practice of Servitude did not favour Propagation, that such immense Numbers of Slaves were daily brought to Rome from Asia & the East' (NLS MS 23159, item 14, p. 23; cf. Mossner, 'Memoranda', p. 514).

34. *The comparison ... cattle*] Comparisons between a population and cattle were features of English political language in the decades before Hume was writing, associated especially with the subject of the stricter forms of hereditary succession and designed to rouse the reader's indignation. Cf., e.g., John Locke: 'he [Filmer, the apologist for hereditary right] speaks of Mankind, as if God had no care of any part of them, but only of their Monarchs, and that the rest of the People, the Societies of Men, were made as so many Herds of Cattle, only for the Service, Use and Pleasure of their Princes' (Locke, *Two Treatises*, 'Second Treatise', § 156; cf. also § 163). This metaphor might also be used to stigmatize foreign forms of despotism, particularly that of the Ottoman Empire (Malcolm, *Useful Enemies*, pp. 207–10). Cf. Hume's glancing comment on this subject in 'Of the Original Contract': 'we find, every where, princes, who claim their subjects as their property' (above, p. 164).

35. *To rear a child ... potatoes*] In this and the following paragraphs, with their explicit reference to Ireland, one may hear echoes of the deliberately shocking language of Swift's *A Modest Proposal* (1729), in which terms coined for animals are applied to human beings. Cf. in particular the question Swift's Proposer poses: 'The question therefore is, how this number shall be reared, and provided for ...' (Swift, *Irish Writings*, p. 148).

36. *If LONDON ... usually computed*] Hume appears to be drawing on the statistics of Charles Davenant, who in 1699 had calculated that 'London requires a Supply of 2000 Souls *per An.* to keep it from decreasing, besides a

further Supply of about 3000 *per Annum* for its Increase at this time. In all 5000, or above half of the Kingdoms neat Increase' (Davenant, *Essay*, p. 20).

37. *manumitted*] i.e. freed.

38. *freedom of the city ... provinces*] By the emperor Caracalla in AD 212.

39. *our planters*] i.e. landowners in the West Indies.

40. *lib. xiv*] 'ἡ δὲ τῶν ἀνδραπόδων ἐξαγωγὴ προὐκαλεῖτο μάλιστα εἰς τὰς κακουργίας, ἐπικερδεστάτη γενομένη· καὶ γὰρ ἡλίσκοντο ῥᾳδίως, καὶ τὸ ἐμπόριον οὐ παντελῶς ἄπωθεν ἦν μέγα καὶ πολυχρήματον, ἡ Δῆλος, δυναμένη μυριάδας ἀνδραπόδων αὐθημερὸν καὶ δέξασθαι καὶ ἀποπέμψαι, ὥστε καὶ παροιμίαν γενέσθαι διὰ τοῦτο· ἔμπορε, κατάπλευσον, ἐξελοῦ, πάντα πέπραται. αἴτιον δ', ὅτι πλούσιοι γενόμενοι Ῥωμαῖοι μετὰ τὴν Καρχηδόνος καὶ Κορίνθου κατασκαφὴν οἰκετείαις ἐχρῶντο πολλαῖς· ὁρῶντες δὲ τὴν εὐπέτειαν οἱ λῃσταὶ ταύτην ἐξήνθησαν ἀθρόως, αὐτοὶ καὶ λῃζόμενοι καὶ σωματεμποροῦντες' (Strabo, *Geography*, XIV.v.2); 'The exportation of slaves induced them most of all to engage in their evil business, since it proved most profitable; for not only were they easily captured, but the market, which was large and rich in property, was not extremely far away, I mean Delos, which could both admit and send away ten thousand slaves on the same day; whence arose the proverb, "Merchant, sail in, unload your ship, everything has been sold." The cause of this was the fact that the Romans, having become rich after the destruction of Carthage and Corinth, used many slaves; and the pirates, seeing the easy profit therein, bloomed forth in great numbers, themselves not only going in quest of booty but also trafficking in slaves.'

41. *cap. 13*] 'Saepenumero civitatis nostrae principes audio culpantes modo agrorum infecunditatem, modo caeli per multa iam tempora noxiam frugibus intemperiem; quosdam etiam praedictas querimonias velut ratione certa mitigantes, quod existiment ubertate nimia prioris aevi defatigatum et effetum solum nequire pristina benignitate praebere mortalibus alimenta' (Columella, *Rei Rusticae*, 'Praefatio', 1); 'Again and again I hear leading men of our state condemning now the unfruitfulness of the soil, now the inclemency of the climate for some seasons past, as harmful to crops; and some I hear reconciling the aforesaid complaints, as if on well-founded reasoning, on the ground that, in their opinion, the soil was worn out and exhausted by the over-production of earlier days and can no longer furnish sustenance to mortals with its old-time benevolence'; 'quod neque fas est existimare rerum Naturam, quam primus ille mundi genitor perpetua fecunditate donavit, quasi quodam morbo sterilitate adfectam; neque prudentis est credere Tellurem, quae divinam et aeternam iuventam sortita communis omnium parens dicta sit, quia et cuncta peperit semper et deinceps paritura sit, velut hominem consenuisse' (ibid., 2); 'for it is a sin to suppose that Nature, endowed with perennial fertility by the creator of the universe, is affected with barrenness as though with some disease; and it is unbecoming to a man of good judgement to believe that Earth, to whose lot was assigned a divine and everlasting

youth, and who is called the common mother of all things – because she has always brought forth all things and is destined to bring them forth continuously – has grown old in mortal fashion'; 'Quo magis prodigio simile est, quod accidit, ut res corporibus nostris vitaeque utilitati maxime conveniens minimam usque in hoc tempus consummationem haberet idque sperneretur genus amplificandi relinquendique patrimonii, quod omni crimine caret' (ibid., 7); 'For this reason, what has come to pass is the more amazing – that the art of the highest importance to our physical welfare and the needs of life should have made, even up to our own time, the least progress; and that this method of enlarging and passing on an inheritance, entirely free from guilt, should be looked upon with scorn'; 'Neque solum antiquior cultura agri, sed etiam melior. Itaque non sine causa maiores nostri ex urbe in agros redigebant suos cives, quod et in pace a rusticis Romanis alebantur et in bello ab his allevabantur' (Varro, *Rerum Rusticarum*, III.i); 'And not only is the tilling of the fields more ancient – it is more noble. It was therefore not without reason that our ancestors tried to entice their citizens back from the city to the country; for in time of peace they were fed by the country Romans, and in time of war aided by them'; 'Iam pauca aratro iugera regiae / moles relinquent' (Horace, *Odes*, II.i.1–2); 'Soon our princely piles will leave only a few acres for the plough'. The reference to Tacitus, *Annales*, III. liv is to a long passage in Tiberius's infamous letter to the Senate, deploring Roman decadence in general terms, but without any specific reference to a decline in agriculture. 'ut tandem annona convaluit, impetum se cepisse scribit frumentationes publicas in perpetuum abolendi, quod earum fiducia cultura agrorum cessaret; neque tamen perseverasse, quia certum haberet posse per ambitionem quandoque restitui. Atque ita posthac rem temperavit, ut non minorem aratorum ac negotiantium quam populi rationem deduceret' (Suetonius, *Deified Augustus*, XLII); 'and when grain at last became more plentiful, he writes: "I was strongly inclined to do away forever with distributions of grain, because through dependence on them agriculture was neglected; but I did not carry out my purpose, feeling sure that they would one day be renewed through desire for popular favour." But from that time on he regulated the practice with no less regard for the interests of the farmers and grain-dealers than for those of the populace'; 'quaenam ergo tantae ubertatis causa erat? ipsorum tunc manibus imperatorum colebantur agri, ut fas est credere, gaudente terra vomere laureato et triumphali aratore, sive illi eadem cura semina tractabant qua bella eademque diligentia arva disponebant qua castra, sive honestis manibus omnia laetius proveniunt quoniam et curiosius fiunt ... at nunc eadem illa vincti pedes, damnatae manus inscriptique vultus exercent, non tam surda tellure quae parens appellatur colique dicitur ut ipso opere ab his adsumpto non invita ea et indignante credatur id fieri. et nos miramur ergastulorum non eadem emolumenta esse quae fuerint imperatorum!' (Pliny the Elder, *Natural History*, XVIII.4 [not 13, as specified by Hume]); 'What therefore was the cause of such great fertility? The fields were tilled in those days by the hands of generals themselves, and we may well believe that the earth rejoiced in a laurel-decked ploughshare and a ploughman who had celebrated a triumph, whether it was that those farmers treated the seed with the same care as they managed their wars and marked out their fields with the same diligence as they arranged a camp, or whether everything prospers better under honourable hands because the work is done with greater attention . . . But nowadays those agricultural operations are performed by slaves with fettered ankles and by the hands of malefactors with branded faces! although the Earth who is addressed as our mother and whose cultivation is spoken of as worship is not so dull that when we obtain even our farm-work from these persons one can believe that this is not done against her will and to her indignation. And we forsooth are surprised that we do not get the same profits from the labour of slave-gangs as used to be obtained from that of generals!'

42. *cap. 7*] 'the free-born were daily fewer' (Tacitus, *Annals*, IV.xxvii).

43. *licentia*] 'scurra' is the Latin word for a dandy or man-about-town. 'Urbanus tibi, Caecili, videris. non es, crede mihi. quid ergo? verna es' (Martial, *Epigrams*, I.xli [not xlii as specified by Hume]); 'You fancy yourself a wit, Caecilius. Believe me, you are not. What then? You are a vulgar buffoon.' 'o noctes cenaeque deum! quibus ipse meique / ante Larem proprium vescor vernasque procaces / pasco libatis dapibus' (Horace, *Satires*, II.vi.65–7); 'O nights and feasts divine! When before my own Lar we dine, my friends and I, and feed the saucy slaves from the barely tasted dishes'. '"O" inquit hominem acutum atque urbanitatis vernaculae fontem' (Petronius, *Satyricon*, XXIV); '"What a very smart gentleman," says she, "– a man of excellent natural wit!" 'Itaque cum videris bonos viros acceptosque diis laborare, sudare, per arduum escendere, malos autem lascivire et voluptatibus fluere, cogita filiorum nos modestia delectari, vernularum licentia, illos disciplina tristiori contineri, horum ali audaciam' (Seneca, *De Providentia*, I.vi); 'And so, when you see that men who are good and acceptable to the gods labour and sweat and have a difficult road to climb, that the wicked, on the other hand, make merry and abound in pleasures, reflect that our children please us by their modesty, but slave-boys by their forwardness; that we hold in check the former by sterner discipline, while we encourage the latter to be bold.'

44. *It is computed . . . recruit them*] In his *Groans of the Plantations* (1698), Edward Littleton had calculated the yearly mortality among a body of slaves at between 8 and 10 per cent: 'He that hath but a hundred *Negroes*, should buy eight or ten every year to keep up his stock' (p. 16).

45. *I shall add . . . freeman*] See item 6 in the list of variants (above, p. 407). This addition perhaps reflects Hume's reading of Adam Smith's *Wealth of Nations* (1776), in which the lower productivity of slave labour is one of the planks of his argument against the prevailing imperial and colonial system.

See Smith, *Wealth*, pp. 387–90 and 684. Smith's general position is that 'The experience of all ages and nations, I believe, demonstrates that the work done by slaves, though it appears to cost only their maintenance, is in the end the dearest of any' (Smith, *Wealth*, p. 387).

46. *The names . . . foreign countries*] Some of these names are given to slaves in comedies by Menander (*c.* 342–291 BC). Syros: *ΔΙΣ ΕΞΑΠΑΤΩΝ* (*Twice a Swindler*); *ΕΠΙΤΡΕΠΟΝΤΕΣ* (*Men at Arbitration*); *ΦΑΣΜΑ* (*The Apparition*). Daos: *ΔΥΣΚΟΛΟΣ* (*The Peevish Fellow*); *ΓΕΩΡΓΟΣ* (*The Farmer*); *ΗΡΩΣ* (*The Guardian Spirit*); *ΚΟΛΑΞ* (*The Fawner*); *ΠΕΡΙΝΘΙΑ* (*The Girl from Perinthus*); *ΠΕΠΙΚΕΙΡΟΜΕΝΗ* (*The Girl with Her Hair Cut Short*). Getas: *ΗΡΩΣ* (*The Guardian Spirit*); *ΔΥΣΚΟΛΟΣ* (*The Peevish Fellow*); *ΜΙΣΟΥΜΕΝΟΣ* (*The Hated Man*).

47. *slaves there*] 'Usus est familia, si utilitate iudicandum est, optima; si forma, vix mediocri. Namque in ea erant pueri litteratissimi, anagnostae optimi et plurimi librarii, ut ne pedisequus quidem quisquam esset qui non utrumque horum pulchre facere posset; pari modo artifices ceteri, quos cultus domesticus desiderat, apprime boni. Neque tamen horum quemquam nisi domi natum domique factum habuit; quod est signum non solum continentiae, sed etiam diligentiae' (Cornelius Nepos, *Vita Attici*, XIII.iii–iv); 'He had slaves that were excellent in point of efficiency, although in personal appearance hardly mediocre; for there were among them servants who were highly educated, some excellent readers and a great number of copyists; in fact, there was not even a footman who was not expert in both those accomplishments. In the same way, the other artisans required by the management of a house were of first-rate quality. In spite of this, however, he possessed no slave who was not born in his house and trained at home, which is a sign, not only of his self-control, but also of his spirit of economy.'

48. *Lib. vii*] 'ἐξ ὧν γὰρ ἐκομίζετο, ἢ τοῖς ἔθνεσιν ἐκείνοις ὁμωνύμους ἐκάλουν τοὺς οἰκέτας, ὡς Λυδὸν καὶ Σύρον, ἢ τοῖς ἐπιπολάζουσιν ἐκεῖ ὀνόμασι προσηγόρευον, ὡς Μάνην ἢ Μίδαν τὸν Φρύγα, Τίβιον δὲ τὸν Παφλαγόνα' (Strabo, VII.iii.12); 'For the Attic people were wont either to call their slaves by the same names as those of the nations from which they were brought (as "Lydus" or "Syrus"), or addressed them by names that were prevalent in their countries (as "Manes" or else "Midas" for the Phrygian, or "Tibius" for the Paphlagonian).'

49. *edit. ALDI*] Demosthenes, *ΚΑΤΑ ΜΕΙΔΙΟΥ* (*Against Meidias*), XLV–L, esp. XLVIII–XL: 'εἴ τις εἰς τοὺς βαρβάρους ἐνεγκὼν τὸν νόμον τοῦτον, παρ᾽ ὧν τὰ ἀνδράποδ᾽ εἰς τοὺς Ἕλληνας κομίζεται, ἐπαινῶν ὑμᾶς καὶ διεξιὼν περὶ τῆς πόλεως εἴποι πρὸς αὐτοὺς ὅτι "εἰσὶν Ἕλληνές τινες ἄνθρωποι οὕτως ἥμεροι καὶ φιλάνθρωποι τοὺς τρόπους ὥστε πόλλ᾽ ὑφ᾽ ὑμῶν ἠδικημένοι, καὶ φύσει τῆς πρὸς ὑμᾶς ἔχθρας αὐτοῖς ὑπαρχούσης πατρικῆς, ὅμως οὐδ᾽ ὅσων ἂν τιμὴν καταθέντες δούλους κτήσωνται, οὐδὲ τούτους ὑβρίζειν ἀξιοῦσιν, ἀλλὰ νόμον δημοσίᾳ τὸν ταῦτα κωλύσοντα τέθεινται τουτονί, καὶ πολλοὺς ἤδη παραβάντας τὸν νόμον τοῦτον ἐζημιώκασι θανάτῳ," εἰ ταῦτ᾽ ἀκούσειαν καὶ συνεῖεν οἱ βάρβαροι, οὐκ ἂν

οἴεσθε δημοσίᾳ πάντας ὑμᾶς προξένους αὐτῶν ποιήσασθαι'; 'Suppose someone carried this law to the barbarous nations from whom we import our slaves; suppose he praised you and described your city to them in these words: "There are in Greece men so mild and humane in disposition that though they have often been wronged by you, and though they have inherited a natural hostility towards you, yet they permit no insult to be offered even to the men whom they have bought for a price and keep as their slaves. Nay, they have publicly established this law forbidding such insult, and they have already punished many of the transgressors with death." If the barbarians heard these words and understood their import, do you not think that they would unanimously appoint you their protectors?'

50. *Panegyr.*] Hume here seems to be inferring Isocrates's attitude towards the barbarians (which is contemptuous and denigratory) rather than reporting a statement of fact in the *Panegyricus*. However, see perhaps sect. CXXXI: 'ἐπεὶ καὶ τοῦτ' ἔχομεν αὐτοῖς ἐπιτιμᾶν, ὅτι τῇ μὲν αὑτῶν πόλει τοὺς ὁμόρους εἰλωτεύειν ἀναγκάζουσι, τῷ δὲ κοινῷ τῷ τῶν συμμάχων οὐδὲν τοιοῦτον κατασκευάζουσιν, ἐξὸν αὐτοῖς τὰ πρὸς ἡμᾶς διαλυσαμένοις ἅπαντας τοὺς βαρβάρους περιοίκους ὅλης τῆς Ἑλλάδος καταστῆσαι'; 'For we have reason to reproach the Lacedaemonians for this also, that in the interest of their own city they compel their neighbours to live in serfdom, but for the common advantage of their allies they refuse to bring about a similar condition, although it lies in their power to make up their quarrel with us and reduce all the barbarians to a state of subjection to the whole of Hellas.'

51. *sub fin.*] There is no relevant passage in Aristotle, *Politics*, VII.x, but cf. these passages from VII.ix and VII.xiii respectively: 'Τοὺς δὲ γεωργήσοντας μάλιστα μέν, εἰ δεῖ κατ' εὐχήν, δούλους εἶναι, μήτε ὁμοφύλων πάντων μήτε θυμοειδῶν (οὕτω γὰρ ἂν πρός τε τὴν ἐργασίαν εἶεν χρήσιμοι καὶ πρὸς τὸ μηδὲν νεωτερίζειν ἀσφαλεῖς), δεύτερον δὲ βαρβάρους περιοίκους παραπλησίους τοῖς εἰρημένοις τὴν φύσιν'; 'Those who are to cultivate the soil should best of all, if the ideal system is to be stated, be slaves, not drawn from people all of one tribe nor of a spirited character (for thus they would be both serviceable for their work and safe to abstain from insurrection), but as a second best they should be alien serfs of a similar nature'; 'διὸ σώφρονα τὴν πόλιν εἶναι προσήκει καὶ ἀνδρείαν καὶ καρτερικήν· κατὰ γὰρ τὴν παροιμίαν, οὐ σχολὴ δούλοις, οἱ δὲ μὴ δυνάμενοι κινδυνεύειν ἀνδρείως δοῦλοι τῶν ἐπιόντων εἰσίν'; 'Therefore it is proper for the state to be temperate, brave and enduring; since, as the proverb goes, there is no leisure for slaves, but people unable to face danger bravely are the slaves of their assailants.'

52. *δουλος*] Aristophanes, ΙΠΠΗΣ (*The Knights*), l. 17: 'ἀλλ' οὐκ ἔνι μοι τὸ θρέττε'; 'But I haven't got an inkling.' The comment of the scholiast means 'he speaks barbarously like a slave'.

53. *orat. 1*] Demosthenes, *ΚΑΤ' ΑΦΟΒΟΥ ΕΠΙΤΡΟΠΗΣ* (*Against Aphobus 1*), IX–XI. Hume draws particularly on IX–X: 'Δῆλον μὲν τοίνυν καὶ ἐκ τούτων ἐστὶ

τὸ πλῆθος τῆς οὐσίας. πεντεκαίδεκα ταλάντων γὰρ τρία τάλαντα τίμημα· ταύτην ἠξίουν εἰσφέρειν τὴν εἰσφοράν. ἔτι δ᾽ ἀκριβέστερον εἴσεσθε τὴν οὐσίαν αὐτὴν ἀκούσαντες. ὁ γὰρ πατήρ, ὦ ἄνδρες δικασταί, κατέλιπε δύ᾽ ἐργαστήρια τέχνης οὐ μικρᾶς ἑκάτερον, μαχαιροποιοὺς μὲν τριάκοντα καὶ δύ᾽ ἢ τρεῖς, ἀνὰ πέντε μνᾶς καὶ ἕξ, τοὺς δ᾽ οὐκ ἐλάττονος ἢ τριῶν μνῶν ἀξίους, ἀφ᾽ ὧν τριάκοντα μνᾶς ἀτελεῖς ἐλάμβανε τοῦ ἐνιαυτοῦ τὴν πρόσοδον, κλινοποιοὺς δ᾽ εἴκοσι τὸν ἀριθμόν, τετταράκοντα μνῶν ὑποκειμένους, οἳ δώδεκα μνᾶς ἀτελεῖς αὐτῷ προσέφερον, ἀργυρίου δ᾽ εἰς τάλαντον ἐπὶ δραχμῇ δεδανεισμένον, οὗ τόκος ἐγίγνετο τοῦ ἐνιαυτοῦ ἑκάστου πλεῖν ἢ ἑπτὰ μναῖ. καὶ ταῦτα μὲν ἐνεργὰ κατέλιπεν, ὡς καὶ αὐτοὶ οὗτοι ὁμολογήσουσιν· ὧν γίγνεται τοῦ μὲν ἀρχαίου κεφάλαιον τέτταρα τάλαντα καὶ πεντακισχίλιαι, τὸ δ᾽ ἔργον αὐτῶν πεντήκοντα μναῖ τοῦ ἐνιαυτοῦ ἑκάστου. χωρὶς δὲ τούτων ἐλέφαντα μὲν καὶ σίδηρον, ὃν κατειργάζοντο, καὶ ξύλα κλίνει· εἰς ὀγδοήκοντα μνᾶς ἄξια, κηκῖδα δὲ καὶ χαλκὸν ἑβδομήκοντα μνῶν ἐωνημένα, ἔτι δ᾽ οἰκίαν τρισχιλίων, ἔπιπλα δὲ καὶ ἐκπώματα καὶ χρυσία καὶ ἱμάτια, τὸν κόσμον τῆς μητρός, ἄξια σύμπαντα ταῦτ᾽ εἰς μυρίας δραχμάς, ἀργυρίου δ᾽ ἔνδον ὀγδοήκοντα μνᾶς᾽; 'From this evidence it is clear what the value of the property was. Three talents is the tax on an estate of fifteen, and this tax they saw fit to pay. But you will see this more clearly if you hear what the property was. My father, men of the jury, left two factories, both doing a large business. One was a sword-manufactory, employing thirty-two or thirty-three slaves, most of them worth five or six minae each and none worth less than three minae. From these my father received a clear income of thirty minae each year. The other was a sofa-manufactory, employing twenty slaves, given to my father as security for a debt of forty minae. These brought him in a clear income of twelve minae. In money he left as much as a talent, loaned at the rate of a drachma a month, the interest of which amounted to more than seven minae a year. This was the amount of productive capital which my father left, as these men will themselves admit, the principal amounting to four talents and five thousand drachmae, and the proceeds to fifty minae each year. Besides this, he left ivory and iron, used in the factory, and wood for sofas, worth about eighty minae; and gall and copper, which he had bought for seventy minae; furthermore, a house worth three thousand drachmae, and furniture and plate, and my mother's jewelry and apparel and ornaments, worth in all ten thousand drachmae, and in the house eighty minae in silver.'

54. *vita* CATONIS] Plutarch, *Lives*, 'Cato Major', XXI.i–ii.
55. *cap.* 43] Tacitus's account of the murder of Pedanius Secundus by one of his slaves is given in *Annals*, XIV.xlii–xlv. Hume refers to a passage in the speech given by the senator Gaius Cassius. However, he omits to mention that the execution of the sentence against Secundus's slaves raised great public discontent, that the emperor had to rebuke the people by edict, and that the slaves had to be marched to execution between lines of soldiers to hold back and control the angry mob.

56. *ever married*] Xenophon, *Oeconomicus*, IX.v: 'ἔδειξα δὲ καὶ τὴν γυναικωνῖτιν αὐτῇ, θύρᾳ βαλανωτῇ ὡρισμένην ἀπὸ τῆς ἀνδρωνίτιδος, ἵνα μήτε ἐκφέρηται ἔνδοθεν ὅ τι μὴ δεῖ μήτε τεκνοποιῶνται οἱ οἰκέται ἄνευ τῆς ἡμετέρας γνώμης. οἱ μὲν γὰρ χρηστοὶ παιδοποιησάμενοι εὐνούστεροι ὡς ἐπὶ τὸ πολύ, οἱ δὲ πονηροὶ συζυγέντες εὐπορώτεροι πρὸς τὸ κακουργεῖν γίγνονται'; 'I showed her the women's quarters too, separated by a bolted door from the men's, so that nothing that ought not to be moved may be taken out, and that the slaves may not breed without our permission. For honest slaves generally prove more loyal if they have produced children, while bad ones, if coupled, become all the more prone to mischief.'

57. *HELOTES*] i.e. the under-class of slaves in ancient Sparta.

58. *obolus*] A copper coin of small value (*OED*, 'obolus', *n.*, 2 b).

59. *family slaves*] Hume refers to Justus Lipsius, *Saturnalium Sermonum Libri Duo* (Antwerp, 1585), I.xiv, p. 57: 'de qua nihil dixerim, præter multiplices in iis ludis minutasque cellas fuisse, in queîs seorsim haberent singuli gladiatores'; 'concerning which I will say nothing, except that at these games there were many small cells, in which individual gladiators lived separately'.

60. *l. 220*] Hesiod, *Works and Days*, ll. 403–7: 'ἀλλά σ' ἄνωγαφράζεσθαι χρειῶν τε λύσιν λιμοῦ τ' ἀλεωρήν. οἶκον μὲν πρώτιστα γυναῖκά τε βοῦν τ' ἀροτῆρα, κτητήν, οὐ γαμετήν, ἥτις καὶ βουσὶν ἕποιτο'; 'I bid you take notice of how to clear your debts and how to ward off famine: a house first of all, a woman, and an ox for plowing – the woman one you purchase, not marry, one who can follow with the oxen.' Ibid., ll. 600–603: 'αὐτὰρ ἐπὴν δὴ πάντα βίον κατάθηαι ἐπάρμενον ἔνδοθι οἴκου, θῆτά τ' ἄοικον ποιεῖσθαι καὶ ἄτεκνον ἔριθον δίζησθαι κέλομαι'; 'When you have laid up all the means of life well prepared inside your house, then I bid you turn your hired man out of your house and look for a serving girl without her own child; for a serving girl with a baby under her flank is a difficult thing.'

61. *lib. viii*] Strabo, VIII.v.4: 'τρόπον γάρ τινα δημοσίους δούλους εἶχον οἱ Λακεδαιμόνιοι τούτους, κατοικίας τινὰς αὐτοῖς ἀποδείξαντες καὶ λειτουργίας ἰδίας'; 'for the Lacedaemonians held the Helots as state-slaves in a way, having assigned to them certain settlements to live in and special services to perform.'

62. *redituum*] Xenophon, *Ways and Means*, IV.xiv: 'πάλαι μὲν γὰρ δήπου οἷς μεμέληκεν ἀκηκόαμεν, ὅτι Νικίας ποτὲ ὁ Νικηράτου ἐκτήσατο ἐν τοῖς ἀργυρείοις χιλίους ἀνθρώπους, οὓς ἐκεῖνος Σωσίᾳ τῷ Θρακὶ ἐξεμίσθωσεν ἐφ' ᾧ ὀβολὸν μὲν ἀτελῆ ἑκάστου τῆς ἡμέρας ἀποδιδόναι, τὸν δ' ἀριθμὸν ἴσους ἀεὶ παρέχειν'; 'Those of us who have given thought to the matter have heard long ago, I imagine, that Nicias son of Niceratus, once owned a thousand men in the mines, and let them out to Socias the Thracian, on condition that Sosias paid him an obol a day per man net and filled all vacancies as they occurred.'

63. *epist. 80*] Cato, *De Re Rustica*, LVI: 'Familiae cibaria. Qui opus facient per hiemem tritici modios IIII, per aestatem modios IIII S, vilico, vilicae,

epistatae, opilioni modios III, conpeditis per hiemem panis P. IIII, ubi vineam fodere coeperint, panis P. V, usque adeo dum ficos esse coeperint, deinde ad P. IIII redito'; 'Rations for the hands: Four modii of wheat in winter, and in summer four and a half for the field hands. The overseer, the housekeeper, the foreman, and the shepherd should receive three. The chain-gang should have a ration of four pounds of bread through the winter, increasing to five when they begin to work the vines, and dropping back to four when the figs ripen.' Donatus, *In Phormion*, I.i.9: 'DE DEMENSO SVO de cibariis *suis*, hoc est quod sibi sit demensum, a metiendo'; 'concerning his ration, that is to say his victuals, that which was doled out to him by measure'. Seneca, *Epistulae*, LXXX.viii: 'servus est, quinque modios accipit et quinque denarios'; 'he is a slave, his wages are five measures of grain and five denarii.'

64. *cap. 10, 11*] Cato, *De Re Rustica*, X–XI: 'Quo modo oletum agri iugera CCXL instruere oporteat. Vilicum, vilicam, operarios quinque, bubulcos III, asinarium I, subulcum I, opilionem I, summa homines XIII . . . Quo modo vineae iugera C instruere oporteat. Vilicum, vilicam, operarios X, bubulcum I, asinarium I, salictarium I, subulcum I, summa homines XVI'; 'This is the proper equipment for an oliveyard of 240 iugera: An overseer, a housekeeper, 5 labourers, 3 teamsters, 1 muleteer, 1 swineherd, 1 shepherd – a total of 13 persons . . . This is the proper equipment for a vineyard of 100 iugera: An overseer, a housekeeper, 10 labourers, 1 teamster, 1 muleteer, 1 willow-worker, 1 swineherd – a total of 16 persons.'

65. *cap. 18*] Varro, *Rerum Rusticarum*, XVIII.iii: 'Horum neuter satis dilucide modulos reliquit nobis, quod Cato si voluit, debuit sic, ut pro portione ad maiorem fundum et minorem adderemus et demeremus. Praeterea extra familiam debuit dicere vilicum et vilicam. Neque enim, si minus CCXL iugera oliveti colas, non possis minus uno vilico habere, nec, si bis tanto ampliorem fundum aut eo plus colas, ideo duo vilici aut tres habendi'; 'Neither of these writers [Cato and Saserna] has left us a very clearly expressed rule. For if Cato wished to do this, he should have stated it in such a way that we add or subtract from the number proportionately as the farm is larger or smaller. Further, he should have named the overseer and the housekeeper outside of the number of slaves; for if you cultivate less than 240 iugera of olives you cannot get along with less than one overseer, nor if you cultivate twice as large a place or more will you have to keep two or three overseers.'

66. *in the family*] Varro, *Rerum Rusticarum*, I.xvii.5: 'Neque eiusdem nationis plures parandos esse; ex eo enim potissimum solere offensiones domesticas fieri'; 'Avoid having too many slaves of the same nation, for this is a fertile source of domestic quarrels.'

67. *cap. 17*] Varro, *Rerum Rusticarum*, XVII.v: 'Praefectos alacriores faciendum praemiis dandaque opera ut habeant peculium et coniunctas conservas, e quibus habeant filios. Eo enim fiunt firmiores ac coniunctiores fundo'; 'The

foremen are to be made more zealous by rewards, and care must be taken that they have a bit of property of their own, and mates from among their fellow-slaves to bear them children; for by this means they are made more steady and more attached to the place.'

68. *cap. 18*] Columella, *Rei Rusticae*, I.viii.5: 'Sed qualicumque vilico contubernalis mulier adsignanda est, quae et contineat eum et in quibusdam rebus tamen adiuvet'; 'But be the overseer what he may, he should be given a woman companion to keep him within bounds and yet in certain matters to be a help to him.'

69. *cap. 44*] Pliny the Elder, *Natural History*, XXXIII.vi.26: 'This is the progress achieved by our legions of slaves – a foreign rabble in one's home, so that an attendant to tell people's names now has to be employed even in the case of one's slaves.' Tacitus, *Annales*, XIV.xliv: 'Suspecta maioribus nostris fuerunt ingenia servorum, etiam cum in agris aut domibus isdem nascerentur caritatemque dominorum statim acciperent. Postquam vero nationes in familiis habemus, quibus diversi ritus, externa sacra aut nulla sunt, conluviem istam non nisi metu coercueris'; 'To our ancestors the temper of their slaves was always suspect, even when they were born on the same estate or under the same roof, and drew in affection for their owners with their earliest breath. But now that our households comprise nations – with customs the reverse of our own, with foreign cults or with none, you will never coerce such a medley of humanity except by terror.'

70. *cap. 10*] Varro, *Rerum Rusticarum*, II.x.6: 'Quod ad feturam humanam pertinet pastorum, qui in fundo perpetuo manent, facile est, quod habent conservam in villa, nec hac venus pastoralis longius quid quaerit. Qui autem in saltibus et silvestribus locis pascunt et non villa, sed casis repentinis imbres vitant, iis mulieres adiungere, quae sequantur greges ac cibaria pastoribus expediant eosque assiduiores faciant, utile arbitrati multi'; 'As to the breeding of herdsmen; it is a simple matter in the case of those who stay all the time on the farm, as they have a female fellow-slave in the steading, and the Venus of herdsmen looks no farther than this. But in the case of those who tend the herds in mountain valleys and wooded lands, and keep off the rains not by the roof of the steading but by makeshift huts, many have thought that it was advisable to send along women to follow the herds, prepare food for the herdsmen, and make them more diligent.'

71. *11. 151*] 'One is the son of a hardy shepherd; another of the neatsherd.'

72. *cap. 8*] Columella, *Rei Rusticae*, I.viii.19: 'Feminis quoque fecundioribus, quarum in subole certus numerus honorari debet, otium, nonnumquam et libertatem dedimus, cum complures natos educassent. Nam cui tres erant filii, vacatio, cui plures, libertas quoque contingebat'; 'To women, too, who are unusually prolific, and who ought to be rewarded for the bearing of a certain number of offspring, I have granted exemption from work and sometimes

even freedom after they had reared many children. For to a mother of three sons exemption from work was granted; to a mother of more her freedom as well.'

73. *the GRACCHI*] Cf. *THN*, II.ii.2, p. 222.

74. *servile war*] The three Servile Wars were slave revolts during the Roman republic. The first happened in Sicily from 135 to 132 BC, and was led by Eunus and Cleon. The second also took place in Sicily, from 104 to 100 BC, and was led by Athenion and Tryphon. The third took place in Italy from 73 to 71 BC, and was led by Spartacus. Hume's reference to 'Eunus and Athenio' suggests that he is conflating the first and second Servile Wars.

75. *CONSTANTINOPLE ... populous*] cf. *Lettres Persanes*, letter 114, on the forced importation of people into Constantinople: 'Constantinople et Ispahan sont les capitales des deux plus grands empires du Monde: c'est là que tout doit aboutir, et que les peuples, attirés de mille manières, se rendent de toutes parts. Cependant elles périssent d'elles-mêmes, et elles seraient bientôt détruites, si les souverains n'y faisaient venir, presque à chaque siècle, des nations entières pour les repeupler' (Montesquieu, *Œuvres*, p. 123). Cf. *Lettres Persanes*, letter 121, on the futility of this practice: 'Tous les transports de peuples faits à Constantinople n'ont jamais réussi' (Montesquieu, *Œuvres*, p. 126).

76. *Mons. MAILLET*] 'son commerce le plus considérable consiste en deux ou trois mille Noirs, qu'elle amene vendre en Egypte' (Maillet, *Description*, letter XIII, vol. II, p. 197). Wallace had also cited Maillet in support of his views (Wallace, *Dissertation*, pp. 49–51).

77. *lib. i*] Appian, *The Civil Wars*, I.vii: 'φερούσης ἅμα καὶ τῆσδε τῆς κτήσεως αὐτοῖς πολὺ κέρδος ἐκ πολυπαιδίας θεραπόντων ἀκινδύνως αὐξομένων διὰ τὰς ἀστρατείας'; 'At the same time the ownership of slaves brought them great gain from the multitude of their progeny, who increased because they were exempt from military service.'

78. *C. GRACCHI*] Plutarch, *Life of Tiberius Gracchus*, VIII.iii: 'ὥστε ταχὺ τὴν Ἰταλίαν ἅπασαν ὀλιγανδρίας ἐλευθέρων αἰσθέσθαι, δεσμωτηρίων δὲ βαρβαρικῶν ἐμπεπλῆσθαι, δι' ὧν ἐγεώργουν οἱ πλούσιοι τὰ χωρία τοὺς πολίτας ἐξελάσαντες'; 'soon all Italy was conscious of a dearth of freemen, and was filled with gangs of foreign slaves, by whose aid the rich cultivated their estates, from which they had driven away the free citizens.' The Greek phrase Hume quotes in the text is drawn from Plutarch, and means 'chained barbarians'.

79. *Lib. vii*] Seneca, *The Controversies*, V.v: 'it is for all this that country once ploughed by whole peoples belongs to single slave-farms and bailiffs have more power than kings.' Pliny, *Natural History*, XVIII.iv: 'But nowadays those agricultural operations are performed by slaves with fettered ankles and by the hands of malefactors with branded faces.' Martial, *Epigrams*, IX.xxii: 'and Tuscan fields clank with countless fettered slaves.' Lucan, *The Civil War*, I.167–70 and VII.402: 'Next they stretched wide the boundaries

of their lands, till those acres, which once were furrowed by the iron plough of Camillus and felt the spade of a Curius long ago, grew into vast estates tilled by foreign cultivators'; 'The cornfields of Italy are tilled by chained labourers.'

80. *cap. 19*] Florus, *Epitomae de Tito Livio*, II.vii.3–4: 'Terra frugum ferax et quodam modo suburbana provincia latifundiis civium Romanorum tenebatur. Hic ad cultum agri frequentia ergastula catenatique cultores materiam bello praebuere'; 'This land, so rich in corn, a province lying, as it were, at our very doors, was occupied by large estates in the possession of Roman citizens. The numerous prisons for slaves employed in tilling the soil and gangs of cultivators who worked in chains provided the forces for the war.'

81. *cap. 8*] Florus, *Epitomae de Tito Livio*, II.xviii.1: 'Sublatis percussoribus Caesaris supererat Pompei domus. Alter iuvenum in Hispania occiderat, alter fuga evaserat contractisque infelicis belli reliquiis, cum insuper ergastula armasset, Siciliam Sardiniamque habebat'; 'Though Caesar's assassins had been thus removed, Pompeius' family still survived. One of his young sons had fallen in Spain, but the other had escaped by flight, and after collecting the survivors of their unsuccessful war and also arming the slave-prisons, was holding Sicily and Sardinia.'

82. *Our modern convents ... commonly imagined*] cf. *Lettres Persanes*, letter 117, where Montesquieu had allowed his imagination to dwell on the suppressing effect on populations exerted by convents and monasteries: 'Ce métier de continence a anéanti plus d'hommes que les pestes et les guerres les plus sanglantes n'ont jamais fait. On voit dans chaque maison religieuse une famille éternelle, où il ne naît personne, et qui s'entretient aux dépens de toutes les autres. Ces maisons sont toujours ouvertes comme autant de gouffres où s'ensevelissent les races futures' (Montesquieu, *Œuvres*, p. 124).

83. *Were the land ... than the convent*] Adam Smith would follow Hume in deploring the wastefulness and frivolity of aristocratic expense: cf. Smith, *Wealth*, III.ii.7, pp. 385–6.

84. *exposing ... disapprobation*] Hume would also draw attention to this custom of antiquity in 'A Dialogue' (*ECPM*, p. 113).

85. *morib. Germ.*] Tacitus, *Germania*, XIX.v: 'numerum liberorum finire aut quemquam ex agnatis necare flagitium habetur'; 'to limit the number of their children, to make away with any of the later children is held abominable.' Hume makes a slight error here: the disapproval was felt by the Germans themselves, not the Roman historian.

86. *cap. 15*] Seneca, *De Ira*, I.xv.2: 'Num quis membra sua tunc odit, cum abscidit? Non est illa ira, sed misera curatio. Rabidos effligimus canes et trucem atque immansuetum bovem occidimus et morbidis pecoribus, ne gregem polluant, ferrum demittimus; portentosos fetus exstinguimus, liberos quoque, si debiles monstrosique editi sunt, mergimus'; 'Does a man hate the members of his own body when he uses the knife upon them? There

is no anger there, but the pitiful desire to heal. Mad dogs we knock on the head; the fierce and savage ox we slay; sickly sheep we put to the knife to keep them from infecting the flock; unnatural progeny we destroy; we drown even children who at birth are weakly and abnormal.' Hume does not provide an entirely accurate summary of what Plutarch says concerning Attalus and Eumenes. A rumour having spread of Eumenes's death, 'Attalus, therefore, the eldest of the king's brothers, an honourable man and more loyal to Eumenes than any of the others, not only took the crown and was proclaimed king, but also married his brother's wife, Stratonicê, and had intercourse with her. But when the news came that Eumenes was alive, and he himself was approaching, Attalus laid aside the crown, took his spears, as had been his custom before, and went with the other guardsmen to meet the king. And Eumenes not only cordially clasped his hand, but also embraced the queen, showing her honour and friendliness; and living a considerable time after his return, without giving a hint of blame or suspicion, he died, leaving to Attalus both his kingdom and his wife. And what did Attalus? When Eumenes was dead, he was unwilling to acknowledge as his own any of the children his wife had borne him, though they were many, but brought up and educated his brother's son and in his own life-time placed the crown upon his head and saluted him as king' (Plutarch, *Moralia*, 'On Brotherly Love', XVIII).

87. *cap.* 24] Sextus Empiricus, *Outlines of Pyrrhonism*, III.xxiv.211: 'ἀλλὰ καὶ τοὺς ἑαυτοῦ παῖδας ὁ Κρόνος ἀναιρεῖν ἔκρινεν, καὶ ὁ Σόλων Ἀθηναίοις τὸν περὶ τῶν ἀκρίτων νόμον ἔθετο, καθ᾽ ὃν φονεύειν ἑκάστῳ τὸν ἑαυτοῦ παῖδα ἐπέτρεψεν. παρ᾽ ἡμῖν δὲ τὸ τοὺς παῖδας φονεύειν ἀπαγορεύουσιν οἱ νόμοι'; 'Moreover, Cronos decided to destroy his own children, and Solon gave the Athenians the law "concerning things immune", by which he allowed each man to slay his own child; but with us the laws forbid the slaying of children.'

88. *CHINA . . . twenty*] cf. Du Halde's account of this Chinese custom: 'Cependant quelque sobre & quelque industrieux que soit le Peuple de la Chine, le grand nombre de ses Habitans y cause beaucoup de misere. On en voit de si pauvres, que ne pouvant fournir à leurs enfans les alimens nécessaires, ils les exposent dans les rues, sur tout lorsque les meres tombent malades, ou qu'elles manquent de lait pour les nourrir. Ces petits innocens sont condamnez en quelque maniere à la mort, presque au même instant qu'ils ont commencé de vivre: cela frappe dans les grandes Villes, comme *Peking*, *Canton*; car dans les autres Villes, à peine s'en apperçoit-on' (Du Halde, *Description*, vol. II, p. 73). Cf. a cancelled note in the 'Early Memoranda': 'Perhaps the Custom of allowing Parents to murder their Infant Children, tho barbarous, tends to render a State more populous, as in China. Many marry by that Inducement; & such is the [force of *inserted above the line*] natural Affection, that none make Use of that Privilege but in extreme Necessity.' (NLS MS 23159, item

14, p. 9; whole note struck through diagonally; cf. Mossner, 'Memoranda', p. 503). Jean-François Melon had also commented on the Chinese custom of infanticide: 'Puisqu'à la Chine il y a tant d'Habitans dans la misere, puisque le meurtre des Enfans y est autorisé, nous dison hardiment que les Chinois ont mal profité de quatre mille ans de paisible Monarchie . . .' (Melon, *Essai politique*, p. 387); as had Richard Cantillon: 'ils sont forcés de fair mourir plusieurs de leurs Enfans dès le berceau, lorsqu'ils ne se voient pas le moïen de les élever, n'en gardant que le nombre qu'ils peuvent nourrir' (Cantillon, *Essai*, p. 89). In *The Wealth of Nations* Adam Smith would also comment on this Chinese practice in terms similar to Hume's: 'Marriage is encouraged in China, not by the profitableness of children [as in the North American colonies], but by the liberty of destroying them. In all great towns several are every night exposed in the street, or drowned like puppies in the water. The performance of this horrid office is even said to be the avowed business by which some people earn their subsistence' (Smith, *Wealth*, p. 90, I.viii.24; cf. Smith, *Jurisprudence*, 'Report of 1762–63', III.80–81, p. 173, where the language is very similar, albeit with the addition of some anticlericalism aimed at the Jesuit missionaries). A similar observation would be made by Adam Ferguson: 'In China, the permission given to parents to kill or to expose their children, was probably meant as a relief from the burden of a numerous offspring. But notwithstanding what we hear of a practice so repugnant to the human heart, it has not, probably, the effects in restraining population, which it seems to threaten; but, like many other institutions, has an influence the reverse of what it seemed to portend. The parents marry with this means of relief in their view, and the children are saved' (Ferguson, *Civil Society*, p. 135). Francis Hutcheson had allowed that '*killing* of their Children . . . is perhaps practis'd, and allow'd from *Self-love*; but I can scarce think it passes for a good Action any where' (Hutcheson, *Inquiry*, p. 186). The alleged right of parents to expose or otherwise kill their children had played a role in late seventeenth-century political argument: see Locke, 'First Treatise', § 56–9 (Locke, *Two Treatises*, pp. 180–83).

89. *Hospitals for foundlings*] The charter establishing Coram's Hospital for foundling children in north London had been signed in 1739.

90. *It is computed . . . educate him*] cf. the note in the 'Early Memoranda': 'A ninth of the Children born in Paris sent to the Enfans Trouvés' (NLS MS 23159, item 14, p. 14; cf. Mossner, 'Memoranda', p. 506). In his *Confessions* (1782) Rousseau reveals that he sent all five of the children born to him by Thérèse Le Vasseur to the Hôpital des Enfants-Trouvés. Voltaire had discovered the fact, and disclosed it in 1764 (Robertson, *Enlightenment*, pp. 443–4).

91. *Before the encrease of the ROMAN power*] For Wallace, too, the rise of the Roman Empire had marked a watershed in the numbers of mankind, and

initiated the decline in population from which, in his opinion, Europe had still not recovered: 'the scarcity of people in later times seems to be not a little owing to the ruin of the antient governments by the *Roman* empire, and the havock the *Romans* made among the smaller states and cities, before they could fully establish their sovereign power'; 'Thus instead of growing more populous, the world declined under the *Roman* yoke, till by the inroads and conquests of the *Goths,* and other barbarous and uncivilized nations, ignorant of industry and agriculture, it was still more miserably distressed. And, by an almost total ruin of antient manners and customs, and the introduction of others, not so well calculated for the increase and improvement of society, the necessary consequence of these inroads, the western parts of the world, which had been well cultivated in antient times, were greatly reduced, and have never been able to regain their antient strength and splendor'; 'the countries we have chiefly in view must have been best peopled ... about the time of *Alexander the Great,* and before the *Roman* empire had enslaved the world' (Wallace, *Dissertation,* pp. 106, 111 and 147).

92. *amore prolis*] Plutarch, *Moralia,* 'On Affection for Offspring', V: 'οἱ μὲν γὰρ πένητες οὐ τρέφουσι τέκνα, φοβούμενοι μὴ χεῖρον ἢ προσήκει τραφέντα δουλοπρεπῆ καὶ ἀπαίδευτα καὶ τῶν καλῶν πάντων ἐνδεᾶ γένηται· τὴν γὰρ πενίαν ἔσχατον ἡγούμενοι κακὸν οὐχ ὑπομένουσι μεταδοῦναι τέκνοις ὥσπερ τινὸς χαλεποῦ καὶ μεγάλου νοσήματος'; 'For when poor men do not rear their children it is because they fear that if they are educated less well than is befitting they will become servile and boorish and destitute of all the virtues; since they consider poverty the worst of evils, they cannot endure to let their children share it with them, as though it were a kind of disease, serious and grievous.'

93. *Enormous cities ... provisions*] cf. 'the exorbitant power and over-grown empire of the *Romans,* as well as the means employed to raise both to so prodigious an height, contributed greatly to the ruin of the world. Indeed this must always be the consequence of too extensive governments'; 'In consequence of this [the growth of empire], great tracts of land being left uncultivated every where; food, and all the necessaries of life, became scarce and dear' (Wallace, *Dissertation,* pp. 114 and 116). Cf. Montesquieu, *Esprit,* book XXIII, chapter 19 and Wallace, *Dissertation,* pp. 249 and particularly 327, where the phrasing is very close to Hume's.

94. *Where each man ... mankind!*] An unexpectedly Rousseauvian passage; in general, Hume is more likely to praise urban refinement than rustic simplicity. Cf. below, p. 463 and n. 199 for similar sentiments and parallel passages in Wallace's *Dissertation.* Adam Ferguson would be struck by this passage, and quoted it (with slight inaccuracy) in his *History of Civil Society* (Ferguson, *Civil Society,* p. 136).

95. *double ... every generation*] See above, p. 97, n. 17.

96. *each soldier . . . four*] cf. the note in the 'Early Memoranda': 'The antient common Soldiers of much better Rank (being Freemen) than the Moderns . . . The Captains got only double pay to the common Soldiers: the Colonels 4 times.' (NLS MS 23159, item 14, p. 24; cf. Mossner, 'Memoranda', pp. 514–15).

97. *ambassadors . . . ambassador*] cf. the note in the 'Early Memoranda': 'The ten Ambassadors sent by Athens to Philip had 1000 Drachmas of Allowance for 6 Months, which Demosthenes calls a considerable Sum περι παραπρεσβειας' (NLS MS 23159, item 14, p. 26; cf. Mossner, 'Memoranda', p. 516).

98. *sometimes two*] cf. the note in the 'Early Memoranda': 'The Athenians gave 2 Drahmas a day to all their Soldiers at the Beginning of the Peloponisian War' (NLS MS 23159, item 14, p. 26; cf. Mossner, 'Memoranda', p. 516).

99. *a drachma . . . foot-soldier*] cf. the note in the 'Early Memoranda': 'Cicero speaks as if Money were not ~~so~~ [in such *inserted above the line*] Plenty in Alexander's Time as in his own; especially at Athens. Yet the common Soldiers Pay from the Athenians was a Groat a day' (NLS MS 23159, item 14, p. 16; cf. Mossner, 'Memoranda', p. 508).

100. *lib. vii*] Xenophon, *Anabasis*, VII.vi.1: 'Ἐν τούτῳ τῷ χρόνῳ σχεδὸν ἤδη δύο μηνῶν ὄντων ἀφικνεῖται Χαρμῖνός τε ὁ Λάκων καὶ Πολύνικος παρὰ Θίβρωνος, καὶ λέγουσιν ὅτι Λακεδαιμονίοις δοκεῖ στρατεύεσθαι ὡς ἐπὶ Τισσαφέρνη, καὶ Θίβρων ἐκπέπλευκεν ὡς πολεμήσων, καὶ δεῖται ταύτης τῆς στρατιᾶς καὶ λέγει ὅτι δαρεικὸς ἑκάστῳ ἔσται μισθὸς τοῦ μηνός, καὶ τοῖς λοχαγοῖς διμοιρία, τοῖς δὲ στρατηγοῖς τετραμοιρία'; 'At this time, when nearly two months had already passed, Charminus the Laconian and Polynicus arrived on a mission from Thibron: they said that the Lacedaemonians had resolved to undertake a campaign against Tissaphernes, that Thibron had set sail to wage the war, and that he wanted this army; also that he said the pay would be a daric per month for every man, twice as much for the captains, and four times as much for the generals.'

101. *considerable sum*] Demosthenes, *De Falsa Legatione*, sect. CLVIII: 'καὶ χιλίας λαβόντες δραχμὰς ἐφόδιον παρ᾽ ὑμῶν'; 'and received from you a thousand drachmas for journey-money'. Demosthenes does not explicitly refer to this as a considerable sum, but the implication that he so regarded it is perhaps sufficiently clear.

102. *lib. iii*] Thucydides, III.xvii.4: 'τήν τε γὰρ Ποτίδαιαν δίδραχμοι ὁπλῖται ἐφρούρουν (αὑτῷ γὰρ καὶ ὑπηρέτῃ δραχμὴν ἐλάμβανε τῆς ἡμέρας), τρισχίλιοι μὲν οἱ πρῶτοι, ὧν οὐκ ἐλάσσους διεπολιόρκησαν, ἑξακόσιοι δὲ καὶ χίλιοι μετὰ Φορμίωνος, οἳ προαπῆλθον'; 'For in the siege of Potidaea the hoplite received a wage of two drachmas a day, one for himself and one for his attendant; and there were at first three thousand of these, and the number was not less than this throughout the siege, besides sixteen hundred who came with Phormio, but went away before the siege was over.'

103. *cap. 37*] Polybius, VI.xxxix.12: 'Ὀψώνιον δ᾽ οἱ μὲν πεζοὶ λαμβάνουσι τῆς ἡμέρας δύ᾽ ὀβολούς, οἱ δὲ ταξίαρχοι διπλοῦν, οἱ δ᾽ ἱππεῖς δραχμήν'; 'As pay the foot soldier receives two obols a day, a centurion twice as much, and a cavalry soldier a drachma.'

104. *alibi passim*] Livy, XL.vii.3 and XL.xiii.7–8: 'Militibus denarios quinos vicenos, duplex centurioni, triplex equiti ambo diviserunt'; 'Both distributed as donatives twenty-five denarii each to the infantry, twice that sum to centurions, and thrice to the cavalry'; 'Militibus in singulos quini deni denarii dati, duplex centurioni, triplex equiti'; 'Each of the infantry received fifteen denarii, the centurions twice, the cavalry each thrice that sum.'

105. *EUROPE ... great monarchies*] Note, however, the positive evaluation of modern monarchies that Hume has put forward in 'Of Civil Liberty': 'though all kinds of government be improved in modern times, yet monarchical government seems to have made the greatest advances towards perfection. It may now be affirmed of civilized monarchies, what was formerly said in praise of republics alone, *that they are a government of Laws, not of Men.* They are found susceptible of order, method, and constancy, to a surprizing degree. Property is there secure; industry encouraged; the arts flourish; and the prince lives secure among his subjects, like a father among his children' (above, vol. 1, p. 81).

106. *absolute princes ... their forces*] During his travels through Germany in 1748 Hume had seen a number of such small states, and had commented on their luxury, albeit less censoriously: 'We have bestow'd half a day in visiting his [the Archbishop of Cologne's] Palace, which is an extensive magnificent Building; & he is certainly the best lodg'd Prince in Europe except the King of France. For besides this Palace, & a sort of Maison de Plaisance near it (the most elegant thing in the World), he has also two Country Houses very magnificent' (*Letters*, vol. I, p. 120); 'Wurtzburgh is a very well-built Town, situated in a fine Valley on the Maine. The Banks of the River are very high and cover'd with Vines. The River runs thro the Town, and is past on a very handsome Bridge. But what renders this Town chiefly remarkable is a Building which surprizd us all, because we had never before heard of it, & did not there expect to meet with such a thing. Tis a prodigious magnificent Palace [i.e. the Residenz] of the Bishop, who is the Sovereign. Tis all of hewn Stone and of the richest Architecture. I do think the King of France has not such a House. If it be less than Versailles, tis more compleat & finish'd. What a surprizing thing it is, that these petty Princes can build such Palaces? But it has been fifty Years a rearing; & tis the chief Expence of Eclesiastics' (*Letters*, vol. I, p. 124). The Prince-bishop of Würzburg was the absolute ruler of the ecclesiastical principality of Würzburg. Construction of the Residenz, which was indeed intended to rival Versailles, had in fact been completed in only twenty five years, between 1719 and 1744.

107. *enlisting themselves*] The following passages from chapter 6 of Stanyan's *Account*, 'Of the People and Dispositions', are relevant: 'The Country is extremely Populous, and the Women the most fertile, I believe, of any in *Europe*. One generally finds Nine or Ten Children in a Family, and sometimes double the Number. Nay there are Men in more than one Canton now alive, who have above an hundred Persons of both Sexes, descended from their Loyns'; 'It is a general Charge against the *Switzers*, that they traffick with Men as with other Merchandize, and sell their Troops to those who will pay best for them, without considering the Merits of the Cause they are to fight for. This is a received Opinion in the World . . .' (Stanyan, *Switzerland*, pp. 143 and 131). Jean-François Melon, whose *Essai politique sur le commerce* Hume would cite in 'Of Commerce', may also have contributed to this observation: 'Les Suisses, avec une bonne Police pour l'augmentation des habitans, ont si peu de terrain, que leur industrie laborieuse ne suffit pas encore pour les nourrir; mais l'Europe ne se trouve plus dans les mêmes circonstances de conquête. Leur voisinage entouré de forteresses les réduit à devenir troupes mercenaires, & à faire la guerre pour le compte d'autrui, sans pouvoir esperer d'augmenter leur terrain . . .' (Melon, *Essai politique*, pp. 34–5). Cf. *Gulliver's Travels*, Part IV, chapter 5: 'There is likewise a Kind of beggarly Princes in *Europe*, not able to make War by themselves, who hire out their Troops to richer Nations for so much a Day to each Man; of which they keep three Fourths to themselves, and it is the best Part of their Maintenance; such are those in many *Northern* Parts of *Europe*' (Swift, *Gulliver's Travels*, p. 365).

108. *SWISSERLAND . . . political institutions*] Hume may again (see above, p. 350, n. 40) be drawing his information from Abraham Stanyan's *An Account of Switzerland* (1714): 'Their Country is crowded with People, which generally make the Riches of other Nations, but for want of Trade, increase the Poverty of this' (Stanyan, *Switzerland*, p. 156); 'We find by Experience in *Holland*, that a Country, tho' it have neither good Havens, nor abound in native Commodities proper for Exportation, may yet drive a prodigious Trade, provided there be great Numbers of Inhabitants employed in Manufactures, and that the Carriage and Transportation of them be cheap and easie. But it is not to be expected, that a Country like this [i.e. Switzerland], should flourish by Trade, that is situated out of the reach of the Sea, and among Mountains passable only by Mules, to Transport their Commodities. So that the Unhappiness of their Situation, and the Difficulty and Expence of Land-Carriage, together with the want of native Commodities to export, or of Industry in the Inhabitants, to supply that Defect by establishing Manufactures, are so many powerful Reasons, that have concurred to discourage Trade in this Country. For it is certain, there is no where so small an Appearance of it as here; and that they think so little of enriching themselves that way, that they are contented to buy of their Neighbours all the Conveniencies, and most of

the Necessaries of Life' (Stanyan, *Switzerland*, pp. 172–3). On the political institutions of the Swiss, see chapter 4 of Stanyan's *Account* (Stanyan, *Switzerland*, pp. 69–114); a text which is also of relevance to Hume's 'Idea of a Perfect Commonwealth' (above, pp. 196–208).

109. *lib. iv*] Appian, *Civil Wars*, IV.xvi.120: 'καὶ τῆς τοιαύτης δ᾿ ὅμως ζημίας ὑμῖν ἕνεκα ἐπιδώσομεν νικητήρια, δραχμὰς ἑκάστῳ στρατιώτῃ πεντακισχιλίας, λοχαγῷ δὲ πεντάκις τοσαύτας, χιλιάρχῃ δὲ τὸ διπλάσιον τοῦ λοχαγοῦ'; 'However, as compensation even for this loss we will give you an additional reward of 5000 drachmas for each soldier, five times as much to each centurion, and twice the latter sum to each tribune.'

110. *in the army*] Caesar, *Gallic War*, VIII.iv: 'Caesar militibus pro tanto labore ac patientia, qui brumalibus diebus itineribus difficillimis, frigoribus intolerandis studiosissime permanserant in labore, ducenos sestertios, centurionibus tot milia nummum praedae nomine condonanda pollicetur legionibusque in hiberna remissis ipse se recipit die xxxx Bibracte'; 'In spite of winter days, the most difficult of marches, and cold weather beyond endurance, the troops had stuck most zealously to their work, and in reward for such effort and hardship Caesar promised them two hundred sesterces apiece, and as many thousand to each centurion, as a free gift in lieu of booty. Then he sent the legions back to cantonments, and himself returned on the fortieth day to Bibracte.' A cartel is a written agreement relating to the exchange or ransom of prisoners (*OED*, 'cartel', *n.*, 3 a).

111. *lib. iii*] Diodorus Siculus, XII.lix.4–5: 'Τραχίνιοι πρὸς Οἰταίους ὁμόρους ὄντας ἔτη πολλὰ διεπολέμουν καὶ τοὺς πλείους τῶν πολιτῶν ἀπέβαλον. ἐρήμου δ᾿ οὔσης τῆς πόλεως ἠξίωσαν Λακεδαιμονίους ὄντας ἀποίκους ἐπιμεληθῆναι τῆς πόλεως. οἱ δὲ καὶ διὰ τὴν συγγένειαν καὶ διὰ τὸ τὸν Ἡρακλέα, πρόγονον ἑαυτῶν ὄντα, ἐγκατῳκηκέναι κατὰ τοὺς ἀρχαίους χρόνους ἐν τῇ Τραχῖνι, ἔγνωσαν μεγάλην αὐτὴν ποιῆσαι πόλιν. διὸ καὶ Λακεδαιμονίων μὲν καὶ τῶν Πελοποννησίων τετρακισχιλίους οἰκήτορας ἐκπεμψάντων, καὶ παρὰ τῶν ἄλλων Ἑλλήνων τοὺς βουλομένους μετέχειν τῆς ἀποικίας προσεδέξαντο· οὗτοι δ᾿ ἦσαν οὐκ ἐλάττους τῶν ἑξακισχιλίων. διὸ καὶ τὴν Τραχῖνα μυρίανδρον ποιήσαντες, καὶ τὴν χώραν κατακληρουχήσαντες, ὠνόμασαν τὴν πόλιν Ἡράκλειαν'; 'The Trachinians had been at war with the neighbouring Oetaeans for many years and had lost the larger number of their citizens. Since the city was deserted, they thought it proper that the Lacedaemonians, who were colonists from Trachis, should assume the care of it. And the Lacedaemonians, both because of their kinship and because Heracles, their ancestor, in ancient times had made his home in Trachis, decided to make it a great city. Consequently the Lacedaemonians and the Peloponnesians sent forth four thousand colonists and accepted any other Greeks who wished to have a part in the colony; the latter numbered not less than six thousand. The result was that they made Trachis a city of ten thousand inhabitants, and after portioning out

the territory in allotments they named the city Heracleia.' Thucydides, III. xcii.2–4: Ὑπὸ δὲ τὸν χρόνον τοῦτον Λακεδαιμόνιοι Ἡράκλειαν τὴν ἐν Τραχινίᾳ ἀποικίαν καθίσταντο ἀπὸ τοιᾶσδε γνώμης. Μηλιῆς οἱ ξύμπαντες εἰσὶ μὲν τρία μέρη, Παράλιοι, Ἱερῆς, Τραχίνιοι· τούτων δὲ οἱ Τραχίνιοι πολέμῳ ἐφθαρμένοι ὑπὸ Οἰταίων ὁμόρων ὄντων, τὸ πρῶτον μελλήσαντες Ἀθηναίοις προσθεῖναι σφᾶς αὐτούς, δείσαντες δὲ μὴ οὐ σφίσι πιστοὶ ὦσι, πέμπουσιν ἐς Λακεδαίμονα ἑλόμενοι πρεσβευτὴν Τεισαμενόν. ξυνεπρεσβεύοντο δὲ αὐτοῖς καὶ Δωριῆς, ἡ μητρόπολις τῶν Λακεδαιμονίων, τῶν αὐτῶν δεόμενοι· ὑπὸ γὰρ τῶν Οἰταίων καὶ αὐτοὶ ἐφθείροντο. ἀκούσαντες δὲ οἱ Λακεδαιμόνιοι γνώμην εἶχον τὴν ἀποικίαν ἐκπέμπειν, τοῖς τε Τραχινίοις βουλόμενοι καὶ τοῖς Δωριεῦσι τιμωρεῖν. καὶ ἅμα τοῦ πρὸς Ἀθηναίους πολέμου καλῶς αὐτοῖς ἐδόκει ἡ πόλις καθίστασθαι· ἐπί τε γὰρ τῇ Εὐβοίᾳ ναυτικὸν παρασκευασθῆναι ἄν, ὥστ᾽ ἐκ βραχέος τὴν διάβασιν γίγνεσθαι, τῆς τε ἐπὶ Θρᾴκης παρόδου χρησίμως ἕξειν. τό τε ξύμπαν ὥρμηντο τὸ χωρίον κτίζειν'; 'It was about this time that the Lacedaemonians established Heracleia, their colony in Tra- chinia, with the following object in view. The people of Malia, considered as a whole, consist of three divisions, Paralians, Hiereans, and Trachinians. Of these the Trachinians, after they had been ruined in war by their neigh- bours the Oetaeans, at first intended to attach themselves to the Athenians, but, fearing that these might not be loyal, sent to Lacedaemon, choosing Teisamenus as their envoy. And envoys from Doris, the mother city of the Lacedaemonians, also took part in the embassy, making the same request, for they too were being ruined by the Oetaeans. After hearing their appeal, the Lacedaemonians were of the opinion that they should send out the colony, wishing to aid both the Trachinians and the Dorians. At the same time, the site of the proposed city seemed to them well adapted for carrying on the war against Athens; for a fleet could be equipped there for an attack upon Euboea and the crossing thus made from a short distance away, and the place would also be useful for expeditions along the coast towards Thrace. In short, they were eager to found the settlement.'

112. *lib. xvi*] Diodorus Siculus, XVI.lxxxii.5: 'κηρύξαντος δ᾽ αὐτοῦ κατὰ τὴν Ἑλλάδα διότι Συρακόσιοι διδόασι χώραν καὶ οἰκίας τοῖς βουλομένοις μετέχειν τῆς ἐν Συρακούσσαις πολιτείας πολλοὶ πρὸς τὴν κληρουχίαν Ἕλληνες ἀπήντησαν· τέλος δὲ οἰκήτορες ἀπεδείχθησαν εἰς μὲν τὴν Συρακοσίαν τὴν ἀδιαίρετον τετρακισμύριοι, εἰς δὲ τὴν Ἀγυριναίαν μύριοι διὰ τὸ μέγεθος καὶ κάλλος τῆς χώρας'; 'He [Timoleon] made proclamation in Greece that the Syracusans would give land and houses to those who wished to come and share in their state, and many Greeks came to receive their allotments. Ultimately forty thousand settlers were assigned to the vacant land of Syracuse and ten thousand to that of Agyrium, because of its extent and quality.'

113. *TIMOL.*] Plutarch, *Life of Timoleon*, XXIII.vi: 'ἤδη δὲ καὶ τῶν ἐξ Ἰταλίας καὶ Σικελίας πολλοὶ τῷ Τιμολέοντι συνεληλύθεισαν· καὶ γενομένοις αὐτοῖς ἑξακισμυρίοις τὸ πλῆθος, ὡς Ἄθανις εἴρηκε, τὴν μὲν χώραν διένειμε'; 'But by

this time many also from Italy and Sicily had flocked to Timoleon; and when their numbers had risen to sixty thousand, as Athanis states, Timoleon divided the land among them.'

114. *disadvantages*] cf. the note in the 'Early Memoranda': 'Tis probable that the Roman Empire ~~was~~ & even Italy was not so well peopled as Europe at present, because Pertinax by an Edict gave the waste Lands to the first Occupier, with Immunities Herodian. Lib 2. C.15' (NLS MS 23159, item 14, p. 23; cf. Mossner, 'Memoranda', p. 514).

115. *correcting all hasty and violent determinations*] On Hume's stance of sceptical reserve, and its moral salutariness as well as the polemical advantages it confers, see above, pp. 419-20, n. 15.

116. *perpetual war*] On the permanent war-footing of the ancient republics, see 'Of Commerce' (above, pp. 3-14).

117. *The maxims . . . invade*] cf. Wallace's comments on the likely consequences of the low moral character of modern European soldiery, on which point he agrees with Hume: Wallace, *Dissertation*, p. 95.

118. *deceitfulness . . . political reasonings*] On the deceptiveness of political appearances, cf. the opening paragraph of 'Of Civil Liberty' (above, vol. 1, pp. 76-7).

119. *rencounters*] Encounters or engagements between two opposing military forces; a battle, a skirmish (*OED*, 'rencounter', *n*., 1a).

120. *The long thin lines . . . sound and entire*] Wallace would deny this characterization of the less destructive nature of modern warfare: 'antient wars were not near so destructive as those in modern times' (Wallace, *Dissertation*, p. 226). Note, however, Hume's disparagement in 'Of Refinement in the Arts' of the bloodless 'battles' fought by Italian mercenaries (above, p. 20).

121. *Instances . . . upon the enemy*] Hume may be thinking of the sieges of Saguntum by the Carthaginians in 219 BC and of Masada by the Romans in AD 73-74, which were both marked by such acts of desperate and suicidal courage on the part of the besieged. Cf. Adam Ferguson on the generous despair of defeated barbarians: 'In their wars they preferred death to captivity. The victorious armies of the Romans, in entering a town by assault, or inforcing an incampment, have found the mother in the act of destroying her children, that they might not be taken; and the dagger of the parent, red with the blood of his family, ready to be plunged at last into his own breast' (Ferguson, *Civil Society*, p. 105). Hume has remarked on the tendency of the ancient Spaniards to commit mass suicide in defeat in 'Of National Characters' (above, p. 163).

122. *cap. 44*] Hume refers to Tacitus's explanation for the carnage after the battle of Bedriacum in AD 69: 'Et media acie perrupta fugere passim Othoniani, Bedriacum petentes. Immensum id spatium, obstructae strage corporum viae, quo plus caedis fuit; neque enim civilibus bellis capti in praedam vertuntur'; 'The Othonians' centre was now broken and they fled in disorder,

making for Bedriacum. The distance to be covered was vast; the roads were blocked with dead, and so the carnage was greater: for in civil wars captives are not turned to profit' (Tacitus, *Histories*, II.xliv).

123. *lib. iv*] Livy, XXXI.xvii.4–5 and xviii.6: 'Quibus cum Philippus nihil pacati nisi omnia permittentibus respondisset, adeo renuntiata haec legatio ab indignatione simul ac desperatione iram accendit ut ad Saguntinam rabiem ... tanta enim rabies multitudinem invasit ut proditos rati qui pugnantes mortem occubuissent, periuriumque alius alii exprobrantes et sacerdotibus maxime, qui quos ad mortem devovissent, eorum deditionem vivorum hosti fecissent, repente omnes ad caedem coniugum liberorumque discurrerent seque ipsi per omnes vias leti interficerent'; 'Philip's reply to them was that no terms were acceptable short of unconditional surrender, and when the results of the delegation were brought back to the people of Abydus indignation and despair roused them to such fury that they resorted to action as insane as that witnessed at Saguntum. . . . Such fury gripped the population of Abydus that, thinking the men who had fallen in battle had been betrayed, they accused each other of perjury, and above all accused the priests, who had delivered alive to the enemy those whom they had by sacred oath marked out for death. They all suddenly ran off to butcher their wives and children and then committed suicide themselves, seeking every possible path to death.' Polybius, XVI.xxxiv.9–12: 'θεωρῶν δὲ τὸ πλῆθος καὶ τὴν ὁρμὴν τῶν σφᾶς αὐτοὺς καὶ τὰ τέκνα καὶ τὰς γυναῖκας ἀποσφαττόντων, κατακαόντων, ἀπαγχόντων, εἰς τὰ φρέατα ῥιπτούντων, κατακρημνιζόντων ἀπὸ τῶν τεγῶν, ἐκπλαγὴς ἦν, καὶ διαλγῶν ἐπὶ τοῖς γινομένοις παρήγγειλε διότι τρεῖς ἡμέρας ἀναστροφὴν δίδωσι τοῖς βουλομένοις ἀπάγχεσθαι καὶ σφάττειν αὑτούς. οἱ δ' Ἀβυδηνοί, προδιειληφότες ὑπὲρ αὑτῶν κατὰ τὴν ἐξ ἀρχῆς στάσιν, καὶ νομίζοντες οἷον εἰ προδόται γίνεσθαι τῶν ὑπὲρ τῆς πατρίδος ἠγωνισμένων καὶ τεθνεώτων, οὐδαμῶς ὑπέμενον τὸ ζῆν, ὅσοι μὴ δεσμοῖς ἢ τοιαύταις ἀνάγκαις προκατελήφθησαν· οἱ δὲ λοιποὶ πάντες ὥρμων ἀμελλήτως κατὰ συγγενείας ἐπὶ τὸν θάνατον'; 'But when he saw the number and the fury of those who destroyed themselves and their women and children, either by cutting their throats, or by burning or by hanging or by throwing themselves into wells or off the roofs, he was amazed, and grieving much thereat announced that he granted a respite of three days to those who wished to hang themselves and cut their throats. The Abydenes, maintaining the resolve they had originally formed concerning themselves, and regarding themselves as almost traitors to those who had fought and died for their country, by no means consented to live except those of them whose hands had been stayed by fetters or such forcible means, all the rest of them rushing without hesitation in whole families to their death.' Appian, *Civil Wars*, IV.x.80: 'Ἀλούσης δὲ τῆς πόλεως οἱ Ξάνθιοι ἐς τὰς οἰκίας συνέτρεχον καὶ τὰ φίλτατα σφῶν κατέκαινον, ἑκόντα τὴν σφαγὴν ὑπέχοντα'; 'When the

city was taken the Xanthians ran to their houses and killed those dearest to them, all of whom willingly offered themselves to the slaughter.'

124. *ARATI*] Plutarch, *Life of Aratus*, VI.i: ʿΗ μὲν οὖν τῶν ὅπλων παρασκευὴ συνήθης ἦν, πάντων, ὡς ἔπος εἰπεῖν, τότε κλωπείαις χρωμένων καὶ καταδρομαῖς ἐπ᾽ ἀλλήλους·'; 'Now the laying in of arms was nothing unusual, since almost everybody at that time indulged in robberies and predatory forays.'

125. *twelve tables*] The foundational codification of Roman law, promulgated in 449 BC.

126. *police*] See above, vol. 1, p. 285, n. 36.

127. *TARTARS*] On the restless way of life of the Tartars, or Scythians, see Gibbon, *Decline and Fall*, vol. I, pp. 1025–32.

128. *cartel*] See above, p. 442, n. 110.

129. *amongst religious parties alone*] cf. 'Of Parties in General': 'the same principles of priestly government continuing, after Christianity became the established religion, they have engendered a spirit of persecution, which has ever since been the poison of human society, and the source of the most inveterate factions in every government' (above, vol. 1, pp. 57–8); but see the whole section from which the quotation is taken, ibid). Hume would revert to the violent intolerance of monotheistical religions in *The Natural History of Religion* (1757), section 9: 'few corruptions of idolatry and polytheism are more pernicious to society than this corruption of theism, when carried to the utmost height. The human sacrifices of the CARTHAGINIANS, MEXICANS, and many barbarous nations, scarcely exceed the inquisition and persecutions of ROME and MADRID. For besides, that the effusion of blood may not be so great in the former case as in the latter; besides this, I say, the human victims, being chosen by lot, or by some exterior signs, affect not, in so considerable a degree, the rest of society. Whereas virtue, knowledge, love of liberty, are the qualities, which call down the fatal vigilance of inquisitors; and when expelled, leave the society in the most shameful ignorance, corruption, and bondage' (*NHR*, p. 62). Cf. the note in the 'Early Memoranda': 'About. 100.000 [Moors *inserted above the line*] condemnd for Apostacy by the Inquisition in 40 Years, 4000 burnt' (NLS MS 23159, item 14, p. 16; cf. Mossner, 'Memoranda', p. 508).

130. *cap. 6*] Justinian, *Institutes*, II.vi: 'Iure civili constitutum fuerat, ut, qui bona fide ab eo, qui dominus non erat, cum crediderit, eum dominum esse, rem emerit vel ex donatione aliave qua iusta causa acceperit, is eam rem, si mobilis erat, anno ubique, si immobilis, biennio tantum in Italico solo usucapiat, ne rerum dominia in incerto essent. et cum hoc placitum erat, putantibus antiquioribus dominis sufficere ad inquirendas res suas praefata tempora, nobis melior sententia resedit, ne domini maturius suis rebus defraudentur neque certo loco beneficium hoc concludatur. et ideo constitutionem super hoc promulgavimus, qua cautum est, ut res quidem mobiles per triennium

usucapiantur, immobiles vero per longi temporis possessionem, id est inter praesentes decennio, inter absentes viginit annis usucapiantur, et his modis non solum in Italia, sed in omni terra quae nostro imperio gubernatur, dominium rerum iusta causa possessionis praecedente adquiratur'; 'By the civil law it was provided, that if anyone by purchase, gift, or any other legal means, had bona fide received a thing from a person who was not the owner, but whom he thought to be so, he should acquire this thing by use if he held it for one year, if it were moveable, wherever it might be, or for two years, if it were an immoveable, but this if it were in the solum Italicum; the object of this provision being to prevent the ownership of things remaining in uncertainty. Such was the decision of the ancients, who thought the times we have mentioned sufficient for owners to search for their property, but we have come to a much better decision, from a wish to prevent owners being despoiled of their property too quickly, and to prevent the benefit of this mode of acquisition being confined to any particular locality. We have, accordingly, published a constitutio providing that movables be acquired by a usus extending for three years, and immovables by the "possession of long time", that is, ten years for persons present, and twenty years for persons absent; and that by these means, provided a just cause of possession precede, the ownership of things may be acquired, not only in Italy, but in every country subject to our empire.'

131. *lib. xx*] Diodorus Siculus, XX.lxxxiv.6: 'καὶ τῶν αἰχμαλώτων τὰ δυνάμενα δοῦναι λύτρον παρεκόμιζον εἰς τὴν πόλιν· συνέθεντο γὰρ οἱ Ῥόδιοι πρὸς τὸν Δημήτριον ὥστε ἀλλήλοις διδόναι λύτρον ἐλευθέρου μὲν χιλίας δραχμάς, δούλου δὲ πεντακοσίας'; 'As for the prisoners, those who could pay a ransom they took into the city, for the Rhodians had made an agreement with Demetrius that each should pay the other a thousand drachmae as ransom for a free man and five hundred for a slave.'

132. *de statu popul.*] Lysias, Oration XXV, *Defence against a Charge of Subverting the Democracy*, sect. xxvii: 'καὶ εἰκότως, ὦ ἄνδρες δικασταί· πᾶσι γὰρ ἤδη φανερόν ἐστιν ὅτι διὰ τοὺς μὲν ἀδίκως πολιτευομένους ἐν τῇ ὀλιγαρχίᾳ δημοκρατία γίγνεται, διὰ δὲ τοὺς ἐν τῇ δημοκρατίᾳ συκοφαντοῦντας ὀλιγαρχία δὶς κατέστη'; 'And with good reason, gentlemen: for it is manifest now to all that the unjust acts of rulers in an oligarchy produce democracy, whereas the trade of slanderers in the democracy has twice led to the establishment of oligarchy.'

133. *There are ... CÆSAR*] cf. the note in the 'Early Memoranda': 'Thrasybulus restoring the People, & Cæsar's Conquest the only Instances in antient History of Revolutions without barbarous Cruelty' (NLS MS 23159, item 14, p. 25; cf. Mossner, 'Memoranda', p. 515).

134. *thirty tyrants*] A violent pro-Spartan oligarchy that held power in Athens 404–403 BC.

135. *sycophants*] cf. Hume's earlier discussion of this term in 'Of the Balance of Trade' (see above, p. 46, n. 1).

136. *poinard*] i.e. dagger.

137. *PHILIP. 1*] Cicero, *Philippic I*, I: 'Nec vero usquam discedebam nec a re publica deiciebam oculos ex eo die quo in aedem Telluris convocati sumus, in quo templo, quantum in me fuit, ieci fundamenta pacis Atheniensiumque renovavi vetus exemplum; Graecum etiam verbum usurpavi quo tum in sedandis discordiis usa erat civitas illa, atque omnem memoriam discordiarum oblivione sempiterna delendam censui'; 'In fact, from that day on which we were summoned to the Temple of Tellus, neither did I withdraw anywhere from, nor did I take my eyes off public affairs. In that temple, so far as was in my power, I laid the foundations of peace and revived the ancient Athenian precedent, even adopting the Greek term [*amnestia*] that was used by that community in laying their quarrels to rest at that time; that is, I proposed that all recollection of disputes should be obliterated and forgotten for all time.'

138. *MANTITH.*] Lysias, Oration XII, *Against Eratosthenes, Who Had Been One of the Thirty*, sect. C: 'οἶμαι δ᾽ αὐτοὺς ἡμῶν τε ἀκροᾶσθαι καὶ ὑμᾶς εἴσεσθαι τὴν ψῆφον φέροντας, ἡγουμένους, ὅσοι μὲν ἂν τούτων ἀποψηφίσησθε, αὐτῶν θάνατον κατεψηφισμένους ἔσεσθαι, ὅσοι δ᾽ ἂν παρὰ τούτων δίκην λάβωσιν, ὑπὲρ αὐτῶν τιμωρίας πεποιημένους'; 'I fancy that they are listening to us, and will know you by the vote that you give; they will feel that those of you who acquit these men will have passed sentence of death on them, while those who inflict the merited penalty will have acted as their avengers.' Lysias, Oration XIII, *Against Agoratus*, sect. XCVI: 'οἱ τριάκοντα τοίνυν τῶν μὲν ἀνδρῶν τούτων, οἳ ἦσαν ὑμέτεροι φίλοι, θάνατον κατέγνωσαν, ὧν δεῖ ὑμᾶς ἀποψηφίζεσθαι· Ἀγοράτου δὲ ἀπεψηφίσαντο, διότι ἐδόκει προθύμως τούτους ἀπολλύναι'; 'Now, the Thirty condemned to death these men, who were your friends, and these you ought to acquit. Agoratus they acquitted, because he was found zealous for their destruction: him you ought to convict.' Lysias's Oration XVI, *In Defence of Mantitheus*, illustrates Hume's point that the restored democracy had pursued even the lesser instruments of the Thirty Tyrants, and had sought to have them capitally punished (as they attempted in the case of Mantitheus).

139. *lib. ii*] Appian, *Civil Wars*, II.xiv.100: 'τῶν δὲ τριακοσίων ὅσους εὗρε διέφθειρεν'; 'Of the 300 [Cato's council of war, the so-called Utican senate] he put to death all that he found.'

140. *Catil.*] Sallust, *Bellum Catilinae*, LI.xxviii–xxxi: 'Lacedaemonii devictis Atheniensibus triginta viros inposuere qui rem publicam eorum tractarent. Ei primo coepere pessumum quemque et omnibus invisum indemnatum necare. Ea populus laetari et merito dicere fieri. Post ubi paulatim licentia crevit, iuxta bonos et malos lubidinose interficere, ceteros metu terrere; ita civitas servitute oppressa stultae laetitiae gravis poenas dedit'; 'The

Spartans, after they had conquered the Athenians, set thirty men over them to administer their state. Those men at first began to put to death without a trial the most wicked and generally hated citizens. The people rejoiced at those executions and declared that they were carried out deservedly. But afterward, when their license gradually increased, the tyrants slew good and bad alike at their pleasure and intimidated the rest. Thus the nation was reduced to slavery and paid a heavy penalty for its foolish rejoicing.'

141. *Orat.* 24] Lysias, Oration XXV, *Defence Against a Charge of Subverting the Democracy,* XIX–XX: 'καὶ εἰ μὲν οἱ τριάκοντα τούτους μόνους ἐτιμωροῦντο, ἄνδρας ἀγαθοὺς καὶ ὑμεῖς ἂν αὐτοὺς ἡγεῖσθε· νῦν δέ, ὅτε ὑπὲρ τῶν ἐκείνοις ἡμαρτημένων τὸ πλῆθος κακῶς ποιεῖν ἠξίουν, ἠγανακτεῖτε, ἡγούμενοι δεινὸν εἶναι τὰ τῶν ὀλίγων ἀδικήματα πάσῃ τῇ πόλει κοινὰ γίγνεσθαι. οὐ τοίνυν ἄξιον χρῆσθαι τούτοις, οἷς ἐκείνους ἑωρᾶτε ἐξαμαρτάνοντας, οὐδὲ ἃ πάσχοντες ἄδικα ἐνομίζετε πάσχειν, ὅταν ἑτέρους ποιῆτε, δίκαια ἡγεῖσθαι, ἀλλὰ τὴν αὐτὴν κατελθόντες περὶ ἡμῶν γνώμην ἔχετε, ἥνπερ φεύγοντες περὶ ὑμῶν αὐτῶν εἴχετε· ἐκ τούτων γὰρ καὶ ὁμόνοιαν πλείστην ποιήσετε, καὶ ἡ πόλις ἔσται μεγίστη, καὶ τοῖς ἐχθροῖς ἀνιαρότατα ψηφιεῖσθε'; 'Now, if the Thirty had kept their punishments for these cases, you would have held them yourselves to be honest men: but when in fact you found them deliberately oppressing the people because of the offences of those persons, you were indignant; for you considered it monstrous that the crimes of the few should be spread over the whole city. It is not right, therefore, that you should resort to those offences which you saw them committing, or regard those deeds, which you deemed unjust when done to you, as just when you do them to others. No: let your feeling towards us after your restoration be the same as you had towards yourselves in your exile; for by this means you will produce the utmost harmony amongst us, the power of the city will be at its highest, and you will vote for what will be most distressing to your enemies.' This passage of Lysias does not seem to make quite the point that Hume imagines it does.

142. *should displease*] Lysias, Oration XXX, *Against Nicomachus,* XIII–XIV: 'καὶ ταῦτα διεπράξαντο διὰ τὸν νόμον ὃν Νικόμαχος ἀπέδειξεν. εἰκὸς τοίνυν, ὦ ἄνδρες δικασταί, ἐνθυμεῖσθαι καὶ ὁπόσοι ὑμῶν ἐνόμιζον Κλεοφῶντα κακὸν πολίτην εἶναι, ὅτι καὶ τῶν ἐν τῇ ὀλιγαρχίᾳ ἀποθανόντων ἴσως τις ἦν πονηρός, ἀλλ' ὅμως καὶ διὰ τοὺς τοιούτους ὠργίζεσθε τοῖς τριάκοντα, ὅτι οὐ τῶν ἀδικημάτων ἕνεκα ἀλλὰ κατὰ στάσιν αὐτοὺς ἀπέκτειναν. ἐὰν οὖν πρὸς ταῦτα ἀπολογῆται, τοσοῦτον μέμνησθε, ὅτι ἐν τοιούτῳ καιρῷ τὸν νόμον ἀπέδειξεν ἐν ᾧ ἡ πολιτεία μεθίστατο, καὶ τούτοις χαριζόμενος οἳ τὸν δῆμον κατέλυσαν, καὶ ταύτην τὴν βουλὴν συνδικάζειν ἐποίησεν ἐν ᾗ Σάτυρος μὲν καὶ Χρέμων μέγιστον ἐδύναντο, Στρομβιχίδης δὲ καὶ Καλλιάδης καὶ ἕτεροι πολλοὶ καὶ καλοὶ κἀγαθοὶ τῶν πολιτῶν ἀπώλλυντο'; 'And they [Satyrus and Chremon] achieved their end because of the law which Nicomachus exhibited. Now you may reasonably reflect, gentlemen, – even those of you who thought Cleophon to be a bad citizen, – that, although among those who perished under the

oligarchy there were perhaps one or two villains, yet it was on account of even such sufferers that you were incensed against the Thirty, as having put them to death, not for their crimes, but for 'motives of party. If, therefore, he tries to rebut this charge, you have merely to remember that he exhibited the law at that very moment when the revolution was being effected, with the aim of gratifying those who had subverted the democracy; and that he included as assessors at the trial that Council in which Satyrus and Chremon had the chief influence, and which put to death Strombichides, Calliades and a number of loyal and upright citizens.'

143. *from the cities*] Isocrates, *To Philip*, XCVI: 'καὶ μὴν καὶ στρατιώτας σὺ μὲν ἐξ ἑτοίμου λήψει τοσούτους ὅσους ἂν βουληθῇς· οὕτω γὰρ ἔχει τὰ τῆς Ἑλλάδος, ὥστε ῥᾷον εἶναι συστῆσαι στρατόπεδον μεῖζον καὶ κρεῖττον ἐκ τῶν πλανωμένων ἢ τῶν πολιτευομένων'; 'Besides, you will find as many soldiers at your service as you wish, for such is now the state of affairs in Hellas that it is easier to get together a greater and stronger army from among those who wander in exile than from those who live under their own polities.'

144. *Lib. iii*] Thucydides, III.lxxxiii.3–4: 'καὶ οἱ φαυλότεροι γνώμην ὡς τὰ πλείω περιεγίγνοντο· τῷ γὰρ δεδιέναι τό τε αὑτῶν ἐνδεὲς καὶ τὸ τῶν ἐναντίων ξυνετόν, μὴ λόγοις τε ἥσσους ὦσι καὶ ἐκ τοῦ πολυτρόπου αὐτῶν τῆς γνώμης φθάσωσι προεπιβουλευόμενοι, τολμηρῶς πρὸς τὰ ἔργα ἐχώρουν. οἱ δὲ καταφρονοῦντες κἂν προαισθέσθαι καὶ ἔργῳ οὐδὲν σφᾶς δεῖν λαμβάνειν ἃ γνώμῃ ἔξεστιν, ἄφαρκτοι μᾶλλον διεφθείροντο'; 'And it was generally those of meaner intellect who won the day; for being afraid of their own defects and of their opponents' sagacity, in order that they might not be worsted in words, and, by reason of their opponents' intellectual versatility find themselves unawares victims of their plots, they boldly resorted to deeds. Their opponents, on the other hand, contemptuously assuming that they would be aware in time and that there was no need to secure by deeds what they might have by wit, were taken off their guard and perished in greater numbers.'

145. *fort. ALEX.*] Dionysius is mentioned twice in Plutarch's 'On the Fortune or the Virtue of Alexander', at I.ix and II.i. But in neither instance is the scale of Dionysius's bloodshed mentioned, so the reason why Hume referred the reader to this essay remains obscure.

146. *lib. xviii, xix*] The deeds of Agathocles are related at length in Diodorus Siculus, XIX.

147. *xxxiv*] Livy's account of the war fought by Titus Quintius Flaminius against the Spartan tyrant Nabis is related in Livy, XXXIV.

148. *says 1300*] Diodorus Siculus, XIV.v.5–7: 'Μετὰ δὲ τὸν τούτου θάνατον οἱ τριάκοντα τοὺς πλουσίους ἐπιλεγόμενοι, τούτοις ψευδεῖς αἰτίας ἐπερρίπτουν, καὶ φονεύοντες τὰς οὐσίας διήρπαζον. ἀνεῖλον δὲ καὶ Νικήρατον τὸν Νικίου τοῦ στρατηγήσαντος ἐπὶ Συρακοσίους υἱόν, ἄνδρα πρὸς ἅπαντας ἐπιεικῆ καὶ φιλάνθρωπον, πλούτῳ δὲ καὶ δόξῃ σχεδὸν πρῶτον πάντων Ἀθηναίων· διὸ καὶ συνέβη πᾶσαν οἰκίαν συναλγῆσαι τῇ τἀνδρὸς τελευτῇ, τῆς διὰ τὴν ἐπιείκειαν

μνήμης προαγούσης εἰς δάκρυα. οὐ μὴν ἔληγόν γε τῆς παρανομίας οἱ τύραννοι, πολὺ δὲ μᾶλλον ἐπίτασιν λαμβανούσης τῆς ἀπονοίας τῶν μὲν ξένων τοὺς πλουσιωτάτους ἑξήκοντα κατέσφαξαν, ὅπως τῶν χρημάτων κυριεύσωσι, τῶν δὲ πολιτῶν καθ᾽ ἡμέραν ἀναιρουμένων οἱ τοῖς βίοις εὐπορούμενοι σχεδὸν ἅπαντες ἔφυγον ἐκ τῆς πόλεως. ἀνεῖλον δὲ καὶ Αὐτόλυκον, ἄνδρα παρρησιαστήν, καὶ καθόλου τοὺς χαριεστάτους ἐπέλεγον. ἐπὶ τοσοῦτο δὲ κατέφθειραν τὴν πόλιν, ὥστε φυγεῖν τοὺς Ἀθηναίους πλείους τῶν ἡμίσεων᾽; 'After the death of Theramenes the Thirty drew up a list of the wealthy, lodged false charges against them, put them to death, and seized their estates. They slew even Niceratus, the son of Nicias who had commanded the campaign against the Syracusans, a man who had conducted himself toward all men with fairness and humanity, and who was perhaps first of all Athenians in wealth and reputation. It came about, therefore, that every house was filled with pity for the end of the man, as fond thoughts due to their memory of his honest ways provoked them to tears. Nevertheless, the tyrants did not cease from their lawless conduct; rather their madness became so much the more acute that of the metics they slaughtered sixty of the wealthiest in order to gain possession of their property, and as for the citizens, since they were being killed daily, the well-to-do among them fled from the city almost to a man. They also slew Autolycus, an outspoken man, and, in a word, selected the most respectable citizens. So far did their wasting of the city go that more than half of the Athenians took to flight.' Isocrates, *Areopagiticus*, LXVI–LXVII: ῾τοὺς δὲ τριάκοντα τῶν μὲν ἀμελήσαντας, τὰ δὲ συλήσαντας, τοὺς δὲ νεωσοίκους ἐπὶ καθαιρέσει τριῶν ταλάντων ἀποδομένους, εἰς οὓς ἡ πόλις ἀνήλωσεν οὐκ ἐλάττω χιλίων ταλάντων; ἀλλὰ μὴν οὐδὲ τὴν πραότητα δικαίως ἄν τις ἐπαινέσειε τὴν ἐκείνων μᾶλλον ἢ τὴν τοῦ δήμου. οἱ μὲν γὰρ ψηφίσματι παραλαβόντες τὴν πόλιν πεντακοσίους μὲν καὶ χιλίους τῶν πολιτῶν ἀκρίτους ἀπέκτειναν, εἰς δὲ τὸν Πειραιᾶ φυγεῖν πλείους ἢ πεντακισχιλίους ἠνάγκασαν· οἱ δὲ κρατήσαντες καὶ μεθ᾽ ὅπλων κατιόντες, αὐτοὺς τοὺς αἰτιωτάτους τῶν κακῶν ἀνελόντες, οὕτω τὰ πρὸς τοὺς ἄλλους καλῶς καὶ νομίμως διῴκησαν, ὥστε μηδὲν ἔλαττον ἔχειν τοὺς ἐκβαλόντας τῶν κατελθόντων᾽; 'while the Thirty neglected the public buildings, plundered the temples, and sold for destruction for the sum of three talents the dockyards upon which the city had spent not less than a thousand talents? And surely no one could find grounds to praise the mildness of the Thirty as against that of the people's rule! For when the Thirty took over the city, by vote of the Assembly, they put to death fifteen hundred Athenians without a trial and compelled more than five thousand to leave Athens and take refuge in the Piraeus, whereas when the exiles overcame them and returned to Athens under arms, these put to death only the chief perpetrators of their wrongs and dealt so generously and so justly by the rest that those who had driven the citizens from their homes fared no worse than those who had returned from exile.' Aeschines, *Against Ctesiphon*, CCXXXV: ῾ἔχαιρε γὰρ κολακευόμενος, ἔπειτ᾽ αὐτὸν οὐχ οὓς ἐφοβεῖτο, ἀλλ᾽

οἷς ἑαυτὸν ἐνεχείριζε, κατέλυσαν· ἔνιοι δὲ καὶ αὐτοὶ τῶν τριάκοντα ἐγένοντο, οἳ πλείους ἢ χιλίους καὶ πεντακοσίους τῶν πολιτῶν ἀκρίτους ἀπέκτειναν, πρὶν καὶ τὰς αἰτίας ἀκοῦσαι ἐφ᾽ αἷς ἔμελλον ἀποθνήσκειν, καὶ οὐδ᾽ ἐπὶ τὰς ἐκφορὰς τῶν τελευτησάντων εἴων τοὺς προσήκοντας παραγενέσθαι'; 'For the people loved to be flattered, and in consequence were overthrown, not by the men whom they feared, but by those in whose hands they had placed themselves. And some of them actually joined the Thirty, who killed more than fifteen hundred of the citizens without trial, before they had even heard the charges on which they were to be put to death, and who would not even allow the relatives to be present at the burial of the dead.' Seneca, *De Tranquillitate Animi*, V.i: 'Numquid potes invenire urbem miseriorem quam Atheniensium fuit, cum illam triginta tyranni divellerent? Mille trecentos cives, optimum quemque occiderant nec finem ideo faciebant, sed irritabat se ipsa saevitia'; 'Can you find any city more wretched than was that of the Athenians when it was being torn to pieces by the Thirty Tyrants? They had slain thirteen hundred citizens, all the best men, and were not for that reason ready to stop, but their very cruelty fed its own flame.'

149. *lib. xv*] Diodorus Siculus, XV.lviii.1–4: Ἡ δ᾽ οὖν στάσις ἐγένετο διὰ τοιαύτας αἰτίας. τῆς πόλεως τῶν Ἀργείων δημοκρατουμένης καί τινων δημαγωγῶν παροξυνόντων τὸ πλῆθος κατὰ τῶν ταῖς ἐξουσίαις καὶ δόξαις ὑπερεχόντων, οἱ διαβαλλόμενοι συστάντες ἔγνωσαν καταλῦσαι τὸν δῆμον. βασανισθέντων δέ τινων ἐκ τῶν συνεργεῖν δοκούντων, οἱ μὲν ἄλλοι φοβηθέντες τὴν ἐκ τῶν βασάνων τιμωρίαν ἑαυτοὺς ἐκ τοῦ ζῆν μετέστησαν, ἑνὸς δ᾽ ἐν ταῖς βασάνοις ὁμολογήσαντος καὶ πίστιν λαβόντος, ὁ μὲν μηνυτὴς τριάκοντα τῶν ἐπιφανεστάτων κατηγόρησεν, ὁ δὲ δῆμος οὐκ ἐλέγξας ἀκριβῶς ἅπαντας τοὺς διαβληθέντας ἀπέκτεινε καὶ τὰς οὐσίας αὐτῶν ἐδήμευσεν. πολλῶν δὲ καὶ ἄλλων ἐν ὑποψίαις ὄντων, καὶ τῶν δημαγωγῶν ψευδέσι διαβολαῖς συνηγορούντων, ἐπὶ τοσοῦτον ἐξηγριώθη τὸ πλῆθος ὥστε πάντων τῶν κατηγορουμένων, ὄντων πολλῶν καὶ μεγαλοπλούτων, καταγνῶναι θάνατον. ἀναιρεθέντων δὲ τῶν δυνατῶν ἀνδρῶν πλειόνων ἢ χιλίων καὶ διακοσίων, καὶ τῶν δημαγωγῶν αὐτῶν ὁ δῆμος οὐκ ἐφείσατο. διὰ γὰρ τὸ μέγεθος τῆς συμφορᾶς οἱ μὲν δημαγωγοὶ φοβηθέντες μή τι παράλογον αὐτοῖς ἀπαντήσῃ, τῆς κατηγορίας ἀπέστησαν, οἱ δ᾽ ὄχλοι δόξαντες ὑπ᾽ αὐτῶν ἐγκαταλελεῖφθαι καὶ διὰ τοῦτο παροξυνθέντες, ἅπαντας τοὺς δημαγωγοὺς ἀπέκτειναν. οὗτοι μὲν οὖν, ὡσπερεί τινος νεμεσήσαντος δαιμονίου, τῆς ἁρμοζούσης τιμωρίας ἔτυχον, ὁ δὲ δῆμος παυσάμενος τῆς λύττης εἰς τὴν προϋπάρχουσαν ἔννοιαν ἀποκατέστη'; 'Now the strife arose from the following causes: the city of Argos had a democratic form of government, and certain demagogues instigated the populace against the outstanding citizens of property and reputation. The victims of the hostile charges then got together and decided to overthrow the democracy. When some of those who were thought to be implicated were subjected to torture, all but one, fearing the agony of torture, committed suicide, but this one came to terms under torture, received a pledge of immunity, and as informer denounced thirty of the most distinguished citizens, and the democracy

without a thorough investigation put to death all those who were accused and confiscated their property. But many others were under suspicion, and as the demagogues supported false accusations, the mob was wrought up to such a pitch of savagery that they condemned to death all the accused, who were many and wealthy. When, however, more than twelve hundred influential men had been removed, the populace did not spare the demagogues themselves. For because of the magnitude of the calamity the demagogues were afraid that some unforeseen turn of fortune might overtake them and therefore desisted from their accusation, whereas the mob, now thinking that they had been left in the lurch by them, were angry at this and put to death all the demagogues. So these men received the punishment which fitted their crimes as if some divinity were visiting its just resentment upon them, and the people, eased of their mad rage, were restored to their senses.'

150. *lib. xiii*] Diodorus Siculus, XIII.xlviii.1–2 and 7: 'Συνέβη δὲ περὶ τοῦτον τὸν χρόνον ἐν τῇ Κορκύρᾳ γενέσθαι μεγάλην στάσιν καὶ σφαγήν, ἣν δι᾽ ἑτέρας μὲν αἰτίας λέγεται γενέσθαι, μάλιστα δὲ διὰ τὴν ὑπάρχουσαν αὐτοῖς πρὸς ἀλλήλους ἔχθραν. ἐν οὐδεμιᾷ γάρ ποτε πόλει τοιοῦτοι πολιτῶν φόνοι συνετελέσθησαν οὐδὲ μείζων ἔρις καὶ φιλονεικία πρὸς ὄλεθρον ἀνήκουσα. δοκοῦσι γὰρ οἱ μὲν ἀναιρεθέντες ὑπ᾽ ἀλλήλων πρὸ ταύτης τῆς στάσεως γεγονέναι περὶ χιλίους καὶ πεντακοσίους, καὶ πάντες οὗτοι πρωτεύοντες τῶν πολιτῶν . . . οἱ δὲ ἑξακόσιοι μετὰ τῶν δημοτικῶν ὁρμήσαντες ἐπὶ τοὺς τὰ Λακεδαιμονίων φρονοῦντας ἐξαίφνης ἀγορᾶς πληθούσης οὓς μὲν συνελάμβανον, οὓς δ᾽ ἐφόνευον, πλείους δὲ τῶν χιλίων ἐφυγάδευσαν· ἐποιήσαντο δὲ τοὺς μὲν δούλους ἐλευθέρους, τοὺς δὲ ξένους πολίτας, εὐλαβούμενοι τό τε πλῆθος καὶ τὴν δύναμιν τῶν φυγάδων'; 'It happened at this time that a serious civil strife occurred in Corcyra accompanied by massacre, which is said to have been due to various causes but most of all to the mutual hatred that existed between its own inhabitants. For never in any state have there taken place such murderings of citizens nor have there been greater quarrelling and contentiousness which culminated in bloodshed. For it would seem that the number of those who were slain by their fellow citizens before the present civil strife was some fifteen hundred, and all of these were leading citizens . . . And the six hundred, setting out unexpectedly with the partisans of the people's party at the time of full market against the supporters of the Lacedaemonians, arrested some of them, slew others, and drove more than a thousand from the state; they also set the slaves free and gave citizenship to the foreigners living among them as a precaution against the great number and influence of the exiles.'

151. *lib. xviii*] Diodorus Siculus, XVIII.viii.5: 'ἦσαν δ᾽ οἱ φυγάδες ἀπηντηκότες ἅπαντες ἐπὶ τὴν πανήγυριν, ὄντες πλείους τῶν δισμυρίων'; 'All the exiles had come together at the festival, being more than twenty thousand in number.'

152. *tyrant in the city*] On the poverty of the Athenians, cf. the note in the 'Early Memoranda': 'To live like an Athenian, was a Proverb for living frugally.' (NLS MS 23159, item 14, p. 21; cf. Mossner, 'Memoranda', p. 512).

153. *raree-shows*] Literally, a set of pictures or a puppet show exhibited in a portable box for public entertainment; a peep show. By extension, any kind of lurid or vulgar entertainment (*OED*, 'raree-show', *n.*, 1 and 2).

154. *all claim and pretension of the younger*] cf. Hume's comments on the practical advantages of the hereditary principle in 'That Politics may be reduced to a Science': 'This chief magistrate may be either *elective* or *hereditary*; and though the former institution may, to a superficial view, appear the most advantageous; yet a more accurate inspection will discover in it greater inconveniencies than in the latter, and such as are founded on causes and principles eternal and immutable. The filling of the throne, in such a government, is a point of too great and too general interest, not to divide the whole people into factions: Whence a civil war, the greatest of ills, may be apprehended, almost with certainty, upon every vacancy' (above, vol. 1, p. 26). Wallace had drawn a different conclusion from the practice of the ancients in respect of inheritance: 'The rules of succession, and the right of primogeniture, by which the eldest son, not only of the most opulent, but even of the middling and inferior families, carries off the greatest part of the father's estate, that the family may be supported in grandeur and affluence, while the younger children get but a small patrimony, may justly be accounted another cause of the scarcity of people in modern times. This was unknown in antient times; for both *Greeks* and *Romans* divided the father's estate more equally among all the children; nor did the antient world in general, as far as I have been able to learn, give so great a proportion to the eldest son' (Wallace, *Dissertation*, p. 92). In so arguing Wallace was following Montesquieu, who in *Lettres Persanes*, letter 119, had made a similar point: 'C'est un esprit de vanité qui a établi chez les Européens l'injuste droit d'aînesse, si défavorable à la propagation, en ce qu'il porte l'attention d'un père sur un seul de ses enfants et détourne ses yeux de tous les autres; en ce qu'il l'oblige, pour rendre solide la fortune d'un seul, de s'opposer à l'établissement de plusieurs; enfin, en ce qu'il détruit l'égalité des citoyens, qui en fait toute l'opulence' (Montesquieu, *Œuvres*, p. 125).

155. *LEUNCLAV.*] Xenophon, *Symposium*, IV.29–32: Ὁ δὲ Καλλίας, Σὸν μέρος, ἔφη, λέγειν, ὦ Χαρμίδη, δι᾽ ὅ τι ἐπὶ πενίᾳ μέγα φρονεῖς. Οὐκοῦν τόδε μέν, ἔφη, ὁμολογεῖται, κρεῖττον εἶναι θαρρεῖν ἢ φοβεῖσθαι καὶ ἐλεύθερον εἶναι μᾶλλον ἢ δουλεύειν καὶ θεραπεύεσθαι μᾶλλον ἢ θεραπεύειν καὶ πιστεύεσθαι ὑπὸ τῆς πατρίδος μᾶλλον ἢ ἀπιστεῖσθαι. ἐγὼ τοίνυν ἐν τῇδε τῇ πόλει ὅτε μὲν πλούσιος ἦν πρῶτον μὲν ἐφοβούμην μή τίς μου τὴν οἰκίαν διορύξας καὶ τὰ χρήματα λάβοι καὶ αὐτόν τί με κακὸν ἐργάσαιτο· ἔπειτα δὲ καὶ τοὺς συκοφάντας ἐθεράπευον, εἰδὼς ὅτι παθεῖν μᾶλλον κακῶς ἱκανὸς εἴην ἢ ποιῆσαι ἐκείνους. καὶ γὰρ δὴ καὶ προσετάττετο μὲν ἀεί τί μοι δαπανᾶν ὑπὸ τῆς πόλεως, ἀποδημῆσαι δὲ οὐδαμοῦ ἐξῆν. νῦν δ᾽ ἐπειδὴ τῶν ὑπερορίων στέρομαι καὶ τὰ ἔγγεια οὐ καρποῦμαι καὶ τὰ ἐκ τῆς οἰκίας πέπραται, ἡδέως μὲν καθεύδω ἐκτεταμένος, πιστὸς δὲ τῇ πόλει γεγένημαι, οὐκέτι δὲ ἀπειλοῦμαι, ἀλλ᾽ ἤδη ἀπειλῶ ἄλλοις, ὡς ἐλευθέρῳ τε ἔξεστί

μοι καὶ ἀποδημεῖν καὶ ἐπιδημεῖν· ὑπανίστανται δέ μοι ἤδη καὶ θάκων καὶ ὁδῶν
ἐξίστανται οἱ πλούσιοι. καὶ εἰμὶ νῦν μὲν τυράννῳ ἐοικώς, τότε δὲ σαφῶς δοῦλος
ἦν· καὶ τότε μὲν ἐγὼ φόρον ἀπέφερον τῷ δήμῳ, νῦν δὲ ἡ πόλις τέλος φέρουσα
τρέφει με. ἀλλὰ καὶ Σωκράτει, ὅτε μὲν πλούσιος ἦν, ἐλοιδόρουν με ὅτι συνῆν,
νῦν δ᾽ ἐπεὶ πένης γεγένημαι, οὐκέτι οὐδὲν μέλει οὐδενί. καὶ μὴν ὅτε μέν γε πολλὰ
εἶχον, ἀεί τι ἀπέβαλλον ἢ ὑπὸ τῆς πόλεως ἢ ὑπὸ τῆς τύχης· νῦν δὲ ἀποβάλλω μὲν
οὐδέν, οὐδὲ γὰρ ἔχω, ἀεὶ δέ τι λήψεσθαι ἐλπίζω᾽; 'But Callias now remarked,
"It's your turn, Charmides, to tell us why poverty makes you feel proud."
"Very well," he said. "Every one agrees about this: confidence is preferable
to fear, freedom to slavery, getting attention to giving it, the trust of one's
country to its distrust. Now, as for my situation in our city, when I was rich,
first of all I dreaded some one tunneling into my house and not only taking
my money but also doing me harm; and second, I paid court to the black-
mailers, quite aware that I was more liable to suffer injury from them than
inflict it. Then too, I was forever being ordered by the government to undertake some expenditure or other, and I could never leave town. Whereas now,
since I'm stripped of my property over the border, get no income from my
holdings in Attica, and my household goods have been sold, I stretch out and
sleep well, I've gained the trust of the city, I get no more threats – I do the
threatening now – and I have the free man's choice of leaving town or staying home. People now actually rise from their seats in deference to me, and
rich men get out of my way in the street. Now I am like a despot; then I was
clearly a slave. Then I paid tribute to the Sovereign People; now I live on the
tribute that the city pays to me. What's more, when I was rich, people used
to vilify me for consorting with Socrates, but now that I'm poor no one cares
about that at all any more. And when my property was large, I was continually losing some of it either to the city or to bad luck, but now I lose nothing
because I have nothing, but I'm always expecting to get something."'

156. *NICOM.*] Lysias, Oration XXX, *Against Nicomachus*, XXV: ʽκαίτοι ἐκεῖνοι
μὲν τοσοῦτον μόνον ὑμᾶς ἔβλαψαν ὅσον ἐν τῷ παρόντι, οὗτοι δ᾽ ἐπὶ τῇ τῶν
νόμων ἀναγραφῇ [καὶ τῶν ἱερῶν] δῶρα λαμβάνοντες εἰς ἅπαντα τὸν χρόνον τὴν
πόλιν ζημιοῦσι᾽; 'Remember that ere now you have put many of the citizens
to death for peculation: yet the injury that they had done you was only for
the passing moment, whereas these men, by taking bribes for the version
that they made of our laws, damage the city for all time.'

157.*Panath.*] Isocrates, *Panathenaicus*, CXXV: ʽὥσθ᾽ ὃ δοκεῖ χαλεπώτατον εἶναι καὶ
σπανιώτατον, εὑρεῖν τινας τῶν οἴκων τῶν τυραννικῶν καὶ βασιλικῶν ἐπὶ τέτταρας
ἢ πέντε γενεὰς διαμείναντας, καὶ τοῦτο συμβῆναι μόνοις ἐκείνοις᾽; 'what is of all
things in the world the most difficult and rare, namely, to find examples of
royal houses or houses of absolute rulers remaining in power through four or
five generations – this too occurred among our ancestors alone.'

158. *violent maxims of government ... GREECE*] Wallace would take strong
exception to Hume's portrait of the moral character of ancient Greece: 'what

can we perceive in our author's representation of this celebrated country, the antient seat of the muses, and the mother of arts and sciences, but the most frightful images of desolation and confusion. Lands depopulated, cities plundered, citizens slaughtered! scarce any vestige of peace and security, or of wise and regular institutions! notwithstanding the learning, philosophy, and politeness of the *Greeks*, their factions are represented as more inflamed, their maxims of assassination more avowed, and party rage more fierce than among the *Irish*, amidst massacre and rebellion! How does such a representation agree with the evidence of authentic history, which proves, that the *Greeks* flourished greatly in the arts of peace, and in numbers of people, from the days of the seven sages, till their states were subdued by *Philip* of *Macedon* and his successors?' (Wallace, *Dissertation*, p. 212). Hume would again survey those features of Greek customs and morality which were at variance with the ideal portrait of Greece common among his contemporaries in 'A Dialogue' (*ECPM*, pp. 110–23). Hume was an early mover in that re-evaluation of Greek culture which would reach its high point in Nietzsche's *The Birth of Tragedy* (1872); cf. also E. R. Dodds, *The Greeks and the Irrational* (Berkeley and Los Angeles, CA: University of California Press, 1951).

159. *singular humanity*] A notorious phrase with a complicated history of usage in the English campaign of the 'Querelle des anciens et des modernes', of which Hume's disagreement with Wallace forms a late skirmish. Charles Boyle, the editor of the Christ Church *Epistles of Phalaris* (Oxford, 1695), had in his preface sardonically thanked Richard Bentley, then Keeper of the King's Library, '*pro singulari sua humanitate*' in denying him (as he alleged) full access to the MS of the text in that library (sig. a4$^v$). In the 'Preface' to the second edition of his *A Dissertation Upon the Epistles of Phalaris* (1713) Bentley had rejected with contempt the imputation concerning his 'singular Humanity' (pp. iii–v).

160. *APPIAN's history*] Appian had composed a history of the Roman civil wars in five books.

161. *lib. xiv*] Diodorus Siculus, XIV.xxxviii.4: Ἐν Ἡρακλείᾳ δὲ τῇ περὶ Τραχῖνα στάσεως γενομένης Ἡριππίδαν ἐξέπεμψαν Λακεδαιμόνιοι καταστήσοντα τὰ πράγματα. ὃς παραγενόμενος εἰς Ἡράκλειαν συνήγαγεν εἰς ἐκκλησίαν τὰ πλήθη, καὶ περιστήσας αὐτοῖς ὁπλίτας συνέλαβε τοὺς αἰτίους καὶ πάντας ἀνεῖλεν, ὄντας περὶ πεντακοσίους'; 'In Trachinian Heracleia civil discord had arisen and the Lacedaemonians sent Herippidas there to restore order. As soon as Herippidas arrived in Heracleia he called an assembly of the people, and surrounding them with his hoplites, he arrested the authors of the discord and put them all to death, some five hundred in number.'

162. *Lib. i*] Dionysius of Halicarnassus, *Roman Antiquities*, I.lxxxix.1: Ἃ μὲν οὖν ἐμοὶ δύναμις ἐγένετο σὺν πολλῇ φροντίδι ἀνευρεῖν Ἑλλήνων τε καὶ Ῥωμαίων συχνὰς ἀναλεξαμένῳ γραφὰς ὑπὲρ τοῦ τῶν Ῥωμαίων γένους, τοιάδ' ἐστίν. ὥστε

θαρρῶν ἤδη τις ἀποφαινέσθω, πολλὰ χαίρειν φράσας τοῖς βαρβάρων καὶ δραπετῶν καὶ ἀνεστίων ἀνθρώπων καταφυγὴν τὴν Ῥώμην ποιοῦσιν, Ἑλλάδα πόλιν αὐτήν'; 'Such, then, are the facts concerning the origin of the Romans which I have been able to discover after reading very diligently many works written by both Greek and Roman authors. Hence, from now on let the reader forever renounce the views of those who make Rome a retreat of barbarians, fugitives and vagabonds, and let him confidently affirm it to be a Greek city.'

163. *RHODES or MARSEILLES*] Marseille (or Massalia) was an independent city-state until 49 BC. Rhodes became a 'permanent ally' of Rome in 164 BC, thus retaining the illusion of technical independence. It was sacked by Cassius in 43 BC. Under the Roman emperors it was favoured by political exiles. Hume would extol the government of modern European republics in a letter of 8 December 1775: 'the Republics in Europe, without Exception, are so well govern'd, that one is at a Loss to which we shoud give the Preference' (*Letters*, vol. II, p. 306). On the improvement of 'all kinds of government' in modern Europe, both republican and monarchical, cf. Hume's comments in 'Of Civil Liberty' (above, vol. 1, p. 81).

164. *Had BRUTUS ... laws and liberty*] Caius Antonius, younger brother of Marcus Antonius the triumvir, was condemned to death by Marcus Brutus in 42 BC. In 63 BC Cicero had ordered the summary execution of five of Catiline's accomplices in the Tullianum prison on the eve of the outbreak of the conspiracy, despite the opposition of Julius Caesar (Sallust, *Bellum Catilinae*, LI.xliii). Sallust, *Bellum Catilinae*, LV.iii–vi: 'Est in carcere locus, quod Tullianum appellatur, ubi paululum ascenderis ad laevam, circiter duodecim pedes humi depressus. Eum muniunt undique parietes atque insuper camera lapideis fornicibus iuncta: sed inculto, tenebris, odore foeda atque terribilis eius facies est. In eum locum postquam demissus est Lentulus, vindices rerum capitalium, quibus praeceptum erat, laqueo gulam fregere. Ita ille patricius ex gente clarissuma Corneliorum, qui consulare imperium Romae habuerat, dignum moribus factisque suis exitium vitae invenit. De Cethego, Statilio, Gabinio, Caepario, eodem modo supplicium sumptum est'; 'In the prison, when you have gone up a little way toward the left, there is a place called the Tullianum, about twelve feet below the surface of the ground. It is enclosed on all sides by walls, and overhead is a vaulted ceiling formed by stone arches; but neglect, darkness, and stench give it a hideous and terrifying appearance. After Lentulus had been let down into this place, the executioners, who had been charged with the task, strangled him with a loop of rope. Thus that patrician, of the very illustrious stock of the Cornelii, who had held consular authority at Rome, found a termination of his life befitting his character and deeds. Punishment was exacted from Cethegus, Statilius, Gabinius, and Caeparius in the same way.'

165. *One general cause ... public offices*] cf. Hume's comments in 'Of Public Credit' on the constitutionally protective function of a natural aristocracy,

which he believed was threatened by the current growth of wealth held in money instruments as opposed to wealth held in the form of land: 'The stocks can be transferred in an instant, and being in such a fluctuating state, will seldom be transmitted during three generations from father to son. Or were they to remain ever so long in one family, they convey no hereditary authority or credit to the possessor; and by this means, the several ranks of men, which form a kind of independent magistracy in a state, instituted by the hand of nature, are entirely lost; and every man in authority derives his influence from the commission alone of the sovereign. No expedient remains for preventing or suppressing insurrections, but mercenary armies: No expedient at all remains for resisting tyranny: Elections are swayed by bribery and corruption alone: And the middle power between king and people being totally removed, a grievous despotism must infallibly prevail' (above, p. 81). The constitutional necessity of a powerful aristocracy was a point on which Wallace concurred: 'in every such government [monarchy], the most dreadful despotism seems unavoidable, where there is not a splendid nobility or gentry' (Wallace, *Dissertation*, p. 92).

166. *census*] In antiquity, a register of citizens and their property for purposes of taxation (*OED*, 'census', *n.*, 1).

167. *in vita SOLON*] Plutarch, *Life of Solon*, XVIII: 'οἱ δὲ λοιποὶ πάντες ἐκαλοῦντο θῆτες, οἷς οὐδεμίαν ἄρχειν ἔδωκεν ἀρχήν, ἀλλὰ τῷ συνεκκλησιάζειν καὶ δικάζειν μόνον μετεῖχον τῆς πολιτείας'; 'All the rest [the poorest fraction of the population of Athens] were called Thetes; they were not allowed to hold any office, but took part in the administration only as members of the assembly and as jurors.'

168. *lib. xviii*] In 322 BC the Macedonian general Antipater had imposed an oligarchical political settlement on Athens. Diodorus Siculus, XVIII.xviii.4: 'τὴν δὲ πολιτείαν μετέστησεν ἐκ τῆς δημοκρατίας καὶ προσέταξεν ἀπὸ τιμήσεως εἶναι τὸ πολίτευμα καὶ τοὺς μὲν κεκτημένους πλείω δραχμῶν δισχιλίων κυρίους εἶναι τοῦ πολιτεύματος καὶ τῆς χειροτονίας'; 'but he changed the government from a democracy, ordering that political power should depend on a census of wealth, and that those possessing more than two thousand drachmas should be in control of the government and of the elections.'

169. *the power in proportion to the property*] The constitutional arrangements devised by Servius Tullius are laid out at length in Livy, I.xliii. In essence, as Hume says, they calibrate political influence by reference to property. His characterization of the correspondence between property and power as 'equal and reasonable' suggests a measure of agreement with the political theory of James Harrington, which was based on a similar equation (see above, vol. 1, p. 230, n. 6), notwithstanding the doubt he levelled at that theory in the opening paragraph of 'Whether the British Government Inclines More to Absolute Monarchy, or to a Republic' (above, vol. 1, p. 48). Given that that essay was written before October 1741 (see headnote, above, vol. 1, p. 242), it may be

that Hume's thinking about the relation between political power and property had moved closer to that of Harrington during the 1740s.

170. *MARSEILLES, RHODES*] See above, p. 457, n. 163.

171. *The only garb . . . became dirty*] On the material immiseration of antiquity, cf. John Arbuthnot, *Tables of Ancient Coins, Weights and Measures* (1727), p. 153: 'I am of M. *Perrault*'s Opinion, that the polite *Augustus* had neither a Shirt to his Back, nor Glass to his Windows.' The reference is to Perrault, *Paralelle*, vol. I, pp. 161–2. It was a detail that would later impress Gibbon (Gibbon, *Decline and Fall*, vol. II, p. 174, n. 33).

172. *the MEDIAN war*] i.e. the series of conflicts between the Hellenes and the Persians that occurred 499–449 BC.

173. *pillars of HERCULES*] i.e. the straits at the western end of the Mediterranean between Gibraltar and north Africa.

174. *ATHENS . . . conceived nothing*] cf. the note on the weakness of Athenian navigation in the 'Early Memoranda': 'The Antient Navigation very defective, as is provd by this remarkable Instance. When the Lacedemonians fortifyd Decelia, they [Athenians *inserted above the line*] were obligd to bring their Corn from Eubœa by Sea turning the Promontory of Sunium, instead of bringing it over Land by Oropus. This they thought a great Inconvenience; tho the Sea Carriage was not above triple the Land, tho the Road was rough, & tho Horses were then very scarce' (NLS MS 23159, item 14, p. 25; cf. Mossner, 'Memoranda', pp. 515–16). Montesquieu had made a similar observation in the *Esprit des Lois*, book XXI, chapter 6: 'Je dis plus, cette navigation [Alexander's discovery of the Indian Ocean] se faisoit sur la côte orientale de l'Afrique; & l'état où étoit la Marine pour lors, prouve assez qu'on n'alloit pas dans des lieux bien reculés' (Montesquieu, *Esprit*, vol. II, p. 34).

175. *Id. ibid.*] Diodorus Siculus, XVIII.xviii.4–5: 'τοὺς δὲ κατωτέρω τῆς τιμήσεως ἅπαντας ὡς ταραχώδεις ὄντας καὶ πολεμικοὺς ἀπήλασε τῆς πολιτείας καὶ τοῖς βουλομένοις χώραν ἔδωκεν εἰς κατοίκησιν ἐν τῇ Θρᾴκῃ. οὗτοι μὲν οὖν ὄντες πλείους τῶν μυρίων καὶ δισχιλίων μετεστάθησαν ἐκ τῆς πατρίδος'; 'He removed from the body of citizens all who possessed less than this amount on the ground that they were disturbers of the peace and warmongers, offering to those who wished it a place for settlement in Thrace. These men, more than twelve thousand in number, were removed from their fatherland.'

176. *Id. ibid.*] Diodorus Siculus, XVIII.lxxiv.3: 'γενομένων δὲ πλειόνων ἐντεύξεων συνέθεντο τὴν εἰρήνην ὥστε τοὺς Ἀθηναίους ἔχειν πόλιν τε καὶ χώραν καὶ προσόδους καὶ ναῦς καὶ τἄλλα πάντα φίλους ὄντας καὶ συμμάχους Κασάνδρου, τὴν δὲ Μουνυχίαν κατὰ τὸ παρὸν κρατεῖν Κάσανδρον, ἕως ἂν διαπολεμήσῃ πρὸς τοὺς βασιλεῖς, καὶ τὸ πολίτευμα διοικεῖσθαι ἀπὸ τιμήσεων ἄχρι μνῶν δέκα, καταστῆσαι δ' ἐπιμελητὴν τῆς πόλεως ἕνα ἄνδρα Ἀθηναῖον ὃν δόξῃ Κασάνδρῳ'; 'After several conferences peace was made on the following terms: the Athenians were to retain their city and territory, their revenues, their fleet, and everything else, and to be friends and allies of Cassander; Munychia was

to remain temporarily under the control of Cassander until the war against the kings should be concluded; the government was to be in the hands of those possessing at least ten minae; and whatever single Athenian citizen Cassander should designate was to be overseer of the city.'

177. *children to* CARTHAGE] Arrian, *Anabasis*, II.xxiv.4: 'ἀπέθανον δὲ τῶν μὲν Τυρίων ἐς ὀκτακισχιλίους, τῶν Μακεδόνων δὲ ἐν τῇ τότε προσβολῇ Ἄδμητός τε ὁ πρῶτος ἑλὼν τὸ τεῖχος, ἀνὴρ ἀγαθὸς γενόμενος, καὶ ξὺν αὐτῷ εἴκοσι τῶν ὑπασπιστῶν· ἐν δὲ τῇ πάσῃ πολιορκίᾳ μάλιστα ἐς τετρακοσίους'; 'Some eight thousand Tyrians fell; in the actual attack the Macedonians lost Admetus, the first to mount on the wall, after he proved himself a brave man, with twenty of the hypaspists; in the entire siege the losses were about four hundred.' Diodorus Siculus, XVII.xlvi.4: 'ὁ δὲ βασιλεὺς τέκνα μὲν καὶ γυναῖκας ἐξηνδραποδίσατο, τοὺς δὲ νέους πάντας, ὄντας οὐκ ἐλάττους τῶν δισχιλίων, ἐκρέμασε. σώματα δ' αἰχμάλωτα τοσαῦτα τὸ πλῆθος εὑρέθη ὥστε τῶν πλείστων εἰς Καρχηδόνα κεκομισμένων τὰ ὑπολειφθέντα γενέσθαι πλείω τῶν μυρίων καὶ τρισχιλίων'; 'The king sold the women and children into slavery and crucified all the men of military age. These were not less than two thousand. Although most of the non-combatants had been removed to Carthage, those who remained to become captives were found to be more than thirteen thousand.'

178. *30,000*] Herodotus, V.xcvii: 'τρεῖς δὲ μυριάδας Ἀθηναίων'; 'thirty thousand Athenians'.

179. *Ib. v*] Herodotus, VIII.cxxxii: 'οἳ προήγαγον αὐτοὺς μόγις μέχρι Δήλου. τὸ γὰρ προσωτέρω πᾶν δεινὸν ἦν τοῖσι Ἕλλησι οὔτε τῶν χώρων ἐοῦσι ἐμπείροισι, στρατιῆς τε πάντα πλέα ἐδόκεε εἶναι, τὴν δὲ Σάμον ἐπιστέατο δόξῃ καὶ Ἡρακλέας στήλας ἴσον ἀπέχειν. συνέπιπτε δὲ τοιοῦτο ὥστε τοὺς μὲν βαρβάρους τὸ πρὸς ἑσπέρης ἀνωτέρω Σάμου μὴ τολμᾶν καταπλῶσαι καταρρωδηκότας, τοὺς δὲ Ἕλληνας, χρηιζόντων Χίων, τὸ πρὸς τὴν ἠῶ κατωτέρω Δήλου· οὕτω δέος τὸ μέσον ἐφύλασσε σφέων'; 'The Greeks brought them as far as Delos, and that not readily; for they feared all that lay beyond, having no knowledge of those parts, and thinking that armed men were everywhere; and they supposed that Samos was no nearer to them than the Pillars of Heracles. So it fell out that the foreigners were too disheartened to dare to sail farther west than Samos, while at the same time the Greeks dared go at the Chians' request no farther east than Delos; thus fear kept the middle space between them.'

180. *Great interest ... infancy*] cf. 'Of Interest': 'an encrease of commerce, by a necessary consequence, raises a great number of lenders, and by that means produces lowness of interest' (above, p. 38). Wallace placed the emphasis differently concerning the state of commerce in antiquity: 'The antients did not neglect trade, but had a greater turn to agriculture; they traded with nations which were not at a great distance, and whose climate better suited their constitutions; but agriculture was their chief employment, and they managed it well' (Wallace, *Dissertation*, p. 96).

181. *My fortune . . . tripled*] Demosthenes, *Against Aphobus 1*, LIX: 'ἐμοὶ δ' ἐκ τεττάρων καὶ δέκα ταλάντων ἐν δέκ' ἔτεσι πρὸς τὸν χρόνον τε καὶ τὴν ἐκείνου μίσθωσιν πλέον ἢ τριπλάσια'; 'But in my case, fourteen talents in ten years, when consideration is given to the time and the terms of his lease, ought to have been more than trebled.'

182. *slaves left by his father*] cf. the note in the 'Early Memoranda': 'Timarchus is spoke of by Æschines as a rich man for possessing 20 Slaves; Demosthenes Father had thirty.' (NLS MS 23159, item 14, p. 26; cf. Mossner, 'Memoranda', p. 517).

183. *for there was higher often paid*] cf. the note in the 'Early Memoranda': 'The Public in Athens payd 20 per Cent for Money. Xenophon' (NLS MS 23159, item 14, p. 19; cf. Mossner, 'Memoranda', p. 511).

184. *The most moderate . . . paid monthly*] cf. the note in the 'Early Memoranda': 'Demosthenes got a Drahma a Month for a Mina; 12 per cent.' (NLS MS 23159, item 14, p. 25; cf. Mossner, 'Memoranda', p. 515).

185. *Interest . . . settlement of the empire*] cf. the note in the 'Early Memoranda': 'The Interest in Rome reducd to 6 per Cent under Tiberius. Tacit.' (NLS MS 23159, item 14, p. 17; cf. Mossner, Memoranda, p. 508).

186. *Among . . . double the land*] See above, p. 459, n. 174, for the note in the 'Early Memoranda' parallel to this passage.

187. *DIAGIT.*] Lysias, Oration XXXII, *Against Diogeiton*, XXV: 'καὶ ἀποπέμψας εἰς τὸν Ἀδρίαν ὁλκάδα δυοῖν ταλάντοιν, ὅτε μὲν ἀπέστελλεν, ἔλεγε πρὸς τὴν μητέρα αὐτῶν ὅτι τῶν παίδων ὁ κίνδυνος εἴη, ἐπειδὴ δὲ ἐσώθη καὶ ἐδιπλασίασεν, αὐτοῦ τὴν ἐμπορίαν ἔφασκεν εἶναι'; 'Again, he dispatched to the Adriatic a cargo of two talents' value, and told their mother, at the moment of its sailing, that it was at the risk of the children; but when it went safely through and the value was doubled, he declared that the venture was his.'

188. *ex edit. ALDI*] Demosthenes, *Against Aphobus 1*, LVIII: 'Κατὰ τούτους τοὺς νόμους Ἀντιδώρῳ μὲν ἐκ τριῶν ταλάντων καὶ τρισχιλίων ἐν ἓξ ἔτεσιν ἓξ τάλαντα καὶ πλέον ἐκ τοῦ μισθωθῆναι παρεδόθη'; 'In the case of Antidorus, as a result of his property having been let in accordance with these laws, there was given over to him, at the end of six years, an estate of six talents and more from an original amount of three talents and three thousand drachmae.'

189. *Id. p. 19*] Demosthenes, *Against Aphobus 1*, IX: 'ὁ γὰρ πατήρ, ὦ ἄνδρες δικασταί, κατέλιπε δύ' ἐργαστήρια τέχνης οὐ μικρᾶς ἑκάτερον, μαχαιροποιοὺς μὲν τριάκοντα καὶ δύ' ἢ τρεῖς, ἀνὰ πέντε μνᾶς καὶ ἕξ, τοὺς δ' οὐκ ἐλάττονος ἢ τριῶν μνῶν ἀξίους, ἀφ' ὧν τριάκοντα μνᾶς ἀτελεῖς ἐλάμβανε τοῦ ἐνιαυτοῦ τὴν πρόσοδον, κλινοποιοὺς δ' εἴκοσι τὸν ἀριθμόν, τετταράκοντα μνῶν ὑποκειμένους, οἳ δώδεκα μνᾶς ἀτελεῖς αὐτῷ προσέφερον, ἀργυρίου δ' εἰς τάλαντον ἐπὶ δραχμῇ δεδανεισμένον, οὗ τόκος ἐγίγνετο τοῦ ἐνιαυτοῦ ἑκάστου πλεῖν ἢ ἑπτὰ μναῖ'; 'My father, men of the jury, left two factories, both doing a large business. One was a sword-manufactory, employing thirty-two or thirty-three slaves, most of them worth five or six minae each and none worth less than three minae. From these my father

received a clear income of thirty minae each year. The other was a sofa-man-ufactory, employing twenty slaves, given to my father as security for a debt of forty minae. These brought him in a clear income of twelve minae. In money he left as much as a talent, loaned at the rate of a drachma a month, the inter-est of which amounted to more than seven minae a year.'

190. *contra* CTESIPH.] Aeschines, *Against Ctesiphon*, CIV: 'ἀναγκαζόμενοι δὲ οἱ Ὠρεῖται καὶ οὐκ εὐποροῦντες, ὑπέθεσαν αὐτῷ τοῦ ταλάντου τὰς δημοσίας προσόδους, καὶ τόκον ἤνεγκαν Δημοσθένει τοῦ δωροδοκήματος δραχμὴν τοῦ μηνὸς τῆς μνᾶς, ἕως τὸ κεφάλαιον ἀπέδοσαν'; 'Now the people of Oreus, pressed for payment and without means, mortgaged to him the public rev-enues as security for the talent, and paid Demosthenes interest on the fruit of his bribery at the rate of a drachma per month on the mina, until they paid off the principal.'

191. *epist. 15*] Cicero, *Letters to Atticus*, XC.vii (IV.xv.7): 'Sequere nunc me in campum. ardet ambitus. 'σῆμα δέ τοι ἐρέω': faenus ex triente Id. Quint. factum erat bessibus'; 'Now follow me to the Campus. Bribery is running riot. "A token I shall tell": interest went up on the Ides of July from 1/3 to 2/3 percent.' The Greek quotation is from the *Iliad*, XXIII.326.

192. *orat. 3*] Cicero, *Against Verres*, II.iii.71: 'Tu, cui publicani ex Carpinatii litteris gratias egerunt, pecunia publica ex aerario erogata, ex vectigalibus populi Romani ad emendum frumentum attributa – fueritne tibi quaestui, pensitaritne tibi binas centesimas? Credo te negaturum; turpis enim est et periculosa confessio'; 'We know that it was you to whom the tax-farmers passed a vote of thanks because of what Carpinatius wrote to them. But when public money had been assigned to you from the treasury, when orders had been made for its payment, out of the nation's revenues, for the purchase of corn – is it true that this money became a source of gain to yourself and brought you in 24 per cent? Doubtless you will deny the charge: to admit the truth of it would be discreditable – and dangerous.'

193. *Essay IV*] i.e. 'Of Interest', above, pp. 36–45, where lowness of interest is associated with the development of commerce.

194. *Lib. vii*] Thucydides, VII.xxviii.1: 'Ή τε τῶν ἐπιτηδείων παρακομιδὴ ἐκ τῆς Εὐβοίας, πρότερον ἐκ τοῦ Ὠρωποῦ κατὰ γῆν διὰ τῆς Δεκελείας θάσσων οὖσα, περὶ Σούνιον κατὰ θάλασσαν πολυτελὴς ἐγίγνετο'; 'There was this further dis-advantage: the bringing in of provisions from Euboea, which had formerly been managed more expeditiously by way of Oropus overland through Deceleia, now became expensive, the route being by sea round Sunium.'

195. AGRIGENTUM] Wallace had also drawn inferences from the populousness of this city (Wallace, *Dissertation*, p. 64).

196. SYBARIS] Wallace had also drawn inferences from the populousness of this city (Wallace, *Dissertation*, p. 58).

197. *The persecutions . . . and of* FRANCE] A reference to the religious persecu-tions in the Low Countries in the later sixteenth century, and in France

following Louis XIV's revocation of the Edict of Nantes (which had afforded a measure of toleration to Protestants) in 1685.

198. *Swisserland ... in Europe*] Here Hume is again drawing on Stanyan's *Account of Switzerland*: 'One may divide the People of *Switzerland* into three Orders or Classes; first, the Peasants; secondly, the Gentry and Vassals; and thirdly, the Citizens. The first are an honest, robust and laborious People, whom Necessity has taught to be excellent Husbandmen, and to make the utmost Advantage of an ungrateful Soil: So that by Application and Industry, some of them arrive at great Riches for People of that Rank, it being no extraordinary thing, to see a Farmer worth forty or fifty thousand Crowns'; 'nay even their Handicraft-Men are, generally speaking, such Bunglers in their Trades, that the better sort of People usually send for their Common Utensils from other Parts' (Stanyan, *Switzerland*, pp. 137–8 and 177–8).

199. *its own little field*] An echo of an earlier passage in this essay: 'Where each man had his little house and field to himself, and each county had its capital, free and independent; what a happy situation of mankind!' (above, p. 110 and n. 94). Wallace had also drawn attention to the probable human fruitfulness of such a frugal situation: 'Hence we may conclude, that when any antient nation divided its lands into small shares, and when even eminent citizens had but a few acres to maintain their families, tho' such a nation had but little commerce, and had learned only a few simple and more necessary arts, it must have abounded greatly in people' (Wallace, *Dissertation*, p. 17; cf. also p. 97 n. \*).

200. *Lib. xiii*] Diodorus Siculus, XIII.lxxxi.4–5: 'κατ' ἐκείνους δὲ τοὺς καιροὺς τήν τε πόλιν καὶ τὴν χώραν τῶν Ἀκραγαντίνων συνέβαινεν εὐδαιμονίας ὑπάρχειν πλήρη· περὶ ἧς οὐκ ἀνάρμοστόν μοι φαίνεται διελθεῖν. καὶ γὰρ ἀμπελῶνες τοῖς μεγέθεσι καὶ τῷ κάλλει διαφέροντες, καὶ τὸ πλεῖστον τῆς χώρας ἐλαίαις κατάφυτον, ἐξ ἧς παμπληθῆ κομιζόμενοι καρπὸν ἐπώλουν εἰς Καρχηδόνα· οὔπω γὰρ κατ' ἐκείνους τοὺς χρόνους τῆς Λιβύης πεφυτευμένης οἱ τὴν Ἀκραγαντίνην νεμόμενοι τὸν ἐκ τῆς Λιβύης ἀντιφορτιζόμενοι πλοῦτον οὐσίας ἀπίστους τοῖς μεγέθεσιν ἐκέκτηντο. πολλὰ δὲ τοῦ πλούτου παρ' αὐτοῖς διαμένει σημεῖα, περὶ ὧν οὐκ ἀνοίκειόν ἐστι βραχέα διελθεῖν'; 'At this time, it so happened, both the city and the territory of the Acragantini enjoyed great prosperity, which I think it would not be out of place for me to describe. Their vineyards excelled in their great extent and beauty and the greater part of their territory was planted in olive-trees from which they gathered an abundant harvest and sold to Carthage; for since Libya at that time was not yet planted in fruit-trees, the inhabitants of the territory belonging to Acragas took in exchange for their products the wealth of Libya and accumulated fortunes of unbelievable size. Of this wealth there remain among them many evidences, which it will not be foreign to our purpose to discuss briefly.'

201. *Lib. xii*] Diodorus Siculus, XII.ix.1–2: 'Καὶ τὰ μὲν κατὰ τὴν Σικελίαν ἐν τούτοις ἦν. κατὰ δὲ τὴν Ἰταλίαν συνέβη κτισθῆναι τὴν τῶν Θουρίων πόλιν δι'

αἰτίας τοιαύτας. ἐν τοῖς ἔμπροσθεν χρόνοις Ἑλλήνων κτισάντων κατὰ τὴν Ἰταλίαν πόλιν Σύβαριν, συνέβη ταύτην λαβεῖν ταχεῖαν αὔξησιν διὰ τὴν ἀρετὴν τῆς χώρας. κειμένης γὰρ ἀνὰ μέσον δυεῖν ποταμῶν, τοῦ τε Κράθιος καὶ τοῦ Συβάριος, ἀφ' οὗ ταύτης ἔτυχε τῆς προσηγορίας, οἱ κατοικισθέντες νεμόμενοι πολλὴν καὶ καρποφόρον χώραν μεγάλους ἐκτήσαντο πλούτους. πολλοῖς δὲ μεταδιδόντες τῆς πολιτείας ἐπὶ τοσοῦτο προέβησαν ὥστε δόξαι πολὺ προέχειν τῶν κατὰ τὴν Ἰταλίαν οἰκούντων, πολυανθρωπίᾳ τε τοσοῦτο διήνεγκαν, ὥστε τὴν πόλιν ἔχειν πολιτῶν τριάκοντα μυριάδας'; 'These, then, were the events in Sicily. And in Italy the city of Thurii came to be founded, for the following reasons. When in former times the Greeks had founded Sybaris in Italy, the city had enjoyed a rapid growth because of the fertility of the land. For lying as the city did between two rivers, the Crathis and the Sybaris, from which it derived its name, its inhabitants, who tilled an extensive and fruitful countryside, came to possess great riches. And since they kept granting citizenship to many aliens, they increased to such an extent that they were considered to be far the first among the inhabitants of Italy; indeed they so excelled in population that the city possessed three hundred thousand citizens.'

202. *But is it . . . of the former*] A recapitulation of the argument of 'Of Commerce': 'The bulk of every state may be divided into *husbandmen* and *manufacturers*. The former are employed in the culture of the land; the latter work up the materials furnished by the former, into all the commodities which are necessary or ornamental to human life. As soon as men quit their savage state, where they live chiefly by hunting and fishing, they must fall into these two classes; though the arts of agriculture employ *at first* the most numerous part of the society. Time and experience improve so much these arts, that the land may easily maintain a much greater number of men, than those who are immediately employed in its culture, or who furnish the more necessary manufactures to such as are so employed' (above, p. 5). Wallace had argued the contrary: 'Hence it follows likewise, contrary perhaps to what many may apprehend, that trade and commerce, instead of increasing, may often tend to diminish the number of mankind, and while they enrich a particular nation and entice great numbers of people into one place, may be not a little detrimental upon the whole, as they promote luxury and prevent many useful hands from being employed in agriculture. The exchange of commodities and carrying them from one country to another by sea or land, does not multiply food; and if such as are employed in this exchange, were employed in agriculture at home, a greater quantity of food would be provided, and a greater number of people might be maintained' (Wallace, *Dissertation*, p. 22).

203. *COLUMELLA hints*] Columella, *On Agriculture*, XI.i.5–6: 'Itaque in Oeconomico Xenophontis, quem M. Cicero Latino sermoni tradidit, egregius ille Ischomachus Atheniensis rogatus a Socrate utrumne, si res familiaris desiderasset, mercari villicum tamquam fabrum, an a se instituere consueverit: "Ego vero, inquit, ipse instituo. Etenim qui me absente in meum

locum substituitur, et vicarius meae diligentiae succedit, is ea, quae ego, scire debet." Sed haec nimium prisca, et eius quidem temporis sunt, quo idem Ischomachus negabat quemquam rusticari nescire'; 'Therefore, in the *Economicus* of Xenophon, which Marcus Cicero translated into Latin, that excellent man Ischomachus the Athenian, when asked by Socrates whether, if his domestic affairs required it, he was in the habit of buying a bailiff, as he would a craftsman, or of training him up himself, answered, "I train him up myself; for he who stands in my place in my absence and acts as a deputy in my activities, ought to know what I know." But this state of affairs dates from too long ago and indeed belongs to a time when the same Ischomachus asserted that everyone knew how to farm.'

204. *the use of bills of exchange*] On which subject, see 'Of the Balance of Trade' (above, pp. 53–5).

205. *police*] See above, vol. 1, p. 285, n. 36.

206. *Oecon.*] Xenophon, *Oeconomicus*, XV.x–xii: 'Ἀλλὰ μήν, ἔφη, ὦ Σώκρατες, οὐχ ὥσπερ γε τὰς ἄλλας τέχνας κατατριβῆναι δεῖ μανθάνοντας πρὶν ἄξια τῆς τροφῆς ἐργάζεσθαι τὸν διδασκόμενον, οὐχ οὕτω καὶ ἡ γεωργία δύσκολός ἐστι μαθεῖν, ἀλλὰ τὰ μὲν ἰδὼν ἂν ἐργαζομένους, τὰ δὲ ἀκούσας, εὐθὺς ἂν ἐπίσταιο, ὥστε καὶ ἄλλον, εἰ βούλοιο, διδάσκειν. οἴομαι δ᾽, ἔφη, πάνυ καὶ λεληθέναι πολλά σε αὐτὸν ἐπιστάμενον αὐτῆς. καὶ γὰρ δὴ οἱ μὲν ἄλλοι τεχνῖται ἀποκρύπτονταί πως τὰ ἐπικαιριώτατα ἧς ἕκαστος ἔχει τέχνης, τῶν δὲ γεωργῶν ὁ κάλλιστα μὲν φυτεύων μάλιστ᾽ ἂν ἥδοιτο, εἴ τις αὐτὸν θεῷτο, ὁ κάλλιστα δὲ σπείρων ὡσαύτως· ὅ τι δὲ ἔροιο τῶν καλῶς πεποιημένων, οὐδὲν ὅ τι ἄν σε ἀποκρύψαιτο ὅπως ἐποίησεν. οὕτω καὶ τὰ ἤθη, ὦ Σώκρατες, ἔφη, γενναιοτάτους τοὺς αὐτῇ συνόντας ἡ γεωργία ἔοικε παρέχεσθαι'; '"Well, Socrates, farming is not a lot of trouble to learn, unlike other arts that the student must study till he is worn out before he can earn his keep by his work. Some of the jobs you can understand by watching men at work, others by just being told, well enough to teach someone else if you wanted. And I believe that you know a good deal about it yourself without being aware of it. The truth is, whereas other artists more or less conceal the most important points in their own art, the farmer who plants best is most pleased when he is being watched, as is the one who sows best. Question him about any piece of work well done and he will tell you exactly how he did it. So farming, Socrates, more than any other calling, seems to produce a very noble disposition in its followers."'

207. *Essay XI*] A slip for Essay XII, 'Of Civil Liberty', where Hume expands on his conviction that 'the internal POLICE of states has also received great improvements within the last century' (above, vol. 1, p. 80).

208. *cap. 26*] Aelius Lampridius, *Historia Augusta*, 'Elagabalus', XXVI.vi: 'Iocabatur sane ita cum servis ut eos iuberet millena pondo sibi aranearum deferre proposito praemio, collegisseque dicitur decem milia pondo aranearum, dicens et hinc intellegendum quam magna esset Roma'; 'He used, too, to play jokes on his slaves, even ordering them to bring him a thousand

pounds of spiders-webs and offering them a prize; and he collected, it is said, ten thousand pounds, and then remarked that one could realize from that how great a city was Rome.'

209. *the numbers of people assigned*] Wallace had reviewed the statistics relating to population in ancient texts at an early stage of his *Dissertation*: see Wallace, *Dissertation*, pp. 35–77. The different ordering of material preferred by Hume is not unrelated to the strategy of his argument.

210. *The free citizens . . . SYBARITES*] Wallace accepts these statistics relating to Sybaris: 'The state of *Sybaris* alone, as *Diodorus* relates, sent an army of 300,000 men against the *Crotonienses*, who met them with 100,000. At this rate, these two neighbouring states had about a million and an half of inhabitants, even supposing they had no more fighting men than they brought to the field, which could scarce have been the case . . . *STRABO* gives the same account of *Sybaris* . . .' (Wallace, *Dissertation*, p. 58).

211. *DIODORUS . . . commodities*] Wallace accepts these classical accounts of the greatness of Agrigentum: '*AGRIGENTUM* in particular is said to have contained natives and strangers, no fewer than 200,000. Now if these are reckoned only the heads of families, or the fighting men, the inhabitants must have been above 800,000; but supposing the whole inhabitants only 200,000, *Agrigentum* was a populous and mighty city. It was likewise splendid, and abounded with sumptuous buildings; and some of its citizens were immensely rich' (Wallace, *Dissertation*, p. 64).

212. *DIODORUS . . . seven millions*] A contradiction noted also by Wallace: 'he [Diodorus Siculus] observes further, that *Egypt* had antiently 18,000 remarkable cities . . . I confess he takes notice, in the same passage, that antiently there were 7,000,000 of people in *Egypt*; and that there were only 3,000,000 in his time . . .' (Wallace, *Dissertation*, p. 45).

213. *PTOLEMY . . . envied and admired*] Wallace devotes considerable space to classical accounts of the population of ancient Egypt, which he corroborates with modern authorities such as Maillet and Templeman: Wallace, *Dissertation*, pp. 41–51. The comment about our willingness to admire distant times is an anticipation of the final observation of the essay (see above, p. 148 and n. 394).

214. *HERODOTUS's wonderful narrations*] Herodotus relates many anecdotes testifying to the immense size of Xerxes's army (e.g. VII.xx–xxi and lvi). He records that it comprised 1,700,000 men, a number arrived at through an ingenious method: Ὅσον μέν νυν ἕκαστοι παρεῖχον πλῆθος ἐς ἀριθμόν, οὐκ ἔχω εἰπεῖν τὸ ἀτρεκές· οὐ γὰρ λέγεται πρὸς οὐδαμῶν ἀνθρώπων· σύμπαντος δὲ τοῦ στρατοῦ τοῦ πεζοῦ τὸ πλῆθος ἐφάνη ἑβδομήκοντα καὶ ἑκατὸν μυριάδες. ἐξηρίθμησαν δὲ τόνδε τὸν τρόπον· συνήγαγόν τε ἐς ἕνα χῶρον μυριάδα ἀνθρώπων, καὶ συννάξαντες ταύτην ὡς μάλιστα εἶχον περιέγραψαν ἔξωθεν κύκλον· περιγράψαντες δὲ καὶ ἀπέντες τοὺς μυρίους αἱμασιὴν περιέβαλον κατὰ τὸν κύκλον, ὕψος ἀνήκουσαν ἀνδρὶ ἐς τὸν ὀμφαλόν· ταύτην δὲ ποιήσαντες

ἄλλους ἐσεβίβαζον ἐς τὸ περιοικοδομημένον, μέχρι οὗ πάντας τούτῳ τῷ τρόπῳ ἐξηρίθμησαν. ἀριθμήσαντες δὲ κατὰ ἔθνεα διέτασσον'; 'What the number of each part of it was I cannot with exactness say; for there is no one who tells us that; but the tale of the whole land army was shown to be a million and seven hundred thousand. The numbering was on this wise: – Ten thousand men were collected in one place, and when they were packed together as closely as might be a line was drawn round them; this being drawn, the ten thousand were sent away, and a wall of stones built on the line reaching up to a man's middle; which done, others were brought into the walled space, till in this way all were numbered. When they had been numbered, they were marshalled according to their several nations' (Herodotus, VII.lx). When passing through Holland in 1748 Hume had observed the preparations for the defence of Breda the following year by an army of 206,000 men, and commented: 'Tis certain so many men are stipulated by the several Powers: The greatest Army, that ever was assembled together in the World, since the Xerxeses & Antaxerxes [sic]; If these coud be called Armies' (Letters, vol. I, p. 118).

215. *Lib. xii*] Diodorus Siculus, XII.ix.5: 'στρατευσάντων δ' ἐπ' αὐτοὺς τῶν Συβαριτῶν τριάκοντα μυριάσιν ἀντετάχθησαν οἱ Κροτωνιᾶται δέκα μυριάσι, Μίλωνος τοῦ ἀθλητοῦ ἡγουμένου καὶ διὰ τὴν ὑπερβολὴν τῆς τοῦ σώματος ῥώμης πρώτου τρεψαμένου τοὺς καθ' αὐτὸν τεταγμένους'; 'When the Sybarites advanced against them with three hundred thousand men, the Crotoniates opposed them with one hundred thousand under the command of Milo the athlete, who by reason of his great physical strength was the first to put to flight his adversaries.'

216. *Lib. vi*] Strabo, VI.i.13: 'τοσοῦτον δ' εὐτυχίᾳ διήνεγκεν ἡ πόλις αὕτη τὸ παλαιόν, ὡς τεττάρων μὲν ἐθνῶν τῶν πλησίον ἐπῆρξε, πέντε δὲ καὶ εἴκοσι πόλεις ὑπηκόους ἔσχε, τριάκοντα δὲ μυριάσιν ἀνδρῶν ἐπὶ Κροτωνιάτας ἐστράτευσε, πεντήκοντα δὲ σταδίων κύκλον συνεπλήρουν οἱ οἰκοῦντες ἐπὶ τῷ Κράθιδι'; 'In early times this city was so superior in its good fortune that it ruled over four tribes in the neighbourhood, had twenty-five subject cities, made the campaign against the Crotoniates with three hundred thousand men, and its inhabitants on the Crathis alone completely filled up a circuit of fifty stadia.'

217. *Lib. xiii*] Diodorus Siculus, XIII.lxxxiv.3: 'κατ' ἐκεῖνον γὰρ τὸν χρόνον Ἀκραγαντῖνοι μὲν ἦσαν πλείους τῶν δισμυρίων, σὺν δὲ τοῖς κατοικοῦσιν ξένοις οὐκ ἐλάττους τῶν εἴκοσι μυριάδων'; 'For at that time the citizens of Acragas numbered more than twenty thousand, and when resident aliens were included, not less than two hundred thousand.'

218. *800,000 inhabitants*] Diogenes Laertius, *Lives of Eminent Philosophers*, VIII.ii.63, 'Empedocles': 'Μέγαν δὲ τὸν Ἀκράγαντα εἰπεῖν φησιν ἐπεὶ μυριάδες αὐτὸν κατῴκουν ὀγδοήκοντα'; 'Timaeus explains that he called Agrigentum great, inasmuch as it had 800,000 inhabitants.'

219. *Idyll. 17*] Theocritus, *Idylls*, XVII.82-85: 'τρεῖς μέν οἱ πολίων ἑκατοντάδες ἐνδέδμηνται, / τρεῖς δ᾽ ἄρα χιλιάδες τρισσαῖς ἐπὶ μυριάδεσσι, / δοιαὶ δὲ τριάδες, μετὰ δέ σφισιν ἐννεάδες τρεῖς· / τῶν πάντων Πτολεμαῖος ἀγήνωρ ἐμβασιλεύει'; 'Three hundred cities are built there, and three thousand in addition to three times ten thousand, and twice three, and thrice nine besides; of all these lord Ptolemy is king.'

220. *Lib. i*] Diodorus Siculus, I.xxxi.6-8: 'Ἡ μὲν οὖν Αἴγυπτος πανταχόθεν φυσικῶς ὠχύρωται τὸν εἰρημένον τρόπον, τῷ δὲ σχήματι παραμήκης οὖσα δισχιλίων μὲν σταδίων ἔχει τὴν παραθαλάττιον πλευράν, εἰς μεσόγειον δ᾽ ἀνήκει σχεδὸν ἐπὶ σταδίους ἑξακισχιλίους. πολυανθρωπίᾳ δὲ τὸ μὲν παλαιὸν πολὺ προέσχε πάντων τῶν γνωριζομένων τόπων κατὰ τὴν οἰκουμένην, καὶ καθ᾽ ἡμᾶς δὲ οὐδενὸς τῶν ἄλλων δοκεῖ λείπεσθαι· ἐπὶ μὲν γὰρ τῶν ἀρχαίων χρόνων ἔσχε κώμας ἀξιολόγους καὶ πόλεις πλείους τῶν μυρίων καὶ ὀκτακισχιλίων, ὡς ἐν ταῖς ἱεραῖς ἀναγραφαῖς ὁρᾶν ἔστι κατακεχωρισμένον, ἐπὶ δὲ Πτολεμαίου τοῦ Λάγου πλείους τῶν τρισμυρίων ἠριθμήθησαν, ὧν τὸ πλῆθος διαμεμένηκεν ἕως 8τῶν καθ᾽ ἡμᾶς χρόνων. τοῦ δὲ σύμπαντος λαοῦ τὸ μὲν παλαιὸν φασι γεγονέναι περὶ ἑπτακοσίας μυριάδας, καὶ καθ᾽ ἡμᾶς δὲ οὐκ ἐλάττους εἶναι τούτων'; 'The land of Egypt, then, is fortified on all sides by nature in the manner described, and is oblong in shape, having a coastline of two thousand stades and extending inland about six thousand stades. In density of population it far surpassed of old all known regions of the inhabited world, and even in our own day is thought to be second to none other; for in ancient times it had over eighteen thousand important villages and cities, as can be seen entered in their sacred records, while under Ptolemy son of Lagus these were reckoned at over thirty thousand, this great number continuing down to our own time. The total population, they say, was of old about seven million and the number has remained no less down to our day.' Diodorus's estimate of the population of Egypt was confirmed a century later by Josephus, who estimated it at 7,500,000 (*Jewish War*, II.ccclxxxv). Diodorus does not, as Hume asserts, say that the population of Egypt has halved in recent times.

221. *first and second PUNIC wars*] i.e. between the end of the First Punic War in 241 BC and the beginning of the Second Punic War in 218 BC.

222. *from the time . . . triumvirates*] i.e. from 264 BC (the beginning of the First Punic War) to 27 BC (the date of the political settlement which marked the beginning of the principate of Augustus).

223. *Orat. funebris*] Lysias, Oration II, *Funeral Oration*, XXVII-XXVIII: 'Μετὰ ταῦτα δὲ Ξέρξης ὁ τῆς Ἀσίας βασιλεύς, καταφρονήσας μὲν τῆς Ἑλλάδος, ἐψευσμένος δὲ τῆς ἐλπίδος, ἀτιμαζόμενος δὲ τῷ γεγενημένῳ, ἀχθόμενος δὲ τῇ συμφορᾷ, ὀργιζόμενος δὲ τοῖς αἰτίοις, ἀπαθὴς δ᾽ ὢν κακῶν καὶ ἄπειρος ἀνδρῶν ἀγαθῶν, δεκάτῳ ἔτει παρασκευασάμενος διακοσίαις μὲν καὶ χιλίαις ναυσὶν ἀφίκετο, τῆς δὲ πεζῆς στρατιᾶς οὕτως ἄπειρον τὸ πλῆθος ἦγεν, ὥστε καὶ τὰ ἔθνη τὰ μετ᾽ αὐτοῦ ἀκολουθήσαντα πολὺ ἂν ἔργον εἴη καταλέξαι· ὃ δὲ μέγιστον σημεῖον τοῦ πλήθους· ἐξὸν γὰρ αὐτῷ χιλίαις ναυσὶ διαβιβάσαι κατὰ τὸ στενότατον τοῦ Ἑλλησπόντου

τὴν πεζὴν στρατιὰν ἐκ τῆς Ἀσίας εἰς τὴν Εὐρώπην, οὐκ ἠθέλησεν, ἡγούμενος τὴν διατριβὴν αὐτῷ πολλὴν ἔσεσθαι᾽; 'Thereafter Xerxes, King of Asia, who had held Greece in contempt, but had been deceived in his hopes, who was dishonoured by the event, galled by the disaster, and angered against its authors, and who was unused to ill-hap and unacquainted with true men, in ten years' time prepared for war and came with twelve hundred ships; and the land army that he brought was so immense in numbers that to enumerate even the nations that followed in his train would be a lengthy task. But the surest evidence of their numbers is this: although he had a thousand ships to spare for transporting his land army over the narrowest part of the Hellespont from Asia to Europe he decided against it, for he judged that it would cause him a great waste of time.'

224. *Lib. ii*] Polybius, II.xxiv.14–17: 'Ῥωμαίων δὲ καὶ Καμπανῶν ἡ πληθὺς πεζῶν μὲν εἰς εἴκοσι καὶ πέντε κατελέχθησαν μυριάδες, ἱππέων δ᾽ ἐπὶ ταῖς δύο μυριάσιν ἐπῆσαν ἔτι τρεῖς χιλιάδες. ὥστ᾽ εἶναι τὸ [κεφάλαιον τῶν μὲν προκαθημένων τῆς Ῥώμης δυνάμεως πεζοὶ μὲν ὑπὲρ πεντεκαίδεκα μυριάδες, ἱππεῖς δὲ πρὸς ἑξακισχιλίους, τὸ δὲ] σύμπαν πλῆθος τῶν δυναμένων ὅπλα βαστάζειν αὐτῶν τε Ῥωμαίων καὶ τῶν συμμάχων πεζῶν ὑπὲρ τὰς ἑβδομήκοντα μυριάδας, ἱππέων δ᾽ εἰς ἑπτὰ μυριάδας. ἐφ᾽ οὓς Ἀννίβας ἐλάττους ἔχων δισμυρίων ἐπέβαλεν εἰς τὴν Ἰταλίαν. περὶ μὲν οὖν τούτων ἐν τοῖς ἑξῆς σαφέστερον ἐκποιήσει κατανοεῖν᾽; 'Of Romans and Campanians there were on the roll two hundred and fifty thousand and twenty-three thousand horse; so that the total number of Romans and allies able to bear arms was more than seven hundred thousand foot and seventy thousand horse, while Hannibal invaded Italy with an army of less than twenty thousand men. On this matter I shall be able to give my readers more explicit information in the course of this work.'

225. *Lib. ii*] Diodorus Siculus, II.v.7: 'Ῥωμαῖοι δὲ μικρὸν πρὸ τῶν Ἀννιβαϊκῶν καιρῶν, προορώμενοι τὸ μέγεθος τοῦ πολέμου, κατέγραψαν τοὺς κατὰ τὴν Ἰταλίαν ἐπιτηδείους εἰς στρατείαν πολίτας τε καὶ συμμάχους, ὧν ὁ σύμπας ἀριθμὸς μικρὸν ἀπέλιπε τῶν ἑκατὸν μυριάδων· καίτοι γ᾽ ἕνεκα πλήθους ἀνθρώπων τὴν Ἰταλίαν ὅλην οὐκ ἄν τις συγκρίνειε πρὸς ἓν ἔθνος τῶν κατὰ τὴν Ἀσίαν. ταῦτα μὲν οὖν ἡμῖν εἰρήσθω πρὸς τοὺς ἐκ τῆς νῦν περὶ τὰς πόλεις οὔσης ἐρημίας τεκμαιρομένους τὴν παλαιὰν τῶν ἐθνῶν πολυανθρωπίαν᾽; 'and the Romans, a little before the time of Hannibal, foreseeing the magnitude of the war, enrolled all the men in Italy who were fit for military service, both citizens and allies, and the total sum of them fell only a little short of one million; and yet as regards the number of inhabitants a man would not compare all Italy with a single one of the nations of Asia. Let these facts, then, be a sufficient reply on our part to those who try to estimate the populations of the nations of Asia in ancient times on the strength of inferences drawn from the desolation which at the present time prevails in its cities.'

226. *CELTICA*] Appian, *Celtica*, I.viii: 'Καῖσαρ δὲ πολεμήσας αὐτοῖς πρῶτον μὲν Ἐλουητίους καὶ Τιγυρίους, ἀμφὶ τὰς εἴκοσι μυριάδας ὄντας, ἐνίκησεν. οἱ Τιγύριοι δ᾽ αὐτῶν χρόνῳ ἔμπροσθεν Πίσωνος καὶ Κασσίου τινὰ στρατὸν ἑλόντες ὑπὸ

ζυγὸν ἐξεπεπόμφεσαν, ὡς ἐν χρονικαῖς συντάξεσι δοκεῖ Παύλῳ τῷ Κλαυδίῳ'; 'Caesar opened his campaigns with a victory over some two hundred thousand of the Helvetii and Tigurini. At an earlier date the Tigurini had captured an army of Piso and Cassius, and had made them walk under the yoke, as Paulus Claudius believes in his annals.' Ibid., I.x–xii; 'Μετὰ τούτους ὁ Καῖσαρ τοῖς καλουμένοις Βέλγαις ἐπιπεσών, ποταμόν τινα περῶσι, τοσούτους ἀπέκτεινεν ὡς τὸν ποταμὸν γεφυρωθέντα τοῖς σώμασι περᾶσαι. Νέρβιοι δὲ αὐτὸν ἐτρέψαντο, ἄρτι στρατόπεδον ἐξ ὁδοιπορίας κατασκευάζοντι αἰφνιδίως ἐπιπεσόντες, καὶ παμπόλλους ἐφόνευσαν, τοὺς δὲ ταξιάρχους καὶ λοχαγοὺς ἅπαντας· καὶ αὐτὸν ἐκεῖνον εἰς λόφον τινὰ μετὰ τῶν ὑπασπιστῶν πεφευγότα περιέσχον κύκλῳ, ὑπὸ δὲ τοῦ δεκάτου τάγματος αὐτοῖς ἐξόπισθεν ἐπιπεσόντος ἐφθάρησαν, ἐξακισμύριοι ὄντες. ἦσαν δὲ τῶν Κίμβρων καὶ Τευτόνων ἀπόγονοι. ἐκράτησε καὶ Ἀλλοβρίγων ὁ Καῖσαρ. Οὐσιπετῶν δὲ καὶ Ταγχαρέων τεσσαράκοντα μυριάδες, στρατεύσιμοί τε καὶ ἀστράτευτοι, συνεκόπησαν'; 'After them, Caesar attacked the so-called Belgae as they were in the process of crossing a river, and killed so many of them that he crossed the river on a bridge of their bodies. The Nervii, however, routed him by attacking unexpectedly as he was making camp just after a march. They killed a large number, including all the tribunes and centurions, and surrounded Caesar himself on a hill where he had taken refuge with his bodyguard. But they were attacked in the rear by the tenth legion and destroyed, although they numbered sixty thousand men. The Nervii were descendants of the Cimbri and Teutones. Caesar also conquered the Allobroges, and cut to pieces four hundred thousand of the Usipites and Tencteri, both soldiers and civilians.'

227. *to two*] Plutarch, *Life of Caesar*, XV: 'ἔτη γὰρ οὐδὲ δέκα πολεμήσας περὶ Γαλατίαν πόλεις μὲν ὑπὲρ ὀκτακοσίας κατὰ κράτος εἷλεν, ἔθνη δὲ ἐχειρώσατο τριακόσια, μυριάσι δὲ παραταξάμενος κατὰ μέρος τριακοσίαις ἑκατὸν μὲν ἐν χερσὶ διέφθειρεν, ἄλλας δὲ τοσαύτας ἐζώγρησεν'; 'For although it was not full ten years that he waged war in Gaul, he took by storm more than eight hundred cities, subdued three hundred nations, and fought pitched battles at different times with three million men, of whom he slew one million in hand to hand fighting and took as many more prisoners.' Julian, *The Caesars*, 321a: 'οὐδενὸς ἔτι τῶν Γαλατικῶν ἐπεμνήσθην, πλεῖν ἢ τριακοσίας ὑπαγόμενος πόλεις, ἀνδρῶν δὲ οὐκ ἐλάσσους ἢ διακοσίας μυριάδας'; 'And still I have said not a word about my campaigns in Gaul, when I conquered more than three hundred cities and no less than two million men!'

228. *cap. 47*] Velleius Paterculus, *Roman History*, II.xlvii.1: 'Per haec insequentiaque et quae praediximus tempora amplius quadringenta milia hostium a C. Caesare caesa sunt, plura capta'; 'During this period, including the years which immediately followed and those of which mention has already been made, more than four hundred thousand of the enemy were slain by Gaius Caesar and a greater number were taken prisoners.'

229. *DIODORUS SICULUS allows . . . incredible*] Diodorus Siculus, II.v.5: "Ἔστι μὲν οὖν ἄπιστον τοῖς αὐτόθεν ἀκούσασι τὸ πλῆθος τῆς στρατιᾶς, οὐ μὴν ἀδύνατόν γε φανήσεται τοῖς ἀναθεωροῦσι τὸ τῆς Ἀσίας μέγεθος καὶ τὰ πλήθη τῶν κατοικούντων αὐτὴν ἐθνῶν'; 'Now at first hearing the great size of the army is incredible, but it will not seem at all impossible to any who consider the great extent of Asia and the vast numbers of the peoples who inhabit it.' Diodorus, however, is speaking principally of the army raised by Ninus to conquer the Bactrians, which is said by Ctesias to have comprised 1,700,000 infantry, 210,000 cavalry and 10,600 chariots. The size of the forces raised by Dionysius are adduced by Diodorus simply to attest the credibility of these numbers.

230. *The GREEK colonies . . . in ITALY*] Wallace also notes the populousness of ancient Sicily, but does not mention its later decline: '*SICILY* was likewise well peopled before the times of *Alexander the Great*, and contained several powerful states' (Wallace, *Dissertation*, p. 63; cf. p. 306).

231. *lib. ii*] Diodorus Siculus, II.v.6: 'κατὰ μὲν οὖν τὴν Σικελίαν ὁ Διονύσιος ἐκ μιᾶς τῆς τῶν Συρακοσίων πόλεως ἐξήγαγεν ἐπὶ τὰς στρατείας πεζῶν μὲν δώδεκα μυριάδας, ἱππεῖς δὲ μυρίους καὶ δισχιλίους, ναῦς δὲ μακρὰς ἐξ ἑνὸς λιμένος τετρακοσίας, ὧν ἦσαν ἔνιαι τετρήρεις καὶ πεντήρεις'; 'In Sicily, for instance, Dionysius led forth on his campaigns from the single city of the Syracusans one hundred and twenty thousand foot-soldiers and twelve thousand cavalry, and from a single harbour four hundred warships, some of which were quadriremes and quinquerernes.' In 'Of Commerce', however, where it suited his argument, Hume had cited without demur the vast size of Dionysius's military establishment, relying on this same passage, noting only in a footnote that the numbers were 'somewhat suspicious' (above, p. 6, n. †).

232. *vita DIONIS*] Plutarch, *Life of Dion*, XXV: 'ὅπλα δέ, χωρὶς ὧν εἶχον οἱ στρατιῶται, δισχιλίας μὲν ἐκόμιζεν ἀσπίδας, βέλη δὲ καὶ δόρατα πολλά, καὶ πλῆθος ἐφοδίων ἄφθονον, ὅπως ἐπιλίπῃ μηδὲν αὐτοὺς ποντοποροῦντας'; 'Moreover, besides the arms which his soldiers had, Dion carried two thousand shields, missiles and spears in great numbers, and a boundless store of provisions, that they might suffer no lack as they traversed the high sea.'

233. *lib. vi*] Strabo, VI.ii.7: 'πρόσεστι δὲ καὶ τὸ ἐγγύθεν· ὡσανεὶ γὰρ μέρος τι τῆς Ἰταλίας ἐστὶν ἡ νῆσος, καὶ ὑποχορηγεῖ τῇ Ῥώμῃ, καθάπερ ἐκ τῶν Ἰταλικῶν ἀγρῶν, ἕκαστα εὐμαρῶς καὶ ἀταλαιπώρως. καὶ δὴ καὶ καλοῦσιν αὐτὴν ταμεῖον τῆς Ῥώμης· κομίζεται γὰρ τὰ γινόμενα πάντα πλὴν ὀλίγων τῶν αὐτόθι ἀναλισκομένων δεῦρο. ταῦτα δ' ἐστὶν οὐχ οἱ καρποὶ μόνον, ἀλλὰ καὶ βοσκήματα καὶ δέρματα καὶ ἔρια καὶ τὰ τοιαῦτα'; 'There is, furthermore, its [Sicily's] propinquity; for the island is a part of Italy, as it were, and readily and without great labour supplies Rome with everything it has, as though from the fields of Italy. And in fact it is called the storehouse of Rome, for everything it produces is brought hither except a few things that are consumed at home, and not the fruits only, but also cattle, hides, wool, and the like.'

234. *ATHENÆUS ... than 40,000*] cf. the note in the 'Early Memoranda': 'That Athens was not so populus as we shoud naturally conclude from its Bulk describd by Thucidides, these Reasons prove. 1. There were ~~but~~ [about *inserted above the line*] 10.000 Houses. Xen. Mem. L. 3. P. 774. 2. There were but 20.000 Citizens, each of which upon an Averrage coud not have 20 Slaves. For. 1. No Rising or Suspicion of a rising is every mentiond by the Historians. 2. Timarchus is spoke of by Æschines as a rich man for possessing 20 Slaves; Demosthenes Father had thirty. 3. Chios is said by Thucidides to have had most Slaves except Sparta of any Greek City. [Lib. 8. Page 581 *inserted above the line*]. Now the Helots were not very numerous as we learn from Plutarch. Besides Sparta had no Trade. 4. Xenophon says there was much empty whn the Walls. περι ποραυς' (NLS MS 23159, item 14, p. 26; cf. Mossner, 'Memoranda', pp. 516–17).

235. *Apolog. SOCR.*] Plato, *Apology of Socrates*, XXIXd: 'Ὦ ἄριστε ἀνδρῶν, Ἀθηναῖος ὤν, πόλεως τῆς μεγίστης καὶ εὐδοκιμωτάτης εἰς σοφίαν καὶ ἰσχύν'; 'Most excellent of men, as an Athenian, a citizen of the greatest of cities and one most distinguished for wisdom and strength . . .'

236. *Orat. 34*] Lysias, Oration XXXIV, *Against the Subversion of the Ancestral Constitution of Athens*, VII–VIII: 'ὁρῶ δὲ καὶ Ἀργείους καὶ Μαντινέας τὴν αὐτὴν ἔχοντας γνώμην τὴν αὐτῶν οἰκοῦντας, τοὺς μὲν ὁμόρους ὄντας Λακεδαιμονίοις, τοὺς δὲ ἐγγὺς οἰκοῦντας, καὶ τοὺς μὲν οὐδὲν ἡμῶν πλείους, τοὺς δὲ οὐδὲ τρισχιλίους ὄντας'; 'And I observe the same attitude in both the Argives and the Mantineans, each inhabiting their own land, – the former bordering on the Lacedaemonians, the latter dwelling near them; in the one case, their number is no greater than ours, in the other it is less than three thousand.'

237. *NICIÆ*] Thucydides, VI.xxxiii.5: 'οὔτε γὰρ πλείους τῶν ἐνοικούντων καὶ ἀστυγειτόνων ἔρχονται (πάντα γὰρ ὑπὸ δέους ξυνίσταται), ἤν τε δι' ἀπορίαν τῶν ἐπιτηδείων ἐν ἀλλοτρίᾳ γῇ σφαλῶσι, τοῖς ἐπιβουλευθεῖσιν ὄνομα, κἂν περὶ σφίσιν αὐτοῖς τὰ πλείω πταίσωσιν, ὅμως καταλείπουσιν'; 'The reason is that they are not, in the first place, superior in numbers to the people against whom they go and the neighbours of these – for fear always brings about union; and if, in the second place, they fail on account of lack of supplies in a foreign land, they leave a proud name to those whom they plotted against, even though their failure be due chiefly to themselves.' Thucydides is reporting the speech of Hemocrates in the Senate of Syracuse concerning the imminent invasion of Sicily by the Athenians. His remarks are a generalization, and despite the use to which Hume puts them, they do not seem immediately to compare the populations of Athens and Syracuse. Plutarch, *Life of Nicias*, XVII: 'Συρακούσας, πόλιν Ἀθηνῶν οὐκ ἐλάττονα'; 'Syracuse, a city fully as large as Athens'.

238. *kind of bay*] Cicero, *Against Verres*, IV.lii: 'Unius etiam urbis omnium pulcherrimae atque ornatissimae, Syracusarum, direptionem commemorabo et in medium proferam'; 'There is still one city, Syracuse, the richest and fairest of all, the tale of whose plundering I will bring forward and relate

to you.' Strabo, VI.ii.4: 'πεντάπολις γὰρ ἦν τὸ παλαιόν, ὀγδοήκοντα καὶ ἑκατὸν σταδίων ἔχουσα τὸ τεῖχος'; 'For in olden times it was a city of five towns, with a wall of one hundred and eighty stadia.'

239. *Lib. vi. cap. 20*] Athenaeus, *The Banquet of the Learned*, VI.272c: 'Κτησικλῆς δ᾽ ἐν τρίτῃ Χρονικῶν κατὰ τὴν ἕπτα καιδεκάτην πρὸς ταῖς ἑκατόν φησιν Ὀλυμπιάδα Ἀθήνησιν ἐξετασμὸν γενέσθαι ὑπὸ Δημητρίου τοῦ Φαληρέως τῶν κατοικούντων τὴν Ἀττικὴν καὶ εὑρεθῆναι Ἀθηναίους μὲν δισμυρίους πρὸς τοῖς χιλίοις, μετοίκους δὲ μυρίους, οἰκετῶν δὲ μυριάδας τεσσαράκοντα'; 'Ctesicles in Book III of the Chronicles says that a census of the inhabitants of Attica was taken in Athens by Demetrius of Phalerum during the 117th Olympiad and that 21,000 Athenians, 10,000 metics, and 400,000 slaves were identified.'

240. *contra ARISTAG.*] Demosthenes, *Against Aristogeiton 1*, LI: 'εἰσὶν ὁμοῦ δισμύριοι πάντες Ἀθηναῖοι'; 'There are something like twenty thousand Athenian citizens in all.'

241. *Lib. v*] Herodotus, V.xcvii: 'πολλοὺς γὰρ οἶκε εἶναι εὐπετέστερον διαβάλλειν ἢ ἕνα, εἰ Κλεομένεα μὲν τὸν Λακεδαιμόνιον μοῦνον οὐκ οἷός τε ἐγένετο διαβάλλειν, τρεῖς δὲ μυριάδας Ἀθηναίων ἐποίησε τοῦτο'; 'Truly it would seem that it is easier to deceive many than one; for he could not deceive Cleomenes of Lacedaemon, one single man, but thirty thousand Athenians he could.'

242. *Lib. viii*] Thucydides, VIII.lxxii.1-2: 'Πέμπουσι δὲ καὶ ἐς τὴν Σάμον δέκα ἄνδρας, παραμυθησομένους τὸ στρατόπεδον καὶ διδάξοντας ὡς οὐκ ἐπὶ βλάβῃ τῆς πόλεως καὶ τῶν πολιτῶν ἡ ὀλιγαρχία κατέστη, ἀλλ᾽ ἐπὶ σωτηρίᾳ τῶν ξυμπάντων πραγμά των, πεντακισχίλιοί τε ὅτι εἶεν καὶ οὐ τετρακόσιοι μόνον οἱ πράσσοντες· καίτοι οὐ πώποτε Ἀθηναίους διὰ τὰς στρατείας καὶ τὴν ὑπερορίαν ἀσχολίαν ἐς οὐδὲν πρᾶγμα οὕτω μέγα ἐλθεῖν βουλεύσοντας, ἐν ᾧ πεντακισχιλίους ξυνελθεῖν'; 'They also sent ten men to Samos to reassure the army there and to explain that the oligarchy had been set up, not for the injury of the city or the citizens, but for the salvation of the whole Athenian cause; and also to explain that there were five thousand, not four hundred only, who were participating in the government, although, because of their military expeditions and their activities abroad, the Athenians had never yet come to consult upon any matter so important that five thousand had assembled.'

243. *but 10,000 houses*] See above, p. 472, n. 234.

244. *much waste ground*] See above, p. 472, n. 234.

245. *insurrection of the slaves*] See above, p. 472, n. 234.

246. *over the negroes*] Hume here echoes Melon: 'Les Colonies sont necessaires à la Nation, & les Esclaves sont necessaires aux Colonies, où leur supériorité de nombre sur les habitans seroit périlleuse, si la douceur ordinaire de la police n'étoit accompagnée de la severité militaire ... Lorsque la supériorité des Maîtres ne laisseroit plus à craindre une révolte, la Loi s'adouciroit pour l'Esclave' (Melon, *Essai politique*, pp. 51-2).

247. *lib. xii*] Thucydides, II.xiii.6: 'χρήμασι μὲν οὖν οὕτω ἐθάρσυνεν αὐτούς· ὁπλίτας δὲ τρισχιλίους καὶ μυρίους εἶναι ἄνευ τῶν ἐν τοῖς φρουρίοις καὶ τῶν παρ᾽ ἔπαλξιν

ἑξακισχιλίων καὶ μυρίων'; 'As to their resources in money, then, he thus sought to encourage them; and as to heavily armed infantry, he told them that there were thirteen thousand, not counting the sixteen thousand men who garrisoned the forts and manned the city walls.' Diodorus Siculus, XII.xl.4: 'Χωρὶς δὲ τῶν χρημάτων τούτων στρατιώτας ἀπεδείκνυεν ὑπάρχειν τῇ πόλει χωρὶς συμμάχων καὶ τῶν ἐν τοῖς φρουρίοις ὄντων ὁπλίτας μὲν μυρίους καὶ δισχιλίους, τοὺς δ' ἐν τοῖς φρουρίοις ὄντας καὶ τοὺς μετοίκους ὑπάρχειν πλείους τῶν μυρίων ἑπτακισχιλίων, τριήρεις τε τὰς παρούσας τριακοσίας'; 'In addition to these financial resources Pericles pointed out that, omitting the allies and garrisons, the city had available twelve thousand hoplites, the garrisons and metics amounted to more than seventeen thousand, and the triremes available to three hundred.'

248. *Mem. lib. ii*] Xenophon, *Memorabilia*, III.vi.14: 'ἀλλ' ἐπεὶ ἡ μὲν πόλις ἐκ πλειόνων ἢ μυρίων οἰκιῶν συνέστηκε'; 'Seeing that our city contains more than ten thousand houses.'

249. *Lib. ii*] Thucydides, II.xiii.7: 'τοῦ τε γὰρ Φαληρικοῦ τείχους στάδιοι ἦσαν πέντε καὶ τριάκοντα πρὸς τὸν κύκλον τοῦ ἄστεως καὶ αὐτοῦ τοῦ κύκλου τὸ φυλασσόμενον τρεῖς καὶ τεσσαράκοντα (ἔστι δὲ αὐτοῦ ὃ καὶ ἀφύλακτον ἦν, τὸ μεταξὺ τοῦ τε μακροῦ καὶ τοῦ Φαληρικοῦ), τὰ δὲ μακρὰ τείχη πρὸς τὸν Πειραιᾶ τεσσαράκοντα σταδίων, ὧν τὸ ἔξωθεν ἐτηρεῖτο, καὶ τοῦ Πειραιῶς ξὺν Μουνιχίᾳ ἑξήκοντα μὲν σταδίων ὁ ἅπας περίβολος, τὸ δ' ἐν φυλακῇ ὂν ἥμισυ τούτου'; 'For the length of the Phalerian wall was thirty-five stadia to the circuit-wall of the city, and the portion of the circuit-wall itself which was guarded was forty-three stadia (a portion being left unguarded, that between the Long Wall and the Phalerian); and the Long Walls to the Peiraeus were forty stadia in extent, of which only the outside one was guarded; and the whole circuit of the Peiraeus including Munichia was sixty stadia, half of it being under guard.'

250. *ratione red.*] Xenophon, *Ways and Means*, II.vi: 'καὶ πολλὰ οἰκιῶν ἔρημά ἐστιν ἐντὸς τῶν τειχῶν'; 'there are many vacant sites for houses within the walls.'

251. *lib. vi*] Athenaeus, *The Banquet of the Learned*, VI.272e–f: 'καὶ αἱ πολλαὶ δὲ αὗται Ἀττικαὶ μυριάδες τῶν οἰκετῶν δεδεμέναι εἰργάζοντο τὰ μέταλλα· Ποσειδώνιος γοῦν, οὗ συνεχῶς μέμνησαι, ὁ φιλόσοφος καὶ ἀποστάντας φησὶν αὐτοὺς καταφονεῦσαι μὲν τοὺς ἐπὶ τῶν μετάλλων φύλακας, καταλαβέσθαι δὲ τὴν ἐπὶ Σουνίῳ ἀκρόπολιν καὶ ἐπὶ πολὺν χρόνον πορθῆσαι τὴν Ἀττικήν'; 'These many tens of thousands of Attic slaves, on the other hand, worked in chains in the mines. The philosopher Posidonius, at any rate, to whom you constantly refer, reports that they revolted and murdered the guards posted at the mines, and then captured the citadel in Sunium and ravaged Attica for an extended period.'

252. *De rep. ATHEN.*] Xenophon (?), *The Constitution of the Athenians*, I.x–xii: 'Τῶν δούλων δ' αὖ καὶ τῶν μετοίκων πλείστη ἐστὶν Ἀθήνησιν ἀκολασία καὶ οὔτε πατάξαι ἔξεστιν αὐτόθι οὔτε ὑπεκστήσεταί σοι ὁ δοῦλος. οὗ δ' ἕνεκέν ἐστι τοῦτο ἐπιχώριον, ἐγὼ φράσω· εἰ νόμος ἦν τὸν δοῦλον ὑπὸ τοῦ ἐλευθέρου τύπτεσθαι ἢ τὸν μέτοικον ἢ τὸν ἀπελεύθερον, πολλάκις ἂν οἰηθεὶς εἶναι τὸν Ἀθηναῖον δοῦλον ἐπάταξεν ἄν· ἐσθῆτά τε γὰρ οὐδὲν βελτίων ὁ δῆμος αὐτόθι ἢ οἱ δοῦλοι καὶ οἱ

μέτοικοι, καὶ τὰ εἴδη οὐδὲν βελτίους εἰσίν. εἰ δέ τις καὶ τοῦτο θαυμάζει ὅτι ἐῶσι τοὺς δούλους τρυφᾶν αὐτόθι καὶ μεγαλοπρεπῶς διαιτᾶσθαι ἐνίους, καὶ τοῦτο γνώμῃ φανεῖεν ἂν ποιοῦντες. ὅπου γὰρ ναυτικὴ δύναμίς ἐστιν, ἀπὸ χρημάτων ἀνάγκη τοῖς ἀνδραπόδοις δουλεύειν, ἵνα λαμβάνων μὲν πράττῃ τὰς ἀποφοράς, καὶ ἐλευθέρους ἀφιέναι· ὅπου δ᾽ εἰσὶ πλούσιοι δοῦλοι, οὐκέτι ἐνταῦθα λυσιτελεῖ τὸν ἐμὸν δοῦλον σὲ δεδιέναι· ἐν δὲ τῇ Λακεδαίμονι ὁ ἐμὸς δοῦλος σ᾽ ἐδεδοίκει· ἐὰν δὲ δεδίῃ ὁ σὸς δοῦλος ἐμέ, κινδυνεύσει καὶ τὰ χρήματα διδόναι τὰ ἑαυτοῦ ὥστε μὴ κινδυνεύειν περὶ ἑαυτοῦ. διὰ τοῦτ᾽ οὖν ἰσηγορίαν καὶ τοῖς δούλοις πρὸς τοὺς ἐλευθέρους ἐποιήσαμεν, καὶ τοῖς μετοίκοις πρὸς τοὺς ἀστούς, διότι δεῖται ἡ πόλις μετοίκων διά τε τὸ πλῆθος τῶν τεχνῶν καὶ διὰ τὸ ναυτικόν· διὰ τοῦτο οὖν καὶ τοῖς μετοίκοις εἰκότως τὴν ἰσηγορίαν ἐποιήσαμεν'; 'Now among the slaves and metics at Athens there is the greatest uncontrolled wantonness; you can't hit them there, and a slave will not stand aside for you. I shall point out why this is their native practice: if it were customary for a slave (or metic or freedman) to be struck by one who is free, you would often hit an Athenian citizen by mistake on the assumption that he was a slave. For the people there are no better dressed than the slaves and metics, nor are they any more handsome. If anyone is also startled by the fact that they let the slaves live luxuriously there and some of them sumptuously, it would be clear that even this they do for a reason. For where there is a naval power, it is necessary from financial considerations to be slaves to the slaves in order to take a portion of their earnings, and it is then necessary to let them go free. And where there are rich slaves, it is no longer profitable in such a place for my slave to fear you. In Sparta my slave would fear you; but if your slave fears me, there will be the chance that he will give over his money so as not to have to worry anymore. For this reason we have set up equality between slaves and free men, and between metics and citizens. The city needs metics in view of the many different trades and the fleet. Accordingly, then, we have reasonably set up a similar equality also for the metics.'

253. *PHILIP.* 3] Demosthenes, *Third Philippic*, III: 'σκοπεῖτε γὰρ ὡδί· ὑμεῖς τὴν παρρησίαν ἐπὶ μὲν τῶν ἄλλων οὕτω κοινὴν οἴεσθε δεῖν εἶναι πᾶσι τοῖς ἐν τῇ πόλει, ὥστε καὶ τοῖς ξένοις καὶ τοῖς δούλοις αὐτῆς μεταδεδώκατε, καὶ πολλοὺς ἄν τις οἰκέτας ἴδοι παρ᾽ ἡμῖν μετὰ πλείονος ἐξουσίας ὅ τι βούλονται λέγοντας ἢ πολίτας ἐν ἐνίαις τῶν ἄλλων πόλεων, ἐκ δὲ τοῦ συμβουλεύειν παντάπασιν ἐξεληλάκατε'; 'For look at it in this way. In other matters you think it so necessary to grant general freedom of speech to everyone in Athens that you even allow aliens and slaves to share in the privilege, and many menials may be observed among you speaking their minds with more liberty than citizens enjoy in other states; but from your deliberations you have banished it utterly.'

254. *STICHO*] Plautus, *Stichus*, III.i.446–48: 'atque id ne uos miremini, homines seruolos / potare, amare, atque ad cenam condicere: / licet haec Athenis nobis'; 'And so that you won't be surprised that slaves drink, make love, and make dinner arrangements, we're allowed to do this in Athens.'

255. *Contra TIMARCH.*] Aeschines, *Against Timarchus*, XLII: 'καὶ ταῦτα οὐκ ὤκνησεν, ἀλλ᾽ ὑπέστη Τίμαρχος οὑτοσί, οὐδενὸς ὢν τῶν μετρίων ἐνδεής· πολλὴν γὰρ πάνυ κατέλιπεν ὁ πατὴρ αὐτῷ οὐσίαν, ἣν οὗτος κατεδήδοκεν, ὡς ἐγὼ προϊόντος ἐπιδείξω τοῦ λόγου'; 'Timarchus did not hesitate, but submitted to it all, though he had income enough to satisfy all reasonable desires. For his father had left him a very large property, which he has squandered, as I will show in the course of my speech.'

256. *Now TIMARCHUS . . . manufactures*] See above, p. 476, n. 255. Cf. also the entry in the 'Early Memoranda': 'Timarchus was said by Æschines to have been left in easy Circumstances by his Father, because he had ten Slaves who gain'd him 2 Oboles apiece a day A Proof that every Citizen of Athens upon an Averrage had not 20 Slaves.' (NLS MS 23159, item 14, p. 25; cf. Mossner, 'Memoranda', p. 516).

257. *DEMOSTHENES . . . considerable manufactory*] Demosthenes, *Against Aphobus 1*, IX–XI: quoted above, pp. 429–30, n. 53.

258. *20,000 slaves deserted*] The desertion of the slaves at Decelea happened in 413 BC.

259. *whole census . . . 6000 talents*] cf. the note in the 'Early Memoranda': 'The Census of the Athenians was 6000 Talents. Περι συμμωριας. Qu Whether was this annual or the whole Stock. If that latter, their Taxes must have been vastly high; since the twelfth Part was sometimes exacted. Id. [It was the Whole Stock as Polybius says expressly. Lib. 2. C. 63 *inserted below the line*]' (NLS MS 23159, item 14, pp. 24–5; cf. Mossner, 'Memoranda', p. 515).

260. *the great number of holidays in ATHENS*] cf. the note in the 'Early Memoranda': 'The Holydays in Athens made two Months in the Year Salmasius.' (NLS MS 23159, item 14, p. 19; cf. Mossner, 'Memoranda', p. 511). In his *Della regolata divozion de' Cristiani* (Venice, 1747) Ludovico Muratori had deplored the number of feast days in Catholic countries, and the consequent economic detriment they inflicted, particularly on the poor (Robertson, *Enlightenment*, p. 405).

261. *Orat. 11*] Lysias, Oration XII, *Against Eratosthenes*, XIX: 'καὶ ἀνδράποδα εἴκοσι καὶ ἑκατόν'; 'also a hundred and twenty slaves'.

262. *Contra APHOB.*] Demosthenes, *Against Aphobus 1*, IX–XI: quoted above, pp. 429–30, n. 53.

263. *Lib. vii*] Thucydides, VII.xxvii.4–5: 'πρότερον μὲν γὰρ βραχεῖαι γιγνόμεναι αἱ ἐσβολαὶ τὸν ἄλλον χρόνον τῆς γῆς ἀπολαύειν οὐκ ἐκώλυον· τότε δὲ ξυνεχῶς ἐπικαθημένων, καὶ ὁτὲ μὲν καὶ πλεόνων ἐπιόντων, ὁτὲ δ᾽ ἐξ ἀνάγκης τῆς ἴσης φρουρᾶς καταθεούσης τε τὴν χώραν καὶ λῃστείας ποιουμένης, βασιλέως τε παρόντος τοῦ τῶν Λακεδαιμονίων Ἄγιδος, ὃς οὐκ ἐκ παρέργου τὸν πόλεμον ἐποιεῖτο, μεγάλα οἱ Ἀθηναῖοι ἐβλάπτοντο. τῆς τε γὰρ χώρας ἁπάσης ἐστέρηντο καὶ ἀνδραπόδων πλέον ἢ δύο μυριάδες ηὐτομολήκεσαν, καὶ τούτων πολὺ μέρος χειροτέχναι, πρόβατά τε πάντα ἀπολώλει καὶ ὑποζύγια· ἵπποι τε, ὁσημέραι ἐξελαυνόντων τῶν ἱππέων, πρός τε τὴν Δεκέλειαν καταδρομὰς ποιουμένων

καὶ κατὰ τὴν χώραν φυλασσόντων, οἱ μὲν ἀπεχωλοῦντο ἐν γῇ ἀποκρότῳ τε καὶ
ξυνεχῶς ταλαιπωροῦντες, οἱ δ᾽ ἐτιτρώσκοντο᾿; 'For before this summer the
enemy's invasions, being of short duration, did not prevent the Athenians
from making full use of the land during the rest of the year; but at this
time, the occupation being continuous, the enemy sometimes invading the
country with a larger force and at others the regular garrison overrunning
the country, as it was compelled to do, and carrying off booty, while Agis,
the king of the Lacedaemonians, who was present in person, carried on the
war in no desultory fashion, the Athenians were suffering great damage.
For they were deprived of their whole territory, more than twenty thousand
slaves had already deserted, a large proportion of these being artisans, and
all their small cattle and beasts of burden were lost; and now that the cavalry were sallying forth every day, making demonstrations against Deceleia
and keeping guard throughout the country, some horses were constantly
going lame because of the rocky ground and the incessant hardships they
had to endure, and some were continually being wounded.'

264. *De rat. red.*] Xenophon, *Ways and Means*, IV.xiii–xxxii. The relevant numbers are given at xxiii–xxiv: Ἦν γε μέντοι τὸ πρῶτον συστῇ διακόσια καὶ χίλια
ἀνδράποδα, εἰκὸς ἤδη ἀπ᾽ αὐτῆς τῆς προσόδου ἐν ἔτεσι πέντε ἢ ἓξ μὴ μεῖον ἂν
τῶν ἑξακισχιλίων γενέσθαι. ἀπό γε μὴν τούτου τοῦ ἀριθμοῦ ἦν ὀβολὸν ἕκαστος
ἀτελῆ τῆς ἡμέρας φέρῃ, ἡ μὲν πρόσοδος ἑξήκοντα τάλαντα τοῦ ἐνιαυτοῦ. ἀπὸ δὲ
τούτων ἦν εἰς ἄλλα ἀνδράποδα τιθῆται εἴκοσι, τοῖς τετταράκοντα ἤδη ἐξέσται
τῇ πόλει χρῆσθαι εἰς ἄλλο ὅ τι ἂν δέῃ. ὅταν δέ γε μύρια ἀναπληρωθῇ, ἑκατὸν
τάλαντα ἡ πρόσοδος ἔσται᾿; 'Assume, however, that the total number of slaves
to begin with is twelve hundred. By using the revenue derived from these the
number might in all probability be raised to six thousand at the least in the
course of five or six years. Further, if each man brings in a clear obol a day,
the annual revenue derived from that number of men is sixty talents. Out
of this sum, if twenty talents are invested in additional slaves, the state will
have forty talents available for any other necessary purpose. And when a
total of ten thousand men is reached, the revenue will be a hundred talents.'

265. *De classibus*] Demosthenes, *On the Navy-Boards*, XIX: ἐπειδὰν δὲ ταῦθ᾽
οὕτως ἔχονθ᾽ ὑπάρχῃ, κελεύω, ἐπειδὴ τὸ τίμημ᾽ ἐστὶ τῆς χώρας ἑξακισχιλίων
ταλάντων᾿; 'When these preliminaries are settled, I propose that your wealth
also should be organized, and that as the ratable value of the country is six
thousand talents . . .'

266. *Lib. ii. cap. 62*] Polybius, II.lxii.7–8: τίς γὰρ ὑπὲρ Ἀθηναίων οὐχ ἱστόρηκε
διότι καθ᾽ οὓς καιροὺς μετὰ Θηβαίων εἰς τὸν πρὸς Λακεδαιμονίους ἐνέβαινον
πόλεμον, καὶ μυρίους μὲν ἐξέπεμπον στρατιώτας, ἑκατὸν δ᾽ ἐπλήρουν τριήρεις,
ὅτι τότε κρίναντες ἀπὸ τῆς ἀξίας ποιεῖσθαι τὰς εἰς τὸν πόλεμον εἰσφορὰς
ἐτιμήσαντο τήν τε χώραν τὴν Ἀττικὴν ἅπασαν καὶ τὰς οἰκίας, ὁμοίως δὲ καὶ τὴν
λοιπὴν οὐσίαν· ἀλλ᾽ ὅμως τὸ σύμπαν τίμημα τῆς ἀξίας ἐνέλιπε τῶν ἑξακισχιλίων
διακοσίοις καὶ πεντήκοντα ταλάντοις. ἐξ οὐκ ἀπεοικὸς ἂν φανείη τὸ περὶ

Πελοποννησίων ἄρτι ῥηθὲν ὑπ᾽ ἐμοῦ᾽; 'Who has not read that when the Athenians, in conjunction with the Thebans, entered on the war against the Lacedaemonians, sending out a force of ten thousand men and manning a hundred triremes, they decided to meet the war expenses by a property tax and made a valuation for this purpose of the whole of Attica including the houses and other property. This estimate, however, fell short of 6,000 talents by 250, from which it would seem that my assertion about the Peloponnese at the present day is not far wide of the mark.'

267. *De rat. red.*] Xenophon, *Ways and Means*, IV.xiv: 'πάλαι μὲν γὰρ δήπου οἷς μεμέληκεν ἀκηκόαμεν, ὅτι Νικίας ποτὲ ὁ Νικηράτου ἐκτήσατο ἐν τοῖς ἀργυρείοις χιλίους ἀνθρώπους, οὓς ἐκεῖνος Σωσίᾳ τῷ Θρᾳκὶ ἐξεμίσθωσεν ἐφ᾽ ᾧ ὀβολὸν μὲν ἀτελῆ ἑκάστου τῆς ἡμέρας ἀποδιδόναι, τὸν δ᾽ ἀριθμὸν ἴσους ἀεὶ παρέχειν'; 'Those of us who have given thought to the matter have heard long ago, I imagine, that Nicias son of Niceratus, once owned a thousand men in the mines, and let them out to Socias the Thracian, on condition that Sosias paid him an obol a day per man net and filled all vacancies as they occurred.'

268. *Contra* APHOBUM] Demosthenes, *Against Aphobus 1*, IX: quoted above, pp. 429–30, n. 53.

269. *780,000*] The reading of 1777a, '78,000', is incorrect: 39,000 Spartan citizens would yield 780,000 slaves, at a ratio of 1:20.

270. *Lib. viii*] Thucydides, VIII.xl.2: 'οἱ γὰρ οἰκέται τοῖς Χίοις πολλοὶ ὄντες καὶ μιᾷ γε πόλει πλὴν Λακεδαιμονίων πλεῖστοι γενόμενοι'; 'For the slaves of the Chians, who were numerous – and indeed the most numerous in any single city except that of the Lacedaemonians.'

271. *vita* LYCURG.] Plutarch, *Life of Lycurgus*, VIII.iii: 'Ἐπάγων δὲ τῷ λόγῳ τὸ ἔργον ἔνειμε τὴν μὲν ἄλλην τοῖς περιοίκοις Λακωνικὴν τρισμυρίους κλήρους, τὴν δὲ εἰς τὸ ἄστυ τὴν Σπάρτην συντελοῦσαν ἐνακισχιλίους· τοσοῦτοι γὰρ ἐγένοντο κλῆροι Σπαρτιατῶν'; 'Suiting the deed to the word, he distributed the rest of the Laconian land among the "perioeci", or free provincials, in thirty thousand lots, and that which belonged to the city of Sparta, in nine thousand lots, to as many genuine Spartans.'

272. *Lib. iv*] Thucydides, IV.lxxx.2–4: 'καὶ ἅμα τῶν Εἱλώτων βουλομένοις ἦν ἐπὶ προφάσει ἐκπέμψαι, μή τι πρὸς τὰ παρόντα τῆς Πύλου ἐχομένης νεωτερίσωσιν. ἐπεὶ καὶ τόδε ἔπραξαν φοβούμενοι αὐτῶν τὴν νεότητα καὶ τὸ πλῆθος (αἰεὶ γὰρ τὰ πολλὰ Λακεδαιμονίοις πρὸς τοὺς Εἵλωτας τῆς φυλακῆς πέρι μάλιστα καθέστηκεν)· προεῖπον αὐτῶν ὅσοι ἀξιοῦσιν ἐν τοῖς πολεμίοις γεγενῆσθαι σφίσιν ἄριστοι, κρίνεσθαι, ὡς ἐλευθερώσοντες, πεῖραν ποιούμενοι καὶ ἡγούμενοι τούτους σφίσιν ὑπὸ φρονήματος, οἵπερ καὶ ἠξίωσαν πρῶτος ἕκαστος ἐλευθεροῦσθαι, μάλιστα ἂν καὶ ἐπιθέσθαι. καὶ προκρινάντων ἐς δισχιλίους οἱ μὲν ἐστεφανώσαντό τε καὶ τὰ ἱερὰ περιῆλθον ὡς ἠλευθερωμένοι, οἱ δὲ οὐ πολλῷ ὕστερον ἠφάνισάν τε αὐτοὺς καὶ οὐδεὶς ᾔσθετο ὅτῳ τρόπῳ ἕκαστος διεφθάρη'; 'Furthermore, the Lacedaemonians were glad to have an excuse for sending out some of the Helots, in order to forestall their attempting a revolt

at the present juncture when Pylos was in the possession of the enemy. Indeed, through fear of their youth and numbers – for in fact most of their measures have always been adopted by the Lacedaemonians with a view to guarding against the Helots – they had once even resorted to the following device. They made proclamation that all Helots who claimed to have rendered the Lacedaemonians the best service in war should be set apart, ostensibly to be set free. They were, in fact, merely testing them, thinking that those who claimed, each for himself, the first right to be set free would be precisely the men of high spirit who would be the most likely to attack their masters. About two thousand of them were selected and these put crowns on their heads and made the rounds of the temples, as though they were already free, but the Spartans not long afterwards made away with them, and nobody ever knew in what way each one perished.'

273. *in Æ GINA*] Athenaeus, *The Banquet of the Learned*, VI.272b–c: 'κἂν τῇ τρίτῃ δὲ τῶν Ἱστοριῶν ὁ Ἐπιτίμαιος ἔφη οὕτως εὐδαιμονῆσαι τὴν Κορινθίων πόλιν ὡς κτήσασθαι δούλων μυριάδας ἓξ καὶ τεσσαράκοντα ... Ἀριστοτέλης δ' ἐν Αἰγινητῶν Πολιτείᾳ καὶ παρὰ τούτοις δφησὶ γενέσθαι ἑπτὰ καὶ τεσσαράκοντα μυριάδας δούλων'; 'And in Book III of his History Epitimaeus claimed that the city of Corinth was so wealthy that its inhabitants owned 460,000 slaves ... Aristotle in the *Constitution of the Aeginetans* claims that they owned 470,000 slaves.'

274. *Lib. ii*] Thucydides, II.xiv.2: 'χαλεπῶς δὲ αὐτοῖς διὰ τὸ αἰεὶ εἰωθέναι τοὺς πολλοὺς ἐν τοῖς ἀγροῖς διαιτᾶσθαι ἡ ἀνάστασις ἐγίγνετο'; 'And the removal was a hard thing for them to accept, because most of them had always been used to live in the country.'

275. *THUCYD. lib. ii*] Thucydides, II.xvii.1: 'Ἐπειδὴ δὲ ἀφίκοντο ἐς τὸ ἄστυ, ὀλίγοις μέν τισιν ὑπῆρχον οἰκήσεις καὶ παρὰ φίλων τινὰς ἢ οἰκείων καταφυγή, οἱ δὲ πολλοὶ τά τε ἐρῆμα τῆς πόλεως ᾤκησαν καὶ τὰ ἱερὰ καὶ τὰ ἡρῷα πάντα πλὴν τῆς ἀκροπόλεως καὶ τοῦ Ἐλευσινίου καὶ εἴ τι ἄλλο βεβαίως κλῃστὸν ἦν· τό τε Πελαργικὸν καλούμενον τὸ ὑπὸ τὴν ἀκρόπολιν, ὃ καὶ ἐπάρατόν τε ἦν μὴ οἰκεῖν καί τι καὶ Πυθικοῦ μαντείου ἀκροτελεύτιον τοιόνδε διεκώλυε, λέγον ὡς "Τὸ Πελαργικὸν ἀργὸν ἄμεινον," ὅμως ὑπὸ τῆς παραχρῆμα ἀνάγκης ἐξῳκήθη'; 'And when they [the country-dwellers] came to the capital, only a few of them were provided with dwellings or places of refuge with friends or relatives, and most of them took up their abode in the vacant places of the city and the sanctuaries and the shrines of heroes, all except the Acropolis and the Eleusinium and any other precinct that could be securely closed. And the Pelargicum, as it was called, at the foot of the Acropolis, although it was under a curse that forbade its use for residence, and this was also prohibited by a verse-end of a Pythian oracle to the following effect: "The Pelargicum unoccupied is better", nevertheless under stress of the emergency was completely filled with buildings.'

276. *no more than 10,000 houses*] See above, p. 472, n. 234.

277. *above twenty miles in extent*] A little earlier, however, Hume has followed Thucydides in stating the length of the walls of Athens to be eighteen miles (above, p. 129).

278. *as we learn from PLINY*] See Pliny the Elder, *Natural History*, VI.xxx.121.

279. *according to PUBLIUS VICTOR*] i.e. in the *Libellus de Regionibus Urbis Romæ* (1505).

280. *lib. xx*] Diodorus Siculus, XX.lxxxiv.2–3: 'ἀριθμὸν δὲ ποιησάμενοι τῶν δυναμένων ἀγωνίζεσθαι πολιτῶν μὲν εὗρον περὶ ἑξακισχιλίους, τῶν δὲ παροίκων καὶ ξένων εἰς χιλίους'; 'When they made a count of those who were able to fight, they found that there were about six thousand citizens and as many as a thousand metics and aliens.'

281. *paneg.*] Isocrates, *Panegyricus*, LXIV: 'τῶν μὲν γὰρ Ἑλληνίδων πόλεων, χωρὶς τῆς ἡμετέρας, Ἄργος καὶ Θῆβαι καὶ Λακεδαίμων καὶ τότ᾽ ἦσαν μέγισται καὶ νῦν ἔτι διατελοῦσι'; 'Of all the Hellenic states, excepting our own, Argos and Thebes and Lacedaemon were at that time the greatest, as they still are to this day.'

282. *lib. vii*] Xenophon, *Hellenica*, VII.ii.1: 'Οὕτω δὲ τούτων προκεχωρηκότων, καὶ τῶν τε Ἀργείων ἐπιτετειχικότων τῷ Φλειοῦντι τὸ ὑπὲρ τοῦ Ἡραίου Τρικάρανον, καὶ τῶν Σικυωνίων ἐπὶ τοῖς ὁρίοις αὐτῶν τειχιζόντων τὴν Θυαμίαν, μάλα ἐπιέζοντο οἱ Φλειάσιοι καὶ ἐσπάνιζον τῶν ἐπιτηδείων· ὅμως δὲ διεκαρτέρουν ἐν τῇ συμμαχίᾳ. ἀλλὰ γὰρ τῶν μὲν μεγάλων πόλεων, εἴ τι καλὸν ἔπραξαν, ἅπαντες οἱ συγγραφεῖς μέμνηνται· ἐμοὶ δὲ δοκεῖ, καὶ εἴ τις μικρὰ πόλις οὖσα πολλὰ καὶ καλὰ ἔργα διαπέπρακται, ἔτι μᾶλλον ἄξιον εἶναι ἀποφαίνειν'; 'When these matters had progressed to this point and the Argives had fortified Mount Tricaranum above the Heraeum, as a base of attack upon Phlius, while the Sicyonians were fortifying Thyamia on its borders, the Phliasians were exceedingly hard pressed and suffered from lack of provisions; nevertheless, they remained steadfast in their alliance. But I will speak further of them; for while all the historians make mention of the large states if they have performed any noble achievement, it seems to me that if a state which is small has accomplished many noble deeds, it is even more fitting to set them forth.'

283. *Id. lib. vii*] Xenophon, *Hellenica*, V.iii.16: 'πολλῶν δὲ λεγόντων Λακεδαιμονίων ὡς ὀλίγων ἕνεκεν ἀνθρώπων πόλει ἀπεχθάνοιντο πλέον πεντακισχιλίων ἀνδρῶν'; 'And when many Lacedaemonians said that merely for the sake of a few individuals they were making themselves hated by a state of more than five thousand men [i.e. Phlius or Phliasia]'.

284. *POLYB. lib. ii*] Polybius, II.lvi.6: 'τὴν ἀρχαιοτάτην καὶ μεγίστην πόλιν τῶν κατὰ τὴν Ἀρκαδίαν'; 'this, the most ancient and greatest city in Arcadia'.

285. *POLYC. lib. ix. cap. 20*] Polybius, IX.xxvi a.1–2: 'Οἱ δὲ πλεῖστοι τῶν ἀνθρώπων ἐξ αὐτῆς τῆς περιμέτρου τεκμαίρονται τὰ μεγέθη τῶν προειρημένων. λοιπὸν ὅταν εἴπῃ τις τὴν μὲν τῶν Μεγαλοπολιτῶν πόλιν πεντήκοντα σταδίων ἔχειν τὸν περίβολον, τὴν δὲ τῶν Λακεδαιμονίων ὀκτὼ καὶ τετταράκοντα, τῷ δὲ μεγέθει διπλῆν εἶναι τὴν Λακεδαίμονα τῆς Μεγάλης πόλεως, ἄπιστον αὐτοῖς εἶναι δοκεῖ

τὸ λεγόμενον'; 'Most people judge of the size of cities simply from their circumference. So that when one says that Megalopolis is fifty stades in circumference and Sparta forty-eight, but that Sparta is twice as large as Megalopolis, the statement seems incredible to them.' 'Polyc.' is a slip for 'Polyb.' (which is the reading found in earlier editions).

286. *orat.* 34] Lysias, Oration XXXIV, *Against the Subversion of the Ancestral Constitution of Athens*, VII–VIII: 'ὁρῶ δὲ καὶ Ἀργείους καὶ Μαντινέας τὴν αὐτὴν ἔχοντας γνώμην τὴν αὐτῶν οἰκοῦντας, τοὺς μὲν ὁμόρους ὄντας Λακεδαιμονίοις, τοὺς δὲ ἐγγὺς οἰκοῦντας, καὶ τοὺς μὲν οὐδὲν ἡμῶν πλείους, τοὺς δὲ οὐδὲ τρισχιλίους ὄντας'; 'And I observe the same attitude in both the Argives and the Mantineans, each inhabiting their own land, – the former bordering on the Lacedaemonians, the latter dwelling near them; in the one case, their number is no greater than ours, in the other it is less than three thousand.'

287. *vita* AUREL.] Flavius Vopiscus, 'Divus Aurelianus', *Historia Augusta*, XXI.9: 'adhibito consilio senatus muros urbis Romae dilatavit'; 'after asking advice from the senate, he extended the walls of the city of Rome'. Ibid., XXXIX.2: 'muros urbis Romae sic ampliavit, ut quinquaginta prope milia murorum eius ambitus teneant'; 'He so extended the wall of the city of Rome that its circuit was nearly fifty miles long.'

288. *9000 citizens*] Xenophon, *Constitution of the Lacedaemonians*, I.i: 'Ἀλλ᾽ ἐγὼ ἐννοήσας ποτέ, ὡς ἡ Σπάρτη τῶν ὀλιγανθρωποτάτων πόλεων οὖσα δυνατωτάτη τε καὶ ὀνομαστοτάτη ἐν τῇ Ἑλλάδι ἐφάνη, ἐθαύμασα, ὅτῳ ποτὲ τρόπῳ τοῦτ᾽ ἐγένετο'; 'It occurred to me one day that Sparta, though among the most thinly populated of states, was evidently the most powerful and most celebrated city in Greece; and I fell to wondering how this could have happened.'

289. *cap.* 20] Polybius, IX.xxvi a.1–2: quoted above, pp. 480–81, n. 285.

290. *lib. xviii*] Diodorus Siculus, XVIII.xxiv.1–2: 'Κατὰ δὲ τούτους τοὺς καιροὺς Ἀντίπατρος καὶ Κρατερὸς ἐπὶ τοὺς Αἰτωλοὺς ἐστράτευσαν, ἔχοντες πεζοὺς μὲν τρισμυρίους, ἱππεῖς δὲ δισχιλίους καὶ πεντακοσίους· οὗτοι γὰρ τῶν ἐν τῷ Λαμιακῷ πολέμῳ διαπολεμησάντων ὑπόλοιποι διέμενον ἀχείρωτοι. οἱ δὲ Αἰτωλοὶ τηλικούτων δυνάμεων ἐπ᾽ αὐτοὺς ὡρμημένων οὐ κατεπλάγησαν ταῖς ψυχαῖς, ἀλλὰ τοὺς μὲν ἀκμάζοντας ταῖς ἡλικίαις ἀθροίσαντες εἰς μυρίους κατέφυγον εἰς τοὺς ὀρεινοὺς καὶ τραχεῖς τόπους, εἰς οὓς τέκνα καὶ γυναῖκας καὶ τοὺς γεγηρακότας καὶ τὸ τῶν χρημάτων πλῆθος ἀπέθεντο'; 'At this time Antipater and Craterus had taken the field against the Aetolians with thirty thousand infantry and twenty-five hundred cavalry; for of those who had taken part in the Lamian War, the Aetolians alone were left unconquered. Although such great forces were sent against them, they were in no panic-stricken mood, but gathering together all who were in the full vigour of manhood to the number of ten thousand, they retired to the mountainous and rough places, in which they placed the children, the women, and the old, together with the greater part of their wealth.'

291. LEGAT.] Polybius, XXIX.xxiv.8–9: 'ἐὰν καὶ δέωνται Ῥωμαῖοι τῆς συμμαχίας, οὐ διὰ τοὺς διακοσίους ἱππεῖς καὶ χιλίους πεζοὺς τοὺς ἀποσταλησομένους

εἰς Ἀλεξάνδρειαν ἀδυνατήσειν τοὺς Ἀχαιοὺς βοηθεῖν Ῥωμαίοις· καλῶς γὰρ ποιοῦντας αὐτοὺς καὶ τρεῖς ἄγειν καὶ τέτταρας μυριάδας ἀνδρῶν μαχίμων'; 'If the Romans did really require their help, the dispatch of the two hundred horse and a thousand foot to Alexandria would not make it impossible for the Achaeans to come to the aid of the Romans; for they could very well raise a force of even thirty or forty thousand men fit to take the field.'

292. *In ACHAICIS*] Pausanias, *Description of Greece*, 'Achaia', VII.xv.7: 'Ἀχαιοῖς δὲ αὖθις ἐπὶ τὴν ἡγεμονίαν τοῦ στρατεύματος παρῆει Δίαιος· καὶ δούλους τε ἐς ἐλευθερίαν ἠφίει, τὸ Μιλτιάδου καὶ Ἀθηναίων βούλευμα τὸ πρὸ τοῦ ἔργου τοῦ ἐν Μαραθῶνι μιμούμενος, καὶ Ἀχαιῶν συνέλεγε καὶ Ἀρκάδων ἀπὸ τῶν πόλεων τοὺς ἐν ἡλικίᾳ· ἐγένετο δέ, ἀναμεμιγμένων ὁμοῦ καὶ οἰκετῶν, τὸ ἀθροισθὲν ἐς ἑξακοσίους μὲν μάλιστα ἀριθμὸν ἱππεῖς, τὸ δὲ ὁπλιτεῦον τετρακισχίλιοί τε καὶ μύριοι'; 'Diaeüs once more came forward to command the Achaean army. He proceeded to set free slaves, following the example of Miltiades and the Athenians before the battle of Marathon, and enlisted from the cities of the Achaeans and Arcadians those who were of military age. The muster, including the slaves, amounted roughly to six hundred cavalry and fourteen thousand foot.'

293. *in CRITONE*] Livy, XXXIV.li.5: 'nec enim temporum modo uitiis ac violentia et licentia regia turbati erant, sed inquieto etiam ingenio gentis, nec comitia nec conventum nec concilium ullum non per seditionem ac tumultum iam inde a principio ad nostram usque aetatem traducentis'; 'For the Thessalians were in turmoil not just because of the problems of the day and the king's violent and wayward behavior, but also because of the turbulent character of their race – from their very beginnings down to our own times they have been able to hold no elections, no meeting and no assembly without dissension and mayhem.' Plato, *Crito*, 53d: 'ἀλλ' ἐκ μὲν τούτων τῶν τόπων ἀπαρεῖς, ἥξεις δὲ εἰς Θετταλίαν παρὰ τοὺς ξένους τοὺς Κρίτωνος· ἐκεῖ γὰρ δὴ πλείστη ἀταξία καὶ ἀκολασία'; 'Well, will you leave these places and come to Thessaly and Crito's friends? Without a doubt there's a great deal of disorder and lawlessness there.' The lawlessness of Thessaly was a common Athenian assumption. See also Xenophon, *Memorabilia*, I.ii.24.

294. *Lib. vii*] Thucydides, IV.iii.2: 'καὶ ἀπέφαινε πολλὴν εὐπορίαν ξύλων τε καὶ λίθων καὶ φύσει καρτερὸν ὂν καὶ ἐρῆμον αὐτό τε καὶ ἐπὶ πολὺ τῆς χώρας· ἀπέχει γὰρ σταδίους μάλιστα ἡ Πύλος τῆς Σπάρτης τετρακοσίους καὶ ἔστιν ἐν τῇ Μεσσηνίᾳ ποτὲ οὔσῃ γῇ, καλοῦσι δὲ αὐτὴν οἱ Λακεδαιμόνιοι Κορυφάσιον'; 'and he showed them that there was at hand an abundance of wood and stone, that the position was naturally a strong one, and that not only the place itself but also the neighbouring country for a considerable distance was unoccupied; for Pylos is about four hundred stadia distant from Sparta and lies in the land that was once Messenia; but the Lacedaemonians call the place Coryphasium.'

295. *Lib. vii*] Herodotus, VII.cxxvi: 'Εἰσὶ δὲ κατὰ ταῦτα τὰ χωρία καὶ λέοντες πολλοὶ καὶ βόες ἄγριοι, τῶν τὰ κέρεα ὑπερμεγάθεα ἐστὶ τὰ ἐς Ἕλληνας φοιτέοντα.

οὖρος δὲ τοῖσι λέουσι ἐστὶ ὅ τε δι᾿ Ἀβδήρων ῥέων ποταμὸς Νέστος καὶ ὁ δι᾿ Ἀκαρνανίης ῥέων Ἀχελῷος᾿; 'There are many lions in these parts, and wild oxen, whose horns are those very long ones which are brought into Hellas. The boundary of the lions' country is the river Nestus that flows through Abdera and the river Achelous that flows through Acarnania.'

296. *cap. 34*] Livy, XLV.xxxiv.6: 'centum quinquaginta milia capitum humanorum abducerentur'; 'one hundred and fifty thousand persons were removed'.

297. *Lib. ix. cap. 5*] Justinus, *Epitomae*, IX.v: 'Compositis in Græcia rebus, Philippus omnium civitatium legatos ad formandum rerum præsentium statum evocari Corinthum iubet. Ibi pacis legem universæ Græciæ pro meritis singularum civitatium statuit; conciliumque omnium, veluti unum senatum, ex omnibus legit. Soli Lacedæmonii, & legem, & regem contempserunt: servitutem non pacem rati, quæ non ipsis civitatibus conveniret, sed à victore ferretur. Auxilia deinde singularum civitatium describuntur, sive adjuvandos ea manu rex oppugnante aliquo foret, seu duce illo bellum inferendum. Neque enim dubium erat, imperium Persarum his apparatibus peti. Summa auxiliorum ducenta millia peditum fuere, & equitum quindecim millia'; 'With matters settled in Greece, Philip ordered the ambassadors of all the states to be summoned to Corinth to shape a political settlement. There he decided the conditions of peace for the whole of Greece according to the deserts of the individual states; and he selected a general council – if you like, a senate – from them all. Only the Spartans despised both the king and his edict: they thought it was slavery, not peace, which was received at the hands of a conqueror rather than agreed by the states themselves. Then the forces of the individual states were assessed, either to assist the king were he attacked by someone, or to wage war under his leadership. Nor was there any doubt that, once these forces were prepared, the kingdom of the Persians would be attacked. The total forces amounted to two hundred thousand infantry and fifteen thousand cavalry.'

298. *by modern writers*] Such as Isaak Vossius and Montesquieu: see the headnote, above, pp. 412–13.

299. *BARTOLI's plans*] Hume had touched on these plans in his letter to John Clephane of April 1750: 'Amongst other topics, it fell in my way to consider the greatness of ancient *Rome*; and in looking over the discourse, I find the following period. "If we may judge by the younger Pliny's account of his house, and by the plans of ancient buildings in Dr. Mead's collection, the men of quality had very spacious palaces, and their buildings were like the Chinese houses, where each apartment is separate from the rest, and rises no higher than a single story." Pray, on what authority are those plans founded? If I remember right, I was told they were discovered on the walls of the baths, and other subterraneous buildings. Is this the proper method of citing them? If you have occasion to communicate this to Dr Mead, I beg that my sincere respects may be joined' (*Letters*, vol. I, p. 140). Hume

reverted to this request for help in his next letter to Clephane of 18 February 1751 (which shows incidentally that Hume was still then improving the text of this essay): 'I asked you a question with regard to the plans of ancient buildings in Dr Mead's collection. Pray, are they authentic enough to be cited in a discourse of erudition and reasoning? have they never been published in any collection? and what are the proper terms in which I ought to cite them? I know you are a great proficient in the *virtu*, and consequently can resolve my doubts' (*Letters*, vol. I, p. 150).

300. CHINESE *houses ... single storey*] Du Halde had observed that even the houses of the rich and noble Chinese commonly 'n'ont que le rez de chaussée' (Du Halde, *Description*, vol. II, p. 85).

301. *Lib. iv*] Dionysius of Halicarnassus, *Roman Antiquities*, IV.xiii.4–5: 'καὶ εἰ μὲν εἰς ταὐτά τις ὁρῶν τὸ μέγεθος ἐξετάζειν βουλήσεται τῆς Ῥώμης, πλανᾶσθαί τ' ἀναγκασθήσεται καὶ οὐχ ἕξει βέβαιον σημεῖον οὐδέν, ᾧ διαγνώσεται μέχρι πού προβαίνουσα ἔτι πόλις ἐστὶ καὶ πόθεν ἄρχεται μηκέτι εἶναι πόλις, οὕτω συνύφανται τὸ ἄστυ τῇ χώρᾳ καὶ εἰς ἄπειρον ἐκμηκυνομένης πόλεως ὑπόληψιν τοῖς θεωμένοις παρέχεται. εἰ δὲ τῷ τείχει, δυσευρέτῳ μὲν ὄντι διὰ τὰς περιλαμβανούσας αὐτὸ πολλαχόθεν οἰκήσεις, ἴχνη δέ τινα φυλάττοντι κατὰ πολλοὺς τόπους τῆς ἀρχαίας κατασκευῆς, βουληθείη μετρεῖν αὐτὴν κατὰ τὸν κύκλον τὸν περιέχοντα Ἀθηναίων τὸ ἄστυ, οὐ πολλῷ τινι μείζων ὁ τῆς Ῥώμης ἂν αὐτῷ φανείη κύκλος'; 'If anyone wishes to estimate the size of Rome by looking at these suburbs he will necessarily be misled for want of a definite clue by which to determine up to what point it is still the city and where it ceases to be the city; so closely is the city connected with the country, giving the beholder the impression of a city stretching out indefinitely. But if one should wish to measure Rome by the wall, which, though hard to be discovered by reason of the buildings that surround it in many places, yet preserves in several parts of it some traces of its ancient structure, and to compare it with the circuit of the city of Athens, the circuit of Rome would not seem to him very much larger than the other.'

302. *Lib. x*] Dionysius of Halicarnassus, *Roman Antiquities*, X.xxxii.5: 'κυρωθέντος δὲ τοῦ νόμου συνελθόντες οἱ δημοτικοὶ τά τε οἰκόπεδα διελάγχανον καὶ κατῳκοδόμουν ὅσον ἕκαστοι τόπον δυνηθεῖεν ἀπολαμβάνοντες. εἰσὶ δ' οἳ σύνδυο καὶ σύντρεις καὶ ἔτι πλείους συνιόντες οἰκίαν κατεσκευάζοντο μίαν, ἑτέρων μὲν τὰ κατάγεια λαγχανόντων, ἑτέρων δὲ τὰ ὑπερῷα'; 'When the law had been ratified, the plebeians assembled, and after drawing lots for the plots of ground, began to build, each man taking as large an area as he could; and sometimes two, three, or even more joined together to build one house, and drawing lots, some had the lower and others the upper stories.'

303. *269, 270*] Juvenal, III.268–72: 'Respice nunc alia ac diversa pericula noctis: / quod spatium tectis sublimibus unde cerebrum / testa ferit, quotiens rimosa et curta fenestris / vasa cadant, quanto percussum pondere signent / et laedant silicem'; 'Now consider the various other dangers of the night.

What a long way it is from the high roofs for a tile to hit your skull! How often cracked and leaky pots tumble down from the windows! What a smash when they strike the pavement, marking and damaging it!'

304. *cap. 72, & c.*] Vitruvius, *On Architecture*, V.xi.1: 'In palaestris peristylia quadrata sive oblonga ita sint facienda, uti duorum stadiorum habeant ambulationis circuitionem, quod Graeci vocant diaulon'; 'Square or oblong cloisters are to be made with a walk round them of two furlongs (this walk the Greeks call diaulos).' Tacitus, *Annals*, XI.iii (the suicide of Asiaticus): 'venas exsolvit, viso tamen ante rogo iussoque transferri partem in aliam, ne opacitas arborum vapore ignis minueretur: tantum illi securitatis novissimae fuit'; 'opened his arteries; but not before he had visited his pyre and given orders for it to be moved to another site, so that his trees with their shady leafage might not be affected by the heat. So complete was his composure to the end!' Suetonius, *Deified Augustus*, LXXII.iii: 'Ampla et operosa praetoria gravabatur. Et neptis quidem suae Iuliae, profuse ab ea exstructa, etiam diruit ad solum, sua vero quamvis modica non tam statuarum tabularumque pictarum ornatu quam xystis et nemoribus excoluit rebusque vetustate ac raritate notabilibus, qualia sunt Capreis immanium beluarum ferarumque membra praegrandia, quae dicuntur gigantum ossa, et arma heroum'; 'He disliked large and sumptuous country palaces, actually razing to the ground one which his granddaughter Julia built on a lavish scale. His own villas, which were modest enough, he decorated not so much with handsome statues and pictures as with terraces, groves, and objects noteworthy for their antiquity and rarity; for example, at Capreae the monstrous bones of huge sea monsters and wild beasts, called the "bones of the giants", and the weapons of the heroes.'

305. *Ancyr.*] *Res Gestae Divi Augusti*, XV: 'et consul undecimum duodecim frumentationes frumento privatim coempto emensus sum, et tribunicia potestate duodecimum quadringenos nummos tertium viritim dedi. quae mea congiaria pervenerunt ad hominum millia nunquam minus quinquaginta et ducenta'; 'In my eleventh consulship I made twelve distributions of food from grain bought at my own expense, and in the twelfth year of my tribunician power I gave for the third time four hundred sesterces to each man. These largesses of mine reached a number of persons never less than two hundred and fifty thousand.'

306. *lib. iii. cap. 48*] Cicero, *Tusculan Disputations*, III.xx.48: 'Et quidem C. Gracchus, cum largitiones maximas fecisset et effudisset aerarium, verbis tamen defendebat aerarium. Quid verba audiam, cum facta videam? L. Piso ille Frugi semper contra legem frumentariam dixerat: is lege lata consularis ad frumentum accipiundum venerat. Animum advertit Gracchus in contione Pisonem stantem; quaerit audiente populo Romano qui sibi constet, cum ea lege frumentum petat, quam dissuaserit. "Nolim" inquit "mea bona, Gracche, tibi viritim dividere libeat, sed si facias, partem petam"'; 'and so too C. Gracchus, after he had granted extravagant doles and poured out the funds

of the treasury like water, none the less, in his words, posed as the protector of the treasury. Why am I to listen to words, seeing that I have the deeds before my eyes? The famous Piso, named Frugi, had spoken consistently against the Corn-law. When the law was passed, in spite of his consular rank, he was there to receive the corn. Gracchus noticed Piso standing in the throng; he asked him in the hearing of the Roman people what consistency there was in coming for the corn under the terms of the law which he had opposed. "I shouldn't like it, Gracchus, to come into your head to divide up my property among all the citizens; but should you do so I should come for my share."'

307. *lib. iii*] Sallust, *Historical Fragments*, III.xlviii.19: 'Nisi forte repentina ista frumentaria lege munia vostra pensantur; qua tamen quinis modiis libertatem omnium aestumavere, qui profecto non amplius possunt alimentis carceris'; 'Unless, perhaps, your public duties have been counterbalanced by that hastily enacted grain law, by which they have valued the freedom of all as being worth five pecks per man, which cannot really be much greater than the rations in a prison.'

308. *frumentaria Roman.*] Nicolaus Hortensius's dissertation 'De re frumentaria' was published as an appendix to vol. IV of Olivet's edition of *M. Tullii Ciceronis Opera* (Paris, 1741), pp. 601–8. The relevant passage reads: 'Si conjecturâ uti licet, quod tamen in re tam obscura necesse est, credam, fœminis exclusis, mares solos, patrem dico, & natos, qui essent ætate militari, admissos ad istam largitionem fuisse, ita ut per capita frumentum quodammodo distribueretur, neque tamen, ut Licinius querebatur, *absolveret curâ familiari tam parva res*, quæ quia minor erat alendæ toti familiæ, marito, inquam, & conjugi cum liberis, plebem ab industria ad desidiam non avocaret'; 'If one may conjecture, as one must in so obscure a subject, I believe that only the men, not the women – I mean the father and the sons of military age – were eligible for this distribution, so that it was in a certain way distributed *per capita*; however it was not the case, as Licinius complained, that "such a small thing extinguished care for the family", because, since it was too meagre to support a whole family (that is to say, a husband, wife and children), it would not have deflected the common people from industry towards idleness' (p. 606).

309. *cap. 40*] 'Populi recensum vicatim egit, ac ne plebs frumentationum causa frequentius ab negotiis avocaretur, ter in annum quaternum mensium tesseras dare destinavit; sed desideranti consuetudinem veterem concessit rursus, ut sui cuiusque mensis acciperet'; 'He revised the lists of the people district by district, and to prevent the commons from being called away from their occupations too often because of the distributions of grain, he determined to give out tickets for four months' supply three times a year; but at their urgent request he allowed a return to the old custom of receiving a share every month' (Suetonius, *Deified Augustus*, XL.ii).

310. *cap. 41*] Suetonius, *Deified Julius*, XLI.iii: 'Recensum populi nec more nec loco solito, sed vicatim per dominos insularum egit atque ex viginti trecentisque milibus accipientium frumentum e publico ad centum quinquaginta retraxit'; 'He made the enumeration of the people neither in the usual manner nor place, but from street to street aided by the owners of blocks of houses, and reduced the number of those who received grain at public expense from three hundred and twenty thousand to one hundred and fifty thousand.'

311. *exact bills of mortality . . . a plague*] cf. the note in the 'Early Memoranda': 'In Nero's time 30.000 buryd in one Autumn, while there was a Plague' (NLS MS 23159, item 14, p. 17; cf. Mossner, 'Memoranda', p. 509).

312. *Nero's golden house*] A lavish palace built by Nero on the Oppian Hill in Rome after the fire of AD 64.

313. *Neronis*] Suetonius, *Nero*, XXXIX.i: 'Accesserunt tantis ex principe malis probrisque quaedam et fortuita: pestilentia unius autumni, quo triginta funerum milia in rationem Libitinae venerunt'; 'To all the disasters and abuses thus caused by the prince there were added certain accidents of fortune; a plague which in a single autumn entered thirty thousand deaths in the accounts of Libitina.'

314. *cap. 42*] Suetonius, *Deified Augustus*, XLII.iii: 'Magna vero quondam sterilitate ac difficili remedio cum venalicias et lanistarum familias peregrinosque omnes exceptis medicis et praeceptoribus partimque servitiorum urbe expulisset, ut tandem annona convaluit, impetum se cepisse scribit frumentationes publicas in perpetuum abolendi, quod earum fiducia cultura agrorum cessaret; neque tamen perseverasse, quia certum haberet posse per ambitionem quandoque restitui. Atque ita posthac rem temperavit, ut non minorem aratorum ac negotiantium quam populi rationem deduceret'; 'Once indeed in a time of great scarcity when it was difficult to find a remedy, he expelled from the city the slaves that were for sale, as well as the schools of gladiators, all foreigners with the exception of physicians and teachers, and a part of the household slaves; and when grain at last became more plentiful, he writes: "I was strongly inclined to do away forever with distributions of grain, because through dependence on them agriculture was neglected; but I did not carry out my purpose, feeling sure that they would one day be renewed through desire for popular favour." But from that time on he regulated the practice with no less regard for the interests of the farmers and grain-dealers than for those of the populace.'

315. *cap. 5*] Herodian, *History of the Empire*, IV.iii.7: 'τῇ τε βασιλείᾳ τῇ αὑτοῦ αὐτάρκη ἔσεσθαι ὑποδοχὴν ὁ Γέτας ἔλεγεν ἢ τὴν Ἀντιόχειαν ἢ τὴν Ἀλεξάνδρειαν, οὐ πολύ τι τῆς Ῥώμης [ὡς ᾤετο] μεγέθει ἀποδεούσας'; 'Geta declared that either Antioch or Alexandria, which were not much smaller than Rome [in his opinion], would be a suitable capital for his empire.'

316. *Lib. xvii*] Diodorus Siculus, XVII.lii.3: 'Τὸν δὲ τύπον ἀποτελῶν χλαμύδι παραπλήσιον ἔχει πλατεῖαν μέσην σχεδὸν τὴν πόλιν τέμνουσαν καὶ τῷ τε μεγέθει

καὶ κάλλει θαυμαστήν· ἀπὸ γὰρ πύλης ἐπὶ πύλην διήκουσα τεσσαράκοντα μὲν σταδίων ἔχει τὸ μῆκος, πλέθρου δὲ τὸ πλάτος, οἰκιῶν δὲ καὶ ἱερῶν πολυτελέσι κατασκευαῖς πᾶσα κεκόσμηται'; 'In shape, it is similar to a chlamys, and it is approximately bisected by an avenue remarkable for its size and beauty. From gate to gate it runs a distance of forty furlongs; it is a plethron in width, and is bordered throughout its length with rich façades of houses and temples.'

317. ελευθεροι . . . πολιται] i.e. freemen and citizens, respectively.

318. *reliqua urbe*] Herodian, IV.i.2: 'ταύτῃ γοῦν καὶ τὴν ὁδοιπορίαν ἔτι μᾶλλον ἤπειγον, ἀδεέστερον ἑκάτερος βιώσεσθαι προσδοκῶν, εἰ ἐν τῇ Ῥώμῃ γένοιντο καὶ τὰ βασίλεια διελόμενοι ἐν πλατείᾳ καὶ πολλῇ οἰκήσει καὶ πάσης πόλεως μείζονι καθ᾽ ἑαυτὸν ἑκάτερος διάγοι ὡς βούλοιτο'; 'Hence there was even greater haste on the journey, since they both believed they would breathe more safely when they reached Rome and divided up the palace, where they could each live their separate lives according to their own interests in a vast, spacious building that was bigger than any city.' Politian, *Opervm Tomvs Secvndvs* (Leiden, 1545), pp. 89–90: 'Ob eamque causam etiam iter properantius faciebant, tutius rati uicturos, ubi iam in urbem pervenissent, diuisaque inter se regia, amplis ac spatiosis ædibus, maioribus etiam reliqua urbe, pro suo uterque arbitrio separatim agitarent.'

319. *ac NERONIS.*] Pliny the Elder, *Natural History*, XXXVI.xxiv.111: 'bis vidimus urbem totam cingi domibus principum Gai et Neronis'; 'Twice have we seen the whole city girdled by imperial palaces, those of Gaius and Nero.'

320. *It appears . . . any taxes*] cf. the note in the 'Early Memoranda': 'Tis probable that the Roman Empire ~~was~~ & even Italy was not so well peopled as Europe at present, because Pertinax by an Edict gave the waste Lands to the first Occupier, with Immunities Herodian. Lib 2. C.15' (NLS MS 23159, item 14, p. 23; cf. Mossner, 'Memoranda', p. 514).

321. *as I have been informed*] Hume has alluded to the remoteness and desolation of parts of Hungary in 'Of the Balance of Power' (above, p. 70).

322. *cap. 15*] Herodian, II.iv.6: 'πρῶτον μὲν γὰρ πᾶσαν τὴν κατ᾽ Ἰταλίαν καὶ ἐν τοῖς λοιποῖς ἔθνεσιν ἀγεώργητόν τε καὶ παντάπασιν οὖσαν ἀργὸν ἐπέρεψεν, ὁπόσην τις βούλεται καὶ δύναται, εἰ καὶ βασιλέως κτῆμα εἴη, καταλαμβάνειν, ἐπιμεληθέντι τε καὶ γεωργήσαντι δεσπότῃ εἶναι'; 'The first of his projects was to make over to private ownership all the land in Italy and the provinces, which was not being farmed and was lying completely fallow, in lots depending on the recipient's requirements and ability to work it. Even if the land was part of the imperial estates, the man who could farm and cultivate it was to become the legal owner.'

323. *cap. 48*] Flavius Vopiscus, 'Divus Aurelianus', XLVIII.ii: 'Etruriae per Aureliam usque ad Alpes maritimas ingentes agri sunt iique fertiles ac silvosi. statuerat igitur dominis locorum incultorum, qui tamen vellent, pretia dare

atque illic familias captivas constituere, vitibus montes conserere atque ex eo opere vinum dare, ut nihil redituum fiscus acciperet, sed totum populo Romano concederet'; 'In Etruria, all along the Aurelian Way as far as the Maritime Alps, there are vast tracts of land, rich and well wooded. He planned, therefore, to pay their price to the owners of these uncultivated lands, provided they wished to sell, and to settle thereon families of slaves captured in war, and then to plant the hills with vines, and by this means to produce wine, which was to yield no profit to the privy-purse but to be given entirely to the people of Rome.'

324. *Lib. xii. cap.* 2] Polybius, XII.ii.4: 'τὸ δὲ τῇ σάλπιγγι πειθαρχεῖν οὐκ ἔστι θαυμάσιον· καὶ γὰρ κατὰ τὴν Ἰταλίαν οἱ τὰς ὗς τρέφοντες οὕτως χειρίζουσι τὰ κατὰ τὰς νομάς. οὐ γὰρ ἕπονται κατὰ πόδας οἱ συοφορβοὶ τοῖς θρέμμασιν, ὥσπερ παρὰ τοῖς Ἕλλησιν, ἀλλὰ προηγοῦνται φωνοῦντες τῇ βυκάνῃ κατὰ διάστημα, τὰ δὲ θρέμματα κατόπιν ἀκολουθεῖ καὶ συντρέχει πρὸς τὴν φωνήν, καὶ τηλικαύτη γίνεται συνήθεια τοῖς ζῴοις πρὸς τὴν ἰδίαν βυκάνην ὥστε θαυμάζειν καὶ δυσπαραδέκτως ἔχειν τοὺς πρώτους ἀκούσαντας. διὰ γὰρ τὴν πολυχειρίαν καὶ τὴν λοιπὴν χορηγίαν μεγάλα συμβαίνει τὰ συβόσια κατὰ τὴν Ἰταλίαν ὑπάρχειν, καὶ μάλιστα τὴν Γαλατίαν, ὥστε τὴν μίαν τοκάδα χιλίους ἐκτρέφειν ὗς, ποτὲ δὲ καὶ πλείους. διὸ καὶ κατὰ γένη ποιοῦνται καὶ καθ' ἡλικίαν τὰς ἐκ τῶν νυκτερευμάτων ἐξαγωγάς. ὅθεν εἰς τὸν αὐτὸν τόπον προαγομένων καὶ πλειόνων συστημάτων οὐ δύνανται ταῦτα κατὰ γένη τηρεῖν, ἀλλά γε συμπίπτει κατά τε τὰς ἐξελασίας καὶ νομὰς ἀλλήλοις, ὁμοίως δὲ κατὰ τὰς προσαγωγάς. ἐξ ὧν αὐτοῖς ἐπινενόηται πρὸς τὸ διακρίνειν, ὅταν συμπέσῃ, χωρὶς κόπου καὶ πραγματείας τὸ κατὰ βυκάνην. ἐπειδὰν γὰρ τῶν νεμόντων ὁ μὲν ἐπὶ τοῦτο τὸ μέρος προάγῃ φωνῶν, ὁ δ' ἐφ' ἕτερον ἀποκλίνας, αὐτὰ δι' αὑτῶν χωρίζεται τὰ θρέμματα καὶ κατακολουθεῖ ταῖς ἰδίαις βυκάναις μετὰ τοιαύτης προθυμίας ὥστε μὴ δυνατὸν εἶναι βιάσασθαι μηδὲ κωλῦσαι μηδενὶ τρόπῳ τὴν ὁρμὴν αὐτῶν. παρὰ δὲ τοῖς Ἕλλησι κατὰ τοὺς δρυμούς, ἐπειδὰν ἀλλήλοις συμπέσῃ διώκοντα τὸν καρπόν, ὁ πλείονας ἔχων χεῖρας καὶ κατευκαιρήσας περιλαβὼν τοῖς ἰδίοις θρέμμασιν ἀπάγει τὰ τοῦ πλησίον. ποτὲ δὲ κλέπτης ὑποκαθίσας ἀπήλασεν, οὐδ' ἐπιγινώσκοντος τοῦ περιάγοντος πῶς ἀπέβαλε, διὰ τὸ μακρὰν ἀποσπᾶσθαι τὰ κτήνη τῶν περιαγόντων, ἁμιλλώμενα περὶ τὸν καρπόν, ὅταν ἀκμὴν ἄρχηται ῥεῖν. πλὴν ταῦτα μὲν ἐπὶ τοσοῦτον'; 'It is by no means surprising that the animals should obey the call of the trumpet; for in Italy those in care of swine manage matters in the same way in pasturing them. The swineherd does not follow behind the animals as in Greece but goes in front and sounds a horn at intervals, the animals following him and responding to the call. They have learned so well to answer to their own horn that those who hear of this for the first time are astonished and loath to believe it. For owing to the large labouring population and the general abundance of food the herds of swine in Italy are very large, especially in Gallia, so that a thousand pigs and sometimes even more are reared from one sow. They, therefore, drive them out from their night quarters in different troops according to their breed and age. Thus when several troops are driven on

to the same place they cannot keep the different classes apart, but they get mixed either when they are being driven out, or when they are feeding, or when they are on the way home. They, therefore, invented the horn call to separate them when they get mixed without trouble or fuss. For when one of the swineherds advances in one direction sounding the horn and another turns off in another direction, the animals separate of their own accord and follow the sound of their own horn with such alacrity that it is impossible by any means to force them back or arrest their course. In Greece, on the contrary, when different herds meet each other in the thickets in their search for acorns, whoever has more hands with him and has the opportunity includes his neighbor's swine with his own and carries them off, or at times a robber will lie in wait and drive some off without the man in charge of them knowing how he has lost them, as the swine become widely separated from their conductors in their race for the acorn when the fruit just begins to fall. But this is enough on this subject.'

325. *inhabitants of* PEKIN] Du Halde had commented on the 'multitude innombrable des Peuples' in Peking (Du Halde, *Description*, vol. I, p. 114).

326. *not citizen*] Aristotle, *Nicomachean Ethics*, IV.x.3–4: 'καὶ οἱ πρὸς ἡδονὴν δὲ ἀρκοῦσιν ὀλίγοι, καθάπερ ἐν τῇ τροφῇ τὸ ἥδυσμα τοὺς δὲ σπουδαίους πότερον <ὡς> πλείστους κατ᾽ ἀριθμόν, ἢ ἔστι τι μέτρον καὶ φιλικοῦ πλήθους, ὥσπερ πόλεως; οὔτε γὰρ ἐκ δέκα ἀνθρώπων γένοιτ᾽ ἂν πόλις, οὔτ᾽ ἐκ δέκα μυριάδων ἔτι πόλις ἐστίν· τὸ δὲ ποσὸν οὐκ ἔστιν ἴσως ἕν τι, ἀλλὰ πᾶν τὸ μεταξὺ τινῶν ὡρισμένων. καὶ φίλων δή ἐστι πλῆθος ὡρισμένον, καὶ ἴσως οἱ πλεῖστοι μεθ᾽ ὧν ἂν δύναιτό τις συζῆν· τοῦτο γὰρ ἐδόκει φιλικώτατον εἶναι· ὅτι δ᾽ οὐχ οἷόν τε πολλοῖς συζῆν καὶ διανέμειν αὑτόν, οὐκ ἄδηλον'; 'Of friends for pleasure also a few are enough, just as a small amount of sweets is enough in one's diet. But should one have as many good friends as possible? Or is there a limit of size for a circle of friends, as there is for the population of a state? Ten people would not make a city, and with a hundred thousand it is a city no longer; though perhaps the proper size is not one particular number, but any number between certain limits. So also the number of one friends must be limited, and should perhaps be the largest number with whom one can constantly associate; since, as we saw, to live together is the chief mark of friendship, but it is quite clear that it is not possible to live with and to share oneself among a large number of people.'

327. *cap. 28*] Pliny the Elder, *Natural History*, VI.xxx.122: 'ferunt ei plebis urbanae d̄c esse'; 'It is said that the population of the city [of Seleucia] numbers 600,000.'

328. *Lib. xvii*] Strabo, XVII.iii.15: 'ὅτε γὰρ ἤρξαντο πολεμεῖν τοῦτον τὸν πόλεμον, πόλεις μὲν εἶχον τριακοσίας ἐν τῇ Λιβύῃ, ἀνθρώπων δ᾽ ἐν τῇ πόλει μυριάδας ἑβδομήκοντα'; 'For when they [the Carthaginians] began to wage this war they had three hundred cities in Libya and seven hundred thousand people in their city.'

329. *Whether the grandeur . . . labour and commodities*] cf. the similar comment in the 'Early Memoranda' on the natural limits to empire: 'There seems to be a natural Course of Things, which brings on the Destruction of great Empires. They push their Conquests till they come to barbarous Nations, which stop their Progress, by the Difficulty of subsisting great Armies. After that, the Nobility & considerable Men of the conquering Nation & best Provinces withdraw gradually from the [frontier *inserted above the line*] Army, by reason of its Distance from the Capital & barbarity of the Country, in which they quarter: They forget the Use of War. Their barbarous Soldiers become their Masters. These have no Law but their Sword, both from their bad Education, & from their Distance from the Sovereign [to whom they bear no Affection *inserted above the line*]. Hence Disorder, Violence, Anarchy, &̶Tyranny, & a Dissolution of Empire.' (NLS MS 23159, item 14, p. 27; cf. Mossner, 'Memoranda', pp. 517–18).

330. *police*] See above, vol. 1, p. 285, n. 36.

331. *sect. 16*] Jean-Baptiste Dubos, *Réflexions critiques sur la poësie et sur la peinture*, 'Seconde partie', section 16 (Paris, 1719), pp. 268–9: 'Les Annales de Rome nous apprennent qu'en l'année 480. de sa fondation, l'hyver y fut si violent que les arbres moururent. Le Tibre y prit dans Rome & la neige y demeura sur terre durant quarante jours. Lorsque Juvenal fait le portrait de la femme superstitieuse, il dit qu'ell fait rompre la glace du Tibre pour y faire ses ablutions. *Hibernum fracta glacie descendet in amnem / Ter matutino Tyberi mergetur. Sat. 6.* ['In winter she will go down to the river of a morning, break the ice, and plunge three times into the Tiber.'] Il parle du Tibre pris dans Rome comme d'un évenement ordinaire. Plusieurs passages d'Horace supposent les ruës de Rome pleines de neiges & de glaces. Nous serions mieux informés si les Anciens avoient eu des Thermométres, mais leurs Ecrivains, quoi qu'ils n'ayent pas songé à nous instruire la dessus, nous en disent encore assez pour nous convaincre que les hyvers étoient autrefois plus rigoureux à Rome qu'ils ne le sont aujourd'hui. Le Tibre ne s'y gele pas plus que le Nil au Caire. On trouve à Rome l'hyver bien rigoureux quand la neige s'y conserve durant deux jours, & quand on y voit durant deux fois vingt quatre heures quelques larmes de glace à une fontaine exposée au Nord.'

332. *Sat. 6*] Juvenal, VI.522–3.

333. *thermometers*] The construction of the first practical thermometer is usually attributed to Robert Fludd, although the first truly reliable instrument was constructed by Daniel Gabriel Fahrenheit in 1714, and used mercury as its expansive medium. So when Hume was writing, the thermometer, and the scale of temperature which it requires in order to measure heat, were still comparatively recent inventions. However, the ancients had been aware of the principle on which the thermometer works, namely that liquids expand when heated.

334. *Colder . . . proverbial expression*] Petronius, *Satyricon*, XIX: 'ego autem frigidior hieme Gallica factus nullum potui verbum emittere'; 'I turned colder than a Swiss winter, and could not utter a syllable.'

335. *Lib. iv*] Diodorus Siculus, V.xxv.2 and 5: 'κειμένη δὲ κατὰ τὸ πλεῖστον ὑπὸ τὰς ἄρκτους χειμέριός ἐστι καὶ ψυχρὰ διαφερόντως. κατὰ γὰρ τὴν χειμερινὴν ὥραν ἐν ταῖς συννεφέσιν ἡμέραις ἀντὶ μὲν τῶν ὄμβρων χιόνι πολλῇ νίφεται, κατὰ δὲ τὰς αἰθρίας κρυστάλλῳ καὶ πάγοις ἐξαισίοις πλήθει, δι᾽ ὧν οἱ ποταμοὶ πηγνύμενοι διὰ τῆς ἰδίας φύσεως γεφυροῦνται· οὐ μόνον γὰρ οἱ τυχόντες ὁδῖται κατ᾽ ὀλίγους κατὰ τοῦ κρυστάλλου πορευόμενοι διαβαίνουσιν, ἀλλὰ καὶ στρατοπέδων μυριάδες μετὰ σκευοφόρων καὶ ἁμαξῶν γεμουσῶν ἀσφαλῶς περαιοῦνται . . . πολλοὶ δὲ καὶ ἄλλοι πλωτοὶ ποταμοὶ κατὰ τὴν Κελτικήν εἰσι, περὶ ὧν μακρὸν ἂν εἴη γράφειν. πάντες δὲ σχεδὸν ὑπὸ τοῦ πάγου πηγνύμενοι γεφυροῦσι τὰ ῥεῖθρα, καὶ τοῦ κρυστάλλου διὰ τὴν φυσικὴν λειότητα ποιοῦντος τοὺς διαβαίνοντας ὀλισθάνειν, ἀχύρων ἐπιβαλλομένων ἐπ᾽ αὐτοὺς ἀσφαλῆ τὴν διάβασιν ἔχουσιν'; 'And the land, lying as it does for the most part under the Bears, has a wintry climate and is exceedingly cold. For during the winter season on cloudy days snow falls deep in place of rain, and on clear days ice and heavy frost are everywhere and in such abundance that the rivers are frozen over and are bridged by their own waters; for not only can chance travellers, proceeding a few at a time, make their way across them on the ice, but even armies with their tens of thousands, together with their beasts of burden and heavily laden wagons, cross upon it in safety to the other side . . . There are also many other navigable rivers in Celtica, but it would be a long task to write about them. And almost all of them become frozen over by the cold and thus bridge their own streams, and since the natural smoothness of the ice makes the crossing slippery for those who pass over, they sprinkle chaff on it and thus have a crossing which is safe.'

336. *anim. lib. ii*] Aristotle, *Generation of Animals*, II.viii.25: 'ἔτι δὲ ψυχρὸν τὸ ζῷον [ὁ ὄνος] ἐστί, διόπερ ἐν τοῖς χειμερινοῖς οὐ θέλει γίνεσθαι τόποις διὰ τὸ δύσριγον εἶναι τὴν φύσιν, οἷον περὶ Σκύθας καὶ τὴν ὅμορον χώραν, οὐδὲ περὶ Κελτοὺς τοὺς ὑπὲρ τῆς Ἰβηρίας'; 'Further, the animal [the ass] is a cold subject; and as it is by nature so sensitive to cold, it is not readily produced in wintry regions, such as Scythia and the neighbouring parts, or the Keltic country beyond Iberia.'

337. *Lib. iv*] Strabo, IV.i.2: 'προϊόντι δ᾽ ἐπὶ τὰς ἄρκτους καὶ τὸ Κέμμενον, ὄρος ἡ μὲν ἐλαιόφυτος καὶ συκοφόρος ἐκλείπει, τἆλλα δὲ φύεται. καὶ ἡ ἄμπελος δὲ προϊοῦσιν οὐ ῥᾳδίως τελεσφορεῖ'; 'As you proceed towards the north and the Cemmenus Mountain, the olive-planted and fig-bearing land indeed ceases, but the other things still grow. Also the vine, as you thus proceed, does not easily bring its fruit to maturity.'

338. *eleg. 7, 9, 10*] Ovid, *Tristia*, III.x.37–50: 'vidimus ingentem glacie consistere pontum, / lubricaque inmotas testa premebat aquas. / nec vidisse sat est; durum calcavimus aequor, / undaque non udo sub pede summa fuit. / si tibi

tale fretum quondam, Leandre, fuisset, / non foret angustae mors tua crimen aquae. / tum neque se pandi possunt delphines in auras / tollere; conantes dura coërcet hiems; / et quamvis Boreas iactatis insonet alis, / fluctus in obsesso gurgite nullus erit; / inclusaeque gelu stabunt in marmore puppes, / nec poterit rigidas findere remus aquas. / vidimus in glacie pisces haerere ligatos, / sed pars ex illis tum quoque viva fuit'; 'I have seen the vast sea stiff with ice, a slippery shell holding the water motionless. And seeing is not enough; I have trodden the frozen sea, and the surface lay beneath an unwetted foot. If thou, Leander, hadst once had such a sea, thy death would not have been a charge against the narrow waters. At such times the curving dolphins cannot launch themselves into the air; if they try, stern winter checks them; and though Boreas may roar and toss his wings, there will be no wave on the beleaguered flood. Shut in by the cold the ships will stand fast in the marble surface nor will any oar be able to cleave the stiffened waters. I have seen fish clinging fast bound in the ice, yet some even then still lived.' Ovid, *Ex Ponto*, IV.vii.1–10: 'Missus es Euxinas quoniam, Vestalis, ad undas, / ut positis reddas iura sub axe locis, / aspicis en praesens, quali iaceamus in arvo, / nec me testis eris falsa solere queri. / accedet voci per te non irrita nostrae, / Alpinis iuvenis regibus orte, fides. / ipse vides certe glacie concrescere Pontum, / ipse vides rigido stantia vina gelu; / ipse vides, onerata ferox ut ducat Iazyx / per medias Histri plaustra bubulcus aquas'; 'Seeing that you have been sent to the Euxine waters, Vestalis, to dispense justice to those lands which lie beneath the pole, you behold face to face in what manner of country I am cast and you will bear witness that I am not wont to utter false complaints. My words will receive through you, young scion of Alpine kings, no idle support. You yourself see the Pontus stiffen with ice, you yourself see the wine standing rigid with the frost; you yourself see how the fierce Iazygian herdsman guides his loaded wagon over the middle of Hister's waters.' Ovid, *Ex Ponto*, IV.ix.85–6: 'mentiar, an coëat duratus frigore Pontus, / et teneat glacies iugera multa freti'; 'whether I am a liar or the Pontus does indeed freeze with the cold and ice covers many acres of the sea'. Ovid, *Ex Ponto*, IV.x.32: 'hic freta vel pediti pervia reddit hiems'; 'here the winter makes even the sea a highway for one on foot.'

339. *a Provençal*] i.e. someone born in Provence, in southern France. Tournefort had been born on 5 June 1656 in Aix-en-Provence.

340. TOURNEFORT . . . *dismal ideas of it*] Joseph Pitton de Tournefort, *Relation d'un voyage du Levant*, 2 vols (Paris, 1717), vol. II, p. 164, 'Lettre XVI': 'Quoiqu'en aient dit les anciens, la mer Noire n'a rien de noir, pour ainsi dire, que le nom; les vent n'y soufflent pas avec plus de furie, & les orages n'y sont gueres plus frequens que sur les autres mers. Il faut pardonner ces exagérations aux Poëtes anciens, & sur tout au chagrin d'Ovide.'

341. *Our northern . . . are felled*] On the greater natural frigidity of the climate in North America for a given latitude, see Paw, *Recherches*, vol. I, p. 8: 'on peut

aisément s'appercevoir que l'air est moi[n]s chaud au Nouveau monde, que dans l'ancien continent. En évaluant, le plus exactement possible, la différence de temperature, je pense qu'on la trouvera de douze degrés de latitude, c'est-à-dire, qu'il fait aussi chaud en Afrique à trente degrés de l'Equateur, qu'à dis-huit degrés seulement de cette Ligne, en Amérique.' De Paw had related this greater frigidity to the prevalence of immense forests in America in language that is close to Hume's: 'Les plus grands espaces sablonneux qu'on connoisse sont en Afrique; les plus grandes forêts de l'univers sont en Amérique: il y en a qui on cinq-cents lieues de diamettre, & chaque arbre y est encore offusqué par des touffes de plantes excroissantes, & parasites, de sorte que jamais la clarté du jour n'a pénétré dans ces affreuses retraites de la nature sauvage. Cela doit beaucoup varier la température de l'air dans des contrées qui ont d'ailleurs les mêmes latitudes, l'expérience ayant démontré que tous les pays à bois sont plus froids que les lieux découverts & défrichés: les arbres ombragent, attirent les nuées, recelent l'humidité dans leurs feuilles, & tous leurs rameaux sont autant de ventilateurs qui agitent la moyenne région de l'air' (vol. I, p. 161). Cf. also Adam Ferguson: 'The climates of America, though taken under the same parallel, are observed to differ from those of Europe. There, extensive marshes, great lakes, aged, decayed, and crouded forests, with the other circumstances that mark an uncultivated country, are supposed to replenish the air with heavy and noxious vapours, that give a double asperity to the winter, and, during many months, by the frequency and continuance of fogs, snow and frost, carry the inconveniencies of the frigid zone far into the temperate' (Ferguson, *Civil Society*, p. 113). Gibbon would apply this insight about the effect of deforestation to explain the greater warmth of modern Germany as compared with the same terrain in antiquity: 'The climate of ancient Germany has been mollified, and the soil fertilized, by the labour of ten centuries from the time of Charlemagne. The same extent of ground which at present maintains, in ease and plenty, a million of husbandmen and artificers, was unable to supply an hundred thousand lazy warriors with the simple necessaries of life.' Gibbon then went on, with a reference to Hume, to reflect on how this disproved the erroneous opinion that 'in the age of Cæsar and Tacitus, the inhabitants of the North were far more numerous than they are in our days' (Gibbon, *Decline and Fall*, vol. I, pp. 238–9).

342. *Lib. iv. cap. 21*] Polybius, IV.xxi.1: 'θεωροῦντες δὲ τὴν τῶν ἠθῶν αὐστηρίαν, ἥτις αὐτοῖς παρέπεται διὰ τὴν τοῦ περιέχοντος ψυχρότητα καὶ στυγνότητα τὴν κατὰ τὸ πλεῖστον ἐν τοῖς τόποις ὑπάρχουσαν'; 'as well as the harshness of character resulting from the cold and gloomy atmospheric conditions usually prevailing in these parts'.

343. *Lib. i. cap. 2*] Varro, *On Agriculture*, I.ii.4: 'Primum cum orbis terrae divisus sit in duas partes ab Eratosthene maxume secundum naturam, ad meridiem versus et ad septemtriones, et sine dubio quoniam salubrior pars

septemtrionalis est quam meridiana, et quae salubriora illa fructuosiora, dicendum utique Italiam magis etiam fuisse opportunam ad colendum quam Asiam, primum quod est in Europa, secundo quod haec temperatior pars quam interior. Nam intus paene sempiternae hiemes, neque mirum, quod sunt regiones inter circulum septemtrionalem et inter cardinem caeli, ubi sol etiam sex mensibus continuis non videtur. Itaque in oceano in ea parte ne navigari quidem posse dicunt propter mare congelatum'; 'Consider first: Eratosthenes, following a most natural division, has divided the earth into two parts, one to the south and the other to the north; and since the northern part is undoubtedly more healthful than the southern, while the part which is more healthful is more fruitful, we must agree that Italy at least was more suited to cultivation than Asia. In the first place, it is in Europe; and in the next place, this part of Europe has a more temperate climate than we find farther inland. For the winter is almost continuous in the interior, and no wonder, since its lands lie between the arctic circle and the pole, where the sun is not visible for six months at a time; wherefore we are told that even navigation in the ocean is not possible in that region because of the frozen sea.'

344. *Lib. iii*] Strabo, III.i.2: 'ταύτης δὴ τὸ μὲν πλέον οἰκεῖται φαύλως· ὄρη γὰρ καὶ δρυμοὺς καὶ πεδία λεπτὴν ἔχοντα γῆν, οὐδὲ ταύτην ὁμαλῶς εὔυδρον, οἰκοῦσι τὴν πολλήν· ἡ δὲ πρόσβορρος ψυχρά τέ ἐστι τελέως πρὸς τῇ τραχύτητι καὶ παρωκεανῖτις, προσειληφυῖα τὸ ἄμικτον κἀνεπίπλεκτον τοῖς ἄλλοις, ὥσθ' ὑπερβάλλει τῇ μοχθηρίᾳ τῆς οἰκήσεως'; 'Now of Iberia the larger part affords but poor means of livelihood; for most of the inhabited country consists of mountains, forests, and plains whose soil is thin – and even that not uniformly well-watered. And Northern Iberia, in addition to its ruggedness, not only is extremely cold, but lies next to the ocean, and thus has acquired its characteristic of inhospitality and aversion to intercourse with other countries; consequently, it is an exceedingly wretched place to live in.'

345. *Lib. i. cap. 1*] Columella, *On Agriculture*, I.i.4–5: 'Multos enim iam memorabiles auctores comperi persuasum habere longo aevi situ qualitatem caeli statumque mutari, eorumque consultissimum astrologiae professorem Hipparchum prodidisse tempus fore, quo cardines mundi loco moverentur, idque etiam non spernendus auctor rei rusticae Saserna videtur adcredidisse. Nam eo libro, quem de agri cultura scriptum reliquit, mutatum caeli situm sic colligit, quod quae regiones antea propter hiemis adsiduam violentiam nullam stirpem vitis aut oleae depositam custodire potuerint, nunc mitigato iam et intepescente pristino frigore largissimis olivitatibus Liberique vindemiis exuberent'; 'For I have found that many authorities now worthy of remembrance were convinced that with the long wasting of the ages, weather and climate undergo a change; and that among them the most learned professional astronomer, Hipparchus, has put it on record that the time will come when the celestial poles will change position, a

statement to which Saserna, no mean authority on husbandry, seems to have given credence. For in that book on agriculture which he has left behind he concludes that the position of the heavens has changed from this evidence: that regions which formerly, because of the unremitting severity of winter, could not safeguard any shoot of the vine or the olive planted in them, now that the earlier coldness has abated and the weather is becoming more clement, produce olive harvests and the vintages of Bacchus in the greatest abundance.'

346. *lib. i. cap. i*] Columella's roll-call of great Roman writers on agriculture (*On Agriculture*, I.i.12) places the two Sasernas after Cato the Censor (234–149 BC) and before Tremelius Scrofa, who was a contemporary of Marcus Terentius Varro and is a speaker in his *De Re Rustica* (116–27 BC). The life of the younger Scipio Africanus (185–129 BC) thus falls between them.

347. *best account of it*] Benoît de Maillet considers the population of Egypt at the end of the first chapter of his *Description* (Maillet, *Description*, pp. 27–31). He begins by noting the large numbers reported by ancient authors: 'Ce que les historiens nous racontent de l'état, où ce pays étoit à cet égard dans les anciens tems, tient du merveilleux. Alors, dit Eusèbe, on y comptoit jusqu'à sept millions cinq cens mille hommes. Les Auteurs Arabes vont encore plus loin, & en mettent jusqu'à vingt millions. Ce nombre est prodigieux sans doute; cependant il ne paroitra pas incroyable, si on fait attention que l'Egypte n'étoit pas alors resserrée & bornée aux seuls terrains aujourd'hui cultivés & habités . . .' (p. 27). But it is so no longer: 'Aujourd'hui les choses ont beaucoup changé de face. J'ai cru, je l'avoüe, pendant un tems que l'Egypte étoit encore de nos jours aussi peuplée qu'elle le fut pendant le régne de ses premiers Rois, ou sous celui des Grecs & les Romains. Mais si je l'ai dit, ou écrit, je ne crains pas de me rétracter' (pp. 27–8). The principal cause of this dwindling of the population is, he believes, the diminished fertility of the Nile, for 'l'ancienne fertilité du Nil a eu des bornes beaucoup plus étendües, que celles qu'elle a aujourd'hui' (p. 29). And he concludes that the effect of depopulation has further exacerbated its cause: 'C'est ainsi que la diminution du nombre des habitans de ce pays fertile a resserré les bornes de sa fecondité, comme il est vrai de dire que les bornes étroites, dans lesquelles elle s'est trouvé resserrée, ont contribué plus que toute autre cause à diminuer le nombre de ses habitans' (p. 31). Cf. above, p. 466, n. 213.

348. *government of the* TURKS *... propagation*] Rycaut had commented on the use of depopulation as a tool of government in the Ottoman Empire: 'The *Turks* have but one sole means to maintain their Countries, which is the same by which they were gained, and that is the cruelty of the sword in the most rigorous way of execution, by killing, consuming and laying desolate the Countries, and transplanting the people unto parts where they are nearest under the command and age [*sic*] of a Governour; being wholly destitute and ignorant of other refined Arts, which more civilized Nations have

in part made serve in the place of violence. And yet the *Turks* have made this course alone answer to all the intents and ends of their Government' (Rycaut, *Present State*, pp. 67–8).

349. *TEUTONS and CIMBRI*] Ancient German tribes.

350. *No one ought to esteem . . . than formerly*] The legend of the 'northern hive' of nations, the profuse offspring of Japheth the son of Noah (Genesis 9:18–19), had been most recently and elaborately expounded by Olaus Rudbeck in his *Atlantica* (Uppsala, 1675–98): for Gibbon's amused account of this work, see Gibbon, *Decline and Fall*, vol. I, p. 234. Hume here echoes Wallace's wording: 'we may justly conclude, that, notwithstanding the numerous swarms which the northern nations sent forth into southern climes, at different times, those northern regions might have, and if barbarous and without agriculture, must have, been ill peopled' (Wallace, *Dissertation*, pp. 15–16). Cf. Montesquieu, *Lettres Persanes*, letter 112: 'Les pays du Nord son fort dégarnis, et il s'en faut bien que les peuples y soient, comme autrefois, obligés de se partager et d'envoyer dehors, commes des essaims de colonies et des nations entières chercher de nouvelles demeures' (Montesquieu, *Œuvres*, p. 121).

351. *lib. iv. cap. 45*] Xenophon, *Anabasis*, VII.iii.10–11 (the speech of Seuthes the Thracian): 'σῖτα δὲ καὶ ποτὰ ὥσπερ καὶ νῦν ἐκ τῆς χώρας λαμβάνοντες ἕξετε· ὁπόσα δ᾽ ἂν ἁλίσκηται ἀξιώσω αὐτὸς ἔχειν, ἵνα ταῦτα διατιθέμενος ὑμῖν τὸν μισθὸν ἐκπορίζω. καὶ τὰ μὲν φεύγοντα καὶ ἀποδιδράσκοντα ἡμεῖς ἱκανοὶ ἐσόμεθα διώκειν καὶ μαστεύειν· ἂν δέ τις ἀνθίστηται, σὺν ὑμῖν πειρασόμεθα χειροῦσθαι'; 'Food and drink you will obtain, just as today, by taking from the country; but whatever may be captured I shall expect to retain for myself, so that by selling it I may provide you your pay. All that flees and hides we shall ourselves be able to pursue and seek out; but if anyone offers resistance, with your help we shall try to subdue him.' Polybius, IV.xlv.6–8: 'οὐ μὴν ἀλλὰ τούτοις τὸ παράπαν κακοῖς παλαίοντες κατὰ γῆν, χωρὶς τῶν ἄλλων τῶν παρεπομένων τῷ πολέμῳ κακῶν, ὑπομένουσί τινα καὶ τιμωρίαν Ταντάλειον κατὰ τὸν ποιητήν. ἔχοντες γὰρ χώραν γενναιοτάτην, ὅταν διαπονήσωσι ταύτην καὶ γένηται τὸ τῶν καρπῶν πλῆθος τῷ κάλλει διαφέρον, κἄπειτα παραγενηθέντες οἱ βάρβαροι τοὺς μὲν καταφθείρωσι τοὺς δὲ συναθροίσαντες ἀποφέρωσι, τότε δή, χωρὶς τῶν ἔργων καὶ τῆς δαπάνης, καὶ τὴν καταφθορὰν θεώμενοι διὰ τὸ κάλλος τῶν καρπῶν σχετλιάζουσι καὶ βαρέως φέρουσι τὸ συμβαῖνον'; 'Nay, such being in general the adverse circumstances against which they [the Byzantines] have to struggle on land, they have in addition to the other evils attendant on war to suffer too something like the torments of Tantalus that Homer describes; for, owners as they are of a most fertile country, when they have carefully cultivated it and a superb harvest is the result, and when the barbarians [i.e. the Thracians] now appear and destroy part of the crops, collecting and carrying off the rest, then indeed, apart from their lost toil and expense, the very beauty of the harvest when they witness its destruction adds to their indignation and distress.' Cf. also Strabo, VII.i.3 and VII.iii.11, for information about the subsistence of the Getae.

352. *lib. vii*] Hume refers to the frequent complaints voiced by Ovid in the collections of poems written in exile, *Tristia* and *Ex Ponto*. Strabo relates what he knows about the Getae in his *Geography*, VII.iii.1–5.

353. *lib. ii. cap. 12*] Polybius, II.xii.6: 'οὐ γὰρ τισὶν, ἀλλὰ πᾶσι, τότε κοινοὺς ἐχθροὺς εἶναι συνέβαινε τοὺς Ἰλλυριούς'; 'for the Illyrians were then not the enemies of this people or that, but the common enemies of all.'

354. *at present*] Note Hume's summary of his impressions of German prosperity, after travelling across the country in 1748: 'Germany is undoubtedly a very fine Country, full of industrious honest People, & were it united it woud be the greatest Power that ever was in the World. The common People are here, almost every where, much better treated & more at their Ease, than in France; and are not very much inferior to the English, notwithstanding all the Airs the latter give themselves. There are great Advantages, in travelling, & nothing serves more to remove Prejudices: For I confess I had entertain'd no such advantageous Idea of Germany: And it gives a Man of Humanity Pleasure to see that so considerable a Part of Mankind as the Germans are in so tolerable a Condition' (*Letters*, vol. I, p. 126). In this paragraph Hume is silently using a principle admitted by Wallace against his general argument: see Wallace, *Dissertation*, pp. 15–16.

355. *the division . . . industry*] Again, Hume here is silently taking issue with an inference made by Wallace: 'if there is very nearly an equal division of the lands, and into such small shares, that they can yield little more than what is necessary to feed and clothe the labourers in a frugal and simple manner; tho', in such a situation, there is little room for commerce with strangers, and none but the most simple and necessary arts can be in use; yet if the country be naturally fertile, it must of necessity be well stored with people. Hence we may conclude, that when any antient nation divided its lands into small shares, and when even eminent citizens had but a few acres to maintain their families, tho' such a nation had but little commerce, and had learned only a few simple and more necessary arts, it must have abounded greatly in people' (Wallace, *Dissertation*, p. 17).

356. *may be ascribed*] Another glance at Wallace's *Dissertation*: 'where the lands are very unequally divided, and are capable of maintaining many more than those who cultivate them, that country must be thinly peopled' (Wallace, *Dissertation*, pp. 17–18).

357. *lib. vi*] Caesar, *Gallic War*, VI.xxiii: 'Civitatibus maxima laus est quam latissime circum se vastatis finibus solitudines habere. Hoc proprium virtutis existimant, expulsos agris finitimos cedere, neque quemquam prope audere consistere; simul hoc se fore tutiores arbitrantur repentinae incursionis timore sublato'; 'Their states account it the highest praise by devastating their borders to have areas of wilderness as wide as possible around them. They think it the true sign of valour when the neighbours are driven to retire from their lands and no man dares to settle near, and at the same time

they believe they will be safer thereby, having removed all fear of a sudden inroad.'

358. *Moribus Germ.*] Tacitus, *Germania*, XVI.i–iii: 'Nullas Germanorum populis urbes habitari satis notum est, ne pati quidem inter se iunctas sedes, colunt discreti ac diversi, ut fons, ut campus, ut nemus placuit. vicos locant non in nostrum morem conexis et cohaerentibus aedificiis: suam quisque domum spatio circumdat, sive adversus casus ignis remedium sive inscitia aedificandi'; 'It is well known that none of the German tribes live in cities, that even individually they do not permit houses to touch each other: they live separated and scattered, according as spring-water, meadow, or grove appeals to each man: they lay out their villages not, after our fashion, with buildings contiguous and connected; everyone keeps a clear space round his house, whether it be a precaution against the chances of fire, or just ignorance of building.'

359. *Lib. vii*] Strabo, VII.i.3: 'κοινὸν δ᾽ ἐστὶν ἅπασι τοῖς ταύτῃ τὸ περὶ τὰς μεταναστάσεις εὐμαρὲς διὰ τὴν λιτότητα τοῦ βίου καὶ διὰ τὸ μὴ γεωργεῖν μηδὲ θησαυρίζειν, ἀλλ᾽ ἐν καλυβίοις οἰκεῖν, ἐφήμερον ἔχουσι παρασκευήν· τροφὴ δ᾽ ἀπὸ τῶν θρεμμάτων ἡ πλείστη, καθάπερ τοῖς Νομάσιν, ὥστ᾽ ἐκείνους μιμούμενοι τὰ οἰκεῖα ταῖς ἁρμαμάξαις ἐπάραντες, ὅπῃ ἂν δόξῃ, τρέπονται μετὰ τῶν βοσκημάτων'; 'It is a common characteristic of all the peoples in this part of the world [Germany] that they migrate with ease, because of the meagreness of their livelihood and because they do not till the soil or even store up food, but live in small huts that are merely temporary structures; and they live for the most part off their flocks, as the Nomads do, so that, in imitation of the Nomads, they load their household belongings on their wagons and with their beasts turn whithersoever they think best.'

360. *Lib. iii. cap. 47*] Herodian, *History of the Empire*, III.xiv.6: 'τὰ γὰρ πλεῖστα τῆς Βρεττανῶν χώρας ἐπικλυζόμενα ταῖς τοῦ ὠκεανοῦ συνεχῶς ἀμπώτισιν ἑλώδη γίνεται'; 'Most of Britain is marshland because it is flooded by the continual ocean tides.'

361. *than the GERMANS*] Caesar, *Gallic War*, VI.xiii: 'Disciplina in Britannia reperta atque inde in Galliam translata esse existimatur, et nunc, qui diligentius eam rem cognoscere volunt, plerumque illo discendi causa proficiscuntur'; 'It is believed that their rule of life was discovered in Britain and transferred thence to Gaul; and today those who would study the subject more accurately journey, as a rule, to Britain to learn it.' Strabo, IV.iv.2: 'νυνὶ μὲν οὖν ἐν εἰρήνῃ πάντες εἰσὶ δεδουλωμένοι καὶ ζῶντες κατὰ τὰ προστάγματα τῶν ἑλόντων αὐτοὺς Ῥωμαίων, ἀλλ᾽ ἐκ τῶν παλαιῶν χρόνων τοῦτο λαμβάνομεν περὶ αὐτῶν ἔκ τε τῶν μέχρι νῦν συμμενόντων παρὰ τοῖς Γερμανοῖς νομίμων. καὶ γὰρ τῇ φύσει καὶ τοῖς πολιτεύμασιν ἐμφερεῖς εἰσι καὶ συγγενεῖς ἀλλήλοις οὗτοι, ὅμορόν τε οἰκοῦσι χώραν, διοριζομένην τῷ Ῥήνῳ ποταμῷ, καὶ παραπλήσια ἔχουσαν τὰ πλεῖστα (ἀρκτικωτέρα δ᾽ ἐστὶν ἡ Γερμανία) κρινομένων τῶν τε νοτίων μερῶν πρὸς τὰ νότια καὶ τῶν ἀρκτικῶν πρὸς τὰ ἀρκτικά'; 'At the present time they

[the Gauls] are all at peace, since they have been enslaved and are living in accordance with the commands of the Romans who captured them, but it is from the early times that I am taking this account of them, and also from the customs that hold fast to this day among the Germans. For these peoples are not only similar in respect to their nature and their governments, but they are also kinsmen to one another; and, further, they live in country that has a common boundary, since it is divided by the River Rhenus, and most of its regions are similar (though Germany is more to the north), if the southern regions be judged with reference to the southern and also the northern with reference to the northern'; VII.i.2: 'Εὐθὺς τοίνυν τὰ πέραν τοῦ Ῥήνου μετὰ τοὺς Κελτοὺς πρὸς τὴν ἕω κεκλιμένα Γερμανοὶ νέμονται, μικρὸν ἐξαλλάττοντες τοῦ Κελτικοῦ φύλου τῷ τε πλεονασμῷ τῆς ἀγριότητος καὶ τοῦ μεγέθους καὶ τῆς ξανθότητος, τἆλλα δὲ παραπλήσιοι, καὶ μορφαῖς καὶ ἤθεσι καὶ βίοις ὄντες οἵους εἰρήκαμεν τοὺς Κελτούς'; 'Now the parts beyond the Rhenus, immediately after the country of the Celti, slope towards the east and are occupied by the Germans, who, though they vary slightly from the Celtic stock in that they are wilder, taller, and have yellower hair, are in all other respects similar, for in build, habits and modes of life they are such as I have said the Celti are.'

362. *Celt. pars 1*] Appian, *Roman History*, IV.i.6: 'Τελευταῖα δὲ καὶ μέγιστα τῶν ἐς Γαλάτας Ῥωμαίοις πεπραγμένων ἐστὶ τὰ ὑπὸ Γαΐῳ Καίσαρι στρατηγοῦντι γενόμενα· μυριάσι τε γὰρ ἀνδρῶν ἀγρίων ἐν τοῖς δέκα ἔτεσιν, ἐν οἷς ἐστρατήγησεν, εἰς χεῖρας ἦλθον, εἴ τις ὑφ' ἓν τὰ μέρη συναγάγοι, τετρακοσίων πλείοσιν καὶ τούτων ἑκατὸν μὲν ἐζώγρησαν, ἑκατὸν δ' ἐν τῷ πόνῳ κατέκανον, ἔθνη δὲ τετρακόσια καὶ πόλεις ὑπὲρ ὀκτακοσίας, τὰ μὲν ἀφιστάμενα σφῶν, τὰ δὲ προσεπιλαμβάνοντες, ἐκρατύναντο'; 'The most recent and greatest of the confrontations between Rome and the Gauls is the campaign under the command of Gaius Caesar. For, in the ten years of his command, Roman armies fought against more than four million fierce opponents (if you count them all together), captured a million of them, and killed another million in battle. They subjected four hundred tribes and more than eight hundred towns, some of which had revolted from us, others were new acquisitions.'

363. *Lib. v*] Diodorus Siculus, V.xxv.1: 'Ἐπεὶ δὲ περὶ τῆς τῶν Γαλατῶν προσηγορίας διήλθομεν, καὶ περὶ τῆς χώρας αὐτῶν δέον ἐστὶν εἰπεῖν. ἡ τοίνυν Γαλατία κατοικεῖται μὲν ὑπὸ πολλῶν ἐθνῶν διαφόρων τοῖς μεγέθεσι· τὰ μέγιστα γὰρ αὐτῶν σχεδὸν εἴκοσι μυριάδας ἀνδρῶν ἔχει, τὰ δ' ἐλάχιστα πέντε μυριάδας, ὧν ἕν ἐστι πρὸς Ῥωμαίους ἔχον συγγένειαν παλαιὰν καὶ φιλίαν τὴν μέχρι τῶν καθ' ἡμᾶς χρόνων διαμένουσαν'; 'Since we have explained the name by which the Gauls are known, we must go on to speak about their land. Gaul is inhabited by many tribes of different size; for the largest number some two hundred thousand men, and the smallest fifty thousand, one of the latter standing on terms of kinship and friendship with the Romans, a relationship which has endured from ancient times down to our own day.'

364. *lib. vi*] Caesar, *Gallic War*, VI.xiii: 'In omni Gallia eorum hominum, qui aliquo sunt numero atque honore, genera sunt duo. Nam plebes paene servorum habetur loco, quae nihil audet per se, nullo adhibetur consilio. Plerique, cum aut aere alieno aut magnitudine tributorum aut iniuria potentiorum premuntur, sese in servitutem dicant nobilibus: in hos eadem omnia sunt iura, quae dominis in servos'; 'Throughout Gaul there are two classes of persons of definite account and dignity. As for the common folk, they are treated almost as slaves, venturing naught of themselves, never taken into counsel. The more part of them, oppressed as they are either by debt, or by the heavy weight of tribute, or by the wrongdoing of the more powerful men, commit themselves in slavery to the nobles, who have, in fact, the same rights over them as masters over slaves.'

365. *Tanistry*] i.e. a system of life-tenure among the ancient Irish and Gaels, whereby the succession to an estate or dignity was conferred by election upon the 'eldest and worthiest' among the surviving kinsmen of the deceased lord (*OED*, 'tanistry', *n.* a).

366. *canton of BERNE . . . many people*] 'there be above Three hundred and Sixty Families of Citizens in *Berne*, and . . . their Canton makes at least a third Part of *Switzerland*' (Stanyan, *Switzerland*, p. 104).

367. *Id. ibid.*] Caesar, *Gallic War*, VI.xv: 'Alterum genus est equitum. Hi, cum est usus atque aliquod bellum incidit (quod fere ante Caesaris adventum quotannis accidere solebat, uti aut ipsi iniurias inferrent aut illatas propulsarent), omnes in bello versantur'; 'The other class are the knights. These, when there is occasion, upon the incidence of a war – and before Caesar's coming this would happen well-nigh every year, in the sense that they would either be making wanton attacks themselves or repelling such – are all engaged therein.'

368. *Lib. iv*] Strabo, IV.i.2: 'τοὺς γὰρ αὐτοὺς ἐκφέρει καρποὺς ἡ Ναρβωνῖτις ἅπασα οὕσπερ ἡ Ἰταλία. προϊόντι δ᾽ ἐπὶ τὰς ἄρκτους καὶ τὸ Κέμμενον, ὄρος ἡ μὲν ἐλαιόφυτος καὶ συκοφόρος ἐκλείπει, τἆλλα δὲ φύεται. καὶ ἡ ἄμπελος δὲ προϊοῦσιν οὐ ῥαδίως τελεσφορεῖ· ἡ δ᾽ ἄλλη πᾶσα σῖτον φέρει πολὺν καὶ κέγχρον καὶ βάλανον καὶ βοσκήματα παντοῖα, ἀργὸν δ᾽ αὐτῆς οὐδέν, πλὴν εἴ τι ἕλεσι κεκώλυται καὶ δρυμοῖς· καίτοι καὶ τοῦτο συνοικεῖται, πολυανθρωπίᾳ μᾶλλον ἢ ἐπιμελείᾳ. καὶ γὰρ τοκάδες αἱ γυναῖκες καὶ τρέφειν ἀγαθαί, οἱ δ᾽ ἄνδρες μαχηταὶ μᾶλλον ἢ γεωργοί· νῦν δ᾽ ἀναγκάζονται γεωργεῖν, καταθέμενοι τὰ ὅπλα'; 'For example, the same fruits are produced by the whole of the province of Narbonitis as by Italy. As you proceed towards the north and the Cemmenus Mountain, the olive-planted and fig-bearing land indeed ceases, but the other things still grow. Also the vine, as you thus proceed, does not easily bring its fruit to maturity. All the rest of the country produces grain in large quantities, and millet, and nuts, and all kinds of livestock. And none of the country is untilled except parts where tilling is precluded by swamps and woods. Yet these parts too are thickly peopled – more because of the

largeness of the population than because of the industry of the people; for the women are not only prolific, but good nurses as well, while the men are fighters rather than farmers. But at the present time they are compelled to till the soil, now that they have laid down their arms.'

369. *lib. ii*] Caesar, *Gallic War*, II.iv: 'Apud eos fuisse regem nostra etiam memoria Diviciacum, totius Galliae potentissimum, qui cum magnae partis harum regionum, tum etiam Britanniae imperium obtinuerit: nunc esse regem Galbam: ad hunc propter iustitiam prudentiamque suam totius belli summam omnium voluntate deferri; oppida habere numero xii, polliceri milia armata quinquaginta; totidem Nervios, qui maxime feri inter ipsos habeantur longissimeque absint; quindecim milia Atrebates, Ambianos decem milia, Morinos xxv milia, Menapios vii milia, Caletos x milia, Veliocasses et Viromanduos totidem, Aduatucos decem et novem milia; Condrusos, Eburones, Caeroesos, Paemanos, qui uno nomine Germani appellantur, arbitrari ad xl milia'; 'Among them, even within living memory, Diviciacus had been king, the most powerful man in the whole of Gaul, who had exercised sovereignty alike over a great part of these districts, and even over Britain. Galba was now king; to him, by reason of his justice and sagacity, the supreme charge of the campaign was delivered by general consent; he had twelve towns, and promised fifty thousand men-at-arms. An equal number were promised by the Nervii, accounted the fiercest among the Belgae, and dwelling farthest away; fifteen thousand by the Atrebates, ten by the Ambiani, five-and-twenty by the Morini, seven by the Menapii, ten by the Caleti, as many by the Veliocasses and the Viromandui, nineteen by the Aduatuci. The Condrusi, Eburones, Caeroesi and Paemani (who are indiscriminately called Germans), had promised, it was thought, some forty thousand men.'

370. *lib. i*] Caesar, *Gallic War*, I.ii: 'Pro multitudine autem hominum et pro gloria belli atque fortitudinis angustos se fines habere arbitrabantur, qui in longitudinem milia passuum ccxl, in latitudinem clxxx patebant'; 'Nay, they could not but consider that the territory they occupied – to an extent of 240 miles long and 180 broad – was all too narrow for their population and for their renown of courage in war.' For Caesar's reckoning of the population of Helvetia, see *Gallic War*, I.xxix, quoted above, p. 144, n. 99.

371. *lib. xxxiv. cap. 17*] Livy, XXXIV.xvii.5–6: 'consul interim rebellione Bergistanorum ictus, ceteras quoque civitates ratus per occasionem idem facturas, arma omnibus cis Hiberum Hispanis adimit; quam rem adeo aegre passi ut multi mortem sibimet ipsi consciscerent, ferox genus, nullam vitam rati sine armis esse'; 'Meanwhile the consul, shocked by the uprising of the Bergistani and thinking the other communities would seize the opportunity to do the same, disarmed all the Spaniards north of the Ebro. The Spaniards were so humiliated by this measure that many took their own lives – they are a headstrong people who feel life is nothing without weapons.' Hume has cited this passage of Livy in 'Of National Characters' (above, p. 144).

372. *In vita Marii*] Plutarch, *Life of Caius Marius*, VI: 'μετὰ δὲ τὴν στρατηγίαν κλήρῳ λαβὼν τὴν ἐκτὸς Ἰβηρίαν λέγεται καθᾶραι λῃστηρίων τὴν ἐπαρχίαν ἀνήμερον οὖσαν ἔτι τοῖς ἐθισμοῖς καὶ θηριώδη, καὶ τὸ λῃστεύειν οὔπω τότε τῶν Ἰβήρων οὐχὶ κάλλιστον ἡγουμένων'; 'After his [Marius's] praetorship, however, the province of Farther Spain was allotted to him, and here he is said to have cleared away the robbers, although the province was still uncivilized in its customs and in a savage state, and robbery was at that time still considered a most honourable occupation by the Spaniards.'

373. *ITALY ... has decayed*] cf. *Lettres Persanes*, letter 112: 'J'ai resté plus d'un an en Italie, où je n'ai vu que le débris de cette ancienne Italie, si fameuse autrefois. Quoique tout le monde habite les villes, elles sont entièrement désertes et dépeuplées: il semble qu'elles ne subsistent encore que pour marquer le lieu où étaient ces cités puissantes dont l'histoire a tant parlé' (Montesquieu, *Œuvres*, p. 121). See also Thomson, *Liberty*, Part I, 'Antient and Modern Italy Compared'.

374. *sportula*] Literally, 'a little basket'; by extension, the dole which great men were accustomed to give their clients, in the form of either food or money. See Martial, I.59 and 80, III.30 and 60, VII.86, VIII.42 and 49, IX.85, X.27 and 75, XIII.123, XIV.125; and Juvenal, I.95, 118 and 128, III.249, X.46, XIII.33.

375. *Bello Hisp.*] Caesar (Hirtius?), *Spanish War*, I.viii: 'Nam fere totius ulterioris Hispaniae regio propter terrae fecunditatem et non minus copiosam aquationem inopem difficilemque habet oppugnationem. Hic etiam propter barbarorum crebras excursiones omnia loca quae sunt ab oppidis remota turribus et munitionibus retinentur, sicut in Africa, rudere, non tegulis teguntur; simulque in his habent speculas et propter altitudinem late longeque prospiciunt'; 'In fact, practically the whole region of Further Spain, fertile as it is and correspondingly well watered, makes a siege a fruitless and difficult task. Here too, in view of the constant sallies of the natives, all places which are remote from towns are firmly held by towers and fortifications, as in Africa, roofed over with rough-cast, not tiles. Moreover, they have watchtowers in them, commanding a view far and wide by reason of their altitude.'

376. *lib. ii. § 90*] Velleius Paterculus, *Roman History*, II.xc.1: 'Hispaniae nunc ipsius praesentia, nunc Agrippae, quem usque in tertium consulatum et mox collegium tribuniciae potestatis amicitia principis evexerat, multo varioque Marte pacatae'; 'The provinces of Spain were pacified after heavy campaigns conducted with varied success now by Caesar in person, now by Agrippa, whom the friendship of the emperor had raised to a third consulship and soon afterwards to a share in the emperor's tribunician power.'

377. *Lib. iii*] Strabo gives his account of the physical and human geography of the Iberian peninsula in Book III of his *Geography*. Hume asserts that the picture he has painted of the moral and material backwardness of the inhabitants 'corresponds exactly' to what Strabo says, but in fact Strabo

(who composed his *Geography* between 60 and 25 BC) locates Spanish backwardness firmly in the past. See, e.g., Strabo, *Geography*, III.ii.15: 'Τῇ δὲ τῆς χώρας εὐδαιμονίᾳ καὶ τὸ ἥμερον καὶ τὸ πολιτικὸν συνηκολούθησε τοῖς Τουρδητανοῖς· καὶ τοῖς Κελτικοῖς δὲ διὰ τὴν γειτνίασιν, ὡς εἴρηκε Πολύβιος, ἢ διὰ τὴν συγγένειαν, ἀλλ᾿ ἐκείνοις μὲν ἧττον· τὰ πολλὰ γὰρ κωμηδὸν ζῶσιν. οἱ μέντοι Τουρδητανοί, καὶ μάλιστα οἱ περὶ τὸν Βαῖτιν, τελέως εἰς τὸν Ῥωμαίων μεταβέβληνται τρόπον, οὐδὲ τῆς διαλέκτου τῆς σφετέρας ἔτι μεμνημένοι. Λατῖνοί τε οἱ πλεῖστοι γεγόνασι, καὶ ἐποίκους εἰλήφασι Ῥωμαίους, ὥστε μικρὸν ἀπέχουσι τοῦ πάντες εἶναι Ῥωμαῖοι. αἵ τε νῦν συνῳκισμέναι πόλεις, ἥ τε ἐν τοῖς Κελτικοῖς Παξαυγούστα καὶ ἡ ἐν τοῖς Τουρδούλοις Αὐγούστα Ἡμερίτα καὶ ἡ περὶ τοὺς Κελτίβηρας Καισαραυγούστα καὶ ἄλλαι ἔνιαι κατοικίαι τὴν μεταβολὴν τῶν λεχθεισῶν πολιτειῶν ἐμφανίζουσι. καὶ δὴ τῶν Ἰβήρων ὅσοι ταύτης εἰσὶ τῆς ἰδέας τογᾶτοι λέγονται· ἐν δὲ τούτοις εἰσὶ καὶ οἱ Κελτίβηρες οἱ πάντων νομισθέντες ποτὲ θηριωδέστατοι. ταῦτα μὲν περὶ τούτων'; 'Along with the happy lot of their country, the qualities of both gentleness and civility have come to the Turdetanians; and to the Celtic peoples, too, on account of their being neighbours to the Turdetanians, as Polybius has said, or else on account of their kinship, but less so the Celtic peoples, because for the most part they live in mere villages. The Turdetanians, however, and particularly those who live about the Baetis, have completely changed over to the Roman mode of life, not even remembering their own language any more. And most of them have become Latins, and they have received Romans as colonists, so that they are not far from being all Romans. And the present jointly settled cities, Pax Augusta in the Celtic country, Augusta Emerita in the country of the Turdulians, Caesar-Augusta near Celtiberia, and some other settlements, manifest the change to the aforesaid civil modes of life. Moreover, all those Iberians who belong to this class are called "Togati". And among these are the Celtiberians, who were once regarded the most brutish of all. So much for the Turdetanians.'

378. *Lib. xliv*] Justinus summarizes the character of the ancient inhabitants of Iberia in XLIV.ii, and he underlines their ferocity: 'Velocitas genti pernix; inquies animus: plurimis militares equi, & arma, sanguine ipsorum cariora'; 'They are a quick and nimble race, and of unquiet mind. For the most part, their horses and weapons are dearer to their soldiers than their own blood' (Justinus, *Epitomae*, p. 279).

379. *robbers in general*] Hume is quoting Cicero, *De Haruspicum Responsis*, IX.xix: 'We have excelled neither Spain in population, nor Gaul in vigour, nor Carthage in versatility, nor Greece in art, nor indeed Italy and Latium itself in the innate sensibility characteristic of this land and its peoples.' He goes on to quote Virgil, *Georgics*, III.408: 'never need you fear restless Spaniards in your rear'.

380. *cap. 42*] Varro, *On Agriculture*, II.praef.3: 'Igitur quod nunc intra murum fere patres familiae correpserunt relictis falce et aratro et manus movere maluerunt in theatro ac circo, quam in segetibus ac vinetis, frumentum

locamus qui nobis advehat, qui saturi fiamus ex Africa et Sardinia, et navibus vindemiam condimus ex insula Coa et Chia'; 'As therefore in these days practically all the heads of families have sneaked within the walls, abandoning the sickle and the plough, and would rather busy their hands in the theatre and in the circus than in the grain-fields and the vineyards, we hire a man to bring us from Africa and Sardinia the grain with which to fill our stomachs, and the vintage we store comes in ships from the islands of Cos and Chios.' Columella, *On Agriculture*, praef., 1–3: 'Saepenumero civitatis nostrae principes audio culpantes modo agrorum infecunditatem, modo caeli per multa iam tempora noxiam frugibus intemperiem; quosdam etiam praedictas querimonias velut ratione certa mitigantes, quod existiment ubertate nimia prioris aevi defatigatum et effetum solum nequire pristina benignitate praebere mortalibus alimenta. Quas ego causas, P. Silvine, procul a veritate abesse certum habeo, quod neque fas est existimare rerum Naturam, quam primus ille mundi genitor perpetua fecunditate donavit, quasi quodam morbo sterilitate adfectam; neque prudentis est credere Tellurem, quae divinam et aeternam iuventam sortita communis omnium parens dicta sit, quia et cuncta peperit semper et deinceps paritura sit, velut hominem consenuisse. Nec post haec reor violentia caeli nobis ista, sed nostro potius accidere vitio, qui rem rusticam pessimo cuique servorum velut carnifici noxae dedimus, quam maiorum nostrorum optimus quisque et optime tractaverat'; 'Again and again I hear leading men of our state condemning now the unfruitfulness of the soil, now the inclemency of the climate for some seasons past, as harmful to crops; and some I hear reconciling the aforesaid complaints, as if on well-founded reasoning, on the ground that, in their opinion, the soil was worn out and exhausted by the over-production of earlier days and can no longer furnish sustenance to mortals with its old-time benevolence. Such reasons, Publius Silvinus, I am convinced are far from the truth; for it is a sin to suppose that Nature, endowed with perennial fertility by the creator of the universe, is affected with barrenness as though with some disease; and it is unbecoming to a man of good judgement to believe that Earth, to whose lot was assigned a divine and everlasting youth, and who is called the common mother of all things – because she has always brought forth all things and is destined to bring them forth continuously – has grown old in mortal fashion. And, furthermore, I do not believe that such misfortunes come upon us as a result of the fury of the elements, but rather because of our own fault; for the matter of husbandry, which all the best of our ancestors had treated with the best of care, we have delivered over to all the worst of our slaves, as if to a hangman for punishment.' Suetonius, *Deified Augustus*, XLII: 'impetum se cepisse scribit frumentationes publicas in perpetuum abolendi, quod earum fiducia cultura agrorum cessaret; neque tamen perseverasse, quia certum haberet posse per ambitionem quandoque restitui'; 'he [Augustus] writes: "I was strongly inclined to do away forever with distributions of grain, because through dependence on them agriculture was neglected; but I did not carry out my purpose, feeling sure that they would one day be renewed through desire for popular favour.'''

381. *parish-rates . . . ENGLAND*] A tax, first imposed during the reign of Elizabeth I, that was collected to support the deserving poor in a particular parish. See E. M. Leonard, *The Early History of English Poor Relief* (Cambridge: Cambridge University Press, 1900) and Paul Slack, *The English Poor Law, 1531–1782* (Cambridge: Cambridge University Press, 1995).

382. *Were I to assign . . . government*] Gibbon would famously be inspired by this judgement (Gibbon, *Decline and Fall*, vol. I, p. 103). As both a trope and a historical assessment, however, it seems to originate with Machiavelli, *Discourses*, I.x: 'Let the times therefore from *Nerva* to *Marcus* be displayed before your Prince, and let him compare them which went before with those which came after, and then make his choice when he would have been born, or when he would have been Soveraign; He will find when good men were at the Helm, the Prince safe in the security of his Subjects; Peace and Justice flourishing in the world; The Senate in Authority; The Magistrates in Esteem; Rich men enjoying their Estates; Nobility and Virtue Exalted; and all things quiet and well; No rancour; No licentiousness; No corruption; No ambition to be found; The times were golden; Every man enjoyed his opinion, and defended it as he pleased; In a word, He will find the world triumphing in felicity, The Prince happy in the reverence and affection of the people; and the people safe in the generosity of their Prince' (Machiavelli, *Works*, p. 282). Cf. also Bacon's praise of the same period between Domitian and Commodus as 'the most happie and flourishing, that euer the Romane Empire, (which then was a modele of the world) enioyed' (Bacon, *Advancement*, p. 40). The trope would be inverted by William Robertson, who in the essay 'A View of the Progress of Society in Europe' that prefaced his *History of Charles V* (1769), would write: 'If a man were called to fix upon the period in the history of the world, during which the condition of the human race was most calamitous and afflicted, he would without hesitation, name that which elapsed from the death of Theodosius the Great, to the establishment of the Lombards in Italy' (vol. I, p. 10).

383. *not the extensive dominion of the ROMANS*] Here Hume is taking issue with the prime cause of depopulation cited by Wallace and Montesquieu; see above, pp. 437–8, n. 91, and p. 438, n. 93.

384. *liv. xxiii. chap. 19*] 'Toutes ces petites Republiques furent englouties dans une grande, & l'on vit insensiblement l'Univers se dépeupler: il n'y a qu'à voir ce qu'étoit l'Italie & la Grèce avant & après les victoires des Romains' (Montesquieu, *Esprit*, vol. II, p. 146).

385. *Orac. Defectus*] Plutarch, *Moralia*, 'The Obsolescence of Oracles', VIII: 'τοῦ δὲ μετρίου καὶ ἱκανοῦ καὶ μηδαμῇ περιττοῦ πανταχῇ δ' αὐτάρκους, μάλιστα τοῖς θείοις πρέποντος ἔργοις, εἰ ταύτην ἀρχὴν λαβὼν φαίη τις ὅτι τῆς κοινῆς

ὀλιγανδρίας, ἣν αἱ πρότεραι στάσεις καὶ οἱ πόλεμοι περὶ πᾶσαν ὁμοῦ τι τὴν οἰκουμένην ἀπειργάσαντο, πλεῖστον μέρος ἡ Ἑλλὰς μετέσχηκε, καὶ μόλις ἂν νῦν ὅλη παράσχοι τρισχιλίους ὁπλίτας, ὅσους ἡ Μεγαρέων μία πόλις ἐξέπεμψεν εἰς Πλαταιέας (οὐδὲν οὖν ἕτερον ἦν τὸ πολλὰ καταλιπεῖν χρηστήρια τὸν θεὸν ἢ τῆς Ἑλλάδος ἐλέγχειν τὴν ἐρημίαν), ἀκριβὲς ἂν οὕτω παράσχοι τι τῆς εὑρησιλογίας. τίνος γὰρ ἦν ἀγαθόν, ἐν Τεγύραις ὡς πρότερον εἶναι μαντεῖον, ἢ περὶ τὸ Πτῷον ὅπου μέρος ἡμέρας ἐντυχεῖν ἔστιν ἀνθρώπῳ νέμοντι'; 'Now moderation, adequacy, excess in nothing, and complete self-sufficiency are above all else the essential characteristics of everything done by the gods; and if anyone should take this fact as a starting-point, and assert that Greece has far more than its share in the general depopulation which the earlier discords and wars have wrought throughout practically the whole inhabited earth, and that today the whole of Greece would hardly muster three thousand men-at-arms, which is the number that the one city of the Megarians sent forth to Plataeae (for the god's abandoning of many oracles is nothing other than his way of substantiating the desolation of Greece), in this way such a man would give some accurate evidence of his keenness in reasoning. For who would profit if there were an oracle in Tegyrae, as there used to be, or at Ptoüm, where during some part of the day one might possibly meet a human being pasturing his flocks?' This is, however, not the opinion of Plutarch himself, but of Ammonius, one of the speakers in the dialogue. For Hume's awareness of the complexities of the dialogue form, and for his understanding that the opinions of the various speakers are not necessarily to be taken for the opinions of the author, see below, p. 522, n. 433.

386. *we have no reason . . . represented*] Again, Hume here is silently taking issue with Wallace and Montesquieu.

387. *lib. i. cap. 2*] Tacitus, *Annals*, I.ii: 'Postquam Bruto et Cassio caesis nulla iam publica arma, Pompeius apud Siciliam oppressus, exutoque Lepido, interfecto Antonio, ne Iulianis quidem partibus nisi Caesar dux reliquus, posito triumviri nomine, consulem se ferens et ad tuendam plebem tribunicio iure contentum, ubi militem donis, populum annona, cunctos dulcedine otii pellexit, insurgere paulatim, munia senatus, magistratuum, legum in se trahere, nullo adversante, cum ferocissimi per acies aut proscriptione cecidissent, ceteri nobilium, quanto quis servitio promptior, opibus et honoribus extollerentur ac novis ex rebus aucti, tuta et praesentia quam vetera et periculosa mallent. Neque provinciae illum rerum statum abnuebant, suspecto senatus populique imperio ob certamina potentium et avaritiam magistratuum, invalido legum auxilio, quae vi, ambitu, postremo pecunia turbabantur'; 'When the killing of Brutus and Cassius had disarmed the Republic; when Pompey had been crushed in Sicily, and, with Lepidus thrown aside and Antony slain, even the Julian party was leaderless but for the Caesar; after laying down his triumviral title and proclaiming himself a simple consul content with tribunician authority to safeguard the commons, he first conciliated the army by

gratuities, the populace by cheapened corn, the world by the amenities of peace, then step by step began to make his ascent and to unite in his own person the functions of the Senate, the magistracy and the legislature. Opposition there was none: the boldest spirits had succumbed on stricken fields or by proscription-lists; while the rest of the nobility found a cheerful acceptance of slavery the smoothest road to wealth and office, and, as they had thriven on revolution, stood now for the new order and safety in preference to the old order and adventure. Nor was the state of affairs unpopular in the provinces, where administration by the Senate and People had been discredited by the feuds of the magnates and the greed of the officials, against which there was but frail protection in a legal system for ever deranged by force, by favouritism, or (in the last resort) by gold.'

388. *Lib. viii. and ix*] Strabo's account of Greece occupies Books VIII to X of his *Geography*.

389. *Numine puniuntur*] A reference to a detail of Thespesius's vision of Nero enduring the torments of the damned in Plutarch, *Moralia*, 'On the Delays of the Divine Vengeance', XXXII: 'ὧν μὲν γὰρ ἠδίκησεν δεδωκέναι δίκας, ὀφείλεσθαι δέ τι καὶ χρηστὸν αὐτῷ παρὰ θεῶν ὅτι τῶν ὑπηκόων τὸ βέλτιστον καὶ θεοφιλέστατον γένος ἠλευθέρωσε'; 'as he had paid the penalty for his crimes, and a piece of kindness too was owing him from the gods, since to the nation which among his subjects was noblest and most beloved of Heaven he had granted freedom'. Nero had emancipated Greece in AD 67.

390. *mercede conductis*] Lucian, *On Salaried Posts in Great Houses*, V: 'Ἐγὼ δ' εἰ μὲν ἑώρων αὐτοὺς φυγήν τινα ὡς ἀληθῶς τῆς πενίας εὑρισκομένους ἐκ τῶν τοιούτων συνουσιῶν, οὐκ ἂν ὑπὲρ τῆς ἄγαν ἐλευθερίας ἐμικρολογούμην πρὸς αὐτούς· ἐπεὶ δὲ – ὡς ὁ καλός που ῥήτωρ ἔφη – τοῖς τῶν νοσούντων σιτίοις ἐοικότα λαμβάνουσι, τίς ἔτι μηχανὴ μὴ οὐχὶ καὶ πρὸς τοῦτο κακῶς βεβουλεῦσθαι δοκεῖν αὐτούς, ἀεὶ μενούσης αὐτοῖς ὁμοίας τῆς ὑποθέσεως τοῦ βίου; πενία γὰρ εἰσαεὶ καὶ τὸ λαμβάνειν ἀναγκαῖον καὶ ἀπόθετον οὐδὲν οὐδὲ περιττὸν εἰς φυλακήν, ἀλλὰ τὸ δοθέν, κἂν δοθῇ, κἂν ἀθρόως ληφθῇ, πᾶν ἀκριβῶς καὶ τῆς χρείας ἐνδεῶς καταναλίσκεται. καλῶς δὲ εἶχε μὴ τοιαύτας τινὰς ἀφορμὰς ἐπινοεῖν αἳ τὴν πενίαν τηροῦσι παραβοηθοῦσαι μόνον αὐτῇ, ἀλλ' αἳ τέλεον ἐξαιρήσουσιν, καὶ ὑπέρ γε τοῦ τοιούτου καὶ εἰς βαθυκήτεα πόντον ἴσως ῥιπτεῖν, εἰ δεῖ, ὦ Θέογνι, καὶ πετρέων, ὡς φῄς, κατ' ἠλιβάτων. εἰ δέ τις ἀεὶ πένης καὶ ἐνδεὴς καὶ ὑπόμισθος ὢν οἴεται πενίαν αὐτῷ τούτῳ διαπεφευγέναι, οὐκ οἶδα πῶς ὁ τοιοῦτος οὐκ ἂν δόξειεν ἑαυτὸν ἐξαπατᾶν'; 'If I saw that they truly found any refuge from poverty in such household positions, I should not quibble with them in behalf of excessive liberty; but when they receive what resembles "the diet of invalids", as our splendid orator once said, how can one avoid thinking that even in this particular they are ill advised, inasmuch as their condition in life always remains the same? They are always poor, they must continue to receive, there is nothing put by, no surplus to save: on the contrary, what is given, even if it is given, even if payment is received in full, is all spent to

the last copper and without satisfying their need. It would have been better not to excogitate any such measures, which keep poverty going by simply giving first aid against it, but such as will do away with it altogether – yes, and to that end perhaps even to plunge into the deep-bosomed sea if one must, Theognis, and down precipitous cliffs, as you say. But if a man who is always poor and needy and on an allowance thinks that thereby he has escaped poverty, I do not know how one can avoid thinking that such a man deludes himself.'

391. *paralogism*] A piece of false or erroneous reasoning, especially one of which the reasoner is unconscious (*OED*, 'paralogism', *n.* 1).

392. *causes no wise proportioned to the effects*] Causal proportionality is an article of faith with Hume; see above, 'Of Interest', p. 37, n. 3.

393. *emptiness and depopulation*] Diodorus Siculus, II.v.7: 'ταῦτα μὲν οὖν ἡμῖν εἰρήσθω πρὸς τοὺς ἐκ τῆς νῦν περὶ τὰς πόλεις οὔσης ἐρημίας τεκμαιρομένους τὴν παλαιὰν τῶν ἐθνῶν πολυανθρωπίαν'; 'Let these facts, then, be a sufficient reply on our part to those who try to estimate the populations of the nations of Asia in ancient times on the strength of inferences drawn from the desolation which at the present time prevails in its cities.'

394. *The humour ... extensive learning*] cf. 'Of Refinement in the Arts': 'To declaim against present times, and magnify the virtue of remote ancestors, is a propensity almost inherent in human nature ...' (above, p. 22). See also Hume's similar lament to Thomas Percy in a letter of 16 January 1773: 'Why still complain of the present times, which, in every respect, so far surpass all the past?' (*New Letters*, p. 199). For a similar sentiment from antiquity, see Thucydides, I.xxi.2. Machiavelli had made a similar observation in Book II of *The Discourses*: 'It is the common practice of Mankind, to commend the ancient, and condemn the present times; but in my judgement not always with reason; for so studiously are they devoted to things of antiquity, that they do not only admire what is transmitted by old Authors, but applaud and cry up when they are old, the passages and occurrences in their youth' (Machiavelli, *Works*, p. 331). Cf. also Sir Thomas Browne, *Pseudodoxia Epidemica* (1646), p. 21: 'And thus is it the humour of many heads to extoll the dayes of their fore-fathers, and declaime against the wickednesse of times present.' Hume's opinion echoes a comment of Fontenelle's in his 'Digression sur les anciens et les modernes' (1688): 'Rien n'arreste tant le progrés des choses, rien ne borne tant les esprits, que l'admiration excessive des Anciens' (Fontenelle, *Poésies*, p. 239). Addison had used the same thought, of the shackles imposed on men's minds by an unjustified reverence for antiquity, as the keynote of his speech at the Oxford University Encaenia in 1693, *Nova Philosophia Veteri Praeferenda Est* (1727): 'Quousque Veterum Vestigiis serviliter insistemus, Academici, ned ultra Patres sapere audebimus? Quousque Antiquitatis ineptias, ut Senum Deliria nunnulli solent, religiose venerabimur? Pudeat sane, dum tam præclarum Ætatis hujusce Specimen

coram Oculis præsens intemur, ad Antiquos Encomia nostra transferre, &
inter priora sæcula quos celebremus sedulo investigare'; 'How long, gentlemen of the university, shall we slavishly tread in the steps of the ancients,
and be afraid of being wiser than our ancestors? How long shall we religiously worship the triflings of antiquity, as some do old wives' stories? It
is indeed shameful, when we survey the great ornament of the present age
[Newton], to transfer our applauses to the ancients, and to take pains to
search into ages past for persons fit for panegyric' (pp. 1–2). Johnson had
touched on 'our Prejudices in favour of Antiquity' in his 'Essay upon Epi-
taphs' (1740) (Womersley, *Johnson*, p. 62). Hume had previously considered
the reasons for this distortion in our judgement in the *Treatise of Human
Nature*, II.iii.7–8 (*THN*, pp. 274–80). Wallace had conceded this point:
'an opinion in favour of antiquity may be carried too far. We may degrade
modern policy too much, and give too great a preference to antient manners
and times. The world is apt to run into parties and factions in this, as in
all other disputable matters; and in such a disposition, 'tis well if truth and
justice be but moderately injured' (Wallace, *Dissertation*, p. 33: cf. also pp.
266–7). Bolingbroke had agreed, but expressed the principle in terms of a
tendency to slight the present rather than magnify the past: 'The sight of the
mind differs very much from the sight of the body, and its operations are frequently the reverse of the other. Objects at a distance appear to the former in
their true magnitude, and diminish as they are brought nearer' (Bolingbroke,
letter 11, *A Dissertation upon Parties*, in Bolingbroke, *Political Writings*, p.
108). Gibbon, too, would invert the insight: 'There exists in human nature a
strong propensity to depreciate the advantages, and to magnify the evils, of
the present times' (Gibbon, *Decline and Fall*, vol. II, p. 207).

395. *regard to them*] 'Quibusdam gentibus numerosam progenerandi sobolem
dedit, ut Aegyptiis et Afris, quibus gemini partus familiares ac paene sol-
lemnes sunt; sed et Italici generis esse voluit eximiae fecunditatis Albanas
Curiatiae familiae trigeminorum matres' (Columella, *On Agriculture*, III.
viii.1–2); 'To some peoples she [nature] has granted the gift of producing
numerous progeny, as to the Egyptians and Africans, with whom the birth
of twins is common and almost an annual occurrence; but of Italian stock,
too, she has willed that there be women of extraordinary fertility – Alban
women of the Curiatian family, mothers of three children at one birth.'

396. *Lib. ii*] Diodorus Siculus, II.v.4: 'συναχθείσης δὲ τῆς στρατιᾶς πανταχόθεν
ἠριθμήθησαν, ὡς Κτησίας ἐν ταῖς ἱστορίαις ἀναγέγραφε, πεζῶν μὲν ἑκατὸν
ἑβδομήκοντα μυριάδες, ἱππέων δὲ μιᾷ πλείους τῶν εἴκοσι μυριάδων, ἅρματα δὲ
δρεπανηφόρα μικρὸν ἀπολείποντα τῶν μυρίων ἑξακοσίων'; 'Accordingly, after
the army had been assembled from every source, it numbered, as Ctesias
has stated in his history, one million seven hundred thousand foot-soldiers,
two hundred and ten thousand cavalry, and slightly less than ten thousand
six hundred scythe-bearing chariots.'

397. *Epist. 122 . . . accustomed*] 'Pedonem Albinovanum narrantem audieramus, erat autem fabulator elegantissimus, habitasse se supra domum S. Papini. Is erat ex hac turba lucifugarum. "Audio," inquit, "circa horam tertiam noctis flagellorum sonum. Quaero, quid faciat; dicitur rationes accipere"' (Seneca, *Epistles*, CXXII.xv); 'I heard Pedo Albinovanus, that most attractive story-teller, speaking of his residence above the town-house of Sextus Papinius. Papinius belonged to the tribe of those who shun the light. "About nine o'clock at night I hear the sound of whips. I ask what is going on, and they tell me that Papinius is going over his accounts."' For Caligula's wish that the Roman people had only one neck, see Suetonius, *Caligula*, XXX.2: 'Infensus turbae faventi adversus studium suum exclamavit: "Utinam p. R. unam cervicem haberet!"'; 'Angered at the rabble for applauding a faction which he opposed, he cried: "I wish the Roman people had but a single neck."' 'Agite dis inmortalibus gratias, quod eum docetis esse crudelem, qui non potest discere'; 'Thank the immortal gods that you are teaching cruelty to a person who cannot learn to be cruel' (Seneca, *Epistles*, VII.5).

398. *contra." Id.*] These five quotations are drawn from Justinian's *Digest* of Roman law, and translate as follows: 'it is not usual for female slaves to be acquired for purposes of breeding'; 'A slave who has been castrated is not, I think, diseased or defective, but sound; just as one who has but one testicle, who is still capable of reproduction'; 'Where however a slave has been castrated in such a way that any part of his body required for the purpose of generation is absolutely absent, he is diseased'; 'The question was asked whether a female slave was diseased who always brought forth dead children. Sabinus says that if this was caused by a uterine infection, she must be so considered'; 'Where a female slave who is pregnant is sold, it is held by all the authorities that she is sound, for it is the greatest and most important function of a woman to conceive and preserve a child. A woman in childbirth is also sound, provided nothing else happens which would cause her some bodily illness. Cœlius says Trebatius makes a distinction in the case of sterility, for if a woman is sterile by nature, she is healthy, but if this occurs through some defect of the body, she is not.' The reference for the final four quotations should be to Book XXI, title 1.

399. *LUCIAN*] See *Dialogues of the Dead*, XV–XIX.

400. *VOLPONE*] Ben Jonson's *Volpone* (1605–6), in which the central character deceives those who aspire to inherit his fortune by leading them to believe that he has named them as his heir.

401. *liberty of divorces in ROME*] cf. *Lettres Persanes*, letter 116 on the wisdom of the Roman practice of permitting divorce: 'Le divorce était permis dans la religion païenne, et il fut défendu aux Chrétiens. Ce changement, qui parut d'abord de si petite conséquence, eut insensiblement des suites terribles, et telles qu'on peut à peine les croire' (Montesquieu, *Œuvres*, p. 123).

402. *Essay XVIII*] A slip for XIX, 'Of Polygamy and Divorces'.

403. *as of some moment*] Hume would revert to the 'unnatural lusts of the ancients' in 'A Dialogue' (*ECPM*, pp. 110–11).

404. *cap. 55*] Pliny the Elder, *Natural History*, XVIII.iv.18: 'Manii quidem Curii post triumphos inmensumque terrarum adiectum imperio nota dictio est perniciosum intellegi civem cui septem iugera non essent satis; haec enim mensura plebei post exactos reges adsignata est'; 'At any rate there is a famous utterance of Manius Curius, who after celebrating triumphs and making a vast addition of territory to the empire, said that a man not satisfied with seven acres must be deemed a dangerous citizen; for that was the acreage assigned for commoners after the expulsion of the kings.' Pliny the Elder, *Natural History*, XVIII.vii.35: 'And if the truth be confessed, large estates have been the ruin of Italy, and are now proving the ruin of the provinces too – half of Africa was owned by six landlords, when the Emperor Nero put them to death.' Tacitus, *Annals*, III.lv: 'per annos centum profusis sumptibus exerciti, paulatim exolevere. Causas eius mutationis quaerere libet. Dites olim familiae nobilium aut claritudine insignes studio magnificentiae prolabebantur. Nam etiam tum plebem, socios, regna colere et coli licitum; ut quisque opibus, domo, paratu speciosus per nomen et clientelas inlustrior habebatur. Postquam caedibus saevitum et magnitudo famae exitio erat, ceteri ad sapientiora convertere. Simul novi homines e municipiis et coloniis atque etiam provinciis in senatum crebro adsumpti domesticam parsimoniam intulerunt, et, quamquam fortuna vel industria plerique pecuniosam ad senectam pervenirent, mansit tamen prior animus'; 'extravagant epicureanism, after being practised for a century, went gradually out of vogue. The causes of that change may well be investigated. Formerly aristocratic families of wealth or outstanding distinction were apt to be led to their downfall by a passion for magnificence. For it was still legitimate to court or be courted by the populace, by the provincials, by dependent princes; and the more handsome the fortune, the palace, the establishment of a man, the more imposing his reputation and his clientèle. After the merciless executions, when greatness of fame was death, the survivors turned to wiser paths. At the same time, the self-made men, repeatedly drafted into the senate from the municipalities and colonies, and even from the provinces, introduced the plain-living habits of their own hearths; and although by good fortune or industry very many arrived at an old age of affluence, yet their prepossessions persisted to the end.'

405. *in GREECE*] Lysias, Oration XXI, *Defence Against a Charge of Taking Bribes*, I–V: 'Περὶ μὲν τῶν κατηγορημένων, ὦ ἄνδρες δικασταί, ἱκανῶς ὑμῖν ἀποδέδεικται· ἀκοῦσαι δὲ καὶ περὶ τῶν ἄλλων ὑμᾶς ἀξιῶ, ἵν᾽ ἐπίστησθε περὶ οἵου τινὸς ὄντος ἐμοῦ ψηφιεῖσθε. ἐγὼ γὰρ ἐδοκιμάσθην μὲν ἐπὶ Θεοπόμπου ἄρχοντος, καταστὰς δὲ χορηγὸς τραγῳδοῖς ἀνήλωσα τριάκοντα μνᾶς καὶ τρίτῳ μηνὶ Θαργηλίοις νικήσας ἀνδρικῷ χορῷ δισχιλίας δραχμάς, ἐπὶ δὲ Γλαυκίππου ἄρχοντος εἰς πυρριχιστὰς Παναθηναίοις τοῖς μεγάλοις ὀκτακοσίας. ἔτι δ᾽ ἀνδράσι χορηγῶν εἰς Διονύσια ἐπὶ τοῦ αὐτοῦ ἄρχοντος ἐνίκησα, καὶ ἀνήλωσα σὺν τῇ τοῦ τρίποδος

ἀναθέσει πεντακισχιλίας δραχμάς, καὶ ἐπὶ Διοκλέους Παναθηναίοις τοῖς μικροῖς κυκλίῳ χορῷ τριακοσίας. τὸν δὲ μεταξὺ χρόνον ἐτριηράρχουν ἑπτὰ ἔτη, καὶ ἓξ τάλαντα ἀνήλωσα. καὶ τοσαύτας δαπάνας δαπανώμενος καὶ καθ᾽ ἡμέραν ὑπὲρ ὑμῶν κινδυνεύων καὶ ἀποδημῶν, ὅμως εἰσφορὰς τὴν μὲν τριάκοντα μνᾶς τὴν δὲ τετρακισχιλίας δραχμὰς εἰσενήνοχα. ἐπειδὴ δὲ κατέπλευσα ἐπὶ Ἀλεξίου ἄρχοντος, εὐθὺς ἐγυμνασιάρχουν εἰς Προμήθεια, καὶ ἐνίκων ἀναλώσας δώδεκα μνᾶς. καὶ ὕστερον κατέστην χορηγὸς παιδικῷ χορῷ καὶ ἀνήλωσα πλέον ἢ πεντεκαίδεκα μνᾶς. ἐπὶ δὲ Εὐκλείδου ἄρχοντος κωμῳδοῖς χορηγῶν Κηφισοδώρῳ ἐνίκων, καὶ ἀνήλωσα σὺν τῇ τῆς σκευῆς ἀναθέσει ἑκκαίδεκα μνᾶς, καὶ Παναθηναίοις τοῖς μικροῖς ἐχορήγουν πυρριχισταῖς ἀγενείοις, καὶ ἀνήλωσα ἑπτὰ μνᾶς. νενίκηκα δὲ τριήρει μὲν ἁμιλλώμενος ἐπὶ Σουνίῳ, ἀναλώσας πεντεκαίδεκα μνᾶς· χωρὶς δὲ ἀρχιθεωρίας καὶ Ἐρρηφορίας καὶ ἄλλα τοιαῦτα, εἰς ἃ ἐμοὶ δεδαπάνηται πλέον ἢ τριάκοντα μναῖ. καὶ τούτων ὧν κατέλεξα, εἰ ἐβουλόμην κατὰ τὰ γεγραμμένα ἐν τῷ νόμῳ λῃτουργεῖν, οὐδ᾽ ἂν τὸ τέταρτον μέρος ἀνήλωσα᾽; 'In regard to the counts of the accusation, gentlemen of the jury, you have been sufficiently informed; but I must ask your attention also for what has yet to be added, so that you may understand what kind of person I am before you give your verdict upon me. I was certified of age in the archonship of Theopompus: appointed to produce tragic drama, I spent thirty minae and two months later, at the Thargelia, two thousand drachmae, when I won a victory with a male chorus; and in the archonship of Glaucippus, at the Great Panathenaea, eight hundred drachmae on pyrrhic dancers. Besides, I won a victory with a male chorus at the Dionysia under the same archon, and spent on it, including the dedication of the tripod, five thousand drachmae; then, in the time of Diocles, three hundred on a cyclic chorus at the Little Panathenaea. In the meantime, for seven years I equipped warships, at a cost of six talents. Although I have borne all these expenses, and have faced daily peril in your service abroad, I have nevertheless made contributions – one of thirty minae and another of four thousand drachmae – to special levies. As soon as I returned to these shores, in the archonship of Alexias, I was producing games for the Promethea, and won a victory after spending twelve minae. Then, later, I was appointed to produce a chorus of children, and spent more than fifteen minae. In the archonship of Eucleides I produced comic drama for Cephisodorus and won a victory, spending on it, with the dedication of the equipment, sixteen minae; and at the Little Panathenaea I produced a chorus of beardless pyrrhic dancers, and spent seven minae. I have won a victory with a warship in the race at Sunium, spending fifteen minae; and besides I had the conduct of sacred missions and ceremonial processions and other duties of the sort, for which my expenses have come to more than thirty minae. Of these sums that I have enumerated, had I chosen to limit my public services to the letter of the law, I should have spent not one quarter. During the time when I had charge of a warship, my vessel was the best found in the whole armament.' In modern editions of Lysias the further speeches to which

Hume refers are numbered differently: Oration XXVI, *On the Scrutiny of Evandros*, and Oration XXXI, *Against Philon*.

406. *common law*] The Swift passage Hume quotes comes from *Gulliver's Travels*, Part III, chapter 6 (Swift, *Gulliver's Travels*, pp. 281–2). The text Hume is using shows that he is referring to an edition of *Gulliver's Travels* published after the Dublin edition of 1735, since the earlier London editions print a bowdlerized version of this passage (for collation and variants, see Swift, *Gulliver's Travels*, p. 695). There are a few deviations from Swift's text in Hume's transcription: in Swift's text the second anagram is 'Langden', a perfect anagram of 'England', and not Hume's 'Langdon', an imperfect anagram of 'London'; in Swift's text the solutions to the anagrams, though transparent, are not supplied; Swift's text reads 'where I had long sojourned', not 'where I had sojourned some time in my travels'; and finally Swift's text reads 'the Bulk of the People consisted wholly', not as Hume has it 'the bulk of the people consist, in a manner, wholly'. The trivial nature of these discrepancies suggests that Hume may be quoting (and slightly misquoting) from memory. If so, this note is important evidence of the deep impression Swift's writings had made upon Hume. On 24 August 1722 Swift's friend Francis Atterbury, sometime Dean of Christ Church, Oxford, and latterly Bishop of Rochester and Dean of Westminster, had been arrested as a Jacobite conspirator, and early the next year, following the successful passage of a bill of pains and penalties, he had been sent into exile and deprived of all preferments and emoluments. A detail of the text of *Gulliver's Travels* immediately following that quoted by Hume alludes to a notorious and ludicrous circumstance of the prosecution against Atterbury (Swift, *Gulliver's Travels*, p. 283 and n. 32).

407. *half of the number*] Pliny the Elder, *Natural History*, VII.xxv.92: 'nam praeter civiles victorias undeciens centena et nonaginta duo milia hominum occisa proeliis ab eo non equidem in gloria posuerim, tantam etiamsi coactam humani generis iniuriam, quod ita esse confessus est ipse bellorum civilium stragem non prodendo'; 'for I would not myself count it to his [Caesar's] glory that in addition to conquering his fellow citizens he killed in his battles 1,192,000 human beings, a prodigious even if unavoidable wrong inflicted on the human race, as he himself confessed it to be by not publishing the casualties of the civil wars.'

408. *these calculations*] Dionysius of Halicarnassus, *Roman Antiquities*, IV.xiii.5: 'εἰ δὲ τῷ τείχει, δυσευρέτῳ μὲν ὄντι διὰ τὰς περιλαμβανούσας αὐτὸ πολλαχόθεν οἰκήσεις, ἴχνη δέ τινα φυλάττοντι κατὰ πολλοὺς τόπους τῆς ἀρχαίας κατασκευῆς, βουληθείη μετρεῖν αὐτὴν κατὰ τὸν κύκλον τὸν περιέχοντα Ἀθηναίων τὸ ἄστυ, οὐ πολλῷ τινι μείζων ὁ τῆς Ῥώμης ἂν αὐτῷ φανείη κύκλος'; 'But if one should wish to measure Rome by the wall, which, though hard to be discovered by reason of the buildings that surround it in many places, yet preserves in several parts of it some traces of its ancient structure, and to

compare it with the circuit of the city of Athens, the circuit of Rome would not seem to him very much larger than the other.'

409. *third rates*] i.e. a middle-ranking ship in the Royal Navy.

410. *loose rhetorical calculations*] Demosthenes, *Against Leptines*, XXXI: 'ἴστε γὰρ δήπου τοῦθ', ὅτι πλείστῳ τῶν πάντων ἀνθρώπων ἡμεῖς ἐπεισάκτῳ σίτῳ χρώμεθα. πρὸς τοίνυν ἅπαντα τὸν ἐκ τῶν ἄλλων ἐμπορίων ἀφικνούμενον ὁ ἐκ τοῦ Πόντου σῖτος εἰσπλέων ἐστίν'; 'For you are aware that we consume more imported corn than any other nation. Now the corn that comes to our ports from the Black Sea is equal to the whole amount from all other places of export.' Lucian, *The Ship, or the Wishes*, V–VI: 'ἀλλὰ μεταξὺ λόγων, ἡλίκη ναῦς, εἴκοσι καὶ ἑκατὸν πήχεων ἔλεγε ὁ ναυπηγὸς τὸ μῆκος, εὖρος δὲ ὑπὲρ τὸ τέταρτον μάλιστα τούτου, καὶ ἀπὸ τοῦ καταστρώματος ἐς τὸν πυθμένα, ᾗ βαθύτατον κατὰ τὸν ἄντλον, ἐννέα πρὸς τοῖς εἴκοσι. τὰ δ᾽ ἄλλα ἡλίκος μὲν ὁ ἱστός, ὅσην δὲ ἀνέχει τὴν κεραίαν, οἵῳ δὲ προτόνῳ συνέχεται, ὡς δὲ ἡ πρύμνα μὲν ἐπανέστηκεν ἠρέμα καμπύλη χρυσοῦν χηνίσκον ἐπικειμένη, καταντικρὺ δὲ ἀνάλογον ἡ πρῷρα ὑπερβέβηκεν ἐς τὸ πρόσω ἀπομηκυνομένη, τὴν ἐπώνυμον τῆς νεὼς θεὸν ἔχουσα τὴν Ἴσιν ἑκατέρωθεν. ὁ μὲν γὰρ ἄλλος κόσμος, αἱ γραφαὶ καὶ τοῦ ἱστίου τὸ παράσειον πυραυγές, καὶ πρὸ τούτων αἱ ἄγκυραι καὶ στροφεῖα καὶ περιαγωγεῖς καὶ αἱ κατὰ τὴν πρύμναν οἰκήσεις θαυμάσια πάντα μοι ἔδοξεν. καὶ τὸ τῶν ναυτῶν πλῆθος στρατοπέδῳ ἄν τις εἰκάσειεν'; 'Incidentally, what a huge ship! A hundred and twenty cubits long, the shipwright said, and well over a quarter as wide, and from deck to bottom, where it is deepest, in the bilge, twenty-nine. Then, what a tall mast, what a yard to carry! What a fore-stay to hold it up! How gently the poop curves up, with a little golden goose below! And correspondingly at the opposite end, the prow juts right out in front, with figures of the goddess, Isis, after whom the ship is named, on either side. And the other decorations, the paintings and the topsail blazing like fire, anchors in front of them, and capstans, and windlasses, and the cabins on the poop – all very wonderful to me. You could put the number of sailors at an army of soldiers. She was said to carry corn enough to feed all Attica for a year.'

411. *bear arms*] Diodorus Siculus, XVII.xiv.1: 'Τῶν δὲ Θηβαίων ἀνῃρέθησαν μὲν ὑπὲρ τοὺς ἑξακισχιλίους, αἰχμάλωτα δὲ σώματα συνήχθη πλείω τῶν τρισμυρίων, χρημάτων δὲ ἄπιστον πλῆθος διεφορήθη'; 'Over six thousand Thebans perished, more than thirty thousand were captured, and the amount of property plundered was unbelievable.'

412. *higher than seventy feet*] cf. the note in the 'Early Memoranda': 'Nero fixt the Houses of Rome to seventy foot high. Vossius' (NLS MS 23159, item 14, p. 23; cf. Mossner, 'Memoranda', p. 514).

413. *cities on the top of cities*] cf. the note in the 'Early Memoranda': 'Vossius says he saw in Rome, that digging forty foot underground they found the Tops of Columns bury'd' (NLS MS 23159, item 14, p. 23; cf. Mossner, 'Memoranda', p. 514).

414. *inconvenient manner*] Strabo, V.iii.7: 'ἐπεμελήθη μὲν οὖν ὁ Σεβαστὸς Καῖσαρ τῶν τοιούτων ἐλαττωμάτων τῆς πόλεως, πρὸς μὲν τὰς ἐμπρήσεις συντάξας στρατιωτικὸν ἐκ τῶν ἀπελευθεριωτῶν τὸ βοηθῆσον, πρὸς δὲ τὰς συμπτώσεις τὰ ὕψη τῶν καινῶν οἰκοδομημάτων καθελὼν καὶ κωλύσας ἐξαίρειν ποδῶν ἑβδομήκοντα τὸ πρὸς ταῖς ὁδοῖς ταῖς δημοσίαις'; 'Now Augustus Caesar concerned himself about such impairments of the city, organizing for protection against fires a militia composed of freedmen, whose duty it was to render assistance, and also to provide against collapses, reducing the heights of the new buildings and forbidding that any structure on the public streets should rise as high as seventy feet.' Vitruvius, *On Architecture*, II.viii.17: 'In ea autem maiestate urbis et civium infinita frequentia innumerabiles habitationes opus est explicare. Ergo cum recipere non possit area planata tantam multitudinem ad habitandum in urbe, ad auxilium altitudinis aedificiorum res ipsa coegit devenire. Itaque pilis lapideis structuris testaceis, parietibus caementiciis altitudines extructae contignationibus crebris coaxatae cenaculorum ad summas utilitates perficiunt despectationes. Ergo moenibus e contignationibus variis alto spatio multiplicatis populus Romanus egregias habet sine inpeditione habitationes'; 'Yet with this greatness of the city and the unlimited crowding of citizens, it is necessary to provide very numerous dwellings. Therefore, since a level site could not receive such a multitude to dwell in the city, circumstances themselves have compelled the resort to raising the height of buildings. And so by means of stone pillars, walls of burnt brick, party walls of rubble, towers have been raised, and these being joined together by frequent board floors produce upper stories with fine views over the city to the utmost advantage. Therefore, walls are raised to a great height through various stories, and the Roman people have excellent dwellings without hindrance.' Aristides, *Regarding Rome*, VIII: 'ωστ ει τις αθελην εθελησειε καθαρως αναπτυξαι και τασ νυν μετεωρους πολεις επι γης ερεισας θειναι αλλην παρ αλλην οσον νυν Ιταλιασ διαλειπον εστιν, αναπληρωθηναι τουτο παν αν μοι δοκει και γενεσθαι πολις συνεχης μια επι τον Ιονιον τεινουσα'; 'Therefore, if someone should wish to unfold all of it and to plant and set the cities, which are now aloft in the air, upon the earth, one beside another, I think that all the now intervening space in Italy would have been filled up and that one continuous city, extending to the Ionian Sea, would have been formed.'

415. *lib. xviii. cap.* 2] Pliny the Younger gives lengthy and detailed descriptions of his seaside house near Ostia and of his country house in Tuscany in his letters (*Letters*, II.xvii and V.vi respectively), from which it is clear that they comprised a maximum of two storeys, and that for much of their extent they had only a single storey. Seneca, *Epistles*, CXIV.ix: 'Deinde in ipsas domos inpenditur cura, ut in laxitatem ruris excurrant, ut parietes advectis trans maria marmoribus fulgeant, ut tecta varientur auro, ut lacunaribus pavimentorum respondeat nitor'; 'Next, they devote attention to their houses – how to take up more space with them, as if they were country houses, how to make

the walls glitter with marble that has been imported over seas, how to adorn a roof with gold, so that it may match the brightness of the inlaid floors.' Valerius Maximus, *Memorable Deeds and Sayings*, IV.iv.7: 'anguste se habitare nunc putat cuius domus tantum patet quantum Cincinnati rura patuerunt'; 'Nowadays anyone whose house covers the same area as Cincinnatus's estate thinks he is living under cramped conditions.' The subsequent references are to the *Natural History* of Pliny the Elder, XXXVI.xxiv.101–25 and XVIII. ii.7, in which impressive Roman buildings are described, and the amount of land necessary to support a Roman citizen (two *iugera*) was specified.

416. *cap. 5*] Pliny the Elder, *Natural History*, III.v.66–7: 'The area surrounded by its walls at the time of the principate and censorship of the Vespasians, in the 826th year of its foundation, measured 13 miles and 200 yards in circumference, embracing seven hills. It is itself divided into fourteen regions, with 265 crossways with their guardian Lares. If a straight line is drawn from the milestone standing at the head of the Roman Forum to each of the gates, which today number thirty-seven (provided that the Twelve Gates be counted only as one each and the seven of the old gates that exist no longer be omitted), the result is a total of 20 miles 765 yards in a straight line. But the total length of all the ways through the districts from the same milestone to the extreme edge of the buildings, taking in the Praetorians' Camp, amounts to a little more than 60 miles. If one were further to take into account the height of the buildings, a very fair estimate would be formed, which would bring us to admit that there has been no city in the whole world that could be compared to Rome in magnitude.' Note that modern editions read 'passuum per directum xx.m.dcclxv', not Hume's '30,775'.

417. *laxiore ambitu*] i.e. in a wider circuit. Vopiscus discusses Aurelian's fortification of Rome twice (*Historia Augusta*, 'Divus Aurelianus', XXI.x and XXXIX.ii), but he does not use this phrase, and does not mention the inclusion of the suburbs north of the Tiber.

418. *from AUGUSTUS to AURELIAN*] i.e. from the accession of Augustus in 31 BC to the assassination of Aurelian in AD 275.

419. *AURELIUS VICTOR*] Sextus Aurelius Victor, *History of the Caesars*, XXI.iv, 'atque aucta urbs magno accessu viae novae et ad lavandum absoluta opera pulchri cultus'; 'the city was enhanced by the magnificent addition of a new road and the construction of a public bath with beautiful fittings.'

420. *sixty or seventy feet under ground*] See above, p. 515, n. 413.

421. *SPARTIAN*] In fact this detail comes not from Spartianus's life of Severus, but from his biography of Severus's predecessor, Didius Julianus: 'corpus eius a Severo uxori Manliae Scantillae ac filiae ad sepulturam est redditum et in proavi monumenta translatum miliario quinto Via Labicana'; 'His body was, by order of Severus, delivered for burial to his wife, Manlia Scantilla, and to his daughter, and it was laid in the tomb of his great-grandfather by the fifth milestone on the Labican Way' (*Historia Augusta*, 'Didius Julianus', VIII.x).

422. *OLYMPIODORUS*] Untraced. Olympiodorus's history of his own times has not survived.

423. *PUBLIUS VICTOR*] In the *Libellus de Regionibus Urbis Romæ* (1505). Hume appears to be offering a rough total of the number of *insulae* (tenements) and *domus* (separate houses) that Publius Victor estimates were found in the various districts of Rome.

424. *LIPSIUS*] In his *De Magnitudine Romana Libri quatuor* (1617), book III, chapters 2–4.

425. *from GRAVESEND to WINDSOR*] i.e. an extent of some 45 miles, from respectively 25 miles to the east of the city of London to 20 miles to the west.

426. *all a town*] i.e. Turin.

427. *well peopled*] Quintus Curtius, *History of Alexander*, IV.viii.2: 'Complexus quidquid soli est inter paludem ac mare octoginta stadiorum muris ambitum destinat et qui exaedificandae urbi praeessent relictis, Memphin petit'; 'Embracing all the ground between the Lake and the sea, he planned a circuit of eighty stadia for the walls, and having left men to take charge of building the city, he went to Memphis.' Strabo, XVII.i.8: ''Εστι δὲ χλαμυδοειδὲς τὸ σχῆμα τοῦ ἐδάφους τῆς πόλεως· οὗ τὰ μὲν ἐπὶ μῆκος πλευρά ἐστι τὰ ἀμφίκλυστα, ὅσον τριάκοντα σταδίων ἔχοντα διάμετρον, τὰ δὲ ἐπὶ πλάτος οἱ ἰσθμοί, ἑπτὰ ἢ ὀκτὼ σταδίων ἑκάτερος, σφιγγόμενος τῇ μὲν ὑπὸ θαλάττης, τῇ δ᾽ ὑπὸ τῆς λίμνης'; 'The shape of the area of the city is like a chlamys; the long sides of it are those that are washed by the two waters, having a diameter of about thirty stadia, and the short sides are the isthmuses, each being seven or eight stadia wide and pinched in on one side by the sea and on the other by the lake.' Diodorus Siculus, XVII.lii.3: 'καὶ τὸν μὲν περίβολον αὐτῆς ὑπεστήσατο τῷ τε μεγέθει διαφέροντα καὶ κατὰ τὴν ὀχυρότητα θαυμάσιον'; 'Alexander also laid out the walls so that they were at once exceedingly large and marvellously strong'; cf. also his comments on its population, XVII.lii.6: 'τὸ δὲ τῶν κατοικούντων οἰκητόρων αὐτὴν πλῆθος ὑπερβάλλει τοὺς ἐν ταῖς ἄλλαις πόλεσιν οἰκήτορας· καθ᾽ ὃν γὰρ ἡμεῖς παρεβάλομεν χρόνον εἰς Αἴγυπτον, ἔφασαν οἱ τὰς ἀναγραφὰς ἔχοντες τῶν κατοικούντων εἶναι τοὺς ἐν αὐτῇ διατρίβοντας ἐλευθέρους πλείους τῶν τριάκοντα μυριάδων, ἐκ δὲ τῶν προσόδων τῶν κατ᾽ Αἴγυπτον λαμβάνειν τὸν βασιλέα πλείω τῶν ἑξακισχιλίων ταλάντων'; 'The number of its inhabitants surpasses that of those in other cities. At the time when we were in Egypt, those who kept the census returns of the population said that its free residents were more than three hundred thousand, and that the king received from the revenues of the country more than six thousand talents.' Ammianus Marcellinus, XXII.xvi.15: 'Sed Alexandria ipsa non sensim (ut aliae urbes), sed inter initia prima aucta per spatiosos ambitus'; 'But Alexandria herself, not gradually (like other cities), but at her very origin, attained her wide extent.' Josephus, *The Jewish War*, II.xvi.385–6: 'καὶ τί δεῖ πόρρωθεν ὑμῖν τὴν Ῥωμαίων ὑποδεικνύναι δύναμιν, παρὸν ἐξ Αἰγύπτου τῆς γειτνιώσης, ἥτις

ἐκτεινομένη μέχρις Αἰθιόπων καὶ τῆς εὐδαίμονος Ἀραβίας, ὅρμος τε οὖσα τῆς Ἰνδικῆς, πεντήκοντα πρὸς ταῖς ἑπτακοσίαις ἔχουσα μυριάδας ἀνθρώπων δίχα τῶν Ἀλεξάνδρειαν κατοικούντων, ὡς ἔνεστιν ἐκ τῆς καθ᾽ ἑκάστην κεφαλὴν εἰσφορᾶς τεκμήρασθαι, τὴν Ῥωμαίων ἡγεμονίαν οὐκ ἀδοξεῖ, καίτοι πηλίκον ἀποστάσεως κέντρον ἔχουσα τὴν Ἀλεξάνδρειαν πλήθους τε ἀνδρῶν ἕνεκα καὶ πλούτου, πρὸς δὲ μεγέθους· μῆκος μέν γε αὐτῆς τριάκοντα σταδίων, εὖρος δ᾽ οὐκ ἔλαττον δέκα, τοῦ δὲ ἐνιαυσιαίου παρ᾽ ὑμῶν φόρου καθ᾽ ἕνα μῆνα πλέον Ῥωμαίοις παρέχει καὶ τῶν χρημάτων ἔξωθεν τῇ Ῥώμῃ σῖτον μηνῶν τεσσάρων· τετείχισται δὲ πάντοθεν ἢ δυσβάτοις ἐρημίαις ἢ θαλάσσαις ἀλιμένοις ἢ ποταμοῖς ἢ ἕλεσιν᾽; 'But why seek so far afield for proofs of the power of Rome, when I can find them at your very door, in Egypt? This country, which extends as far as Ethiopia and Arabia Felix, which is the port for India, which has a population of seven million five hundred thousand souls, exclusive of the inhabitants of Alexandria, as may be estimated from the poll-tax returns, this country, I say, does not disdain to submit to Roman domination; and yet what an incentive to revolt she has in Alexandria, so populous, so wealthy, so vast! The length of that city is thirty furlongs, its breadth not less than ten; the tribute which she yields to Rome in one month surpasses that which you pay in a year; besides money she sends corn to feed Rome for four months; she is protected on all sides by trackless deserts, by seas without ports, by rivers or lagoons.'

428. *Hic dabat*] Suetonius, *Nero*, XXXI.i: 'Non in alia re tamen damnosior quam in aedificando domum a Palatio Esquilias usque fecit, quam primo transitoriam, mox incendio absumptam restitutamque auream nominavit. De cuius spatio atque cultu suffecerit haec rettulisse. Vestibulum eius fuit, in quo colossus CXX pedum staret ipsius effigie; tanta laxitas, ut porticus triplices miliarias haberet; item stagnum maris instar, circumsaeptum aedificiis ad urbium speciem; rura insuper arvis atque vinetis et pascuis silvisque varia, cum multitudine omnis generis pecudum ac ferarum'; 'There was nothing, however, in which he was more ruinously prodigal than in building. He made a palace extending all the way from the Palatine to the Esquiline, which at first he called the House of Passage, but when it was burned shortly after its completion and rebuilt, the Golden House. Its size and splendour will be sufficiently indicated by the following details. Its vestibule was large enough to contain a colossal statue of the emperor a hundred and twenty feet high; and it was so extensive that it had a triple colonnade a mile long. There was a pond too, like a sea, surrounded with buildings to represent cities, besides tracts of country, varied by tilled fields, vineyards, pastures and woods, with great numbers of wild and domestic animals.' Flavius Vopiscus, 'Divus Aurelianus', XLIX.ii: 'milliarensem denique porticum in Hortis Sallustii ornavit'; 'he built a portico in the Gardens of Sallust one thousand feet long.' Horace, *Odes*, II.xv.14–16: 'nulla decempedis / metata privatis opacam / porticus excipiebat Arcton'; 'No colonnades measured out by private rods trapped the cool shade of the northerly Bear.' Horace, *Satires*,

I.viii.12: 'mille pedes in fronte, trecentos cippus in agrum / hic dabat'; 'Here a pillar assigned a thousand feet frontage and three hundred of depth.'

429. *LATIN original*] Julius Caesar, *Gallic War*, I.xxix: 'In castris Helvetiorum tabulae repertae sunt litteris Graecis confectae et ad Caesarem relatae, quibus in tabulis nominatim ratio confecta erat, qui numerus domo exisset eorum, qui arma ferre possent, et item separatim pueri, senes mulieresque. Quarum omnium rerum summa erat capitum Helvetiorum milia cclxiii, Tulingorum milia xxxvi, Latobrigorum xiiii, Rauracorum xxiii, Boiorum xxxii; ex his, qui arma ferre possent, ad milia nonaginta duo. Summa omnium fuerunt ad milia ccclxviii. Eorum qui domum redierunt censu habito, ut Caesar imperaverat, repertus est numerus milium c et x'; 'In the camp of the Helvetii were found, and brought to Caesar, records written out in Greek letters, wherein was drawn up a nominal register showing what number of them had gone out from their homeland, who were able to bear arms, and also separately children, old men and women. On all these counts the total showed 263,000 persons of the Helvetii, 36,000 of the Tulingi, 14,000 of the Latobrigi, 23,000 of the Rauraci, 32,000 of the Boii; of these there were about 92,000 able to bear arms. The grand total was about 368,000. Of those who returned home a census was taken in accordance with Caesar's command, and the number was found to be 110,000.'

430. *to more early times*] Strabo, IV.i.5: 'ἐξημερουμένων δ᾽ ἀεὶ τῶν ὑπερκειμένων βαρβάρων, καὶ ἀντὶ τοῦ πολεμεῖν τετραμμένων ἤδη πρὸς πολιτείας καὶ γεωργίας διὰ τὴν τῶν Ῥωμαίων ἐπικράτειαν, οὔτ᾽ αὐτοῖς ἔτι τούτοις συμβαίνοι ἂν περὶ τὰ λεχθέντα τοσαύτη σπουδή'; 'But since, on account of the overmastery of the Romans, the barbarians who are situated beyond the Massiliotes became more and more subdued as time went on, and instead of carrying on war have already turned to civic life and farming, it may also be the case that the Massiliotes themselves no longer occupy themselves so earnestly with the pursuits aforementioned.' Pliny the Elder, *Natural History*, XIV.i.2: 'For who would not admit that now that intercommunication has been established throughout the world by the majesty of the Roman Empire, life has been advanced by the interchange of commodities and by partnership in the blessings of peace, and that even things that had previously lain concealed have all now been established in general use?' Pliny the Elder, *Natural History*, III.v.39: 'chosen by the providence of the gods to make heaven itself more glorious, to unite scattered empires, to make manners gentle, to draw together in converse by community of language the jarring and uncouth tongues of so many nations, to give mankind civilization, and in a word to become throughout the world the single fatherland of all the races.' Tertullian, *On the Soul*, XXX.iii–iv: 'A glance at the face of the earth shows us that it is becoming daily better cultivated and more fully peopled than in olden times. There are few places now that are not accessible; few, unknown; few, unopened to commerce. Beautiful farms now cover what

once were trackless wastes, the forests have given way before the plough, cattle have driven off the beasts of the jungle, the sands of the desert bear fruit and crops, the rocks have been ploughed under, the marshes have been drained of their water, and, where once there was but a settler's cabin, great cities are now to be seen. No longer do lonely islands frighten away the sailor nor does he fear their rocky coasts. Everywhere we see houses, people, stable governments, and the orderly conduct of life. The strongest witness is the vast population of the earth to which we are a burden and she scarcely can provide for our needs; as our demands grow greater, our complaints against nature's inadequacy are heard by all.' Hume supplies an accurate translation of Aristides, *Regarding Rome*, XCVII. Diodorus Siculus, I.xxxi.6: quoted above, p. 468, n. 220. Josephus, *The Jewish War*, II.xvi.385: quoted above, pp. 518–19, n. 427. Strabo, XVII.i.12: 'Ἐπαρχία δὲ νῦν ἐστι, φόρους μὲν τελοῦσα ἀξιολόγους, ὑπὸ σωφρόνων δὲ ἀνδρῶν διοικουμένη τῶν πεμπομένων ἐπάρχων ἀεί. ὁ μὲν οὖν πεμφθεὶς τὴν τοῦ βασιλέως ἔχει τάξιν· ὑπ' αὐτῷ δ' ἐστὶν ὁ δικαιοδότης, ὁ τῶν πολλῶν κρίσεων κύριος· ἄλλος δ' ἐστὶν ὁ προσαγορευόμενος ἰδιόλογος, ὃς τῶν ἀδεσπότων καὶ τῶν εἰς Καίσαρα πίπτειν ὀφειλόντων ἐξεταστής ἐστι· παρέπονται δὲ τούτοις ἀπελεύθεροι Καίσαρος καὶ οἰκονόμοι, μείζω καὶ ἐλάττω πεπιστευμένοι πράγματα. ἔστι δὲ καὶ στρατιωτικοῦ τρία τάγματα, ὧν τὸ ἓν κατὰ τὴν πόλιν ἵδρυται, τἆλλα δ' ἐν τῇ χώρα· χωρὶς δὲ τούτων ἐννέα μέν εἰσι σπεῖραι Ῥωμαίων, τρεῖς μὲν ἐν τῇ πόλει, τρεῖς δ' ἐπὶ τῶν ὅρων τῆς Αἰθιοπίας ἐν Συήνῃ, φρουρὰ τοῖς τόποις, τρεῖς δὲ κατὰ τὴν ἄλλην χώραν. εἰσὶ δὲ καὶ ἱππαρχίαι τρεῖς ὁμοίως διατεταγμέναι κατὰ τοὺς ἐπικαιρίους τόπους. τῶν δ' ἐπιχωρίων ἀρχόντων κατὰ πόλιν μὲν ὅ τε ἐξηγητής ἐστι, πορφύραν ἀμπεχόμενος καὶ ἔχων πατρίους τιμὰς καὶ ἐπιμέλειαν τῶν τῇ πόλει χρησίμων, καὶ ὁ ὑπομνηματογράφος καὶ ὁ ἀρχιδικαστής, τέταρτος δὲ ὁ νυκτερινὸς στρατηγός. ἦσαν μὲν οὖν καὶ ἐπὶ τῶν βασιλέων αὗται αἱ ἀρχαί, κακῶς δὲ πολιτευομένων τῶν βασιλέων ἠφανίζετο καὶ ἡ τῆς πόλεως εὐκαιρία διὰ τὴν ἀνομίαν'; 'Egypt is now a Province; and it not only pays considerable tribute, but also is governed by prudent men – the prefects who are sent there from time to time. Now he who is sent has the rank of the king; and subordinate to him is the administrator of justice, who has supreme authority over most of the lawsuits; and another is the official called Idiologus, who inquires into all properties that are without owners and that ought to fall to Caesar; and these are attended by freedmen of Caesar, as also by stewards, who are entrusted with affairs of more or less importance. There are also three legions of soldiers, one of which is stationed in the city and the others in the country; and apart from these there are nine Roman cohorts, three in the city, three on the borders of Aethiopia in Syenê, as a guard for that region, and three in the rest of the country. And there are also three bodies of cavalry, which likewise are assigned to the various critical points. Of the native officials in the city, one is the Interpreter, who is clad in purple, has hereditary prerogatives, and has charge of the interests of the city; and another the Recorder; and another the Chief Judge; and the fourth the Night Commander. Now these officers existed also in the time of the kings, but, since the kings were carrying on a bad government, the prosperity of the city was also vanishing on account of the prevailing lawlessness.' Athenaeus, *The Banquet of the Learned*, I.xxxiii d: ὅτι ὁ Μαρεώτης οἶνος ὁ Ἀλεξανδρεωτικὸς τὴν μὲν προσηγορίαν ἔχει ἀπὸ τῆς ἐν Ἀλεξανδρείᾳ λίμνης Μαρείας καὶ τῆς παρ᾽ αὐτὴν πόλεως ὁμωνύμου, ἢ πρότερον μὲν ἦν μεγίστη, νῦν δὲ κώμης περιείληφε μέγεθος, τὴν προσηγορίαν λαβοῦσα ἀπὸ Μάρωνος ἑνὸς τῶν μετὰ Διονύσου τὰς στρατείας πεποιημένων'; 'Mareotic wine from Alexandria gets its name from Lake Mareia in Alexandria and from the city called Mareia beside it. The city was formerly quite large, but is now only as big as a village; it took its name from Maron, who was one of Dionysus's companions during his campaigns.' Suidas, 'Augustus': 'και ευρισκονται οι την Ρωμαιων οικουντες και αις ανδρες' ('Suidas', *Lexicon*, ed. Ada Adler, 5 vols [Leipzig: Teubner, 1928–38], vol. I, p. 410).

431. *direct assertions*] Polybius, II.lxii.3–5: ἐγὼ γὰρ οὐ λέγω κατ᾽ ἐκείνους τοὺς χρόνους, ἐν οἷς ὑπό τε τῶν ἐν Μακεδονίᾳ βασιλέων, ἔτι δὲ μᾶλλον ὑπὸ τῆς συνεχείας τῶν πρὸς ἀλλήλους πολέμων ἄρδην κατέφθαρτο τὰ Πελοποννησίων, ἀλλ᾽ ἐν τοῖς καθ᾽ ἡμᾶς καιροῖς, ἐν οἷς πάντες ἓν καὶ ταὐτὸ λέγοντες μεγίστην καρποῦσθαι δοκοῦσιν εὐδαιμονίαν, ὅμως ἐκ Πελοποννήσου πάσης ἐξ αὐτῶν τῶν ἐπίπλων χωρὶς σωμάτων οὐχ οἷόν τε συναχθῆναι τοσοῦτο πλῆθος χρημάτων'; 'For, not speaking of those times, when the Peloponnese had been utterly ruined by the Macedonian kings and still more by continued intestinal wars, but in our own times, when all are in complete unison and enjoy, it is thought, very great prosperity, I assert that a sale of all the goods and chattels, apart from slaves, in the whole Peloponnese would not bring in such a sum.'

432. *last book de republica*] A reference to the story of Er, and his vision of judgement after death and the moral governance of creation in Book X of Plato's *Republic* (614a–621d).

433. *The absurdities . . . maintaining*] cf. however, Hume's comment on the distribution of opinions in a dialogue in his letter to Gilbert Elliott of Minto of 10 March 1751: 'I have often thought, that the best way of composing a Dialogue, wou'd be for two Persons that are of different Opinions about any Question of Importance, to write alternately the different Parts of the Discourse, & reply to each other. By this Means, that vulgar Error woud be avoided, of putting nothing but Nonsense into the Mouth of the Adversary . . .' (*Letters*, vol. I, p. 154). For comment on the general subject of philosophical dialogues in the eighteenth century, see Michael Prince, *Philosophical Dialogue in the British Enlightenment: Theology, Aesthetics and the Novel* (Cambridge: Cambridge University Press, 1996). Chapter 5 (pp. 136–60) discusses Hume's dialectical practice.

434. *Histoire des oracles*] For examples of Fontenelle's discussion of Plutarch on oracles, see his *Histoire des Oracles* (Paris, 1686); translated into

English as *The History of Oracles and the Cheats of the Pagan Priests* (1688), pp. 9, 17, 27, 28, 30, 35, 87, 89, 101, 112, 119, 156–8, 162, 165, 169, 207–9, 211.

## XII. OF THE ORIGINAL CONTRACT

Published in: *1748, 1753, 1758, 1760, 1764, 1767, 1768, 1770, 1772, 1777a*
Significant revisions:

1) *1748–1768* read: '. . . invested an *Elizabeth* or a *Harry*\* with Authority, did also, . . .' (*1748*, p. 291; cf. above, p. 162). The footnote reads: '\**Harry* the 4th of *France*.' (*1748*, p. 291, n.\*).

2) *1748–1768* omit 'or something approaching equality,' (above, p. 163).

3) *1748–1772* omit the paragraph 'Yet even this . . . in the people.' (above, p. 163).

4) *1748* omits the two paragraphs 'The ACHÆANS . . . consent and promise!' (above, pp. 166–7).

5) *1748* omits the two paragraphs 'My intention here . . . the controversy.' (above, p. 167).

6) *1748–1772* omit the paragraph 'Did one generation . . . every government.' (above, pp. 169–70).

7) *1748* reads: 'The House of *Lancaster* rul'd in *England* about sixty Years: The present Establishment has taken Place very near the same Time.' (*1748*, p. 302; cf. above, p. 171).

8) *1748* omits 'Several cases, no doubt . . . changes of government.' (above, pp. 173–6).

9) *1748* reads:

'. . . Forms of Government. The Discussion of these Matters would lead us entirely beyond the Compass of these Essays. 'Tis sufficient for our present Purpose, if we have been able to determine, in general, the Foundation of that Allegiance, which is due to the establish'd Government, in every Kingdom and Commonwealth \*.

'\*When there is no legal Prince, who has a Title to a Throne, I believe it may safely be determined to belong to the first Occupier. This was frequently the Case with the *Roman* Empire. When any Race of Princes expires, the Will or Destination of the last Prince will be regarded as a Title. Thus the Edict of *Louis* the XIVth, who call'd the Bastard Princes to the Succession, in Case of Failure of all the legitimate Princes, would, in such an Event, have some Authority. The Cession of the ancient Proprietor, especially when join'd to Conquest, is likewise esteem'd a very good Right. The general Bond or Obligation, that binds us to Government, is the Interest and Necessities of Society; and this Obligation is very strong. The Determination of it to this or that particular Prince or Form of Government is frequently more uncertain

and dubious. Present Possession has considerable Authority in these Cases, and greater than in private Property; because of the Disorders, that attend all Revolutions and Changes of Government.' (*1748*, pp. 306–7 and n. *).
In later editions, much of the information in this footnote is given a little later in the text proper (see above, pp. 175–6).

10) *1753–1768* read: '... our historian, *Rapin*, allows, that ...' (*1753*, vol. I, p. 321; cf. above, p. 173).

11) *1753–1758* omit: 'Thus the will ... monarchy.' (above, p. 175).

12) *1753–1768* print as a footnote cued to '... changes of government.' (above, p. 176; cf. *1753*, vol. I, p. 325) the following text, which in *1770–1777* forms the final paragraph of the essay:
'† The crime of rebellion, amongst the ancients, was commonly markt by the terms νεωτεριζειν, *novas res moliri*.' (*1753*, vol. I, p. 325, n. †).

13) *1753–1768* print 'The only passage ... such foundation.' (above, p. 176) as a footnote cued to '... to determine.' (*1753*, vol. I, p. 326, n. ‡).

The reallocations of material between text proper and footnotes in the final section of this essay may be the result of compositorial error, or they may show Hume experimenting with a more aphoristic style. Either way, these movements of material were allowed to stand by Hume in later editions, and so they are retained here.

Copy text: *1777a*
Headnote:

This essay was composed probably in the summer of 1747 and was finished by early 1748, together with its companion pieces 'Of Passive Obedience' and 'Of the Protestant Succession'. On 8 January 1748 Hume wrote to the Jacobite Lord Elibank asking him to 'peruse a few Essays I intend to add to those already publish'd'. One of these was 'Of the Original Contract', which Hume particularly drew to Elibank's attention, presumably because he was likely to find its argument congenial: 'I shall be very much mortify'd, if you do not approve, in some small degree, of the Reasonings with regard to the original Contract, which, I hope, are new & curious, & form a short, but compleat Refutation of the political Systems of Sydney, Locke, and the Whigs, which all the half Philosophers of the Nation have implicitely embrac'd for near a Century; tho' they are plainly, in my humble Opinion, repugnant to Reason and the Practice of all Nations' (Mossner, 'New Letters', p. 437). Hume stated in a letter to Charles Erskine of 13 February 1748, just as he was about to embark for the continent: 'You must know, that Andrew Millar is printing a new Edition of certain Essays, that have been ascrib'd to me; and as I threw out some, that seem'd frivolous and finical, I was resolv'd to supply their Place by others, that shou'd be more instructive. One is against the original Contract, the System of the Whigs, another against passive Obedience, the System of the Tories: A third upon the Protestant Succession, where I suppose a man to deliberate, before the

Establishment of that Succession, which Family he shou'd adhere to, & to weigh the Advantages and Disadvantages of each' (*Letters*, vol. I, p. 112). In the quest for greater intellectual substance, Hume had turned back to the *Treatise*, for the 'germ of the arguments of all three essays can be found in the sections on allegiance in Book III of the *Treatise*, and they are thus to be seen as a part of the repackaging of the arguments of the *Treatise* in more digestible essay form' (Harris, *Hume*, p. 237).

Hume's purpose and method in these three essays are well expressed at the beginning of a slightly later essay, 'Of the Coalition of Parties': 'There is not a more effectual method of promoting so good an end [i.e. a coalition of parties], than to prevent all unreasonable insult and triumph of the one party over the other, to encourage moderate opinions, to find the proper medium in all disputes, to persuade each that its antagonist may possibly be sometimes in the right, and to keep a balance in the praise and blame, which we bestow on either side' (below, p. 181). Hence the tart *obiter dictum* in this essay: 'philosophers, who have embraced a party (if that be not a contradiction in terms) . . .' (above, p. 163).

The use made of examples drawn from English history in this essay, and in particular the reference to Paul Rapin de Thoyras (below, p. 539, n. 49), perhaps indicates that already in 1747 Hume had begun the research for his *History of England*, composition of which would be seriously under way by September 1752 (*Letters*, vol. I, pp. 167–9 and 170–71). Cf. James Harris's judgement, that the 'speed with which the *History* was written makes it unlikely that Hume began his historical research in the spring of 1752 when he took up his position at the Advocates' Library' (Harris, *Hume*, p. 325). It is perhaps significant that early in 1747, in a letter to Henry Home, Hume had mentioned with frustrated enthusiasm his '*historical projects*' (*Letters*, vol. I, p. 99; cf. also p. 109). As Duncan Forbes noted, it is a curious feature of both this essay and 'Of Passive Obedience' that Hume 'never seems to have realized, or refused to allow, that these systems had any pedigree, or European or classical ancestry. Both of them he regarded, or professed to regard, as British, parochial and recent' (Forbes, *Politics*, p. 92).

When composing this essay, Hume perhaps had in mind Bolingbroke's summary of the character of a Whig in letter 1 of *A Dissertation upon Parties*: 'The power and majesty of the people, an original contract, the authority and independency of Parliament, liberty, resistance, exclusion, abdication, deposition; these were ideas associated, at that time ['a few years ago'] to the idea of a Whig, and supposed by every Whig to be incommunicable, and inconsistent with the idea of a Tory' (Bolingbroke, *Political Writings*, p. 5). But if so, Hume was nevertheless taking issue with Bolingbroke, who in letter 9 of *A Dissertation upon Parties* had asserted: 'The settlements, by virtue of which he [the king of England] governs, are plainly original contracts' (Bolingbroke, *Political Writings*, p. 83). And Bolingbroke would nail

his argumentative colours still more firmly to the mast of an original contract in letter 13: 'Our original contract hath been recurred to often, and as
many cavils as have been made, as many jests as have been broke about this
expression, we might safely defy the assertors of absolute monarchy and
arbitrary will, if there were any worth our regard, to produce any one point
of time, since which we know anything of our constitution, wherein the
whole scheme of it would not have been one monstrous absurdity, unless an
original contract had been supposed. They must have been blinded therefore
by ignorance, or passion, or prejudice, who did not always see that there is
such a thing necessarily, and in the very nature of our constitution; and that
they might as well doubt whether the foundations of an ancient, solid building were suited and proportioned to the elevation and form of it, as whether
our constitution was established by composition and contract' (ibid., pp.
123–4). However, the *locus classicus* of the Whig notion of an original
contract was formulated by Locke in the 'Second Treatise', § 97: 'And thus
every Man, by consenting with others to make one Body Politick under one
Government, puts himself under an Obligation to every one of that Society,
to submit to the determination of the *majority*, and to be concluded by it;
or else this *original Compact*, whereby he with others incorporates into *one
Society*, would signifie nothing, and be no Compact, if he be left free, and
under no other ties, than he was in before in the State of Nature' (Locke,
*Two Treatises*, p. 332).

Hume's defence of the political utility of custom and of settled habitual
possession in this essay marks a further point of challenge to the political thought of Locke, who in § 58 of the 'First Treatise' had attacked
custom as too often a mere crystallizing of error or corruption: 'when
Fashion hath once Established, what Folly or craft began, Custom makes
it Sacred, and 'twill be thought impudence or madness, to contradict or
question it. He that will impartially survey the Nations of the World, will
find so much of their Governments, Religions, and Manners brought in
and continued amongst them by these means, that he will have but little
Reverence for the Practices which are in use and credit amongst Men,
and will have Reason to think, that the Woods and Forests, where the
irrational untaught Inhabitants keep right by following Nature, are fitter
to give us Rules, than Cities and Palaces, where those that call themselves
Civil and Rational, go out of their way, by the Authority of Example'
(Locke, *Two Treatises*, p. 183).

Finally, consider what Hume says on this subject in the *History of England*,
in the context of 1688: 'It happens unluckily for those, who maintain an original contract between the magistrate and the people, that great revolutions
of government, and new settlements of civil constitutions, are commonly
conducted with such violence, tumult, and disorder, that the public voice can
scarcely ever be heard; and the opinions of the citizens are at that time less

attended to than even in the common course of administration' (*History of England*, vol. VI, p. 528).

1. *that violence and hurry, in which it was raised*] A surprising comment, since both the doctrine of the divine origin of government and the doctrine of the legitimacy of government resting on consent are of great antiquity. Neither was created *ex nihilo* in England in the seventeenth century. However, in the phrase 'violence and hurry' Hume perhaps refers to the haste with which these venerable doctrines were applied to the emergent English situation.

2. *The one party . . . smallest article*] i.e. *jus divinum* or divine right: the principle on which Stuart kings had rested their kingly authority. Cf. Figgis, *Divine Right*. For an argument asserting the survival and only gradual decline of divine-right sentiment (as ideology if not practical politics) after the events (1688 and 1714) which had seemed to sound its death-knell, see Clark, *English Society*, pp. 119–98. In his *The Idea of a Patriot King*, Bolingbroke had poured scorn on this doctrine and its associated superstitions concerning monarchy: 'the notions concerning the divine institution and right of kings, as well as the absolute power belonging to their office, have no foundation in fact or reason, but have risen from an old alliance between ecclesiastical and civil policy. The characters of king and priest have been sometimes blended together: and when they have been divided, as kings have found the great effects wrought in government by the empire which priests obtain over the consciences of mankind, so priests have been taught by experience, that the best method to preserve their own rank, dignity, wealth, and power all raised upon a supposed divine right, is to communicate the same pretension to kings, and, by a fallacy common to both, impose their usurpations on a silly world' (Bolingbroke, *Political Writings*, p. 224). In 'Whether the British Government Inclines More to Absolute Monarchy, or to a Republic' Hume had also argued that the divine sanction of monarchy was now an exploded doctrine: 'The mere name of *king* commands little respect; and to talk of a king as GOD's vicegerent on earth, or to give him any of those magnificent titles, which formerly dazzled mankind, would but excite laughter in every one' (above, vol. 1, pp. 50–51). When travelling through Holland in 1748 Hume noticed triumphal arches bearing mottos supportive of the House of Orange. One of these was 'Vox populi, vox Dei', and he commented: 'I shall only say, if this last Motto be true the Prince of Orange is the only *Jure divino* Monarch in the Universe' (*Letters*, vol. I, p. 116).

3. *The other party . . . entrusted him*] cf. the *Treatise of Human Nature*, III.ii.9, where Hume gives the following account of the origin of contract theory, which follows closely the thought of Locke: 'Those political writers, who have had recourse to a promise, or original contract, as the source of our allegiance to government, intended to establish a principle, which is perfectly just and reasonable; tho' the reasoning, upon which they endeavour'd to

establish it, was fallacious and sophistical. They wou'd prove, that our submission to government admits of exceptions, and that an egregious tyranny in the rulers is sufficient to free the subjects from all ties of allegiance. Since men enter into society, say they, and submit themselves to government, by their free and voluntary consent, they must have in view certain advantages, which they propose to reap from it, and for which they are contented to resign their native liberty . . . But when instead of protection and security, they meet with tyranny and oppression, they are freed from their promises . . . and return to that state of liberty, which preceded the institution of government' (*THN*, p. 352); cf. Locke, *Two Treatises*, 'Second Treatise', chapters 17–19.

4. *That the DEITY . . . all his creatures*] For Hume's complicated and guarded stance towards the notion of a providential design superintended by a benevolent and omnipotent deity, see above, p. 356, n. 51. He would again derive unexpected consequences from this principle in 'Of Suicide' (see above, pp. 248–52).

5. *an ANGRIA*] Hume may have read of the Indian pirate Tulagee Angria in Clement Downing, *A Compendious History of the Indian Wars; with an Account of the Rise, Progress, Strength and Forces of Angria the Pyrate* (1737). The pattern of revision to this essay suggests that later accounts, such as the anonymous *An Authentick & Faithful History of that Arch-Pyrate Tulagee Angria* (1756) and *A Genuine History of that Noted Pyrate Tulagee Angria* (1757), probably did not influence Hume.

6. *When we consider . . . that influence*] This paragraph can be read in parallel with Hume's explanation in the first paragraph of 'Of the First Principles of Government' of the sovereign importance of opinion (rather than strict right or justice) in the political life of communities (above, pp. 36–7).

7. *The chieftain . . . civil government*] An idea on which Hume had also touched in 'Of the Origin of Government': 'Government commences more casually and imperfectly. It is probable, that the first ascendant of one man over multitudes begun during a state of war; where the superiority of courage and of genius discovers itself most visibly, where unanimity and concert are most requisite, and where the pernicious effects of disorder are most sensibly felt' (above, vol. 1, p. 42). Cf. also the *Treatise of Human Nature*, III.ii.8: 'Hence we may give a plausible reason, among others, why all governments are at first monarchical, without any mixture and variety; and why republics arise only from the abuses of monarchy and despotic power. Camps are the true mothers of cities; and as war cannot be administred, by reason of the suddenness of every exigency, without some authority in a single person, the same kind of authority naturally takes place in that civil government, which succeeds the military' (*THN*, p. 346).

8. *But philosophers . . . no other foundation*] Hume here has principally in mind the arguments mounted by Locke in the 'Second Treatise' (see headnote). But

it should be remembered that these arguments were endlessly repeated and recycled by more vulgar Whig political writers, so that the doctrine of the original contract was to be found not only on the summits of political theory but also in the journalistic undergrowth which choked its foothills. Later in the century it would recur in the political philosophy associated with Rational Dissent, e.g. the writings of Richard Price. For Hume's characterization of the philosopher as estranged from party as a matter of intellectual principle, cf. 'Of the Protestant Succession': 'It belongs, therefore, to a philosopher alone, who is of neither party . . .' (above, p. 191).

9. *nothing that . . . corresponds to their ideas*] cf. Sir William Temple, 'An Essay upon the Original and Nature of Government': 'From this Principle [the tendency of power to follow authority], and from the Discovery of some natural Authority, may perhaps be deduced a truer Original of all Governments among Men, than from any Contracts: Tho' these be given us by the great Writers concerning Politicks and Laws' (Temple, *Works*, vol. I, p. 99).

10. *claim their subjects as their property*] cf. Locke, *Two Treatises*, 'Second Treatise', § 156: 'he [Filmer, the apologist for hereditary right] speaks of Mankind, as if God had no care of any part of them, but only of their Monarchs, and that the rest of the People, the Societies of Men, were made as so many Herds of Cattle, only for the Service, Use and Pleasure of their Princes' (cf. also § 163). In the first volume of *The Decline and Fall* (1776) Gibbon would draw attention to the speciousness of this vulgar Whig language in relation to hereditary monarchy, before revealing the solid advantages of the institution: 'Of the various forms of government, which have prevailed in the world, an hereditary monarchy seems to present the fairest scope for ridicule. Is it possible to relate, without an indignant smile, that, on the father's decease, the property of a nation, like that of a drove of oxen, descends to his infant son, as yet unknown to mankind and to himself; and that the bravest warriors and the wisest statesmen, relinquishing their natural right to empire, approach the royal cradle with bended knees and protestations of inviolable fidelity? Satire and declamation may paint these obvious topics in the most dazzling colours, but our more serious thoughts will respect a useful prejudice, that establishes a rule of succession, independent of the passions of mankind; and we shall cheerfully acquiesce in any expedient which deprives the multitude of the dangerous, and indeed the ideal, power of giving themselves a master' (Gibbon, *Decline and Fall*, vol. I, p. 187).

11. *On the contrary . . . allegiance*] A recapitulation of the account of the origin of allegiance that Hume had advanced in the *Treatise of Human Nature*, III. ii.8: 'were you to ask the far greatest part of the nation, whether they had ever consented to the authority of their rulers, or promis'd to obey them, they wou'd be inclin'd to think very strangely of you; and wou'd certainly reply, that the affair depended not on their consent, but that they were born to such an obedience' (*THN*, p. 351). Cf. ibid., III.ii.10: 'We naturally

suppose ourselves born to submission; and imagine, that such particular persons have a right to command, as we on our part are bound to obey' (*THN*, p. 355).

12. *being so ancient . . . any authority*] Notwithstanding its ostensible blandness of expression, this was provocative in the mid-eighteenth century, when ideas of the ancient constitution as a precious legacy of the past, to be venerated in spirit if not absolutely followed in the smallest detail, could still be a powerful presence in public discourse. Duncan Forbes captured the importance of the doctrine for the Whigs: 'ancient constitutionalism was Whig orthodoxy in the eighteenth century, meaning by this a compelling need to assert and defend the essential continuity of the English form of government – hence the search for feudalism, or at least something like it, in England before the conquest, hence the notion of William I as not a usurper, but a tyrant, a man who was forced to act like a conqueror later, but who never claimed a right of conquest, hence the view of Magna Carta as not merely or mainly a feudal document of post-conquest provenance and so on' (Forbes, *Politics*, p. 249).

13. *(which republican writers will never allow)*] A general reference to the argument mounted by Locke against Filmer's patriarchal politics in the first treatise of his *Two Treatises*.

14. *Almost all . . . subjection of the people*] cf. the *Treatise of Human Nature*, III. ii.10: ''Tis certain, that if we remount to the first origin of every nation, we shall find, that there scarce is any race of kings, or form of a commonwealth, that is not primarily founded on usurpation and rebellion, and whose title is not at first worse than doubtful and uncertain' (*THN*, p. 356).

15. *When an artful . . . partizans*] Most immediately a reference to Oliver Cromwell and his ascent to the Lord Protectorship. Hume would reflect on Cromwell's political adroitness in his *History of England*: 'It seems to me, that the circumstance of Cromwel's life, in which his abilities are principally discovered, is his rising, from a private station . . . to a high command and authority in the army. . . . To incite such an army to rebellion against the parliament, required no uncommon art or industry: To have kept them in obedience had been the more difficult enterprize. When the breach was once formed between the military and civil powers, a supreme and absolute authority, from that moment, is devolved on the general; and if he be afterwards pleased to employ artifice or policy, it may be regarded, on most occasions, as great condescension, if not as superfluous caution . . . An army is so forcible, and at the same time so coarse a weapon, that any hand, which wields it, may, without much dexterity, perform any operation, and attain any ascendant, in human society' (*History of England*, vol. VI, pp. 108–9). On the ratio of ruler to ruled of one to a hundred, cf. 'Of Commerce': 'It is computed, that, in all EUROPEAN nations, the proportion between soldiers and people does not exceed one to a hundred' (above, p. 6).

16. *disposed of . . . their rulers*] See above, p. 424, n. 34.

17. *the Revolution*] i.e. the Glorious Revolution of 1688. In the *History of Eng-land* Hume would acknowledge a broader significance in the settlement of 1688: 'The convention annexed to this settlement of the crown a declar-ation of rights, where all the points, which had, of late years, been disputed between the king and people, were finally determined; and the powers of royal prerogative were more narrowly circumscribed and more exactly defined, than in any former period of the English government' (*History of England*, vol. VI, p. 530).

18. *seven hundred*] A round figure for those who attended the Convention Parliament.

19. *near ten millions*] A plausible estimate of the total population of Great Brit-ain in 1688: cf. Wallace, *Characteristics*, p. 185. Hume would, however, present the events of 1688 in a different light in the *History of England*: 'It happens unluckily for those, who maintain an original contract between the magistrate and people, that great revolutions of government, and new settle-ments of civil constitutions, are commonly conducted with such violence, tumult, and disorder, that the public voice can scarcely ever be heard; and the opinions of the citizens are at that time less attended to than even in the common course of administration. The present transactions in England [the events of 1688–9], it must be confessed, are a singular exception to this observation' (*History of England*, vol. VI, p. 528).

20. *The republic . . . of conquest*] Hume here draws on the research he had done in preparation for writing 'Of the Populousness of Ancient Nations': see above, pp. 95–160.

21. *Lib. ii. cap. 38*] Polybius, II.xxxviii.6–7: 'ἰσηγορίας καὶ παρρησίας καὶ καθόλου δημοκρατίας ἀληθινῆς σύστημα καὶ προαίρεσιν εἰλικρινεστέραν οὐκ ἂν εὕροι τις τῆς παρὰ τοῖς Ἀχαιοῖς ὑπαρχούσης. αὕτη τινὰς μὲν ἐθελοντὴν αἱρετιστὰς εὗρε Πελοποννησίων, πολλοὺς δὲ πειθοῖ καὶ λόγῳ προσηγάγετο· τινὰς δὲ βιασαμένη σὺν καιρῷ παραχρῆμα πάλιν εὐδοκεῖν ἐποίησεν αὐτῇ τοὺς ἀναγκασθέντας'; 'One could not find a political system and principle so favorable to equality and freedom of speech, in a word so sincerely democratic, as that of the Achaean league. Owing to this, while some of the Peloponnesians chose to join it of their own free will, it won many others by persuasion and argument, and those whom it forced to adhere to it when the occasion presented itself sud-denly underwent a change and became quite reconciled to their position.'

22. *HARRY the IVth . . . their authority*] In *The Art of Lawgiving* Harrington had noted that Henry VII had been 'conscious of infirmity in his title', and had in consequence embarked on that policy of diminishing the power of the peers which had in the end broken the old English constitution by gradually and progressively separating the exercise of political power from the ownership of land (Harrington, *Works*, pp. 606–7). More generally, Bacon's *Historie of the Raigne of King Henry the Seventh*, first published in 1622, had been republished in 1676, and this may have served to refresh interest in his reign.

Bacon had also commented on the complexities and deficiencies of Henry's title: 'The King immediately after the Victory . . . was himselfe with generall applause, and great Cries of Ioy, in a kind of *Militar Election*, or *Recognition*, saluted King . . . But King HENRY in the very entrance of his Reigne, and the instant of time, when the Kingdome was cast into his Armes, met with a Point of great difficultie, and knotty to solue, able to trouble and confound the wisest King in the newnesse of his Estate; and so much the more, because it could not endure a *Deliberation*, but must be at once deliberated and determined. There were fallen to his lot, and concurrent in his Person, three seuerall *Titles* to the Imperiall Crowne. The first, the Title of the Lady *Elizabeth*, with whom, by precedent Pact with the Partie that brought him in, he was to marry. The second, the ancient and long disputed Title (both by *Plea*, and *Armes*) of the House of *Lancaster*, to which he was Inheritour in his owne Person. The third, the Title of the *Sword* or *Conquest*, for that he came in by victorie of Battaile, and that the King in possession was slaine in the Field . . . But the King out of the greatnesse of his own minde, presently cast the Die, and the inconueniences appearing vnto him on all parts; and knowing there could not be any *Interreigne* or suspension of Title; and preferring his affection to his own Line and Bloud, and liking that Title best which made him independent; and being in his Nature and constitution of minde not very apprehensiue or forecasting of future Euents a-farre off, but an Intertainer of Fortune by the Day; resolued to rest vpon the Title of *Lancaster* as the *Maine*, and to vse the other two, that of *Marriage*, and that of *Battaile*, but as *Supporters*, the one to appease secret Discontents, and the other to beate downe open murmur and dispute: not forgetting that the same Title of *Lancaster* had formerly maintained a possession of three Discents in the Crowne, and might haue proued a *Perpetuitie*, had it not ended in the weakenesse and inabilitie of the last Prince. Whereupon the King presently that very day, being the two and twentieth of August, assumed the Stile of King in his owne name, without mention of the Lady ELIZABETH at all, or any relation thereunto. In which course hee euer after persisted, which did spin him a threed of many seditions and troubles' (Bacon, *Henry VII*, pp. 1–6). Whig writers such as John Somers had placed the emphasis differently when writing of Henry IV: 'Then [on the resignation of Richard II] did the Parliament proceed to choose *Henry* the Fourth King; And upon this Title onely did he rely, though he mentioned some other trifling ones, as that he challenged it, being then void, by Force, as Descended to him from King *Henry* the Third . . . And he plainly shewed what a good Opinion he had of a Parliamentary Title to the Crown, when in the *7th* year of his Reign, he procured an Act of Parliament to pass, whereby the Inheritance of the Crown and Realms of *England* and *France* were setled upon himself for Life, and the Remainder entail'd upon his four Sons by name, and the Issue of their Bodies begotten' (Somers, *Succession*, p. 7). In letter 8 of his *A Dissertation upon*

*Parties* Bolingbroke had drawn attention to the compromised and defective nature of Henry VII's title (Bolingbroke, *Political Writings*, p. 73).

23. *Strange ... consent and promise!*] cf. the *Treatise of Human Nature*, III.ii.8: 'we do not commonly esteem our allegiance to be deriv'd from our consent or promise' (*THN*, p. 351).

24. *conquest or usurpation*] Hume here is silently encroaching on what, in seventeenth-century English political debate, had been a most important question, namely what had been the character of the Norman Conquest and its implications for English law, politics and monarchy. This had been a perennial topic for common lawyers since the time of Sir Edward Coke. Common lawyers had tended to argue that, in legal terms, the Conquest had made no breach in the continuity of English legal history, since one of the first acts of William I had been to confirm and codify the laws of his Saxon predecessor, Edward the Confessor – an argument which relied on documents we know now to be inauthentic (judged by Maitland to be 'bad and untrustworthy': F. Pollard and F. W. Maitland, *The History of English Law Before the Time of Edward I* [Cambridge: Cambridge University Press, 1968], vol. I, pp. 103–4). See, e.g., Edward Cooke, *A Seasonable Treatise* (1689) and for comment, see Janelle Greenberg, 'The Confessor's Laws and the Radical Face of the Ancient Constitution', *EHR*, 104 (1989), pp. 611–37. If on the other hand William had really made a conquest, and in consequence had been king by *jus conquestus*, all his acts – including the confirmation of the Saxon laws he had found here – had been made out of the plenitude of his unfettered, absolute, sovereignty; and therefore the English monarchy to this day retained that absolutist character. This had been the view of Thomas Hobbes, and it had drawn down upon him the opprobrium of his old friend Edward Hyde (Hobbes, *Leviathan*, chapter 24, p. 172; G. A. J. Rogers [ed.], *Leviathan: Contemporary Responses to the Political Theory of Thomas Hobbes* [Bristol: Thoemmes Press, 1995], pp. 245–50). Hence the desire of the common lawyers from Coke to Blackstone to present William not as a conqueror but rather as a claimant to the Crown under ancient law who had vindicated his claim by trial of battle; see, e.g. Philip Hunton, *A Treatise of Monarchy* (1643), in Wootton, *Divine Right*, pp. 198–9. It is interesting that Royalist writers until late in the seventeenth century had also tended to downplay the significance of the Conquest, being uneasy with such appeals to the sword. They had preferred instead to rest their defences of Stuart monarchy on the presence of the royal prerogative within the scope of the ancient constitution. However, Robert Brady and Sir William Dugdale, writing in opposition to William Petyt and William Atwood, had represented William as in every respect a conqueror of the most high-handed kind, who had imported feudalism into England, thereby displacing the earlier Saxon tenures and creating a watershed in English legal history: 'Though we have many *Laws* and *Customs* from the *Northern* People, and North parts of *Germany*, from whence

both Saxons and Normans came: yet after the *Conquest*, the Bulk and Maine of our Laws were brought hither from *Normandy*, by the Conqueror. For from whence we received our Tenures, and the Manner of holding our Estates in every respect, from thence also we received the Customs incident to those *Estates*. And likewise the quality of them, being most of them *Feudal*, and enjoyed under several Military Conditions, and Services, and of necessary consequence from thence, we must receive the *Laws* also by which these Tenures, and the Customs incident to them were regulated, and by which every mans right in such Estates was secur'd according to the nature of them. But from *Normandy* (and brought in by the *Conqueror*) we received most, if not all our ancient *Tenures*, and manner of holding and enjoying our *Lands* and *Estates*, as will appear by comparing our *Ancient Tenures* with theirs' (Brady, *A Full and Clear Answer* [1681], p. 31). In 1686 Nathaniel Johnston had gone further, arguing in *The Excellency of Monarchical Government* that the Conqueror had been an absolute monarch, and that in consequence all post-Conquest English laws and liberties were the result of grants and concessions made by other absolute monarchs. The most recent scholarly treatment of this complex and fascinating question is George Garnett, *The Norman Conquest in English History. Volume I, A Broken Chain?* (Oxford: Oxford University Press, 2020).

25. *a tacit consent*] In *Behemoth* Hobbes had argued that, given the possibility of emigration, continued residence in a state entailed an implicit promise of obedience. In dialogue I speaker 'A' asks: 'Must tyrants also be obeyed in everything actively? Or is there nothing wherein a lawful King's command may be disobeyed? What if he should command me with my own hands to execute my father, in case he should be condemned to die by the law?' Speaker 'B' replies: 'if such a command as you speak of were contrived into a general law . . . you were bound to obey it, unless you depart the kingdom after the publication of the law, and before the condemnation of your father' (Hobbes, *Behemoth*, p. 51).

26. *carried on board while asleep*] Hume has discussed the pressing of seamen in 'Of Some Remarkable Customs' (above, pp. 93–4).

27. *What if . . . that emperor?*] cf. the note in the 'Early Memoranda': 'In the Roman Government, there was a great Restraint on Liberty, since a Man coud not leave his Colony or live where he pleasd. Lib. ~~40~~ [39 *inserted above the line*]. Cap. 3' (NLS MS 23159, item 14, p. 20; cf. Mossner, 'Memoranda', p. 511). The reference is to Livy.

28. *ancient MUSCOVITES*] The restrictions on movement in Russia had been noted by Guy Miège: 'it is prohibited upon pain of death to any man to Travail out of that Country, unless they be the *Tzars* Merchants, or Ministers of State, which he sends to other Princes in quality of Ambassadors. The reason is, lest by their Travails into other parts, they should bring back some new customes at their return, and having tasted the sweetness of the liberty other

Nations injoy, they should some time or other break asunder the chains of their own Servitude' (Miège, *Embassies*, p. 61).

29. *cap. 14*] Tacitus, *Annals*, VI.xiv: 'At Rubrio Fabato, tamquam desperatis rebus Romanis Parthorum ad misericordiam fugeret, custodes additi. Sane is repertus apud fretum Siciliae retractusque per centurionem nullas probabiles causas longinquae peregrinationis adferebat'; 'On the other hand, Rubrius Fabatus was placed under surveillance on the ground that, in despair at the state of Rome, he was contemplating flight to the mercy of the Parthians. Certainly he was discovered in the neighbourhood of the Sicilian Strait, and, when haled back by a centurion, could give no plausible reasons for his distant pilgrimage.'

30. *A company . . . native freedom*] Most immediately, a reference to the Puritan emigrations to America in the early seventeenth century, concerning which Hume would write in his *History of England*: 'The puritans, restrained in England, shipped themselves off for America, and laid there the foundations of a government, which possessed all the liberty, both civil and religious, of which they found themselves bereaved in their native country. But their enemies, unwilling that they should any where enjoy ease and contentment, and dreading, perhaps, the dangerous consequences of so disaffected a colony, prevailed on the king to issue a proclamation, debarring these devotees access even into those inhospitable deserts. Eight ships, lying in the Thames, and ready to sail, were detained by order of the council; and in these were embarked Sir Arthur Hazelrig, John Hambden, John Pym, and Oliver Cromwel, who had resolved for ever to abandon their native country, and fly to the other extremity of the globe; where they might enjoy lectures and discourses of any length or form which pleased them. The king had afterwards full leisure to repent this exercise of his authority' (*History of England*, vol. V, pp. 241–2).

31. *their prince . . . new settlement*] As indeed George III did, until the American colonies declared independence in 1776, and obtained it in 1783.

32. *silk-worms and butterflies*] An image of the transience and heedlessness of human life, recently used memorably by Thomas Gray in his 'Ode on the Spring' (1742): 'The insect youth are on the wing, / Eager to taste the honied spring, / And float amid the liquid noon: / Some lightly o'er the current skim, / Some shew their gayly-gilded trim / Quick-glancing to the sun. / To Contemplation's sober eye / Such is the race of Man: / And they that creep, and they that fly, / Shall end where they began. / Alike the Busy and the Gay / But flutter thro' life's little day, / In fortune's varying colours drest: / Brush'd by the hand of rough Mischance, / Or chill'd by age, their airy dance / They leave in dust to rest.'

33. *violent innovations . . . and accident*] Hume's stance towards the right of resistance to, and the habit of deference towards, established authority was complex and changeable. The fluidity of his thought on the matter is

crystallized in a cancelled note in the 'Early Memoranda': ~~Men have much oftener errd from too great Respect to Government than from too little~~ (NLS MS 23159, item 14, p. 13; cf. Mossner, 'Memoranda', p. 506). Cf. also the *Treatise of Human Nature*, III.ii.10: 'But tho', on some occasions, it may be justifiable, both in sound politics and morality, to resist supreme power, 'tis certain, that in the ordinary course of human affairs nothing can be more pernicious and criminal; and that besides the convulsions, which always attend revolutions, such a practice tends directly to the subversion of all government, and the causing an universal anarchy and confusion amongst mankind. As numerous and civiliz'd societies cannot subsist without government, so government is entirely useless without an exact obedience. We ought always to weigh the advantages, which we reap from authority, against the disadvantages; and by this means we shall become more scrupulous of putting in practice the doctrine of resistance. The common rule requires submission; and 'tis only in cases of grievous tyranny and oppression, that the exception can take place' (*THN*, p. 354).

34. *The violent innovations ... authority*] In his *History of England* Hume would expand on the tyrannical nature of Henry VIII's rule, where violent authority would once again be the keynote of the analysis: 'No prince in Europe was possessed of such absolute authority as Henry, not even the pope himself, in his own capital, where he united both the civil and ecclesiastical powers ...' (*History of England*, vol. III, p. 212); 'The absolute, uncontrouled authority which he [Henry VIII] maintained at home, and the regard which he acquired among foreign nations, are circumstances, which entitle him, in some degree, to the appellation of a *great* prince; while his tyranny and barbarity exclude him from the character of a *good* one ... A catalogue of his vices would comprehend many of the worst qualities incident to human nature: Violence, cruelty, profusion, rapacity, injustice, obstinacy, arrogance, bigotry, presumption, caprice ... The extensive powers of his prerogative, and the submissive, not to say slavish, disposition of his parliaments, made it the more easy for him to assume and maintain that entire dominion, by which his reign is so much distinguished in the English history' (*History of England*, vol. III, pp. 321–2).

35. *faction and fanaticism*] i.e. political disaffection and dissenting, or otherwise anti-episcopal, religion. In his *History of England* Hume would draw attention to the confluence of political and religious causes in the English Civil Wars: 'When two names, so sacred in the English constitution as those of KING and PARLIAMENT, were placed in opposition; no wonder the people were divided in their choice, and were agitated with most violent animosities and factions ... The city of London ... and most of the great corporations, took part with the parliament, and adopted with zeal those democratical principles, on which the pretensions of that assembly were founded. The government of cities, which even under absolute monarchies, is commonly

republican, inclined them to this party: The small hereditary influence, which can be retained over the industrious inhabitants of towns; the natural independence of citizens; and the force of popular currents over these more numerous associations of mankind; all these causes gave, there, authority to the new principles propagated throughout the nation . . . The genius of the two religions, so closely at this time interwoven with politics, corresponded exactly to these divisions. The presbyterian religion was new, republican, and suited to the genius of the populace: The other had an air of greater show and ornament, was established on ancient authority, and bore an affinity to the kingly and aristocratical parts of the constitution. The devotees of presbytery became of course zealous partizans of the parliament: The friends of the episcopal church valued themselves on defending the rights of monarchy' (*History of England*, vol. V, pp. 386–7).

36. *Suppose . . . tyrant and usurper*] An anonymized and compressed account of English constitutional history between the execution of Charles I in 1649 and the restoration of Charles II in 1660.

37. *The prætorian . . . controversy*] cf. Hume's account of the complicated situation which preceded the accession of the emperor Severus (above, pp. 174–5).

38. *When we assert . . . inevitable*] Hume here gives a *précis* of Roman imperial history from the death of Augustus until broadly the adoption of the Antonines in AD 138. The Praetorians were the personal bodyguard of the Roman emperors, and consisted of picked veterans who enjoyed better pay and conditions than ordinary legionaries. They had been created by Augustus, and originally comprised nine cohorts each of 1,000 men. At first stationed in different parts of Italy, the Praetorians were eventually concentrated by Sejanus into a single camp on the north side of Rome, which increased their effectiveness as an instrument of internal intimidation. In book I, chapter 4 of *The Art of War* Machiavelli had identified the creation of the Praetorian corps as a turning point in the trajectory of Roman decline: 'For *Octavian* first, and afterwards *Tiberius* (preferring their private power before the profit of the publick) began to disarm the people (that thereby they might have them more easily at command) and to keep standing Armies upon the Frontiers of their Empire. But because they thought them insufficient to curb the people, and awe the Senate of Rome; they established another Army (which they called the *Pretorian*) which was quartered always about the City, and intended as a guard. But when afterwards the Emperors permitted them who were listed in those Bands, to lay aside all other professions, and devote themselves to War, they grew insolent immediately, and became not only terrible to the Senate, but pernicious to the Emperors, insomuch that many of them were put to death by the fury and insolence of those Soldiers, who created, and deposed their Emperors as they pleased; and sometimes it fell out that at the same time several Emperors were created

by the several Armies, which occasioned the division first, and by degrees the destruction of the Empire' (Machiavelli, *Works*, p. 440). Cf. Harrington, *Oceana*, 'The Second Part of the Preliminaries' (Harrington, *Works*, p. 189), and Sidney, *Discourses*, p. 155, and pp. 455 and 508 (on the sufferings of the Romans under the sway of a 'mad corrupted soldiery'). Of the twenty-six Roman emperors who reigned from Augustus (63–14 BC) to Alexander Severus (AD 208–235), only ten died from natural causes: Augustus, Vespasian, Titus, Nerva, Trajan, Hadrian, Antoninus Pius, Lucius Verus, Marcus Aurelius and Septimius Severus. However, the remaining sixteen were not all assassinated by their own Praetorians: that was a fate reserved for Caligula, Galba, Domitian, Commodus, Pertinax, Caracalla and Elagabalus. In chapter 19 of *The Prince* Machiavelli had given extended consideration to the deaths of the Roman emperors, noting that it was their particular misfortune to be obliged to 'endure the cruelty and avarice of the soldiers', and that 'some of them always lived nobly and demonstrated great strength of character, yet nevertheless lost their empire or were killed by their own soldiers who plotted against them' (Machiavelli, *Prince*, pp. 65–71; quotations on pp. 66 and 65). Cf. also Juvenal, X.112; Machiavelli, *Discourses*, I.x and *The Art of War*, Book I; Neville, *Plato Redivivus*, p. 110; and Sidney, *Discourses*, p. 50.

39. *about sixty years*] From 1399 until 1461.

40. *white rose*] i.e. the adherents of the rival house of York.

41. *The present establishment*] Hume must be reckoning from 1688, which gives a period of exactly sixty years until the first publication of this essay. The House of Hanover had come to the throne only thirty-four years previously, in 1714.

42. *the abdicated family*] i.e. the Stuarts. To call the Stuarts 'abdicated' is a sign of Whiggism, and implies a justification of 1688, since it suggests that James II was not driven from the throne, and that therefore the nation might legitimately act to fill the place he had vacated by his flight (hence Hume's insistence that the Stuarts were 'justly expelled' immediately below). This was the official retrospective interpretation of 1688 enshrined in the preamble to the Bill of Rights (1689): 'And whereas the said late King James the Second having abdicated the government and the throne being thereby vacant . . .'. This interpretation had a number of important advantages, among which the most important were: 1) it cleared those who had resisted James II of any charge of rebellion; 2) it conferred on William and Mary a parliamentary title to the throne, not an alarming title by conquest, of which the powers might be vast, undefined and precarious. For a scholarly narrative and analysis, see J. P. Kenyon, *Revolution Principles: The Politics of Party 1689–1720* (Cambridge: Cambridge University Press, 1977). In letter 8 of his *A Dissertation upon Parties*, however, Bolingbroke had been loftily dismissive of the importance of such language and the debates it had inspired: 'The disputes about the words abdicate, or desert, and about the vacancy of the throne,

were indeed fitter for a school than a house of Parliament, and might have been expected in some assembly of pedants, where young students exercised themselves in disputation, but not in such an august assembly as that of the Lords and Commons, met in solemn conference upon the most important occasion' (Bolingbroke, *Political Writings*, p. 67).

43. *Have all views . . . imaginary loyalty*] Most immediately a reference to the very recent Jacobite rebellion of 1745. For a modern scholarly review of the persistence and enduring appeal of Jacobitism well into the eighteenth century, and long after it had ceased to be a serious political option, see Clark, *English Society*, pp. 119–98, esp. pp. 132–3.

44. *All moral duties . . . two kinds*] The final section of this essay draws on book III, part ii, of the *Treatise of Human Nature*, albeit with some important changes of vocabulary. For comment, see Harris, *Hume*, pp. 237–8.

45. *natural duties of justice and fidelity*] cf. *Treatise of Human Nature*, III.ii.8, 'Of the Source of Allegiance'.

46. *But to whom . . . infinite discussions*] cf. *Treatise of Human Nature*, III.ii.10, 'Of the Objects of Allegiance'.

47. *usurpation and violence*] See above, pp. 533–4, n. 24.

48. *The questions . . . arbitrary*] cf. *Treatise of Human Nature*, III.ii.3, 'Of the Rules, which determine Property'.

49. *our historian . . . war and violence*] Hume refers to 'A Dissertation on the Salick-Law, and the Dispute between Philip of Valois and Edward III', which forms part of Book IX of Rapin's *History of England* (Rapin, *History*, vol. IV, pp. 343–68) and is appended to his account of the reign of Edward III. The Salic Law excluded women and their descendants from succession to the Crown of France. Rapin asserts that, when Edward III (whose claim to the French Crown was based on the fact that he was the son of a princess of France) disputed the succession with Philip of Valois, the Salic Law was as yet not fully established as a settled principle of succession: 'Ever since that Point [the dispute between Edward and Philip] was decided, the present Notion of the *Salick-Law* is just and certain; but I will venture to say that it was doubtful at that Time, and this is what I hope plainly to make appear in the following Dissertation' (Rapin, *History*, vol. IV, p. 344). After reviewing at length the history and substance of the Salic Law, Rapin turns to the dispute between Edward and Philip, which he summarizes as follows: '*Edward* pleaded that he was the nearest Male-Relation of the late King. *Philip* grounded his Claim upon the *Salick-Law*, which, according to him, excluded not only the Women, but also their Descendants from the Succession to the Crown . . . The Business therefore at present is to examine the Rights of both Parties separately from the Events and Philip's Possession. This will be the only Means to enable us to judge whether the War which this Affair occasioned was just or unjust, or whether, as it is my Opinion, there were on both Sides, sufficient Reasons to justify the Attack and the Defence' (ibid.,

vol. IV, p. 362). Rapin insists that, as the nature of the Salic Law had not yet been clarified, each side might justly try to explicate it in the sense that supported their own claim: 'the point in Question had never been decided. Each Party therefore was at Liberty before the Decision, to explain the *Salick-Law*, and put that Sense upon it as he judged for his Purpose, without being liable to be taxed with Rashness' (ibid., vol. IV, p. 364). Rapin's conclusion, as Hume says, was that the question was properly decided by the sword: 'the two Kings had each very plausible Reasons, and that consequently it was just Matter of Process' (ibid., vol. IV, p. 368). In his *History of England*, however, Hume dissents from Rapin's opinion, saying of Edward's claim: 'There could not well be imagined a notion weaker or worse grounded. The principle of excluding females was of old an established opinion in France, and had acquired equal authority with the most express and positive law: It was supported by ancient precedents: It was confirmed by recent instances, solemnly and deliberately decided: And what placed it still farther beyond controversy; if Edward was disposed to contest its validity, he thereby cut off his own pretensions; since the three last kings had all left daughters, who were still alive, and who stood before him in the order of succession … [Edward's claim] was so contrary to the established principles of succession in every country of Europe, was so repugnant to the practice both in private and public inheritances, that no body in France thought of Edward's claim' (*History of England*, vol. II, p. 198).

50. *Who shall tell me … usurpation?*] This paragraph is taken almost verbatim from the *Treatise of Human Nature*, III.ii.10 (*THN*, p. 360).

51. *a pretty long succession of excellent emperors*] Hume refers to the sequence of Roman emperors from the adoption of Trajan in AD 96 to the death of Marcus Antoninus in AD 180: Trajan, Hadrian, Titus Antoninus Pius and Marcus Aurelius Antoninus.

52. *his wench and her gallant*] Commodus was strangled in a drunken stupor by a wrestler, who had been suborned to assassinate the emperor by Marcia, Commodus's favourite concubine, Eclectus his chamberlain and Laetus his Praetorian prefect (see Gibbon, *Decline and Fall*, vol. I, p. 120).

53. *Prætorian Præfect*] Originally, and during the reign of Commodus, the commander of the Praetorian Guard, the emperor's personal bodyguard made up of selected veterans from the legions; later a high-ranking administrative official and chief counsellor to the emperor.

54. *inferior to the imperial crown*] Gibbon would disagree: 'Mr. Hume, in supposing that the birth and dignity of Severus were too much inferior to the Imperial crown, and that he marched in Italy as general only, has not considered this transaction with his usual accuracy' (Gibbon, *Decline and Fall*, vol. I, p. 135, n. 30).

55. *Inter hæc … præsenti*] Julius Capitolinus, *Historia Augusta*, 'Maximus and Balbinus', XIV.vii: 'In the meantime Gordian Caesar was lifted up by the

soldiers and hailed emperor (that is, Augustus), there being no one else at hand.' These events occurred in AD 238.

56. *ALEXANDER's successors*] i.e. the so-called 'Diadochi', a transliteration of the Greek word for 'successors'; namely, the generals, relations and associates of Alexander the Great, who divided up his empire after his death in 323 BC, and who fought a series of wars between themselves from 319 to 275 BC. The various kingdoms of the Diadochi which emerged from these wars lasted from 275 to 30 BC, when the Romans conquered Ptolemaic Egypt. The entire period from 323 to 30 BC is referred to as the Hellenistic period of Mediterranean history.

57. *the edict of LEWIS the XIVth*] By the Edict of Marly of July 1714 Louis had granted the right to succeed to the French throne to two of his bastard sons by his mistress, Mme de Montespan: the Duc du Maine and the Comte de Toulouse. The succession to the throne of France had required reinforcement after three Dauphins (the Grand Dauphin; the Petit Dauphin, the Duc de Bourgogne; and his son Louis, Duc de Bretagne) had died of smallpox within eleven months, between 14 April 1711 and 8 March 1712. After Louis's death the edict had been reversed in 1717 by the Parlement de Paris. Henri de Boulainvilliers had been a posthumous participant in perhaps the most momentous eighteenth-century political argument in France before 1789. His *Histoire de l'ancien gouvernement de la France* (1727–8) expounded the 'thèse nobiliaire' of the origins of the French monarchy. According to Boulainvilliers, the French aristocracy were the heirs and descendants of Frankish invaders who had overrun Gaul. Their descendants still ruled those territories by right of conquest, and in consequence the French monarchy was more barbaric than Roman and more feudal than imperial, reflecting its origin in an arrangement by which a pre-eminent warlord was given a limited and contractual authority by his fellow chiefs, whom he ruled as *primus inter pares*. Boulainvilliers had been answered by the Abbé Dubos, whose *Histoire critique de l'établissement de la monarchie françoise* (1734) laid out the 'thèse royale'. According to Dubos, the Gauls had been free subjects of the Romans, the Franks had been their protectors rather than their conquerors, and Clovis's acceptance of the consulship demonstrated that, at its point of origin, the French monarchy was an offshoot of Roman *imperium*, the absolutist character and privileges of which it therefore naturally retained. Hume refers to Boulainvilliers rather bluntly as 'a noted republican'. Certainly Boulainvilliers's historical enquiries and his political inclinations led him to resist royal absolutism and to desire an increase in the political influence of the French aristocracy. His controversial and swiftly suppressed *Memoire pour la noblesse de France, contre les ducs et pairs* (1717) had argued against the peers being allowed to form a separate class of nobility, and accordingly it was easy for him to associate himself with the cause of the bastard princes, since that too served to close the distance between noble blood and royal

blood. The text in which Boulainvilliers explicitly addressed the case of the bastard princes was his 'Memoire, Touchant l'affaire de Mrs. les Princes du Sang', printed in his *Etat de la France*, vol. III ('Londres', 1728), pp. 527–38. Boulainvilliers discusses the circumstances that led to Hugh Capet ascending the throne of France on pp. 532–3, and he summarizes his view as follows: 'Dira-t'on sur cet exposé que l'Histoire justifie dans toutes ses circonstances, que les suffrages des François libres de se choisir un Maître par l'extinction de la Maison régnante, ayent élevé Hugue Capet sur le trône? Ne voit-on pas, au contraire, que la France a eu le sort commun de tous les Empires de longue durée, dans le changement de races qui y ont régné, & où les plus forts, & les plus habiles à profiter des circonstances, ont chassé les plus foibles, & ont occupé leurs places?' (p. 532).

58. *CHARLES the Second ... monarchy*] Shortly before his death, Charles II of Spain had been prevailed upon to alter his will so as to leave the whole of the Spanish monarchy to Louis XIV's grandson, Philip of Anjou, who thereby became Philip V of Spain. Louis XIV's acceptance of the terms of the will flouted the various Partition Treaties he had agreed with William III of England, and it thereby triggered the War of the Spanish Succession (1701–14).

59. *lib. ii*] Book II of Herodian's *History of the Empire* covers the period from the assassination of Commodus to Severus's successful descent on Rome in AD 193, the events of which Hume summarizes in this paragraph.

60. *obey the laws*] Hume refers to Plato, *Crito*, 50c–54e. The passage at 53a, in which Socrates imagines the laws of Athens addressing him, is particularly apposite: 'οὕτω σοι διαφερόντως τῶν ἄλλων Ἀθηναίων ἤρεσκεν ἡ πόλις τε καὶ ἡμεῖς οἱ νόμοι δῆλον ὅτι· τίνι γὰρ ἂν πόλις ἀρέσκοι ἄνευ νόμων; νῦν δὲ δὴ οὐκ ἐμμενεῖς τοῖς ὡμολογημένοις'; 'Thus it's clear that the city satisfied you far more than the rest of the Athenians, and presumably so did we the Laws. For, who would a city without laws satisfy? So now after all this, aren't you going to stand by what's been agreed?'

61. *νεωτερίζειν, novas res moliri*] respectively, Greek and Latin for to innovate. Hume may be thinking of a comment by Socrates in Plato's *Republic*, IV.424b, describing the duties of the guardians: 'Ὡς τοίνυν διὰ βραχέων εἰπεῖν, τούτου ἀνθεκτέον τοῖς ἐπιμεληταῖς τῆς πόλεως, ὅπως ἂν αὐτοὺς μὴ λάθῃ διαφθαρὲν ἀλλὰ παρὰ πάντα αὐτὸ φυλάττωσι, τὸ μὴ νεωτερίζειν περὶ γυμναστικήν τε καὶ μουσικὴν παρὰ τὴν τάξιν, ἀλλ᾽ ὡς οἷόν τε μάλιστα φυλάττειν, φοβουμένους ὅταν τις λέγῃ ὡς τὴν ἀοιδὴν μᾶλλον ἐπιφρονέουσ᾽ ἄνθρωποι, ἥτις ἀειδόντεσσι νεωτάτη ἀμφιπέληται'; 'Well then, to put it briefly: what those in charge of our state must cling to so that it is not corrupted through carelessness without their noticing it, but must guard above all else is this: they must not introduce innovations that contravene what is prescribed for physical and intellectual education, but preserve it as far as possible and feel alarm whenever anyone says that: Men have a higher regard for the song which is the

latest the singers bring with them'; and also perhaps of a comment in Tacitus, *Annals*, II.xxvii: 'Sub idem tempus e familia Scriboniorum Libo Drusus defertur moliri res novas'; 'Nearly at the same time a charge of revolutionary activities was laid against Libo Drusus, a member of the Scribonian family' (for another Latin example of the phrase, see, e.g., Livy, XXXIV.lxi). Cf. the comment Hume placed in the mouth of his imagined Royalist sitting in the Long Parliament in 'Of the Coalition of Parties': 'The spirit of innovation is in itself pernicious, however favourable its particular object may sometimes appear' (above, p. 183).

62. *chap. vii. § 90*] Locke, *Two Treatises*, 'Second Treatise', § 90: 'Hence it is evident, that *Absolute Monarchy*, which by some Men is counted the only Government in the World, is indeed *inconsistent with Civil Society*, and so can be no Form of Civil Government at all. For the *end of Civil Society*, being to avoid, and remedy those inconveniencies of the State of Nature, which necessarily follow from every Man's being Judge in his own Case, by setting up a known Authority, to which every one of that Society may Appeal upon any Injury received, or Controversie that may arise, and which every one of the Society ought to obey; where-ever any persons are, who have not such an Authority to Appeal to, for the decision of any difference between them, there those persons are still *in the state of Nature*. And so is every *Absolute Prince* in respect of those who are under his *Dominion*' (Locke, *Two Treatises*, p. 326).

63. *138, 139, 140*] See Locke, *Two Treatises*, pp. 360–62. Hume seems to have the following passages particularly in mind: 'The *Supream Power cannot take* from any Man any part of his *Property* without his own consent. For the preservation of Property being the end of Government, and that for which Men enter into Society, it necessarily supposes and requires, that the People should *have Property*, without which they must be suppos'd to lose that by entring into Society, which was the end for which they entered into it, too gross an absurdity for any Man to own' (ibid., p. 360); ''Tis true, Governments cannot be supported without great Charge, and 'tis fit every one who enjoys his share of the Protection, should pay out of his Estate his proportion for the maintenance of it. But still it must be with his own Consent, *i.e.* the Consent of the Majority, giving it either by themselves, or their Representatives chosen by them. For if any one shall claim a *Power to lay* and levy *Taxes* on the People, by his own Authority, and without such consent of the People, he thereby invades the *Fundamental Law of Property*, and subverts the end of Government. For what property have I in that which another may by right take, when he pleases to himself?' (ibid., p. 362).

64. *time alone . . . violence*] cf. Boulainvilliers, on the durability of the title seized by Hugh Capet: 'Une possession constante de plus de sept cents ans est un titre si puissant & si demonstratif, que toute la malice des hommes n'y sauroit donner atteinte . . .' (*Etat de la France*, vol. III, p. 533).

## XIII. OF PASSIVE OBEDIENCE

Published in: *1748, 1753, 1758, 1760, 1764, 1767, 1768, 1770, 1772, 1777a*
Significant revisions:

1) *1748* reads: '. . . against a *Nero*, or a *Caracalla*, so infatuated . . .' (*1748*, p. 309; cf. above, p. 178).

2) *1753–1768* read: '. . . against a *Nero*, or a *Philip*, so infatuated . . .' (*1753*, p. 328; cf. above, p. 178).

Copy text: *1777a*
Headnote:

Composed in the summer of 1747 (see above, headnote to 'Of the Original Contract', pp. 524–7). 'Passive Obedience' was originally a phrase coined to refer to the submission of Christ to the will of his Father, leading to his suffering and death upon the Cross. It was applied by extension to the duty of the subject not to resist the supreme power in the state (*OED*). Although it was claimed by the Stuarts and their apologists to be a perpetual, divine and natural law of obligation (see, for instance, Abednego Seller, *The History of Passive Obedience* [1689]), the idea of passive obedience had in the later seventeenth century been subjected to a withering Whig critique, which had exposed both its conceptual deformity and its relative novelty as a political doctrine. Locke had eloquently mocked the ethical monstrosity concealed within it: 'Who would not think it an admirable Peace betwixt the Mighty and the Mean, when the Lamb, without resistance, yielded his Throat to be torn by the imperious Wolf? *Polyphemus*'s Den gives us a perfect Pattern of such a Peace, and such a Government, wherein *Ulysses* and his Companions had nothing to do, but quietly to suffer themselves to be devour'd. And no doubt *Ulysses*, who was a prudent Man, preach'd up *Passive Obedience*, and exhorted them to a quiet Submission, by representing to them of what concernment Peace was to Mankind; and by shewing the inconveniencies might happen, if they should offer to resist *Polyphemus*, who had now the power over them' (Locke, *Two Treatises*, p. 417). Writing of the Middle Ages, Roger Coke had observed that the 'Doctrines of *Passive Obedience*, and submitting to the *Absolute Will and Pleasure* of the King, were Strangers to those Days'; and he traced the inception of this, to his eyes, incoherent political doctrine to no earlier than 1678: 'The *Tories* had got a new invented Doctrine of inconsistible Terms, called, *Passive Obedience*: I would willingly be informed in the Grammatical Construction of these two Words, how a Noun Adjective or Participle, can alter the Signification of a Noun Substantive; for if any one be subject to another, and be commanded or forbidden by this other, it is Disobedience if he does not the Command of this other: How therefore Passive joined to Disobedience, can make it Obedience, had need of a better Interpretation than what the *Tories* give; which is, if you cannot obey, you must suffer: But this is another Proposition; and so Disobedience here is Disobedience still; and the true Construction of *Passive Obedience*, is Disobedience, and be hang'd for it' (Coke, *Detection*, pp. 206 and 531–2). Cf. also Sidney, *Discourses*, p. 15, and *Whole Kingdoms*, pp. 44–67. In *The Freeholder*, no. 10 (23 January 1716), Addison had exposed passive obedience and its associated concepts to a devastating critique: 'the Gross of the People, who are imposed upon by Terms which they do not comprehend, are *Whigs* in their Hearts. They are made to believe, that Passive-Obedience and Non-Resistance, Unlimited Power and Indefeasible Right, have something of a venerable and religious meaning in them; whereas in Reality they only imply, that a King of *Great Britain* has a Right to be a Tyrant, and that his Subjects are obliged in Conscience to be Slaves' (Addison, *Freeholder*, p. 82); and in no. 22 (5 March 1716) the fox-hunting squire whom Addison makes the mouthpiece for crude Tory prejudices says that travel is good for nothing except (*inter alia*) to teach a man 'to talk against Passive-Obedience' (Addison, *Freeholder*, p. 132). In letter 8 of his *A Dissertation upon Parties* Bolingbroke had argued that these doctrines had expired in 1688: 'The slavish principles of passive obedience and non-resistance, which had skulked perhaps in some old homily before King James the First, but were talked, written and preached into vogue in that inglorious reign, and in those of his three successors, were renounced at the Revolution by the last of the several parties who declared for them' (Bolingbroke, *Political Writings*, p. 66).

This essay should be read in conjunction with the *Treatise of Human Nature*, III.ii.9, 'Of the Measures of Allegiance'. Cf. particularly: ''Tis certain, therefore, that in all our notions of morals we never entertain such an absurdity as that of passive obedience, but make allowances for resistance in the more flagrant instances of tyranny and oppression' (*THN*, pp. 353–4). It is worth also juxtaposing this essay with the brief, contemptuous comments on passive obedience to be found in the earlier, longer final section of 'Of the Parties of Great Britain' printed in editions up to and including *1768* (above, vol. 1, pp. 253–7).

Compare also Bolingbroke's summary of the character of a Tory, in letter 1 of his *A Dissertation upon Parties*: 'Divine, hereditary, indefeasible right, lineal succession, passive-obedience, prerogative, non-resistance, slavery, nay and sometimes property too, were associated in many minds to the idea of a Tory, and deemed incommunicable and inconsistent in the same manner, with the idea of a Whig' (Bolingbroke, *Political Writings*, p. 5).

1. *fiat Justitia & ruat Cœlum*] 'let justice be done, though the heavens fall'. Apparently not a phrase drawn from classical Latin, it had however been frequently quoted in the pamphlet and polemical literature of the Exclusion Crisis: see *Fiat Justitia, & Ruat Coelum* (1679); *A Plea to the Duke's Answers* (1680); *A List of Abhorrors* (1681); *The Lion's Elegy* (1681); George Savile, *A Seasonable Addresse* (1681); Thomas Barlow, *The Original of Kingly and*

*Ecclesiastical Government* (1681); and Henry Care, *The History of Popery* (1682). Cf. Hume's letter to Francis Hutcheson of 17 September 1739 (quoting Horace, *Satires*, III.98): 'I have never call'd Justice unnatural, but only artificial. *Atque ipsa utilitas justi prope mater & aequi.* Says one of the best Moralists of Antiquity' (*Letters*, vol. I, p. 33). However, the importance of separating questions of justice from questions of utility is an important theme in the legal and philosophical thinking of antiquity, from which therefore Hume is here separating himself: cf., e.g., Cicero, *De Legibus*, I.42–3. In the next century Henry Sidgwick would characterize this phrase as an 'intuitionist' maxim (Sidgwick, *Ethics*, p. 20).

2. *binds us to obedience . . . public utility*] Hobbes had concluded *Leviathan* by insisting to his reader that the primary purpose of the book had been nothing more than to 'set before mens eyes the mutuall Relation between Protection and Obedience' (Hobbes, *Leviathan*, p. 491).

3. *Salus populi suprema Lex*] i.e. 'the safety of the people is the supreme law'. See, e.g., Cicero, *De Legibus*, III.iii.8. This maxim had been much relied upon in late-sixteenth-century French resistance theory, such as Hotman's *Franco-Gallia* (Figgis, *Divine Right*, pp. 118–19). For conspicuous seventeenth-century English invocations of this ultimately utilitarian principle, see Sir Francis Bacon, 'Of Judicature': *'Judges* ought above all to remember the Conclusion of the *Roman Twelve Tables*; *Salus Populi Suprema Lex*; And to know, that Lawes, except they bee in Order to that End, are but Things Captious, and Oracles not well Inspired' (Bacon, *Essayes*, p. 169); and also Hobbes, *Leviathan*, chapter 30: 'The Office of the Soveraign . . . consisteth in the end, for which he was trusted with the Soveraign Power, namely the procuration of the safety of the people' (Hobbes, *Leviathan*, p. 231; cf. 'Introduction', ibid., p. 9; see also Hobbes, *Behemoth*, p. 68). Note also the endorsement by Locke in the 'Second Treatise', § 158: '*Salus Populi Suprema Lex*, is certainly so just and fundamental a Rule, that he, who sincerely follows it, cannot dangerously err' (Locke, *Two Treatises*, p. 373). The implications of the saying had been explored from diverse political perspectives in the middle decades of the seventeenth century. Henry Parker had invoked the principle in his *Observations* of 1642 (p. 3); as had Sir Robert Filmer in his *The Anarchy of a Limited or Mixed Monarchy* (1648) (Filmer, *Patriarcha*, p. 149); and John Warr in 1649 had asserted that the 'end of just laws is the safety and freedom of a people' (Wootton, *Divine Right*, p. 152; and cf. also p. 47). It was, however, an extremely common political maxim, often quoted in Parliament during the 1650s and after the Restoration (e.g. Burton, *Diary*, vol. I, pp. 234, 240–41, 261, 281; vol. III, pp. 108, 569; vol. IV, pp. 47, 94; Grey, *Debates*, vol. I, p. 113; vol. VI, p. 329; vol. IX, pp. 98 and 101; cf. also Algernon Sidney, *Court Maxims*, ed. Hans W. Blom *et al.* (Cambridge: Cambridge University Press, 1996), p. 126, and *State-Tracts*, vol. II, pp. 23 and 24). See, e.g.: Robert Sanderson, *Nine Cases of Conscience* (1678), p. 169; Charles

Blount, *An Appeal from the Country to the City* (1679), tp; William Denton, *The Ungrateful Behaviour of the Papists* (1679), p. 123; Sir Robert Filmer, *The Free-Holders Grand Inquest* (1679), p. 281; Thomas Hobbes, *Behemoth* (1679), p. 67; Sir Roger L'Estrange, *The Case Put, Concerning the Succession* (1679), p. 16; Bethel Slingsby, *The Interest of Princes and States* (1680), p. 262; Buckingham, *An Essay upon Satyr* (1680), p. 49; Robert Constable, *God and the King* (1680), p. 31; Thomas Hobbes, *The Last Sayings* (1680), p. 1; John Humfrey, *A Peaceful Resolution of Conscience* (1680), p. 102; Sir John Monson, *A Discourse Concerning Supreme Power* (1680), p. 141; and Thomas Otway, *The Poet's Complaint of His Muse* (1680), p. 16. In his *A Dissertation upon Parties*, letter 9, Bolingbroke had expressed the same sentiment: 'Necessity and self-preservation are the great laws of nature, and may well dispense with the strict observation of the common forms of any particular constitution' (Bolingbroke, *Political Writings*, p. 81). In *The Idea of a Patriot King* he had invoked the maxim explicitly: '*Salus reipublicae suprema lex esto* is a fundamental law' (ibid., p. 232: silently echoing Hobbes, *Behemoth*, p. 68). The maxim is also invoked in Jean-François Melon's *Essai politique sur le commerce* (Melon, *Essai politique*, p. 156), who goes on to remark: 'Ce seroit une Histoire bien interessante & bien utile, que celles des malheurs causés par l'imprudente, ou la fausse application de cette Maxime' (p. 157). Hume refers to the principle in Section III, Part 2, of *An Enquiry Concerning the Principles of Morals*: 'The safety of the people is the supreme law: All other particular laws are subordinate to it, and dependent on it' (*ECPM*, p. 22).

4. *the insurrections ... the undertakers*] Nero was dethroned after a series of insurrections originating in the provinces, and terminating in the 'Year of the Four Emperors', AD 69. Philip II of Spain faced a prolonged rebellion in the Low Countries, the so-called 'Eighty Years' War' (1568–1648). Cf. the *Treatise of Human Nature*, III.ii.10: 'the establish'd liberty of the *Dutch* is no inconsiderable apology for their obstinate resistance to *Philip* the Second' (*THN*, p. 362).

5. *our high monarchical party*] i.e. the high-flying wing of the Tories.

6. *the last refuge*] cf. the digression on the right to resistance to which the execution of Charles I moves Hume in the *History of England*: 'If ever, on any occasion, it were laudable to conceal truth from the populace; it must be confessed, that the doctrine of resistance affords such an example; and that all speculative reasoners ought to observe, with regard to this principle, the same cautious silence, which the laws, in every species of government, have ever prescribed to themselves. Government is instituted, in order to restrain the fury and injustice of the people; and being always founded on opinion, not on force, it is dangerous to weaken, by these speculations, the reverence, which the multitude owe to authority, and to instruct them beforehand, that the case can ever happen, when they may be freed from their duty of allegiance. Or should it be found impossible to restrain the licence of human

disquisitions, it must be acknowledged, that the doctrine of obedience ought alone to be *inculcated*, and that the exceptions, which are rare, ought seldom or never to be mentioned in popular reasonings and discourses. Nor is there any danger, that mankind, by this prudent reserve, should universally degenerate into a state of abject servitude. When the exception really occurs, even though it be not previously expected and descanted on, it must, from its very nature, be so obvious and undisputed, as to remove all doubt, and overpower the restraint, however great, imposed by teaching the general doctrine of obedience' (*History of England*, vol. V, p. 544). Locke had defended himself against the imputation that the political theory of the *Two Treatises* was an invitation to perpetual unrest by insisting that people would be reluctant to overthrow a government unless grievously provoked: 'Nor let any one say, that mischief can arise from hence, as often as it shall please a busie head, or turbulent spirit, to desire the alteration of Government. 'Tis true, such Men may stir, whenever they please, but it will be only to their own just ruine and perdition. For till the mischief be grown general, and the ill designs of the Rulers become visible, or their attempts sensible to the greater part, the People, who are more disposed to suffer, than right themselves by Resistance, are not apt to stir. The examples of particular Injustice, or Oppression of here and there an unfortunate Man, moves them not. But if they universally have a perswasion, grounded upon manifest evidence, that designs are carrying on against their Liberties, and the general course and tendency of things cannot but give them strong suspicions of the evil intention of their Governors, who is to be blamed for it? Who can help it, if they, who might avoid it, bring themselves into this suspicion? Are the People to be blamed, if they have the sence of rational Creatures, and can think of things no otherwise than as they find and feel them? And is it not rather *their fault*, who puts things in such a posture that they would not have them thought, to be as they are?' ('Second Treatise', § 230, in Locke, *Two Treatises*, pp. 417–18).

7. *For besides . . . of society*] Hume here seems to have in mind two passages from Hobbes's *Leviathan*, from chapters 18 and 29 respectively: 'the greatest pressure of Sovereign Governours, proceedeth not from any delight, or profit they can expect in the dammage, or weakening of their Subjects, in whose vigor, consisteth their own strength and glory; but in the restiveness of themselves, that unwillingly contributing to their own defence, make it necessary for their Governours to draw from them what they can in time of Peace, that they may have means on any emergent occasion, or sudden need, to resist, or take advantage of their Enemies' (Hobbes, *Leviathan*, pp. 128–9); 'And as to Rebellion in particular against Monarchy; one of the most frequent causes of it, is the Reading of the books of Policy, and Histories of the antient Greeks, and Romans; from which, young men, and all others that are unprovided of the Antidote of solid Reason, receiving a strong, and delightfull impression, of the great exploits of warre, atchieved by the Conductors of their

Armies, receive withall a pleasing Idea, of all they have done besides; and imagine their great prosperity, not to have proceeded from the aemulation of particular men, but from the vertue of their popular forme of government: Not considering the frequent Seditions, and Civill warres produced by the imperfection of their Policy. From the reading, I say, of such books, men have undertaken to kill their Kings, because the Greek and Latine writers, in their books, and discourses of Policy, make if lawfull, and laudable, for any man so to do, provided before he do it, he call him Tyrant. For they say not *Regicide*, that is, killing of a King, but *Tyrannicide*, that is, killing of a Tyrant is lawfull' (ibid., pp. 225–6). Note also Hume's very similar comments on the inutility of tyrannicide in *An Enquiry Concerning the Principles of Morals*, Section II, Part 2: '*Tyrannicide*, or the assassination of usurpers and oppressive princes, was highly extolled in ancient times; because it both freed mankind from many of these monsters, and seemed to keep the others in awe, whom the sword or poinard could not reach. But history and experience having since convinced us, that this practice encreases the jealousy and cruelty of princes, a TIMOLEON and a BRUTUS, though treated with indulgence on account of the prejudices of their times, are now considered as very improper models for imitation' (Hume, *ECPM*, p. 11).

8. *as obedience ... may be allowed*] cf. the *Treatise of Human Nature*, III. ii.10: 'No maxim is more conformable, both to prudence and morals, than to submit quietly to the government, which we find establish'd in the country where we happen to live, without enquiring too curiously into its origin and first establishment' (*THN*, p. 357).

9. *that party among us*] It is clear that here Hume has in mind the Whigs, since by the 'antagonists' who exalted the principle of obedience he can mean only the Tories. However, this characterization of the two parties ignores the fact that, during the first half of the eighteenth century in Britain, arguments for resistance were often found on the lips of Jacobites. John Pocock has described this curious exchange of ideological clothing which occurred in the first half of the eighteenth century: 'We encounter yet again the problem that Tory language, which ought to have been and often was High Church and Jacobite, ought not to have been but often was radical and republican, Commonwealth as well as country. There are Jacobite manifestos of 1745 that sound not unlike Monmouth's manifestos of 1685' ('The Varieties of Whiggism from Exclusion to Reform', in J. G. A. Pocock, *Virtue, Commerce, and History* [Cambridge: Cambridge University Press, 1985], p. 245).

10. *It is ... by him*] A reference to the principle that the king can do no wrong. This principle is often misinterpreted as meaning that the king is 'legibus solutus' and possesses a freedom of action unconstrained by law or moral principle. In fact, however, the principle is a brake on royal power, because it means that a servant of the Crown can never plead a royal instruction as a justification for committing an illegal action.

11. *This is . . . indiscretion*] Hume had given general consideration to the events of 1688 in the *Treatise of Human Nature*, III.ii.10, where he had justified resistance to James II on the grounds that, in 'the late *revolution*', 'all the rights and privileges, which ought to be sacred to a free nation, were at that time threaten'd with the utmost danger' (*THN*, p. 361). In his *History of England* he would present 1688 as the natural outcome of a collision between James II's arbitrary inclinations and the embryonic fences against encroachments by the Crown which were already present in the English constitution: 'jealousy of royal power was the very basis of the English constitution, and the principle, to which the nation was beholden for all that liberty, which they enjoy above the subjects of other monarchies. That this jealousy, though, at different periods, it may be more or less intense, can never safely be laid asleep, even under the best and wisest princes. That the character of the present sovereign afforded cause for the highest vigilance, by reason of the arbitrary principles, which he had imbibed; and still more, by reason of his religious zeal, whith it is impossible for him ever to gratify, without assuming more authority than the constitution allows him' (*History of England*, vol. VI, p. 454). And in his summary of James's character, Hume would depict a man brought down by the conjunction of the mediocrity of his virtues and his culpable indifference towards the constitution: 'Thus ended the reign of a prince, whom, if we consider his personal character rather than his public conduct, we may safely pronounce more unfortunate than criminal. He had many of those qualities, which form a good citizen . . . What then was wanting to make him an excellent sovereign? A due regard and affection to the religion and constitution of his country. Had he been possessed of this essential quality, even his middling talents, aided by so many virtues, would have rendered his reign honourable and happy. When it was wanting, every excellency, which he possessed, became dangerous and pernicious to his kingdoms' (ibid., vol. VI, p. 520). Nevertheless, note Duncan Forbes's shrewd insight about the awkwardness of Hume's position on 1688: 'although Hume can defend, quite unambiguously and consistently with his general principles, the present establishment, he cannot unambiguously and consistently defend those who brought it about' (Forbes, *Politics*, p. 100).

### XIV. OF THE COALITION OF PARTIES

Published in: *1760, 1764, 1767, 1768, 1770, 1772, 1777a*
Significant revisions:

    1) *1760–1772* read: '. . . regard to the *philosophical* controversies . . .' (*1760*, vol. II, p. 324; cf. above, p. 181).

    2) *1760–1768* insert the following note, cued to '. . . rule of administration.' (*1760*, vol. II, p. 328; cf. above, p. 184):

'*The author believes that he was the first writer who advanced that the family of TUDOR possessed in general more authority than their immediate predecessors: An opinion, which, he hopes, will be supported by history, but which he proposes with some diffidence. There are strong symptoms of arbitrary power in some former reigns, even after signing of the charters. The power of the crown in that age depended less on the constitution than on the capacity and vigour of the prince who wore it.' (*1760*, vol. II, pp. 328–9).

3) *1760–1768* read: '. . . barbarous and GOTHIC constitution . . .' (*1760*, vol. II, p. 329; cf. above, p. 184).

Copy text: *1777a*

Headnote:

Composed towards the end of 1759, as Hume's letter to Andrew Millar of 18 December 1759 reveals: 'I am surprizd that Strahan had not printed the Essay on the Coalition of Parties. He was very near it when I left London; & his Press must have stopd other wise it had been printed off in a week after' (*Letters*, vol. I, p. 317). Hume seems to have left London at the beginning of November 1759. For an interpretation of this essay as a summary of the historical and political vision of Hume's *History of England*, see Harris, *Hume*, pp. 386–7. Duncan Forbes describes this essay as 'an apologia for the first volume of the *History* published four years previously' (Forbes, *Politics*, p. 265).

1. *above a century past*] Hume refers to the English Civil Wars (1642–51).
2. *there have appeared . . . party distinctions*] cf. Hume's letter to William Strahan on the accession of George III in 1760: 'I was glad to observe what our King says, that Faction is at an End and Party Distinctions abolish'd' (*Letters*, vol. I, p. 336; cf. also pp. 368 and 385). Hume here builds upon an insight of Bolingbroke's, articulated in his *A Dissertation upon Parties*, that the party identities forged at the end of the seventeenth century had probably since 1688, and certainly by the early 1730s (the individual letters of the *Dissertation* were first published between October 1733 and December 1734), begun to lose their distinctness: 'These associations are broken; these distinct sets of ideas are shuffled out of their order; new combinations force themselves upon us; and it would actually be as absurd to impute to the Tories the principles, which were laid to their charge formerly, as it would be to ascribe to the projector and his faction the name of Whigs, whilst they daily forfeit that character by their actions. The bulk of both parties are really united; united on principles of liberty, in opposition to an obscure remnant of one party, who disown those principles [presumably the Jacobites], and a mercenary detachment from the other, who betray them [presumably the Commonwealthmen, or radical Whigs]' (Bolingbroke, *Political Writings*, p. 5; cf. also the headnote to 'Of the Parties of Great Britain', above, vol. 1, pp. 257–58).

The terms 'Whig' and 'Tory' would remain in use throughout the eighteenth century, but their propositional content became ever more elusive. On 7 August 1790 Gibbon would write to his friend Lord Sheffield and reproach him for using 'those foolish obsolete, odious, words Whig and Tory. In the American War they might have some meaning, and then your Lordship was a Tory; since the coalition [between Fox and Pitt], all general principles have been confounded' (Gibbon, *Letters*, vol. III, p. 195).

3. *the name of whigs*] cf. 'Of the Parties of Great Britain' (above, vol. 1, pp. 63–5). In the *History of England* Hume described the origin of party in the Exclusion Crisis of 1680–81: 'Thus the nation came to be distinguished into *petitioners* [those who wished to exclude the Duke of York] and *abhorrers* [those who viewed such attempts at exclusion with abhorrence]. Factions indeed were at this time extremely animated against each other. The very names, by which each party denominated its antagonist, discover the virulence and rancour, which prevailed. For besides petitioner and abhorrer, appellations which were soon forgotten, this year [1680] is remarkable for being the epoch of the well-known epithets of WHIG and TORY, by which, and sometimes without any material difference, this island has been so long divided. The court party reproached their antagonists with their affinity to the fanatical conventiclers in Scotland, who were known by the name of whigs: The country party found a resemblance between the courtiers and the popish banditti in Ireland, to whom the appellation of tory was affixed. And after this manner, these foolish terms of reproach came into public and general use; and even at present seem not nearer their end than when they were first invented' (*History of England*, vol. VI, p. 381).

4. *specious*] Alluring or attractive; at this time, a word without any necessary pejorative implication.

5. *precedents in favour of prerogative*] See above, p. 326, n.30. In letter 12 of *A Dissertation upon Parties* Bolingbroke had written contemptuously of 'men who persisted long in the attempt to talk and write that chimera called prerogative into vogue; to contend that it was something real, a right inherent in the crown, founded in the constitution of our government; and equally necessary to support the just authority of the prince, and to protect the subject' (Bolingbroke, *Political Writings*, p. 119).

6. *that parliament … began the civil wars*] i.e. the Long Parliament, which had convened on 3 November 1640 and had continued in existence, with interruptions, until 16 March 1660. In the *History of England* Hume had described the mood of anticipation which attended its inception: 'The eager expectations of men with regard to a parliament, summoned at so critical a juncture, and during such general discontents; a parliament, which, from the situation of public affairs, could not be abruptly dissolved, and which was to execute every thing left unfinished by former parliaments; these motives, so

important and interesting, engaged the attendance of all the members; and the house of commons was never observed to be, from the beginning, so full and numerous. Without any interval, therefore, they entered upon business, and by unanimous consent they immediately struck a blow, which may, in a manner, be regarded as decisive [the impeachment of Strafford]' (*History of England*, vol. V, pp. 285–6). This Parliament's 'violent encroachments on the crown' included the impeachments of the Earl of Strafford and Archbishop Laud, the Grand Remonstrance of 1641, the abolition of Star Chamber in 1641, the Militia Ordinance of 1642, whereby Parliament asserted control over the appointment of officers in the army and navy, and the Self-Denying Ordinance of 1645. By the end, when its dissolution was engineered by General Monck, 'all men, however different in affections, expectations, and designs, united in their detestation of the long parliament' (*History of England*, vol. VI, p. 133).

7. *The spirit of innovation is in itself pernicious*] cf. the concluding sentence of 'Of the Original Contract' (above, p. 176).

8. *A truth ... ancient liberties of the people*] The doctrine of ancient constitutionalism had fuelled much seventeenth-century resistance to Stuart kingship. Royalists tended to see such claims as a figleaf for republicanism, and attempted to turn the flank of their parliamentary opponents by invoking the ancient constitution themselves (as in, for instance, the king's answers to Parliament's resolutions of 20 May 1642).

9. *the accession of the House of TUDOR*] In 1485, with the accession of Henry VII.

10. *the reign of the Emperor ADRIAN*] Hadrian ruled from AD 117 to AD 138. The Roman republic had been extinguished when Augustus assumed sole power in 31 BC.

11. *still subsisting*] Gibbon would define the imperial system of government artfully framed by Augustus as 'an absolute monarchy disguised by the forms of a commonwealth' (Gibbon, *Decline and Fall*, vol. I, p. 93).

12. *scarcely ... historians and politicians*] Here Hume takes silent issue with James Harrington and his followers, such as Henry Neville. For Harrington, the reign of Henry VII had marked the watershed between a preceding period when power had been broadly aligned with property, and a subsequent period when property had migrated towards fractions of society hitherto largely excluded from a say in government: 'Henry the Seventh ... was the richest in money of English princes. Nevertheless this accession of revenue did not at all preponderate on the king's part, nor change the balance. But while, making farms of a standard, he increased the yeomanry and, cutting off retainers, he abased the nobility, he began that breach in the balance of land, which proceeding, hath ruined the nobility and in them that government' (*The Prerogative of Popular Government*, in Harrington, *Works*, p. 408, and cf. also p. 436; cf. also *The Art of Lawgiving* [1659], in

ibid., pp. 606 and 659; and *The Prologue in Answer to Mr Wren's Preface*, in ibid., p. 709). Neville had sketched this periodization of English political history in Parliament on 8 February 1659: 'The Barons got a great share, and having a considerable part of the land, and not part in the Government, they began to stir and ruffle with the King; and in fine got authority, and gave laws both to King and Commons, until King Henry VII's time. He designed to weaken the hands of the nobility and their power' (Burton, *Diary*, vol. III, p. 133). And he would repeat the point in his *Plato Redivivus* (1680; second, substantially revised edition, 1681). However, by September 1752 Hume had already formed the view that the reign of Henry VII had been exaggerated as a watershed in English history, as he explained to Adam Smith: 'I was once of the same Opinion with you, & thought that the best Period to begin an English History was about Henry the 7th. But you will please to observe, that the Change, which then happen'd in public Affairs, was very insensible, and did not display its Influence till many Years afterwards' (*Letters*, vol. I, pp. 167–8). However, in May 1757, as he began composition of the Tudor volumes of his *History*, Hume's ideas on the significance of this reign had shifted back towards his earlier position, as he explained to Andrew Millar: 'at present I begin with the Reign of Henry the 7th. It is properly at that Period modern History commences. America was discoverd: Commerce extended: The Arts cultivated: Printing invented: Religion reform'd: And all the Governments of Europe almost chang'd. I wish therefore I had begun here at first. I shoud have obviated many Objections, that were made to the other Volumes' (*Letters*, vol. I, p. 249; cf. also the very similar letter to William Strahan, ibid., p. 251, and the similar sentiments in the letter to John Clephane, ibid., p. 264). In the *History of England* Hume would distinguish Henry's reign as 'a kind of epoch in the English constitution' and as marking the advent of a more extensive absolutism (*History of England*, vol. III, p. 74).

13. *PLANTAGENETS*] i.e. the kings of England drawn from the house of Anjou; also known as the Angevins. The first Plantagenet king of England was Henry II, who acceded in 1154. The last was Richard II, whose reign ended in 1399.

14. *Under what . . . ancient constitution?*] In the *History of England* at the end of chapter 23 Hume included a review of the English constitution up to 1485 and the accession of Henry VII, and he concluded: 'Those who, from a pretended respect to antiquity, appeal at every turn to an original plan of the constitution, only cover their turbulent spirit and their private ambition under the appearance of venerable forms; and whatever period they pitch on for their model, they may still be carried back to a more ancient period, where they will find the measures of power entirely different, and where every circumstance, by reason of the greater barbarity of the times, will appear still less worthy of imitation. Above all, a civilized nation, like the English, who have happily established the most perfect and most accurate system of liberty that was ever found compatible with government, ought to

be cautious in appealing to the practice of their ancestors, or regarding the maxims of uncultivated ages as certain rules for their present conduct. An acquaintance with the ancient periods of their government is chiefly *useful* by instructing them to cherish their present constitution, from a comparison or contrast with the condition of those distant times' (*History of England*, vol. II, p. 525).

15. *magna charta*] Magna Carta and the Carta de foresta had long been prized by common lawyers as the foundations of English liberty (see the commentary on Magna Carta which begins the second part of the *Institutes*: Coke, *Selected Writings*, vol. II, pp. 755–913). During the 1690s the Whig clergyman and agitator Samuel Johnson had studied Magna Carta and published his findings in *The Second Part of the Confutation of the Ballancing Letter* (1700), arguing that it pre-dated the time of King John and was untainted by rebellion. However, technically Magna Carta and the Carta de foresta were not laws, because they were grants of the Crown rather than acts of Parliament. (For an example of the popular Whiggish ignorance of the legal status of Magna Carta, see Henry Care, *English Liberties* [1680], p. 19, where he seems to think that Magna Carta is an act of Parliament.) Robert Brady had exploited this fact in an attempt to undermine the popular belief that Magna Carta could be used to curb the power of the Crown, arguing that the charter itself was an act of the Crown, and so could not be used to restrict the power from which it had proceeded: '*all the* Liberties *and* Priviledges *the People can pretend to, were the* Grants *and* Concessions *of the* Kings *of this Nation, and were Derived from the Crown*' (Brady, *A Complete History of England* [1685], 'To the Reader', sig. A4r). In *Politicaster* Harrington had presented Magna Carta as the site of repeated struggles between Crown and people: 'If in England there have ever been any such thing as a government of laws, was it not Magna Charta? Well, and have not our kings broken Magna Charta some thirty times? I beseech you, sir, did the law govern when the law was broken? Or was that a government of men? On the other side, hath not Magna Charta been as often repaired by the people? And the law being so restored, was it not a government of laws, and not of men?' (Harrington, *Works*, p. 715).

16. *house of commons . . . an existence*] The antiquity or otherwise of the House of Commons had been a fiercely disputed battleground in seventeenth-century politics, and especially so during the Exclusion Crisis of 1680–81. Filmer's *Freeholder's Grand Inquest*, republished in 1680, had argued against the antiquity of the House of Commons, noting that the earliest extant writ to the house was dated 1265, during the reign of Henry III (Filmer, *Patriarcha*, pp. 76, 80 and 84: drawing on John Selden's *Priviledges of the Baronage of England* [1642]). In his reply, *The Antient Right of the Commons of England Asserted* (1680), William Petyt had assembled a range of early medieval materials to present the image of an ancient, pre-Conquest Parliament that

had possessed and exercised (and whose successors therefore still possessed and might exercise) the right to alter the succession. In the cause of defending the antiquity and authority of Parliament, Petyt had been joined by his friend and associate William Atwood, whose *Jani Anglorum Facies Nova* (1680) and *Jus Anglorum ab antiquo* (1681) had argued in a similar direction. In the *History of England*, however, Hume argued consistently against what he represents as ill-founded and exaggerated claims for the antiquity of the House of Commons, and of its rights and privileges. In his appendix on 'The Feudal and Anglo-Norman Government and Manners', he observed: 'So far the nature of a general council or ancient parliament is determined without any doubt or controversy. The only question seems to be with regard to the commons, or the representatives of counties and boroughs; whether they were also, in more early times, constituent parts of parliament? This question was once disputed in England with great acrimony: But such is the force of time and evidence, that they can sometimes prevail even over faction; and the question seems, by general consent, and even by their own, to be at last determined against the ruling party. It is agreed, that the commons were no part of the great council, till some ages after the conquest; and that the military tenants alone of the crown composed that supreme and legislative assembly' (*History of England*, vol. I, p. 467).

17. *The property ... ancestors enjoyed*] A glance at the theory associated most closely with James Harrington, namely that, in a balanced political system, power naturally flows from the ownership of property (see above, vol. 1, p. 230, n. 6). For commentary on Hume's dissociation of himself from this axiom, see Forbes, *Politics*, pp. 229-30.

18. *the present established practice of the age*] cf. similar statements in the *History of England*: 'the only rule of government, which is intelligible or carries any authority with it, is the established practice of the age' (*History of England*, vol. II, p. 525); 'If any other rule than established practice be followed, factions and dissentions must multiply without end' (*History of England*, vol. IV, p. 355).

19. *Had we no other monuments ... her government*] Hume's narrative of the reign of Elizabeth I in his *History of England* nevertheless relied heavily on the antiquarian William Camden; but it was checked and reinforced by various collections of state papers. As recently as 2 August 1758 Hume had written to Horace Walpole, and had reminded him of the profusion of original materials relating to the reign of Elizabeth: 'The original books, which instruct us in the reign of Q. Elizabeth alone, would require six months reading at the rate of ten hours a day' (*Letters*, vol. I, p. 285). Hume summarized Elizabeth's accomplishments of rule as follows: 'Her singular talents for government were founded equally on her temper and on her capacity. Endowed with great command over herself, she soon obtained an uncontrouled ascendant over her people; and while she merited all their esteem by her real virtues, she also

engaged their affections by her pretended ones. Few sovereigns of England succeeded to the throne in more difficult circumstances; and none ever conducted the government with such uniform success and felicity. Though unacquainted with the practice of toleration, the true secret for managing religious factions, she preserved her people, by her superior prudence, from those confusions, in which theological controversy had involved all the neighbouring nations: And though her enemies were the most powerful princes of Europe, the most active, the most enterprising, the least scrupulous, she was able by her vigour to make deep impressions on their states: Her own greatness, meanwhile, remained untouched and unimpaired' (*History of England*, vol. IV, p. 352).

20. *If the origin . . . from the people*] The doctrine of constituent power residing in the people, although present in antiquity (see, e.g., Cicero, *On Agrarian Law*, II.xi.27), had flourished in the mid-seventeenth century, and had in particular been explored during the Interregnum by the Levellers: 'Wee are your Principalls, and you our Agents; it is a Truth which you cannot but acknowledge' (Richard Overton, *A Remonstrance of Many Thousand Citizens* [1646], p. 3; cf. Lorenzo Sabbadini, 'Popular Sovereignty and Representation in the English Civil War', in Richard Bourke and Quentin Skinner [eds], *Popular Sovereignty in Historical Perspective* [Cambridge: Cambridge University Press, 2017], pp. 164–86). See also William Walwyn, *Englands Lamentable Slaverie* (1645): 'a Parliamentary authority is a power intrusted by the people (that chose them) for their good, safetie and freedome; and . . . therefore a Parliament cannot justlie do any thing to make the people lesse safe or lesse free then they found them' (p. 3; and cf. Wootton, *Divine Right*, pp. 51–2), and Roger Williams, *The Bloudy Tenent of Persecution* (1644): 'the sovereign, original and foundation of civil power lies in the people' (Wootton, *Divine Right*, p. 243). It was a doctrine closely associated with regicide. On 4 January 1649, shortly before the execution of Charles I, Parliament had asserted that 'the people are, under God, the original of all just power' (quoted in Scott, *Commonwealth Principles*, p. 252). In the Putney Debates the pamphleteer John Wildman had said plainly that 'all government is in the free consent of the people' (Wootton, *Divine Right*, p. 299), and in 1653 John Streater would insist that 'power is essentially in the people' (Streater, *A Glympse of that Jewel*, p. 2; cf. Burton, *Diary*, vol. I, p. xxix). But in Carolean England the doctrine of popular sovereignty remained unsurprisingly deeply heterodox to those associated with the Court. As Sir Leoline Jenkins had said in the Commons on 11 November 1680, 'I have always taken it, that the Government had it's original, not from the People, but from God' (Grey, *Debates*, vol. VII, p. 447). In July 1683 the first of the 'damnable doctrines' that would be condemned by the University of Oxford was the proposition that 'All civil authority is derived originally from the people' (Kenyon, *Stuart Constitution*, pp. 471–4; Wootton, *Divine Right*, p. 121). The contrary position was also vigorously held, for instance by the author of *The Character*

*of a Popish Successour*, who argued that monarchy could arise in only two ways: either by conquest, or 'By the Choice of the People, who frequently in the beginning of the World, out of the natural desire of Safety, for the securing peaceful Community and Conversation, chose a single Person to be their head, as a proper Supreme Moderator in all Differences that might arise to disquiet that Community. Thus were Kings made for the People, and not the People for the King' (*State-Tracts*, vol. I, p. 162). In *The Art of Lawgiving* Harrington's subtle position had been that popular sovereignty was a necessary, fundamental, and yet also extra-constitutional element in a well-ordered commonwealth: 'An assembly of the people sovereign! Nay, and an assembly of the people consisting in the major vote of the lower sort! Why sure, it must be a dull, an unskilful thing. But so is the touchstone in a goldsmith's shop a dull thing, and altogether unskilled in the trade; yet without this would even the master be deceived' (Harrington, *Works*, p. 676). In letter 12 of *A Dissertation upon Parties* Bolingbroke had asserted that 'As all government began, so all government must end by the people' (Bolingbroke, *Political Writings*, p. 112). On the deep historical roots and early-modern flourishing of the doctrine of popular sovereignty, see most recently Daniel Lee, *Popular Sovereignty in Early Modern Constitutional Thought* (Oxford: Oxford University Press, 2016), esp. chapter 9; and for a survey by many hands of the concept over the *longue durée* from antiquity to the present, see Richard Bourke and Quentin Skinner (eds), *Popular Sovereignty in Historical Perspective* (Cambridge: Cambridge University Press, 2017). Cf. Joseph de Maistre, *On the Origins of Sovereignty*, book I, chapter 1: 'The people is a sovereign which cannot exercise sovereignty' (Joseph de Maistre, *Collected Works*, ed. Richard Lebrun [Charlottesville, VA: InteLex Corporation, 2008], 'Against Rousseau', p. 45).

21. *is now openly struck at*] i.e. in 1640, as the Long Parliament assembled: see above, p. 543, n. 61.

22. *But the people ... despotic tyrants*] The most vivid recent instance of this transition from sedition to military despotism in English history had occurred in 1655, when Cromwell had established a military government that in the *History of England* Hume described in terms close to those of this essay: 'the protector [Cromwell] instituted twelve major-generals; and divided the whole kingdom of England into so many military jurisdictions. These men, assisted by commissioners, had power to subject whom they pleased to decimation, to levy all the taxes imposed by the protector and his council, and to imprison any person who should be exposed to their jealous or suspicion; nor was there any appeal from them but to the protector himself and his council. Under colour of these powers, which were sufficiently exorbitant, the major-generals exercised an authority still more arbitrary, and acted as if absolute masters of the property and person of every subject. All reasonable men now concluded, that the very masque of

liberty was thrown aside, and that the nation was for ever subjugated to military and despotic government, exercised not in the legal manner of European nations, but according to the maxims of eastern tyranny. Not only the supreme magistrate owed his authority to illegal force and usurpation: He had parcelled out the people into so many subdivisions of slavery, and had delegated to his inferior ministers the same unlimited authority, which he himself had so violently assumed' (*History of England*, vol. VI, pp. 73-4).

23. *the present fury of the people . . . the fanaticism of religion*] Hume's sensitivity to popular agitation in England had perhaps been heightened by the Whig response to the Tudor volumes of his *History of England*, concerning which he wrote to Adam Smith on 28 July 1759: 'The Whigs, I am told, are anew in a Rage against me; tho' they know not how to vent themselves: For they are constrain'd to allow all my Facts' (*Letters*, vol. II, p. 313). Hume's tracing of political unrest to the root of 'the fanaticism of religion' has been endorsed by some recent scholars: 'all forms of radicalism in early-modern England had a religious origin. This was true both doctrinally and practically. Doctrinally, the problem for the disaffected within a Christian-monarchical polity was precisely that of rejecting Trinitarian orthodoxy, the intellectual underpinning of Church, King and Parliament. It could not be ignored or disregarded; the difficulty was to find an intellectual strategy which would permit escape from a political theology whose theoretical power and widespread reception walled in the dissident' (Clark, *English Society*, p. 277).

24. *a principle . . . law, reason, or authority*] Hume had previously described the particular perniciousness of party conflicts that are fuelled by religious sentiment and belief in the concluding section of 'Of Parties in General' (above, vol. 1, pp. 57-8).

25. *the malcontent party*] i.e. the Jacobites.

26. *They now find . . . human nature*] For the role played by Addison in this detoxification of Whiggism, see the 'Introduction' (above, vol. 1, pp. xv-xvi).

27. *abdicated family*] i.e. the House of Stuart. On the important political implications of the word 'abdicated', see above, p. 538-9, n. 42.

28. *the reproach of faction and innovation*] cf. the final sentence of 'Of the Original Contract' (above, p. 176).

29. *enure*] accustom, habituate (*OED*, 'enure', *v.* 1, 1 a).

## XV. OF THE PROTESTANT SUCCESSION

Published in: *1752a, 1752b, 1753, 1758, 1760, 1764, 1767, 1768, 1770, 1772, 1777a*

Significant revisions:

1) *1752a-1760* read: '. . . of the old *Gothic* militia, and . . .' (*1752a*, p. 266; cf. above, p. 189).

2) *1752a–1768* omit 'It appears . . . any government.' (above, p. 190).

3) *1752a–1768* append the following note, cued to '. . . powers and preroga-tives.' (*1752a*, p. 266; cf. above, p. 190):

'*IT appears from the speeches, and proclamations, and whole train of king *James* the I.'s actions, as well as his son's, that they consider'd the *English* government as a simple monarchy, and never imagin'd that any considerable part of their subjects entertain'd a contrary idea. This made them discover their pretensions, without preparing any force to support them; and even without reserve or disguise, which are always employ'd by those, who enter upon any new project, or endeavour to innovate in any government. King *James* told his parliament plainly, when they med-dled in state affairs, *Ne sutor ultra crepidam.* He us'd also, at his table, in promiscuous companies, to advance his notions, in a manner still more undisguis'd: As we may learn from a story told in the life of Mr. *Waller*, and which that poet us'd frequently to repeat. When Mr. *Waller* was young, he had the curiosity to go to court; and he stood in the circle, and saw king *James* dine, where, amongst other company, there sat at table two bishops. The king, openly and aloud, propos'd this question, *Whether he might not take his subjects money, when he had occasion for it, without all this formality of parliament.* The one bishop readily replied, *God forbid you shou'd not: For you are the breath of our nostrils.* The other bishop declin'd answering, and said he was not skill'd in parliamentary cases: But upon the king's urging him, and saying he wou'd admit of no evasion, his lordship replied very pleasantly, *Why then, I think your majesty may lawfully take my brother's money: For he offers it.* In Sir *Walter Raleigh*'s preface to the history of the world, there is this remarkable passage. *Philip the II. by strong hand and main force, attempted to make himself, not only an* absolute monarch *over the* Netherlands, *like unto the kings and sovereigns of* England *and* France; *but* Turk-like *to tread under his feet all their natural and fundamental laws, privileges and antient rights.* Spenser, speaking of some grants of the *English* kings to the *Irish* corporations, says, "All which, tho', at the time of their first grant, they were tolerable, and perhaps reasonable, yet now are most unreasonable and inconvenient. But all these will easily be cut off with the superior power of her maj-esty's prerogative, against which her own grants are not to be pleaded or enforc'd." *State of Ireland*, page 1537, Edit. 1706.

'As these were very common, tho' not, perhaps, the universal notions of the times, the two first princes of the house of *Stuart* were the more excus-able for their mistake. And *Rapin*, the most judicious of historians, seems sometimes to treat them with too much severity upon account of it.' (*1752a*, pp. 266–8, n. *).

*1758–1768* read: 'And RAPIN, suitable to his usual malignity and partiality, seems . . .' (*1758*, p. 267, n. k).

4) *1752a–1760* read: '... farther blinded them; and above all ...' (*1752a*, p. 267; cf. above, p. 190).

5) *1752a–1768* read: 'And the glory of the nation has spread itself all over *Europe*; while we stand the bulwark against oppression, and the great antagonist of that power, which threatens every people with conquest and subjection. So long ...' (*1752a*, pp. 271–2; cf. above, p. 192).

6) *1752a–1768* append the following note to '... a precarious establishment.' (*1752a*, p. 273; cf. above, p. 193):

'*THOSE who consider how universal this pernicious practice of funding has become all over *Europe* may perhaps dispute this last opinion. But we lay under less necessity than other states.' (*1752a*, p. 273, n. *).

7) *1752a–1768* insert the following paragraph after that ending '... sickly patient' (above, p. 193):

'THE advantages, which result from a parliamentary title, preferably to an hereditary one, tho' they are great, are too refin'd ever to enter into the conception of the vulgar. The bulk of mankind wou'd never allow them to be sufficient for committing what wou'd be regarded as an injustice to the prince. They must be supported by some gross, popular, and familiar topics; and wise men, tho' convinc'd of their force, wou'd reject them, in compliance with the weakness and prejudices of the people. An encroaching tyrant or deluded bigot alone, by his misconduct, is able to enrage the nation, and render practicable what was always, perhaps, desirable.' (*1752a*, p. 274).

8) *1752a–1768* insert the following paragraph after that ending '... our natural ally.' (above, p. 194):

'In the last war, it has been of service to us, by furnishing us with a considerable body of auxiliary troops, the bravest and most faithful in the world. The elector of *Hanover* is the only considerable prince in the empire, who has drove no separate end, and has rais'd up no stale pretensions, during the late commotions of *Europe*; but has acted, all along, with the dignity of a king of *Britain*. And ever since the accession of that family, 'twou'd be difficult to show any harm we have ever receiv'd from the electoral dominions, except that short disgust in 1718, with *Charles* the twelfth, who, regulating himself by maxims very different from those of other princes, made a personal quarrel of every public injury.' (*1752a*, pp. 275–6).

In *1764–1768* the following note is appended: '*This was published in the year 1752.' (*1764*, vol. I, p. 536, n. *).

9) *1752a–1760* read: '... abate the virulent acrimony of opposite ...' (*1752a*, p. 277; cf. above, p. 194).

10) *1752a–1768* add the following passage to the paragraph now ending '... entirely trusted.' (above, p. 194): 'The conduct of the *Saxon* family, where the same person can be a catholic king and a protestant elector, is, perhaps, the first instance, in modern times, of so reasonable and prudent a behaviour. And the gradual progress of the catholic superstition does, even there,

prognosticate a speedy alteration: After which, 'tis justly to be apprehended, that persecutions will put a speedy period to the protestant religion in the place of its nativity.' (*1752a*, p. 277).

11) *1752a–1768* add the following passage to the paragraph now ending '. . . hard to determine.' (above, p. 194): 'For my part, I esteem liberty so invaluable a blessing in society, that whatever favours its progress and security, can scarce be too fondly cherish'd by every one, who is a lover of human kind.' (*1752a*, pp. 277–8).

Copy text: *1777a*
Headnote:

Composed in late 1747, along with 'Of the Original Contract' and 'Of Passive Obedience' (see above, headnote to 'Of the Original Contract', pp. 524–5); however, first published only in the *Political Discourses* of 1752.

Hume, about to leave for the continent in the retinue of General St Clair, had entrusted his friend Charles Erskine with the decision of whether or not to publish 'Of the Protestant Succession', which Hume recognized might be controversial. His dispassionate, philosophical approach to this question – and, in particular, the measured and unideological consideration he gave to pro-Jacobite arguments – could, he realized, in the aftermath of the 1745 rebellion, be thought tepid to the point of disaffection: 'I hope I have examin'd this Question as coolly & impartially as if I were remov'd a thousand Years from the present Period: But this is what some People think extremely dangerous, & sufficient, not only to ruin me for ever, but also throw some Reflection on all my Friends, particularly those which whom I am connected at present' (*Letters*, vol. I, p. 112; cf. Harris, *Hume*, pp. 239–41, and the similar comments in Hume's letter to Lord Elibank of 8 January 1748 [Mossner, 'New Letters', p. 437]). A few days before Hume had struck the same note to Henry Home: 'I leave here two works going on, a new edition of my *Essays*, all of which you have seen, except one, *Of the Protestant Succession*, where I treat that subject as coolly and indifferently, as I would the dispute betwixt Caesar and Pompey. The conclusion shows me a Whig, but a very sceptical one' (*Letters*, vol. I, p. 111).

In the context of its likely reception, it is relevant to consider the possibility of an interaction between this essay and Robert Wallace's *Dissertation*. The final section of that work reads very much like an answer by Wallace to this essay of Hume's, which Wallace had been permitted to read in 1752 (*New Letters*, p. 30). Cf. especially Wallace's eulogy to Hanoverian kingship, in the context of the suppression of the '45: 'Indeed 'tis impossible to express, how great obligations every loyal subject to his Majesty, every zealous friend to the Protestant Succession, and every sincere assertor of the liberty of *Britain* has to those, whose hearty regard to the interest of their country has produced the happy prospect we have at present, of living for the future in peace, and seeing liberty penetrate into the most remote parts of the island' (Wallace, *Dissertation*, p. 156).

It is possible to detect in this essay a certain hardening and growing asperity of tone which would become one of the hallmarks of Hume's later style, evident also in the unpublished, post-1773, essay on the poems of Ossian (above, pp. 272–81). The movement from the suavity and stylistic elaborateness of the earlier essays to the occasional sarcasm and undisguised bitterness of the essays written later is perhaps a corollary of the darkening of Hume's assessment of British public life which has been noted by scholars. On the 'apocalyptic note' that Hume struck with increasing frequency in the last decade or so of his life, see Harris, *Hume*, pp. 437–8. Cf. also Hume's early comments on 'open or concealed . . . satire' in the *Treatise of Human Nature*, I.iii.13 (*THN*, pp. 102–3).

1.  *I suppose . . . consideration*] Twelve years later Hume would revert to this device of imagining the thoughts of a hypothetical actor at a moment of historical crisis when composing 'Of the Coalition of Parties' (above, pp. 181–7).
2.  See p. 552, n. 4, above.
3.  *It is in vain . . . fighting about*] cf. Sir William Temple, *Miscellanea*: 'those are the best Governments, where the best Men govern; and . . . the difference is not so great in the Forms of Magistracy, as in the Persons of Magistrates'; 'were the Constitution of any Government never so perfect, the Laws never so just, yet if the Administration be ill, ignorant, or corrupt, too rigid, or too remiss, too negligent or severe, there will be more just Occasion given of Discontent and Complaint, than from any Weakness or Fault in the original Conception or Institution of Government. For it may perhaps be concluded, with as much Reason as other Theams of the like Nature, That those are generally the best Governments where the best Men govern; and let the Sort or Scheme be what it will, those are ill Governments where ill Men govern, and are generally employ'd in the Offices of State' (Temple, *Works*, vol. I, pp. 105 and 259); cf. too *A Copy of a Letter from an Officer of the Army in Ireland* (1656), p. 18, where the maxim is quoted with powerful aversion: 'it matters not who Governs so they Govern well.' Hume perhaps also has in mind the famous lines on government from Pope's *An Essay on Man*, Epistle III, ll. 303–4: 'For Forms of Government let fools contest; / Whate'er is best administer'd is best.' Pope himself seems to be invoking a proverbial Latin maxim, 'res nolunt diu male administrari', current in English since the Venerable Bede: cf. Thomas Barlow, *The Genuine Remains* (1693), pp. 235–6. A distant and speculative source for the idea has been suggested in Aristotle, *Metaphysics*, XII.x.14:

'οὐ βούλεται πολιτεύεσθαι κακῶς', 'the world must not be governed badly'; cf. Sir Peter Pett, *The Happy Future State of England* (1688), p. 250. Cf. also Cicero, *De Inventione*, I.xxxiv. The maxim was frequently cited in the later seventeenth century: Sir William Petty, *A Treatise of Taxes and Contributions* (1662), sig. A3ᵛ, and *A Discourse Made Before the Royal Society* (1674), 'The Epistle Dedicatory'; Henry Neville, *Plato Redivivus* (1680), tp; William Payne, *The Unlawfulness of Stretching Forth the Hand* (1683), p. 31; William Penn, *A Perswasive to Moderation* (1685), p. 42. Walter Moyle reported that the maxim was a favourite of Robert Harley, Earl of Oxford (Walter Moyle, 'An Essay on the Lacedaemonian Government', in his *Whole Works* [1727], p. 60). By 1729, however, when Swift quoted it in a letter to Bolingbroke, it had evidently become trite: 'Pray will you please to take your pen and blot me out that political maxim from whatever book it is in: that *Res nolunt diu male administrari*; the commonness makes me not know who is the author, but sure he must be some Modern' (Swift, *Correspondence*, vol. III, p. 230; cf. vol. II, p. 78; and Swift, *Prose Writings*, vol. VIII, p. 180, and vol. XII, p. 309).

4. *How could . . . wars and convulsions?*] From the outset of his career Hume had been convinced of the real disadvantages of elective monarchy, notwithstanding its specious attractions. In the *Treatise of Human Nature*, III. ii.10, he had explained the naturalness of hereditary succession: 'When neither long possession, nor present possession, not conquest take place, as when the first sovereign, who founded any monarchy, dies; in that case, the right of *succession* naturally prevails in their stead, and men are commonly induc'd to place the son of their late monarch on the throne, and suppose him to inherit his father's authority. The presum'd consent of the father, the imitation of the succession to private families, the interest, which the state has in choosing the person, who is most powerful, and has the most numerous followers; all these reasons lead men to prefer the son of their late monarch to any other person' (*THN*, pp. 357–8). It was a point to which he had returned in 'That Politics may be reduced to a Science': 'This chief magistrate may be either *elective* or *hereditary*; and though the former institution may, to a superficial view, appear the most advantageous; yet a more accurate inspection will discover in it greater inconveniencies than in the latter, and such as are founded on causes and principles eternal and immutable. The filling of the throne, in such a government, is a point of too great and too general interest, not to divide the whole people into factions: Whence a civil war, the greatest of ills, may be apprehended, almost with certainty, upon every vacancy' (above, vol. I, p. 26). He would again return to the inconveniences of elective monarchy in 'Of the Original Contract': 'Nor can any thing be more unhappy than a despotic government of this kind; where the succession is disjointed and irregular, and must be determined, on every vacancy, by force or election' (above, p. 175). In taking this

line, Hume was following Bolingbroke, who had made a similar point in his *The Idea of a Patriot King*: 'Nothing can be more absurd, in pure speculation, than an hereditary right in any mortal to govern other men: and yet, in practice, nothing can be more absurd than to have a king to choose at every vacancy of a throne' (Bolingbroke, *Political Writings*, p. 229); cf. also Bolingbroke's observation that among the Saxons 'birth, instead of merit, became, for the sake of order and tranquillity, a title to the throne' (ibid., p. 115). In 1776 (and probably influenced more by Hume than by Bolingbroke) Gibbon would echo this prudential argument for hereditary succession in the opening sentences of chapter 7 of *The Decline and Fall*: 'Of the various forms of government, which have prevailed in the world, an hereditary monarchy seems to present the fairest scope for ridicule. Is it possible to relate, without an indignant smile, that, on the father's decease, the property of a nation, like that of a drove of oxen, descends to his infant son, as yet unknown to mankind and to himself; and that the bravest warriors and the wisest statesmen, relinquishing their natural right to empire, approach the royal cradle with bended knees and protestations of inviolable fidelity? Satire and declamation may paint these obvious topics in the most dazzling colours, but our more serious thoughts will respect a useful prejudice, that establishes a rule of succession, independent of the passions of mankind; and we shall cheerfully acquiesce in any expedient which deprives the multitude of the dangerous, and indeed the ideal, power of giving themselves a master' (Gibbon, *Decline and Fall*, vol. I, p. 187). For discussion of the survival in England throughout the eighteenth century of the hereditary principle, see Clark, *English Society*, pp. 119–98.

5. *the ROMAN empire . . . to be envied*] cf. Hume's expanded comments on the disruptions in the Roman Empire leading up to and following changes of ruler in 'Of the Original Contract' (above, pp. 173–5). Cf. Machiavelli, *The Prince*, chapter 19 (Machiavelli, *Works*, pp. 223–7).

6. *Eastern nations . . . soldiery*] The instability of the despotic governments of the eastern Mediterranean, particularly the Ottoman Empire, whose sultans were often at the mercy of their elite soldiery, the Janissaries, was a topic in early-modern European political thought (on which see Malcolm, *Useful Enemies*, pp. 237–8, 242, 353, 367, 369 and 410). In *The Present State of the Ottoman Empire* (third edition, 1670), Paul Rycaut had noted that the Grand Signior and his principal ministers had frequently suffered fatally from the mutinies of the Janissaries (p. 193), and had reported that the 'present *Sultan Mahomet* still retaining the memory and impression of the amazement he suffered in his infancy on occasion of a dangerous combination and conspiracy of the *Janizaries*, will never confide himself to their guard' (pp. 198–9). It is possible that Hume's information about the instability of the Ottoman Empire derives most immediately from the *Relation d'un voyage du Levant*, 2 vols (Paris, 1717), of Joseph Pitton de

Tournefort, which he had cited in 'Of the Populousness of Ancient Nations' (above, p. 141): 'Les Sultans de crainte qu'on ne les trouvât desarmez, se sont fait des chaînes à eux-mêmes & à leur posterité, en instituant une milice formidable, qui subsiste également en temps de paix & en temps de guerre. Les Janissaires & les Spahis balancent tellement la puissance du Prince, quelqu absolu qu'il soit, qui'ils on quelquefois l'insolence de lui demander sa tête. Ils déposent les Empereurs & en créent de nouveaux avec plus de facilité que les troupes Romaines ne le faisoient dans leurs temps: c'est un frein pour les Sultans qui empêche la Tyrannie' (vol. II, p. 4).

7. *It is but a foolish wisdom . . . mankind*] cf. also the comments in 'Whether the British Government Inclines More to Absolute Monarchy, or to a Republic' on the waning of deference in English political life since 1688: 'Most people, in this island, have divested themselves of all superstitious reverence to names and authority: The clergy have much lost their credit: Their pretensions and doctrines have been ridiculed; and even religion can scarcely support itself in the world. The mere name of *king* commands little respect; and to talk of a king as GOD's vicegerent on earth, or to give him any of those magnificent titles, which formerly dazzled mankind, would but excite laughter in every one' (above, vol. 1, pp. 50–51). In his letter to Lord Minto of 1 May 1760, writing a propos Frederick II's publication of his unguarded views of Christianity, Hume commented: 'These Freedoms surely belong not to any body; much less, to People that are in such a precarious & dependant Situation as Kings: They ought at least to leave them to their Betters' (*Letters*, vol. I, p. 327). A few months later, after the accession of George III on 25 October 1760, Hume struck the same note in a letter to William Strahan: 'I wonder how Kings dare be so free: They ought to leave that to their Betters; to Men who have no Dependance on the Mob, or the Leaders of the Mob. As to poor Kings they are obligd sometimes to retract and to deny their Writings' (*Letters*, vol. I, p. 336). However, Hume was not in fact so well armoured against the strong charm of monarchy. When he was introduced to Louis XV in October 1763, he reported to Adam Smith: 'The King said nothing particular to me, when I was introducd to him; and (can you imagine it) I was become so silly as to be a little mortify'd by it, till they told me, that he never says any thing to any body, the first time he sees them' (*Letters*, vol. I, p. 408). This slight change in Hume's attitude towards monarchs is also suggested by his deletion after *1768* of the passage towards the end of 'Of the Parties of Great Britain' concerning the 'Weakness, Folly, and Arrogance of Monarchs', who are said to be 'nothing superior, if not rather inferior, to the rest of Mankind' (above, vol. 1, pp. 256–7).

8. *it violates hereditary right . . . dignity*] This was not, however, how the Hanoverians themselves saw their title. Although George I had been fifty-eighth in line to the throne in 1714, he had begun his first speech to Parliament

by claiming that it had 'pleased Almighty God, of his good Providence, to call me to the throne of my ancestors' (quoted in Clark, *English Society*, p. 134). In *The Idea of a Patriot King* Bolingbroke had poured scorn on the project of reconciling the tenure of the Hanoverians with the principle of hereditary right: 'I have an imperfect remembrance, that some scribbler was employed, or employed himself, to assert the hereditary right of the present royal family. A task so unnecessary to any good purpose, that, I believe, a suspicion arose of its having been designed for a bad one' (Bolingbroke, *Political Writings*, p. 246).

9. *It is evident ... establishment*] Hume seems to date the rise in the political importance of the commons from the Reformation; cf. what he would say about the 'property, acquired of late by the commons' in 'Of the Coalition of Parties' (above, p. 184). The point owes a broad debt to Harrington and the emphasis he had placed on changing patterns of property ownership (see above, vol. 1, p. 230, n. 6).

10. *mercenary armies*] Hume here touches on the subject of standing armies and militias, which had been a topic of controversy in England since 1698, a matter of political sensitivity before that, and was not an entirely spent issue as late as 1747. See most recently David Womersley (ed.), *Writings on Standing Armies* (Indianapolis, IN: Liberty Fund, 2020).

11. *some of our BRITISH sovereigns*] i.e. the Stuarts.

12. *It appears ... contrary idea*] In the *History of England*, Hume would go some way towards justifying the expansive notions that James I entertained of his kingly authority. He notes that, at the moment of James's accession on 24 March 1603, 'a great many' of the people believed 'monarchy, simple and unmixed, was ... the government of England; and those popular assemblies were supposed to form only the ornament of the fabric, without being, in any degree, essential to its being and existence' (*History of England*, vol. V, p. 127). As a result of 'these exalted ideas of kingly authority, the prerogative, besides the articles of jurisdiction, founded on precedent, was, by many supposed to possess an inexhaustible fund of latent powers, which might be exerted on any emergence. In every government, necessity, when real, supersedes all laws, and levels all limitations: But, in the English government, convenience alone was conceived to authorize any extraordinary act of regal power, and to render it obligatory on the people. Hence the strict obedience required to proclamations, during all periods of the English history; and, if James has incurred blame on account of his edicts, it is only because he too frequently issued them at a time, when they began to be less regarded, not because he first assumed or extended to an unusual degree that exercise of authority' (ibid., pp. 127–8). And he concluded: 'Upon the whole, we must conceive that monarchy, on the accession of the house of Stuart, was possessed of a very extensive authority: An authority, in the judgment of all, not exactly

limited; in the judgment of some, not limitable. But, at the same time, this authority was founded merely on the opinion of the people, influenced by ancient precedent and example. It was not supported either by money or by force of arms. And, for this reason, we need not wonder, that the princes of that line were so extremely jealous of their prerogative; being sensible, that, when those claims were ravished from them, they possessed no influence, by which they could maintain their dignity, or support the laws' (ibid., p. 128).

13. *that of the clergy ... arbitrary power*] Once again, Hume had slightly modified his position on this point by the time he came to write the *History of England*: 'the principles in general which prevailed during that age, were so favourable to monarchy, that they bestowed on it an authority almost absolute and unlimited, sacred and indefeasible ... The prerogative of the crown was represented by lawyers as something real and durable; like those eternal essences of the schools, which no time or force could alter. The sanction of religion was, by divines, called in aid; and the monarch of heaven was supposed to be interested in supporting the authority of his earthly vicegerent. And though it is pretended, that these doctrines were more openly inculcated and more strenuously insisted on during the reign of the Stuarts, they were not then invented; and were only found by the court to be more necessary at that period, by reason of the opposite doctrines, which *began* to be promulgated by the puritanical party' (*History of England*, vol. V, p. 127).

14. *choose a prince ... privileges of the people*] For the different conception of their title entertained by the Hanoverians, see above, pp. 566–7, n. 8. Such disillusioned comments would undoubtedly have been found inflammatory in 1747, so soon after the Jacobite rebellion of 1745. Gibbon, however, would find Hume's dispassionate analysis of the impurity of the Hanoverian title (being at once elective and hereditary) attractive in 1790 when composing his *Antiquities of the House of Brunswick*, which begins: 'An English subject may be prompted, by a just and liberal curiosity, to investigate the origin and story of the House of Brunswick, which, after an alliance with the daughters of our kings, has been called by the voice of a free people to the legal inheritance of the Crown' (Edward Gibbon, *Miscellaneous Works*, 2 vols [1796], vol. II, p. 637).

15. *the lineal heir*] i.e. the son of James II, James Francis Edward Stuart, known as the Old Pretender.

16. *foreign dominions*] The continental commitments of the Hanoverians were indeed from time to time a source of political difficulty and resentment in England after 1714. For an authoritative account of a particularly fraught episode in the relationship between Hanover and England later in the century, see T. C. W. Blanning, '"That Horrid Electorate" or "Ma Patrie Germanique"? George III, Hanover and the *Fürstenbund* of 1785',

*Historical Journal*, XX (1977), pp. 311–44, and note his comment on p. 314: '"Chained to a rotting corpse" is not perhaps quite the image for the relationship between Electorate and Kingdom – however much certain English politicians would have relished the description.'

17. *a philosopher alone, who is of neither party*] cf. 'Of the Original Contract': 'philosophers, who have embraced a party (if that be not a contradiction in terms) . . .' (above, p. 163).

18. *Or if he indulges . . . unfit judges*] Another instance of Hume's later asperity of tone. Such outspoken contempt for the judgement of the multitude makes an interesting contrast with Hume's own statement of the original purpose of these essays, which was precisely to forge connections and links between the worlds of learning and society at large, thereby to render learning more social and society more learned. See the 'Advertisement' to *1741* (above, pp. 285–6).

19. *above eighty years*] i.e. from the accession of James I in 1603 to the abdication of James II in 1688.

20. *a foreign power*] i.e. France, which began to dominate Europe during the reign of Louis XIV.

21. *with our assistance*] It was notorious that Cromwell – for whom on religious grounds the principal European enemy was Spain – had negotiated two treaties of mutual aid and assistance with Cardinal Mazarin, one signed on 24 October 1655 and the other on 13/23 March 1657 (the Treaty of Paris). Cromwell had been concerned that the French would support domestic attempts to unseat him, and on 10 April 1655 Mazarin wrote to Bordeaux, the French ambassador in England, asking him to assure Cromwell that 'we are not to be persuaded to be interested in all those attempts, which are made to weaken his authority . . . we would never hearken here, directly or indirectly, to any propositions of commotions in England' (*A Collection of the State Papers of John Thurloe*, 7 vols [1742], vol. III, p. 327). The second of these treaties contained secret articles providing for mutual military aid. For censure of Cromwell's policy towards France, see Slingsby Bethel, *The World's Mistake in Oliver Cromwell* (1668), reprinted in *State-Tracts*, vol. I, pp. 366–74, relevant passages on pp. 370–71. For modern scholarly commentary on the question of Interregnum diplomacy, see David L. Smith, 'Diplomacy and the Religious Question: Mazarin, Cromwell, and the Treaties of 1655 and 1657', *e-Rea*, 11, 2 (2014); François Saulnier, 'La diplomatie française et la République d'Angleterre, 1649–1658', Diss. Université de Paris IV Sorbonne, 1999; and Steven Pincus, *Protestantism and Patriotism: Ideologies and the Making of English Foreign Policy, 1650–1668* (Cambridge: Cambridge University Press, 1996). This caressing of France would continue after the restoration of the Stuarts in 1660. On 22 May 1670 Charles II had signed the secret Treaty of Dover with France, under the terms of

which he received payments from Louis XIV in return for military help against the Dutch, and a public declaration of his conversion to Roman Catholicism. Bolingbroke had insisted that these negotiations and receipts of money from Louis XIV 'were the King's negotiations', not those of his ministers (Bolingbroke, *Political Writings*, p. 33).

22. *these last sixty years*] i.e. since 1688.

23. *two rebellions*] In 1715 and 1745.

24. *plots and conspiracies without number*] Besides the two actual rebellions of 1715 and 1745 and the attempted invasions of Scotland by French forces in 1708, 1719 and 1722, there were potentially serious Jacobite plots and conspiracies in the 1690s (the Ailesbury plot of 1691–2, the Fenwick plot of 1695, and the assassination plot of 1696) and throughout the reigns of George I and George II, including the Atterbury plot of 1722. There is a large and growing literature on Jacobitism, but on this particular aspect of it, see Bruce Lenman, *The Jacobite Risings in Britain 1689–1746* (London: Eyre Methuen, 1980). In letter 6 of his *A Dissertation upon Parties* Bolingbroke had, however, noted that the allegation of Jacobitism might be flung about indiscriminately: 'any man who declares against a certain person . . . is sure to be followed by the cry of Jacobitism' (Bolingbroke, *Political Writings*, p. 49).

25. *the narrow genius . . . establishment*] By 'narrow genius' Hume may be alluding to the Stuarts' inflexible adherence to the theory of divine-right monarchy. The conversion of the Young Pretender, Charles Edward Stuart, to Protestantism in 1750 would demonstrate that he at least had realized Roman Catholicism posed an insuperable obstacle to ascending the English throne.

26. *not yet antiquated*] In 1747 the Jacobite threat remained practically viable, and the claim of the Stuarts to the throne of England was still acknowledged by many as superior to that of the Hanoverians. As late as 1777 Samuel Johnson would insist that 'the state of the country is this: the people knowing it to be agreed on all hands that this King [George III] has not the hereditary right to the crown, and there being no hope that he who has it [Charles Edward Stuart, the Young Pretender] can be restored, have grown cold and indifferent upon the subject of loyalty, and have no warm attachment to any King. They would not, therefore, risk any thing to restore the exiled family. They would not give twenty shillings a piece to bring it about. But, if a mere vote could do it, there would be twenty to one; at least, there would be a very great majority of voices for it' (Boswell, *Life of Johnson*, pp. 606–7). In *The Idea of a Patriot King* Bolingbroke had stigmatized 'every Jacobite, at this time [a useful parenthesis, given his own past, compromised, conduct]' as 'a rebel to the constitution under which he is born, as well as to the prince on the throne. The law of his country has settled the right of succession in a new family. He resists this law, and

asserts, on his own private authority, not only a right in contradiction to it, but a right extinguished by it' (Bolingbroke, *Political Writings*, p. 267). Gibbon, however, located the extinguishing of the remnants of Jacobite sentiment (which had been strong in his family, and which as a teenager he had shared) to the late 1750s and to the accession of George III in 1760: 'The most beneficial effect of this institution [the militia] was to eradicate among the Country gentlemen the relicks of Tory, or rather of Jacobite prejudice. The accession of a British king [George III] reconciled them to the government, and even to the court; but they have been since accused of transferring their passive loyalty from the Stuarts to the family of Brunswick; and I have heard Mr. Burke exclaim in the House of Commons, "They have changed the Idol, but they have preserved the Idolatry"' (Gibbon, *Autobiographies*, p. 182).

27. *by the late peace*] The Treaty of Aix-la-Chapelle (18 October 1748) had concluded the War of the Austrian Succession (1740–48). This detail must therefore have been added after the main body of the essay had been written in the summer of 1747.

28. *the pernicious practice . . . incumbrances*] The growth in the public debt had drawn dismayed comments from Hume in 'Of Civil Liberty' and 'Of Public Credit' (above, vol. 1, p. 82 and vol. 2, pp. 75–87). See the headnote to 'Of Public Credit' (above, pp. 386–8), and cf. Harris, *Hume*, pp. 436–7.

29. *that parliament which recalled the royal family*] i.e. the Convention Parliament of 1660.

30. *Duke of York*] i.e. the future James II.

31. *Duke of . . . Gloucester*] The younger brother of Charles II and the Duke of York, who died of smallpox on 13 September 1660, less than four months after the Restoration of May 1660.

32. *like a quack with a sickly patient*] Given Hume's familiarity with the writings of Swift, it is possible that this image of a mischievous and irresponsible physician owes a general debt to Swift's satire against physicians in *Gulliver's Travels*, Part IV, chapter 6, whom Gulliver describes as 'a Sort of People bred up among us, in the Profession or Pretence of curing the Sick': 'One great Excellency in this Tribe is their Skill at *Prognosticks*, wherein they seldom fail; their Predictions in real Diseases, when they rise to any Degree of Malignity, generally portending *Death*, which is always in their Power, when Recovery is not: And therefore, upon any unexpected Signs of Amendment, after they have pronounced their Sentence, rather than be accused as false Prophets, they know how to approve their Sagacity to the World by a seasonable Dose' (*Gulliver's Travels*, pp. 377–8 and 380–81). Cf. also the image of the timid physician at the beginning of 'Whether the British Government Inclines More to Absolute Monarchy, or to a Republic' (above, vol. 1, p. 48). The image of the politician as a state physician has a definite Whig pedigree: see, e.g., Neville, *Plato*, p. 10.

NOTES TO PP. 193–4

This had been noted at the time, as the title of Thomas Goddard's attack on Neville, *Plato's Demon: or, the State-Physician Unmaskt* (1684), sufficiently shows.

33. *on account of their religion*] i.e. their Roman Catholicism: an issue that Charles Edward Stuart would address in 1750 by his conversion to the Church of England (see above, p. 570, n. 25).

34. *no foreign dominions*] On the political consequences of the German territories held by the Hanoverians, see above, pp. 568–9, n. 16.

35. *the laws of the empire*] The internal constitutional arrangements of the Holy Roman Empire had been settled by the Peace of Westphalia (1648).

36. *AUSTRIA, our natural ally*] In the first half of the eighteenth century British foreign policy had tended to see Austria as Britain's natural European partner in a shared strategy of containment of Bourbon France; but this traditional alliance would be disrupted during the Seven Years' War by the British alliance with Prussia. See D. B. Horn, *Great Britain and Europe in the Eighteenth Century* (Oxford: Clarendon Press, 1967).

37. *on a foreigner*] i.e. the Pope. As king of England George II was also Supreme Governor of the Church of England, thereby uniting in his own person the regal and the sacerdotal office.

38. *But the settlement . . . actually taken place*] Hume would explain his prescriptive understanding of political legitimacy to Catherine Macaulay on 29 March 1764: 'I look upon all kinds of subdivision of power, from the monarchy of France to the freest democracy of some Swiss Cantons, to be equally legal, if established by custom and authority' (*New Letters*, p. 81). This was no new opinion for Hume, since it can be traced back to the *Treatise of Human Nature*, III.ii.10: 'The *first* of those principles I shall take notice of, as a foundation of the right of magistracy, is that which gives authority to almost all the establish'd governments of the world: I mean, *long possession* in any one form of government, or succession of princes. 'Tis certain, that if we remount to the first origin of every nation, we shall find, that there scarce is any race of kings, or form of a commonwealth, that is not primarily founded on usurpation and rebellion, and whose title is not at first worse than doubtful and uncertain. Time alone gives solidity to their right; and operating gradually on the minds of men, reconciles them to any authority, and makes it seem just and reasonable'; 'Time and custom give authority to all forms of government, and all successions of princes; and that power, which at first was founded only on injustice and violence, becomes in time legal and obligatory' (*THN*, pp. 356 and 362). A passage from letter 9 of Bolingbroke's *A Dissertation upon Parties*, affirming the political watershed formed by 1688, is also apposite: 'Our constitution is no longer a mystery; the power of the crown is now exactly limited, the chimera of prerogative removed, and the rights of the subject are no longer problematical, though some things necessary

to the more effectual security of them may be still wanting. Under this constitution the greatest part of the men now alive were born. They lie under no pretence of obligation to any other, and to the support of this they are bound by all the ties of society, and all the motives of interest' (Bolingbroke, *Political Writings*, p. 78).

39. *called to mount our throne*] A deft phrase that evidently impressed Gibbon, who in his *Antiquities of the House of Brunswick* would echo it in describing how the then reigning royal family 'has been called by the voice of a free people to the legal inheritance of the Crown' (Edward Gibbon, *Miscellaneous Works*, 2 vols [1796], vol. II, p. 637).

40. *They have ... laws and constitution*] This bland attribution to the Hanoverians of 'mildness, equity, and regard to the laws and constitution' is an implicit rebuttal of a strain of Jacobite rhetoric, which after the suppression of the 1715 and 1745 rebellions had presented George I and George II as bloodthirsty tyrants, often through the mordantly ironic description of them as clement: see, e.g. *An Address to the People of England, Shewing the Unworthiness of their Behaviour to King George* (1715), pp. 23-4. For discussion, see Ian Higgins, *Swift's Politics* (Cambridge: Cambridge University Press, 1994), pp. 175-6. Swift wrote bitterly to Robert Cope on 9 October 1722, after the discovery of the conspiracy of Francis Atterbury, Bishop of Rochester and Dean of Westminster, to restore the House of Stuart: 'It is a wonderful thing to see the Tories provoking his present majesty, whose clemency, mercy, and forgiving temper, have been so signal, so extraordinary, so more than humane, during the whole course of his reign' (Swift, *Correspondence*, vol. II, p. 432).

41. *Not to mention ... disputed title*] The Hanoverians had been on the throne since 1714, a mere thirty-three years before the composition of this essay. In the *Treatise of Human Nature*, III.ii.10, Hume had required a much longer passage of time to establish a new dynasty: 'a century is scarce sufficient to establish any new government, or remove all scruples in the minds of the subjects concerning it' (*THN*, p. 356). The recent Jacobite rebellion in 1745 had shown that 'all scruples' concerning Hanoverian kingship had indeed not yet been removed.

42. *A calamity ... bring upon us*] Hume's late letters occasionally echo this gloomy prediction: 'I am delighted to see the daily and hourly Progress of Madness and Folly and Wickedness in England. The Consummation of these Qualities are the true Ingredients for making a fine Narrative in History; especially if followd by some signal and ruinous Convulsion, as I hope will soon be the Case with that pernicious People [i.e. the English]'; 'You say I am of a desponding Character: On the contrary, I am of a very sanguine Disposition. Notwithstanding my Age, I hope to see a public Bankruptcy, the total Revolt of America, the Expulsion of the English from the East Indies, the Diminution of London to less than a half, and the Restoration of the

Government to the King, Nobility, and Gentry of this Realm' (*Letters*, vol. II, pp. 208 and 210).

## XVI. IDEA OF A PERFECT COMMONWEALTH

Published in: *1752a, 1752b, 1753, 1754, 1758, 1760, 1764, 1767, 1768, 1770, 1772, 1777a*

Significant revisions:

1) *1752a–1768* read: 'OF all mankind, there are none so pernicious as political projectors, if they have power; nor so ridiculous, if they want it: As on the other hand, a wise politician is the most beneficial character in nature, if accompany'd with authority, and the most innocent, and not altogether useless, even if depriv'd of it. 'Tis not with forms of government . . .' (*1752a*, p. 281; cf. above, p. 196).

2) *1752a–1752b* read: 'Let all the freeholders in the country parishes, and those who pay scot and lot in the town parishes, meet annually . . .' (*1752a*, p. 285; cf. above, p. 198).

*1753–1768* read: 'Let all the freeholders of ten pounds a-year in the country, and all the householders worth 200 pounds in the town parishes, meet annually . . .' (*1753*, vol. IV, p. 253).

3) *1752a–1768* read: '. . . a number of people, Good sense is one thing: But follies are numberless; and every man has a different one. The only way of making people wise is to keep them from uniting into large assemblies.' (*1752a*, p. 295; cf. above, p. 203).

4) *1752a–1768* read: '. . . to prevent brigue and faction . . .' (*1752a*, p. 296; cf. above, p. 204).

5) *1752a–1758* read: 'Not to mention their annual election, by almost the whole body of the people.' (*1752a*, p. 298; cf. above, p. 205).

6) *1752a–1768* read: '. . . of the United provinces, formerly one of the wisest and most renown'd governments, that ever was in the world.' (*1752a*, p. 299; cf. above, p. 205).

7) *1752a–1768* read: '. . . The plan of the republican parliament ought to be . . .' (*1752a*, p. 300; cf. above, p. 206).

8) *1752a–1752b* read: '. . . who possess not a hundred a year.' (*1752a*, p. 300; cf. above, p. 206).

9) *1752a–1768* read: '. . . ought to be remov'd, whose behaviour, *in former parliaments*, destroy'd entirely the authority of that house: The number . . .' (*1752a*, p. 300; cf. above, p. 206).

10) *1752a–1768* read: '. . . keeping up a standing army. 'Tis evident, that this is a mortal distemper in the *British* government, of which it must at last inevitably perish. I must, however, confess, that *Sweden* seems, in some measure, to have remedy'd this inconvenience, and to have a militia, along

with its limited monarchy, as well as a standing army, which is less dangerous than the *British*.' (*1752a*, pp. 301–2; cf. above, p. 206).

Copy text: *1777a*

Headnote:

With this essay Hume took his place in the long line of thinkers who have sketched ideal political constitutions. Important predecessors in this project include Plato (*The Republic*) and Sir Thomas More (*Utopia*). In Book II of *Politics* Aristotle gives a survey of such ideal commonwealths, and he notes that Hippodamus, the son of Euryphon, was 'the first man not engaged in politics who attempted to speak on the subject of the best form of constitution' (*Politics*, II.v.i). The heroic legislators of antiquity – Lycurgus, Solon, Numa – were also unmistakably involved in the project of constitutional design. For Hume's antipathy to these figures, see Meehan, *Liberty*, p. 63.

In 'Whether the British Government Inclines More to Absolute Monarchy, or to a Republic' Hume had written, it seemed dismissively, of 'any fine imaginary republic, of which a man may form a plan in his closet' (above, vol. 1, p. 51). In adopting this stance Hume was following in the footsteps of both Machiavelli and Locke. In chapter 15 of *The Prince* Machiavelli had explained how his purpose in writing about politics was distinct from the Utopian tradition: 'my intention being to write for the benefit and advantage of him who understands, I thought it more convenient to respect the essential verity, than the imagination of the thing (and many have fram'd imaginary Commonwealths and Governments to themselves which were never seen, nor had any real existence) for the present manner of living is so different from the way that ought to be taken, that he who neglects what is done, to follow what ought to be done, will sooner learn how to ruine, than how to preserve himself' (Machiavelli, *Works*, p. 219). Locke, in the 'First Treatise', § 81, had asserted something similar: 'Ideas of Government in the Fancy, though never so perfect, though never so right, cannot give Laws, nor prescribe Rules to the Actions of Men . . .' (Locke, *Two Treatises*, p. 202). The same cautionary note would be struck later, in a more elaborate manner, by Adam Smith, whose comments on political idealism, added to *The Theory of Moral Sentiments* in the sixth edition of 1790, are apposite, and may guide us in our attempts to grasp the deeper purpose of Hume's essay: 'The man of system . . . is apt to be very wise in his own conceit; and is often so enamoured with the supposed beauty of his own ideal plan of government, that he cannot suffer the smallest deviation from any part of it. He goes on to establish it completely and in all its parts, without any regard either to the great interests, or to the strong prejudices which may oppose it. He seems to imagine that he can arrange the different members of a great society with as much ease as the hand arranges the different pieces upon a chess-board . . . Some general, and even systematical, idea of the perfection of policy and law, may no doubt be necessary for directing the views of the statesman. But to insist upon establishing, and upon establishing all at once, and in spite of all opposition, every thing which that idea may seem to require, must often be the highest degree of arrogance. It is to erect his own judgment into the supreme standard of right and wrong. It is to fancy himself the only wise and worthy man in the commonwealth, and that his fellow-citizens should accommodate themselves to him and not he to them' (Smith, *Theory*, VI.ii.2.17–18, pp. 233–4).

Nevertheless, Hume chose to end *Political Discourses* (1752) with a sketch of just such an imaginary constitution, modelled in certain respects on that described in great detail by James Harrington in *Oceana* (1656): for commentary, see Harris, *Hume*, pp. 286–8. This essay may have drawn an implicit retort from Robert Wallace, who in his *Dissertation* had asserted that 'it would be the greatest degree of madness to exchange the present happy constitution of this country, for the most perfect ideal one, which imagination could delineate' (Wallace, *Dissertation*, p. 106). (In the year preceding publication of the *Dissertation* Hume had arranged for Wallace to be sent a copy of *Political Discourses* [*New Letters*, p. 30].) In letter 13 of *A Dissertation upon Parties* Bolingbroke had reported Tacitus as holding the view that the design of a mixed form of government made up of the three simple forms was 'rather a subject of fine speculation than of practice' (Bolingbroke, *Political Writings*, p. 128). And in his *Idea of a Patriot King*, Bolingbroke had attacked constitutional idealism with even more vigour: 'We must tell ourselves once for all, that perfect schemes are not adapted to our imperfect state; that Stoical morals and Platonic politics are nothing better than amusements for those who have had little experience in the affairs of the world, and who have much leisure' (Bolingbroke, *Political Writings*, p. 230).

According to Nicholas Phillipson, this essay is 'Hume's reply to Harrington, providing an imaginary model of a modern British polity in a post-Walpolian era to replace Harrington's image of a post-Cromwellian republic' (Phillipson, 'Propriety', p. 319). Given Hume's evident wariness about such imaginary models, might not this essay, however, be pursuing its goals in a more subtle and oblique manner? Might it not be that Hume, implicitly replying to those such as Bolingbroke who tirelessly and tediously praised the English constitution as an ideal (e.g. Bolingbroke, *Political Writings*, p. 163), constructed such an ideal, and then allowed its difference from the actual English constitution to sink in. Nevertheless, one should not forget Hume's comments in a letter of December 1775 to his nephew: 'I cannot but agree with Mr Millar, that the Republican Form of [Government] is by far the best. The antient Republics were somewhat ferocious, and torn [internally] by bloody Factions; but they were still much more preferable to the Monarchies or [Aristocracies] which seem to have been quite intolerable. Modern Manners have corrected this Abuse; and all the Republics in Europe, without Exception, are so well govern'd, that one is at a Loss to which we shoud give the Preference. But what is this general Subject of Speculation to our Purpose?' (*Letters*, vol. II, p. 306).

On the general siren-subject of constitutional design, the tart comment of Jacob Burckhardt (written in full awareness of the constitution of the United States) is still salutary: 'The great modern fallacy that a constitution can be made, can be manufactured by a combination of existing forces and tendencies, was constantly cropping up [among the Florentines] in stormy times; even Machiavelli is not wholly free from it. Constitutional artists were never wanting who by an ingenious distribution and division of political power, by indirect election of the most complicated kind, by the establishment of nominal offices, sought to found a lasting order of things, and to satisfy or deceive the rich and the poor alike' (Burckhardt, *Renaissance*, p. 54).

1. *engine*] A contrivance or means (not necessarily mechanical in nature): see *OED*, 'engine', *n.*, I 2.
2. *infinite advantage ... established*] cf. the similar sentiments in 'Of the Protestant Succession' (above, pp. 194–5) and perhaps particularly at the end of 'Of the Original Contract' (above, pp. 176).
3. *The mathematicians ... discovery*] Huygens had investigated ship design as part of his work for the French government between 1665 and 1681. Columbus had discovered America on 12 October 1492, and Drake had circumnavigated the globe between 1577 and 1580.
4. *A long dissertation ... chimerical*] Perhaps a reference to Harrington's *Oceana* (1656), which entered into sometimes fantastic and redundant detail. Cf. Hume's comment on this author and his work in the *History of England*: 'Harrington's Oceana was well adapted to that age, when the plans of imaginary republics were the daily subjects of debate and conversation; and even in our time it is justly admired as a work of genius and invention. The idea, however, of a perfect and immortal commonwealth will always be found as chimerical as that of a perfect and immortal man. The style of this author wants ease and fluency; but the good matter, which his work contains, makes compensation' (*History of England*, vol. VI, p. 153). In 1776 he would substantially endorse this judgement, in the process once again revisiting the language of this essay ('chimerical'): '[Ha]rrington is an Author of Genius; but chimerical. No Laws, however rigorous, [woud ma]ke his Agrarian practicable' (*Letters*, vol. II, p. 306).
5. *All plans ... plainly imaginary*] cf. the opening sentence of 'Of the Independency of Parliament': 'Political writers have established it as a maxim, that, in contriving any system of government, and fixing the several checks and controuls of the constitution, every man ought to be supposed a *knave*, and to have no other end, in all his actions, than private interest' (above, vol. 1, p. 44; and for commentary see also vol. 1, pp. 237–9, n. 1).

6. *Its rotation*] i.e. the Venetian principle of the rota, which had made so strong an impression on Harrington. See, in particular, Harrington's *The Manner and Use of the Ballot* (1660) (Harrington, *Works*, pp. 361–7).

7. *Its Agrarian*] A law intended to prevent the accumulation of very large amounts of landed property by the expedient of continual and repeated redistributions. Note, however, that the 'fundamental law against conquests' that Hume wishes to see adopted in his perfect commonwealth would have some of the same effect as an agrarian, in that it would curb the amassing of preponderant wealth by individuals. For Hume's scepticism about agrarian laws, see the *Enquiry Concerning the Principles of Morals*, III, 'Of Justice' (*ECPM*, pp. 20–21).

8. *As his negative . . . little consequence*] cf. the similarly dismissive comments on the royal assent in 'Of the Independency of Parliament' (above, vol. 1, p. 45). However, the last occasion on which the Royal assent had been withheld was comparatively recent. In 1707 Queen Anne had withheld assent from a bill relating to the Scottish militia.

9. *lords of the articles*] i.e. the Committee of Articles of the Scots Parliament, which had been abolished in 1689–90. In the *History of England* Hume described the purpose and curious composition of this body: 'The lords of articles were an ancient institution in the Scottish parliament. They were constituted after this manner. The temporal lords chose eight bishops: The bishops elected eight temporal lords: These sixteen named eight commissioners of counties, and eight burgesses: And without the previous consent of the thirty-two, who were denominated lords of articles, no motion could be made in parliament. As the bishops were entirely devoted to the court, it is evident, that all the lords of articles, by necessary consequence, depended on the king's nomination; and the prince, besides one negative after the bills had passed through parliament, possessed indirectly another before their introduction; a prerogative of much greater consequence than the former' (*History of England*, vol. V, p. 333).

10. *A government . . . original principles*] A reference to Machiavelli, *Discourses*, III.i: "Tis a certain truth, that the things of this World are determined, and a set time appointed for their duration; but those run thorow the whole course which is assigned them by their Stars, who keep their body in such order, that it may not alter at all, or if it does, it is for the better. I speak now of mixt bodies, as Common-wealths, and Sects, and I say that those alterations are salutiferous, which reduce them towards their first principles; and therefore the best ordered, and longest liv'd are they who (by their own orders) may be often renewed, or else by some accident (without the help of the said orders) may tend to renovation: 'tis as clear as the day, that no bodies of men are of long duration, unless they be renewed; and the way to renew them (as is said before) is to reduce them to their principles. For the Fundamentals of all Sects, Common-wealths and Kingdoms have always something of good in them, by means of which they recover their first reputation and grandeur. And because in process of time that goodness corrupts, that body must of

necessity die, unless something intervenes that reduces it to its first principles' (Machiavelli, *Works*, p. 377).

11. *twenty pounds*] Note variant 2 (above, p. 574), which shows how Hume steadily increased the property requirement for voting. Hume's eventual threshold of £20 would have, in his own day, greatly reduced the franchise. Prior to the 1832 Reform Act only those owning land with a rental value of £2 or more a year could vote.

12. *county representatives*] Hume's arithmetic seems to have gone awry. If the county magistrates (including the senators) have the authority of county representatives, then the total number of county representatives should be 11,100 (i.e. 10,000 + 1,100).

13. *in a conclave, like the cardinals*] A conclave is, literally, a lockable room; but 'conclave' is also the name given to the assembly of cardinals met for the election of a Pope (*OED*, 'conclave', *n.* 3 a). The etymology of the word ('clavis' is the Latin word for a key) reflects the circumstances of this most special meeting: for the cardinals are locked in a room until they have settled on the name of the new Pope.

14. *an intricate ballot . . . MALTA*] The Venetian ballot had been often described, attention focusing in particular on its incorporation of an element of randomness to counteract the natural self-interestedness of the voters. In an English context, an important description had been that offered by James Harrington in *The Manner and Use of the Ballot* (1660) (Harrington, *Works*, pp. 361–7). Other significant accounts include: Contarini, *The Commonwealth and Gouernment of Venice* (1599), pp. 51–6; James Howell, *A Survay of the Signorie of Venice* (1651), p. 34; Amelot de la Houssaye, *The History of the Government of Venice* (1677), pp. 39–40; Paul Hay du Chastelet, *The Policy and Government of the Venetians* (1671), pp. 60–61. For a description of the intricate balloting that was specified for the election of the Grand Master of the Maltese Knights, see Vertot, *Malta*, vol. II, pp. 139–43.

15. *a protector*] A striking echo of the language of the Interregnum, for almost half of which (1653–8) Oliver Cromwell had served as head of state with the title of Lord Protector.

16. *two secretaries of state*] This mirrors the post-Restoration administration in England, in which provision was made for two secretaries of state: one for the northern and one for the southern department.

17. *session and suffrage*] i.e. the right to vote: see *OED*, 'suffrage', *n.*, 8 a, quoting this passage.

18. *The magistrates . . . any presbyter*] A subordination of religious to civil authority that may in part have been dictated by Hume's experience of the powerful influence of religious authority in Scotland during his lifetime.

19. *The militia . . . insist upon it*] Hume is presumably silently referring his reader to Abraham Stanyan's *An Account of Switzerland* (1714), in which chapter 10 (pp. 190–205) deals with the militia. Rousseau would recommend the

Swiss example as a model for a republican militia in his *Considérations sur le gouvernement de Pologne* (composed, 1770–71; published posthumously, 1782), chapter 12, pp. 129–44.

20. *correcting all inequalities*] A form of Machiavellian *ricorso*: see above, pp. 578–9, n. 10.

21. *the nobles in POLAND*] In *Esprit des Lois*, book II, chapter 3, Montesquieu had commented on the oppressive nature of the Polish aristocracy: 'La plus imparfaite de toutes, est celle où la Partie du Peuple qui obéit est dans l'Esclavage civil de celle qui commande, comme l'Aristocratie de *Pologne*, où les Païsans sont esclaves de la Noblesse' (Montesquieu, *Esprit*, vol. I, p. 23). In *The Wealth of Nations* Adam Smith would illustrate his argument that feudalism operated as a suppressant of economic progress by citing the example of contemporary Poland: 'Poland, where the feudal system still continues to take place, is at this day as beggarly a country as it was before the discovery of America' (Smith, *Wealth*, vol. I, p. 256, I.xi.n.1).

22. *as HARRINGTON observes*] Not a precise quotation so much as a paraphrase of a recurrent topic in Harrington's political thought, which is preoccupied by the relation between wisdom and honesty: 'From the beginning of the world unto this day, you never found a commonwealth where the leaders, having honesty enough, wanted skill enough to lead her unto her true interest at home or abroad; that which is necessary unto this end is not so much skill as honesty, and let the leaders of Oceana be dishonest if they can. In the leading of a commonwealth aright this is certain: wisdom and honesty are all one, and though you shall find defects in their virtue, those that have had the fewest have ever been and forever shall be the wisest' (*The Prerogative of Popular Government*, book I, chapter 12, in Harrington, *Works*, p. 495). In *Oceana*, the necessity of a bicameral legislation is expressed through the homely example of the two girls sharing a cake: one divides, the other chooses. (Hume had invoked this principle in a jocular spirit in a letter to John Clephane of 18 June 1747: 'Perhaps you . . . will reproach me with both dividing and choosing' [*Letters*, vol. I, p. 101].) Applying this to the practice of government, Harrington stipulates that the senate divides (i.e. proposes legislation), on which the popular assembly chooses (i.e. votes either to adopt or to discard). The benefits of bicameralism are there explained by Harrington in language that comes close to Hume's summary of his understanding of the need for a senate, or upper house: 'The wisdom of the few may be the light of mankind, but the interest of the few is not the profit of mankind, nor of a commonwealth; wherefore, seeing we have granted interest to be reason, they must not choose, lest it put out their light; but as the council dividing consisteth of the wisdom of the commonwealth, so the assembly or council choosing should consist of the interest of the commonwealth. As the wisdom of the commonwealth is in the aristocracy, so the interest of the commonwealth is in the whole body of the people, and whereas this, in case

the commonwealth consist of an whole nation, is too unwieldy a body to be assembled, this council is to consist of such a representative as may be equal, and so constituted as can never contract any other interest than that of the whole people . . .' (Harrington, *Works*, p. 173).

23. *carves*] Perhaps a reference to Harrington's celebrated example of two girls dividing a cake, intended to illustrate the salutariness of a separation of political functions (dividing and choosing): see Harrington, *Works*, pp. 172–3.

24. *Cardinal . . . the least motive*] 'I have often said, that all companies are but like a mob which can be relied upon only for the present instant' (*Memoirs of the Cardinal de Retz*, 4 vols [Dublin, 1777], vol. I, p. 250).

25. *an undistinguishing rabble, like the ENGLISH electors*] Hume's eventual contempt for the English is plain in his letters of the later 1760s and early 1770s: 'I am delighted to see the daily and hourly Progress of Madness and Folly and Wickedness in England . . . that pernicious People'; 'it has been my Misfortune to write in the Language of the most stupid and factious Barbarians in the World'; 'those wicked, abandon'd Madmen'; 'that deluded People'; 'Our Government has become a Chimera; and is too perfect in point of Liberty, for so vile a Beast as an Englishman, who is a Man, a bad Animal too, corrupted by above a Century of Licentiousness'; 'what abandon'd Madmen there are in England!'; 'The Madness and Wickedness of the English . . . appear astonishing'; 'For as to any Englishman, that Nation is so sunk in Stupidity and Barbarism and Faction that you may as well think of Lapland for an Author' (*Letters*, vol. II, pp. 208, 209, 214, 215, 216, 218, 226 and 269).

26. *men of fortune and education*] For Hume's tendency to increase the property qualification for voting in this ideal commonwealth, see above, p. 579 and n. 11.

27. *The senate of VENICE . . . such resolutions*] In *Oceana* Harrington had also insisted on the principle of rotation as necessary for political health: 'for in motion consisteth life, and the motion of a commonwealth will never be current, unless it be circular . . . for if it be not in rotation both as to persons and things, it will be very sick' (Harrington, *Works*, p. 248). Venice, albeit Harrington thought that its rotation was not perfect, served as his model (Harrington, *Works*, p. 182).

28. *A small . . . little commonwealth*] 'The virtue of such a constitution, according to Hume, was that it had the capacity to combine the transparency and accountability of government in small city republics with the power and stability of a large monarchy. Hume's intention was to sever the traditional connection – recently reaffirmed by Montesquieu in Book VIII of the *Esprit des Lois* – between a republic's freedom and its smallness of size' (Harris, *Hume*, p. 287). See below, p. 583, n. 36. Adam Ferguson would reassert the view that the small republics of antiquity had enjoyed special advantages: 'The small republics of Greece, indeed, by their subdivisions, and the balance

of their power, found almost in every village the object of nations. Every little district was a nursery of excellent men, and what is now the wretched corner of a great empire, was the field on which mankind have reaped their principal honours. But in modern Europe, republics of a similar extent, are like shrubs, under the shade of a taller wood, choked by the neighbourhood of more powerful states' (Ferguson, *Civil Society*, p. 61). In 'Of the Populousness of Ancient Nations' Hume had praised to the point of lyricism a state of society in which 'each man had his little house and field to himself, and each county had its capital, free and independent; what a happy situation of mankind! How favourable to industry and agriculture; to marriage and propagation!' (above, p. 110); cf. also the parallel passage in 'Of Commerce' where Hume considers more dispassionately the consequences of a state of affairs in which 'every field, belonging to a different proprietor, was able to maintain a family, and rendered the numbers of citizens very considerable, even without trade and manufactures' (above, p. 8).

29. *The DUTCH ... formerly*] cf. Sir William Temple: 'This Office [Burgomaster] is a Charge of the greatest Trust, Authority, and Dignity; and so much the greater, by not being of Profit or Advantage, but only as a way to other constant Employments in the City, that are so. The Salary of a Burgomaster of *Amsterdam* is but five hundred Gilders a Year, though there are Offices worth five thousand in their Disposal; but yet none of them known to have taken Mony upon such occasions, which would lose all their Credit in the Town, and thereby their Fortunes by any Publick Employments' (Temple, *Works*, vol. I, p. 31).

30. *the natural ambition of mankind*] A principle of human nature also deployed by Hume as a solvent of historical misunderstanding in 'Of the Coalition of Parties': 'Is it not known, that, though representatives received wages from their constituents; to be a member of the lower house was always considered as a burden, and an exemption from it as a privilege? Will they persuade us, that power, which, of all human acquisitions, is the most coveted, and in comparison of which even reputation and pleasure and riches are slighted, could ever be regarded as a burden by any man?' (above, p. 184).

31. *the resemblance ... United Provinces*] The Stadtholderate had been restored in the Low Countries after the French invasion of 1747, and thereafter assumed a hereditary form until its abolition in 1813. Hume had expressed his faith in the new Dutch government in a letter to John Home of 3 March 1748 from The Hague: 'this we may venture to say, that Holland was undoubtedly ruin'd by its Liberty; & has now a Chance of being sav'd by its Prince: Let Republicans make the best of this Example they can' (*Letters*, vol. I, pp. 115–16).

32. *The plan of CROMWELL's parliament*] As provided for in the Instrument of Government of December 1653.

33. *the Bishops ... ought to be removed*] The bishops of the Church of England were one of the three estates of which the English Parliament was composed

(the others being the Lords and the Commons). The political role of the bishops sitting in the House of Lords had become freshly controversial during the later seventeenth century in the context of the impeachment of the Earl of Danby: 'Upon this [Danby's impeachment] a famous debate arose, concerning the Bishops right of voting in any part of a trial for treason. It was said, that, tho' the bishops did not vote in the final judgment, yet they had a right to vote in all preliminaries ... Many books were writ on both sides ... The truth was, they [the bishops] desired to have withdrawn, but the King would not suffer it. He was so set on maintaining the pardon [he had sealed for Danby], that he would not venture such a point on the votes of the temporal Lords. And he told the Bishops, they must stick to him, and to his prerogative, as they would expect that he should stick to them, if they came to be push'd at. By this means they were exposed to the popular fury' (Burnet, *History*, vol. I, p. 460; cf. also pp. 462–5, for Burnet's precis of the arguments deployed by both sides in the debate; Sydney, *Letters*, pp. 70–71; and Grey, *Debates*, vol. VII, p. 303; John Brydall, *A New-Years-Gift* [1682]; the same issue had arisen in relation to the trial of Strafford in 1641). Cf. particularly Denzil Holles, *Letter of a Gentleman to his Friend Shewing that Bishops are not to be Judges in Parliament in Cases Capital* (1679), and Edward Stillingfleet, *The Grand Question, Concerning the Bishops Right to Vote in Parliament* (1680).

34. *Such an aristocracy ... against it*] cf. Hume's comments in 'Of Public Credit' on the protective function of an aristocracy (above, p. 81).

35. *standing army*] See above, vol. 1, p. 336, n. 89.

36. *We shall conclude ... small territory*] A reference to Montesquieu, *Esprit*, part I, book IV, chapter 7; cf. above, pp. 581–2, n. 28.

37. *first concoction*] A phrase drawn from the old physiology, where it referred to the digestion of food in the stomach and intestines preliminary to its conversion into blood (second concoction) and its eventual secretion (third concoction) (*OED*, 'concoction', *n.*, 1 b); here used metaphorically to refer to a preliminary stage (ibid., 1 c).

38. *Man and for ever!*] cf. Pope, *Second Epistle of the Second Book of Horace Imitated by Mr. Pope*, ll. 246–63: 'The Laws of God, as well as of the Land, / Abhor, a *Perpetuity* should stand: / Estates have wings, and hang in Fortune's pow'r / Loose on the point of ev'ry wav'ring Hour; / Ready, by force, or of your own accord, / By sale, at least by death, to change their Lord. / *Man?* and *for ever?* Wretch, what wou'dst thou have? / Heir urges Heir, like Wave impelling Wave: / All vast Possessions (just the same the case / Whether you call them Villa, Park, or Chace) / Alas, my BATHURST! what will they avail? / Join *Cotswold* Hills to *Saperton*'s fair Dale, / Let rising Granaries and Temples here, / There mingled Farms and Pyramids appear, / Link Towns to Towns with Avenues of Oak, / Enclose whole Downs in Walls, 'tis all a joke! / Inexorable Death shall level all, / And Trees, and Stones, and Farms, and

Farmer fall.' Although it is clear that Pope is Hume's source for this particular phrase, the transience of human artifice is a commonplace with a rich hinterland. Cf. Dryden, 'Mac Flecknoe' (1682), l. 1, 'All human things are subject to decay'; Waller, 'Of the Danger His Majesty . . . escaped', ll. 163–4, 'All human things / Of dearest value hang on slender strings' (an allusion to Ovid, *Ex Ponto*, IV.iii.35, 'omnia sunt hominum tenui pendentia filo'). The observation is also to be found in prose writers who influenced Hume: cf. Hobbes, *Leviathan*, chapter 29, 'Of those things that Weaken, or tend to the DISSOLUTION of a Common-wealth': 'Though nothing can be immortall, which mortals make; yet, if men had the use of reason they pretend to, their Common-wealths might be secured, at least, from perishing by internall diseases' (Hobbes, *Leviathan*, p. 221). In letter 12 of *A Dissertation upon Parties* Bolingbroke had exclaimed that the English constitution 'is better fitted than any, ancient or modern, ever was, not only to preserve liberty, but to provide for its own duration, and to become immortal, if any thing human could be so' (Bolingbroke, *Political Writings*, p. 121). However, in *The Idea of a Patriot King* the same mercurial author had insisted that 'Absolute stability is not to be expected in any thing human . . .' (Bolingbroke, *Political Writings*, p. 252). Compare also Adam Smith, *Wealth of Nations*, V.ii.c.6: 'But though empires, like all the other works of men, have all hitherto proved mortal, yet every empire aims at immortality' (Smith, *Wealth*, p. 830) and Montesquieu, *Esprit*, vol. I, p. 260. Cf. also the entry in the 'Early Memoranda': NLS MS 23159, item 15, p. 55: 'Most of the Inventions of Men are subject to Change. They depend upon Humour & Caprice. They have a Vogue for a Time, & then sink into Oblivion.'

39. *The world itself . . . immortal*] Philo and Cleanthes debate the eternity or otherwise of the world in Part VI of *Dialogues Concerning Natural Religion* (*Hume on Religion*, pp. 197–201); cf. also the beginning of 'Of the Populousness of Ancient Nations' (above, pp. 95–6).

40. *consuming plagues*] cf. 'Of the Populousness of Ancient Nations', above, p. 96.

41. *extensive conquests . . . free government*] cf. the note on the natural tendency of empires to impermanence in the 'Early Memoranda': 'There seems to be a natural Course of Things, which brings on the Destruction of great Empires. They push their Conquests till they come to barbarous Nations, which stop their Progress, by the Difficulty of subsisting great Armies. After that, the Nobility & considerable Men of the conquering Nation & best Provinces withdraw gradually from the [frontier *inserted above the line*] Army, by reason of its Distance from the Capital & barbarity of the Country, in which they quarter: They forget the Use of War. Their barbarous Soldiers become their Masters. These have no Law but their Sword, both from their bad Education, & from their Distance from the Sovereign [to whom they bear no Affection *inserted above the line*]. Hence Disorder, Violence, Anarchy, &̶ Tyranny, & a Dissolution of Empire.' (NLS MS 23159, item 14, p. 27; cf. Mossner, 'Memoranda', pp. 517–18).

# *Withdrawn Essays*

On Hume's reasons for withdrawing some essays, see his comments to William Strahan in a letter of 7 February 1772: 'I suppress'd these Essays, not because they coud give any Offence, but because, I thought, they coud neither give Pleasure nor Instruction: They were indeed bad Imitations of the agreeable *Triffling* of Addison' (*Letters*, vol. II, p. 257). Nevertheless, as M. A. Box has acutely observed, the withdrawn essays possess a peculiar value for the student of Hume, even if in their author's eyes they came to be negligible: 'it is precisely the jettisoned essays, now displaced from their original settings in the table of contents, that best show Hume's initial conception for his second book' (Box, *Suasive Art*, p. 112). Box also notes that all the withdrawn essays fall on the moral side of the collection, none on the political (ibid., p. 123).

## I. OF ESSAY-WRITING

Published in: *1742a*
Significant revisions: none
Copy text: *1742a*
Headnote:
> One of the three essays (the others were 'Of Moral Prejudices' and 'Of the Middle Station of Life') which Hume had excised in *1748a* as being 'frivolous and finical' (*Letters*, vol. I, p. 112).
>
> In arguing that the essay, at least in its early eighteenth-century English form, furnished a bridge between the learned and the conversible, Hume was echoing Addison (see below, n. 3). 'Of Essay-Writing' also shows Hume trying to imitate Addison's easy style and informal manner. The withdrawal of the essay shows that Hume was not satisfied for long with this exercise in imitation, which indeed does not ring true even in its own terms, and which swiftly fell out of alignment with Hume's more mature ambitions for the essay as a literary form.

1. *The Separation . . . and Company*] See below, n. 3.
2. *Stun'd . . . said that*] Matthew Prior, *Alma, or the Progress of the Mind* (1718), canto III, ll. 524–5.
3. *a Kind of Resident or Ambassador*] cf. Addison's Mr. Spectator, who aspired 'to have it said of me, that I have brought Philosophy out of Closets and Libraries, Schools and Colleges, to dwell in Clubs and Assemblies, at Tea-Tables and in Coffee-Houses' (Addison, *Spectator*, no. 10, 12 March 1711, vol. I, p. 44). Cf. Cicero, *Tusculan Disputations*: 'Socrates autem primus philosophiam devocavit e caelo et in urbibus collocavit et in domus etiam introduxit et coëgit de vita et moribus rebusque bonis et malis quaerere'; 'Socrates on the other hand was the first to call philosophy down from the heavens and set her in the cities of men and bring her also into their homes and compel her to ask questions about life and morality and things good and evil' (V.iv.10).
4. *The Balance of Trade . . . both Sides*] A jocular invocation of a prevalent notion in contemporary economics on which Hume would in 1750 and 1758 formulate some strongly independent views: see above, pp. 46–63, 'Of the Balance of Trade' and 'Of the Jealousy of Trade'.
5. *delicate Affections*] For Hume's views on the felicity of having a delicate taste, see above, vol. 1, pp. 17–20, 'Of the Delicacy of Taste and Passion': 'delicacy of taste is as much to be desired and cultivated as delicacy of passion is to be lamented, and to be remedied, if possible' (p. 18).
6. *a neighbouring Nation*] i.e. France.
7. *Mr. Addison's . . . mystic Devotion*] *Spectator* papers written by Addison which deal with religious subjects include nos. 159 (1 September 1711) and 543 (22 November 1712). Hume may have paid particular attention to this latter paper, because in it Addison had mounted an argument for providence on the basis of anatomy. However, Hume may also have had in mind Addison's *Evidences of the Christian Religion* (1730).
8. *Otway's Tragedies*] Otway's tragedies, such as *Venice Preserv'd* (1682), were still performed on the eighteenth-century stage.
9. *the Rants of Mr. Dryden*] e.g. the rodomontade characteristic of Almanzor in *The Conquest of Granada* (1672).
10. *sacrifice the Substance to the Shadow*] Proverbial, and most obviously an allusion to the Aesopian fable of the dog who steals some meat, but then loses it when crossing a river because he also tried to grab its reflection in the water: 'Dives for the Shadow, lets the Substance fall' (*Aesop's Fables, with their morals* [1706], p. 6). But possibly also we have here a recollection of what Bacon had said in *De Dignitate et Augmentis Scientiarum* (1623) about the relation between poetry and history: 'videtur *Poesis* hæc humanæ Naturæ largiri, quæ Historia denegat; atque Animo Vmbris rerum vtcunque satisfacere, cùm Solida haberi non possint'; 'Poesie seems to endow human nature with that which history denies; and to give satisfaction to the mind, with, at least, the shadow of things, where the substance cannot be had' (p. 108).

## II. OF MORAL PREJUDICES

Published in: *1742a*
Significant revisions: none
Copy text: *1742a*
Headnote:

> Composed before 4 June 1739, when it was one of the two draft essays that Hume sent to Henry Home (*New Letters*, p. 5; Harris, *Hume*, pp. 154–5; the reference to the story of Diogenes in Cicero [*New Letters*, p. 7] identifies it as such). Harris finds that in this essay of Addisonian imitation Hume 'proposes a compromise position between a purely sceptical view of human beings as blind and selfish and an overly optimistic view of them as able to transcend their limitations by means of rational self-discipline' (Harris, *Hume*, p. 155).

1. *There is … insipid Raillery*] Hume perhaps has in mind the followers of a moral sceptic such as Bernard Mandeville.
2. *And even … chimerical and romantic*] cf., however, Hume's more acceptant description of the undeferential spirit that had established itself in Britain since 1688 in 'Whether the British Government Inclines More to Absolute Monarchy, or to a Republic' (above, vol. 1, p. 50–51; and cf. above, vol. 1, pp. 243–4, n. 12).
3. *a free Constitution … Corruption*] On the role of self-interest in political life, see Hume's comments in 'Of the First Principles of Government' (above, vol. 1, p. 36).
4. *that grave philosophic Endeavour after Perfection*] To which Hume himself had succumbed as a young man (see the headnote to 'Of the Delicacy of Taste and Passion', and above, vol. 1, pp. 207–8, n. 10).
5. *useful Byasses*] cf. Hume's use of this mechanical metaphor at the end of 'Of the Parties of Great Britain' (above, vol. 1, p. 65).
6. *I wish … this Particular*] Hume's 'The Stoic' (above, vol. 1, pp. 119–25), together with its companion essays, can be read as dissuading its readers from both an imitation of the philosophical sects of antiquity, and an adoption of the medicinal concept of philosophy those sects espouse.
7. *the GOD-like Stroke*] i.e. the assassination of Julius Caesar in 44 BC.
8. *That all Men … Head about them*] 'ὁ δὲ Στατίλιος ἔφη τῷ σοφῷ καὶ νοῦν ἔχοντι διὰ φαύλους καὶ ἀνοήτους κινδυνεύειν καὶ ταράττεσθαι μὴ καθήκειν'; 'and Statilius had declared that it did not become a wise and sensible man to be thrown into turmoil and peril for the sake of feeble and foolish folk' (Plutarch, *Life of Brutus*, XII.iii).
9. *an antient Philosopher*] The anecdote is related by Plutarch, in his *Moralia*, 'On Brotherly Love', IV: 'Οἶδα γοῦν ἐμαυτὸν ἐν Ῥώμῃ δυεῖν ἀδελφῶν ἀναδεξάμενον δίαιταν, ὧν ἅτερος ἐδόκει φιλοσοφεῖν· ἦν δ᾽ ὡς ἔοικεν οὐ μόνον ἀδελφὸς ἀλλὰ καὶ φιλόσοφος ψευδεπίγραφος καὶ ψευδώνυμος· ἐμοῦ γὰρ ἀξιοῦντος αὐτὸν ὡς ἀδελφὸν ἀδελφῷ καὶ ἰδιώτῃ φιλόσοφον προσφέρεσθαι, "ταῦτ᾽," εἶπεν, "ὡς πρὸς ἰδιώτην ἀληθῶς, ἐγὼ δ᾽ οὐ σεμνὸν οὐδὲ μέγα ποιοῦμαι τὸ ἐκ τῶν αὐτῶν μορίων

γεγονέναι"'; 'I remember, for instance, that in Rome I undertook to arbitrate between two brothers, of whom one had the reputation of being a philosopher. But he was, as it appears, not only as a brother but also as a philosopher, masquerading under a false name and appellation; for when I asked him to conduct himself as brother to brother and as philosopher to layman, "What you say," said he, "as to his being a layman, is correct, but I account it no momentous or important matter to have sprung from the same loins."' There is nothing in Plutarch's Greek phrase 'the same loins' (or perhaps 'the same natural organ') which could give rise to Hume's scruple about the anecdote not being 'proper to repeat'. It may therefore be that Hume's awareness of this anecdote is mediated *via* Montaigne, where it is more coarsely expressed: 'Je n'en fais pas, dict-il, plus grand estat pour estre sorty de mesme trou.' 'He matters no more to me for having come out of the same hole' ('De l'amitié', in Montaigne, *Œuvres*, p. 183).

10. *When your ... Perfection of Wisdom*] Ὅταν κλαίοντα ἴδῃς τινὰ ἐν πένθει ἢ ἀποδημοῦντος τέκνου ἢ ἀπολωλεκότα τὰ ἑαυτοῦ, πρόσεχε μή σε ἡ φαντασία συναρπάσῃ ὡς ἐν κακοῖς ὄντος αὐτοῦ τοῖς ἐκτός, ἀλλ᾽ εὐθὺς ἔστω πρόχειρον ὅτι "τοῦτον θλίβει οὐ τὸ συμβεβηκός (ἄλλον γὰρ οὐ θλίβει), ἀλλὰ τὸ δόγμα τὸ περὶ τούτου." μέχρι μέντοι λόγου μὴ ὄκνει συμπεριφέρεσθαι αὐτῷ, κἂν οὕτω τύχῃ, καὶ συνεπιστενάξαι· πρόσεχε μέντοι μὴ καὶ ἔσωθεν στενάξῃς'; 'When you see someone weeping in sorrow, either because a child has gone on a journey, or because he has lost his property, beware that you be not carried away by the impression that the man is in the midst of external ills, but straightway keep before you this thought: "It is not what has happened that distresses this man (for it does not distress another), but his judgement about it." Do not, however, hesitate to sympathize with him so far as words go, and, if occasion offers, even to groan with him; but be careful not to groan also in the centre of your being' (Epictetus, *Encheiridion*, XVI).

11. *Diogenes ... Temper*] 'Durior Diogenes et is quidem idem sentiens, sed ut Cynicus asperius, proiici se iussit inhumatum. Tum amici: Volucribusne et feris? Minime vero, inquit, sed bacillum propter me quo abigam ponitote. Qui poteris? illi, non enim senties. Quid igitur mihi ferarum laniatus oberit nihil sentienti?'; 'Diogenes was rougher; his feeling it is true was the same, but like a Cynic he spoke more harshly and required that he should be flung out unburied. Upon which his friends said: "To the birds and wild beasts?" "Certainly not," said he, "but you must put a stick near me to drive them away with." "How can you, for you will be without consciousness?" they replied. "What harm, then, can the mangling of wild beasts do me if I am without consciousness?"' (Cicero, *Tusculan Disputations*, I.xliii.104). Cf. *Letters*, vol. I, p. 32, and *New Letters*, pp. 6–7.

12. *Eugenius*] As James Harris suggests, this is an imitation of the fictionalized exemplary biographies that Hume would have encountered in early eighteenth-century periodicals such as *The Spectator* (Harris, *Hume*, pp. 155–6). Etymologically, 'Eugenius' means 'nobly born'.

13. *the general Debt to Nature*] i.e. she died.
14. *a Letter from a Friend*] Such fictional letters were another common feature in *The Spectator* and similar publications.
15. *Matter of Fact*] It is possible that Hume had heard of this story, or something like it, during his early period of residence in France, 1734–7. It is recorded in François Gayot de Pitaval's *Causes celebres*, vol. VIII (Paris, 1739), at which date it was still evidently unresolved: 'Je ne sçai point comment ce procès fut terminé' (account on pp. 560–65; quotation on p. 565).
16. *Parterre*] In a theatre, that part which we now call the stalls. Cf. Hume's account of the *coup de foudre* which struck Lord Marchmont in the theatre in 1748 (*Letters*, vol. I, p. 110).

## III. OF THE MIDDLE STATION OF LIFE

Published in: *1742a*
Significant revisions: none
Copy text: *1742a*
Headnote:

> In this essay Hume follows in the footsteps of Addison, who in *The Spectator* had also recommended the middle station of life as best suited to those who wished to improve themselves in both learning and virtue (see below, n. 5). In the context of Hume's political philosophy more generally, this championing of the middle station resonates with his encouragement to his readers to avoid extreme and polarized positions. Note, however, the more substantive reason for the essay's withdrawal hinted at by Duncan Forbes: 'Hume's change of view about the middling rank is one of the most clear and indisputable and significant changes in his political and social theory' (Forbes, *Politics*, p. 94).

1. *the following Fable*] cf. William Somervile, *The Two Springs, a Fable* (1725).
2. *the Danube or the Rhine*] cf. Somervile, *Two Springs*, p. 8.
3. *the most eligible of all others*] cf. the advice given to Robinson Crusoe by his father: 'He told me ... that mine was the middle State, or what might be called the upper Station of *Low Life*, which he had found by long Experience was the best State in the World, the most suited to human Happiness, not exposed to the Miseries and Hardships, the Labour and Sufferings of the mechanick Part of Mankind, and not embarass'd [*sic*] with the Pride, Luxury, Ambition and Envy of the upper Part of Mankind' (Daniel Defoe, *Robinson Crusoe*, ed. Thomas Keymer [Oxford: Oxford University Press, 2007], p. 6).
4. *too much immers'd in Pleasure*] In 1768 Hume would write to Turgot pointing out that 'the rich have so many more alluring Appetites to gratify than

that for Knowledge, and the poor are occupyed in daily Labour, and Industry' (*Letters*, vol. II, p. 181).

5. *Agur's Prayer*] See Proverbs 30:7–9. A popular text in the earlier eighteenth century: see, e.g., Daniel Defoe, *Moll Flanders*, ed. G. A. Starr and Linda Bree (Oxford: Oxford University Press, 2011), p. 160. In *The Spectator*, no. 464 (22 August 1712) Addison had praised the 'middle condition' as 'most eligible to the Man that would improve himself in Virtue', and had quoted this biblical text (Addison, *Spectator*, vol. IV, p. 139). In no. 287 (29 January 1712) Addison had also praised the middle state as the most propitious to learning.

6. *It has been . . . obliging them too far*] The bitter insight, that no good deed goes unresented, had most recently been expressed by Hobbes in *Leviathan*, part I, chapter 11: 'To have received from one, to whom we think our selves equall, greater benefits than there is hope to Requite, disposeth to counterfeit love; but really secret hatred; and puts a man into the estate of a desperate debtor, that in declining the sight of his creditor, tacitely wishes him there, where he might never see him more. For benefits oblige; and obligation is thraldome; and unrequitable obligation, perpetuall thraldome; which is to ones equall, hatefull' (Hobbes, *Leviathan*, p. 71). Cf. Tacitus, *Annals*, IV.xviii: 'Nam beneficia eo usque laeta sunt, dum videntur exsolvi posse: ubi multum antevenere, pro gratia odium redditur'; 'For services are welcome as far as it seems possible to requite them: when that prospect greatly recedes, the response is hatred rather than gratitude.'

7. *Wisdom and Ability*] cf. *Spectator*, no. 287 (above, n. 5).

8. *A certain Pope . . . governs itself*] Urban VIII, as reported by Pierre Bayle: 'Pope *Urban* VIII. was not altogether wrong in saying, *That the World in a great measure govern'd it self*' (*Miscellaneous Reflections*, 2 vols [1708], vol. II, p. 503). In *Cato's Letters*, no. 48 (14 October 1721) a similar remark is attributed to 'Pope Aeneas Sylvius' (Pius II) (*Cato's Letters*, p. 320). Note that Hume recognized that in these early essays he had 'committed some Mistakes . . . by trusting to my Memory' (*New Letters*, p. 7).

9. *Harry IV.*] Presumably the French king Henri IV, who ruled 1589–1610, and whose reign brought the French Wars of Religion to a close.

10. *A happy Talent . . . Prodigy among Men*] cf. Hume's contention, in 'Of the Rise and Progress of the Arts and Sciences', that 'curiosity, or the love of knowledge, has a very limited influence, and requires youth, leisure, education, genius, and example, to make it govern any person' (above, vol. 1, p. 94).

## IV. OF IMPUDENCE AND MODESTY

Published in: *1741, 1742b, 1748a, 1753, 1758, 1760*
Significant revisions:

1) *1741–1742b* insert the following paragraph after that ending '. . . resembles it.' (above, p. 225):

'I WAS lately lamenting to a Friend of mine, who loves a Conceit, that popular Applause should be bestowed with so little Judgment, and that so many empty forward Coxcombs should rise up to a Figure in the World: Upon which he said there was nothing surprising in the Case. *Popular Fame*, says he, *is nothing but Breath or Air; and Air very naturally presses into a Vacuum.*' (*1741*, p. 21).

Copy text: *1760*

Headnote:

This essay was withdrawn after 1760, together with 'Of Love and Marriage' and 'Of the Study of History'. Hume would explain to Strahan in 1772 that he had withdrawn these essays 'not because they coud give any Offence, but because, I thought, they coud neither give Pleasure nor Instruction: They were indeed bad Imitations of the agreeable *Triffling* of Addison' (*Letters*, vol. II, p. 257).

1. *good or bad qualities . . . generally imagined*] Hume had defended this position more fully in Part 2 of the conclusion to the *Enquiry Concerning the Principles of Morals* (*ECPM*, pp. 79–82).

2. *a benevolent disposition . . . love and esteem*] See the note on the 'moral sense' school of philosophy, with which Hume associated himself, in the annotation to 'Of the Standard of Taste' (above, vol. 1, pp. 374–5, n. 1).

3. *to put himself off for*] To pass oneself off, with connotations of fraudulence or deceptiveness (*OED*, 'to put off', 9 a).

4. *A decent assurance . . . attendant of virtue*] cf. the similar judgement in the *Enquiry Concerning the Principles of Morals*, section 8: 'A small biass towards modesty, even in the internal sentiment, is favourably regarded, especially in young people; . . . In short, a generous spirit and self-value, well founded, decently disguised, and courageously supported under distress and calumny, is a great excellency, and seems to derive its merit from the noble elevation of its sentiment' (*ECPM*, pp. 69–70).

5. *Riches . . . modesty of their behaviour*] Hume had touched on our natural tendency to admire the rich in the *Treatise of Human Nature*, II.ii.4–5, in the course of examining the causes of love and hatred: 'The same passions arise from bodily accomplishments, such as beauty, force, swiftness, dexterity; and from their contraries; as likewise from the external advantages and disadvantages of family, possessions, cloaths, nation and climate' (*THN*, pp. 214–15).

6. *the following allegory*] Hume's fondness for allegory in these early essays (cf. the allegory of the two streams in 'Of the Middle Station of Life') is an aspect of his imitation of Addison. In *Spectator*, no. 501 (4 October 1712), Addison confessed his ambition to make this form of writing once again current: 'As some of the finest Compositions among the Ancients are in Allegory, I have endeavoured, in several of my Papers, to revive that way of

Writing, and hope I have not been altogether unsuccessful in it: For I find there is always a great Demand for those particular Papers, and cannot but observe that several Authors have endeavoured of late to excell in Works of this Nature' (Addison, *Spectator*, vol. IV, p. 275); the complimentary reference is to Thomas Parnell. Johnson too would incorporate allegories in *The Rambler*. However, Hume was conscious that allegory was a difficult mode of writing to master, as he stated in *The Natural History of Religion*, section 5: 'Allegories, indeed, entirely perfect, we ought not to expect as the productions of ignorance and superstition; there being no work of genius, that requires a nicer hand, or has been more rarely executed with success' (*NHR*, p. 50).

## V. OF LOVE AND MARRIAGE

Published in: *1741, 1742b, 1748a, 1753, 1758, 1760*
Significant revisions: none
Copy text: *1760*
Headnote:

> Hume discussed his dissatisfaction with this essay in a letter to Adam Smith of 24 September 1752, and in so doing disclosed something of its secret history: 'I am just now diverted for a Moment by correcting my Essays moral & political, for a new Edition. If any thing occur to you to be inserted or retrench'd, I shall be obliged to you for the Hint. In case you shou'd not have the last Edition by you, I shall send you a Copy of it. In that Edition [i.e. the 1748 edition], I was engag'd to act contrary to my Judgement in retaining the 6th & 7th Essays [i.e. 'Of Love and Marriage' and 'Of the Study of History'], which I had resolv'd to throw out, as too frivolous for the rest, and not very agreeable neither even in that trifling manner: But Millar, my Bookseller, made such Protestations against it, & told me how much he had heard them praisd by the best Judges; that the Bowels of a Parent melted, & I preserv'd them alive' (*Letters*, vol. I, p. 168).

1. *more a friend to truth*] Here Hume playfully reapplies Aristotle's famous remark about Plato, 'amicus Plato sed magis amica veritas': 'Plato is my friend, yet truth is still more my friend.' Cf. *Nicomachean Ethics*, 1096a 1: 'δόξειε δ᾿ ἂν ἴσως βέλτιον εἶναι, καὶ δεῖν ἐπὶ σωτηρίᾳ γε τῆς ἀληθείας καὶ τὰ οἰκεῖα ἀναιρεῖν, ἄλλως τε καὶ φιλοσόφους ὄντας· ἀμφοῖν γὰρ ὄντοιν φίλοιν ὅσιον προτιμᾶν τὴν ἀλήθειαν'; 'Still perhaps it would appear desirable, and indeed it would seem to be obligatory, especially for a philosopher, to sacrifice even one's closest personal ties in defence of the truth. Both are dear to us, yet it is our duty to prefer the truth.'

2. *love of dominion*] cf. Pope, *Moral Essays*, 'To a Lady', ll. 207–10: 'In men, we various ruling passions find; / In women, two almost divide the kind; /

Those, only fixed, they first or last obey, / The love of pleasure, and the love of sway.'

3. *We are told ... suspected*] A number of ancient authors relate inform-ation about the Scythians, and Hume seems to have assembled details from Pliny the Elder (*Natural History*, VI.vii: rule by women), Herodotus (IV.i–iii: copulating with blinded slaves) and Justin (*Epitome*, II.iv: secession by women) to forge this legend. There is a possible contemporary parallel in Anon, *Selecta Historica: or, a Curious Collection of Useful and Instructive Histories on Moral Subjects, selected partly from the sacred writings, but mostly from the best Greek, Roman, and other ancient authors* (1741), pp. 174–7.

4. *their SCYTHIAN ancestors*] A reference to the tradition that the Scots and Irish were descended from the Scythians. See, e.g., Edmund Spenser, *A View of the Present State of Ireland*: 'For not of one nation was it [Ireland] peopled as it is, but of sundry people of different conditions and manners, but the chiefest which have first possessed and inhabited it, I suppose to be Scyth-ians, which at such time as the Northern nations overflowed all Christendom, came down to the sea coast, where inquiring for other countries abroad and getting intelligence of this country of Ireland, finding shipping convenient, passed over thither and arrived in the North part thereof, which is now called Ulster; which first inhabiting, and afterwards stretching themselves forth into the land as their numbers increased, named it all of themselves Scuttenland – which more briefly is called Scutlande, or Scotland' (Spenser, *Ireland*, pp. 37–8). On 2 June 1767 Edward Murphy had written to Hume in a jocu-lar manner, touching on this ethnographical theory: 'history proves that we native Irish (whom you, and other mistaken mortals reckon savages, because we have wings and tails, and eat human flesh when we can get it good) – we, I say, are proved by history to be Scythians by descent, or rather Σκυθαι or Skyths, which word has been corrupted into Scots; with which people we never have had the least intercourse' (Burton, *Letters*, p. 171).

5. *Tyrants ... in their turn*] Perhaps an anonymized reference to the career of Oliver Cromwell, similar to the parallel passage in 'Of the Original Contract' (above, pp. 165–6).

6. *PLATO's account ... marriage*] A reference to *Symposium*, 189c–193d, where Aristophanes relates this fable. In *The Examiner*, no. 31 (8 March 1710) Swift had also applied this fable to the birth of party (Swift, *Prose Writings*, vol. III, pp. 101–5). Swift's reapplication of the fable provides a precedent for Hume's similar extension of it.

7. *ANDROGYNES*] Hume had initially made an error here, by trusting to his memory: 'I suppose, that instead of the Hydrogenes, I should have said the Androgynes of Plato' (*Letters*, vol. I, p. 32; *New Letters*, p. 7). Cf. Plato, *Symposium*, 189e.

8. *LOVE and HYMEN*] Another attempt at allegory: see above, pp. 591–2, n. 6.

## VI. OF THE STUDY OF HISTORY

Published in: *1741, 1742b, 1748a, 1753, 1758, 1760*
Significant revisions:

> 1) *1741–1748a* omit the attribution to Lucretius of the final quotation (cf. above, p. 237).

Copy text: *1760*
Headnote:

> See headnote to 'Of Love and Marriage' for the circumstances surrounding the withdrawal of this essay.
>
> It is not surprising that Hume should have wanted to write an essay on this subject. But it is surely surprising that, given the seriousness and depth of his historical interests, he could not have written something better. In particular, it is remarkable that Hume does not here give adequate treatment to the vital contribution made by history to the emergent 'science of man'. The bantering opening section of the essay, in which Hume attempts a would-be gallant address to 'female readers', reveals just how distorting the early ambition to imitate Addison had been. In the case of this essay, the snare of Addisonian imitation almost entirely suppresses the genuinely interesting discussion of this subject that Hume was certainly capable of writing.

1. *Among other important truths*] The study of history was commonly recommended as inculcating wisdom and practical morality; as philosophy teaching by examples (in the famous formulation of Bolingbroke, in his *Letters on the Study and Use of History* [1752], pp. 15 and 57); as an illustration and vindication of the providential government of the world; or as a revelation of the secrets of rule, the 'arcana imperii' (Tacitus, *Annals*, II.xxxvi). Here Hume is attempting, perhaps without great success, a playful lightness.

2. *I remember . . . against her*] Presumably a fiction.

3. *secret history*] The phrase 'secret history' is equivalent to 'anecdotes', and so reaches back to the *Anecdota* (or 'Things Unpublished') composed by the Byzantine historian Procopius of Caesarea, a scandalous insider's account of the court of the emperor Justinian which defamed the emperor, his empress Theodora, and their chief military commander Belisarius. The manuscript of the *Anecdota* had been discovered in the Vatican before 1623, when the first bowdlerized Latin translation of it as *Arcana Historia* ('The Secret History') was published at Lyon by Nicolaus Alemannus. Hence 'Anecdotes' came to be synonymous with 'Secret History'. Modern imitations had begun with Antoine Varillas, *Anekdota Heterouiaka* (1685), a secret history of the Medicis translated into English by Ferrand Spence in 1686. In England 'secret history' flourished as originally a Whig literary

form in which the misdemeanours of the Stuarts were luridly portrayed: cf. *The Secret History of the Four Last Monarchs of Great Britain* (1691) and John Somers's *True Secret History of the Reigns of All the Kings and Queens of England* (1702). The genre had received a Tory twist when Delarivier Manley published *The New Atalantis* (1709). Swift was contemptuous of the genre, as catering to the literary tastes of women: 'His [Burnet's] Secret History is generally made up of coffee-house scandals, or at best from reports at the third, fourth, or fifth hand. The account of the Pretender's birth, would only become an old woman in a chimney corner' (Swift, *Prose Writings*, vol. V, p. 183; cf. also p. 228). On the applications of secret history in England at this time, see Rebecca Bullard, *The Politics of Disclosure 1674–1725: Secret History Narratives* (London: Pickering and Chatto, 2009).

4. *handle my subject more seriously*] But note that Hume nevertheless does not discuss history as a justification of divine providence.

5. *to observe … arts and sciences*] The favourite Enlightenment theme of the 'progress of society'. Recent salient examples include the prefatory essay 'A View of the Progress of Society in Europe' with which William Robertson had introduced his *History of Charles V* (1769), vol. I, pp. 1–192. Hume's own 'Of the Rise and Progress of the Arts and Sciences' (above, vol. 1, pp. 93–112) is itself of course a notable contribution to the subject; as is his unpublished 'An Historical Essay on Chivalry and modern Honour' (above, pp. 265–71). The Enlightenment consensus that the development of arts and sciences had been a boon to mankind and had encouraged human flourishing would soon be vigorously challenged by Rousseau's *Discours* (Geneva, 1750), on the question 'Si le rétablissement des Sciences & des Arts a contribué à épurer les Mœurs', which had been set by the Académie de Dijon.

6. *To remark the rise … empires*] cf. the note on the natural tendency of empires to impermanence in the 'Early Memoranda': 'There seems to be a natural Course of Things, which brings on the Destruction of great Empires. They push their Conquests till they come to barbarous Nations, which stop their Progress, by the Difficulty of subsisting great Armies. After that, the Nobility & considerable Men of the conquering Nation & best Provinces withdraw gradually from the [frontier *inserted above the line*] Army, by reason of its Distance from the Capital & barbarity of the Country, in which they quarter: They forget the Use of War. Their barbarous Soldiers become their Masters. These have no Law but their Sword, both from their bad Education, & from their Distance from the Sovereign [to whom they bear no Affection *inserted above the line*]. Hence Disorder, Violence, Anarchy, & Tyranny, & a Dissolution of Empire.' (NLS MS 23159, item 14, p. 27; cf. Mossner, 'Memoranda', pp. 517–18).

7. *In reality … choice of pleasures*] This description of the pleasures of the mental prospect afforded by history recalls the fallacious description of the

pleasures of immortality that Swift had attributed to Gulliver: 'if it had been my good Fortune to come into the World a *Struldbrugg*; as soon as I could discover my own Happiness by understanding the Difference between Life and Death, I would first resolve by all Arts and Methods whatsoever to procure myself Riches: In the Pursuit of which, by Thrift and Management, I might reasonably expect in about two Hundred Years, to be the wealthiest Man in the Kingdom. In the second Place, I would from my earliest Youth apply myself to the Study of Arts and Sciences, by which I should arrive in time to excel all others in Learning. Lastly, I would carefully record every Action and Event of Consequence that happened in the Publick, impartially draw the Characters of the several Successions of Princes, and great Ministers of State; with my own Observations on every Point. I would exactly set down the several Changes in Customs, Languages, Fashions, Dress, Dyet and Diversions. By all which Acquirements, I should be a living Treasury of Knowledge and Wisdom, and certainly become the Oracle of the Nation ... Add to all this, the Pleasure of seeing the various Revolutions of States and Empires; the Changes in the lower and upper World; antient Cities in Ruins, and obscure Villages become the Seats of Kings. Famous Rivers lessening into shallow Brooks; the Ocean leaving one Coast dry, and overwhelming another: The Discovery of many Countries yet unknown. Barbarity overrunning the politest Nations, and the most barbarous becoming civilized. I should then see the Discovery of the *Longitude*, the *perpetual Motion*, the *universal Medicine*, and many other great Inventions brought to the utmost Perfection' (Swift, *Gulliver's Travels*, pp. 312-14).

8. *for ever children*] Echoing a famous remark of Cicero's: 'Nescire quid ante quam natus sis acciderit id est semper esse puerum'; 'To be ignorant of what happened before you were born is to be a perpetual child' (*Orator*, XXIV. cxx).

9. *to deny the reality of all moral distinctions*] Most immediately, a glance at the school of moral scepticism associated with Mandeville.

10. *that remark of HORACE ... return upon you*] 'Naturam expelles furca, tamen usque recurret, / et mala perrumpet furtim fastidia victrix'; 'You may drive out nature with a pitchfork, yet she will return, and will disrupt your foolish contempt in triumph' (*Epistles*, I.x.24-5).

11. *a just medium*] This placing of the study of history between the *vita activa* of a man of business and the *vita contemplativa* of a philosopher is interesting in relation to Hume's turn towards the writing of history, already substantially accomplished before this essay was withdrawn.

12. *LUCRET.*] *De Rerum Natura*, III.57-8: 'only then are truthful words drawn from the depths of the heart'.

## VII. OF AVARICE

Published in: *1741, 1742b, 1748a, 1753, 1758, 1760, 1764, 1767, 1768*
Significant revisions: none
Copy text: *1768*
Headnote:

> Another example of Hume's desire in these early essays to reinforce the 'common sense of its time' in an 'interesting and unusual way' (Harris, *Hume*, p. 161). It was important, however, that these new justifications of received moral positions should be 'natural', and therefore free of any basis in theology.

1. *has often been compared*] Despite Hume's confident assertion that this was a common comparison, no example of it has been traced.
2. *Two men . . . end of his story*] See *1 Henry IV*, II.iv.200.
3. *Among the fables . . . ingenious author*] 'L'Avare et Minos', in *Fables nouvelles* (Paris, 1719), pp. 57–61. These fables were translated in 1721 as *One Hundred New Court Fables*.
4. *Styx . . . Charon*] In classical mythology respectively, the river separating Hades from the world of the living, and the ferryman who carried the dead over the Styx to Hades for the fare of one penny. In conversation Hume would playfully imagine his own crossing and his conversation with Charon (above, vol. 1, pp. 11–12).
5. *Prometheus*] For the crime of giving fire to mankind Prometheus was chained to a rock and had his liver devoured daily by an eagle, before it regrew overnight to be consumed once more the following day.
6. *Danaides*] The daughters of Danaus were punished for murdering their husbands by being made to pour water into a leaky urn (Horace, *Odes*, III. xi.21–52).
7. *Sisyphus*] Sisyphus was condemned for ever to roll a boulder up a slope, without ever reaching the summit (Homer, *Odyssey*, XI.593–600). Hume has slightly curtailed the number of possible punishments Minos was encouraged to consider; in La Motte's original the punishments of Tantalus and Ixion are also recommended (La Motte, *Fables*, p. 60).
8. *Minos*] In classical mythology, one of the three judges of the dead.
9. *Damn'd . . . slave that hides*] See Pope, *Epistles to Several Persons*, epistle III, 'Of the Use of Riches', ll. 109–10.
10. *ransack her very bowels for hidden treasure*] Hume's language here is close to that of Milton's account of how Mammon encouraged men to mine for precious metals: 'By him first / Men also, and by his suggestion taught, / Ransacked the center, and with impious hands / Rifled the bowels of their mother earth / For treasures better hid' (*Paradise Lost*, I.684–8). On the

general topos of the violent impiety of mining, cf. also Ovid, *Metamorphoses*, I.125–42; Spenser, *Faerie Queene*, II.vii.17; and Sidney, *Arcadia*, p. 135.

11. *bury and conceal their riches*] cf. perhaps the incident of the Yahoo who buried some jewels only to have them stolen (Swift, *Gulliver's Travels*, Part IV, chapter 7, p. 392).

## VIII. A CHARACTER OF SIR ROBERT WALPOLE

Published in: *1742a*
Significant revisions: none; but see the 'Headnote' below
Copy text: *1742a*
Headnote:

In editions of the *Essays* subsequent to *1742a*, and up to and including *1768* (i.e. in *1748a*, *1753*, *1758*, *1760*, *1764*, *1767* and *1768*), this character of Walpole was printed not as a separate essay but rather as a footnote at the end of 'That Politics may be reduced to a Science'. From *1748a* to *1768* the text of the portrait was introduced with the following remarks: '*What our Author's Opinion was of the famous Minister here pointed at, may be learn'd from that Essay, printed in the former Edition, under the Title of* A Character of Sir ROBERT WALPOLE. *It was as follows:*' (*1748a*, p. 36). After the text of the character, Hume added the following: '*The Author is pleased to find, that after Animosities are laid, and Calumny has ceas'd, the whole Nation almost have return'd to the same moderate Sentiments with regard to this great Man; if they are not rather become more favourable to him, by a very natural Transition, from one Extreme to another. The Author would not oppose these humane Sentiments towards the Dead; tho' he cannot forbear observing, that the not paying more of our public Debts was, as hinted in this Character, a great, and the only great, Error in that long Administration*' (*1748a*, pp. 37–8). In *1742a* it had been introduced with the following remarks in the 'Advertisement' prefacing the whole volume: 'The Character of Sir ROBERT WALPOLE was drawn some Months ago, when that Great MAN was in the Zenith of his Power. I must confess, that, at present, when he seems to be upon the Decline, I am inclin'd to think more favourably of him, and to suspect, that the Antipathy, which every true born *Briton* naturally bears to Ministers of State, inspir'd me with some Prejudice against him. The impartial READER, if any such there be; or Posterity, if such a Trifle can reach them, will best be able to correct my Mistakes in this Particular' (pp. iii–iv; and above, p. 286). Cf. Hume's jocular reference to this essay in his letter to William Mure of 14 November 1742 (*Letters*, vol. I, p. 44). For the textual history of the portrait, see Robert C. Elliott, 'Hume's "Character of Sir Robert Walpole": Some Unnoticed Additions', *Journal of English and Germanic Philology*, XLVIII (1949), pp. 367–70.

There are two references to Walpole and his political career in the 'Early Memoranda': 'The Pension Bill fail'd passing along with the Triennial in a Whig Courtier Parliament only by some Idle Disputes about the Expression of the King & his Heirs & Successors' and 'S. R. W. was more considerable before he was Prime Minister than any private Man since. His Change in one Night about the Mutiny Bill in 1717 augmented the ~~Mutiny Bill~~ [Majority *inserted above the line*] by 80' (NLS MS 23159, item 14, p. 11; cf. Mossner, 'Memoranda', p. 504). In 'Of Eloquence' Hume illustrated the modern lack of interest in parliamentary oratory by reporting that 'When old CIBBER is to act, the curiosity of several is more excited, than when our prime minister is to defend himself from a motion for his removal or impeachment' (above, vol. 1, p. 85). These events took place in early 1742.

A comment in 'Of Refinement in the Arts' is relevant to Hume's distancing of himself in this essay from the allegations of corruption that were regularly levelled at Walpole: 'And though corruption may seem to encrease of late years; this is chiefly to be ascribed to our established liberty, when our princes have found the impossibility of governing without parliaments, or of terrifying parliaments by the phantoms of prerogative' (above, p. 21). Cf. the note on 'private *bribery*' to 'Of the Independency of Parliament' (above, vol. 1, p. 47).

1. *more earnestly and openly canvassed*] For an overview of the eighteenth-century debate on Walpole's character and the tendency of his ministry, see Christine Gerrard, *The Patriot Opposition to Walpole: Politics, Poetry, and National Myth, 1725–1742* (Oxford: Clarendon Press, 1994).

2. *Twenty Years*] i.e. since 1721.

3. *not virtuous*] Walpole had a reputation for lax sexual morals.

4. *not attended with Frugality*] A hint of Hume's concerns about the growth of the national debt: see above, p. 395, n. 38.

5. *He would have been … never possest it*] An allusion to Tacitus's famous lapidary judgement on Galba: 'omnium consensu capax imperii nisi imperasset'; 'in the opinion of all capable of being emperor, had he never become emperor' (*Histories*, I.xlix).

6. *Learning gone to Ruin*] That Walpole had failed to offer patronage to writers of talent, and instead had directed public money towards those who were prepared to write in support of his administration and policies, was a common criticism levelled at the first minister. In a note to *The Dunciad*, II.314, Pope had complained that 'One Minister … expended, for the current dulness of ten years in Britain, double the sum which gained Louis XIV. so much honour, in annual Pensions to Learned men all over Europe. In which, and in a much longer time, not a Pension at Court, nor Preferment in the Church or Universities, of any Consideration, was bestowed on any man distinguished for his Learning separately from Party-merit, or Pamphlet-writing.' It was a

criticism that stuck. As late as 1759, in his *An Inquiry into the Present State of Polite Learning*, Goldsmith would regret that the connection between literary accomplishment and political power that had been forged during the ascendancy of Lord Somers had more recently been destroyed: 'Since the days of a certain prime minister of inglorious memory [i.e. Walpole], the learned have been kept pretty much at a distance. A jockey, or a laced player, supplies the place of the scholar, poet, or the man of virtue. Those conversations, once the result of wisdom, wit, and innocence, are now turned to humbler topics, little more being expected from a companion than a laced coat, a pliant bow, and an immoderate friendship for – a well-served table' (*The Miscellaneous Works of Oliver Goldsmith* [London: Macmillan, 1925], p. 435).

7. *St. James's*] Then the principal royal residence in London, to which the Prime Minister would naturally have easy access.

8. *Houghton-Hall*] Walpole's country house in Norfolk.

# Posthumously Published Essays

## OF SUICIDE

Published in: *1777b*
Significant revisions: none
Copy text: NLS MS 509, pp. 203–21
Headnote:

This essay and 'Of the Immortality of the Soul' have a complicated history of composition and eventual, much delayed, publication. It is however worth tracing that history in some detail, because it sheds light on the informal constraints on the dissemination of heterodox material in Britain even after the lapse of the Licensing Act in 1695, which is so often assumed (mistakenly) to have opened the floodgates of uncensored publication. In fact, after 1695 post-publication censorship remained in full force under the provisions of legislation designed to prevent seditious libel (on which, see Thomas Keymer, *Poetics of the Pillory* [Oxford: Oxford University Press, 2019]). In addition, informal machinery to suppress the dissemination of heterodox material remained effective, as the publication history of these essays shows.

In a letter to William Strahan of 25 January 1772, Hume related how 'Of Suicide' and 'Of the Immortality of the Soul' had been printed in 1755 but had then been suppressed. A rumour had gone about in London in 1772 that these two essays were now at last to be published, and it was this rumour which impelled Hume to write to Strahan: 'These I suppose are two Essays of mine, one on Suicide and another on the Immortality of the Soul, which were printed by Andrew Millar about seventeen Years ago, and which from my abundant Prudence I suppress'd and would not now wish to have revivd. I know not if you were acquainted with this Transaction. It was this: I intended to print four Dissertations, the natural History of Religion, on the Passions, on Tragedy, and on the metaphisical Principles of Geometry. I sent them up to Mr Millar; but before the last was printed, I happend to meet with Lord Stanhope, who was in this Country, and he convincd me, that either there was some Defect in the Argument or in its perspicuity; I forget which; and I wrote to Mr Millar, that I woud not print that Essay; but upon

601

his remonstrating that the other Essays woud not make a Volume, I sent him up these two [i.e. the essays 'Of Suicide' and 'Of the Immortality of the Soul'], which I had never intended to have publishd. They were printed; but it was no sooner done than I repented; and Mr Millar and I agreed to suppress them at common Charges, and I wrote a new Essay on the Standard of Taste, to supply their place. Mr Millar assurd me very earnestly that all the Copies were suppress'd, except one which he sent to Sir Andrew Mitchell, in whose Custody I thought it safe. But I have since found that there either was some Infidelity or Negligence in the case; for on Mr Morehead's Death, there was found a Copy, which his Nephew deliverd up to me. But there have other Copies got abroad; and from one of these, some rascally Bookseller is, it seems, printing this Edition' (*Letters*, vol. II, pp. 252–4). On Stanhope's European-wide reputation as a mathematician, see the letter to Hume from D'Alembert of 14 January 1769 (Burton, *Letters*, pp. 215–16).

The rumoured pirated edition of these two essays in 1772 did not in fact appear. 'Of Suicide' and 'Of the Immortality of the Soul' were first printed posthumously in 1777 as *Two Essays*, without any indication on the title page as to either author or printer. By a codicil to his will of 7 August 1776 Hume had left his manuscripts to Strahan, specifying that 'I desire, that my Dialogues concerning natural Religion may be printed and published any time with two Years after my Death; to which, he [i.e. Strahan] may add, if he thinks proper, the two Essays formerly printed but not published' (*Letters*, vol. II, p. 453); and the surviving proof copy of the 1755 *Five Dissertations*, including the texts of the essays on suicide and the immortality of the soul, with corrections in Hume's hand (NLS MS 509), was inscribed by Hume as follows: 'This book is to be considerd as a manuscript and to be deliverd to Mr Strahan according to my will.' Strahan did not in the event publish the *Dialogues Concerning Natural Religion*, which had to wait until 1779 to be published at the instigation of David Hume the Younger (see *Letters*, vol. II, p. 454).

There are three textual witnesses to the texts of these essays: 1) the proof copy of the suppressed 1755 *Five Dissertations*, corrected by Hume (NLS MS 509); 2) the posthumous and unattributed *Two Essays* (1777), hereafter referred to as *1777b*; and 3) *Essays on Suicide, and the Immortality of the Soul, Ascribed to the Late David Hume* (1783), hereafter referred to as *1783*.

The corrections Hume made to the 1755 proofs of these essays were relatively few and modest, and can be grouped under the following four headings: 1) corrections of compositional errors (4); 2) eliminations of archaisms (13); 3) adjustments to punctuation (3); 4) substantive changes to wording (15). However, none of these corrections affects in the slightest the argument of either essay. It is also important to recognize that we do not know when Hume made these corrections, just as we also do not know when he composed the essays themselves (Harris, *Hume*, p. 359); although it may be significant that section XI of the *Enquiry Concerning Human Understanding*, on a particular providence and a future state, is plainly relevant to both essays. The thorough elimination of archaisms and archaic contractions suggests that the correction of proof may have been some time after 1755, since presumably Hume had been satisfied with these spellings and stylistic features in the MS he had sent to Millar earlier that year. NLS MS 509 might therefore be the copy of *Five Dissertations* returned to Hume by Morehead's nephew after Morehead's death some years afterwards, and which Hume then corrected to his later satisfaction (*Letters*, vol. II, pp. 253–4, n. 3).

Comparison of the readings in NLS MS 509 with the text published in *1777b* supports the following inferences about the relationship between these two witnesses: 1) *1777b* was printed in ignorance of the corrections Hume had made to the 1755 proof, since none of its readings was adopted; and, 2) some of the variants in *1777b* suggest that the compositor did not fully understand what he was typesetting, and that the proofreader (if any) was at moments similarly confused. For the most part, the differences between *1777b* and the 1755 texts of these essays involve accidental matters of paragraphing, spelling and punctuation. So it seems reasonable to conclude that *1777b* was set from one of the 'escaped' copies of *Five Dissertations* (1755), but not the copy corrected by Hume (NLS MS 509). However, one variant may possess a further significance. *1777b* reads '*Varro*' instead of the 1755 reading '*Nero*'. This may suggest that *1777b* was set from an *earlier* proof of 1755, and that the corrected proof preserved in NLS MS 509 is a second or subsequent proof. *1783* was evidently set from a copy of *1777b*, as the preserved misreading '*Varro*' in *1783* indicates (see *1777b*, p. 39, and *1783*, p. 36). This perhaps increases the likelihood that the origin of *1777b* was an early, escaped, proof of the 1755 volume.

It follows that both *1777b* and *1783* have no independent textual authority. They do, however, have a clear historical importance, since they preserve the only versions of these two essays that were known to the readers of the nineteenth and early twentieth centuries. Two further inferences are possible. The authorial inscription inside NLS MS 509, that it is to be treated as a MS and conveyed to Strahan on Hume's death, perhaps implies either that Hume's wishes were disregarded, or that the publisher of *1777b* was not Strahan; or possibly both of those. Certainly *1777b*, which is crudely printed, does not look like the other refined products of Strahan's publishing house.

It is worth recalling that suicide was not merely an abstract question for Hume. In 1746 he had witnessed the suicide of a distant relative, Alexander Forbes, an officer serving alongside Hume under General St Clair. Anxious over whether he would be able to do his duty, Forbes had succumbed to depression: 'returning to his Room early next Morning, I found him with small Remains of Life, wallowing in his own Blood, with the Arteries of his Arm cut asunder. I immediatly sent for a Surgeon, got a Bandage ty'd to his Arm, & recoverd him entirely to his Senses & Understanding. He liv'd above four & twenty hours after, & I had several Conversations with him. Never a man exprest a more steady Contempt of Life nor more determind philosophical Principles, suitable to his Exit. He beg'd of me to unloosen his Bandage & hasten his Death, as the last Act of Friendship I coud show him: But alas! we live not in Greek or Roman times' (*Letters*, vol. I, p. 97).

However, what were Hume's deepest and original (not necessarily the same thing, of course) intentions for these essays? The comment in his letter to Strahan that these were essays 'which I had never intended to have publishd' encourages us to reflect more widely on the anomalousness of their spare stylistic manner, when compared with Hume's other essays. Earlier sympathetic discussions of suicide – for instance, Donne's *Biathanatos* (1644) or John Robeck's *Exercitatio Philosophica de ... Morte Voluntaria Philosophorum et Bonorum Virorum etiam Iudaeorum et Christianorum* (Rintelii, 1736) – had relied on a piling up of examples more than on an analysis of underlying arguments. As Robeck had said: 'Mors voluntaria ex iis, quas indicauimus, caussis oppetita, omnium populorum, Graecorum, Romanorum, Afrorum, Asiaticorum sensibus, moribus ac institutis congruens, infinitis exemplis est probata' ['Infinite examples show that voluntary death, from the causes I have indicated, was approved of by the united sentiments, customs, and precepts of all peoples – Greeks, Romans, Africans, and Asiatics']; and he did not stint himself in accumulating and rehearsing these 'infinita exempla' (p. 178). Donne also had drawn attention to the lavishness of his examples: 'Every branch which is excerpted from other authors, and engrafted here, is not written for the readers faith, but for illustration and comparison. Because I undertooke the declaration of such a proposition as was controverted by many, and therefore was drawne to the citation of many authorities, I was willing to goe all the way with company, and to take light from others, as well in the iourney as at the journeys end. If therefore in multiplicity of not necessary citations there appeare vanity, or ostentation, or digression my honesty must make my excuse and compensation, who acknowledg as *Pliny* doth [*That to chuse rather to be taken in a theft, then to gaue every man due, is* obnoxii animi, et infelicis ingenii.] I did it the rather because scholastique and artificiall men use this way of instructing; and I made account that I was to deale with such, because I presume that naturall men are at least enough inclinable of themselves to this doctrine' (p. 23). Abundance of citation is the early-modern way when talking of voluntary death, because (so it would seem) it offers valuable camouflage to the author on this most sensitive of topics. 'These are not necessarily my opinions on suicide,' the anthologizing author such as Donne or Robeck seems to say; 'I am merely reporting and arranging the evidence.' Hume takes quite a different tack in 'Of Suicide' and 'Of the Immortality of the Soul'. Here we find no examples, but rather an unswerving focus on premises, inferences and arguments. The rhetorical element of these arguments is completely pared away.

If these were indeed, as the letter to Strahan seems to suggest, private papers in which Hume, in a skeletal way, had clarified and made precise his thinking about two issues which were related to a whole series of philosophical questions (identity, substance, justice, religion, superstition) that lay at the centre of his philosophical life, and which moreover touched on some of the most neuralgic ethical, political and theological points in the British culture of his day, then they open a window on the fascinating process whereby Hume's thoughts were at first transmitted to paper, and thence eventually, sometimes, became publications. The implication in the letter to Strahan seems to be that Hume had these papers to hand, in a more or less finished form, in the mid-1750s. In a moment of weakness, he sent them to London to satisfy Andrew Millar's importunity. They may have been composed some long time before 1755; the points of contact with entries in the 'Early Memoranda', noted in the annotation below, show that Hume had been thinking hard about these questions as a young man. If that hypothesis is correct, then the rhetorical thinness of these essays might be to some degree explained by the fact that they were little more than the heads of arguments the younger Hume had drawn up on these subjects, and which he had originally composed purely for his private satisfaction. As Michael MacDonald observes, these essays are simply 'a series of answers to objections that were commonplace in the early eighteenth century' (MacDonald, *Sleepless Souls*, p. 161). Their composition might therefore mark the discursive watershed between the earlier legalistic discussion of the permissibility or otherwise of suicide (which they embody), and the later Romantic and sentimental treatment of the subject that was both crystallized and popularized in Goethe's *The Sorrows of Young Werther* (1774) before being systematized by Mme de Staël in her *Reflections on Suicide* (1813) (MacDonald, *Sleepless Souls*, pp. 176–7; Robertson, *Enlightenment*, p. 337).

These two essays are linked by more than just the accidents of their publication history, for the topics of suicide and the immortality of the soul had been entangled from the earliest antiquity. If it is true that Pythagoras was the originator of the simile that would be invoked so often by later writers against suicide, namely that God has placed us here as a sentinel, and it is not open to us to quit our post (as reported by Cicero, *De Senectute*, LXXIII), then this condemnation of suicide may be a corollary of the Pythagorean doctrine of metempsychosis, which clearly assumes the immortality of the soul. In the *Phaedo*, Socrates's voluntary death is preceded by arguments asserting both the impermissibility of suicide and the immortality of the soul. The story of the suicide of Cato the Younger, which allegedly followed a reading of the *Phaedo* (Plutarch, *Cato the Younger*, LXVIII), had been dramatized by Addison in *Cato* (1713), a celebrated early eighteenth-century play in which the immortality of the soul and the nobility of suicide had come together memorably in Cato's speech at the beginning of Act V, scene i (itself a fascinating *rifacimento* of Hamlet's soliloquy 'To be, or not to be'): 'It must be so – Plato, thou reason'st well! – / Else whence this pleasing hope, this fond desire, / This longing after immortality? / Or whence this secret dread, and inward horror, / Of falling into nought? why shrinks the soul / Back on herself, and startles at destruction?' (Addison, *Cato*, p. 88).

However, the relationship between these two topics, though almost perennial, was not stable. In pagan antiquity, it might be the case (but, given the range of attitudes towards suicide in pagan antiquity, it might not necessarily and inevitably be the case) that a persuasion of the immortality of the soul, imprisoned within the material body, might serve as an encouragement to suicide: the examples of Cato, Seneca and Thrasea Paetus seem to illustrate this (Griffin, 'Roman Suicide', p. 65). But once suicide had in late antiquity been condemned by Christendom as a mortal sin, a persuasion of the immortality of the soul (which might receive eternal punishment) would surely have dissuaded men from committing suicide. So, in the legal, confessional and moral dispensation within which Hume was writing, the arguments of these two essays fitted together snugly. Suicide, Hume argues, is not in any discoverable sense a crime; and even if it were, there is no afterlife in which the soul could be punished, since we have no reason to believe that the soul is immortal.

Hume threw a simple and dichotomous historical schema over the topics of both these essays. It was the advent of Christendom, he claims, that both condemned suicide in defiance of the toleration of the practice of voluntary death in pagan antiquity, and that promulgated the doctrine of the immortality of the soul.

In respect of both suicide and the immortality of the soul, however, Hume is factually wrong. The ancient Greeks and Romans did not condone all forms of suicide (see below, pp. 611–13, n. 4); and they certainly entertained a notion of the immortality of the soul. Plato's *Phaedo*, a dialogue it is inconceivable that Hume did not know well (for instance, he refers to it in the *Natural History of Religion* [*NHR*, p. 74]), is in itself striking evidence of both these facts. Moreover, the Christian condemnation of suicide began no earlier than Augustine, and was crystallized into canon law as late as 452 at the Council of Arles (the early Christian legislation regarding suicide is summarized in C. A. Kerin, *The Privation of Christian Burial: An Historical Synopsis and Commentary*, Catholic University of America Canon Law Studies, 136 [Washington DC, 1941]; cf. also Nils Retterstøl, *Suicide: A European Perspective* [Cambridge: Cambridge University Press, 1993], p. 17). Furthermore, an entry in the 'Early Memoranda' demonstrates that Hume was well aware that in ancient Greece the corpses of suicides might suffer mutilation and degradation: 'It was a Custom among the Greeks, if a Person killd himself, to cut off his hand, & bury it apart from the Body. Id.' (NLS MS 23159, item 14, p. 25; cf. Mossner, 'Memoranda', p. 515).

Prior to St Augustine's *City of God* the culture of Christendom had been receptive to, at moments even enthusiastic about, voluntary death. The Passion had been interpreted as a voluntary death by Tertullian and others, following the implication of Christ's words in John 10:17–18: 'Therefore doth the Father love me, because I lay down my life, that I may take it again. No one taketh it away from me, but I lay it down of myself. I have power to lay it down, and I have power to take it again.' (On the point of the Passion as a voluntary death, see also Donne, *Biathanatos*, p. 58.) Other scriptural texts which seem to endorse suicide, such as 2 Maccabees 14:37–46, Philippians 1:23 and Romans 7:24, were cited further to condone the practice. Donne had noted the widespread scriptural silence about suicide: 'when I entred into the examination of places of Scriptures, it seemed to me to have some weight, that in all the Judiciall and Ceremoniall Law, there was no abomination of *Selfe-homicide* ... in relating the Histories of them who killed themselves, the phrase of Scripture never diminishes them by any aspersion or imputation for that fact, if they were otherwise vertuous, nor aggravates thereby their former wickednesse, if they were wicked' (Donne, *Biathanatos*, p. 195). Accordingly, Hamlet had spoken carelessly when he complained that 'the Everlasting had ... fixed / His canon 'gainst self-slaughter (*Hamlet*, I.ii.131–2; and cf. *Cymbeline*, III.iv.75–7). The Christian prohibition of suicide is not scriptural, but patristic.

Accordingly, early Christian sects such as the Donatists (against whom the miso-suicide Augustine had ranged himself: his arguments against suicide had been forged as weapons in a clerical wrestle for supremacy with Petilian, the Donatist bishop of Cirta, who had contended that Judas was a martyr on the grounds of his self-slaughter) had blurred the line between genuine martyrdom and suicide (on the Donatists, see Gibbon, *Decline and Fall*, vol. I, p. 823). Indeed, the vehemence of Augustine's attack on suicide in the *City of God*, I.xi–xxvii, can be read as an oblique witness to the prevalence and deep-rootedness of the culture of voluntary death in early Christianity. For as Donne would shrewdly observe, 'wheresoever you finde many and severe Lawes against an offence it is not safe from thence to conclude an extreame enormity or hainousnesse in the fault, but a propensnesse of that people, at that time, to that fault' (Donne, *Biathanatos*, p. 93; cf. Robeck, *Exercitatio*, p. 276, where the approval of suicide among 'priscos Christianos' ['the first Christians'] is noted).

Moreover, early Christianity had also accommodated sects that asserted the mortality of the soul, and this heresy had revived with some vigour in England in the mid-seventeenth century: see, e.g., Richard Overton, *Mans Mortalitie* ('Amsterdam', 1644), and for commentary see Nicholas McDowell, 'Dead Souls and Modern Minds? Mortalism and the Early Modern Imagination, from Marlowe to Milton', *Journal of Medieval and Early Modern Studies*, vol. XL (2010), pp. 559–92.

In the recent past, arguments against suicide had been advanced on grounds different from ecclesiastical doctrinal fiat. In chapter 14 of *Leviathan* Hobbes had, in passing, seemed to condemn self-murder as a contravention of natural law: 'A LAW OF NATURE, (*Lex Naturalis*,) is a Precept, or generall Rule, found out by Reason, by which a man is forbidden to do, that, which is destructive of his life, or taketh away the means of preserving the same' (Hobbes, *Leviathan*, p. 91). For Locke, suicide was forbidden because it conflicted with the implications of his theory of property. Contrary to what men might think, they were the property of the God who had created them, and hence had no property in themselves: 'But though this [the state of nature] be a *State of Liberty*, yet it is *not a State of Licence*, though Man in that State have an uncontroleable Liberty, to dispose of his Person or Possessions, yet he has not Liberty to destroy himself, or so much as any Creature in his Possession, but where some nobler use, than its bare Preservation calls for it . . . For Men being all the Workmanship of one Omnipotent, and infinitely wise Maker; All the Servants of one Sovereign Master, sent into the World by his order and about his business, they are his Property, whose Workmanship they are, made to last during his, not one anothers Pleasure.' The upshot is that 'Man, [does not have] the Power of his own Life . . .' ('Second Treatise', §§ 6 and 23, Locke, *Two Treatises*, pp. 270–71 and 284).

What then might explain Hume's simplification of the relationship between pagan antiquity and Christendom in relation to both suicide and the immortality of the soul? It is perhaps not coincidental that in the summer of 1755 Hume had come under renewed attack from the Popular Party in the Church of Scotland. In such an adversarial setting, nuance and scholarly precision might suffer: see Harris, *Hume*, pp. 355–61. As MacDonald says: 'The debate over suicide was one campaign in the war between the champions of 'modern paganism' and traditional Christianity' (MacDonald, *Sleepless Souls*, p. 148). That said, it is probably a mistake to view Hume in these two essays as a lonely and pioneering voice for humanity and moderation, since according to the careful research of MacDonald humanity and moderation had been in the ascendant in attitudes towards suicide since the Restoration. Rather, in these essays Hume emerges as a spokesman for the new humane orthodoxy that was ever more successfully resisting moral and clerical revanchism. As Jeffrey Watt has noted, the philosophic defence of suicide was in the rear of, rather than leading, the trend of popular opinion: 'The decline in penalties cannot be attributed to the influence of Voltaire, Montesquieu, and other Enlightenment writers who criticized these judicial practices. Sentences that went beyond the denial of burial rites were becoming less common already in the mid-seventeenth century, well before these critics raised their voices.' Therefore, they should be seen as 'more an expression of changing mentalities already under way than the agents of change themselves' (Jeffrey R. Watt [ed.], *From Sin to Insanity: Suicide in Early*

*Modern Europe* [Ithaca, NY: Cornell University Press, 2004], p. 5). It was therefore a sign of the times that, when John 'Estimate' Brown had committed suicide in 1766, he had been quietly buried in St James's Church.

It is possible that Hume's treatment of suicide was influenced by Montesquieu, who had discussed suicide on three occasions. Two of these instances have little detectable relation to Hume's essay. In chapter 12 of book XIV of the *Esprit des Lois* Montesquieu had considered the supposed inclination of the English towards suicide as 'l'effet d'une maladie', a disorder of the 'filtration du suc nerveux' (Montesquieu, *Esprit*, vol. I, p. 377). In chapter 12 of the *Considérations sur les causes de la grandeur des Romains et de leur décadence* he had reflected in a paradoxical and curiously unengaged manner on the Roman custom of suicide, concluding that: 'L'amour-propre, l'amour de notre conservation, se transforme en tant de manières, et agit par des principes si contraires, qu'il nous porte à sacrifier notre être pour l'amour de notre être; et tel est le cas que nous faisons de nous-mêmes, que nous consentons à cesser de vivre, par un instinct nature et obscur qui fait que nous nous aimons plus que notre vie même' (Montesquieu, *Œuvres*, p. 459).

That sense of disengagement is curious, however, because in letter 76 of *Lettres Persanes* Montesquieu had placed in the mouth of Usbek a series of powerful, at moments indignant, criticisms of the European condemnation of suicide (Montesquieu, *Œuvres*, p. 103); and here we can finally see an affinity with Hume's essay. Some of Usbek's criticisms and the wording in which they are expressed are close to Hume's criticisms, and they are noted in the annotation below.

The influence of Hume's essay is detectable in the language of Gibbon's comments on the Roman stance towards suicide: 'The powers of this world have indeed lost their dominion over him who is resolved on death; and his arm can only be restrained by the religious apprehension of a future state. Suicides are enumerated by Virgil among the unfortunate, rather than the guilty; and the poetical fables of the infernal shades could not seriously influence the faith or practice of mankind. But the precepts of the gospel, or the church, have at length imposed pious servitude on the minds of Christians, and condemn them to expect, without a murmur, the last stroke of disease or the executioner' (Gibbon, *Decline and Fall*, vol. II, p. 8). Adam Smith inserted an extended discussion of suicide into the sixth, 1790, edition of the *Theory of Moral Sentiments*, which in some respects challenges, in others endorses, Hume's essay (Smith, *Theory*, VII.ii.1.27–37, pp. 281–9; for the relation to Hume, see p. 287, n. 36).

The story related by Charles Moore, that Hume lent a copy of this essay to a friend who then shot himself, is unsupported (Moore, *Inquiry*, vol. II, p. 66, n. x). It seems to be an imitation of the anecdote preserved in a poem by Callimachus, that Cleombrotus of Ambracia leapt to his death after reading the *Phaedo* (A. S. F. Gow and D. L. Page, *The Greek Anthology: Hellenistic*

*Epigrams*, 'Callimachus' no. 53); or (possibly) of the later report that Eustace Budgell, before throwing himself into the Thames, had left a note which pointed to a literary impulse behind his suicide: 'What Cato did and Addison approved / Must sure be right' (quoted in David Francis Taylor, 'What Cato Did: Suicide, Sentimentalism, and the Drama of Emulation', *Eighteenth-Century Life*, vol. XLVI [2022], pp. 56–78; quoted on p. 56).

The bibliography of suicide is very large, but noteworthy contributions include the following: Al Alvarez, *The Savage God* (London: Weidenfeld and Nicolson, 1971); Nils Retterstøl, *Suicide: A European Perspective* (Cambridge: Cambridge University Press, 1993); Marzio Barbagli, *Farewell to the World: A History of Suicide* (Cambridge: Polity, 2015); M. Pabst Battin (ed.), *The Ethics of Suicide: Historical Sources* (Oxford: Oxford University Press, 2015); Émile Durkheim, *Le suicide* (Paris, 1897); Jennifer Michael Hecht, *Stay: A History of Suicide and the Philosophies Against It* (New Haven, CT, and London: Yale University Press, 2013); Paul Seaver et al., *The History of Suicide in England, 1650–1850*, 8 vols (London: Pickering and Chatto, 2012–13); Kelly McGuire, *Dying to be English: Suicide Narratives and National Identity, 1721–1814* (London: Pickering and Chatto, 2012); Ian Marsh, *Suicide: Foucault, History and Truth* (Cambridge: Cambridge University Press, 2010); R. A. Houston, *Punishing the Dead: Suicide, Lordship, and Community in Britain, 1500–1830* (Oxford: Oxford University Press, 2010); Eric Francis Langley, *Narcissism and Suicide in Shakespeare and His Contemporaries* (Oxford: Oxford University Press, 2009); Jeffrey R. Watt (ed.), *From Sin to Insanity: Suicide in Early Modern Europe* (Ithaca, NY: Cornell University Press, 2004); Alexander Murray, *Suicide in the Middle Ages*, 2 vols (Oxford: Oxford University Press, 2008–11); Georges Minois, *Histoire du suicide: la société occidentale face à la mort volontaire* (Paris: Fayard, 1995); Michael MacDonald and Terence R. Murphy, *Sleepless Souls: Suicide in Early Modern England* (Oxford: Clarendon Press, 1990); W. Wynn Westcott, *Suicide, Its History, Literature, Jurisprudence, Causation, and Prevention* (London, 1885); Albert Camus, *Le mythe de Sisyphe* (Paris: Gallimard, 1942); Erwin Stengel, *Suicide and Attempted Suicide* (London: MacGibbon and Kee, 1965); Robin Fedden, *Suicide: A Social and Historical Study* (London: P. Davies Ltd, 1938).

For commentary on this theme in Hume's writings in particular, see: Max Grober, '"A Steady Contempt of Life": Suicide Narratives in Hume and Others', *Journal of Scottish Philosophy*, 10 (2012), pp. 51–68. Tom Beauchamp has published an analysis of this essay as a rebuttal of Aquinas: Tom L. Beauchamp, 'An Analysis of Hume's Essay "On Suicide"', *Review of Metaphysics*, XXX (1976), pp. 73–95. For contemporary responses delivered from different standpoints, see G. Horne, *A Letter to Adam Smith* (Oxford, 1777) and *Letters on Infidelity* (Oxford, 1784); and S. J. Pratt, *An Apology for the Life and Writings of David Hume* (1777).

1. *Of Suicide*] The etymology of the word 'suicide' is impure: 'The word "suicide" is derived from Latin but is not an actual Latin compound (*suus* not being used in compounds). In Latin, it would mean "the killing of a pig"' (Griffin, 'Roman Suicide', p. 68).

2. *De Divin. lib. ii.*] 'Nam, ut vere loquamur, superstitio, fusa per gentis, oppressit omnium fere animos atque hominum imbecillitatem occupavit . . . Instat enim et urget et, quo te cumque verteris, persequitur, sive tu vatem sive tu omen audieris, sive immolaris sive avem aspexeris, si Chaldaeum, si haruspicem videris, si fulserit, si tonuerit, si tactum aliquid erit de caelo, si ostenti simile natum factumve quippiam'; 'Speaking frankly, superstition, which is widespread among the nations, has taken advantage of human weakness to cast its spell over the mind of almost every man . . . For superstition is ever at your heels to urge you on; it follows you at every turn. It is with you when you listen to a prophet, or an omen; when you offer sacrifices or watch the flight of birds; when you consult an astrologer or a soothsayer; when it thunders or lightens or there is a bolt from on high; or when some so-called prodigy is born or is made' (Cicero, *De Divinatione*, II.lxxii).

3. *The superstitious man . . . future calamities*] cf. the comment in 'The Sceptic' on the character of the passions that make for happiness: 'To be happy, the passion must be chearful and gay, not gloomy and melancholy. A propensity to hope and joy is real riches: One to fear and sorrow, real poverty' (above, vol. 1, p. 135).

4. *all the antient philosophers*] Too sweeping a statement, as MacDonald notes: 'The Greeks had been deeply ambivalent about the question [of the permissibility of suicide]; and even the Romans had been less favourable than most eighteenth-century thinkers realised' (MacDonald, *Sleepless Souls*, p. 153). In *The Laws* Plato singles out certain kinds of suicide for shameful treatment after death: 'τὸν δὲ δὴ πάντων οἰκειότατον καὶ λεγόμενον φίλτατον ὃς ἂν ἀποκτείνῃ, τί χρὴ πάσχειν; λέγω δὲ ὃς ἂν ἑαυτὸν κτείνῃ, τὴν τῆς εἱμαρμένης βίᾳ ἀποστερῶν μοῖραν, μήτε πόλεως ταξάσης δίκῃ, μήτε περιωδύνῳ ἀφύκτῳ προσπεσούσῃ τύχῃ ἀναγκασθείς, μηδὲ αἰσχύνης τινὸς ἀπόρου καὶ ἀβίου μεταλαχών, ἀργίᾳ δὲ καὶ ἀνανδρίας δειλίᾳ ἑαυτῷ δίκην ἄδικον ἐπιθῇ. τούτῳ δὴ τὰ μὲν ἄλλα θεὸς οἶδεν ἃ χρὴ Dνόμιμα γίγνεσθαι περὶ καθαρμούς τε καὶ ταφάς, ὧν ἐξηγητάς τε ἅμα καὶ τοὺς περὶ ταῦτα νόμους ἐπανερομένους χρὴ τοὺς ἐγγύτατα γένει ποιεῖν αὐτοῖσι κατὰ τὰ προσταττόμενα· τάφους δ' εἶναι τοῖς οὕτω φθαρεῖσι πρῶτον μὲν κατὰ μόνας μηδὲ μεθ' ἑνὸς ξυντάφου, εἶτα ἐν τοῖς τῶν δώδεκα ὁρίοισι μερῶν τῶν ὅσα ἀργὰ καὶ ἀνώνυμα, θάπτειν ἀκλεεῖς αὐτούς, μήτε στήλαις μήτε ὀνόμασι δηλοῦντας τοὺς τάφους'; 'Now he that slays the person who is, as men say, nearest and dearest of all, – what penalty should he suffer? I mean the man that slays himself, – violently robbing himself of his Fate-given share of life, when this is not legally ordered by the State, and when he is not compelled to it by the occurrence of some intolerable and inevitable misfortune, nor by falling into some disgrace that is beyond remedy

or endurance, – but merely inflicting upon himself this iniquitous penalty owing to sloth and unmanly cowardice. In this case, the rest of the matters – concerning the rules about rites of purification and of burial – come within the cognizance of the god, and regarding these the next of kin must seek information from the interpreters and the laws dealing with these matters, and act in accordance with their instructions: but for those thus destroyed the tombs shall be, first, in an isolated position with not even one adjacent, and, secondly, they shall be buried in those borders of the twelve districts which are barren and nameless, without note, and with neither headstone nor name to indicate the tombs' (Plato, *Laws*, IX, 873c–d): cf. also Aristotle, *Nicomachean Ethics*, III.vii.11–13 for a discussion of when suicide is shameful rather than virtuous. Turning to Roman authors: Cicero uses the metaphor of not abandoning one's station to suggest that suicide should not be undertaken lightly: 'Sed haec et vetera et a Graecis. Cato autem sic abiit e vita, ut causam moriendi nactum se esse gauderet: vetat enim dominans ille in nobis deus iniussu hinc nos suo demigrare: cum vero causam iustam deus ipse dederit, ut tunc Socrati, nunc Catoni, saepe multis, ne ille, medius fidius, vir sapiens laetus ex his tenebris in lucem illam excesserit, nec tamen illa vincla carceris ruperit – leges enim vetant – , sed tamquam a magistratu aut ab aliqua potestate legitima, sic a deo evocatus atque emissus exierit. Tota enim philosophorum vita, ut ait idem, commentatio mortis est'; 'This, however, is ancient history and Greek history too: but Cato departed from life with a feeling of joy in having found a reason for death; for the God who is master within us forbids our departure without his permission; but when God Himself has given a valid reason as He did in the past to Socrates, and in our day to Cato, and often to many others, then of a surety your true wise man will joyfully pass forthwith from the darkness here into the light beyond. All the same he will not break the bonds of his prison-house – the laws forbid it – but as if in obedience to a magistrate or some lawful authority, he will pass out at the summons and release of God. For the whole life of the philosopher, as the same wise man says, is a preparation for death' (Cicero, *Tusculan Disputations*, I.xxx.74). The final reference is to Plato, *Phaedo*, 67d: 'καὶ τὸ μελέτημα αὐτὸ τοῦτό ἐστιν τῶν φιλοσόφων, λύσις καὶ χωρισμὸς ψυχῆς ἀπὸ σώματος· ἢ οὔ'; 'and just this is the proper practice of the philosophers: the freeing and separation of soul from body, or isn't it?' In the *Aeneid* Virgil places suicides in a mournful area of the underworld, a locale it is hard to reconcile with a heroic concept of voluntary death: 'proxima deinde tenent maesti loca, qui sibi letum / insontes peperere manu lucemque perosi / proiecere animas. quam vellent aethere in alto / nunc et pauperiem et duros perferre labores! / fas obstat tristisque palus inamabilis undae / alligat et noviens Styx interfusa coercet'; 'The region thereafter is held by those sad souls who in innocence wrought their own death and, loathing the light, flung away their lives. How gladly now, in the air above, would they bear both want and harsh distress! Fate withstands; the unlovely mere with its dreary water enchains them and Styx imprisons with his ninefold circles' (*Aeneid*, VI.434–9). Plutarch records the firmness of Cleomenes, who resolved to abstain from suicide 'while there remains a finger's breadth of hope' (Plutarch, *Life of Cleomenes*, XXXI.v–vi; cf. Montaigne, *Œuvres*, p. 335). On the kinds of suicide that were condemned in classical antiquity, see Durkheim, *Suicide*, pp. 295–7. However, the idea that pagan antiquity uniformly condoned suicide is an error characteristic of philosophic opinion in Hume's day. Voltaire, for instance, in the article 'De Caton, et du suicide' in the *Dictionnaire Philosophique*, says: 'Le suicide est défendu chez nous par le droit canon. Mais les décrétales, qui font la jurisprudence d'une partie de l'Europe, furent inconnues à Caton, à Brutus, à Cassius, à la sublime Arria, à l'empereur Othon, à Marc-Antoine, et à cent héros de la véritable Rome, qui préférèrent une mort volontaire à une vie qu'ils croyaient ignominieuse.' This is strictly speaking correct, in that of course none of these ancient Romans could possibly have had knowledge of canon law; but it is misleading in its implication that suicide was universally condoned in pagan antiquity. The most authoritative survey is the two-part article by Miriam Griffin, 'Philosophy, Cato, and Roman Suicide', in *Greece and Rome*, XXXIII (1986), pp. 64–77 and 192–202.

5. *All events . . . of the universe*] Hume had also made mischievous and creative use of the doctrine of providential design in 'Of the Original Contract' (see above, pp. 161–2).

6. *The revolutions . . . or tempest*] But cf. what Hume has suggested elsewhere concerning the natural history of empire in 'Of Money' (above, pp. 25–6), 'Of the Balance of Trade' (above, p. 50), 'Of the Balance of Power' (above, pp. 69–70) and 'Idea of a Perfect Commonwealth' (above, pp. 207–8). The seed of this insight into the natural determinism of political bodies is to be found in the 'Early Memoranda': 'There seems to be a natural Course of Things, which brings on the Destruction of great Empires. They push their Conquests till they come to barbarous Nations, which stop their Progress, by the Difficulty of subsisting great Armies. After that, the Nobility & considerable Men of the conquering Nation & best Provinces withdraw gradually from the [frontier *inserted above the line*] Army, by reason of its Distance from the Capital & barbarity of the Country, in which they quarter: They forget the Use of War. Their barbarous Soldiers become their Masters. These have no Law but their Sword, both from their bad Education, & from their Distance from the Sovereign [to whom they bear no Affection *inserted above the line*]. Hence Disorder, Violence, Anarchy, & Tyranny, & a Dissolution of Empire.' (NLS MS 23159, item 14, p. 27; cf. Mossner, 'Memoranda', pp. 517–18). Cf. also Rousseau, *Contrat*, book II, chapter 9 (pp. 62–6).

7. *Has not every one . . . his own life?*] cf. Donne: 'mee thinks I have the keyes of my prison in mine owne hand, and no remedy presents it selfe so soone to

my heart, as mine own sword' (Donne, *Biathanatos*, p. 18). Montaigne had also been drawn to the metaphor of holding the key to one's prison: 'C'est ce qu'on dit, que le sage vit tant qu'il doit, non pas tant qu'il peut; et que le present que nature nous ait fait le plus favorable, et qui nous oste tout moyen de nous pleindre de nostre condition, c'est de nous avoir laissé la clef des champs' (Montaigne, *Œuvres*, p. 331: cf. also Cicero, *Tusculan Disputations*, V.xiv.42; Seneca, *Epistles*, LXIX–LXXVIII, esp. LXX; and Seneca, *Phoenissae*, ll. 151–3).

8. *But the life of man . . . an oyster*] cf. the similarly deflating comparison that Hume employs in section 12 of the *Dialogues Concerning Natural Religion*: 'I next turn to the Atheist, who, I assert, is only nominally so, and can never possibly be in earnest; and I ask him, whether, from the coherence and apparent Sympathy in all the parts of this world, there be not a certain degree of analogy among all the operations of Nature, in every situation and in every age; whether the rotting of a Turnip, the generation of an animal, and the structure of human thought be not energies that probably bear some remote analogy to each other' (*Hume on Religion*, p. 249). In *Lettres Persanes*, letter 76, Montesquieu had also traced one of the roots of the condemnation of suicide back to the principle of deluded human self-importance: 'Toutes ces idées, mon cher Ibben, n'ont d'autre source que notre orgueil: nous ne sentons point notre petitesse, et, malgré qu'on en ait, nous voulons être comptés dans l'Univers, y figurer et y être un objet important. Nous nous imaginons que l'anéantissement d'un être aussi parfait que nous dégraderait toute la nature, et nous ne concevons pas qu'un homme de plus ou de moins dans le Monde – que dis-je? – tous les hommes ensemble, cent millions de terres comme la nôtre, ne sont qu'un atome subtil et délié, que Dieu n'aperçoit qu'à cause de l'immensité de ses connaissances' (Montesquieu, *Œuvres*, p. 103).

9. *Were the disposal . . . its destruction*] Here Hume is engaging with an argument advanced by John Adams in his *Essay Concerning Self-Murther* (1700). In the *Two Treatises* Locke had argued against suicide on the grounds that, as the workmanship of God, we were his property and therefore could not dispose of ourselves (see the headnote, above, p. 608). Adams had refined this argument to say that man had a '*Right of Use*, but *not a Right of absolute Propriety*' over his life (Adams, *Self-Murther*, p. 10). Socrates had also entertained an argument against suicide based on the premise that human beings are the possessions of a god or gods (Plato, *Phaedo*, 62 b).

10. *If I turn aside . . . assigned to it*] cf. Montesquieu, *Lettres Persanes*, letter 76: 'vous troublez l'ordre de la Providence. Dieu a uni votre âme avec votre corps, et vous l'en séparez. Vous vous opposez donc à ses desseins, et vous lui résistez . . . Troublé-je l'ordre de la Providence, lorsque je change les modifications de la matière et que je rends carrée une boule que les premières lois de mouvement, c'est à dire les lois de la création et de la conservation, avaient faite ronde? Non, sans doute: je ne fais qu'user du droit qui m'a été donné; et, en ce sens,

je puis troubler à ma fantaisie toute la nature, sans que l'on puisse dire que je m'oppose à la Providence' (Montesquieu, *Œuvres*, p. 103). Cf. also Donne: 'we may safely infer, that nothing which we call sinne is so against nature, but that it may be sometimes agreeable to nature' (Donne, *Biathanatos*, p. 37).

11. *A hair, a fly, an insect*] John Robeck had also found in the fragility of human life the grounds of some natural recommendation of suicide: 'Deinde, vt modo demonstratum, mors voluntaria in tanta leuitate et incertitudine rerum humanarum, et in tanta imbecillitate generis humani, est certissimum ac tutissimum tranquillitatis animi praesidium et firmamentum'; 'So, as has just been proved, amidst the inconstancy and uncertainty of human affairs, and the surpassing weakness of the human race, a voluntary death is the most certain and the safest defence and support of tranquillity of mind' (Robeck, *Exercitatio*, pp. 182–3).

12. *a few ounces of blood*] cf., perhaps, Montaigne, 'Coustume de l'Isle de Cea': 'Pourquoy n'est la vaine du gosier autant à nostre commandement que la mediane?' (Montaigne, *Œuvres*, p. 332). 'Le gosier' and 'la mediane' are both technical terms for veins in French anatomy.

13. *prolong ... shame and poverty*] The mention of poverty suggests that Hume may have in mind here Swift's portrait of the curse of eternal life in the form of the Struldbrugs, who after the age of eighty 'are looked on as dead in Law; their Heirs immediately succeed to their Estates, only a small Pittance is reserved for their Support; and the poor ones are maintained at the publick Charge' (Swift, *Gulliver's Travels*, Part III, chapter 10, pp. 309–21; quotation on p. 318).

14. *Epist. xii*] 'let us thank God that no man can be kept in life' (Seneca the Younger, *Epistles*, XII.x).

15. *If my life ... like motives*] Hume here draws attention to the way our common manner of praising those who place themselves in danger implies that our lives are indeed our own. That we are the owners of our own lives is a common argument among defenders of suicide, such as Montaigne in 'Coustume de l'Isle de Cea': 'Comme je n'offense les loix qui sont faictes contre les larrons, quand j'emporte le mien, et que je me coupe ma bourse; ny des boutefeux, quand je brusle mon bois; aussi ne suis je tenu aux lois faictes contre les meurtriers pour m'avoir osté ma vie' (Montaigne, *Œuvres*, p. 332).

16. *But you are ... displeasure*] A notable commonplace, that has its deepest source in a saying of Pythagoras (recorded by Cicero in *De Senectute*, LXXIII), and that passes thence to Plato's *Phaedo*, LXII b–c, and Cicero's *Tusculan Disputations*, I.lxxiv. Thereafter it flows through St Augustine, *City of God*, I.xxii; Erasmus, *Adages*, IV, VI, LXXXI, 'Nemo sibi nascitur'; Tiraquellus, *De Nobilitate*, XXXI; and Montaigne, 'Coustume de l'Isle de Cea' (Montaigne, *Œuvres*, pp. 332–3). Hume's language here comes close to that of Samuel Clarke's *A Discourse Concerning the Unchangeable Obligations of Natural Religion* (1706), in the course of which Clarke had asserted the 'Unlawfulness of Self-murder' (pp. 97–103) on, inter alia, the following grounds: 'for

the same Reason that a Man is obliged not to depart wilfully out of this Life, which is the *general Station* that God has appointed him; he is obliged likewise to attend the Duties of that *particular Station* or condition of life, whatsoever it be, wherein Providence has *at present* placed him; with diligence, and contentment; Without being either uneasy and discontented, that others are placed by Providence in different and superiour Stations in the World' (pp. 103–4); and see also the comparison with a 'Centinel' on p. 101. Boswell reports Hume acknowledging that after he had begun to read Locke and Clarke he 'never had entertained any belief in religion' (James Boswell, *Boswell in Extremes: 1776–1778*, ed. Charles McC. Weis and Frederick A. Pottle, 'The Yale Edition of the Private Papers of James Boswell' [London: Heinemann, 1971], p. 11). Resistance to the analogy with a sentinel had a clear freethinking pedigree. For example, Charles Gildon, in 'An Account of the Life and Death of the Author', with which he prefaced the *Miscellaneous Works* (1695) of his friend, the freethinker and suicide Charles Blount, had been impatient with it: 'I know *Cicero* brings a Simile for an Argument against this point: A Centinel, says he, that is plac'd in his Station, ought not to leave it till reliev'd by his Commander that plac'd him there. But first a Simile is no Proof, especially when there is no parallel in the cases, as there is not betwixt a Centinel at his Post, and a Man in this Life; for first the Soldier (at least in free Countries) is not forc'd to that Station without his consent, he knows before he lists himself the Conditions of a Soldier's Life, and then submits himself to those Conditions, a very substantial Reason, why he should stay till relieved at his Post. But what Man had his free choice, or indeed could have, whether he would *be* or not *be*, before he was? Then 2dly, what will they agree is a relieving us from the Post of Life? Nothing but dying on a Bed?' (sigs. A7$^v$–A8$^r$). Samuel Clarke had turned aside in his Boyle lectures on natural religion to deride Gildon's argument as 'weak and childish' (*A Discourse Concerning the Unchangeable Obligations of Natural Religion* [1706], p. 101).

17. *I owe my birth . . . actions of men*] cf. the apposite entry in the 'Early Memoranda': 'It seems to be a kind of Objection against the Immortality of the Soul to consider the trifling Accidents of Marriage, Copulation &c that bring Men into Life.' (NLS MS 23159, item 14, p. 34; cf. Mossner, 'Memoranda', p. 502). This also suggests how closely interrelated for Hume were the questions of suicide and the immortality of the soul: the same considerations might be influential in both cases.

18. *Ann. lib. i*] 'optume rebus mortalium consuluisse naturam, quae sua ora fluminibus, suos cursus, utque originem, ita finis dederit; spectandas etiam religiones maiorum, qui sacra et lucos et aras patriis amnibus dicaverint; quin ipsum Tiberim nolle prorsus accolis fluviis orbatum minore gloria fluere'; 'Nature had made the best provision for the interests of humanity, when she assigned to rivers their proper mouths – their proper courses – their limits as well as their origins. Consideration, too, should be paid to the faith of their

fathers, who had hallowed rituals and groves and altars to their country streams. Besides, they were reluctant that Tiber himself, bereft of his tributary streams, should flow with diminished majesty' (Tacitus, *Annals*, I.lxxix).

19. *the principles ... individual creature*] Note the defiant materialism of this restatement of the Epicurean doctrine of the imperishability of matter. Cf. Montesquieu, *Lettres Persanes*, letter 76: 'Pensez-vous que mon corps, devenu un épi de blé, un ver, un gazon, soit changé en un ouvrage de la Nature moins digne d'elle? et que mon âme, dégagée de tout ce qu'elle avait de terrestre, soit devenue moins sublime?' (Montesquieu, *Œuvres*, p. 103).

20. *a breach of our duty to our neighbour and to society*] The classical condemnation of suicide on the grounds that it is injurious to society occurs in Aristotle's *Nicomachean Ethics*: 'οἷον οὐ κελεύει ἀποκτιννύναι ἑαυτὸν ὁ νόμος (ἃ δὲ μὴ κελεύει, ἀπαγορεύει)· ἔτι ὅταν παρὰ τὸν νόμον βλάπτῃ (μὴ ἀντιβλάπτων) ἑκών, ἀδικεῖ (ἑκὼν δὲ ὁ εἰδὼς καὶ ὃν καὶ ᾧ)· ὁ δὲ δι᾽ ὀργὴν ἑαυτὸν σφάττων ἑκὼν τοῦτο δρᾷ (παρὰ τὸν ὀρθὸν λόγον), ὃ οὐκ ἐᾷ ὁ νόμος. ἀδικεῖ ἄρα· ἀλλὰ τίνα; ἢ τὴν πόλιν, αὑτὸν δ᾽ οὔ; ἑκὼν γὰρ πάσχει, ἀδικεῖται δ᾽ οὐθεὶς ἑκών. διὸ καὶ ἡ πόλις ζημιοῖ, καί τις ἀτιμία πρόσεστι τῷ ἑαυτὸν διαφθείραντι ὡς τὴν πόλιν ἀδικοῦντι'; 'For instance, the law does not sanction suicide (and what it does not expressly sanction, it forbids). Further, when a man voluntarily (which means with knowledge of the person affected and the instrument employed) does an injury (not in retaliation) that is against the law, he commits injustice. But he who kills himself in a fit of passion, voluntarily does an injury (against the right principle) which the law does not allow. Therefore the suicide commits injustice; but against whom? It seems to be against the state rather than against himself; for he suffers voluntarily, and nobody suffers injustice voluntarily. This is why the state exacts a penalty; suicide is punished by certain marks of dishonour, as being an offence against the state' (1138a, 2–4). This Aristotelian view of suicide had been revived in *De legibus naturae* (1672) by Richard Cumberland: '*Civil Laws* ... usually judge a *Self-Murderer* injurious, not to *himself alone*, but to the *Publick* also, which he robs of a *Subject*; and that Fact is justly reckon'd among the greatest Crimes' (*A Treatise of the Laws of Nature*, tr. J. Maxwell [1727], p. 337). John Adams agreed: 'there is scarce any Wretch but may be some way or other beneficial to the Publick, even by *his being alive alone*' (Adams, *Self-Murther*, p. 108). In the final sentence of this essay Hume would turn the tables on this argument, and defend suicide as in certain circumstances an act 'useful to society' (above, p. 255).

21. *All our obligations ... bound any longer*] cf. Montesquieu, *Lettres Persanes*, letter 76: 'Pourquoi veut-on que je travaille pour une société dont je consens de n'être plus? que je tienne, malgré moi, une convention qui s'est faite sans moi? La société est fondée sur un avantage mutuel. Mais lorsqu'elle me devient onéreuse, qui m'empêche d'y renoncer? La vie m'a été donnée comme une faveur; je puis donc la rendre lorsqu'elle ne l'est plus: la cause cesse; l'effet doit donc cesser aussi' (Montesquieu, *Œuvres*, p. 103).

22. *Why then . . . to society?*] cf. Montesquieu, *Lettres Persanes*, letter 76: 'Quand je suis accablé de douleur, de misère, de mépris, pourquoi veut-on m'empêcher de mettre fin à mes peines, et me priver cruellement d'un remède qui est en mes mains?' (Montesquieu, *Œuvres*, p. 103).

23. *Strozzi of Florence*] Strozzi had led a *coup d'état* in Florence, was defeated, and imprisoned. He committed suicide rather than reveal his accomplices. For further comment, see Melissa Meriam Bullard, *Filippo Strozzi and the Medici* (Cambridge: Cambridge University Press, 1980).

24. *I believe . . . while it was worth keeping*] cf. Mandeville on the presumed rationality of suicide: 'He that makes Death his choice, must look upon it as less terrible than what he shuns by it; for whether the Evil dreaded be present or to come, real or imaginary, no body would kill himself wilfully but to avoid something' (Mandeville, *Fable*, vol. I, p. 209). Christianity, however, with its promises of an afterlife might align suicide and self-preservation, as Donne had observed: 'Besides, *Selfe-preservation*, which wee confesse to be the foundation of generall naturall Law, is no other thing then a naturall affection and appetition of good, whether true or seeming. For certainly the desire of Martyrdome, though the body perish, is a *Selfe-preservation*, because thereby, out of our election our best part is advanc'd' (Donne, *Biathanatos*, p. 49).

25. *not a single text of scripture*] St Paul's injunction to 'abide in the flesh' (Philippians 1:24) was, however, sometimes taken to prohibit suicide. Cf. Michael MacDonald: 'Following the example of Augustine, Protestant writers repeatedly declared that self-murder was contrary to divine law. The fact that both the Bible and the early church afforded them few proofs of this conviction only deepened the clergy's determination to popularize Augustine's insistence that suicide was forbidden by the Sixth Commandment and that the early martyrs who killed themselves were not examples for ordinary Christians to emulate' (MacDonald, *Sleepless Souls*, p. 32).

26. *Thou shalt not kill . . . no authority*] St Augustine had argued otherwise, and had placed the sixth commandment at the centre of his prohibition of suicide: 'Neque enim frustra in sanctis canonicis libris nusquam nobis divinitus praeceptum permissumve reperiri potest, ut vel ipsius adipiscendae inmortalitatis vel ullius cavendi carendive mali causa nobismet ipsis necem inferamus. Nam et prohibitos nos esse intellegendum est, ubi lex ait: Non occides, praesertim quia non addidit: "proximum tuum" sicut falsum testimonium cum vetaret: Falsum, inquit, testimonium non dices adversus proximum tuum. Nec ideo tamen si adversus se ipsum quisquam falsum testimonium dixerit, ab hoc crimine se putaverit alienum, quoniam regulam diligendi proximum a semet ipso dilector accepit, quando quidem scriptum est: Diliges proximum tuum tamquam te ipsum'; 'Not for nothing is it that in the holy canonical books no divinely inspired order or permission can be found authorizing us to inflict death upon ourselves, neither in order to acquire immortality nor in order to avert or divert some evil. For we must certainly understand

the commandment as forbidding this when it says: "Thou shalt not kill", particularly since it does not add "thy neighbour", as it does when it forbids false witnessing. It says: "Thou shalt not bear false witness against thy neighbour." No one should, however, think that he is free from this charge if he has borne false witness only against himself, for he who loves his neighbour has received a rule of love based on himself, since indeed Scripture says: "Thou shalt love thy neighbour as thyself"' (*City of God*, I.xx).

27. *practice of magistrates . . . letter of this law*] As had been noted by Donne: 'For though the words be generall, *Thou shalt not kill*, we may kill beasts; Magistrates may kill men; and a private man in a just warre, may not onely kill, contrary to the sound of this Commandement, but hee may kill his Father, contrary to another' (Donne, *Biathanatos*, p. 165).

28. *the law of Moses is abolished*] A reference to the abolition by Christ of the Old Testament law promulgated by Moses: 'For Christ is the end of the law unto righteousness to every one that believeth' (Romans 10:4); 'having abolished in his flesh the enmity, even the law of commandments contained in ordinances' (Ephesians 2:15).

29. *Lib. ii. Cap. 7*] 'inperfectae vero in homine naturae praecipua solatia, ne deum quidem posse omnia, – namque nec sibi potest mortem consciscere, si velit, quod homini dedit optimum in tantis vitae poenis, nec mortales aeternitate donare aut revocare defunctos, nec facere ut qui vixit non vixerit, qui honores gessit non gesserit, – nullumque habere in praeterita ius praeterquam oblivionis, atque (ut facetis quoque argumentis societas haec cum deo copuletur) ut bis dena viginti non sint aut multa similiter efficere non posse: per quae declaratur haut dubie naturae potentia, idque esse quod deum vocemus'; 'But the chief consolations for nature's imperfection in the case of man are that not even for God are all things possible – for he cannot, even if he wishes, commit suicide, the supreme boon that he has bestowed on man among all the penalties of life, nor bestow eternity on mortals or recall the deceased, nor cause a man that has lived not to have lived or one that has held high office not to have held it – and that he has no power over what is past save to forget it, and (to link our fellowship with God by means of frivolous arguments as well) that he cannot cause twice ten not to be twenty or do many things on similar lines: which facts unquestionably demonstrate the power of nature, and prove that it is this that we mean by the word "God" (Pliny the Elder, *Natural History*, II.v.27).

## OF THE IMMORTALITY OF THE SOUL

Published in: *1777b*
Significant revisions: none.
Copy text: NLS MS 509, pp. 225–40

Headnote:

>    For what we know of the composition and publication of this essay, see the head-
>    note to 'Of Suicide' (above, pp. 601–3). It is worth bearing in mind what Hume
>    had said on this topic in the *Treatise of Human Nature*, I.iii.9: 'And indeed the
>    want of resemblance in this case [the doctrine of a future state of rewards and
>    punishments] so entirely destroys belief, that except those few, who upon cool
>    reflection on the importance of the subject, have taken care by repeated medita-
>    tion to imprint in their minds the arguements for a future state, there scarce are
>    any, who believe the immortality of the soul with a true and establish'd judg-
>    ment; such as is deriv'd from the testimony of travellers and historians' (*THN*,
>    p. 79). The *Treatise of Human Nature*, I.iv.5, 'Of the Immateriality of the Soul',
>    is also of relevance, especially the final paragraph (*THN*, pp. 152–64). In 'The
>    Stoic' Hume has his *persona* dismiss the topic of immortality and life after death
>    as irrelevant to the moral deliberations of a truly virtuous man: 'Let speculative
>    reasoners dispute, how far this beneficent being extends his care, and whether
>    he prolongs our existence beyond the grave, in order to bestow on virtue its just
>    reward, and render it fully triumphant' (above, vol. 1, p. 125).
>
>    For classical and pagan arguments for the immortality of the soul, and
>    Christian mortalist arguments, see the headnote to 'Of Suicide' (above, pp.
>    605–8). However, the question of the immortality of the soul had, in the
>    course of the seventeenth century, become closely attached to the question of
>    personal identity: on this subject, see Udo Thiel, *The Early Modern Subject:
>    Self-Consciousness and Personal Identity from Descartes to Hume* (Oxford:
>    Oxford University Press, 2011), pp. 81–5 and 166–9. Once Hume's essay
>    is returned to this context, its anticlericalism is slightly muted, and its con-
>    tinuities with a suite of philosophical topics in which Hume had serious,
>    non-polemical and long-standing interests emerge more clearly.
>
>    The subject of personal immortality would be to the fore in the conver-
>    sation James Boswell had with the dying Hume on 7 July 1776; and at a
>    number of moments the topics and language recorded by Boswell come close
>    to the topics and language of this essay. Boswell pressed Hume on the question
>    of life after death:
>
> > I had a strong curiosity to be satisfied if he persisted in disbelieving a
> > future state even when he had death before his eyes. I was persuaded
> > from what he now said, and from his manner of saying it, that he did
> > persist. I asked him if it was not possible that there might be a future
> > state. He answered it was possible that a piece of coal put upon the fire
> > would not burn; and he added that it was a most unreasonable fancy
> > that we should exist for ever. That immortality, if it were at all, must
> > be general; that a great proportion of the human race has hardly any
> > intellectual qualities; that a great proportion dies in infancy before being
> > possessed of reason; yet all these must be immortal; that a porter who

gets drunk by ten o'clock with gin must be immortal; that the trash of every age must be preserved, and that new universes must be created to contain such infinite numbers. This appeared to me an unphilosophical objection, and I said, 'Mr Hume, you know spirit does not take up space.'

I asked him if the thought of annihilation never gave him any uneasiness. He said not the least; no more than the thought that he had not been. 'Well,' said I, 'Mr Hume, I hope to triumph over you when I meet you in a future state; and remember that you are not to pretend that you was joking with all this infidelity.' 'No, no', said he. 'But I shall have been so long there before you come that it will be nothing new.' In this style of good humour and levity did I conduct the conversation. Perhaps it was wrong on so awful a subject. But as nobody was present, I thought it could have no bad effect . . .

He had once said to me, on a forenoon while the sun was shining bright, that he did not wish to be immortal. This was a most wonderful thought. The reason he gave was that he was very well in this state of being, and that the chances were very much against his being so well in another state; and he would rather not be more than be worse. I answered that it was reasonable to hope he would be better; that there would be a progressive improvement. I tried him at this interview with that topic, saying that a future state was surely a pleasing idea. He said no, for that it was always seen through a gloomy medium; there was always a Phlegethon or a hell.

(Boswell, *Edinburgh Journals*, pp. 257–8; for Johnson's dismissive response, see Boswell, *Life of Johnson*, p. 605)

1. *the gospel, and the gospel alone*] But Plato's *Phaedo* advances a non-Christian argument for the immortality of the soul. In the 'Early Memoranda' Hume had noted that 'Plato & Cicero maintain'd the Eternity of the Soul a parte ante as well as a parte post; & ought also to have maintain'd that of Beasts.' (NLS MS 23159, item 14, p. 33; cf. Mossner, 'Memoranda', p. 501).

2. *the soul is immaterial*] In the *Treatise of Human Nature*, I.iv.5, Hume had explored some of the difficulties in which this traditional notion was, on careful inspection, enmeshed: 'It appears, then, that to whatever side we turn, the same difficulties follow us, and that we cannot advance one step towards the establishing the simplicity and immateriality of the soul, without preparing the way for a dangerous and irrecoverable atheism' (*THN*, p. 160): by which he meant, mischievously, the 'hideous hypothesis' of Spinoza (ibid., p. 158) (and he would adhere to this position in the anonymous defence of the doctrine of the *Treatise*, the *Letter from a Gentleman* [*THN*, p. 423]). Hume was able, therefore, to conclude: 'the question concerning the substance of the soul is absolutely unintelligible' (*THN*, p. 163). However, there is one striking contrast between what Hume says on this subject in the *Treatise* and what he implies in this essay. In the *Treatise*, Hume states that his argument about

the immateriality of the soul is without implication for religion: 'If my philosophy, therefore, makes no addition to the arguments for religion, I have at least the satisfaction to think it takes nothing from them, but that every thing remains precisely as before' (*THN*, p. 164). In 'Of the Immortality of the Soul', however, Hume's anticlericalism is biting and overt, while the essay's final paragraph is the most insultingly perfunctory of fig leaves.

3. *it is impossible for thought to belong to a material substance*] Hume must have been aware of Locke's carefully worded suggestion in *An Essay Concerning Human Understanding*, book IV, chapter 3, §6, that God may have endowed matter with a power of thought: 'We have the *Ideas* of *Matter* and *Thinking*, but possibly shall never be able to know, whether any mere material Being thinks, or no; it being impossible for us, by the contemplation of our own *Ideas*, without revelation, to discover, whether Omnipotency has not given to some Systems of Matter fitly disposed, a power to perceive and think, or else joined and fixed to Matter so disposed, a thinking immaterial Substance: It being, in respect of our Notions, not much more remote from our Comprehension to conceive, that GOD can, if he pleases, superadd to Matter a Faculty of Thinking, than that he should superadd to it another Substance, with a Faculty of Thinking; since we know not wherein Thinking consists, nor to what sort of Substances the Almighty has been pleased to give that Power, which cannot be in any created Being, but merely by the good pleasure and Bounty of the Creator' (Locke, *Essay*, pp. 540–41). Locke went on to say that his hypothesis of 'thinking matter' would not 'any way lessen the belief of the Soul's Immateriality', and that in any case 'All the great Ends of Morality and Religion, are well enough secured, without philosophical Proofs of the Soul's Immateriality' (Locke, *Essay*, pp. 541 and 542). This speculation on Locke's part provoked many responses from more orthodox thinkers, for whom the immateriality and the immortality of the soul were closely associated doctrines, and who saw in the notion of thinking matter an implicit attack on that traditional position. Examples of such resistance include Richard Bentley's second Boyle lecture, *Matter and Motion Cannot Think* (1692), Edward Stillingfleet's *Answer* (1697), Lawrence Smith, *Evidence of Things Not Seen* (1701; second, much enlarged, edition 1703), Henry Lee, *Anti-Scepticism* (1702), John Broughton, *Psychologia* (1703), Benjamin Hampton, *The Existence of the Human Soul after Death* (1711), Samuel Clarke, *A Collection of Papers* (1717), Peter Brown, *The Procedure, Extent and Limits of Human Understanding* (1728) and Andrew Baxter, *An Enquiry into the Nature of the Human Soul* (1733). Later in the century Locke's hypothesis was challenged by Giacinto Sigismondo Gerdil in his *L'Immatérialité de l'âme* (Turin, 1747): it is possible that Hume may have come across this book during his residence in Turin in 1748. Further resistance was offered by Malcolm Flemyng, *A New Critical Examination* (1751). It is probable that the notice taken of Locke's suggestion by Voltaire

in his *Letters Concerning the English Nation* (1733) (pp. 94–108) did little
to calm the breasts of the orthodox. Those engaging on the materialist side
included William Coward, *The Grand Essay* (1704). In 1759, in chapter 48
of *Rasselas*, Johnson would weigh in on the traditional, immaterialist, side of
the question (Womersley, *Johnson*, pp. 708–10; see Gwin J. Kolb, 'The Intellectual Background of the Discourse on the Soul in *Rasselas*', *Philological
Quarterly*, LIV [1975], pp. 357–69). For much of the century the 'thinking
matter' debate was mired in sterile charge and counter-charge, before Joseph
Priestley's *Disquisitions Relating to Matter and Spirit* (1777) marked a turning point by reconceptualizing what was meant by matter: 'Since the only
reason why the principle of thought, or sensation, has been imagined to be
incompatible with matter, goes upon the supposition of impenetrability being
the essential property of it, and consequently that *solid extent* is the foundation of all the properties that it can possibly sustain, the whole argument for
an immaterial thinking principle in man, on this new supposition, falls to the
ground; matter, destitute of what has hitherto been called *solidity*, being no
more incompatible with sensation and thought, than that substance, which,
without knowing any thing farther about it, we have used to call *immaterial*'
(p. 18). By 1781 the materialist philosophy was so far in the ascendant that
Lord Monboddo could in that year write to Richard Price, 'the prejudice is
so great in favour of the Mechanical Philosophy at Present, that I did not
expect you were to be convinced by anything I have said against it' (William
A. Knight [ed.], *Lord Monboddo and Some of His Contemporaries* [London,
1900], p. 147). Cf. the entry in the 'Early Memoranda': 'Strato's Atheism
the most dangerous of the Antient, holding the Origin of the World from
Nature, or a Matter endu'd with Activity' (NLS MS 23159, item 14, p. 32;
cf. Mossner, 'Memoranda', p. 501). For commentary, see John W. Yolton,
*Thinking Matter: Materialism in Eighteenth-Century Britain* (Minneapolis,
MI: University of Minnesota Press, 1983).

4. *the notion of substance . . . unknown something*] cf. Hume's scepticism concerning substance in the *Treatise of Human Nature*: 'We have therefore no
idea of substance, distinct from that of a collection of particular qualities,
nor have we any other meaning when we either talk or reason concerning
it' (*THN*, I.i.6, p. 16). In the *Enquiry Concerning Human Understanding*,
Hume's phrasing of this position seems if anything more extreme: 'Bereave
matter of all its intelligible qualities, both primary and secondary, you in a
manner annihilate it, and leave only a certain unknown, inexplicable *something*, as the cause of our perceptions; a notion so imperfect, that no sceptic
will think it worth while to contend against it' (*ECHU*, XII.i, p. 116).

5. *the etherial fire of the Stoics*] Stoics conceived of the universe as a material
reasoning substance, in which passive matter is animated by an intelligent
aether or primordial fire. In Cicero's *De Natura Deorum* an account of the
doctrine is attributed to Chrysippus: 'ait enim vim divinam in ratione esse

positam et in universae naturae animo atque mente, ipsumque mundum deum dicit esse et eius animi fusionem universam, tum eius ipsius principatum qui in mente et ratione versetur, communemque rerum naturam [universam] atque omnia continentem, tum fatalem vim et necessitatem rerum futurarum, ignem praeterea [et] eum quem ante dixi aethera, tum ea quae natura fluerent atque manarent, ut et aquam et terram et aëra, solem lunam sidera unitatemque rerum qua omnia continerentur, atque etiam homines eos qui inmortalitatem essent consecuti'; 'he says that divine power resides in reason, and in the soul and mind of the universe; he calls the world itself a god, and also the all-pervading world-soul, and again the guiding principle of that soul, which operates in the intellect and reason, and the common and all-embracing nature of things; and also the power of Fate, and the Necessity that governs future events; beside this, the fire that I previously termed aether; and also all fluid and soluble substances, such as water, earth, air, the sun, moon and stars, and the all-embracing unity of things; and even those human beings who have attained immortality' (I.xxxix). In the 'Early Memoranda' Hume had referred to 'the Stoics, who maintain'd their God to be fiery & compound' (NLS MS 23159, item 14, p. 32; cf. Mossner, 'Memoranda', p. 501).

6. *She employs . . . a new form*] A statement of the Epicurean doctrine of the imperishability of matter.

7. *material substance . . . minds*] Another defiantly materialistic touch which strikes at orthodox Christian doctrine. Cf. *Hamlet*, III.vi.16–30: 'A man may fish with the worm that hath ate of a king, and eat of the fish that hath fed of that worm . . . a king may go a progress through the guts of a beggar.'

8. *Only to gain a livelihood . . . this world*] An unusually plain and unadorned expression of Hume's anticlericalism. In contrast to this outspokenness, one might juxtapose the laborious irony of the *Treatise of Human Nature*, I.iv.5: 'There is only one occasion, when philosophy will think it necessary and even honourable to justify herself, and that is, when religion may seem to be in the least offended; whose rights are as dear to her as her own, and are indeed the same. If any one, therefore, shou'd imagine that the foregoing arguments are any ways dangerous to religion, I hope the following apology with remove his apprehensions' (*THN*, pp. 163–4).

9. *every thing . . . ordained by him*] Another mischievous application of the doctrine of providential design: see above, p. 528, n. 4.

10. *lib. vi. cap. 5*] 'Ille venantium modo latibula scrutatus plerosque confodit, ad ultimum circumire saltum milites iubet, ut, si qua pateret, irrumperent. Sed ignotis locis plerique oberrabant, exceptique sunt quidam, inter quos equus regis – Bucephalam vocabant – , quem Alexander non eodem quo ceteras pecudes animo aestimabat. Namque ille nec in dorso insidere suo patiebatur alium, et regem, cum vellet escendere, sponte genua submittens excipiebat credebaturque sentire quem veheret. Maiore ergo quam decebat ira simul ac

dolore stimulatus, equum vestigari iubet et per interpretem pronuntiari, ni reddidisset, neminem esse victurum. Hac denuntiatione territi, cum ceteris donis equum adducunt'; 'Alexander, tracing them to their lairs as hunters do, slew many of them, and finally ordered the soldiers to encircle the forest, and to rush in if they could find an opening anywhere; but in the unknown country many of them strayed and lost their way, and some were captured, among them the king's horse – they called him Bucephalas – which Alexander valued more highly than all other animals. For he would not allow anyone else to sit upon his back, and when the king wished to mount him, he knelt down of its own accord to receive him, and seemed to know whom he was carrying. Therefore aroused with greater anger than was seemly and at the same time with grief, the king gave orders that the horse should be traced, and that proclamation should be made through an interpreter, that unless it should be returned, not a man would be left alive' (Quintus Curtius, *History of Alexander*, VI.v.17–19).

11. *August. cap. 3*] A slip for chapter 33: 'Ipse ius dixit assidue et in noctem nonnumquam, si parum corpore valeret lectica pro tribunali collocata, vel etiam domi cubans. Dixit autem ius non diligentia modo summa sed et lenitate, siquidem manifesti parricidii reum, ne culleo insueretur, quod non nisi confessi adficiuntur hac poena, ita fertur interrogasse: "Certe patrem tuum non occidisti?"'; 'He himself administered justice regularly and sometimes up to nightfall, having a litter placed upon the tribunal, if he was indisposed, or even lying down at home. In his administration of justice he was both highly conscientious and very lenient; for to save a man clearly guilty of parricide from being sewn up in the sack, a punishment which was inflicted only on those who pleaded guilty, he is said to have put the question to him in this form: "You surely did not kill your father, did you?"' (Suetonius, *Deified Augustus*, XXXIII.i).

12. *The chief source . . . interests of human society*] A glance at the utilitarian ethics that Hume had elaborated in the *Enquiry Concerning the Principles of Morals*. Cf. 'Usefulness is agreeable, and engages our approbation. This is a matter of fact, confirmed by daily observation. But, useful? For what? For some body's interest, surely. Whose interest then? Not our own only: For our approbation frequently extends farther. It must, therefore, be the interest of those, who are served by the character or action approved of; and these we may conclude, however remote, are not totally indifferent to us' (*ECPM*, p. 37).

13. *Nature has . . . state*] The natural weakness and vulnerability of human infants were cited as evidence in the context of Epicurean denials of the existence of providence: see, e.g., Lucretius, *De Rerum Natura*, V.222–34: 'Tum porro puer, ut saevis proiectus ab undis / navita, nudus humi iacet, infans, indigus omni / vitali auxilio, cum primum in luminis oras / nixibus ex alvo matris natura profudit, / vagituque locum lugubri complet, ut aequumst

/ cui tantum in vita restet transire malorum. / at variae crescunt pecudes armenta feraeque, / nec crepitacillis opus est, nec cuiquam adhibendast / almae nutricis blanda atque infracta loquella, / nec varias quaerunt vestes pro tempore caeli, / denique non armis opus est, non moenibus altis, / qui sua tutentur, quando omnibus omnia large / tellus ipsa parit naturaque daedala rerum'; 'Then further the child, like a sailor cast forth by the cruel waves, lies naked upon the ground, speechless, in need of every kind of vital support, as soon as nature has spilt him forth with throes from his mother's womb into the regions of light, and he fills all around with doleful wailings – as is but just, seeing that so much trouble awaits him in life to pass through. But the diverse flocks and herds grow, and wild creatures; they need no rattles, none of them wants to hear the coaxing and broken babytalk of the foster-nurse, they seek no change of raiment according to the temperature of the season, lastly they need no weapons, no lofty walls to protect their own, since for them all the earth herself brings forth all they want in abundance, and nature the cunning fashioner of things.' More recently, human imbecillity had been a topic that Swift had found useful in his mortification of complacency and pride: see Swift, *Gulliver's Travels*, Part II, chapter 7 (p. 198), and Part IV, chapter 4 (pp. 357–8). However, Adam Smith would put forward a recuperative account of human weakness, as a circumstance that had summoned into existence the energies that had led to the progress of society (see Smith, *Jurisprudence*, pp. 487–8; cf. Phillipson, *Adam Smith*, pp. 116 and 175).

14. *Metempsychosis*] i.e. the doctrine that souls are immortal, and migrate to a new (and possibly non-human) body on the death of the old. It is a view associated with Pythagoras. It flies in the face of all Christian doctrines of the soul, and had been explicitly rejected by Locke in his account of personal identity: 'He that shall place the *Identity* of Man in any thing else, but like that of other Animals in one fitly organized Body taken in any one instant, and from thence continued under one Organization of Life in several successively fleeting Particles of Matter, united to it, will find it hard, to make an *Embryo*, one of Years, mad, and sober, the same Man, by any Supposition, that will not make it possible for *Seth, Ismael, Socrates, Pilate*, St. *Austin*, and *Cæsar Borgia* to be the same Man. For if the *Identity* of Soul alone makes the same Man, and there be nothing in the Nature of Matter, why the same individual Spirit may not be united to different Bodies, it will be possible, that those Men, living in distant Ages, and of different Tempers, may have been the same Man: Which way of speaking must be from a very strange use of the Word *Man*, applied to an *Idea*, out of which Body and Shape is excluded: And that way of speaking would agree yet worse with the Notions of those Philosophers, who allow of Transmigration, and are of Opinion that the Souls of Men may, for their Miscarriages, be detruded into the Bodies of Beasts, as fit Habitations with Organs suited to the satisfaction of their Brutal Inclinations. But yet I think no body, could he be sure that the

Soul of *Heliogabalus* were in one of his Hogs, would yet say that Hog were a *Man* or *Heliogabalus*' (Locke, *Essay*, II.xxvii, p. 332). Even so, the doctrine had clearly fascinated Christians who cannot have been unaware of the challenge it posed to the dogmas to which their faith obliged them to adhere. For example, in his *Fables* Dryden had chosen to include 'Of the Pythagorean Philosophy', a version of that section of Ovid's *Metamorphoses* which describes the metempsychosis (Dryden, *Poems on Various Occasions* [1701], pp. 501–30). Nevertheless, Hume's bland willingness to entertain the possibility of the metempsychosis is an aspect of the anti-Christian stance he adopts in this essay. Locke's theory of personal identity had been explicitly framed to be consistent with the Christian doctrine of the Resurrection of the body, and thus had explicitly resisted the metempsychosis: 'And thus we may be able without any difficulty to conceive, the same Person at the Resurrection, though in a Body not exactly in make or parts the same which he had here, the same consciousness going along with the Soul that inhabits it' (Locke, *Essay*, II.xxvii.15, p. 340). However, others were prepared to take it more seriously, as a thought-experiment at least: see, e.g. Peter Brown, *The Procedure, Extent and Limits of Human Understanding* (1728), pp. 165–73.

15. *Nothing . . . indissoluble*] cf. the similar comments which open 'Of the Populousness of Ancient Nations' (above, pp. 95–6).

16. *Lib. vii. cap. 55*] 'But how much easier and safer for each to trust in himself, and for us to derive our idea of future tranquillity from our experience of it before birth!' (Pliny the Elder, *Natural History*, VII.lv.190).

17. *defend the negative*] cf. what Hume says in his letter of April 1750 to John Clephane about his strategy in 'Of the Populousness of Ancient Nations', which he characterizes as 'not altogether in opposition to *Vossius* and *Montesquieu* . . . but, starting some doubts, and scruples, and difficulties, sufficient to make us suspend our judgment on that head' (*Letters*, vol. I, p. 140).

18. *Nothing . . . great and important truth*] cf. the similarly feline irony of the conclusion of 'Of Miracles': 'the CHRISTIAN religion not only was at first attended with miracles, but even at this day cannot be believed by any reasonable person without one. Mere reason is insufficient to convince us of its veracity: And whoever is moved by *Faith* to assent to it, is conscious of a continued miracle in his own person, which subverts all the principles of his understanding, and gives him a determination to believe what is most contrary to custom and experience' (*ECHU*, sect. 10, p. 99). In the *Treatise of Human Nature*, I.iii.9, Hume had identified custom as the source of 'all belief and reasoning' (*THN*, p. 80).

# Unpublished Essays

## AN HISTORICAL ESSAY ON CHIVALRY AND MODERN HONOUR

Copy text: NLS MS 23159 (4)

Headnote:

> The text printed here is a 'clean' reading text, with the occasional few corrections in the MS adopted without comment. It thus represents Hume's final intentions. The manuscript breaks off abruptly owing to the loss of one or more leaves.
>
> Transcriptions of this essay have been published twice previously: E. C. Mossner, 'David Hume's "An Historical Essay on Chivalry and Modern Honour"', *Modern Philology*, 45 (1947), pp. 54–60 (an unreliable transcription); and John P. Wright, 'Hume on the Origin of "Modern Honour": A Study in Hume's Philosophical Development', in Ruth Savage (ed.), *Philosophy and Religion in Enlightenment Britain: New Case Studies* (Oxford: Oxford University Press, 2012), pp. 187–209. On the reasons for dating the manuscript to the early 1730s, see M. A. Stewart, 'The Dating of Hume's Manuscripts', in Paul Wood (ed.), *The Scottish Enlightenment: Essays in Reinterpretation* (Rochester: University of Rochester Press, 2000), pp. 267–314.
>
> Chivalric values and practices (notably duelling) survived into the eighteenth century under the guise of gallantry, although the tension between them and Christian values and practices was unignorable. For commentary, see Clark, *English Society*, pp. 93–118, 'The Social Theory of Elite Hegemony'; Markku Peltonen, *The Duel in Early Modern England: Civility, Politeness and Honour* (Cambridge: Cambridge University Press, 2003); and Maurice Keen, *Chivalry* (New Haven, CT, and London: Yale University Press, 1984).
>
> In Shaftesbury's 'The Moralists', I.ii, Philocles reports that Palemon has disparaged gallantry as '*a modern Growth*': 'this whole Order and Scheme of Wit you condemn'd absolutely, as *false*, *monstrous*, and GOTHICK; quite out of the way of Nature, and sprung from the mere Dregs of *Chivalry* or *Knight-Errantry*; a thing which in it-self you prefer'd, as of a better Taste

than that which reigns at present in its stead. For at a time when this Mystery of *Gallantry* carry'd along with it the Notion of doughty Knighthood; when *the Fair* were made Witnesses, and, in a manner, Partys to Feats of Arms, enter'd into all the Points of War and Combat, and were won by dint of Launce and manly Prowess; 'twas not altogether absurd (you thought) on such a foundation as this, to pay 'em Homage and Adoration, make 'em the Standard of Wit and Manners, to bring Mankind under their Laws' (Shaftesbury, *Characteristicks*, vol. II, pp. 9–10). It may be that in this essay Hume is responding to and exploring further the implications of this passage. He would certainly refer later to this passage of Shaftesbury, in 'Of the Rise and Progress of the Arts and Sciences': 'If the superiority in politeness should be allowed to modern times, the modern notions of *gallantry*, the natural produce of courts and monarchies, will probably be assigned as the causes of this refinement. No one denies this invention to be modern: But some of the more zealous partizans of the ancients, have asserted it to be foppish and ridiculous, and a reproach, rather than a credit to the present age' (above, vol. 1, p. 107). It is interesting to see Hume referring to Shaftesbury as one of the 'more zealous partizans of the ancients'.

It is also likely that in this essay Hume is engaging with what Mandeville had said about modern honour in his *An Enquiry into the Origin of Honour, and the Usefulness of Christianity in War* (1732). Here Mandeville had revived the speakers in the dialogues of *The Fable of the Bees*, Cleomenes and Horatio, and used them to put forward a strongly anticlerical interpretation of the origins of chivalry and honour. According to Cleomenes, chivalry and honour arise from the belated understanding, on the part of the Church Fathers of the second century, that in order to acheive their temporal objectives they needed to find a way of accommodating the pacific doctrine of their religion to militarism: 'The Divines of those Days were most of them become arrant Priests, and saw plainly, that a Religion, which would not allow its Votaries to assist at Courts or Armies, and comply with the vain World, could never be made National; consequently, the Clergy of it could never acquire any considerable Power upon Earth' (Mandeville, *Honour*, pp. 33–4). Honour, a later derivative from virtue, was accordingly much better adapted to the failings of human nature: 'It is manifest then, that there are Allurements in the Principle of Honour, to draw in Men of the lowest Capacity, and even the vicious, which Virtue has not' (Mandeville, *Honour*, p. 44). And he went on: 'What I would demonstrate, is, that there are many Allowances, gross Indulgences to Human Nature in the Principle of Honour, especially of modern Honour, that are always exclaim'd against by the Voice of Virtue, and diametrically opposite to the Doctrine of *Christ*' (Mandeville, *Honour*, p. 45). Turning to chivalry, Cleomenes unmasked it as a 'deep-laid Plot for enslaving the Laity' of the Church of Rome: 'The various Orders of Knighthood were so many Bulwarks to defend the Temporals of the Church', and the purpose of these orders was 'to reconcile, in outward Shew, the Principle of Honour with that of the Christian Religion' (Mandeville, *Honour*, p. 46). Modern honour and gallantry were simply the dwindled afterlife of this tremendous stroke of priestcraft that had been executed in late antiquity and institutionalized in the Middle Ages: 'There is certainly a great Difference between the Men of Honour in former Ages and many of those, who now-a-days assume the Title. A Man in whom Justice, Integrity, Temperance and Chastity are join'd with Fortitude, is worthy of the highest Esteem; but that a debauch'd Fellow, who runs in every Tradesman's Debt, and thinks himself not obliged to pay any Thing but what is borrow'd or lost at Play, should claim the same Regard from us, for no other Reason than because he dares to Fight, is very unreasonable' (Mandeville, *Honour*, p. 90).

As James Harris has noted, Hume does not follow Mandeville down the path of anticlericalism, although his argument in this essay (to the extent that we can discern it, given the surviving essay's incompleteness) is broadly compatible with Mandeville's (Harris, *Hume*, pp. 58–60). However, Hume looks for the origins of honour and chivalry in a more natural process, set in motion when barbarian psychology collided with the remnants of empire and the humane ideals of the new religion. Whereas Mandeville's Cleomenes saw chivalry and honour as stupendous triumphs of clerical imposture and encroachment, Hume sees, not ecclesiastical conspiracy, but a process which exemplifies the natural, historical development of manners. A further point of divergence is that, whereas Mandeville saw honour as an accommodation for human weakness and vice, Hume understands how it might equally operate to restrain the violent passions from which it arose.

The topic of chivalry would remain of historical and philosophical interest throughout the eighteenth century, sustained in part by the mid- and late-eighteenth-century fashions for the medieval and the faux-medieval in architecture, decorative arts and poetry.

In the *Esprit des Lois*, book III, chapters 6 and 7, Montesquieu would identify honour as the principle which animated monarchy. The history and institutions of chivalry would be explored and defended in the five 'mémoires' on the subject by Curne de Ste Palaye, published in the *Mémoires de l'Académie des Inscriptions et Belles Lettres*, vol. XX (1753), pp. 597–847. Richard Hurd, the bishop of Worcester, in his *Letters on Chivalry and Romance* (1762) silently resisted the anticlerical interpretation of chivalry advanced by Mandeville. For Hurd (who refers to and draws on Curne de Ste Palaye: Hurd, *Chivalry and Romance*, pp. 24–5), 'Chivalry was no absurd and freakish institution, but the natural and even sober effect of the feudal policy; whose turbulent genius breathed nothing but war, and was fierce and military even in its amusements' (Hurd, *Chivalry and Romance*, p. 10). Insofar as the Church had encouraged chivalry, it was a matter not of worldly policy so much as self-defence: 'the Christian world . . . had been harrassed by long wars, and had but just recovered a breathing-time from the brutal ravages of the Saracen armies. The remembrance of what they had lately suffered from these grand enemies of the faith, made it natural and even necessary to engage a new military order on the side of religion' (Hurd, *Chivalry and Romance*, p. 20).

Adam Ferguson in his *History of Civil Society* (1767) would take a more philosophical approach. For Ferguson, chivalry had guided and directed the turning point from antiquity to modernity: 'chivalry, uniting with the genius of our policy, has probably suggested those peculiarities in the law of nations, by which modern states are distinguished from the ancient. And if our rule in measuring degrees of politeness and civilization is to be taken from hence, or from the advancement of commercial arts, we shall be found to have greatly excelled any of the celebrated nations of antiquity' (Ferguson, *Civil Society*, p. 193).

For commentary, see Harris, *Hume*, pp. 58–60 and 74–5; Ryan P. Hanley, 'David Hume and the Modern Problem of Honor', *The Modern School-man*, 84 (2007), pp. 295–312; Donald T. Siebert, 'Chivalry and Romance in the Age of Hume', *Eighteenth-Century Life*, 21 (1997), pp. 62–79; and Ryu Susato, 'The Idea of Chivalry in the Scottish Enlightenment: The Case of David Hume', *Hume Studies*, 33 (2007), pp. 155–78. Hanley states the importance of this early essay most forcefully, contending that it inaugurates 'Hume's life-long investigation of the nature of the difference between antiquity and modernity, and his attempt to promote within the Enlightenment an accommodation, if not a restoration, of that which it ostensibly sought to replace', and that it 'represents Hume's first salvo in his extensive project to reconcile his competing attachments to the classical ethical virtues of magnanimity and courage and the modern ethical virtues of benevolence and humanity – the reconciliation of which would prove to be one of the animating themes of his mature political thought' (p. 296).

Hume would pick up the topic of modern gallantry once more in 'Of the Rise and Progress of the Arts and Sciences' (above, vol. 1, pp. 93–112): 'If the superiority in politeness should be allowed to modern times, the modern notions of *gallantry*, the natural produce of courts and monarchies, will probably be assigned as the causes of this refinement. No one denies this invention to be modern …' (above, vol. 1, p. 107). Note also the passage Hume deleted from 'Of the Rise and Progress of the Arts and Sciences', in which he asserts the modernity of the separation of honour and virtue (variant 15, above, vol. 1, pp. 303–4); a point clearly relevant to this essay.

1. *these Barbarians, who overspread the Roman Empire*] The undermining and eventual overthrow of the Roman Empire in the West by the northern barbarians had long been recognized as one of the great turning points in human history: see, e.g., Machiavelli, *History of Florence*, Book I (Machiavelli,

*Works*, pp. 1–7). Gibbon's *Decline and Fall* would be in part an exploration of the far-reaching consequences of this process.

2. *Conquest over their Conquerors*] An allusion to Horace's famous statement of how Greece, though militarily conquered, nevertheless subdued the victorious Romans with her arts, and thus drove underground the native rustic strain in Latin poetry: 'Graecia capta ferum victorem cepit et artis / intulit agresti Latio'; 'Greece, the captive, made her savage victor captive, and brought the arts into rustic Latium' (Horace, *Epistles*, II.i.156–7). Hume would revert to this famous passage in 'Of Civil Liberty' (above, p. 282 and n. 25). Probably a few years after Hume had composed this essay, Pope would imitate these lines of Horace and apply them to England and France: 'We conquer'd France, but felt our captive's charms; / Her Arts victorious triumph'd o'er our Arms' ('The First Epistle of the Second Book of Horace Imitated. To Augustus', ll. 263–4). The notion of the stealthy conquest of the victors by the subtle arts of the defeated became a commonplace: see, e.g., Thomson, *Liberty*, III.372–5.

3. *reject their own Religion*] The Goths and Visigoths had been converted by Ulphilas in the late fourth century AD. Gibbon would narrate the process of conversion and explore its consequences in chapter 37 of *The Decline and Fall* (Gibbon, *Decline and Fall*, vol. II, pp. 429–50).

4. *The antient . . . inventing new ones*] cf. Gibbon on the extinguishing of creative energy in the later, and as he thought, intellectually moribund, periods of the Roman Empire: 'They held in their lifeless hands the riches of their fathers, without inheriting the spirit which had created and improved that sacred patrimony: they read, they praised, they compiled, but their languid souls seemed alike incapable of thought and action. In the revolution of ten centuries [from the fall of the Roman Empire in the West to the fall of Constantinople], not a single discovery was made to exalt the dignity or promote the happiness of mankind. Not a single idea has been added to the speculative systems of antiquity, and a succession of patient disciples became in their turn the dogmatic teachers of the next servile generation. Not a single composition of history, philosophy or literature has been saved from oblivion by the intrinsic beauties of style or sentiment, of original fancy, or even of successful imitation. In prose, the least offensive of the Byzantine writers are absolved from censure by their naked and unpresuming simplicity: but the orators, most eloquent in their own conceit, are the farthest removed from the models whom they affect to emulate. In every page our taste and reason are wounded by the choice of gigantic and obsolete words, a stiff and intricate phraseology, the discord of images, the childish play of false or unseasonable ornament, and the painful attempt to elevate themselves, to astonish the reader, and to involve a trivial meaning in the smoke of obscurity and exaggeration' (Gibbon, *Decline and Fall*, vol. III, p. 410).

5. *Grecian Philosophy ... Christian Religion*] However, Hobbes had detected the infection of Greek philosophy in the doctrines of Christianity. This hybridization would be one of the sources of that intellectual darkness, which arose 'by mixing with the Scripture divers reliques of the Religion, and much of the vain and erroneous Philosophy of the Greeks, especially of Aristotle' (Hobbes, *Leviathan*, p. 418). This allegation of pagan Greek contamination in Christianity would become a mainstay of the later deistic attack on the new religion. The doctrine of purgatory was a particularly egregious theological fruit pollinated by 'contagion of the Daemonology of the Greeks' (Hobbes, *Leviathan*, p. 426); while the doctrine of the Trinity was regularly denounced as nothing more than a Christian copy of an originally Platonic notion.

6. *such fairy-ground*] i.e. insubstantial and delusory. There is perhaps a flavour here of the language in which Hobbes had mocked the papacy by comparing it with the '*Kingdome of Fairies*' (Hobbes, *Leviathan*, p. 480). Equally, however, and given both the demonstrable importance of Prior's poetry to Hume and the chivalric subject of the essay, we may find here also an echo of Prior's imitation of Spenser, the *Ode, Humbly Inscrib'd to the Queen*: 'He [Spenser] travell'd ENGLAND o'er on Fairy Ground, / In Mystic Notes to Sing his Monarch's Praise' (Prior, *Works*, vol. I, p. 232).

7. *The same thing ... by Nature*] Most immediately a reference to that severe disciplining of the natural characteristic of Stoic philosophy. This essay was probably composed in the aftermath of a recent attempt by Hume to live his life on arduous Stoic principles, which had gone badly wrong: see above, vol. 1, pp. 207–8, n. 10.

8. *No Engine ... our Tip-toes*] A common illustration of groundless human confidence; cf. Samuel Johnson, *The History of Rasselas, Prince of Abissinia*, 2 vols (1759), chapter 6, 'A dissertation on the art of flying', in Womersley, *Johnson*, pp. 645–7.

9. *as the Grecians did the Romans*] cf. above, p. 632, n. 2.

10. *lick it into any Form*] A turn of phrase which derives from the tradition that reaches back to antiquity (cf. Ovid, *Metamorphoses*, XV.379–81) and is enshrined in medieval bestiaries, that bear cubs are born shapeless and are then licked into shape by their mother. Sir Thomas Browne had dismissed the belief with conspicuous and unnecessary learning (*Pseudodoxia Epidemica* [1646], book III, chapter 6, pp. 116–17).

11. *descended from the Moors & Arabians*] The speculation that the manners and customs of chivalry had taken their rise from the cohabitation of the Arabs and the Goths in the Iberian peninsula after the Islamic invasion and settlement of the early eighth century AD had been advanced by the greatest English orientalists of the seventeenth century, such as Edward Pococke and Simon Ockley. It would still be repeated by Herder at the end of the eighteenth century: 'the more refined customs of chivalry were evidently

brought into Europe by the arabs ... this gayer spirit of chivalry was first introduced among the christians in Spain, where the arabs and goths lived together for centuries. Here ... the spirit of chivalry was so deeply imprinted in the character of the Spaniards, that even knights errant, and chevaliers of love, perfectly in the arabian style, were not with them mere creatures of the imagination. The romaunt, or historical poem, particularly as dedicated to the adventurers of love and chivalry; and probably the romance, as the old Amadis, and others; were the offspring of their language and way of thinking, in which Cervantes found in latter days the materials for that incomparable national romance, Don Quixote de la Mancha' (J. G. Herder, *Outlines of a Philosophy of the History of Man*, tr. T. Churchill [London, 1800], pp. 607–8). Richard Hurd, however, would see in chivalry not the hybridizing influence of Arabian manners, but Christian resistance to the unwanted presence of the Saracens in Spain: 'And here, by the way, the reason appears why the Spaniards, of all the Europeans, were furthest gone in every characteristic madness of true chivalry. To all the other considerations, here mentioned, their fanaticism in every way was especially instigated and kept alive by the memory and neighbourhood of their old infidel invaders' (Hurd, *Chivalry and Romance*, pp. 21–22).

12. *comparing the Gothic with the Grecian*] cf. Pope's similar comparison of these two different kinds of architecture in the 'Preface' to his edition of Shakespeare (quoted above, 'Of Simplicity and Refinement in Writing', vol. 1, p. 348, n. 5).

13. *All Ideas of Merit ... of the Nation*] The thinkers of antiquity had suspected that civil society had begun in the loyalty felt by soldiers towards a successful commander: 'ducis boni imperatoriam virtutem esse' (Tacitus, *Agricola*, XXXIX.ii).

14. *Hence in Rome ... deriv'd from it*] cf. Hume's comment in his letter to Francis Hutcheson of 17 September 1739: '*Virtus* signify'd chiefly Courage among the *Romans*' (*Letters*, vol. I, p. 33). This is a point of contact with Mandeville: 'We have Reason to think, that, at First, Nothing was meant by Virtus, but Daring and Intrepidity, right or wrong' (Mandeville, *Honour*, 'Preface', p. iv.).

15. *some Foundation*] Hume refers to the manner of interpreting myth devised by Euhemerus of Messina, called euhemerism after its founder, in which myth was presented as misremembered or embroidered history, and hence the heathen gods and the events of pagan mythology turned out to be memories of earthly heroes and their deeds. See Frank E. Manuel, *The Eighteenth Century Confronts the Gods* (New York: Atheneum, 1967), pp. 103–5. Cf. Adam Ferguson: 'Hercules, who perhaps was an eminent warrior, became a god with posterity, and his race was set apart for royalty and sovereign power' (Ferguson, *Civil Society*, p. 98).

16. *Upon this ... refin'd Courage*] Adam Ferguson would also note this discrepancy of manners: 'The hero of Greek poetry proceeds on the maxims of animosity and hostile passion. His maxims in war are like those which prevail in the woods of America. They require him to be brave, but they allow him to practise against his enemy every sort of deception. The hero of modern romance professes a contempt of stratagem, as well as of danger, and unites in the same person, characters and dispositions seemingly opposite; ferocity with gentleness, and the love of blood with sentiments of tenderness and pity' (Ferguson, *Civil Society*, p. 191). Hume would rely on this once more in his essay on Ossian: see below, pp. 645–6, n. 15. Hurd, however, would insist that the manners of the Homeric heroes and those of chivalric knights displayed 'a remarkable correspondency' (Hurd, *Chivalry and Romance*, p. 26; cf. also p. 31).

17. *So that a Mistress ... Devotee*] cf. Adam Ferguson: 'The system of chivalry, when completely formed, proceeded on a marvellous respect and veneration to the fair sex ... The Germans, even in their native forests, paid a kind of devotion to the female sex' (Ferguson, *Civil Society*, pp. 191–2).

18. *submiss*] submissive, humble, ready to obey (*OED*, 'submiss', *adj.*, 1 a).

19. *Parcere ... debellare superbos*] 'to spare the defeated and to lay low the proud'; the expression of Roman destiny that Virgil had placed in the mouth of Anchises when visited by Aeneas in the underworld (*Aeneid*, VI.853).

20. *Hence arises ... Violence of Giants*] cf. *ECHU*, XII, 'Of the Academical or Sceptical Philosophy': 'The knights-errant, who wandered about to clear the world of dragons and giants, never entertained the least doubt with regard to the existence of these monsters' (p. 112).

21. *betraying with a Kiss*] An allusion to the betrayal of Jesus by Judas: see Matthew 26:48–9; Mark 14:44–6; Luke 22:47–8.

22. *He salutes you ... Courage*] cf. Hume's mockery of the examples of such extravagant chivalry in the poems of Ossian (above, pp. 274–5).


## OF THE POEMS OF OSSIAN

Copy text: NLS MS 23159 (17)
Headnote:

> The manuscript of this essay is heavily corrected. The text printed here is a 'clean' reading text, with the substantial corrections in the MS adopted without comment. It thus represents Hume's final intentions.
>
> The text of the essay has been previously published on two occasions: Hill Burton, *Life*, vol. I, pp. 471–80; and Green and Grose, vol. II, pp. 415–24.
>
> This is a late essay, composed at some point after the spring of 1773, since Hume refers to Macpherson's recently published translation of the *Iliad* (cf.

also *Letters*, vol. II, p. 280). It may indeed be even later, as there are striking similarities of tone and phrasing between this essay and Hume's comments about Ossian in a letter to Edward Gibbon of 18 March 1776. In volume I of *The Decline and Fall* Gibbon had reserved judgement on the authenticity of the Ossianic poems without actually disputing their authenticity, but Hume thought this hesitation a misplaced courtesy: 'I see you entertain a great Doubt with regard to the Authenticity of the Poems of Ossian. You are certainly right in so doing. It is, indeed, strange, that any men of Sense coud have imagin'd it possible, that above twenty thousand Verses, along with numberless historical Facts, could have been preservd by oral Tradition during fifty Generations, by the rudest, perhaps, of all European Nations; the most necessitous, the most turbulent, and the most unsettled. Where a Supposition is so contrary to common Sense, any positive Evidence of it ought never to be regarded. Men run with great Avidity to give their Evidence in favour of what flatters their Passions, and their national Prejudices. You are, therefore, over and above indulgent to us in speaking of the Matter with Hesitation' (*Letters*, vol. II, pp. 310–11). However, in 1775 Macpherson had published his *The History of Great Britain from the Restoration to the Accession of the House of Hanover*, which Hume had castigated to William Strahan as 'one of the most wretched *Productions* that ever came from your Press' (*Letters*, vol. II, p. 304). It is difficult to believe that, had Hume been aware of this history when he wrote this essay, he would have failed to add it to the list of Macpherson's misdemeanours in print. So for the composition of this essay we may reasonably suggest a *terminus a quo* of April 1773, and a *terminus ad quem* of November 1775.

In 1760 James Macpherson (1736–1796), a schoolteacher from the Highlands of Scotland, had published *Fragments of Ancient Poetry*, which he boldly presented as 'translations' of Gaelic originals: 'The public may depend on the following fragments as genuine remains of ancient Scottish poetry' (Macpherson, *Fragments*, p. iii). The slim volume (sixty pages of poetry, prefaced with a short introductory essay of ten pages) was received with great excitement, as it met the public taste for new forms of poetry that had been growing since the death of Pope in 1744, and that would soon be fed further by, inter alia, Thomas Percy's *Reliques of Ancient English Poetry* (1765). As Thomas Warton, the historian of English literature, would write to Percy in 1762, 'the Public ought to have their Attention called to Poetry in new forms; to Poetry endued with new Manners & new Images' (*The Correspondence of Thomas Warton*, ed. D. Fairer [Athens, GA: University of Georgia Press, 1995], p. 126). Macpherson's later publications, in which he was assisted in various ways by the Scottish man of letters Hugh Blair (*Fragments* was followed, after a tour of the Highlands to collect further raw materials, by *Fingal* [1762], *Selma* [1762] and *Temora* [1763]), certainly gratified this appetite for poetic novelty (for a brief account of the circumstances of recovery and publication, see Blair, *Dissertation*, pp. 117–19; and for the encouragement by Blair, 'a gentleman, who has himself made a figure in the poetical world', of Macpherson, see Macpherson, *Fingal*, p. xiv). The impact of these poems, allegedly snatched from the maw of oblivion and published under the patronage of the Earl of Bute (Macpherson, *Fingal*, p. xv, and 'Advertisement'), was immediate and immense both in Great Britain and on the continent.

These 'recovered' Gaelic poems had of course a particular appeal for Scottish readers. They could be seen as evidence for Scotland's parity of cultural dignity with England at a time when the political and military events of the past fifty years had threatened to reduce Scotland to a condition of political, economic, and cultural dependency: 'After the experiences of the 1707 Union, the Jacobite Risings and, more immediately, the militia crisis, it was particularly urgent that England's great epic poet [Milton] should be matched by a Scot. And although *Paradise Lost* was hard to surpass in terms of quality, *The Poems of Ossian* at least scored highly on antiquity' (Fiona Stafford, '*Fingal* and the Fallen Angels: Macpherson, Milton and Romantic Titanism', in Fiona Stafford and Howard Gaskill [eds], *From Gaelic to Romantic: Ossianic Translations* [Amsterdam and Atlanta, GA: Rodopi, 1998], p. 164).

In England, the initial rapture provoked by these poems began to yield to doubts and scruples over their authenticity. Thomas Gray's enthusiasm, for instance, soon curdled into scepticism. He had been initially 'charmed' by the pre-publication specimens he had received from Horace Walpole in the spring of 1760. But by June of that year Gray was clearly torn between on the one hand his desire to believe them genuine and on the other the difficulties of so believing: 'I was so struck, so *extasié* with their infinite beauty, that I writ into Scotland to make a thousand enquiries. the letters I have in return are ill-wrote, ill-reason'd, unsatisfactory, calculated (one would imagine) to deceive one, & yet not cunning enough to do it cleverly. in short, the whole external evidence would make one believe these fragments ... counterfeit: but the internal is so strong on the other side, that I am resolved to believe them genuine, spite of the Devil & the Kirk. it is impossible to convince me, that they were invented by the same Man, that writes me these letters. on the other hand it is almost as hard to suppose, if they are original, that he should be able to translate them so admirably. what can one do?' (Gray, *Correspondence*, vol. II, pp. 664, 680; cf. pp. 690 and 771).

Hugh Blair's *A Critical Dissertation on the Poems of Ossian* (1763; second and third editions, 1765) was intended to lay such doubts to rest. But by widening the field of debate so that it now touched the largest questions of the progress of society from antiquity to modernity, Blair's defences of the poems only drew attention to new areas of vulnerability. In the 'Appendix' to his *Dissertation*, Blair had denounced disbelief of the authenticity of the Ossianic poems as an English prejudice, since in 'Scotland, their authenticity

was never called in question': 'Yet in England, it seems, an opinion has prevailed with some, that an imposture has been carried on; that the poems
which have been given to the world, are not translations of the works of any
old Galic Bard, but modern compositions, formed, as it is said, upon a higher
plan of poetry and sentiment than could belong to an age and a country
reputed barbarous' (Blair, *Dissertation*, pp. 117 and 119). However, it is precisely this accusation that Hume revives and presses in his essay. And indeed,
from start to finish (as the annotation below makes clear) Hume's essay is in
sustained, extensive and adversative dialogue with the arguments and language of Blair's *Dissertation*; with the various dissertations and prefatory
essays that Macpherson had attached to the published volumes of Ossianic
poetry; and even, at moments, with his own earlier comments on the subject
of Ossian in letters to friends.

Modern scholarship, guided particularly by D. S. Thomson's *The Gaelic
Sources of Macpherson's 'Ossian'* (Edinburgh: Oliver and Boyd, 1952), has
settled on the consensus that Macpherson was dealing with authentic Gaelic
fragments and traditions which, however, he 'worked up' with varying
degrees of intensity and intrusiveness to produce texts which are as much,
perhaps at times more, of the 1760s as they are of the third century AD. Thus
the Ossianic poems present fragmentary images of Gaelic antiquity refracted
through a medium of later literary sophistication. (One of the paradoxes of
the Ossian affair is that Macpherson's stature as a creative, imaginative force
in European letters depends on the Ossianic poems being much more than
the simple verbatim 'translations' of Gaelic originals that Macpherson dog-
gedly insisted that they were.)

The publication of the Ossianic poems might almost have been designed
to catch Hume between wind and water. On the one hand, Hume's admiration for John Home's tragedy *Douglas* (1756), and his leaping to the defence
of William Wilkie's would-be Homeric *Epigoniad* in 1757, had both recently
demonstrated his desire for the advancement of Scottish literature, and his
receptiveness to attempts to revive older literary forms for modern times. In
this perspective, Macpherson's publications must have been welcome confir-
mations of the perennial merit of Scottish letters.

But on the other hand, Hume's commitment to the progress of society and
his allegiance to modernity (clear in essays such as 'Of the Rise and Progress
of the Arts and Sciences', 'Of Refinement in the Arts' and 'Of the Populousness of Ancient Nations'), while it disposed him to welcome a modern
rival to Homer, would equally make him shrink from the primitivism that
might naturally accompany such poems (and that had indeed accompanied Macpherson's). After all, Macpherson (whose early experiences of the
suppression of the '45 had probably made him at least a sentimental Jacobite) had prefaced *Fingal* with an elegy for the Highland past: 'The genius
of the highlanders has suffered a great change within these few years. The

communication with the rest of the island is open, and the introduction of trade and manufactures has destroyed that leisure which was formerly dedicated to hearing and repeating the poems of ancient times. Many have now learned to leave their mountains, and seek their fortunes in a milder climate; and though a certain *amor patriæ* may sometimes bring them back, they have, during their absence, imbibed enough of foreign manners to despise the customs of their ancestors. Bards have been long disused, and the spirit of genealogy has greatly subsided. Men begin to be less devoted to their chiefs, and consanguinity is not so much regarded. When property is established, the human mind confines itself to the pleasure it procures. It does not go back to antiquity, or look forward to succeeding ages. The cares of life increase, and the actions of other times no longer amuse. Hence it is, that the taste for their ancient poetry is at a low ebb among the highlanders. They have not, however, thrown off the good qualities of their ancestors. Hospitality still subsists, and an uncommon civility to strangers. Friendship is inviolable, and revenge less blindly followed than formerly' (Macpherson, *Fingal*, p. xv; cf. Blair, *Dissertation*, p. 123 – the two passages are very similar, and so perhaps are evidence of Blair guiding the pen of his protégé). The whole tendency of Hume's social philosophy had been to present as welcome refinements the very social developments (commerce in its broadest sense; cosmopolitanism and a loosening of merely local attachments; the erosion of atavism) that Macpherson (or perhaps Blair) in this passage deplores. For a further example of Macpherson's occasionally Rousseauvian ethical primitivism, see Macpherson, *Temora*, p. 76 n. *.

The awkwardness of the Ossianic poems for Hume was only intensified once questions had arisen concerning their authenticity. In his essays and in his *History of England* Hume had made, and would continue to make, heavy intellectual investments in a particular understanding of the relationship between antiquity and modernity. Following in the footsteps of Fontenelle, Hume had repeatedly stigmatized as a mere prejudice mankind's tendency to magnify and admire the distant past (e.g., in 'Of Refinement in the Arts', above, p. 22; and in the final sentence of 'Of the Populousness of Ancient Nations', above, p. 148). He had distanced himself from the 'virtue' politics promoted by extollers of Roman antiquity, such as Machiavelli. The luxury of a commercial society, which had been deplored by civic humanists as moral and political corruption, Hume had re-described as a healthy and welcome refinement that posed no threat to the flourishing of human society. However, that whole edifice of carefully argued praise for commercial modernity might be endangered were it to be shown that Hume's sense of the difference between the ancient and the modern was so vague and insecure that he had been willing to recognize modern forgeries as authentic Gaelic poetry.

That possibility might have been all the more present to Hume's thoughts because one of the great episodes in the English campaign of the 'Querelle des anciens et des modernes' had turned on an exactly analogous point. In his 'Essay upon Ancient and Modern Learning' (1690) Sir William Temple had praised the epistles of Phalaris as exemplifying the superlative quality of genuinely ancient literature: 'the oldest Books we have, are still in their kind the best . . . so I think the Epistles of *Phalaris* to have more Race, more Spirit, more Force of Wit and Genius than any others I have ever seen, either Ancient or Modern' (Temple, *Works*, vol. I, p. 166). Encouraged by such remarks, and guided by Henry Aldritch, Dean of Christ Church, Oxford, Charles Boyle prepared an edition of these epistles (1695) on the basis that they were indeed the authentic compositions of the legendary Sicilian tyrant of the sixth century BC.

In 1697 Richard Bentley published a hand grenade disguised as a book, his *A Dissertation upon the Epistles of Phalaris*. In this work Bentley deployed his exceptional philological and historical knowledge to demonstrate that these epistles were in fact composed long after the death of Phalaris. Instead, they were probably examples of a literary game of a much later period, to which the Sophists had been addicted, namely the fabrication of speeches and letters for historical figures (Bentley, *Dissertation*, p. 8). In reading them, he said, and notwithstanding Temple's extravagant praise, 'you feel, by the emptiness and deadness of them, that you converse with some dreaming Pedant with his elbow on his desk; not with an active, ambitious Tyrant, with his Hand on his Sword, commanding a Million of Subjects' (Bentley, *Dissertation*, p. 63).

Hume refers to Bentley's *Dissertation* explicitly towards the end of this essay (above, p. 279), and other passages suggest that Bentley's language and polemical vigour are in Hume's thoughts as he writes (e.g., below, p. 645, n.13). Well might Bentley have haunted Hume as he wrestled over the difficult problem with which the Ossianic poems had presented him. His initial acceptance of the authenticity of these poems was a matter of public knowledge, as was his later retreat from that position. Might not a shrewd antagonist, who wished to resist or discredit Hume's larger arguments concerning the relation of antiquity to modernity, have noted that this change of heart on Hume's part revealed that he, just like Sir William Temple and Charles Boyle, had no infallible sagacity for when he was in the presence of something ancient or something modern? If so, what reliance was to be placed on those provocative arguments about the superiority of modernity to the earlier ages of human society that Hume had so confidently advanced? Surely Hume's tergiversation over Ossian had demonstrated that he might easily be confused on this point. Hence, perhaps, the unusual asperity of tone we detect in this essay, as well as the heavily corrected state of the manuscript, which bespeaks a certain agitation of mind on the part of its author – precisely the kind of inward agitation that we can imagine would overtake someone who found himself embodying in his own experience both poles of the 'Querelle'.

For Hume's initial acceptance of the authenticity of the poems of Ossian, and his early complimentary view of the character of Macpherson, see the long and enthusiastic letter of 16 August 1760 to Sir David Dalrymple (*Letters*, vol. I, pp. 328–31), where Hume's only reservation concerns 'the regular plan which appears in some of these pieces, and which seems to be the work of a more cultivated age' (p. 330). Hume was so far convinced of the authenticity of the poems and of the trustworthiness of Macpherson that on 9 February 1761 he wrote a letter of introduction and recommendation to Strahan, saying that Macpherson was 'a sensible, modest young Fellow, a very good Scholar, and of unexceptionable Morals' (*Letters*, vol. I, pp. 342–3; quotation on p. 343).

By 19 September 1763, however, Hume's assessment had undergone an important change. In a long letter to Macpherson's defender, Hugh Blair, who had just published the first edition of his *Critical Dissertation on the Poems of Ossian* (1763), Hume explained his reasons for now doubting the authenticity of the poems – reasons which closely match the arguments deployed in this essay (*Letters*, vol. I, pp. 398–401; cf. also ibid., pp. 497, 513–14 and 516). Hume's view of Macpherson's character had also changed by October 1763, when he told Blair he found Macpherson 'so strange and heteroclite a mortal, than whom I have scarce ever known a man more perverse and unamiable' (*Letters*, vol. I, p. 403; *New Letters*, p. 72).

For the time being, however, Hume reserved his doubts for his Scottish friends; he was still ready to defend the authenticity of the Ossianic poems to their European admirers. On 9 November 1763 he wrote to Adam Ferguson from Fontainebleau: 'Tell Dr Blair that I have conversed here twice or thrice with the Duchesse d'Aiguillon, who has been amusing herself with translating passages of Ossian; and I have assured her that the authenticity of these poems is to be proved soon beyond all contradiction' (*Letters*, vol. I, p. 413). By 1773, after the publication in 1772 of Macpherson's work on early British history, Hume's opinion, though still negative, had perhaps softened slightly: 'Macpherson has Style and Spirit; but is hot-headed, and consequently without Judgement' (*Letters*, vol. II, p. 269). When Hume had tea with Boswell on 6 March 1775, however, he was in no doubt that the poems were forgeries. Boswell reports Hume explaining that 'he disbelieved not so much for want of testimony, as from the nature of the thing according to his apprehension. He said if fifty barea—d highlanders should say that *Fingal* was an ancient Poem, he would not believe them. He said it was not to be believed that a people who were continually concerned to keep themselves from starving or from being hanged, should preserve in their memories a Poem in six books . . . He said the highlanders, who had been famed as a warlike people, were so much flattered to have it thought that they had a great Poet among them that they all tried to support the fact, and their wish to have it so made them even ready to persuade themselves into it' (quoted in Mossner, *Life*, p. 418). By February 1776 Hume's views of the poems and their author had hardened still further into contempt. A pamphlet, *The Claims of Great Britain Asserted*, was reputed to be by Macpherson, but Hume doubted it, on the grounds that 'I neither find in it the Effrontery nor the Absurdity by which that learned Gentleman's Writings are so eminently distinguished' (*New Letters*, p. 210).

It is worth noting that Sir John Pringle had written to Hume on 9 August 1765, and had questioned the authenticity of the Ossian poems on much the same grounds as Hume, at least eight years later, does in this essay: 'I thank you for your ingenious criticism on Fingal; but it was not satisfactory. I do not think it probable that any Scottish bard, about the age of chivalry, would endeavour to sink his own name in order the better to preserve his poems; or that he could improve so far upon his contemporaries, as to make his works pass for those of an author who had lived so many hundred years before; or, though he had, by having been abroad, entered into the spirit of chivalry himself, he could likewise make his barbarous countrymen relish such refinements of sentiment and manners. I shall add, that I do not even acknowledge those sentiments and manners in Ossian's Poems to be the same with those we read in the old romances (so far at least as I can judge of them from what I have read of them in Don Quixote, for I never saw the originals.) There are no giants, no enchantments, no Christians and Moors, no castles, no sublimated love for ladies, but politeness to them, some fidelity, and a good deal of the sensuality joined . . . I must, in short, believe that they were either all or in part the production of a poet who lived before Constantine, or that most of them have been cooked up in our own time, notwithstanding all the Highland evidence to the contrary' (Burton, *Letters*, pp. 267–8).

A comment from the *Treatise of Human Nature*, I.iii.10, is relevant to the Ossian controversy, and goes some way towards suggesting why Hume was so intensely engaged with it: 'Poets themselves, tho' liars by profession, always endeavour to give an air of truth to their fictions; and where that is totally neglected, their performances, however ingenious, will never be able to afford much pleasure' (*THN*, p. 83). This is a general principle that Macpherson seems to flout.

For further commentary, see Mossner, *Life*, pp. 417–20; Mossner, *Forgotten Hume*, pp. 83–102; Harris, *Hume*, pp. 440–42; and David Raynor, 'Ossian and Hume', in Howard Gaskill (ed.), *Ossian Revisited* (Edinburgh: Edinburgh University Press, 1991), pp. 147–63. On the Ossian controversy more generally, see: Fiona Stafford, *The Sublime Savage: James Macpherson and the Poems of Ossian* (Edinburgh: Edinburgh University Press, 1988); Howard Gaskill (ed.), *Ossian Revisited* (Edinburgh: Edinburgh University Press, 1991); Fiona Stafford and Howard Gaskill (eds), *From Gaelic to Romantic: Ossianic Translations* (Amsterdam and Atlanta, GA: Rodopi, 1998). For the European reception, see Howard Gaskill, *The Reception of Ossian in Europe* (London and New York:

Thoemmes, 2004); and for the German reception in particular (where no less a figure than Goethe took a lead), see W. G. Schmidt and Howard Gaskill (eds), '*Homer des Nordens' und 'Mutter der Romantik': James Macphersons Ossian und seine Rezeption in der deutschsprachigen Literatur*, 4 vols (Berlin and Boston: De Gruyter, 2012). For the text of the celebrated and controversial poems themselves, see Howard Gaskill (ed.), *The Poems of Ossian* (Edinburgh: Edinburgh University Press, 1996).

1. *tiresome, insipid, Performance*] As early as the winter of 1763 Hume had expressed to Blair his opinion that the Ossianic poems were 'a little tedious by reason of their Uniformity' (*Letters*, vol. II, p. 419).

2. *an obscure Highlander*] Macpherson had been born in Ruthven, near Kingussie, the son of a farmer. He had attended King's College and Marischal College, Aberdeen, and the University of Edinburgh. Prior to the publication of *Fragments of Ancient Poetry* he had worked as a family tutor and as a corrector of the press, and had dabbled in literature. Hume's characterization of Macpherson's background is obviously disparaging, but not therefore inaccurate.

3. *a royal Bard*] Ossian was one of the sons of Fingal, the ruler of Morven, or the Highlands, 'the last of the race of Fingal' (Macpherson, *Fragments*, p. 37).

4. *several languages of Europe*] The European vogue for the Ossianic poems was remarkable, particularly in France and Germany. It is reviewed in Howard Gaskill, *The Reception of Ossian in Europe* (London and New York: Thoemmes, 2004).

5. *Molly Mog*] A light-hearted poem principally attributed to John Gay, but with contributions from Pope and Swift, written in praise of a landlord's pretty daughter, the Molly Mog of the title, and published in 1726. The metre of the poem is dactylic trimeters, with the final dactyl in lines two and four of each stanza replaced by a trochee. The insistent rhymes on 'Mog', and the frequent use of feminine rhymes, create a sense of burlesque.

6. *goes on a Mission*] See Blair, *Dissertation*, pp. 117–19.

7. *Orlando Furioso*] An Italian epic poem on a chivalric subject by Ludovico Ariosto, published between 1516 and 1532. It became very popular throughout Europe, and remained influential well into the seventeenth century.

8. *Lusiade*] Or *Os Lusíadas*, a Portuguese epic poem by Luís Vaz de Camões published in 1572, and celebrating the discovery of the sea route to India by the Portuguese navigator Vasco de Gama (*c.* 1469–1524).

9. *faithfully transmitted . . . unsettled*] cf. the very similar phrasing in the letter to Gibbon of 18 March 1776 quoted in the headnote above (p. 636). In the prefatory 'Dissertation' to *Fingal*, Macpherson had acknowledged the apparent force of this objection: 'The strongest objection to the authenticity of the poems now given to the public under the name of Ossian, is the improbability of

their being handed down by tradition through so many centuries. Ages of barbarism some will say, could not produce poems abounding with the disinterested and generous sentiments so conspicuous in the compositions of Ossian; and could those ages produce them, it is impossible but they must be lost, or altogether corrupted in a long succession of barbarous generations.' Macpherson answers this objection by reference to the vigorous bardic culture of the ancient north Britons (Macpherson, *Fingal*, p. x).

10. *such Countries as ... Music*] Tahiti is the largest of the Windward Islands in the central Pacific, which had recently become celebrated in Britain following the visit by Captain Samuel Wallis in 1767, the publication in 1771 (English translation, 1772) of the account of the visit by the French explorer Louis-Antoine de Bougainville in 1768, and most of all the first visit by Captain James Cook in 1769, which had been described by John Hawkesworth in his *An Account of the Voyages*, 3 vols (1773). Malacca is a coastal city in modern-day Malaysia, which since the sixteenth century had been an important centre of the European spice trade, controlled by first the Portuguese and then the Dutch. Concerning Tahiti, Hume appears to be following the characterization of the inhabitants and their way of life given by Bougainville: 'L'air qu'on respire, les chants, la danse presque toujours accompagnée de postures lascives, tout rappelle à chaque instant les douceurs de l'amour, tout crie de s'y livrer. Ils dansent au son d'une espece de tambour, & lorsqu'ils chantent, ils accompagnent la voix avec une flûte très-douce à trois ou à quatre trous, dans laquelle, comme nous l'avons déjà dit, ils soufflent avec le nez ... Cette habitude de vivre continuellement dans le plaisir, donne aux Taitiens un penchant marqué pour cette douce plaisanterie fille du repos & de la joie' (Louis-Antoine de Bougainville, *Voyage autour du monde* [Paris, 1771], p. 220). Concerning Malacca, Hume may be drawing on Dryden's translation of Dominique Bouhours's *Life of St Francis Xavier* (1688), where the Malaccese are described as pure hedonists and addicted to music: 'Amongst all the Nations of *Asia* there is not any, more inclin'd to pleasure; and this seems chiefly to proceed, from the mild temper of the air. For there is an eternal Spring, notwithstanding the neighbourhood of the Line. The Inhabitants follow the natural bent of their complexion; their whole business is Perfumes, Feasts, and Musique; to say nothing of Carnal Pleasures, to which they set no bound. Even the Language, which they speak, participates of the softness of the Country. 'Tis call'd the *Malaya Tongue*, and of all the Orient, 'tis the most delicate, and sweet of Pronunciation' (p. 205).

11. *peculiar Advantages*] Macpherson had emphasized particular features of the Celtic language to explain the faithful transmission of the Ossianic poems: 'The use of letters was not known in the North of Europe till long after the institution of the bards: the records of the families of their patrons, their own, and more ancient poems were handed down by tradition. Their poetical compositions were admirably contrived for that purpose. They were

adapted to music; and the most perfect harmony observed. Each verse was so connected with those which preceded or followed it, that if one line had been remembered in a stanza, it was almost impossible to forget the rest. The cadences followed in so natural a gradation, and the words were so adapted to the common turn of the voice, after it is raised to a certain key, that it was almost impossible, from a similarity of sound, to substitute one word for another. This excellence is peculiar to the Celtic tongue, and is perhaps to be met with in no other language' (Macpherson, *Fingal*, p. xii).

12. *Lapland and Runic Odes*] Thomas Gray had shared the mid-century enthu-siasm for the ancient poetry of northern Europe: see the long headnote to 'The Fatal Sisters. An Ode' in Roger Lonsdale (ed.), *The Poems of Gray, Collins and Goldsmith* (London: Longman, 1969), pp. 210–14. The printed sources for these poems were two late seventeenth-century Danish public-ations: Thomas Bartholin, *Antiquitatum Danicarum de Causis Contemptæ a Danis Adhuc Gentilibus Mortis* (Copenhagen, 1689), and Thormodus Torfaeus, *Orcades seu Rerum Orcadensium Historiae* (Copenhagen, 1697). Blair had himself drawn attention to the difference in manners between Ossian and the ancient Scandinavian poetry preserved in runic inscriptions (Blair, *Dissertation*, pp. 7–21), and concluded: 'But when we open the works of Ossian, a very different scene presents itself. There we find the fire and the enthusiasm of the most early times, combined with an amazing degree of regularity and art. We find tenderness, and even delicacy of sentiment, greatly predominant over fierceness and barbarity. Our hearts are melted with the softest feelings, and at the same time elevated with the highest ideas of magnanimity, generosity, and true heroism. When we turn from the poetry of Lodbrog [which Blair has just quoted at length] to that of Ossian, it is like passing from a savage desart, into a fertile and cultivated country. How is this to be accounted for?' (Blair, *Dissertation*, p. 21).

13. *But this . . . assume*] Perhaps a memory of Bentley's emphatic dismissal of the *Epistles of Phalaris*, quoted in the headnote, can be detected here (see above, p. 640).

14. *The manners . . . Authenticity*] In *Fragments of Ancient Poetry*, Macpherson had unguardedly asserted that the poems he had placed before the public 'abound with those ideas, and paint those manners, that belong to the most early state of society' (Macpherson, *Fragments*, p. iii). He had retreated from this exposed position in important ways by the time of the publication of *Fingal* in 1762.

15. *We see nothing . . . artificial Modes of thinking*] A similar point about the contrast between ancient heroism and chivalric scruple had been made by Adam Ferguson in part IV, section 4, of his *An Essay on the History of Civil Society* (1767): 'The hero of the Greek fable, endued with superior force, courage, and address, takes every advantage of an enemy, to kill with safety to himself; and actuated by a desire of spoil, or by a principle of revenge, is

never stayed in his progress by interruptions of remorse or compassion . . . Our modern fable, or romance, on the contrary, generally couples an object of pity, weak, oppressed, and defenceless, with an object of admiration, brave, generous, and victorious; or sends the hero abroad in search of mere danger, and of occasions to prove his valour. Charged with the maxims of a refined courtesy, to be observed even towards an enemy; and of a scrupulous honour, which will not suffer him to take any advantages by artifice or surprise; indifferent to spoil, he contends only for renown, and employs his valour to rescue the distressed, and to protect the innocent. If victorious, he is made to rise above nature as much in his generosity and gentleness, as in his military prowess and valour . . . The hero of modern romance professes a contempt of stratagem, as well as of danger, and unites in the same person, characters and dispositions seemingly opposite; ferocity with gentleness, and the love of blood with sentiments of tenderness and pity' (Ferguson, *Civil Society*, p. 191). Note the parallel observation in Hume's much earlier 'An Historical Essay on Chivalry and modern Honour' (above, pp. 269–70).

16. *a nocturnal Incursion . . . sleeping Foe*] See, e.g., Homer, *Iliad*, X.476–502 (the night raid by Diomedes and Odysseus on the Trojan camp); Virgil, *Aeneid*, IX.224–445 (the night raid by Nisus and Euryalus on the Rutulian camp). Blair had attempted to extenuate the presence of touches of chivalry in the Ossianic poems: 'Lathmon is peculiarly distinguished by high generosity of sentiment. This is carried so far, particularly in the refusal of Gaul, on one side, to take the advantage of a sleeping foe; and of Lathmon, on the other, to overpower by numbers the two young warriors, as to recall into one's mind the manners of Chivalry; some resemblance to which may perhaps be suggested by other incidents in this collection of Poems. Chivalry, however, took rise in an age and country too remote from those of Ossian, to admit the suspicion that the one could have borrowed any thing from the other. So far as Chivalry had any real existence, the same military enthusiasm, which gave birth to it in the feudal times, might, in the days of Ossian, that is, in the infancy of a rising state, through the operation of the same cause, very naturally produce effects of the same kind on the minds and manners of men' (Blair, *Dissertation*, pp. 71–2). In contrasting the manners of the Ossianic heroes with those of the Homeric heroes, and associating them rather with the extravagant code of honour found in later romance writing, Hume is silently rejecting the earlier assertion of Richard Hurd, that the manners of ancient Greece and of the chivalric Middle Ages exhibited 'a remarkable correspondency': 'Greek antiquity very much resembles the Gothic . . . what are the Grecian Bacchus, Hercules, and Theseus but Knights-errant, the exact counter-parts of Sir Launcelot and Amadis de Gaule?' (Hurd, *Chivalry and Romance*, pp. 26 and 31).

17. *Orlando . . . defend himself*] Untraced.

18. *Gaul & Oscar ... kill them*] Hume refers to an episode in 'Lathmon: A Poem', where however it is Gaul and Ossian, not Oscar, who attack the enemy camp at night. Gaul 'spoke the words of the valiant' in refusing to kill an unawakened enemy: 'Shall the son of Fingal rush on a sleeping foe? Shall he come like a blast by night when it overturns the young trees in secret? ... Strike, Ossian, strike the shield of battle, and let their thousands rise. Let them meet Gaul in his first battle, that he may try the strength of his arm.' Macpherson appended a note to the episode, explicitly comparing it to Homer and Virgil: 'This proposal of Gaul is much more noble, and more agreeable to true heroism, than the behaviour of Ulysses and Diomed in the Iliad, or that of Nisus and Euryalus in the Æneid. What his valour and generosity suggested became the foundation of his success. For the enemy being dismayed with the sound of Ossian's shield, which was the common signal of battle, thought that Fingal's whole army came to attack them; so that they fly in reality from an army, not from two heroes; which reconciles the story to probability' (Macpherson, *Fingal*, p. 235 and n. *). Hume here may be implicitly recalling the distinction he had drawn in 'Of the Standard of Taste' between the moral visions of Homer and Fénelon: 'HOMER's general precepts, where he delivers any such, will never be controverted; but it is obvious, that, when he draws particular pictures of manners, and represents heroism in ACHILLES and prudence in ULYSSES, he intermixes a much greater degree of ferocity in the former, and of cunning and fraud in the latter, than FENELON would admit of. The sage ULYSSES in the GREEK poet seems to delight in lies and fictions, and often employs them without any necessity or even advantage: But his more scrupulous son, in the FRENCH epic writer, exposes himself to the most imminent perils, rather than depart from the most exact line of truth and veracity' (above, vol. 1, p. 184).

19. *Amadis de Gaul or Lancelot du Lake*] Amadis de Gaula is the hero of a Spanish chivalric romance of the same name first published in 1508. It was the favourite book of Don Quixote. Lancelot du Lake is a hero of the Arthurian romances.

20. *Nay, Fingal ... attack the Enemy*] For Blair, this circumstance had been one of the great moral beauties of *Fingal*, and a stroke of art which revealed Ossian to be fully the equal of Homer when it came to aggrandizing the character of his hero: 'Nothing could be more happily imagined for this purpose than the whole management of the last battle, wherein Gaul the son of Morni, had besought Fingal to retire, and to leave to him and his other chiefs the honour of the day. The generosity of the king in agreeing to this proposal; the majesty with which he retreats to the hill, from whence he was to behold the engagement, attended by his Bards, and waving the lightning of his sword; his perceiving the chiefs overpowered by numbers, but from unwillingness to deprive them of the glory of victory by coming in person to their assistance, first sending Ullin, the Bard to animate their courage; and

at last, when the danger becomes more pressing, his rising in his might, and interposing, like a divinity, to decide the doubtful fate of the day; are all circumstances contrived with so much art, as plainly discover the Celtic Bards to have been not unpractised in Heroic poetry' (Blair, *Dissertation*, p. 43).

21. *Nay, Fingal ... Return of Light*] Hume summarizes the events related in Book IV of *Fingal* (Macpherson, *Fingal*, pp. 49–60). Similar events occur in Book III of *Temora* (Macpherson, *Temora*, pp. 47–62). For discussion, see Macpherson, *Temora*, pp. 108–9 n.* and 164 n.*.

22. *The Gallantry ... and Regard*] Blair had drawn attention to this delicacy towards women as a sign of authenticity: 'Ossian's heroes have all the gallantry and generosity of those fabulous knights, without their extravagance; and his love scenes have native tenderness, without any mixture of those forced and unnatural conceits which abound in the old romances' (Blair, *Dissertation*, p. 72). In 1760 Hume himself had been willing to accept that the gallantry shown by Ossian's heroes was no necessary indication of spuriousness: 'I own, that my first and chief objection to the authenticity of these fragments, was not on account of the noble and even tender strokes which they contain; for these are the offspring of genius and passion in all countries ...' (*Letters*, vol. I, p. 330).

23. *no Giants ... or Activity*] Macpherson had cited the frequency of such elements in the Irish poetry of Fion as a sign of spuriousness and relatively recent composition: 'They are entirely writ in that romantic taste, which prevailed two ages ago. – Giants, enchanted castles, dwarfs, palfreys, witches and magicians for the whole circle of the poet's invention. The celebrated *Fion* could scarcely move from one hillock to another, without encountering a giant, or being entangled in the circles of a magician. Witches, on broomsticks, were continually hovering about him, like crows; and he had freed enchanted virgins in every valley in Ireland' (Macpherson, *Temora*, p. xxiii).

24. *the School of Epicurus*] Epicurus (341–270 BC) had taught that, although the gods exist, they take no part in human life, and so should be neither feared nor placated. Blair had also commented on the absence of religion from the Ossianic poems, but as a feature that suggested their authenticity: 'There are, besides, two other circumstances to be attended to, still of greater weight, if possible, against this hypothesis [that the poems are counterfeited]. One is the total absence of religious ideas from this work; for which the translator has, in his preface, given a very probable account, on the footing of its being the work of Ossian. The druidical superstition was, in the days of Ossian, on the point of its final extinction; and for particular reasons, odious to the family of Fingal; whilst the christian faith was not yet established. But had it been the work of one, to whom the ideas of christianity were familiar from his infancy; and who had superadded to them also the bigotted superstition of a dark age and country; it is impossible but in some passage or other, the traces of them would have appeared' (Blair, *Dissertation*, p. 34;

cf. also p. 61). Macpherson explains the absence of religion from the Ossianic poems not in the 'Preface' to *Fingal*, but in the 'Dissertation Concerning the Antiquity, &c. of the Poems of Ossian the Son of Fingal' that follows (Macpherson, *Fingal*, pp. iv–vii). He had also touched on this aspect of the Ossianic poems in *Fragments of Ancient Poetry* (Macpherson, *Fragments*, p. iv). For the natural theology of the Caledonians, see Macpherson, *Temora*, pp. 149–50 n.*.

25. *To account ... Species of Religion*] cf. Macpherson, *Fragments*, pp. iv–v; Macpherson, *Fingal*, pp. v–vi.

26. *we attached Ourselves ... Hatred of the Old*] Hume's remarks on the psychology of religion among the English following Elizabeth I's restoration of Protestantism are apposite: 'Though the catholic religion, adapting itself to the senses, and enjoining observances, which enter into the common train of life, does at present lay faster hold on the mind than the reformed, which, being chiefly spiritual, resembles more a system of metaphysics; yet was the proportion of zeal, as well as of knowledge, during the first ages after the reformation, much greater on the side of the protestants. The catholics continued, ignorantly and supinely, in their ancient belief, or rather their ancient practices: But the reformers, obliged to dispute on every occasion, and inflamed to a degree of enthusiasm by novelty and persecution, had strongly attached themselves to their tenets; and were ready to sacrifice their fortunes and even their lives, in support of their speculative and abstract principles' (*History of England*, vol. IV, p. 14).

27. *his Literature*] Here used in the more expansive early-modern sense of learning or knowledge of literature (*OED*, 'literature', *n.*, 1).

28. *We know ... in the Woods*] In the *History of England*, Hume states that the ancient Britons 'dwelt in huts, which they reared in the forests and marshes, with which the country was covered' (*History of England*, vol. I, p. 5).

29. *But a stately ... with fire*] A detail from 'Carthon: A Poem': 'I have seen the walls of Balclutha, but they were desolate. The fire had resounded in the halls: and the voice of the people is heard no more. The stream of Clutha was removed from its place, by the fall of the walls. – The thistle shook, there, its lonely head: the moss whistled to the wind. The fox looked out, from the windows, the rank grass of the wall waved round his head.' In a footnote Macpherson himself drew attention to the parallel with Isaiah (Macpherson, *Fingal*, p. 132 and n. *). Blair had boldly claimed that the Ossianic poems were free from such anachronisms: 'no modern allusion drops from him' (Blair, *Dissertation*, p. 31). In the *History of England* Hume had stated that the ancient Britons 'had not, without the assistance of the Romans, art of masonry sufficient to raise a stone rampart for their own defence' (*History of England*, vol. I, p. 14; cf. p. 12). Macpherson, however, had insisted that in 'Caledonia they begun very early to build with stone' (Macpherson, *Temora*, p. 36 n. †).

30. *borrowd from the Scripture*] Isaiah 13:21–2, foretelling the destruction of Babylon: 'But wild beasts of the desert shall lie there; and their houses shall be full of doleful creatures; and ostriches shall dwell there, and satyrs shall dance there. And wolves shall cry in their castles, and jackals in the pleasant palaces: and her time is near to come, and her days shall not be prolonged.' The Hebrew word 'Shuai' can refer to either a fox or a jackal. There are a number of biblical texts which associate foxes with dilapidation: e.g., Nehemiah 4:3; Lamentations 5:18; and Psalm 63:10.

31. *no Shipping but Currochs*] Hume regarded it as axiomatic that 'the naval arts can flourish among a civilized people alone' (Hume, *History of England*, vol. I, p. 16). In the *History of England* Hume noted that the ancient Britons, following the collapse of the Roman Empire in the West, had been 'removed from the fury' of the barbarian incursions which followed that collapse because Britain was 'secured by the sea against the inroads of the greater tribes of the barbarians' (*History of England*, vol. I, p. 11). This circumstance argues against any great barbarian maritime competence in the fifth century; however, Hume also records that the Scots had long infested the Roman settlements in Great Britain 'by pyracy and rapine', which suggests at least a meagre maritime presence (*History of England*, vol. I, p. 12; cf. also p. 16, on the piratical tendencies of the Anglo-Saxons). Macpherson, however, was of a different opinion: 'The Caledonians, most certainly, acquired a considerable knowledge in navigation, by their living on a coast intersected with many arms of the sea, and, in islands, divided, one from another, by wide and dangerous firths. It is, therefore, highly probable, that they, very early, found their way to the north of Ireland, which is within sight of their own country' (Macpherson, *Temora*, p. vii; cf. also p. 118 n.*). Larthon was allegedly the inventor of Caledonian shipbuilding (Macpherson, *Temora*, pp. 130–31 n.*). In *The Wealth of Nations*, I.iii.3–6, Adam Smith would reflect on the role of shipping in developing human society, and on the consequent correlation between a competence in shipping and commercial advancement (Smith, *Wealth*, vol. I, pp. 33–5).

32. *entirely by Hunting*] Macpherson argues for a more mixed mode of subsistence, in which hunting was supplemented by pasturage and rudimentary agriculture: 'If we make allowance of the backward state of agriculture, the valleys were not unfertile ... His table was supplied by his own herds, and what his numerous attendants killed in hunting' (Macpherson, *Temora*, p. xv).

33. *from the Experience of America*] Hume's information concerning the precariousness and, in terms of extent of territory required, the wastefulness, of the subsistence derived by the American Indians from hunting is possibly drawn from Cornélius de Paw, *Recherches philosophiques sur les Americains*, 2 vols ('London', 1771), where the perennial wars between tribes of Indians are attributed to anxiety over 'la subsistance de chaque peuplade en particulier, à qu'il falloit un immense terrein inculte, pour équivalent d'un

petit terrein cultivé ... Le grand intérêt qui divisoit donc tous ces peuples chasseurs, étoit la chasse même: c'étoit la source de l'éternelle discorde qui armoit une tribu contre une autre, dès qu'elles étoient assez rapprochées, pour s'intercepter mutuellement le gibier' (Paw, *Recherches*, vol. I, p. 99). Cf. William Robertson, *History of America* (1777), vol. II, pp. 80–81. Another possible source is Locke's 'Second Treatise', § 37, where Locke considers the much greater productivity of enclosed and improved land over wasteland: 'For I aske whether in the wild woods and uncultivated wast of America left to Nature, without any improvement, tillage or husbandry, a thousand acres will yield the needy and wretched inhabitants as many conveniencies of life as ten acres of equally fertile land doe in Devonshire where they are well cultivated?' (Locke, *Two Treatises*, p. 294). On the extent of territory necessary to support a non-commercial population, cf. Aristotle's acerbic comment on the ideal republic of Plato (Aristotle, *Politics*, 1265a), cited by Smith in *The Wealth of Nations* (Smith, *Wealth*, p. 388, III.ii.9; cf. Hont, *Jealousy of Trade*, p. 443). Smith would recur to the subject of the 'very great' difference between 'the number of shepherds and that of hunters whom the same extent of equally fertile territory can maintain' in Smith, *Wealth*, p. 634, IV.vii.c.100 and pp. 691–2, V.i.a.5; cf. Smith, *Jurisprudence*, iv.38–9. Kant would make a similar observation in *The Metaphysics of Morals* (Kant, *Metaphysics*, pp. 125–6). For further comment and context, see Hont, *Jealousy of Trade*, p. 96.

34. *unacquainted with Fishing*] Macpherson, however, draws attention to the fact that the waters of the Highlands 'swarmed with variety of fish' (Macpherson, *Temora*, p. xv).

35. *Wind or Water Mill*] Untraced in the Ossianic poems. For the late development of cereal agriculture by the Scots, see Macpherson, *Temora*, p. xiii. Windmills were invented in Asia Minor, and their first recorded use in western Europe was in Normandy in 1105, according the antiquarian P. J.-B. Legrand d'Aussy, in his *Histoire de la vie privée des Français* (Paris, 1782), vol. I, pp. 42–3, citing Charles du Fresne Ducange, *Glossarium ad Scriptores Mediæ et Infimæ Latinitatis, sv* 'molendinum': cf. Gibbon, *Decline and Fall*, vol. III, p. 726, n. 65. Macpherson refers to the ancient Britons' use of 'handmills' in his *An Introduction to the History of Great Britain and Ireland* (Macpherson, *Introduction*, p. 213). Adam Smith would surely err in dating the adoption of this technology in western Europe much later: 'Neither wind nor water mills of any kind were known in England so early as the beginning of the sixteenth century, nor, so far as I know, in any other part of Europe north of the Alps' (Smith, *Wealth*, p. 263, I.xi.o.12).

36. *the best Antiquaries*] Presumably a reference to Charles du Fresne Ducange: see above, n. 35.

37. *all kinds of Metals*] Hume has in mind the occasional mentions of furnaces and forging in the Ossianic poems: see, e.g., Macpherson, *Fragments*, p. 24;

Macpherson, *Fingal*, pp. 14, 55, 62, 199 and 207; and Macpherson, *Temora*, pp. 120 n.* and 128 n.*. In 1760 Hume's scepticism had not been alarmed by what Ossian relates of the ancient Caledonians' skills in metalwork: 'I remember Mr Macpherson told me, that the heroes of this Highland epic were not only, like Homer's heroes, their own butchers, bakers, and cooks, but also their own shoemakers, carpenters, and smiths. He mentioned an incident which put this matter in a remarkable light. A warrior has the head of his spear struck off in a battle; upon which he immediately retires behind the army, where a forge was erected; makes a new one; hurries back to the action; pierces his enemy, while the iron, which was yet red-hot, hisses in the wound. This imagery you will allow to be singular, and so well imagined, that it would have been adopted by Homer, had the manners of the Greeks allowed him to have employed it' (*Letters*, vol. I, pp. 330–31). That a people should be skilled in metalwork before acquiring a competency in agriculture seems like an inversion of the apparently natural order (see Ronald L. Meek, *Social Science & the Ignoble Savage* [Cambridge: Cambridge University Press, 1976]). However, in his *Discours sur l'origine et les Fondements de l'inegalité* ('Amsterdam', 1755), Rousseau had argued that it may just as easily have happened that the smelting of metals had stimulated the growth of agriculture, and had therefore necessarily preceded it: 'L'invention des autres arts fut donc nécessaire pour forcer le Genre-humain de s'appliquer à celui de l'agriculture. Dès qu'il fallut des hommes pour fondre & forger le fer, il fallut d'autres hommes pour nourrir ceux-là. Plus le nombre des ouvriers vint à se multiplier, moins il y eut de mains employées à fournir à la subsistance commune, sans qu'il y eut moins de bouches pour la consommer; & comme il fallut aux uns des denrées en échange de leur fer, les autres trouvérent enfin le secret d'employer le fer à la multiplication des denrées. De là naquirent d'un côté le labourage & l'agriculture, & de l'autre l'art de travailler les métaux, & d'en multiplier les usages' (pp. 122–3). For examples of the Rousseauvian colouring of Macpherson's understanding of the development of human society, see Macpherson, *Temora*, pp. xii, 107 n.*, and 172 n.* (although cf. also p. 128 n.*).

38. *Stridenti ... carmen*] A quotation from Menalcas's rebuke to Damoetas in Virgil's *Eclogues* (III.26–7): 'Wasn't it you, you dunce, that at the crossroads was wont to murder a sorry tune on a scrannel straw?'

39. *The Irish Scoti ... antient people*] Hume here relies, most recently, on the arguments of Thomas Innes: '*the* Scots *in* Britain ... *by the consent of all the learned, unquestionably came in at first from* Ireland' (Innes, *Critical Essay*, vol. I, p. xl; cf. also pp. 174–83). Macpherson, however, resisted allowing precedence to the Irish: 'The colony [of Celts] from Gaul possessed themselves, at first, of that part of Britain which was next to their own country; and spreading northward, by degrees, as they increased in numbers, peopled the whole island. Some adventurers passing over from those parts of Britain

that are within sight of Ireland, were the founders of the Irish nation: which is a more probable story than the idle fables of Milesian and Gallician colonies. Diodorus Siculus mentions it as a thing well known in his time, that the inhabitants of Ireland were originally Britons; and his testimony is unquestionable, when we consider that, for many ages, the language and customs of both nations were the same' (Macpherson, *Fingal*, pp. ii–iii). In the 'Dissertation' prefacing *Temora* Macpherson had referred to the notion that the Scots derived from the Irish as one of 'the vulgar errors of the times', asserting instead 'That Ireland was first peopled from Britain is certain' and that the Ossianic poems preserve 'the history of the first migration of the Caledonians into Ireland' (Macpherson, *Temora*, pp. iii, vii–viii and ix; and for a more extended rebuttal of Irish precedency, in which the 'favourite chimæra, that Ireland is the mother-country of the Scots, is totally subverted and ruined', at least to Macpherson's satisfaction, see pp. xx–xxxiv; quotation on p. xxii). Innes was acutely aware of the sensitive nature of this subject, at least to Scottish ears: see Innes, *Critical Essay*, vol. I, p. xlii.

40. *They represent ... these Traditions*] For Macpherson's different interpretation of the significance of these features of Irish traditions, see above, pp. 652–3, n. 39.

41. *The Songs ... they are natural*] By 'Senachees' Hume means exclusively the bards of ancient Ireland, although the term can also be applied to the household bards and historians of the Scottish Highlands (see Johnson, *Journey*, pp. 92–4, and Macpherson, *Temora*, p. 176 n. †). Hume probably derives his understanding of the crudity and barbarousness of their poetry from Thomas Innes: see Innes, *Critical Essay*, vol. II, pp. 428–78.

42. *The same ... Celtic Nation*] Johnson also believed that the Welsh and the Scots were the descendants of the original Celtic settlers who had been driven into the mountains by the Saxons: 'It sometimes happens that by conquest, intermixture, or gradual refinement, the cultivated parts of a country change their language. The mountaineers then become a distinct nation, cut off by dissimilitude of speech from conversation with their neighbours. Thus in Biscay, the original Cantabrian, and in Dalecarlia, the old Swedish still subsists. Thus Wales and the Highlands speak the tongue of the first inhabitants of Britain, while the other parts have received first the Saxon, and in some degree afterwards the French, and then formed a third language between them' (Johnson, *Journey*, p. 34).

43. *the Socratic Age*] Lucian and Longinus were writers of the second and first centuries AD, respectively. The 'Socratic Age' fell in the fifth century BC.

44. *To the Poem ... Highlands*] See Macpherson, *Fingal*, pp. 155–6 n. *.

45. *that the Turks ... Solomon's Guard*] A reference to the 'Alexander Romance', a family of texts which derived from an ancient original, but which proliferated wildly in late antiquity and the Middle Ages, and in which the events of Alexander's life were embroidered with romance and its core of historical

fact perverted and diluted. Since the late sixteenth century this conflation of biblical and classical history had been often cited as evidence of Turkish ignorance of chronology. It had figured in the account of his travels in Turkey written by the Flemish diplomat Ogier Ghiselin de Busbecq: 'For, the Truth is, the *Turks* keep no just Account either of Times or Ages, but makes [*sic*] a confused Hodge-podge of all History. When they have a Mind to it, they scruple not to say, *That* Job *was Master of the Horse to King* Solomon, *and that* Alexander the Great *was General if* [*sic*] *his Army*; with such-like Stuff' (Ogier Ghiselin de Busbecq, *Travels into Turkey* [1744], p. 71). For later recyclings of the allegation in popular works of the eighteenth century, see, e.g., Thomas Brett, *A Chronological Essay on the Sacred History* (1729): 'the Want of this has caused the *Turks* to be so shamefully put upon in the History of ancient Times, as to be made believe that *Alexander* the Great was the General of *Solomon*'s Army, and *Julius Cæsar* the Master of his Horse' (p. 2); cf. also Samuel Derrick, *A Collection of Travels* (1762), p. 145 and Rycault, *Present State*, p. 6. On Ottoman interest in Alexander the Great, which could extend beyond the fabulous, see Malcolm, *Useful Enemies*, pp. 27-8.

46. *Greek and Roman ... Absurdity*] As Macpherson himself had pointed out in the 'Dissertation' which prefaces *Fingal*: 'Hence it is that we find so much of the marvellous in the origin of every nation; posterity being always ready to believe any thing, however fabulous, that reflects honour on their ancestors. The Greeks and Romans were remarkable for this weakness. They swallowed the most absurd fables concerning the high antiquities of their respective nations' (Macpherson, *Fingal*, p. i).

47. *Cicerone*] A guide who explains the antiquities or curiosities of a place to strangers (*OED*, 'cicerone', *n.*).

48. *the Scotch fabulous History*] Principally John Fordun, Hector Boece and George Buchanan. For Innes's dismissal of the story of the forty ancient kings of Scotland before Fergus II, see Innes, *Critical Essay*, vol. I, pp. 172-5.

49. *Fergus the second*] i.e. Fergus the son of Earc; *d.* 501.

50. *Father Innes ... of the Nation*] Hume refers to Thomas Innes's *A Critical Essay on the Ancient Inhabitants of the Northern Parts of Britain or Scotland* (1729), in which the mythical history of Scotland is discredited (for a summary of the argument, see the 'Preface' to vol. I; and esp. p. xviii). However, Innes, a crypto-Jacobite, was motivated in this work less by a scholarly devotion to truth than by a desire to establish the legitimacy of the Stuart dynasty, following his discovery in 1694 of a charter of Robert II which appeared to do so (see Innes, *Critical Essay*, vol. I, pp. xxx-xxxi, and Appendix VIII).

51. *the Sophist ... Epistles*] See the headnote, above, pp. 639-40.

52. *Cicero's Consolation*] The *Consolatio* is a lost work by Cicero, fragments of which survived in the works of later writers such as Lactantius and St

Jerome. In 1583 the Italian humanist Carlo Sigonio (*c.* 1524–1584) claimed to have found an integral text of this work, which he published in Venice in 1583. Suspicions arose immediately about its authenticity, and it is now believed, on the basis of stylometric analysis, to be spurious.

53. *Fragments of Petronius*] The genuine text of Petronius's *Satyricon* (*c.* AD 60) survives only in fragments. In the seventeenth century two attempts were made to pass off modern fabrications as rediscovered, authentic text. José Antonio González de Salas (1588–1654) published in 1629 an edition of the *Satyricon* which incorporated new material that Salas falsely claimed was taken from an earlier edition published in Paris. In 1690 François Nodot (*c.* 1650–1710) claimed that a manuscript containing missing portions of the *Satyricon* had been discovered during the sack of Belgrade in 1688. Nodot incorporated these discoveries into his edition of the *Satyricon* (Paris, 1693), and they were initially accepted as genuine. However, Pieter Burmann the Elder conclusively demonstrated that they were spurious, and published his own edition of Petronius (Trajecti ad Rhenum, 1709).

54. *an antient History of Britain*] Macpherson's *Introduction to the History of Great Britain and Ireland* had been published in 1772. Hume commented on it in a letter to the Alexander Dow, the historian of Hindustan: 'My compliments to Ossian. He has given us a work last winter, which contains a great deal of genius and good writing; but I cannot assent to his system. I must still adhere to the common opinion regarding our origin, or rather your origin; for we are all plainly Danes or Saxons in the low countries' (*Letters*, vol. II, p. 267).

55. *Belgæ, Cimbri, and Sarmatæ*] All ancient tribes occupying land in northern Europe.

56. *the History . . . Livy*] Livy's narrative of the First Punic War (264–241 BC) occupied Books XVI–XIX of *Ab Urbe Condita*, and has not survived; that of the Second Punic War (218–201 BC) occupies Books XXI–XXX and has survived intact; that of the Third Punic War (149–146 BC) occupied Books XLVIII–XLIX, and has not survived.

57. *mention'd by Tacitus*] In the *Germania* and the *Agricola*.

58. *a Translation of Homer*] i.e. *The Iliad of Homer*, translated by James Macpherson, 2 vols (London, 1773). On 10 April 1773 Hume wrote tartly to Adam Smith: 'Have you seen Macpherson's Homer? It is hard to tell whether the Attempt or the Execution be worse. I hear he is employd by the Booksellers to continue my History: But in my Opinion, of all men of Parts, he has the most anti-historical Head in the Universe' (*Letters*, vol. II, p. 280). The rumour that a continuation of his *History of England* was planned by Strahan had caused Hume anxiety earlier in the year, and had led temporarily to strained relations between the two men (*Letters*, vol. II, pp. 276 and 279–80).

59. *the Translation of Pope*] Pope had published a translation of *The Iliad* in six volumes spread over five years (1715–20). A translation of *The Odyssey* had followed in five volumes spread over two years (1725–6); although not all of this later translation was by Pope himself (see Maynard Mack, *Alexander Pope: A Life* [New Haven, CT, and London: Yale University Press, 1985], pp. 412–17).

60. *the Age of Severus*] Septimius Severus was Roman emperor from 193 to 211. Macpherson dated the Ossianic poems to the age of Severus on the basis of their mention of Caracul (i.e. Caracalla) as the 'Son of the King of the World', or Roman emperor (Macpherson, *Fingal*, pp. vii–viii). Gibbon, however, was alert to the implausibility of this: 'That the Caracul of Ossian is the Caracalla of the Roman history, is, perhaps, the only point of British antiquity in which Mr. Macpherson and Mr. Whitaker are of the same opinion; and yet the opinion is not without difficulty. In the Caledonian war, the son of Severus was known only by the appellation of Antoninus; and it may seem strange, that the Highland bard should describe him by a nick-name, invented four years afterwards, scarcely used by the Romans till after the death of that emperor, and seldom employed by the most ancient historians' (Gibbon, *Decline and Fall*, vol. I, p. 152 n. 14).

61. *external positive Evidence*] i.e. the testimonies collected by Blair, and first published as an appendix to the second edition of his *Dissertation* (London, 1765), pp. 221–48.

62. *the present Highlanders*] Hume's admiration for Highland character, at least in its moral aspect, was sincere and of long standing. On 8 October 1754 he had encouraged John Wilkes to visit the Highlands: 'You woud there have seen human Nature in the golden Age, or rather, indeed, in the Silver: For the Highlanders have degenerated somewhat from the primitive Simplicity of Mankind' (*Letters*, vol. I, p. 195). For Hume's idea of the golden age, see the *Enquiry Concerning the Principles of Morals*, III, 'Of Justice' (*ECPM*, pp. 16–17).

63. *not even excepting the Swiss*] cf. Stanyan's tribute to Swiss character: 'the *Switzers* are a People equally brave in Arms, and faithful to their Engagements' (Stanyan, *Switzerland*, p. 155).

64. *On such Occasions . . . Ossian*] Hume here refers back to material he had adduced in, and more generally to the overall argument of, *An Enquiry Concerning Human Understanding*, section 10, 'Of Miracles'. There too he had discussed the miracles attributed to the Jansenist Abbé Paris. He also at moments closely echoes his earlier language: 'There surely never was a greater number of miracles ascribed to one person, than those, which were lately said to have been wrought in FRANCE upon the tomb of Abbé PARIS, the famous JANSENIST, with whose sanctity the people were so long deluded. The curing of the sick, giving hearing to the deaf, and sight to the blind, were every where talked of as the usual effects of

that holy sepulchre. But what is more extraordinary; many of the miracles were immediately proved upon the spot, before judges of unquestioned integrity, attested by witnesses of credit and distinction, in a learned age, and on the most eminent theatre that is now in the world. Nor is this all: A relation of them was published and dispersed every where; nor were the JESUITS, though a learned body, supported by the civil magistrate, and determined enemies to those opinions, in whose favour the miracles were said to have been wrought, ever able distinctly to refute or detect them. Where shall we find such a number of circumstances, agreeing to the corroboration of one fact? And what have we to oppose to such a cloud of witnesses, but the absolute impossibility or miraculous nature of the events, which they relate? And this surely, in the eyes of all reasonable people, will alone be regarded as a sufficient refutation' (*ECHU*, section 10, 'Of Miracles', pp. 93–4). The supposed miracles of the Jansenist Abbé Paris occurred at his tomb in the graveyard of the chapel of St Médard in Paris beginning in 1731, some years after his death on 1 May 1727. They quickly became a cause célèbre for a Jansenist movement that had come under pressure since 1713 and the publication of the papal bull *Unigenitus* (against which Abbé Paris had himself written); and they were vigorously defended in the clandestine Jansenist periodical *Nouvelles Ecclesiastiques*. These miracles are thus likely to have been topics of conversation when Hume arrived in La Flèche in 1734; and it was during this period of residence in France that he wrote the first version of his own essay on miracles (*Letters*, vol. I, p. 24; *New Letters*, p. 2; and for Hume's later recollection of how the key argument against miracles occurred to him while he was in conversation with a learned Jesuit, see ibid., p. 361). It is therefore curious that, in the *Treatise of Human Nature*, I.iii.9, Hume should assert that a 'man, whose memory presents him with a lively image of the *Red-Sea*, and the *Desert*, and *Jerusalem*, and *Galilee*, can never doubt of any miraculous events, which are related either by *Moses* or the *Evangelists*' (*THN*, pp. 76–7). Conyers Middleton's *A Free Enquiry into the Miraculous Powers* (1749), which Hume mentions in 'My Own Life' (above, vol. 1, p. 5), also discusses the miracles associated with the Abbé Paris (pp. 223–6). Robert Wallace had written an essay entitled 'Observations on the Account of the Miracles of the Abbé Paris' (Edinburgh University Library, Laing MSS, Box II. 620, item 20).

65. *President Forbes ... second Sight*] i.e. a supposed power by which occurrences in the future or things at a distance are perceived as though they were actually present (*OED*, 'second sight', *n.*). Duncan Forbes (1685–1747), Lord President of the Court of Session; Scottish politician and lawyer.

66. *finite added to finite ... Testimony*] Another echo of the language and argumentation of 'Of Miracles': 'there is no testimony for any [miracle], even those which have not been expressly detected, that is not opposed by an

infinite number of witnesses; so that not only the miracle destroys the credit of testimony, but the testimony destroys itself' (*ECHU*, section 10, 'Of Miracles', p. 91). Hume here alludes aggressively to the 'Appendix' first attached by Blair to the second edition of his *Dissertation*, in which various testimonies to the authenticity of the Ossianic poems were assembled (Blair, *Dissertation*, pp. 123–30). However, in the winter of 1763 Hume had written more encouragingly to Blair about the impact such testimony might produce: 'I approve very much of your Plan for ascertaining the Authenticity of Ossian's Poems; and I doubt not of your Success. I do not think you can publish all the Letters you receive, which no body would read. A Summary of them will do better; but endeavour to be as particular, as you can, with regard to Names of Persons and Passages: For the force of your Argument will lie there' (*Letters*, vol. I, p. 418). In 1760 Hume had implied to Sir David Dalrymple that positive testimony might corroborate the authenticity of the poems (*Letters*, vol. I, p. 329).

# *Appendices*

### APPENDIX 2

1. *Letters*, vol. I, pp. 219–20.
2. *Letters*, vol. I, p. 252.
3. *Letters*, vol. I, pp. 253–5.
4. *Letters*, vol. I, p. 258.
5. *Letters*, vol. I, p. 262.
6. *The Critical Review*, July 1757, pp. 27–35.
7. See *An Essay on Criticism*, l. 357 (the famous line on the defects of the alexandrine).
8. *The Critical Review*, pp. 28, 29 and 34.
9. *Letters*, vol. I, p. 266.
10. *Letters*, vol. I, pp. 268–9.
11. *The Critical Review*, April 1759, pp. 323–34.

# Index

Page numbers in roman refer to pages in volume 1; page numbers in *italic* refer to pages in volume 2

Louis XII (1462–1515), king of
France: 55, 222
Louis XIV (1638–1715), king of
France: 94, 215, 272, 299, 346,
364, 29, 122, 175, 177, 222, 309,
321, 337, 366, 374, 396, 417,
463, 523, 541, 542, 569–70, 599
Louis XV (1710–1774), king of
France: 395, 396, 417, 566
Louvestein faction: 62, 259
love: 19, 31, 41, 54, 75, 99, 101, 105,
107, 109, 115, 118, 123, 131,
137, 139, 144, 150–53, 169–70,
179, 181, 199, 18, 104, 171, 172,
217–19, 225, 229–33, 234, 235,
239, 247, 257, 262, 270
Lucan (AD 39–65), Roman poet: 107,
434–5
Lucian of Samosata (c. AD 125–c.
180), Syrian satirist and
rhetorician: 11, 108, 110, 142,
146, 250, 322, 340, 147, 150,
153, 160, 277, 508, 511, 515,
653
Lucretius Carus, Titus (c. 99–c. 55
BC), Roman poet: 105, 156, 276,
304, 316, 318, 327, 328, 330,
332, 341, 369, 223–4, 416, 594,
625
luxury: 18, 49, 77, 102, 291, 4–6,
9–11, 15–24, 31, 45, 72, 81, 100,
106, 136, 139, 313, 316–19,
324, 349, 375–6, 412, 440, 464,
589, 639
Lycia: 72, 378
Lycurgus (fl. c. 820 BC), legendary
legislator of ancient Sparta: 212,
246, 53, 131, 312, 348–9, 478,
575
Lyons: 139, 321
Lysias (c. 440–c. 380 BC), Attic
orator: 90, 114–15, 117, 121,
126, 130, 132, 447, 448, 449,

455, 461, 468, 472, 476, 481,
512, 513–14

Macedonia: 35, 106, 107, 295, 299,
310, 311, 319, 320, 340, 56, 64,
66, 75, 110, 133, 291, 354, 356,
362, 363, 364, 365, 388, 389,
398, 410, 456, 458, 460, 522
Machiavelli, Niccolò (1469–1527),
statesman, historian, and political
theorist: xxv–xxvi, 29, 34, 35,
76, 198, 216, 218, 220–21, 229,
237–8, 246, 250, 279–80, 283,
331, 377, 198, 237, 309, 322–3,
325, 329, 359, 402, 411–12, 415,
506, 509, 537–8, 565, 575, 577,
578–9, 580, 631–2, 639
Macpherson, James (1736–1796),
'discoverer' and publisher of
'Ossian': 272–81, 635–52
his other publications: 278–9
his unreliability: 278–80
Madrid: 152, 446
Magna Carta: 213, 184, 404–5, 530,
555
magnanimity: 184, 329, 332, 645
Maillet, Benoit de (1656–1738),
French diplomat, whose postings
included acting as consul
to Egypt and Tuscany; his
publications include Description
de l'Egypte (1735) and Idée du
gouvernement ancien et moderne
de l'Egypte (1743): 107, 142,
434, 466, 496
Malcolm, Noel: xxxi, 215, 313, 424,
565, 654
Malebranche, Nicolas (1638–1715),
French theologian and
philosopher: 314
Malta: 199, 579
Mandeville, Bernard (1670–1733),
physician and writer on